W9-DFJ-524

"The name 'Jungmann' is synonymous with the history of the Mass. Have a question about the origins of some part of the Sunday Eucharist? 'Look it up in Jungmann,' people will say. These volumes are both historical and historic. This new edition will make this timeless research more available to the eager reader."

Rev. Paul Turner
Author of *Glory in the Cross*

"What a delight to have this classic work in print again! It still remains the most reliable and detailed guide to the evolution of the Roman mass, to which every student of liturgical history should turn."

Paul Bradshaw
Professor of Liturgy
University of Notre Dame

Joseph A. Jungmann, S.J. (1889–1975), an Austrian Roman Catholic priest and scholar, was ordained to the priesthood in 1913 and entered the Society of Jesus (the Jesuits) four years later. He spent most of his career as professor of pastoral theology at the University of Innsbruck, where he taught both catechetics and liturgy. With the exception of the years during which Hitler closed down the theological faculty (1939–45), Jungmann's entire teaching career was spent at Innsbruck, where for a time he also served as rector of the community of Jesuits.

Jungmann is best known for his contributions to Catholic catechetics and liturgical studies. In particular, he is associated with the renewal of the Eucharistic liturgy and served on the Second Vatican Council's commission that produced *Sacrosanctum Concilium*, a document on liturgy and worship, in 1964. He authored many books, including *Liturgical Worship*, *Christian Prayer through the Centuries*, and *The Mass of the Roman Rite*.

The Mass
of the Roman Rite:

ITS ORIGINS AND DEVELOPMENT

(Missarum Sollemnia)

By
Rev. JOSEPH A. JUNGMANN, S. J.
Professor of Theology,
University of Innsbruck

Translated by
Rev. FRANCIS A. BRUNNER, C. SS. R.

VOLUME TWO

Christian Classics *Notre Dame, Indiana*

First published in English in 1951. Translated from the German revised edition of *Missarum Solemnia*, 1949.

"The Commingling," published here as an appendix to volume 2, was part of the revised and abridged edition of *The Mass of the Roman Rite*, Burns and Oates, London, 1959.

Imprimi Potest: Francis J. Fagen, C.Ss.R.
Provincial, St. Louis Province of Redemptorist Fathers
March 10, 1950

Nihil Obstat: Cardinal Francis Spellman
Archbishop of New York
Given at New York, September 22, 1950

The Nihil Obstat and *Imprimatur* are official declarations that a book or pamphlet is free of doctrinal or moral error. No implication is contained therein that those who have granted the *Nihil Obstat* or *Imprimatur* agree with its contents, opinions, or statements expressed.

Christian Classics™, Ave Maria Press®, Inc., P.O. Box 428, Notre Dame, IN 46556.

Founded in 1865, Ave Maria Press is a ministry of the United States Province of Holy Cross.

www.christian-classics.com

	Hardcover Edition	Paperback Edition
Complete Set	ISBN-10 0-87061-271-9	ISBN-10 0-87061-274-3
	ISBN-13 978-0-87061-271-8	ISBN-13 978-0-87061-274-9
Volume 1	ISBN-10 0-87061-272-7	ISBN-10 0-87061-275-1
	ISBN-13 978-0-87061-272-5	ISBN-13 978-0-87061-275-6
Volume 2	ISBN-10 0-87061-273-5	ISBN-10 0-87061-276-X
	ISBN-13 978-0-87061-273-2	ISBN-13 978-0-87061-276-3

Cover image © CBW / Alamy.

Cover and text design by John R. Carson.

Printed and bound in the United States of America, 2012.

ABBREVIATIONS

AAS	:	Acta Apostolicæ Sedis
CE	:	The Catholic Encyclopedia
CSEL	:	Corpus Scriptorum Ecclesiasticorum Latinorum
DACL	:	Dictionnaire d'Archéologie Chrétienne et de Liturgie
DThC	:	Dictionnaire de Théologie Catholique
Eph. liturg.	:	Ephemerides Liturgicæ. Analecta historico-ascetica.
GCS	:	Die Griechischen Christlichen Schriftsteller
HBS	:	Henry Bradshaw Society
JL	:	Jahrbuch für Liturgiewissenschaft
LF	:	Liturgiegeschichtliche Forschungen
LQ	:	Liturgiegeschichtliche Quellen
LQF	:	Liturgiegeschichtliche Quellen und Forschungen
LThK	:	Lexikon für Theologie und Kirche
MGH	:	Monumenta Germaniæ Historica
Periodica	:	Periodica de re morali, canonica, liturgica
PG	:	Migne, Patrologia Græca
PL	:	Migne, Patrologia Latina
RAC	:	Reallexikon für Antike and Christentum
SRC	:	(Decree of) The Congregation of Sacred Rites
StZ	:	Stimmen der Zeit
TU	:	Texte und Untersuchungen
ZkTh	:	Zeitschrift für katholische Theologie

TABLE OF CONTENTS

Part IV

THE MASS CEREMONIES IN DETAIL
THE SACRIFICE

I. The Offertory

1. The Offertory Procession of the Faithful

WHEN THE LESSONS HAVE BEEN CONCLUDED WITH THE PRAYER of those assembled, and when all who are not fully competent members of the congregation have departed, it is possible to proceed to the main event in the celebration, the renewal of Christ's institution. The Master had inaugurated the eucharistic mystery under the tokens of bread and wine—bread, such as was to be found on the table of the Last Supper, and the cup which stood before Him, these He took and changed into the heavenly gift. Bread and wine must therefore be ready at hand when the celebration of the Mass is to begin.

This readying of bread and wine need not, of course, be a ritual action. It might be taken care of, some way or other, by anyone before the beginning of the ceremonies. In the most ancient accounts, in fact, we find no traces of a special stressing of this preparatory activity. As long as the Eucharist was joined to the fraternal meal there was scarcely any occasion for such special stress, because the gifts were already on the table. Even in Justin's description the matter is recounted simply and impersonally: bread is brought in, and wine and water. No particular formalities are observed, no symbolism introduced into the movement. This ties in with the strict aloofness which the nascent Church in the first two centuries showed towards material matters, preferring to emphasize, in opposition to pagan and Jewish sacrificial customs, the spiritual character of Christian cult.[1] Passing over the earthly bread and wine, the Church's attention focused on the spiritual, not to say heavenly, gift which proceeds from her *Eucharistia,* and on the thanksgiving which pours out heavenward from the hearts of men—a worship which is indeed "in spirit and in truth."

But near the end of the second century we begin to see a trend away from this severe attitude. To oppose the repudiation of matter, which was a doctrine of the growing Hellenistic Gnosis, it was necessary to stress the value of the earthly creation, even in divine worship. The peril then no

[1] See Vol. I, p. 26 f.

1

longer lay in the materialism of heathen sacrificial practices, but in the spiritualism of a doctrine that hovered just on the borderline of Christianity.

So the Eucharist also appeared in a new light. The heavenly gift had an earthly origin; it was from the "firstlings of creation" that it proceeded. In Irenæus, as we saw, this point was emphasized for the first time. The approach towards God, this movement in which the Lord's body and blood was offered up, begins to include the presentation of material gifts which were thus drawn into the liturgical activity. In Tertullian we see the faithful bringing their gifts, and their action is described as an *offerre* directed to God.[2] Similarly, in Hippolytus of Rome not only are the bread and wine (brought in by the deacons before the *eucharistia* of the bishop) called *oblatio*,[3] but the consecrated gifts are designated *oblatio sanctæ Ecclesiæ*.[4] In another place, describing the liturgy of Baptism, we see that the faithful—at least the newly baptized—"offer up" their gifts for the Eucharist.[5]

By the time we reach Cyprian it has already become a general rule that the faithful should present gifts at the eucharistic solemnity. This is evident from Cyprian's scolding a rich woman for her lack of charity: *dominicum celebrare te credis . . . quæ in dominicum sine sacrificio venis, quæ*

---

[2] Tertullian, *De exhort. cast.*, c. 11 (CSEL LXX, 146 f.): [he is addressing a man who had married a second time, in reference to his first wife] . . . *pro qua oblationes annuas reddis. Stabis ergo ad Dominum cum tot uxoribus, quot in oratione commemores? Et offeres pro duabus, et commendabis illas duas per sacerdotem . . . et ascendet sacrificium tuum libera fronte?* Cf. for this Elfers, *Die Kirchenordnung Hippolyts*, 294 f.

[3] Dix, 6: *illi* [sc. *episcopo*] *vero offerant diacones oblationem.* The word *offerant* does not here mean an oblation to almighty God.

[4] Dix, 9. Cf. *supra*, I, 29.

Also in a prayer at the consecration of a bishop, there is a plea that the newly consecrated may προσφέρειν σοι τὰ δῶρα τῆς ἁγίας σου Ἐκκλησίας (Dix, 5).

[5] These should "bring along no other vessel but that for the Eucharist; for it is fitting for each then to bring his gift (προσφορά)." Hippolytus, *Trad. Ap.* (Dix, 32; cf. Hennecke, *Neutestamentl. Apokryphen*, 579: " . . . for it is fitting for what has been worthily accomplished that he offer up." We are dealing here with a text to be derived from divergent oriental trans-

lations). Besides, the terms *oblatio* and *offerre* or their oriental equivalents are often used in the "Apostolic Tradition" in a wider sense. The agape as a unit is called *oblatio*. Likewise within the plan of the agape the blessing of the cup by the individuals is designated as *offerre* (Dix, 46: *calicem singuli offerant*), and also the blessing of the bread at the beginning by the presiding cleric seems to be identified with an *offerre* (Dix, 48: all should receive the *benedictio* from his hands; cf. Dix, 46: *qui offert* should remember the host). Obviously the word is used here to signify that these objects are hallowed by the prayer of benediction and so in a way dedicated to God. It is possible, too, that in addition an offering was actually put into words, as in the following case: When the first-fruits are brought to the bishop (again the word *offerre*, προσενεγκεῖν) is used to express the idea; incidentally there is no connection here with the celebration of the Eucharist), the latter should offer them up (*offerre*) and for this purpose a formula is submitted: *Gratias tibi agimus, Deus, et offerimus tibi primitias fructuum . . .* (Dix, 53 f.; also preserved in Greek: προσφέρομεν). But this *offerre* also has ref-

partem de sacrificio quod pauper obtulit sumis.[5] Apparently, then, the individual worshiper was bound not only to contribute to the community poor box *(corban)* but also to make an offering for the altar, and from Cyprian's words it is quite clear that this offering was nothing more nor less than the bread and wine of the sacrifice.

The evolution must have been such that the offerings which had always been made for the needs of the Church and the poor were gradually drawn more closely into the liturgical pattern. The tie-in with the eucharistic celebration was all the easier since it had been customary to think of every gift to the Church and the poor as a gift to God, or even to designate it as an offering, an oblation.[7] Thus, such gifts of Christian charity were joined to the offering of the Eucharist.[8] It was, then, but a step to connect the offering made by the faithful with the ritual preparation of the gifts for the eucharistic sacrifice—a step which would be taken naturally in an age which was liturgically alive.[9] Thus we find in almost all the liturgies

---

erence to the blessing of the fruit, as the continuation of the text shows : *Benedicuntur quidem fructus, id est . . .* (the enumeration follows; Dix, 54). Furthermore the fact that these firstlings are brought to the bishop already implies a certain hallowing of the gifts, just as in the offering of bread and wine before the eucharistic prayer, so that even this *offerre* acquires a religious coloring.

Cf. J. Coppens, *Les prières de l'offertoire* (Cours et Conférences, VI; Louvain, 1928), 189-192; but the author does not pursue the connection between blessing and *oblatio*.

[6] Cyprian, *De opere et eleemos.*, c. 15 (CSEL, III, 384). The same idea later in Cæsarius of Arles, *Serm.* 13 (Morin, 63; PL, XXXIX, 2238). A detailed evaluation of the many references to the oblation in Cæsarius is presented in a work (still in manuscript) on Cæsarius as a liturgico-historical source, written by Dr. Karl Berg (Salzburg); I was able to look into and utilize this work.

The actual offertory procession is attested by the beginning of the 4th century by the synods of Elvira and Nicea; see *infra*, p. 20, note 108.

[7] Phil. 4:18. Cf. E. Peterson, *Apostel und Zeuge Christi* (Freiburg, 1940), 38 f.: The Church gets support not in the form of taxes but in the form of a gift to God, "a sacrifice that breathes out fragrance."

In Hermas, *Pastor,* Simul. V, 3, 8, an

alms combined with fasting is called a θυσία and a λειτουργία pleasing to God.

The word *operari (opus, operatio),* which in the language of pagan worship was used in the sense of *sacris operari = sacrificari,* and from which comes the German word *opfern,* "to offer (up)" (the word must have been borrowed already at the beginning of the period of Roman missionizing, some time in the sixth century, as the sound-shaft indicates), was employed in the Latin of the Christians since Tertullian's time for the Christian work of mercy; cf. the title of Cyprian's tract cited in the previous note. However, *offerre (oblatio)*—whence the Old English *offrian* ᛋ *offer*—was also used in the same sense. Both expressions are found together in Tertullian, *De idolol.,* c. 22 (CSEL, XX, 55). But it must be admitted that with regard to *operari* the basic meaning of *opus bonum* had a distinct influence; H. Janssens, *Kultur und Sprache. Zur Geschichte der alten Kirche im Spiegel der Sprachentwicklung von Tertullian bis Cyprian* (Nijmegen, 1938), 217-224; cf. 104-110.

[8] Irenæus, *Adv. hær.,* IV, 31, 5 (Harvey, II, 209); cf. Tertullian, *De or.,* c. 28 (CSEL, XX, 198 f.); *Ad uxor.,* II, 8 (CSEL, LXX, 124).

From a later period, Augustine, *Enchiridion,* c. 110 (PL, XL, 283) : For the dead *sacrificia sive altaris sive quarumcumque eleemosynarum* were offered up.

[9] G. P. Wetter, *Altchristliche Liturgien, II. Das christliche Opfer* (Forschungen zur

since the fourth century an offering (in some form or other) of gifts directed towards the Eucharist. As a passing custom it was practically universal in the Church. In the Orient, it is true, only fragmentary vestiges have survived.[10] There the connection with the gift-offering at Mass was not very close. At any rate this holds true of the Antiochene-Byzantine area.

The offerings could be made, for instance, before the beginning of the service, being placed in a side-room specially designated for this pur-

Religion u. Literatur des A. und N. T., N. F., 17; Göttingen, 1922), turns the whole process of development topsy-turvy. Without further proof Wetter considers the offering of natural gifts made to God directly—his material is gathered in the main from the offertory prayers of early medieval texts—as a remnant from the customs of the primitive Church, where the faithful brought contributions for the agape connected with the Eucharist. From this offering, which (according to him) was conceived as a sacrifice in the full sense of the word, the idea of an offering was taken over into the Eucharist. Cf. the critical examination of the question by J. Coppens, "L' offrande des fidèles dans la liturgie eucharistique ancienne," *Cours et Conférences*, VI (Louvain, 1927), 99-123, along with the same author's treatment of the study, "Les prières de l'offertoire et le rite de l'offrande," *Cours et Conférences*, VI (Louvain, 1927), 185-196; A. Arnold, *Der Ursprung des christlichen Abendmahles*, 84-100, who describes Wetter's wild methods thoroughly (p. 95 ff.); still his reliance on Wetter's results within the limitation presented, p. 100, is not sufficiently well founded.

[10] So far there has been no comprehensive investigation of the offering of gifts by the faithful in the Orient. An enumeration of the sources to be considered in Hanssens, III, 279-282, who is himself inclined to think that in the Orient there was no offertory procession of the faithful, at least in the narrower sense of a presentation of bread and wine at the start of each individual celebration. E. Bishop, in his addendum to Connelly, *The Liturgical Homilies of Narsai*, 116 f., is less negative in his judgment.—In Egypt an offering of gifts by the people, related in some way to the Eucharist, must have persisted for a long

time. The eucharistic prayer of Serapion includes a plea for the offerers (Quasten, *Mon.*, 64). In the 6th century the term εὐχαριστήριον here meant an offering (of the people) for the dead; see E. Peterson, "Die alexandrinische Liturgie bei Kosmas Indikopleustes," *Eph. liturg.*, 46 (1932), 66-74.—There is evidence that among the Copts the practice of the faithful bringing bread and wine for the Eucharist to church continued into modern times; J. Bute, *The Coptic Morning Service* (London, 1908), 133; Cl. Kopp, *Glaube und Sakramente der koptischen Kirche* (Orientalia christiana, 75; Rome, 1932), 120.

As regards Syria, the Testamentum Domini in the 5th century furnishes evidence of offerings by the faithful; a special room was set aside for them (I, 19; see the following note); candidates for Baptism were not to bring anything along *præter unum panem ad eucharistiam* (II, 8; Rahmani, 127); the bread of the catechumens was not to be accepted (I, 23; Rahmani, 37). Cf. further Jacob of Batnä (James of Sarugh, d. 521), *Poem on the Mass for the Dead* (BKV, 6 [1919], 305-315); he speaks about bread and wine which the faithful carry in procession to the altar.

Theodoret, *Hist. eccl.*, V, 17 (PG, LXXXII, 1236 CD) tells of the offertory procession of the Emperor Theodosius, who for this purpose entered the sanctuary; true, this took place in Milan, but it presupposes a similar custom in Constantinople (ὥσπερ εἰώθει). Similarly Gregory of Nazianzus, *Or.*, 43, 52 (PG, XXXVI, 564 A), tells of an offering of gifts by the Emperor Valens (but see the critical remarks of Bishop, *op. cit.*, 116, and also the defense by Dix, *The Shape of the Liturgy*, 123, note 3). Cf. also the Trullan Synod (692), c. 69 (Mansi, XI, 973).

pose.[11] Thence the things necessary for the Eucharist were transferred to the altar at the beginning of the sacrifice. The ceremonial accompanying this transfer, first seen in the work of pseudo-Dionysius,[12] expanded gradually into the Great Entrance which takes the place of our offertory and is a climax in the Byzantine liturgy. Preceded by torches and incense, the deacon and priest carry the host and the chalice, reverently covered, from the *prothesis*[13] through the nave of the church and back into the sanctuary. Meanwhile, in the procession the King of all, surrounded by hosts of angels unseen, is greeted and honored in song.[14] Similar forms of a ceremonial transfer of the sacrificial gifts are to be found in other liturgies of this cycle, or at least they can be reconstructed from the vestiges that remain.[15]

In the Gallo-Frankish Church the same had been in use for a long time in a fully-developed form.[16] Obviously, with an elaborate form such as this, an offering on the part of the people within the Mass itself was entirely out of the question. But this does not mean that they made no offering at all. By no means.

For it is precisely from the Gallic Church of this period that we have clear evidence of the part the people took in this, among other things a directive of the National Council of Macon (585), in which the offering of the faithful—consisting of bread and wine—is re-emphasized, with

[11] Thus the direction in the Testamentum Domini, I, 19 (Rahmani, 23; Quasten, *Mon.*, 237): *Diaconicon sit a dextera ingressus qui a dexteris est, ut eucharistiæ sive oblationes quæ offeruntur possint cerni.* This *diaconicon* corresponds to one of the two παστοφόρια mentioned in the Apostolic Constitutions, II, 57 (Quasten, 181), although here the rooms have already been transferred to the vicinity of the sanctuary.

[12] Ps.-Dionysius, *Eccl. hierarch.*, III, 2 (Quasten, *Mon.*, 294).

[13] The Prothesis, that is, the place for the preparation of the oblation gifts, is at present generally found next to the sanctuary or else is a table actually in the sanctuary, to the north of the altar. Brightman, 586.

[14] The Patriarch Eutychius (d. 565), *De Pasch.*, c. 8 (PG, LXXXVI, 2400 f.), had already expressed doubts about this proleptic veneration of bread and wine; others after him did the same. Hanssens, III, 286-289. It is possible to suggest that this veneration was originally directed to Christ as represented by the consecrated priest; but the sources give no hint of such a thing. A different explanation in Dix, *The Shape of the Liturgy*, 284 f.

[15] Baumstark, *Die Messe im Morgenland*,

112; Hanssens, III, 272-277; 285-293.— In the Syrian area the thought that Christ thus makes His entry in order to suffer or to be offered up (προέρχεται σφαγιασθῆναι) puts in an early appearance; Hanssens, III, 291 f.

Only in Egypt was there question here rather of a procession around the altar; this took place at the start of the fore-Mass and therefore did not necessarily involve a special place distinct from the altar for the preparation of the gifts; cf. Hanssens, III, 31-33.

[16] The oldest account comes from Gregory of Tours, *De gloria mart.*, c. 86 (PL, LXXI, 781 f.). The offertory procession is next mentioned in the *Expositio* of the ancient Gallican Mass (ed. Quasten, 17 f.). It is also found in the pseudo-Roman Mass of the 8th century, see *Capitulare eccl. ord.* and its monastic parallels (Silva-Tarouca, 206): After the reading the offerings are carried by the priest and the deacon in turret-shaped vessels (called *turres*) and in the chalice from the *sacrarium* to the altar. Here the offerings are called *oblationes,* whereas the sources mentioned previously speak proleptically of the body of the Lord. During the transfer to the altar

special reference to the fact that the usage was traditional.[17] The faithful made their offering before the beginning of the service in the place set aside for this purpose.[18] Similar arrangements must be presupposed in the Orient, too, wherever there is mention of offerings by the people.[19]

In the ancient Milanese [20] and Roman liturgies, and probably also in the North African, the offering of the faithful was very closely bound up with the eucharistic sacrifice. From the last of these, the North African liturgy, we get our oldest accounts of the offering of the faithful, and the customs connected with it are quite fully expounded, especially in St. Augustine.[21] In Africa it was possible to bring one's offerings to the altar day after day, as Monica was wont to do.[22] The priest himself received what was offered by the people, and in turn he offered these things to God.[23] Thus the offering and the oblation of the gifts was built into the very structure of the Mass. This is also certified by the report of the singing of psalms which was introduced at this time *ante oblationem* as well as at the communion.[24]

How the offertory was conducted at the papal stational service in seventh century Rome, we know in fullest detail.[25] Here the gifts were not

---

the so-called *sonus* was sung. For an explanation of the data, in part previously misunderstood, see Nickl, *Der Anteil des Volkes*, 37-42.

[17] Can. 4 (Mansi, IX, 951) : ... *Propterea decernimus ut omnibus dominicis diebus altaris oblatio ab omnibus viris et mulieribus offeratur, tam panis quam vini.*—Cf. Cæsarius of Arles, *Serm.* 13 (Morin.—63; PL, XXXIX, 2238) : *Oblationes quæ in altario consecrentur offerte. Erubescere debet homo idoneus, si de aliena oblatione communicaverit.*

[18] Nickl, 36 ff. For this Nickl cites a story in Gregory of Tours, *De gloria confess.*, c. 65 (PL, LXXI, 875 C) : For a whole year a widow had Mass said daily for her deceased husband and each time offered for this purpose a sixth of the best wine; however, the subdeacon who accepted the gifts cheated her, substituting cheap wine and keeping the good for himself, until one day the lady unexpectedly communicated and so discovered the fraud. It would hardly have been possible to perpetrate such a deception except in the *sacrarium*, a room apart, from which the oblation would be carried to the altar.

[19] For Syria cf. *supra,* note 11. The side-room which was designated for the reception of the offerings of the faithful has become general throughout the Orient since the second half of the 6th century; Baum-

stark, *Die Messe im Morgenland,* 109 f.

[20] Ambrose, *In ps. 118,* prol. 2 (CSEL, LXII, 4) ; cf. *infra,* p. 20, note 112.

[21] Clear evidence of the gifts of the faithful on the altar is given by Optatus of Mileve, *Contra Parmen.,* VI, 1 (CSEL, XXVI, 142) : The Donatists overturned altars *in quibus et vota populi et membra Christi portata sunt.* Victor of Vita, *Hist. pers. Afric.,* II, 51 (CSEL, VII, 44), tells of one individual instance of this.

[22] Augustine, *Confessiones,* 5, 9 (CSEL, XXXIII, 104) ; cf. *Ep.,* 111, 8 : The ladies and virgins who had fallen into the hands of the barbarians could no longer *ferre oblationem ad altare Dei vel invenire ibi sacerdotem, per quem offerant Deo* (CSEL, XXXIV, 655). The first phrase must refer to the offertory procession *(ferre oblationem)* at a public celebration, the second to a votive Mass requested privately; cf. *supra,* I, 219 f.

[23] Augustine, *Enarr. in ps.,* 129, 7 (PL, XXXVII, 1701).—Cf. also Roetzer, 116.

[24] See *infra,* p. 26.

[25] *Ordo Rom. I,* n. 13-15 (PL, LXXVIII, 943 f.). Cf. the later revision of this text in *Ordo Rom.* III, n. 12-14 (PL, LXXVIII, 980 f.). A dissertation studying this text and its bearing on modern practice, G. J. Booth, *The Offertory Procession in the Ordo Romanus Primus* (Washington, 1948), contributes little of

brought by the people to the altar, but were collected by the celebrant and his retinue. After the Gospel the pope and his assistants first approached the nobility and received from them, according to their rank, their offerings of bread, while the archdeacon who followed accepted the wine (which was presented in special flasks or cruets [26] and poured it into a large chalice which was held by a subdeacon who, in turn, emptied this into a still larger vessel *(scyphus)*. In the same manner the pope handed the breads to a subdeacon accompanying him, who laid them in a large cloth (perhaps a linen sack) held by two acolytes. One of the bishops, assisted by a deacon, then took over and continued to collect the offerings. Meanwhile, the pope left the men's side, and moved to the *confessio* where on feast days he received the offerings of the higher court officials; then he proceeded to the women's side to receive the gifts of the ladies of the nobility. It was then the duty of the archdeacon to prepare the bread offerings on the altar, with the help of subdeacons who handed him the breads which had been collected. He laid out as much as seemed to be needed for the Communion of the people. After this was done the pope himself took up the bread gifts of the assisting clergy and laid on the altar his own offering, which consisted of two breads [27] which the *subdiaconus oblationarius* [28] had brought along. For the chalice, only the offering presented by the pope himself and his group was used, or perhaps a little was taken out of the large vessel containing the wine offered by the people, and this was poured into the *calix sanctus.* [29] After the water, offered by the singing-boys, was commingled with the wine, the chalice was placed on the altar, to the right of the bread offered by the pope.

The general outlines of this oblation rite are still to be discerned some five hundred years later. [30]

Of the many gifts which were thus gathered, we can readily understand that only a small portion could be used for the altar. What was done with the rest? Where, first of all, was it kept during the service? Amongst the gold and silver objects which the Lateran basilica acquired from Con-

value, but reprints the pertinent passages. —Note that there is no documentary evidence of an "offertory *procession*" at Rome. See V. L. Kennedy, "The Offertory Rite," (*Orate Fratres*, 12 [1937-8], 193-198), 198.

[26] Drawing of *amulæ* in Beissel, *Bilder*, 317 f. These are special little flasks, ornamented with religious pictures, made for this particular purpose.

[27] Regarding the number two, cf. Amalar, *De eccl. off.*, III, 19 (PL, CV, 1130 D): *unam [oblationem] pro se et alteram pro diacono.*

[28] Regarding this office, see Eichmann, *Die Kaiserkrönung*, II, 246.

[29] In pouring the wine from the larger vessel into the sacred chalice a special colander or strainer was used. Thus, *inter alia,* the *Ordo* of St. Amand (Duchesne, 460); a more detailed description in *Ordo Rom.* VI, n. 8 (PL, LXXVIII, 992).—This *colatorium*—also called *colum, sia* ("strainer") or *cochlear* (from its ladle shape)— is mentioned in general as long as the practice of the people offering wine continued. Further details regarding the liturgical strainer in Braun, *Das christliche Altargerät*, 448-454. Illustration of a *colatorium* in Beissel, 318.

[30] *Ordo eccl. Lateran.* (Fischer, 82): As soon as the offertory chant is started the

stantine, the *Liber pontificalis* lists *altaria septem ex argento purissimo.*[31] There was but one altar in any one church, as we know full well. These, then, must have been tables to hold the offertory gifts. The fact that they were seven coincides with the fact that there were seven deacons who were called upon "to bestow their care upon tables" as once the deacons did in Jerusalem.[32] On these tables, which were set up somewhere in the forepart of the basilica,[33] the gifts of bread and wine were laid as an oblation to God.[34] Then, in so far as the needs of the clergy did not require them, they were set aside primarily for the poor, whose care was amongst the chief duties of the deacons.[35]

bishop goes *ad accipiendam oblationem in consueto loco, mansionario ante eum præcedente.* No further details are given regarding this acceptance of the offering, but immediately afterwards the paten prepared *cum hostia* is handed to the bishop at the altar.—However, the rite must have disappeared within the next few decades, for no mention is made of it in the commentary of Innocent III. True, offerings are mentioned for Christmas in *Ordo Rom.* XIV and XV, but they no longer disturb the course of the papal Mass; cf. *infra*, note 35.

[31] Duchesne, *Liber pont.*, I, 172.

[32] Acts 6: 2.—In accordance with this number seven for the deacons—which was also retained in other episcopal cities — Rome was divided into seven regions for the care of the poor. If further assistance was required, it was ready at hand in the institution of subdeacons.

[33] Th. Klauser, "Die konstantinischen Altäre in der Lateranbasilika," *Röm. Quartalschrift*, 43 (1935), 179-186, gives it as his opinion that there is a connection between this and the origin of the transepts in the Constantinian basilicas. Room had to be made for setting up each table. Cf., on the other hand, J. P. Kirsch, "Das Querschiff in den stadtrömischen christlichen Basiliken des Altertums," *Pisciculi, F. J. Dölger dargeboten* (Münster, 1939), 148-156.

[34] This harmonizes with the fact that the formulas of the *oratio super oblata* in the *Sacramentarium Leonianum,* as well as in our own missal, for that matter, repeatedly mention a plurality of altars on which the offerings of the people are laid: *tua, Domine, muneribus altaria cumulamus* (Muratori, I, 324). On the other hand, in the

formulas of the post-communion the *mensa* is referred to exclusively in the singular. Klauser, 185 f.

[35] Here again we see the close connection between the notion of alms and the offering; cf. *supra*, p. 2. — With the disappearance, *resp.* the transformation, of the offerings in the Middle Ages this meaning seems to have vanished; the thought of the poor recedes completely into the shade; cf. Schreiber, *Gemeinschaften des Mittelalters,* 468 b (register). From the *Ordo ecclesiæ Lateranensis* (Fischer, 141, 1. 2) we learn that in the twelfth century at the start of the night office on the titular feast June 24) a liberal drink *(defertur potus honorifice et sufficienter)* was to be served *de oblatione altaris maioris* to the assisting clergy, to be handed to them by those *qui oblationem altaris custodiunt* (*ibid.*, 140, 1. 3). Now the offerings were connected with a particular place, a particular altar, and a distinction was made between those which were to go *sub altari* and those which were to go *desuper* (Fischer, 52, 95 f.) ; the distribution to the clergy was made according to this distinction.—Even a late *Ordo* like that of Petrus Amelii (d. 1403) = *Ordo Rom.* XV., n. 9 (PL, LXXVIII, 1278 D) contains this regulation for the papal service: *quidquid offertur sive ad manus papæ vel pedes vel super altare, capellanorum commensalium est, excepto pane et vino, quod acolythorum est, et quidquid venit per totam missam super altare.* Cf. *Ordo Rom.* XIV, n. 70 f. (PL, LXXVIII, 1184, 1187). Therefore, besides the gifts which the pope receives in person, there are those gifts which may be laid down anywhere in the church during the further course of the Mass—the *Ordo eccl. Lateran.* (Fischer,

In other churches of the West,[36] and more especially in the Roman liturgy after it was transplanted to Frankish countries, the oblation[37] was metamorphosed into an offertory procession of the faithful. After the *Credo* a line was formed, which wended its way to the altar. First came the men, then the women; the priests and deacons joined in after them, with the archdeacon bringing up the rear. Frankish interpreters compared the procession to the parade of the multitude that went out to meet and acclaim our Lord on Palm Sunday.[38]

Here, too, bread and wine form the offertory gift of the faithful.[39] The English Synod of Cealychythe (Chelsea, 787) stresses the prescription that the offering should be bread, not cake.[40] As a rule the bread was carried to the altar in a little white cloth;[41] but mention is made also of woven baskets.[42] The celebrant and his assistants went down to meet the offerers at the spot dictated by custom.[43] We learn that the gifts were placed on a large paten carried by an acolyte.[44] But even when they were offered up at the altar they were no longer set down on the altar itself, but *post altare.*[45] For even when they still consisted of bread and wine, they were no longer intended for consecration.[46] The reception of Communion had sunk to such

95 f.) also mentions offerings made during Rogation processions; to all appearances such offerings were laid principally on the mensa of a side altar. All these offerings apparently fell under the designation *ad pedes;* cf. Acts 4: 35, 37; 5: 2; Durandus, IV, 30, 38. The offerings of bread and wine, which had lost their importance, fell to the lot of the acolytes.

[36] For Aquileia cf. *infra*, p. 10.

[37] Here it was insisted on from the start; see Synod of Mainz (813), can. 44 (Mansi, XIV, 74).

[38] Amalar, *Expositio* of 813-814 (Gerbert, *Monumenta*, II, 152 f.) ; *Expositio "Missa pro multis,"* ed. Hanssens (*Eph. liturg.,* 1930), 36 f.; *De eccl. off.,* III, 19 (PL, CV, 1128 B, 129 D). This analogy to Palm Sunday recurs in later commentators, for example Honorius Augustod., *Gemma an.,* I, 26 (PL, CLXXII, 553), and Sicard of Cremona, *Mitrale,* III, 5 (PL, CCXIII, 114 B, 116 A).

[39] Amalar, *De eccl. off.,* III, 19 (PL, CV, 1129 D).

[40] Can. 10 (Mansi, XII, 942).

[41] *Expositio "Missa pro multis,"* ed. Hanssens (*Eph. liturg.,* 1930), 38 ; *Eclogæ* (PL, CV, 1324) ; *Ordo Rom.* II, n. 9 (PL, LXXVIII, 973) : *cum fanonibus candidis.* Similarly in the monasteries: *Udalrici Consuetud. Clun.,* III, 12 (PL, CIL,

756 A).

[42] Christian of Stablo, *In Matth.* (after 865), c. 35 (PL, CVI, 1393 A).

[43] According to Herard of Tours, *Capitula* (from the year 858), c. 82 (Hardouin, V, 455), laics were not permitted to enter the sanctuary and the offerings therefore had to be received *foris septa.* Similarly the collection of capitularies of Benedictus Levita (dated about 850), I, 371 (PL, XCVII, 750) ; and so also, at an earlier date, the II Synod of Braga (563), can. 13 (Mansi, IX, 778).—On the other hand, Theodulf of Orleans (d. 821), *Capitulare,* I, c. 6 (PL, CV, 193 f.), excludes only women from the sanctuary. For this praxis there is also later evidence: Martène, 1, 4, 6, 7 (I, 387 f.) ; cf. 1, 3, 9, 8-10 (I, 341-344).—At present wherever the offertory procession is customary, no distinction, so far as I know, is made for women.

[44] *Ordo Rom.* VI, n. 9 (PL, LXXVIII, 992 C) : *patena.* This *patena* was apparently a large plate. Such plates were still in use in France up to very recent times; Corblet, II, 229.

[45] Regino of Prüm, *De synod. causis,* I, 62 (PL, CXXXII, 204).

[46] They were turned over to the *custos ecclesiæ* [the sexton] *ad observandum;* so *Ordo Rom.* VI, n. 9 (PL, LXXVIII, 993 A). Cf. *supra,* note 35.—A portion of

a minimum that the bread offered by the faithful was superfluous. Besides, usually only unleavened bread was used for the altar, and this was generally procured in some other way ;[47] in the years to follow, special regulations were made regarding its preparation.[48] Nevertheless, the offertory procession survived for quite some time, or rather, to put it more correctly, an outgrowth and development of it now put in an appearance almost everywhere.

Granting the principle that, besides the Eucharist, material gifts also could be presented to God, it was not long before the offerings consisted of objects other than bread and wine.[49] From the era of Constantine we have the mosaic from the floor of the large double church excavated at Aquileia; here is the representation of an offertory procession in which men and women are bringing not only bread and wine, but also grapes, flowers, and a bird.[50] For that reason, it became necessary from early times to make regulations specifying in what manner these offerings could be made. A synod of Hippo in 393 says categorically: "At the Sacrament of the Body and Blood of Christ nothing is to be offered except bread and wine mixed with water."[51] About the same time the Apostolic Canons stipulate: "When a bishop or priest, contrary to the institutions of the Lord about the sacrifice at the altar, offers up something else: honey or milk, or, in place of [the right kind], wine turned to vinegar, or fowl, or any type of beast or vegetable, in opposition to the mandate, he should be deposed. Aside from ears of wheat and grapes in season and oil for the lamps and incense, nothing should be brought to the altar at the time of the sacrifice. All other fruits should (as firstlings) be sent to the bishop or the priests at their home and not to the altar; it is clear that the bishop and priests distribute these too among the deacons and the other clergy."[52] These ordinances were repeated and expanded also in the West during the ensuing centuries.[53] Amongst the objects meriting the honor of being

---

the bread was blessed and distributed after the service; see the pertinent visitation questions in Regino, I, inquis. 61 (PL, CXXXII, 190 A) : *Si de oblationibus, quæ a populo offeruntur, die dominico et in diebus festis expleta missa eulogias plebi tribuat.*—More details regarding the eulogiæ, *infra,* p. 452.

[47] *Ordo Rom.* VI, n. 9 (PL, LXXVIII, 992 f.), still makes reference to bread offered by the faithful (cf. the argument for washing the hands, which follows), but on the altar is placed only what is needed from the offerings of the clerics and from the *oblatæ a nullo immolatæ* (ibid.).

[48] In the charters we find the obligation of supplying the *annona missalis* for the house of God. Examples since the 13th century

in K. J. Merk, *Abriss einer liturgiegeschichtlichen Darstellung des Mesz-Stipendiums* (Stuttgart, 1928), 12, note 23.

[49] See *supra* 2 f.

[50] See the account in *JL*, 2 (1922), 156 f; illustration in Righetti, *Manuale,* II, 29.

[51] Can. 23 (Mansi, III, 922) ; an exception continues to be made for milk and honey at the Easter Baptism Mass (cf. *supra,* I, 15) and for the *primitiæ* of grapes and grain.—The distinction which Augustine, *Ep.* 149, 16 (CSEL, 44, 362) makes appears to correspond to this : *voventur autem omnia, quæ offeruntur Deo, maxime sancti altaris oblatio.*

[52] *Canones Apostolorum,* 2 - 4 = *Const. Ap.,* VIII, 47, 2-4 (Funk, I, 564).

[53] They are still found in Regino of Prüm,

allowed to be brought to the altar, there appear, in addition to the oil for the lamps,[54] especially wax and candles.[55] Even at the present time, during the Mass of ordination, the newly ordained bring the bishop a lighted candle, which is presented to him.

Next we hear that in many churches *pretiosa ecclesiæ utensilia* destined for the church were laid on the altar at the offertory procession on great feasts.[56] Even the transfer of immovable property was often executed by handing over a deed or voucher at the offertory.[57] From the eleventh century on, the offering of money began to come to the fore.[58] Peter Damian tells, as something still out of the ordinary, that two prominent ladies offered goldpieces at his Mass.[59] But more and more the offering of bread and wine was made by the clerics alone,[60] and in monastic churches by

De synod. causis, I, 63-65 (PL, CXXXII, 204), and therefore they cannot be looked upon here as simply an expression of contemporary praxis, as Netzer, 226, considers them.

[54] At Rome even the oil which was consecrated on Maundy Thursday was taken from the offerings; *Sacramentarium Gregorianum,* ed. Lietzmann, n. 77, 4: *levantur de ampullis quæ offerunt populi.*

[55] Cæsarius of Arles, *Serm.* 13 (Morin, 13; PL, XXXIX, 2238), makes mention of wax and oil, but without stressing the point that they were conveyed to the altar.—On an Exultet roll from Gaeta there is a miniature which goes back to a much earlier design that illustrated the Exultet text in the earlier Gelasianum; it presents an offertory procession in which one of the front figures hands a small bottle of wine to the deacon who carries the chalice, while the other figure offers the bishop two rings of wax, apparently for the Easter candle; Th. Klauser, "Eine rätselhafte Exultetillustration aus Gaeta," *Corolla, L. Curtius zum 60. Geburtstag dargebracht* (Stuttgart, 1937), 168-176 (with illustration; also in L. A. Winterswyl, *Gestaltswandel der Caritas* [Freiburg, 1939], 12-13). Klauser refers to an Exultet text in a Florence missal (10th c.) which includes a petition for the offerer: *cereum, Domine, quod tibi offert famulus tuus ille;* Ebner, 27.—A loaf and a candle also appear as the customary offering in the twelfth century in the legend of the buried miner who was saved from death by the weekly Mass at which his wife made an offering; Franz, *Die Messe im deutschen Mittelalter,* 8 f. The legend, in turn,

was a leading factor in the production of a change in the offertory gifts. Cf. also the section on candles and wax as offerings in E. Wohlhaupter, *Die Kerze im Recht* (Forschungen zum deutschen Recht, IV, 1 [Weimar, 1940]), 29-35.— The offering of bread and a candle was so much a part of English parochial practice that it was revived in the time of Queen Mary; see Gasquet, *Parish Life in Medieval England,* 158.

[56] John Beleth, *Explicatio,* c. 41 (PL, CCII, 50 D). According to a decree of the Congregation of Rites published on Jan. 26, 1658, it is still permitted to take up *oblationes intortitiorum et calicis* at the offertory: *Decreta auth., SRC,* n. 1052.

[57] Martène, 1, 4, 6, 2 (I, 385 C).—One Christmas, after presenting a precious chalice at the midnight Mass, Emperor Henry II made a further gift at the high Mass when, during the offertory, he laid on the altar a gift certificate for the property of Erwitte; *Vita* of Bishop Meinwerk of Paderborn (d. 1036), n. 182 (MGH, Scriptores, XI, 149). — Regarding this practice of making gifts by laying them on the altar, and the forms observed in so doing, see Bona, II, 8, 8 (703-706).

[58] Merk, *Abrisz,* 92 f.; *ibid.,* 11, note 22, a charter from Vendôme dated 1046-49, in which someone transfers his own private church and along with it *nummorum etiam offerende medietatem.* — In Spain money offerings played a part already in the 7th century; see *infra,* p. 16.

[59] Petrus Damiani, *Ep.,* V, 13 (PL, CXLIV, 359 D): *byzanteos obtulerunt.*

[60] Thus Ivo of Chartres, *De conven.* (PL, CLXII, 550 C): *hostiam* [later identified

the monks.[61] Only in unusual circumstances was the presentation of the bread and wine by lay people continued, as, for instance, at the coronation of Kings,[62] or at the consecration of virgins,[63] perhaps also on certain great feasts[64] and, in some instances, at the burial services for the

as bread and wine for the consecration] *accipit a ministris et diversi generis oblationem a populis.*—The Mass-*ordo* of Séez (PL, LXXVIII, 248 A) generally mentions only the *oblationes offerentium presbyterorum et diaconorum.*

[61] Gradually this was restricted to a procession with the hosts. With a gold or silver spoon the sacristan lifted the hosts one by one from a large plate and handed them to each monk, who received them in a little cloth. A second sacristan poured wine into each one's cup. Priest-monks were permitted to pour the wine themselves into the large altar chalice. Whatever was not needed for the consecration was set aside as eulogia and distributed later in the refectory. William of Hirsau, *Const.*, I, 84; II, 30 (PL, CL, 1011, 1014 f., 1083 f.), and the analogous ordinances in other monasteries; see St. Hilpisch, "Der Opfergang in den Benediktinerklöstern des Mittelalters," *Studien u. Mitteilungen z. Geschichte des Benediktinerordens*, 59 (1941-2), 86-95, esp. 91 f.—In many Franciscan convents similar practices existed as late as the 18th century. In St. Vaast near Arras at the conventual Mass each day bread on a paten and wine in a chalice were offered by the superior in the name of the community. After the *Oremus* he was greeted by the celebrant with a *Pax tecum, reverende Pater* as he approached the altar with these offerings, kissed the maniple which was held out to him, and placed the bread on the altar paten and poured the wine into the altar chalice. Elsewhere, as at Cluny, only the communicants, each in turn, placed a host on the priest's paten; Hilpisch, 94 f. Cf. also de Moléon, 149, 239; Lebrun, *Explication*, I, 252 f.

[62] Cod. Ratoldi (10th cent.; PL, LXXVIII, 260 C).—E. S. Dewick, *The coronation book of Charles V of France* (HBS, 16; London, 1899), 43: *debet offerre panem unum, vinum in urceo argenteo, tresdecim bisantos aureos.*—W. Maskell, *Monumenta ritualia ecclesiæ Anglicanæ*, III, (London,

1847), 42: The king offers bread and wine, and then *marcam auri* (a late Middle Age direction).—According to the 12th century *Ordo* for the coronation of the emperor (Ordo C) the emperor offers at the throne of the pope *panem simul et cereos et aurum, singillatim vero imperator vinum, imperatrix aquam, de quibus debet ea die fieri sacrificium;* Eichmann, *Die Kaiserkrönung im Abendland*, I, 178; cf. 215. According to Ordo D which was in use since the 13th century and goes back to Innocent III, the emperor offers only *aurum quantum sibi placuerit;* Eichmann, I, 264; cf. 285; II, 273 f. This last arrangement is also prescribed in the *Pontificale Romanum* I, *De bened. et cor. regis.*

[63] So in England even around 1500: Each of the virgins had her hands covered with a cloth. In the right she carried a paten with a host and in the left a cruet with wine for the altar. She slipped the host onto the paten which the deacon held, the cruet she handed to the bishop, whose hand she kissed. The wine was put into a chalice and administered after the Communion. W. Maskell, *Monumenta*, II (London, 1846), 326 f.—The same rite was used for the dedication of oblate boys, in the customs of the Piedmontese monastery of Fruttuaria (11th c.): Albers, *Consuetudines*, IV, 154. The precedents for this usage are already in St. Benedict's Rule, ch. 59.— The *Pontificale Romanum* I, *De bened. et consecr. virginum*, recognizes only the offering of a burning candle.

[64] Regarding the offering of bread and wine at a papal Mass, cf. *supra*, note 30. According to the *Ordinarium* of Nantes of the year 1263 *luminarii* were offered at the first Mass on Christmas, bread at the second and money at the third; E. Martène, *Tractatus de antiqua ecclesiæ disciplina* (Lyons, 1706), 90. Durandus, *Rationale*, IV, 30, 40, mentions an offering of bread by the people on Christmas.— There is a comparatively late reference to an unrestricted offering of bread and wine in the cession of a church to the monastery

dead.[65] So, since the twelfth century, in explaining the offertory, the enumeration of offerings usually begins with gold: Some offer gold, like the Wise Men from the East, others silver, like the widow in the Temple, still others *de alia substantia;* only after that are bread and wine mentioned [66] as gifts of the clerics, who have always formed the last in the ranks of offerers. In later writings, there is no mention at all of bread and wine in this connection. Only at an episcopal consecration does the Roman liturgy still contain a vestige of this practice: the newly consecrated bishop presents two altar breads, two small casks of wine, and two candles.[67] And at a papal Mass, on the occasion of a solemn canonization, an offering is made of two breads, two barrels of wine and water, five

of St. Denis in the year 1180; the former owner hands over, amongst others, *omnia ad altare pertinentia cum offerenda panis et vini, lini, canapi et candele;* Merk, *Abrisz,* 13, note 27; cf. 87, note 11. A contemporary record from Tours mentions *panis, vinum, denarius, candela* as the usual offertory materials.

[66] In Champagne even as late as the first half of the 19th century it was still a custom at a burial service for the next of kin to offer up a loaf on a serviette, and wine in a special flagon, along with a candle; by 1860-70 instead of wine only an empty canister and money were presented. The rest of the ladies offered bread and candle, the men money. This information comes from the youthful memories of A. Loisy, as recorded in Wetter, *Altchristliche Liturgien,* II (*supra,* note 9) 77 f.—The same custom is reported in the beginning of the 18th century in Orleans: de Moléon, 215 f.; there is also the example of a parish where on All Souls Day 50 to 60 ladies took part in his offertory procession; *ibid.;* cf. also 239, 408, 409, 410.—De Moléon, 173, 187, 427, also describes another procession, still current at that time in certain cathedrals, where the canons at a solemn service for the dead formed a proeession with paten and chalice. Corblet, I, 225, witnesses to the custom, still in vogue in Normandy in his day (1885), where the respective family at a service for the dead presented a flask of wine and a loaf of bread which were then offered up by two altar boys at the offertory.—Regarding the offering of bread or meal which in present-day Bavarian parishes is deposited on the altar-rail before a funeral Mass, and also regarding the custom of

alms bread, cf. V. Thalhofer-L. Eisenhofer, *Handbuch der katholischen Liturgik,* II (Freiburg, 1912), 121, note 3. I have been told about a Regensburg country parish where a tin cup is placed on the tumba and formerly a loaf of bread was set beside it (L. Schlosser, 1931). Another account comes to me from Kœssen in the Lower Inn valley; here it is still the custom at solemn funeral services to set up a pan of meal and three tin pitchers which are filled after the Mass with gifts for the priest (P. Werner).—The rapport with the Mass is less close in other accounts of an offering of bread for the poor after a funeral service; such practices were customary even in our own century in places like my native South Tyrol.

[66] Honorius Augustod., *Gemma an.,* I, 27 (PL, CLXXII, 553); cf. Sicard of Cremona, *Mitrale,* III, 5 (PL, CCXIII, 115); Durandus, IV, 30, 34. Another enumeration of the Mass offerings usual in the 12th century reads: *Panis, vinum, denarius et candela;* Martène, 1, 4, 6, 6 (I, 387A).

[67] *Pontificale Rom.,* De consecr. ep.; similarly at the Blessing of an Abbot. Likewise in the Roman Pontifical of the 13th century and (also at the consecration of cardinal priests and deacons) in that of the 12th century; Andrieu, II, 349, 364 f.; I, 137, 151 f.—Even at present at the cathedral of Lyons the first two priests on each side of the choir bring bread and wine to the altar on the ferias of Lent; J. Baudot, *Le Missel Romain* (Paris, 1912), 101. Cf. de Moléon, 246. As late as 1700 the canons of Angers still conducted an offertory procession; *ibid.,* 89.

candles, and three cages containing pigeons, turtle-doves, and other birds.[68]

Shortly after this it was pointed out that clerics do not generally have an obligation to make an offering.[69] Other means had long since been devised of procuring the elements of bread and wine, while in the offertory procession the chief concern was a domestic one, to obtain support for the clergy. This offering served, as they said, *ut inde sibi victum habeant sacerdotes.*[70] And since money gradually superseded almost all other gifts, and since many objects were already excluded from the offertory proper because of the holiness of the place, there was soon no distinction at all, in intent and disposition, between free-will offerings and those made according to strict ecclesiastical prescription. And inversely, the latter offerings were all the more consciously drawn into the offertory procession and all the more plainly considered as gifts made to God. Even the presentation of the tithes was designated as an *offerre.*[71] Under the concept of oblation were listed all the products of rural industry and all objects of ecclesiastical and domestic use; and in regard to all of these, in so far as it was practicable, an effort was made to integrate them, in some way, with the offertory procession.[72]

Besides, one of the features of the older Gallican rite recurs again— offering up all sorts of things for the altar *before* the services. Because of the richness of such gifts, it so happened that—especially when the churches were privately owned—the landlord would lay hands on the offerings and even demand the majority for himself, claiming that he was already taking care of the church and its priests. As early as 572 the Synod of Braga had ordained that no bishop was to consecrate a church which

[68] J. Brinktrine, *Die feierliche Papstmesse,* 54-56. The first evidence of this offertory procession at a canonization is in 1391; see Th. Klauser, "Die Liturgie der Heiligsprechung," *Heilige Uberlieferung* (Münster, 1938), 212-233; esp. 223 ff. The allegorical intent in the choice of the gifts is explained in H. Chirat, "Psomia diaphora," *Mélanges E. Podechard* (Lyons, 1945), 121-126.

[69] *Ordo Rom.* VI (10th c.), n. 9 (PL, LXXVIII, 993 A; Hittorp, 8): *quos non tam patrum instituta iubent quam proprium arbitrium immolare suadet.* John Beleth, *Explicatio,* c. 41 (PL, CCII, 59): *Clerici enim non offerunt nisi in exequiis mortuorum et in nova celebratione sacerdotis. Nam inhumanum videretur, si ii offerre tenerentur, qui ex oblationibus vivunt aliorum.*—Durandus, IV, 30, 36, appends to the exceptions: *et in quibusdam præcipuis sollemnitatibus,* and extends the exemption to *monachi.*

[70] John Beleth, *Explicatio,* c. 17 (PL,

CCII, 30). In the same sense Durandus, IV, 30, 9, distinguishes between *donum* and *sacrificium;* he says: *donum dicitur quicquid auro vel argento vel qualibet alia specie offertur,* while *sacrificium* is what serves for the consecration.

[71] G. Schreiber, *Untersuchungen zum Sprachgebrauch des mittelalterlichen Oblationswesens* (Wörishofen, 1913), 19 f. Schreiber tells about a spiritualizing that set in regarding the discharge of tithes.

[72] At a First Mass in the diocese of Eichstätt during the 15th century it was customary for all the people to take part in an offertory procession in which they presented not only money and natural products but also all sorts of household goods like cooking utensils and bedding as an endowment for the new priest; J. B. Götz, *Die Primizianten des Bistums Eichstätt aus den Jahren 1493-1557* (Reformationsgeschichtliche Studien und Texte, 63; Münster, 1934), 18.—In certain parishes in the lower Alpine region of Bavaria it

some landlord had built in order to snatch half the oblations.[73] The struggle against these and similar claims went on for centuries.[74] It even affected the altar oblation proper, which was now grounded on a much wider basis and whose ecclesiastical disposition, in its more ancient modest range, had hardly been imperiled.[75]

In the interval during which the ancient offering of bread and wine was being displaced by the other objects at the offertory procession—the ninth and the tenth centuries—the effort was made to establish a strict distinction between the former offering and the latter. Only bread and wine are to be offered up according to the traditional form at the offertory of the Mass, while candles and the rest are to be presented before Mass or be-

was customary on specified feast days, right down to modern times, to make offerings of flax and sheaves of wheat in church, while other products were brought to the churchyard. In one parish on Martinmas (Nov. 11) every farmer "offered" a goose, later (till 1903) a hen; the animals were kept in a cage near the cemetery during the church services and afterwards were auctioned off for the benefit of the parish treasury. G. Rückert, "Alte kirchliche Opfergebräuche im westlichen bayerischen Voralpenland," *Volk und Volkstum*, I (1936), 263-269.—We hear of similar practices at present among Slovenes of Carinthia. In the Gail valley at a wedding service natural products are offered, like the wine which is blessed and handed to the married couple. At St. Jacob in Neuhaus there is a special room next to the sacristy where on Sundays the offertory gifts which are presented before Mass are kept; after services they are auctioned off by the church treasurer. Few are the Sundays on which nothing—lambs, shoats or fowl—is forthcoming. In some churches where these customs prevail the offerer walks around the altar to symbolize that his gift is made to God. (From a notation by a former pupil of mine, chaplain Christian Srienc.).

[73] Can. 6 (Mansi, IX, 840) ; cf. III Synod of Toledo (589), c. 19 (*ibid.*, 998).

[74] Jonas of Orleans (d. 843), *De inst. laicali*, II, 19 (PL, CVI, 204 f.) ; Synod of Ingelheim (948), can. 8 (Mansi, XVIII, 421) ; *Decretum Gratiani*, III, 1, 10 (Friedberg, I, 1296).—In the course of a transfer of churches to monasteries and bishops, as we ascertain from source docu-

ments (deeds and charters) since the 9th century, the rights ceded often included the *oblationes, offerentiæ* or *offerendæ* (the last especially is a regular designation for altar offerings; see Schreiber, *Untersuchungen*, 24 ff. ; cf. French "offrande"), frequently with the stipulation that a specified number of the clergymen who went with the transfer must be retained. Examples in Merk, *Abrisz*, 48 ff. ; G. Schreiber, "Mittelalterliche Segnungen und Abgaben" (*Zeitschrift d. Savigny-Stiftung*, 63 [1943], 191-299), 245 f., 280 f., 283, 289 note. (= Schreiber, *Gemeinschaften des Mittelalters*, 247 f., etc. ; see *ibid.*, 467 f., Index *s.v.* "Oblationen").— Exact settlements between the canonesses and the priest-canons who worked in the church are continued, e.g., in the *Liber ordinarius* of the capitular church of Essen (14th c.), ed. by F. Arens (Paderborn, 1908), 126-128 ; cf. 200-204.

[75] In the *Const. Ap.*, VIII, 31 (Funk, I, 532 f.) there is a clue to how the "Blessing" left over at the mysteries (τὰς περισσευούσας ἐν τοῖς μυστικοῖς εὐλογίας) was to be distributed among the ranks of the clergy. Manifestly bread and wine are meant. Further instances from the Orient in Funk, *loc. cit.*—Gregory the Great, *Dial.*, IV, 55 (PL, LXXVII, 417 B), tells about a priest to whom someone wanted to give *duas oblationem coronas,* which are thereafter labeled *panis sanctus.* Cf. also *supra*, p. 8, note 34.—The allotment to bishop, clergy, church buildings and the poor—frequently mentioned since the 5th century—refers to the distribution of the church revenues as a whole, and not directly to the altar offerings.

fore the Gospel.[76] As a matter of fact, the ensuing years witness a great deal of hesitancy regarding the proper place for this remodeled offertory procession. In Bavarian country parishes an offertory procession before the Gospel has survived right down to the present.[77] An offertory procession at the *Kyrie eleison* was also a common practice which continued[78] for a long time.[79] In Spain it was customary, even in earlier times, to offer money at the Communion procession,[80] a custom which also existed elsewhere or was formed anew.[81] And again there was repeated occasion for sharp prohibitions against simoniacal dealings.[82] Later, in Spain, we meet with an offertory procession inserted between the priest's offering of bread and wine and the washing of his hands. This is done in the Mozarabic liturgy,[83] and even in the Roman liturgy this addition is admitted to a certain

[76] Hincmar of Reims, *Capitula*, I, c. 16 (PL, CXXV, 777 f.). Similarly Regino of Prüm, *De synod. causis, inquis.* 72 f. (PL, CXXXII, 190 C).

[77] Thalhofer-Eisenhofer, *Handbuch der katholischen Liturgik*, II, 121, note 3. Besides this offertory procession right after the collects, there is generally a second one at funeral services, after the Gospel. At both money is offered.—This dual procession at services for the dead also in Ingolstadt in the 16th century; Greving, *Johann Ecks Pfarrbuch*, 83, 113 f., 118, note 1. The same custom also obtained at that time in Biberach; Schreiber *Untersuchungen*, 15, note 1, following A. Schiller (Freiburg Diocesan Archives, 1887).

[75] So according to a commentary in a 15th century Stuttgart MS.; Franz, *Die Messe*, 704 f.

[79] It was still mentioned in 1909 as a contemporary custom at a wedding Mass; L. von Hörmann, *Tiroler Volksleben* (Stuttgart, 1909), 371. But I myself have had no acquaintance with the practice.

[80] Isidore of Seville, *Ep. ad Leudefredum*, n. 12 (PL, LXXXIII, 896).—Synod of Merida (666), can. 14 (Mansi, XI, 83): *communicationis tempore a fidelibus pecuniam novimus poni*. Cf. the remarks of A. Lesley regarding the *Missale mixtum* (PL, LXXXV, 537 f.).

[81] E. G. about 1400 in Rome: *Ordo Rom.* XV, n. 85 (PL, LXXVIII, 1332 C). In the memoranda of the Mainz parish priest Florentius Diel (1491-1518), ed. by F. Falk, (*Erläuterungen zu Janssens Geschichte des deutschen Volkes*, IV, 3 [Freiburg, 1904], 15, 46), it is opposed as an abuse: The faithful ought not to lay the money on the Communion cloth.

[82] Synod of Trullo (692), can. 23 (Mansi, XI, 953); synod of Worcester (1240), can. 29 (Mansi, XXIII, 536): *parochianos suos, cum communicant, offerre compellunt, propter quod simul communicant et offerunt, per quod venalis videtur . . . hostia pretiosa.* Further examples in Browe, *Die häufige Kommunion im Mittelalter*, 136 f.—What led to this practice was the desire, quite understandable, to lessen the disturbance caused by the repeated comings and goings, by combining the offertory and Communion processions. —There is a possible connection between the fact that even in modern times the traditional offertory processions are conducted after the Communion, and the ordinance of Joseph II, of June 24, 1785, which sought to do away with the commotion caused by the offertory procession during Mass. This ordinance placed the procession before Mass, and enjoined only money and no burning candles; *K.k. Verordnungen welche über Gegenstände in Materiis publico-ecclesiasticis 1784 u. 1785 sind erlassen worden* (Augsburg, 1786), 22.—Regarding the custom in Vorarlberg, see L. Jochum, "Religiöses und kirchliches Brauchtum in Vorarlberg," *Montfort*, 1 (Bregenz, 1946), 263 ff., especially 271.

[83] *Missale mixtum* (PL, LXXXV, 537). According to the rubric for the first Sunday of Advent, the incensing of the altar and the *Adiuvate me fratres* also come before the procession.

extent.[84] The author of the *Micrologus* denounces this arrangement as inverted.[85] As a rule, the offertory, even in its new dress, assumes its old place after the *Oremus*, while the *offertorium* is being sung, its gladsome tone spurring one on to joyful giving.[86] It is presupposed as taking place in this spot in the Mass *ordo* of Burchard of Strassburg, printed in 1502,[87] and here, too, it is to be found wherever the old custom still survives.[88]

Burchard's *ordo*, which always notes the rubrics with great exactness, also describes the rite for the priest in these circumstances. After he has read the offertory from the missal, he goes to the Epistle side, takes the maniple from his arm and extends it to each of the offerers to be kissed, at the same time blessing them with a special formula.[89] The same rite is presupposed in Spanish Mass books of the fifteenth and sixteenth centuries.[90] In Spain the rite is an ancient tradition,[91] and here, too, it has survived to this day, with the exception of the blessing which had to be sacrificed in 1881 as the result of a decree of the Congregation of Sacred Rites.[92] The main outlines of the rite are also to be found elsewhere up to

[84] For France see the numerous instances from the 11th to the 18th centuries in Lebrun, I, 254 f.—For England see the instruction regarding Mass in the Vernon MS. (about 1375), in Simmons, *The Lay Folks Mass Book*, 142.—The rubric in the 1547 Missal of Vich also seems to assert the same; Ferreres, 121.

[85] Bernold of Constance, *Micrologus*, c. 10 (PL, CLI, 983 C).

[86] Alexander of Hales, *Summa theol.*, p. IV, 10, 5, 2, and following him William of Melitona, *Opusculum super missam*, ed. van Dijk (*Eph. liturg.*, 1939), 327.

[87] Legg, *Tracts*, 149.

[88] For Spain see Ferreres, 121 f.—B. Gavanti, too, thinks it appropriate that the offertory procession which is sometimes performed at present should be inserted here; Gavanti-Merati, II, 7, 5 (I, 260).—As a matter of fact, however, the procession which is still in vogue in country churches often begins a bit later, and then, if there are many offerers, it frequently lasts during the whole Mass, with just a short break at the consecration.

[89] Legg, *Tracts*, 149: *dicto offertorio, si sint volentes offerre, celebrans accedit ad cornu epistolæ, ubi stans detecto capite, latere suo sinistro altari verso, deponit manipulum de brachio sinistro, et accipiens illud in manum dextram porrigit summitatem eius singulis offerentibus osculandum dicens singulis: Acceptabile sit sacrificium tuum omnipotenti Deo, vel:*

Centuplum accipias et vitam æternam possideas. Also in Franz, *Die Messe*, 614, note 1. — According to two Mass books from the neighborhood of Monte Cassino (11-12th cent.), after the priest has taken up the *oblationes singulorum*, he recites the words: *Suscipe s. Trinitas hanc oblationem, quam tibi offert famulus tuus, et præsta ut in conspectum tuum tibi placens ascendat;* Ebner, 309, 340; cf. 346. The same formula, and probably for the same purpose, found already in the first half of the 11th century in the *Missa Illyrica* and the missal of Troyes: Martène, 1, 4, IV; VI (I, 508 D, 532 C), and at the other end still occurs in the Missal of St. Lambrecht (Köck, 120), written in 1336.—The blessing: *Acceptabilis sit omnipotenti Deo oblatio tua,* appears also in the *Missa Illyrica,* but is said by the bishop when he receives the *oblata* for the Eucharist, and similarly by the deacon; Martène, 1, 4, IV (I, 508); cf. Mass *ordo* of Séez (PL, LXXVIII, 248 A).

[90] Ferreres, 120 f.

[91] Cf. *Missale mixtum* (PL, LXXXV, 529 A): The priest says to each: *Centuplum accipias et vitam æternam possideas in regno Dei. Amen.*

[92] Decision of Dec. 30, 1881; *Decreta auth. SRC,* n. 3535, 1. Still the blessing has not disappeared entirely; see Kramp, "Messgebräuche der Gläubigen in den ausserdeutschen Ländern" (*StZ,* 1927, II), 362.—Either the maniple or the stole or

very recent times.[93] In many places, instead of the maniple or the stole,[94] the offerer (after handing over his gift)[95] kissed the hand of the celebrant,[96] or, in other places, the corporal[97] or even an extended paten.[98] Sometimes the offerer accompanied his gift with a word of blessing.[99] According to a Mass *ordo* of the fifteenth century the priest was finally to bless the peo-

(before 1881) a particle of the True Cross was presented to be kissed. In the diocese of Urgel the blessing was worded: *Oblatio tua accepta sit Deo.* After renewed representations the kissing of the stole was permitted also at a funeral Mass: June 15, 1883; *Decreta auth. SRC,* n. 3579. Ferreres, 121 f.—Cf. G. Martinez de Antoñana, *Manual de liturgia sagrada,* I (5th ed., Madrid, 1938), 496 f.; here is a rubric book that takes the offertory procession into consideration.

[93] In Vorarlberg the priest stood at the epistle side during the offertory procession. However, only a vestige was left of the older practice of presenting the maniple to be kissed: as each gift was offered the priest merely waved his maniple and pronounced a blessing, e.g., *Pax tecum;* Jochum (see *supra,* note 82), 272.—In St. Gall nearby a synod of 1690 determined that only the men should kiss the maniple, while it was laid on the heads of the women. K. Steiger, *JL,* 2 (1922), 176. Cf. the note following.

[94] Ferreres, 121 f. Each of the canonesses at the capitular church in Essen, upon handing the oblation to the priest (who came to the choir with a whole retinue of assistants according to a fixed order), kiss his stole; Arens, *The Liber ordinarius,* 18, 200 f.—According to the parish book of Biberach, about 1530, ed. by A. Schilling, *Freiburger Diözesanarchiv,* 1887, the priest presented the stole to the nobles to be kissed, but merely placed it on the heads of others; Schreiber, *Untersuchungen,* 15 note 1.

[95] The references are to offerings made *ad altare, ad librum, ad stolam, ad manum;* Merk, *Abrisz,* 33 f.; cf. 34, note 4, an Obendorf Mass foundation of 1474: "the offering is thus placed on the altar or given and laid in his [the chaplain's] hand or book."—John Beleth, *Explicatio,* c. 41 (PL, CCII, 50 D), objects to the priest's holding a *pyxis* or something of the sort in his hand, on the ground that it could

easily give the impression of avariciousness.—Durandus, IV, 30, 38, pretends to know that except at Masses for the dead the pope always received *ad manum* only the oblation of bread, while all else was laid *ad pedes;* cf. *supra,* note 35. So, too, the oblations which were offered *ad manum episcopi* were accepted by the subdeacon because the bishop was not supposed to busy himself with his own hands in worldly matters.

[96] Durandus, IV, 30, 35.

[97] According to a report from Lübeck dated about 1350: P. Browe, *Hist. Jahrbuch,* 49 (1929), 481.

[98] The custom was forbidden by Pius V; likewise in Milan it was prohibited by the provincial synod of 1574. At Rouen, however, it was continued at least for great feasts; de Moléon, 366. In Belgium kissing the paten, at Masses for the dead, continued to be practiced even to the present; Kramp. *op. cit.,* 358.—C. M. Merati proposes a crucifix or some other image in place of the paten; Gavanti-Merati, II, 7, 5, XXI (I, 263).—In Upper Silesia it is (or was) the custom to kiss the foot of a large crucifix while marching around the altar (which was generally part of the offertory procession); A. Stasch, S.J., 1947.

[99] In the *Missa Illyrica:* Martène, 1, 4, IV (I, 508 B) the offerer says the words: *Tibi Domino creatori meo offero hostiam pro remissione omnium peccatorum meorum et cunctorum fidelium tuorum vivorum ac defunctorum.* Two other formulas which voice a special intention, *ibid.* It stands to reason that phrases such as these would be expected generally only from the clergy. In the Mass *ordo* of Séez (PL, LXXVII, 248 A) it is actually designated only for the priest and deacon; similarly in later MSS. in Martène, 1, 4, XVI (I, 598) and in Ebner, *Quellen,* 346. Also in the missal of Troyes (about 1050), where a second formula follows: *Hanc oblationem, clementissime Pater, defero ad manus sacer-*

ple with the words: *Centuplum accipiatis et vitam æternam possideatis, in nomine Patris . . .*[100]

A very festive rite of offertory procession is still in use at the solemn papal Mass which is celebrated on the occasion of a canonization. The offerers step up to the pope's throne in three groups, each led by a cardinal. In each group two noblemen precede the cardinal and two other people follow—the four gift-bearers. The gifts borne by the nobles, two heavy candles, two breads, two cruets of wine and water, are handed to the Holy Father by the respective cardinal; in doing so he kisses the pope's hand and stole, and his Holiness in turn blesses the gifts and turns them over to his master of ceremonies. The other gifts (candles, cages with birds) are handed over by the bearers to the cardinal procurator; the latter holds them out to the pope for his blessing.[101]

However, the general attitude of the later Roman liturgy towards the offertory procession, the attitude of reserve and even avoidance, has led to the very singular result that the celebrant as a rule takes no notice of the procession even when it still occurs.[102] This conduct is to be found even earlier in the declining years of the Middle Ages.[103] In such cases the people brought their gifts and laid them in a plate or box standing near the altar. In other instances two places were set apart—perhaps for two different purposes—one on the Gospel side, the other on the Epistle; the faithful presented part of their gift at the first location, circled the altar (where this was possible), and then made their second offering at the second place.[104]

Since the third century, then, it very quickly became a fixed rule that the faithful should offer their gifts at a common eucharistic celebration, but because of the close connection with the performance of the sacred mystery it was from the very start recognized as a right restricted to those who were full members of the Church, just like the reception of the Sacrament. In the Syrian Didascalia there is a long discussion outlining the duty of the bishops and deacons to watch out from whom they accept a

---

dotis tui, ut offerat eam tibi Deo Patri omnipotenti pro cunctis peccatis meis et pro totius populi delictis. Amen. Martène, 1, 4, VI (I, 532 C).—The Sacramentary of Fonte Avellana (PL, CLI, 886), which could not have been written much before 1325, still introduces the first formula with the rubric: *Quando quis offert oblationem presbytero dicat.*

[100] Pontifical of Noyons: V. Leroquais, *Les Pontificaux,* I (Paris, 1937), 170.

[101] Brinktrine, *Die feierliche Papstmesse,* 55 f. Cf. *supra,* p. 13—A similarly solemn cortege accompanied the king of France when he made his offering on coronation day; see Corblet, I, 223.

[102] But even as cautious a rubricist as B. Gavanti thinks that the present rubrics do not require so narrow an interpretation; where it is the custom the priest could present his hand to be kissed (except at Masses for the dead); therefore he could at least pause. But Gavanti debars the practice sometimes seen at First Masses where the neo-priest was wont *circuire ecclesiam ad oblationem.* Gavanti-Merati, II, 7, 5 q. (I, 260 f.).

[103] This was understood, of course, when the procession started at the beginning of Mass; see *supra,* p. 15.

[104] Thus often in Alpine countries; see, e.g., the account in the *Korrespondenzblatt*

gift;[106] the gifts of all who openly lived in sin were to be refused, whether they were the unchaste or thiefs or usurers or even Roman officials who had stained their hands with blood. Similar regulations recur more than once in the ensuing years in both the East and the West.[106] At the beginning of the sixth century the *Statuta Ecclesiæ antiqua,* which stem from the neighborhood of Arles, insist that nothing is to be accepted from dissenting brethren, whether in *sacrario* or in *gazophylacio.*[107] Penitents, too, were deprived of this right,[108] and it was not restored to them until their reconciliation.[109] Similarly, the gifts of those Christians who lived at enmity were refused.[110] As late as the fifteenth century a preacher, Gottschalk Hollen, made principles of this sort his own.[111]

On the other hand, the congregation was expected to make an offering every Sunday,[112] and the wish for even a daily oblation found utterance.[113] In monasteries, after the reform of Benedict of Aniane (d. 821), a daily offering was actually incorporated into the order of service.[114] But

für den katholischen Klerus, 54 (Vienna, 1935), 73.

[106] *Didascalia,* IV, 5-8 (Funk, I, 222-228). To be sure, the chief argument proposed for prompting such action is that the widows supported by the donations could pray for obdurate sinners. But at the same time the gifts were also, at least in theory, linked with the altar; cf. IV, 7, 1, 3; IV, 5, 1, and the heading over the last of these passages in the parallel Greek text of the *Apostolic Const.:* "With what care the Sunday contributions are to be received" (Funô, 222).

[106] See a whole series of references in Funk, 224, note on IV, 6, 1; Bona, II, 8, 5 (693 f.); Corblet, I, 218 f.

[107] Can. 93, al. 49 (PL, LVI, 834): *Oblationes discordantium fratrum neque in sacrario neque in gazophylacio recipiantur.* Those gifts which were destined for the altar were deposited in the *sacrarium.*

[108] Council of Nicea (325), can. 11 (Mansi, II, 673); Felix III, *Ep.* 7, al. 13 (PL, LVIII, 926 A; Thiel, 263).—The possessed (in a wide sense) were also excluded: Council of Elvira, can. 29 (Mansi, II, 10). Cf. Dölger, *Antike u. Christentum,* 4 (1933), 110-137.

[109] Cf. in the Spanish *Liber ordinum* (Férotin, 98) the prayer at the reconciliation: *ut liceat deinceps sacrificia laudum per manus sacerdotum tuorum sincera mente offerre et ad cibum mensæ cælestis accedere.*

[110] XI Synod of Toledo (675), can. 4

(Mansi, XI, 139). On the other hand, Gregory the Great, *Ep.* VI, 43 (PL, LXXVII, 831 B), mentions his admonition to a bishop that he should not accept a gift from an opponent of his merely on account of a dispute. [111] Franz, 22.

[112] Theodulf of Orleans, *Capitulare,* I, c. 24 (PL, CV, 198): *Concurrendum est* [on Sunday] *etiam cum oblationibus ad missarum sollemnia.* — Benedictus Levita, *Capitularium collectio* (9th c.), I, 371 (PL, XCVII, 750): *Et hoc populo nuntietur, quod per omnes dies dominicos oblationes Deo offerant et ut ipsa oblatio foris septa altaris recipiatur.* Cf. *ibid.,* II, 170 (PL, XCVII, 768). As a matter of fact, in the 8th and 9th centuries even neoconverts were expected to participate in the offertory procession; see Pirminius, *Scarapsus,* c. 30 (G. Jecker, *Die Heimat des hl. Firman* [Münster, 1927] 69); J. M. Heer, *Ein karolingischer Missionskatechismus* (Freiburg, 1911), 81, 94.

[113] Benedictus Levita, *Capitularium Collectio,* II, 170 (PL, XCVII, 768). In such cases the regulations had in mind principally the offerings of those for whose intention the Mass was being celebrated; cf. *infra,* p. 22 f. The German Queen Mathilda (d. 968) had such an offertory procession every day: *quotidie sacerdoti ad Missam præsentare oblationem panis et vini; Vita,* c. 19 (MGH, SS, IV, 296).

[114] *Capitula monachorum ad Augiam directa* (Albers, *Consuetudines,* III, 105; cf. p. XX): *sunt equidem cottidie sex per*

the Sunday offering was an ancient custom, and is still kept up here and there even at the present.[115]

After the change from natural goods to money had set in, and the obvious symbolism of the offering of bread and wine had given way before more practical economic considerations, the Sunday oblation seems to have lost favor. In fact it could be pointed out that the necessary income of the Church was assured for the most part by fixed possessions and by taxes which were definitely prescribed. Still, it did seem right that the symbolic activity of the offertory procession should be kept up, at least within modest limits. The Roman reform synod of 1059 deplored the neglect of the oblations (understood here in a somewhat wider sense) and threatened the refusal of Communion.[116] In 1078 Pope Gregory VII reaffirmed the old obligation: *ut omnis Christianus procuret ad missarum sollemnia aliquid Deo offerre*,[117] pointing to Exodus 23:15 and ancient

---

brevem deputati fratres sacram offerentes oblationem. Further evidence for the zeal with which the oblation was made in these circles is found in the rules for recluses of Grimlaich, *Reg.* (9th c.), c. 16 (PL, CIII, 594 B): The cell of the anchorite should be so designed that the priest can receive the oblation through the window. Under the influence of Cluny a custom grew up, lasting into the 12th and 13th centuries, that at the early Mass on ferial days all should make an offering, and at the principal Mass each half of the choir alternately; of those who made the offering at the principal Mass a certain number were allowed to go to Communion. On feast days the superior alone made the offering. *Consuetudines monasteriorum Germ.*, n. 33; 43 (Albers, V, 28; 47); William of Hirsau, *Const.*, II, 30 (PL, CL, 1083); cf. Hilpisch, "Der Opfergang" (*Studien u. Mitteilungen*, 1941-42), 88 ff. More detailed regulations determining when one, when two, or when half of the brethren or all (as on All Souls) should make the offering, found in the *Consuetudines* of Farfa (11th c.): Albers, I, see register, p. LVI. At Masses for the dead it was everywhere customary for all the monks to take part in the offertory procession, probably to intensify the power of the intercession; Hilpisch, 90; 93. At a private Mass, according to William of Hirsau, *Const.*, I, 86 (PL, CL, 1017), the server or someone else, *si iste non vult communicare*, should make the offering. In all these cases it is commonly the offering of hosts and

wine that is meant; cf. *supra*, note 61.

[115] Through my own occasional inquiries I have found that the Sunday offertory procession, in which the whole congregation takes part, is still customary along the northern borders of the Alps, especially in many parishes of Vorarlberg and Upper Bavaria, but also in the vicinity of Schneidemühl. The proceeds belong to the church. In certain country parishes in the neighborhood of Freising (and likewise, I am told, in both the German and the Polish parts of Upper Silesia) an offertory procession is also customary on weekdays; one of the members of the family for which the Mass is being celebrated starts the procession, the others follow, in the order and degree of relationship.—I have also heard of such processions being held on Sundays about twice a month in rural parishes of the diocese of Zips in Slovakia, but here they are for a special purpose or under the auspices of a particular society (the Rosary confraternity) whose members march around the altar with burning candles.—Kramp, *op. cit.*, 361, gives accounts of Sunday offertory processions in Spanish dioceses; in some places there the practice has undergone a certain change, in that only the village or city officials take part each Sunday. A similar custom of having the superiors represent the community was to be found here and there in monasteries and convents even in modern times; Hilpisch, 93 f.

[116] Can. 6 (Mansi, XIX, 908 f.).

[117] Can. 12 (Mansi, XX, 510). Schreiber,

tradition as his endorsement.[118] But no special day was mentioned. Actually, since the eleventh century it had become more and more customary to hold the offertory procession on certain specified feast days, and even to regard it as obligatory on such days. The number of these days fluctuated at first.[119] In the later Middle Ages they were usually the greater feasts, Christmas, Easter and Pentecost, to which was added All Saints[120] or the Assumption, or the feast of the dedication of the church, or the church's patronal feast. In the many source documents in which arrangements are made for the proper carrying out of the offering, frequent reference is therefore made to the offering of the *quattuor* or *quinque festivitates*, of the four-time offering or simply the *quattuor offertoria*.[121] Even in the course of the Catholic Reform during the sixteenth and seventeenth centuries an effort was made to retain these offertory processions or to revive them.[122] But they seem to have disappeared more completely, even, than the old Sunday offerings.[123] Why these efforts at restoration miscarried is not easy to understand; the main reason, perhaps, lay in the opposition to feast day offertory processions which had become entangled in the financial overgrowths of the late Middle Ages, an opposition which, after the Council of Trent, outweighed the desire to restore the ancient symbolical rite.[124]

Gemeinschaften des Mittelalters, 306-322, offers a commentary on this legislation.

[118] This rule found also in the *Corpus Juris Canonici, Decretum Gratiani*, III, 1, 69 (Friedburg, I, 1312 f.)—Durandus, IV, 30, 32 f., stresses the obligation with great emphasis, citing many Old Testament passages.—As many later synods pointed out in more detail, the obligation embraced all those who had reached the *anni discretionis* or who had completed their 14th year or who had received their First Communion; Merk, *Abrisz*, 6, note 14.

[119] Examples since the 11th century with three to seven feast days, in Merk, *Abrisz*, 18 ff.—*Ibid.*, 14 (with note 28), a statement of Bishop Manasses of Troyes, of the year 1185, which takes for granted that the Sunday oblations are still held in many churches.

[120] The obligation is already restricted to these four days in John Beleth (d. about 1165), *Explicatio*, c. 17 (PL, CCII, 30).

[121] Schreiber, *Untersuchungen*, 7; 12 f.; 38; Merk, *Abrisz*, 18-21. A larger number of feast days is still mentioned in 1364 in an enactment of the bishop of Ermland, in Merk, 104 f.

[122] Synod of Arras (1570), *Statuta prædec.* 9 (Hartzheim, VIII, 255 f.). The synod

makes a reference to the wording of those secret prayers which commend to God the *oblationes populi*. Cf., *inter alia*, also the synod of Cologne, 1549 (Hartzheim, VI, 557), and even Constance, 1609 (*ibid.*, VIII, 912 f.).

[123] E. Martène, around 1700, still knows of offertory processions being held on certain days in French churches here and there, but they were, in part at least, restricted either to communicants or to the clergy; Martène, 1, 4, 6, 9 (I, 388 f.). Cf. Corblet, I, 222-225.—A well-known instance of the offertory procession is that which still survives at the cathedral of Milan, in a manner stately if somewhat formal: two men and two women from the *Scuolo di Sant' Ambrogio*, dressed in special attire, march to the entrance of the choir, holding in their right hand wafers or hosts, in their left a caster of wine; the celebrant accepts both. Righetti, *Manuale*, III, 253. Similarly in the 12th century, but then the men went up to the altar; M. Magistretti, *Beroldus* (Milan, 1894), 52.

[124] Cf. Jedin, "Das Konzil von Trient und die Reform des römischen Meszbuches" (*Liturg. Zeitschrift*, 1939), 59.—In the Age of Enlightenment, too, the only things

But in addition to the prescribed processions of the great feast days, the Middle Ages introduced numerous free-will oblations on those occasions when certain specific groups gathered at the Mass: at funeral Masses and the succeeding memorial Masses for the dead, at weddings, at the departure of pilgrims, and the anniversary feasts of guilds and fraternities.[125] It is precisely on such occasions that the offertory procession is often retained in country places right down to the present.[126] Of even greater import were the oblations at Votive Masses which an individual or a family ordered to be celebrated for special intentions: for the sick, for friends, for a good harvest, in honor of a saint, in manifold dangers.[127] Generally the persons concerned made an offering, as the *secreta* and the special *Hanc igitur* formulas in many cases indicate. Besides, the faithful who might be present could always bring their oblation to the altar and thus join more closely in the sacrifice. In this way arose the *oblationes cotidianœ fidelium* of which medieval documents make mention.[128]

But then it was here precisely that the close connection between participation and presentation broke down—between a sharing in the sacri-

---

that seemed to be noticed in the offertory procession were the abuses; see Vierbach, 228-233; cf. *supra*, note 82.

[125] At the beginning of the 16th century, for example, it was the custom in Ingolstadt for the members of the Hatmakers' Guild, along with their wives and servants, to form an offertory procession on the feast of St. Barbara, their patron. At academic services it was the duty of the rector of the university to see that all the prominent members of the university, the doctors, licentiates, masters and noble students, took part in the offertory procession; if they were absent he had to impose a fine of two groats. Greving, *Johann Ecks Pfarrbuch*, 115 ff., 168.

[126] Even in the dominion of Joseph II, who forbade processions precisely of this type (in the ordinance cited *supra*, note 82). Unfortunately there is no survey of present-day usages. Some instances are found in J. Kramp, "Meszgebräuche der Gläubigen in der Neuzeit" (*StZ*, 1926, II), 216; 219; *idem*, "Meszgebräuche der Gläubigen in den auszerdeutschen Ländern" (*ibid.*, 1927, II), 357 g.; 261 f. The offertory procession at services for the dead seems to be customary wherever German is the native tongue; it also exists in Holland, Belgium and Spain.—At weddings it still survives in the eastern portion of Germany, especially in upper

Silesia; R. Adamsky, in *Seelsorger*, 6 (Vienna, 1929-30), 381. Likewise in Vorarlberg, where the whole bridal party marches around the altar; Jochum (see *supra*, note 82), 266. It is also found among the Carinthian Slovenes, where the groomsman takes the lead (according to Srienc; see *supra*, note 72). In some places, as in my own native parish of Taufers in South Tyrol, it is a traditional custom to celebrate the feasts of the various trades unions with an offertory procession; the head of the union leads the procession; the offering represents the annual contribution to the church. — Elsewhere, too, the designation of a particular person to head the procession appears to be part of the offertory procession rite; cf. L. A. Veit., *Volksfrommes Brauchtum und Kirche im deutschen Mittelalter* (Freiburg, 1936), 96, where we read the following regarding a present-day custom: "In Swabia at the Herd-Mass which is celebrated before the cattle are driven out to pasture, the whole congregation parades around the altar with the herd's boy in the lead."

[127] Examples from the 14th century in Merk, 28 f., with notes 55, 56; 108.—For modern times see the account regarding Freising, *supra*, note 115.

[128] Merk, 22 f. According to Schreiber, *Gemeinschaften des Mittelalters*, 307, they

fice and the offering of gifts during that sacrifice. Just as had long been the case in regard to foundations whereby, through the gift of a larger sum, the repeated celebration of Mass was guaranteed for a period of time,[129] so now, even for individual Masses, the custom grew of quietly handing the priest a gift beforehand,[130] without thereby prejudicing the right of other offerers. The latter could still, as ever, take part at the regular offertory procession or even, for their part, secure a special share in the Mass by their own private gifts.[131] At the same time, however, the Mass stipend properly so-called makes its appearance—an honorarium paid in advance to obligate the priest to celebrate exclusively for the intention of the donor.[132] For this negotiation the ordinary term employed was *comparatio missæ, missam comparare.*[133] But the system of stipends was not adopted wholeheartedly at once, for as long as the notions were not made clear and precise enough, scrupulous hesitation and opposition were not wanting.[134]

were also called *oblationes peculiares* to distinguish them from the *oblationes communes* of Sundays and feasts.

[129] Examples of large Mass-foundations since the 11th century in Merk, 37 ff. Further discussion in Bridgett, 123-140. Early examples of the establishment of Mass-foundations in E. Bishop, *Liturgica Historica* (Oxford, 1918), 368.

[130] This is the *occulte offerre,* the *denarius secretalis.* Examples from the 14th century in Merk, 35 f. The same procedure is presupposed even earlier in two documents of 1176 and 1268 which treat of gifts *pro missis* which are donated in the church *vel extra;* Merk 40 f.; notes 15, 16.

[131] These latter represent the *recommendationes missæ* which make an appearance since the 12th century; to these *recommendationes* was frequently coupled an obligation for the priest to make mention of the name in the *Memento* or to insert a special oration. Merk, 45 f., 74, 88 f.

[132] It would be difficult to set an exact date for the first appearance of the Mass stipend. If a money gift is the essential in the notion of a stipend, then that essential can be discovered already in such cases as that mentioned by St. Augustine (*supra,* note 22), cases that must have been duplicated long before. Further, there is the account found in Epiphanius, *Adv. hær.,* XXX, 6 (PG, XLI, 413), where someone gives the bishop who had just baptized him a sum of money with the request: προσφερε υπερ εμου. — However,

the Mass stipend grew enormously in importance near the end of the Middle Ages, when the number of priests increased, and with them the number of private Masses; cf. *supra,* I, 223 ff. Thus it became possible more and more for an individual to secure the celebration of Mass for his own intention by handing the priest a present.—So far no one has written a satisfactory history of the development of the Mass stipend system. As an introduction see Merk, *Abrisz,* especially his summary, p. 91 ff. This book, which is so valuable for the documentary materials it supplies, is not always trustworthy in its historical exposition or its conclusions. A wealth of material is also gathered in Fr. de Berlendis, *De oblationibus ad altare* (Venice, 1743).

[133] Evidence since the 13th century in Merk; see the index under *comparatio.* But the word *comparare* in the Latin of the period had also the meaning "to buy." —The technical word in German at the time was *"Messe vruemen"* (that is, *frumen* or *frommen*), which signifies nothing more than to engage or order; the word does not seem to have been given the meaning "to acquire an advantage or gain" (Merk, 96); cf. Grimm, *Deutsches Wörterbuch,* IV, 1 (1878), 246 f.; J. B. Schoepf, *Tirolisches Idiotikon* (Innsbruck, 1866), 157.

[134] At Würzburg in 1342 a Magister Konrad Heger, who had impugned the *"Messe frumen"* as simoniacal, was forced to

At the Council of Trent, where one of the chief concerns was the removal of abuses regarding ecclesiastical monetary matters, this question of stipends came to the fore. But in the end the Council did nothing more than issue a general admonition to the bishops,[135] and this in turn was amplified by subsequent canonical legislation. In this later amplification the rift between gift and oblation was obviously made even wider, for according to more recent decisions it is no longer forbidden to accept a stipend from non-Catholics, even from heathens who can in no wise become offerers of the oblation of the Church.[136] Of course this does not prevent at least the stipend of the faithful—viewed in the light of ecclesiastical tradition—from continuing to be the gift to God which, like the bread and wine, is directed immediately to the sacrifice of the New Covenant. The priest accepts it with the obligation (*ratione rei detentæ*) of consummating the sacrifice for the benefit of the donor, and with the right to use for his own support whatever money is not required for the expense of celebration.[137] The faithful, however, were always to be aware of the priesthood that is theirs through baptism and confirmation, and were therefore to regard their offering of the stipend as only the start of their participation in the sacrifice, much as the Christians of an earlier era did when they not only brought their gifts to the altar but also continued to follow the celebration and partook of the Body of the Lord as a return gift.[138]

The ancient offering of the faithful survives also in another metamorphosis, the offertory collection.[139] There is no reason why this should

swear *quod actus "messefrumen" seu misse comparatio ex sui natura est oblatio . . . item quod . . . non est "messekaufen" seu misse emptio,* and so was allowed. The text in Merk, 98-100.—Others opposed Mass stipends without calling their lawfulness into question; thus Heinrich von Pflummern of Biberach (d. 1531); L. A. Veit, *Volksfrommes Brauchtum und Kirche* (Freiburg, 1936), 211. The Society of Jesus originally accepted no Mass stipends; *Constitutiones S.J.,* VI, 2, 7 (Institutum S.J., II [Florence, 1893], 96).—The Franciscans were even stricter; from the start they did not permit even *oblationes manuales;* Salimbene, *Chronik* (MGH, SS, 32, p. 422; 425).

[135] *Conc. Trid.,* sessio *XXII,* decretum de observandis: in particular the bishops were to severely forbid *importunas atque illiberales eleemosynarum exactiones potius quam postulationes.*

[136] Roman decisions in this sense since 1848, in Hanssens, *Institutiones,* II, 64 f. Hanssens considers that from the 16th

century on there came into being a new concept of the Mass stipend, by virtue of which the donor of the stipend is no longer necessarily a *missæ oblator.*—Still it seems to me we are doing justice to the facts if, with M. de la Taille, *The Mystery of the Faith,* II (transl., Archpriest Jos. Carroll; London & New York, 1950), 292 f., we view these decisions as treating certain borderline cases where the Mass stipend in its true concept as a contractual engagement is not under consideration at all, but simply an alms which is accepted and in view of which a promise is made to offer the sacrifice for the intentions expressed.

[137] M. de la Taille, *The Mystery of Faith and Human Opinion* (London, 1934), 81-197; 221-223. Other discussions of stipends can be found in the works of the canonists; e.g. Ch. F. Keller, *Mass Stipends* (Catholic University dissertation 27, Washington, 1925).

[138] Cf. *supra,* 2 f. and note 17 f.

[139] In Germany the so-called *Klingelbeutel*

not be permitted to serve a more than merely utilitarian purpose, no reason why it should not be given a deeper spirit and a more vivid form than it ordinarily presents—a spirit, by harking back to the living roots of this contribution which is primarily intended as a gift to God and which is destined for the earthly recipient only through and over the altar; a form, by confining the collection to the time of the offertory and clothing the activity with dignified and appropriate ceremonial.[140] Even though this is a collection and not an offertory procession, the basic idea of a genuine oblation is not excluded any more than it was at the rite in vogue in the stational services of the city of Rome.

2. The Offertory Chant

The entrance of the clergy at the start of Mass was made to the accompaniment of the introit sung by the *schola cantorum*. It was then but a natural application of the same principle that suggested that the "procession" of the people at the offertory and communion—both interruptions during the audible part of the Mass—should be enlivened and enriched by psalmodic song.

That this was the meaning and purpose of the offertory chant was well understood all during the Middle Ages. The chanting was called by the same name that was given to the presentation of the oblation gifts: *offertorium*,[1] *offerenda*.[2] Even in the Middle Ages the commentators stressed

or offertory basket is passed around only on certain occasions to receive the voluntary money contributions of the faithful, but in North America (the United States and Canada particularly) the collection is part and parcel of every Sunday and feast-day Mass, since the needs of the church are provided for almost exclusively in this fashion.—Regarding the criticisms leveled against the use of the collection basket in the era of the Enlightenment, see Vierbach, 232 f.

[140] One Paris pastor has the servers take up a collection on twelve collection plates which they then hold in their hands on either side of the altar during the recitation of the *secreta*. G. Chevrot, "Restauration de la Grand' messe dans une paroisse de Paris," *Etudes de Pastorale liturgique* (*Lex orandi*, I; Paris, 1944), 269-292, esp. 286 f. A discussion by Jos P. Donovan, C.M., of a similar ceremony in one of the U. S. churches, in *Homiletic & Pastoral Review*, 47 (1946), 221-222. A private response of the SRC outlawing two other such American innovations is printed in G. J. Booth, *The Offertory Rite*

in the *Ordo Romanus Primus* (Washington, 1948), 48.

[1] The name *offertorium* for the chant appears regularly even in the earliest MSS. of the Mass chant books, so that it goes back at least to the 17th century; see Hesbert, *Antiphonale missarum sextuplex*. The full title, *antiphona ad offertorium*, is less frequent; cf. Wagner, Einführung, I, 107, 121; III, 418. In the first place the word *offertorium* designated the rite of *offerre*, that is, the presentation of the offertory gifts by people and clergy; thus in the description of the course of the Mass in the *Sacramentarium Gregorianum* (Lietzmann, n. 1) and in the *Ordo Romanus* I, n. 16 (PL, LXXVIII, 944); cf. the paraphrase in the Maundy Thursday rite in the older Gelasianum, I, 39 (Wilson, 67): *Post hæc offert plebs*. Transferred to the chant, the term appears first in Isidore of Seville, *De eccl. off.*, I, 14 (PL, LXXXIII, 751): *De offertoriis*.

[2] Thus in the MS redacted by G. M. Tommasi (Tommasi-Vezzosi, V, 3 ff.); see also Amalar, *De eccl. off.*, III, 19 (PL,

this connection: the chant (they said in substance) should signify the jubilance of heart with which the faithful proffer their gifts, for (as they quoted) "God loves the cheerful giver."[3]

When all the gifts had been presented, a signal was given the singers to conclude their chanting.[4] And whenever the *oratio super oblata* was not immediately pronounced aloud—as had been customary in the early Middle Ages—complete quiet set in, a conscious silence which foreshadowed the beginning of the priestly activity of oblation,[5] although only preparatory actions immediately followed—actions like washing the hands, incensing, silent prayer. This silence was also made the object of special commentary and explanation.[6] Not till the turn of the medieval epoch, when an understanding of this silence vanished, and when in addition—as the result of the disappearance of even the feast-day procession—the chant was reduced to the antiphon as we have it at present, only then did the masters of polyphony turn their attention on greater feasts to this song—in contrast to introit and communion—and by their art they lengthened and extended it to cover the other rites which are at present comprehended under the term offertory; thus the offertory song became a connecting link with the preface.

The earliest accounts of an offertory chant come from North Africa. It seems to have been introduced there in the time of St. Augustine, first at Carthage, later at Hippo through Augustine's own efforts. In a review of his own literary activity the saint mentions that he wrote a work, now lost, taking issue with a certain Hilarius who had opposed the practice, then recently introduced, of singing psalms during the offering of the gifts and at the communion.[7] At Rome, too, the practice must have gained an entry very early, perhaps about the same time.[8] Nevertheless, on Holy Saturday the offertory chant is missing, as are the other chants of the *schola,* for this Mass retains the features of a more ancient usage. How-

---

CV, 1126 D) ; Remigius of Auxerre, *Expositio* (PL, CI, 1251 D) Pontificale of Poitiers: Martène, 4, 22, 5 (III, 300 C). —The expression appears principally in the French area and then as a designation of the offertory procession; cf. Schreiber, *Untersuchungen,* 21 ff. It survives in the French word "offrande," offering, offertory procession.

[3] II Cor. 9: 7.—Innocent III, *De s. alt. mysterio,* II, 53 (PL, CCXVII, 831) ; Durandus, IV, 27, 5.—Cf. *supra,* p. 17.

[4] *Ordo Rom.* I, n. 15 (PL, LXXVIII, 944) ; cf. *Ordo Rom.* II, n. 9 (PL, LXXVIII, 973), where the signal is given before the *Orate.*

[5] It is significant that in William of Melitona, *Opusculum,* ed. van Dijk (*Eph.*

liturg., 1939), 327, the offertory procession and the offertory chant, being purely preparatory, are still attached to the first part of the Mass; see *supra,* I, 114.

[6] Innocent III, *op. cit.,* II, 54 (PL, CCXVII, 831) : De silentio post offertorium.—Cf. *supra,* I, 108 ff.

[7] Augustine, *Retractationes,* II, 37 (CSEL, 36, 144) : *ut hymni ad altare dicerentur de psalmorum libro sive ante oblationem, sive cum distribueretur populo, quod fuisset oblatum.*

[8] But J. Brinktrine, "De origine offertorii in missa Romana," *Eph. liturg.,* 40 (1926), 15-20 ; *idem., Die hl. Messe,* 125 f., thinks differently. However, the grounds alleged by Brinktrine for a late origin of the Roman offertorium (8th c.), especially the

ever, to all appearances Rome had but a modest store of offertory chants even in the sixth century, as we can gauge from the Milanese Mass, which has preserved its antique form to the present, and in which the offertory chants give every indication of having been borrowed from Rome. In the Roman Mass itself, however, this modest store was later richly augmented by Gregory the Great and his successors.[9]

At first the offertory chant probably had the same antiphonal design as the chant at the introit: the *schola,* divided into two choirs, sang a psalm alternately, with an antiphon as prelude.[10] The psalm varied from celebration to celebration, taking into account, as far as possible, the church year with its festivals and seasons.

It is a striking fact that at a very early period the antiphonal performance of the offertory was abandoned and a responsorial style substituted for it. Even the ancient substructure of Roman offertories preserved at Milan, as mentioned above, had this responsorial design. Among these, for instance, is the offertory which the present Roman Missal assigns to the eleventh Sunday after Pentecost (also used on Ash Wednesday); in the oldest sources it has the following form:

> *Exaltabo te, Domine, quoniam suscepisti me, nec delectasti inimicos meos super me. [Refrain:] Domine clamavi ad te et sanasti me.*
>
> V. *Domine abstraxisti ab inferis animam meam, salvasti me a descendentibus in lacum. [Refrain]: Domine clamavi ad te et sanasti me.*
>
> V. *Ego autem dixi in mea abundantia: non movebor in æternum. Domine in voluntate tua præstitisti decori meo virtutem. [Refrain:] Domine, clamavi [ad te et sanasti me].*[11]

Here, just as in the chants interpolated before the Gospel, a refrain is repeated several times.[12] In line with this, the verse (as found in the oldest manuscripts with neums) is treated as a solo and consequently provided

recurrence of the same text in various formularies, rather support an earlier introduction.

[9] O. Heiming, "Vorgregorianisch-römische Offertorien in der mailändischen Liturgie," *Liturg. Leben,* 5 (1938), 152-159.

[10] The designation that occasionally appears in the sources, *antiphona ad offertorium* (see note 1 above), points to this.

[11] Antiphonary of Compiègne (Hesbert, n. 37 b; cf. n. 183).—The words in brackets are filled out in conformity with Heiming, 156. To justify this expansion we point to the fact that only the second half of the first verse is repeated at the end.—The Milanese liturgy employs this offertory chant, using the verse and the refrain on one Sunday, the second verse and the

refrain on another Sunday; the refrain in each case is set to the same melody. Heiming, 156.—The responsorial character of the offertories is marked with special clarity in the MS of Compiègne: Hesbert, n. 3 ff.

[12] In the offertories, even in the oldest texts, there is still another notable repetition that appears: within the text itself individual words or phrases are sung twice, three times or more, and they are sometimes so written even in MSS without neums. Thus in the antiphonary of Senlis the fourth verse of the 21st Sunday after Pentecost begins: *Quoniam, quoniam, quoniam non revertetur;* Hesbert, n. 196 a. There is no explanation for this exceptional usage. The Vatican *Graduale* has retained the texts thus shaped as long as they are traditional. Wagner, I, 109-111.

with the greatest melodic richness.[13] A few of the manuscripts devoted to
the solo chants therefore contain the verse of the offertory while merely
indicating the texts that pertain to the choir, namely, the initial section
and the refrain.[14] Apparently the *Gloria Patri* was not appended to these
verses.

And now we may well ask how this remarkable development came
about. It is almost certain that the main consideration was to give the
offertory chant a certain lengthiness, in view (obviously) of the people's
procession. True, this extra length could also have been achieved by having the psalm sung antiphonally right down to the end, and then repeating the antiphon which stands at the start. Perhaps the responsorial form
was chosen to make it easier for the singers to take part in the offertory
procession.[15] Besides, the main point in singing at all was not so much to
render the text of a complete psalm, but rather to achieve a festive mood,
which could be done more readily by musical means. This resulted, therefore, in a shortening of the psalm, along with a corresponding compensa-
tion both by the enrichment of the melody of the verse sung as a solo, and
by the repetition of the antiphon or a part thereof, after the manner of a
refrain. This refrain could, of course, have been turned over to the people,
but by this time there was obviously little interest in such participation
of the people in responsorial chanting, at least in the greater stational
services. We already noted in the history of the intervenient chants how
early the art of the special singers preponderated even in responsorial
song.[16] So the refrain at the offertory was from the very start reserved
to the singing choir.

It is in this responsorial form that the offertory chant regularly appears
in the choral books of the early Middle Ages. The number of psalm verses
fluctuates between one and four.[17]. That is patently more than in the other
Mass chants. The extension must be explained, as already indicated, by
the length of the offertory procession.[18] Whereas at the introit only a single
group, the clergy, wended through the church, and whereas the reception
of Communion, for which the communion chant was intended, had become since the close of the ancient era nearly everywhere a rare and
slight affair, the whole congregation continued to take part in the offertory
procession Sunday after Sunday till at least the year 1000. Not till the
eleventh century was there any noticeable drop in the regularity of this
procession; after that it was gradually limited to the greater festivals.
And, as a matter of fact, it is in the eleventh century that the offertory
verses begin to disappear from many manuscripts. By the following century this omission has become a general rule, although exceptions are to

[13] Wagner, I, 108. [14] *Ibid.*
[15] Thus Wagner, I, 108. However, for the
procedure in this offertory rite cf. *supra*,
I, 71-72. [16] *Supra,* I, 425 f.
[17] For particulars see Wagner, I, 111.

[18] For this connection see, about 1080,
Udalrici Consuet. Clun., I, 6 (PL, CIL,
652) : the *præcentor* should intone one
verse or all of them, as he sees fit, *maxime
propter offerentes.*

be found till the very end of the Middle Ages.[19] The portion which had originally been the antiphon was considered sufficient. In the Missal of Pius V only the Mass for the Dead retained a verse, and with it a refrain: *Hostias et preces* and *Quam olim Abrahœ;* this fits in once again with the fact that it was precisely at the Requiem that the offertory procession continued in use. On the other hand, the Milanese Mass has retained the offertory verse even to the present, and similarly the Mozarabic Mass.[20]

As already pointed out, the offertory was always performed by a choral group.[21] And because their singing prevented the choristers from personally taking part in the offertory procession, their place was taken by one of the members; at Rome it was the *archiparaphonista* whose duty it was to offer the water.[22] Since in the churches of the later Middle Ages the singing choir usually represented a part of the clerical choir, it was really only a nominal difference when sometimes the *clerus*[23] was mentioned and sometimes the *chorus*.[24] A reminiscence of the fact that the offertory was a chant sung by the choir survived in some of the Mass *ordos* of the Middle Ages where the texts were appointed to be recited at the high Mass, not only by the celebrant alone, but by the deacon and subdeacon along with him.[25]

As for the texts of the offertory, they are taken as a rule from Holy Scripture; for the most part, in fact, from the Psalms, as the psalmodic origin of the chant would naturally imply. One would expect that the texts chosen would be expressive of the idea of oblation and so suggest the meaning of the offertory procession. But actually this is only the exceptional case: examples of this sort are found in the offertory of the Dedication of a Church: *Domine Deus, in simplicitate cordis mei lœtus obtuli universa;* on Epiphany: *Reges Tharsis et insulœ munera offerent;* on Pentecost: . . . *tibi offerent reges munera;* on Corpus Christi: *Sacerdotes Domini incensum et panes offerunt Deo.* The offertory of the Mass for the Dead also belongs to this class; notice the verse: *Hostias et preces tibi Domine laudis offerimus.*[26] But most of the texts have a very general character or dwell on the theme of the feast being celebrated. This is true

---

[19] Wagner, I, 112.—*Ibid.,* 112, note 2, citing two MSS from the 15-16th centuries which still have offertory verses for the Christmas Mass; cf. *supra,* p. 22. The Sarum missal of the last years of the Middle Ages still presents two verses for the offertory in several Masses, but according to an adjoining rubric only one verse was then used on week-days in Advent and after Septuagesima; Ferreres, 118.—Even Durandus, IV, 27, 4, for his part, has this to say of the verses: *hodie plerisque locis omittuntur.*

[20] Here the chant is called *sacrificium*: *Missale mixtum* (PL, LXXXV, 536 A).

[21] *Supra,* p. 28.

[22] *Ordo Rom.* I, n. 14 (PL, LXXVIII, 944) ; Amalar, *De eccl. off.,* III, 19 (PL, CV, 1131 C) ; Ps.-Alcuin, *De div. off.* (PL, CI, 1246 A).

[23] Rabanus Maurus, *De inst. cler.,* I, 33 (PL, CVII, 322).

[24] *Ordo Rom.* VI, n. 9 (PL, LXXVIII, 992 C) ; Durandus, IV, 27, 3.

[25] *Liber ordinarius* of Liége: Volk, 92; Mass-*ordo* of York (ab. 1425) : Simmons, 98; so also in the present rite of the Dominicans: *Missale O.P.* (1889), 27; see also the apparatus in Volk, *loc. cit.*

[26] Because of the language it uses to de-

also of the verses which once were appended here; they regularly belonged to the same psalm or the same scriptural text as the initial verse. As a matter of fact, a reference to what was happening at the offertory procession was superfluous so long as the practice itself was alive. The chief purpose then was not, as it is in our present-day Mass chants, to explain what was already plain enough in itself; the chief thing was to give it a religious dedication.

3. The Matter for the Sacrifice

The vicissitudes which befell the offertory procession were dependent, to a large extent, on the requirements regarding the condition of the elements for the sacrifice. There can be little doubt that the bread used by Christ our Lord at the Last Supper was the unleavened bread prescribed for the paschal meal, a bread made of fine wheat flour. But the very way the accounts read readily indicates that no importance was attached to the particular paschal practice of using unleavened bread;

scribe the state of the souls departed, this offertory has been the object of much discussion; see the survey of the main solutions in Gihr, 542 f. New attempts are to be found also in *Eph. liturg.*, 50 (1936), 140-147; in the *Theol. prakt. Quartalschrift*, 91 (1938), 335-337.—One thing is sure, namely, that ideas of the hereafter are depicted here which have not had the benefit of thorough theological clarification and which, in particular, fail to distinguish plainly between hell and purgatory. Things are said about the deliverance of the departed that could easily be understood to refer to deliverance from hell. To come to details, critics point out, with disapproval, that the offertory presents the ancient and yet Christian picture of the passage of the soul through the skyey realm where the good and the bad angels battle for it; J. Stiglmayr, "Das Offertorium in der Requiemmesse und der 'Seelendurchgang,'" *Der Katholik*, 93 (1913), I, 248-255. That St. Michael plays a role in this struggle is an inference from biblical data. St. Michael frequently appears in Coptic sepulchre art; he weighs the merits of the dead, and is also the one who leads them to light (cf. *signifer sanctus Michael repraesentet eas in lucem sanctam*). A Coptic grave inscription of the year 409 prays for rest for the soul of a deceased person διὰ τοῦ ἀγίου καὶ φωταγωγοῦ ἀρχαγγέλου Μιχαῆλ.—Cf. also, from the article by H. Leclercq, "Anges," DACL, I, 2080-2161, the section on "Les Anges psychagogues" and "Les Anges psychopompes," esp. col. 2137 ff.—Our offertory originated in Gallic territory. Various elements of the text appear here in the 8th to 10th centuries; see R. Podevijn, "Het Offertorium der Doodenmis," *Tijdschrift voor Liturgie*, 2 (1920), 338-349; 3 (L921), 249-252; reviewed in *JL*, 2 (1922), 147. Cf. the additional bibliographical references in *JL*, 15 (1941), 364.—For the phrase *de profundo lacu*, etc., cf. H. Rahner, "Antenna crucis," II (*ZkTh*, 1942), 98, plus note 77; 113, note 175. Franz, *Die Messe*, 222, draws upon medieval representations of purgatory as a means of clarification.—Among the matters proposed as *abusus missæ* at the Council of Trent, our offertory was one of the things pointed out as requiring alteration: *Concilium Tridentinum*, ed. Goerres, VIII, 917. A detailed interpretation of this offertory, reconciling the wording with Catholic dogma, in Eisenhofer, II, 138 f. A study of the whole matter, sum-

what our Lord took into his hands is simply called ἄρτος, a word which could designate not only the unleavened bread used at the paschal feast but also the leavened kind which was otherwise in use among Jews as well as pagans.[1] The latter kind was therefore from earliest times considered at least licit for the Eucharist. Thus it was all the less difficult for the faithful to be able to make an offering of the bread for the altar; they just took bread from their domestic supply and brought it for divine service.[2] Both literary accounts and pictorial illustrations show us that the shape of the eucharistic bread did not differ from the shape of bread used for domestic purposes.[3] The only distinction, if distinction it was, consisted in this, that the finest and best formed loaves were selected, as was only natural. In two mosaics at Ravenna, in which the eucharistic altar is shown, the bread appears in the form of a chaplet or crown, that is, twisted like a braid and then wound into a circlet about four inches across.[4] This is the *corona* referred to by St. Gregory the Great;[5] being an out-

marizing all the above, is found in B. M. Serpelli, *L'offertorio della Messa dei defunti* (Rome, 1946); see the review in *Eph. liturg.*, 61 (1947), 245-252.

[1] Gossens, *Les origines,* 117. — Present usage requires bread made of wheaten flour, and therefore flour ground from rye, oats, barley or maize—though these are all classified as grain (*frumentum*)—is invalid. R. Butin, "The Bread of the Bible," *The Ecclesiastical Review,* 59 (1918), 113-125, concludes that nothing definite can be deduced from the scriptural narratives of the Last Supper, for although ἄρτος was generally used in classical Greek for wheaten bread, it is probably here only a translation of the Hebrew *lehem* (or rather the Aramaic *lahma*), which referred to any kind of bread. An uninterrupted tradition, however, has always favored wheaten bread.

[2] Cf. the accounts *supra*, p. 2 ff. Ambrose, *De sacramentis*, IV, 4 (Quasten, *Mon.*, 158), is quite unmistakable when he puts these words upon his hearer's lips: *meus panis est usitatus*, that is, the bread I have received in Communion is the bread I am accustomed to use every day.—It is recounted of the Egyptian monk and Monophysite bishop, Peter the Iberian (d. 487), that for the Eucharist he had a bakery produce loaves that were beautiful and white and fit for the sacrifice, and very small in circumference; these he let harden —they were therefore leavened bread— and thus he used them from time to time

as he celebrated the holy sacrifice. Dölger, *Antike u. Christentum*, 1 (1929), 33 f.; further references, *ibid.*, 34 ff.—The story in John the Deacon, *Vita s. Gregorii,* II, 41 (PL, LXXV, 103), about the lady who recognized in the particle given her at Communion the same bread she had herself baked and brought along, and who thereupon laughed and received a reprimand for so doing, is probably only a legend of the 9th century, as the formula for distribution shows (see *infra*).

In the West the XVI Synod of Toledo (693) demanded that the host-bread be prepared specially; can. 6 (Mansi, XII, 73 f.).

[3] Dölger, *Antike u. Christentum,* 1 (1929), 1-46: "Heathen and Christian bread stamp with religious symbols," esp. 33 ff. R. M. Wooley, *The Bread of the Eucharist* (Alcuin Club Tracts, 10; London, 1913).

[4] San Vitale: illustration in Braun, *Der christliche Altar,* I, plate 6; Sant' Apollinare in Classe: illustration in Dölger, *Antike u. Christentum,* 1 (1929), plate 10.

[5] *Supra*, p. 15, note 75.—The *Liber pontificalis* (under Zephyrinus: Duchesne, I, 139), mentions the *corona consecrata* that is distributed for Communion. In the *Ordo* of St. Amand (9th c.), too, the host is once referred to as *corona;* Duchesne, *Christian Worship,* 461.—The host-breads on the ivory tablet in Frankfort are also in the form of a crown; illustration, DACL,

standing product of the baker's skill, it is known to us since the third century.[6] Or sometimes the center hole of the crown was filled in, and so the bread had the form of a disk.[7] Perhaps the form most frequently used was a round loaf divided into four parts by a cross-notch (panis quadratus, panis decussatus);[8] its form easily lent itself to a Christian explanation, and so was even considered indispensable,[9] although the shape had been developed merely for a very practical reason—easier breaking—and for precisely this reason had been in common use even in pre-Christian culture.[10] Along with this there was a practice, already known in ancient times, of stamping the bread with a symbol or inscription. A breadstamp from the fourth or fifth century shows a superimposed XP symbol;[11] however, there is no proof that a bread so inscribed was intended precisely for the Eucharist. Still, in the years that followed, many of the Oriental rites formed the practice of using just such stamps or irons, although their use for leavened bread (which was less firm) was not a matter of course.[12] In most of these instances the stamp consisted of a repetition of the Cross in various patterns. In the eucharistic stamp of the Byzantine rite the somewhat larger round bread is impressed with a square which is divided into four fields by the Cross, and on these are distributed the symbols of the inscription: 'I (ησοῦς) X (ριστός) νικᾷ.

In the West, various ordinances appeared from the ninth century on, all demanding the exclusive use of unleavened bread for the Eucharist.[13] A growing solicitude for the Blessed Sacrament and a desire to employ only

III, 2476-77; Braun, Das christliche Altargerät, plate 6.

[6] Dölger, 37, note 152.

[7] Thus one of the two loaves in the representation of the altar at Sant' Apollinare; a cross is depicted in the center. Cf. supra, note 4.

[8] A. de Waal, "Hostie," in Kraus, Realencyclopädie, I (Freiburg, 1882), 672. The shape and size were about like those of a hot-cross bun.

[9] Cf. Gregory the Great, Dial., I, 11 (PL, LXXVII, 212).

[10] Dölger, 39-43. In one ancient representation of the Last Supper is seen a loaf divided into three sections by three ray-like gashes starting at the center (panis trifidus), the type which Paulinus of Nola describes as usual in his neighborhood, and which he interprets in terms of the Trinity; Dölger, Antike u. Christentum, 1 (1929), 44 f.; 6 (1940), 67.

[11] Dölger, Antike u. Christentum, 1 (1929), 17-20, with plate 9.—Similarly a bread stamp of the 6th century from Carthage, which bears, in addition, the inscription:

Hic est flos campi et lilium; H. Leclercq, DACL, V, 1367.

[12] Dölger, 21-29, along with the illustrations on plate 3-8.—The host-breads of the Orientals, excepting perhaps the East Syrians, are somewhat larger than our own large hosts and, because of the yeast, thicker, about the thickness of a finger (except in the Byzantine rite); Hanssens, II, 174-178. Thus they can always be broken.

[13] Alcuin, Ep. 69 (alias 90; PL, C, 289): panis, qui corpus Christi consecratur, absque fermento ullius alterius infectionis debet esse mundissimus. However, the point directly insisted on here is that there be no admixture (fermentum) of salt.—Rabanus Maurus, De inst. cler., I, 31 (PL, CVII, 318 D): panem infermentatum.—The oft-cited quotation from Venerable Bede is not relevant; for this and other supposed references see J. R. Geiselmann, Die Abendmahlslehre an der Wende der christlichen Spätantike, 21-36. Nevertheless Geiselmann grants that the use of unleavened bread was recognized towards

the best and whitest bread,[14] along with various scriptural considerations[15] —all favored this development.[16] Still, the new custom did not come into exclusive vogue until the middle of the eleventh century.[17] Particularly in Rome it was not universally accepted till after the general infiltration of various usages from the North. In the Orient there were few objections to this usage during olden times.[18] Not till the discussions that led to the schism of 1054 did it become one of the chief objections against the Latins.[19] At the Council of Florence (1439), however, it was definitely established that the Sacrament could be confected *in azymo sive fermentato pane.*[20] Therefore, as we well know, the various groups of Orientals who are united with Rome continue to use the type of bread traditional among them.

Reverence for the Blessed Sacrament, however, soon took a new turn both in the East and in the West, namely, in the effort to remove the bread destined for the altar farther and farther from the sphere of the merely profane. In the Orient the making of the breads was committed

the end of the 8th century. A. Michel, *Byzant. Zeitschrift,* 36 (1936), 119 f., assigns a substantially greater antiquity for unleavened bread in the West.

[14] Cf. XVI Synod of Toledo (693), can. 6 (Mansi, XII, 73 f.); cf. also note 2, *supra,* the example of Peter the Iberian.

[15] Contributing factors included, besides the consideration of our Lord's own example at the Last Supper, the interpretation of leaven as an ignoble admixture (esp. I Cor. 5: 7 f.). In addition, the early Middle Ages grew increasingly conscious of the importance of Old Testament prescriptions (Lev. 2: 4, 11; 6: 16 f., etc.; cf. also Mal. 1: 11).

[16] F. Cabrol, "Azymes," DACL, I, 3254-3260.—The opinion put forward by J. Mabillon, *Dissertatio de pane eucharistico* (Paris, 1674; = PL, CXLIII, 1219-1278), in his answer to the Jesuit J. Sirmond, *Disquisitio de azymo* (Paris, 1651), namely, that in the West it was always the practice to use only unleavened bread, is no longer tenable.

[17] J. Geiselmann, *Die Abendmahlslehre,* 38 ff.—The three little breads twisted into the form of a crown which are seen lying before the celebrant on the ivory tablet in the Frankfort municipal library (9-10th century; cf. *supra,* note 5), obviously represent leavened bread.

[18] A. Michel, *Humbert und Kerullarius,* II

(Paderborn, 1930), 112 ff., especially 117 f., 122.—The Armenians used unleavened bread as early as the 6th century, and both dissidents and Catholics have continued to adhere to the practice. However, the Council of Trullo (692), which occupied itself repeatedly with the peculiarities of the Armenians, makes no mention of this; Hanssens, II, 156 f. Among the Syrians, too, unleavened bread appears to have received the preference already in the 5th century; this practice is strictly followed by the Maronites at present; it has certainly been the custom since the plenary synod of 1736, but whether as an uninterrupted tradition from olden times is uncertain. For the rest, however, leavened bread became the rule in the Orient; Hanssens, II, 134 ff. For a thorough discussion of all the prescriptions and controversies in the oriental rites, see *ibid.,* II, 121-217. For the East Syrians (Chaldeans), see D. de Vries, *Sakramententheologie bei den Nestorianern* (Orientalia Christ. anan. 133; Rome, 1947), 193 ff.

[19] The ἄζυμα are properly ἄψυχα and imply a denial of Christ's soul; they are a relapse into the Old Testament; Christ Himself used only leavened bread. Therefore a Eucharist with unleavened bread is invalid. Geiselmann, 42 ff. Later the criticism again became less severe.

[20] Denzinger-Umberg, n. 693.

as a rule only to clerics; in any case—according to present practice—women are excluded. The baking is done in a church building to the accompaniment of prayer, and as far as possible on the day of the celebration itself.[21] Among the East Syrians there is a special rite, divided into two parts: the preparation of the dough, and the baking, both encircled with many prayers and psalms; this rite is considered a portion of the Mass-liturgy.[22] Among the Abyssinians each church has for the same purpose a little side building called *beth-lechem* ("House of Bread"), from which three freshly-baked breads are borne to the altar in solemn procession at the beginning of service.[23]

In the West, too, the making of bread was for a time given a liturgical form, particularly within the ambit of the Cluniac reform movement. According to the customs of the monastery of Hirsau in the Black Forest (eleventh century), the wheat had to be selected kernel for kernel; the mill on which it was to be ground had to be cleaned, then hung about with curtains; the monk who supervised the milling had to don alb and humeral. The same vesture was worn by the four monks to whom the baking of the hosts was confided; at least three of these monks were to be in deacon's orders or even higher rank. While working they were to keep strict silence, so that their breath might not touch the bread.[24] According to the instructions in other monasteries, on the other hand, the monks were to combine their work with the singing of psalms according to a precise plan.[25] It might be added that such a solemn act did not take place every day, but only a few times in the year.[26] Recalling the instructions regarding the Old Testament bread of proposition,[27] the desire was expressed that even outside the monasteries only the priest should prepare and bake the host;[28] in France this order was in many instances faithfully

[21] Hanssens, II, 206-217.
[22] *Ibid.*, II, 208 f.; Brightman, 247-249.
[23] Hanssens, II, 210 f. For the Mass itself only one of the three breads is selected.
[24] Bernardus, *Ordo Clun.*, I, 53 (Herrgott, Vetus disciplina monastica, 249); William of Hirsau, *Const.*, II, 32 (PL, CL, 1086 f.). Cf. Udalricus, *Consuet. Clun.*, III, 13 (PL, CIL, 757 f.), and the description of the Evesham customs in Bridgett, *History of the Holy Eucharist in Great Britain*, 76-77.
[25] Consuetudines of Fruttuaria (11th c.; Albers, *Consuetudines*, IV, 138); Lanfranc (d. 1089), *Decreta pro O.S.B.*, c. 6 (PL, CL, 488 f.). Further references in Corblet, I, 176 f.
[26] William of Hirsau, *Const.*, II, 32 (PL, CL, 1087 A): there was no regulation *quot vicibus in anno;* cf. Bernardus, *Ordo Clun.*, I, 53 (Herrgott, 249): especially

before Christmas and Easter.
[27] I Par. 9: 32.
[28] Sicard of Cremona, *Mitrale*, III, 6 (PL, CCXIII, 119 A). Even the accompanying *melodia psalmorum* is mentioned as a general regulation; Humbert of Silva Candida, *Adv. Græcorum calumnias*, n. 21 (PL, CXLIII, 946; C. Will, *Acta et scripta de controversiis ecclesiæ græcæ et latinæ s. XI* [Leipzig, 1861], 104).—Already in the canons of Theodore of Canterbury, II, 7, 4 (Finsterwalder, 322), it is expressly stated that according to Roman practice—it was different with the Greeks—the host-bread was not allowed to be prepared by women. In Theodulf of Orleans (d 821), *Capitulare*, I, c. 5 (PL, CV, 193), the preparation is reserved to priests or at least clerics: *Panes, quos Deo in sacrificium offertis, aut a vobis aut a vestris pueris coram vobis nitide ac studiose fiant.*

followed even as late as the eighteenth century.[29] Elsewhere, at an earlier period, it was thought sufficient if there was some guarantee that the pertinent ecclesiastical prescriptions were fully carried out by the persons entrusted with the operation.[30] As a result, the preparation of the hosts was done mostly in the houses of religious, more especially in convents of women.

The drift away from selecting the bread destined for the altar just from the gifts of the faithful, and towards providing for it carefully in some other way is to be noticed occasionally even at an early period.[31] But with the substitution of unleavened bread the exclusion of the faithful became a matter of course. At first the thin disks of the unleavened wheat bread were made in a larger size and were brought thus to the altar where they were broken up for the Communion of the people.[32] But since this Communion came under consideration almost only on the greatest feast days, it soon became the practice, even in the twelfth century, to shape the priest's host in the more modest size it has today, *in modum denarii.*[33] This form was then retained even on Communion days, and in order to avoid breaking up the species the custom grew of preparing the "particles"[34] for the Communion of the faithful ahead of time. And since the thin cakes from which the hosts were cut had to be baked in a metal form, the altar-bread irons,[35] it was not hard to impress at least the large hosts with some sort of decorative stamp. At first this was simply the traditional Cross; soon this became the figure of the Crucified or some other image of Christ,[36] and since there was never any general regulation in this re-

---

[29] Eisenhofer, II, 132; Corblet, I, 177 f.

[30] *Ibid.*

[31] Cf. *supra*, note 14. Venantius Fortunatus recounts how the holy queen Radegundis (d. 587) baked host-bread every year during Lent and distributed it to the churches: *Vita*, n. 16 (MGH, Scriptores Merov., II, 369 f.).—Further data in Merk, *Abriss*, 3, note 7.

[32] Humbert of Silva Candida (d. 1061), *Adv. Græcorum calumnias*, n. 33 (PL, CXLIII, 952 B): *tenues oblatas ex simila præparatas integras et sanas sacris altaribus nos quoque superponimus, et ex ipsis post consecrationem fractis cum populo communicamus.* Cf. *ibid.*, n. 32 (951 B). This explains Udalricus, *Consuet. Clun.*, III, 12 (PL, CIL, 755 D), where he tells us how even on Sundays when quite a few went to Communion, only five *hostiæ* were placed on the altar. Even as late as 1140 it was customary at the Lateran basilica to consecrate *integræ oblatæ*, which were then broken; *Ordo eccl. Lateran.* (Fischer, 48, 11. 2, 21).

[33] Honorius Augustod., *Gemma an.*, I, 35; 66 (PL, CLXXII, 555; 564).—Ernulf of Rochester (d. 1124), *Ep. ad Lambertum* (d'Achery, *Spicilegium*, 2nd ed. III, 471): *in forma nummi.*—Cf. F. de Berlandis, *De oblationibus ad altare* (Venice, 1743), 22 f.

[34] Similar designations were, of course, as ancient as Christianity itself; see E. Peterson, ["Μερίς. Hostienpartikel und Opferanteil," *Eph. liturg.*, 61 (1947), 3-12; Chr. Mohrmann, *Vigiliæ christianæ*, 1 (1947), 247 f.

[35] First mentioned in the *Miracula s. Wandregisili* (9th c.), n. 53; J. Braun, "Hostieneisen," *LThK*, V, 157. Also in Bishop Idlefons (c. 845), *Revelatio* (PL, CVI, 889). The Latin term for this mold is *ferrum* or *ferramentum;* the older English term was "bult" or "singing-iron" (the latter a name never satisfactorily explained).

[36] Honorius Augustod., *Gemma an.*, I, 35 (PL, CLXXII, 555): *imago Domini cum litteris.*

gard, many other representations made their appearance in later years, not to mention various inscriptions and legends which are found quite early.[37]

The term we now employ for the wafers destined for the Eucharist is the proleptic expression "hosts."[38] The word *hostia* was originally used only for a living thing, the sacrificial victim that was "slaughtered" *(hostio = ferio,* I strike, I kill). It could therefore be understood in the first instance only of Christ, who had become for us a *hostia (cf.* Eph. 5:2), a sacrificial Lamb. More ancient is the use of the word *oblata* for the bread offered up.[39] In other liturgies, too, we find for the still unconsecrated elements a similar use of names which signify the offering, the sacrifice.[40] The exact parallel to the transfer of meaning which we have in the word "host" is found in the Byzantine liturgy where the piece of bread selected in the *proskomide* and destined for the consecration is called "Lamb."[41]

In regard to the second element, the wine, there are also a number of questions that had to find their solution in the course of history. But only in small part do they concern the constitution of the wine itself. In the Orient, red wine was preferred, and occasionally this was also the case in the West since thus any accidental confusion with the water was more surely avoided.[42] But there was at no time any regulation that was uni-

---

[37] Cf. Ildefons, *Revelatio* (PL, CVI, 883 f., 888 f.).—These marks include the IHC or the Alpha-Omega, and the like.

[38] Instances of *hostia* in this sense since the 13th century in Du Cange-Favre, IV, 243 f. Examples from the 11th century on, in Ebner, 296, 298, 300, etc. Further references in Eisenhofer, II, 130. Perhaps we ought to cite in this connection Amalar, *De eccl. off.,* Præfatio altera (PL, CV, 990 B): *sacerdos componit hostiam in altari.*—On the other hand, cf. the more ancient meaning of the word in our canon of the Mass, where it embraces also the body and blood of Christ: *hostiam puram, hostiam sanctam, hostiam immaculatam.*

[39] See e.g., *supra,* note 32. But even in *Ordo Rom. I,* n. 13-15 (PL, LXXVIII, 943 f.), the words *oblatio* and *oblata* are already used. Cf. also XVI Synod of Toledo (693), can. 6 (Mansi, XII, 74 A): not large loaves of bread, *sed modica tantum oblata* are to be brought to the altar.—The medieval English terms, used down to the Reformation, were derived from these: "oblete," from Latin *oblata;* and "obley" ("oble" or "uble"), from the French *oublie* and the low Latin *oblea.*

[40] Brightman, 571 f.

[41] Brightman, 571: ἀμνός. The Copts, too, call the host "Lamb," Arabic *alhamal.* The designation appears in the Egyptian area in the *Canones Basilii,* c. 98 (Riedel, 275 f.), where the paschal lamb is introduced as a figure of the stainlessness of the offertory bread.—Among the Syrians the host is called "the first-born"; Brightman, 571 f. Because of the marks stamped on the bread, the host was also named "seal"; thus among the Greeks (σφραγίς) and the West Syrians. The consecrated host is called by the Syrians "(glowing coal." The same expression (ἄνθραξ) in the region of Antioch as early as the fourth century; J. E. Eschenbach, *Die Auffassung der Stelle Is. 6 : 6, 7 bei den Kirchenvätern und ihre Verwendung in der Liturgie* (Würzburger theol. Preisaufgabe: Würzburg, 1927), esp. 34 ff. —The designation μαργαρίτης, *margarita,* "pearl" is also used in the same sense by Syrians and Greeks, and in the Byzantine liturgy, especially for the consecrated particles distributed to the faithful; Brightman, 585, *s.v.* "Pearl." The designation is traceable to early Christian tradition; Dekkers, *Tertullianus,* 46, note 3.

[42] A Paris synodal decree (ab. 1210) found

versally obligatory. When, later on, the use of the purificator became general, that is, since the sixteenth century, white wine has been commonly preferred because it leaves fewer traces in the linen.⁴³

In some few districts of the Orient where wine is hard to get—especially among the Copts and Abyssinians—a substitute was and is created by softening dried grapes (raisins, that is) in water and then pressing them out; this process is permitted even among Catholics, with the proviso that at least the start of fermentation is awaited.⁴⁴

Much more profound were the discussions regarding the mixture of the wine. According to ancient rule some water must be mingled with the wine. This was not, indeed, a native Palestinian custom, but a Greek practice which was observed in Palestine in Christ's time.⁴⁵ As early as the second century this admixture for the Eucharist is expressly mentioned.⁴⁶ Later, under pressure of Gnostic circles that rejected all wine-drinking, there was a trend here and there to replace the wine entirely by water.⁴⁷ In one of his detailed writings Cyprian repudiated such a procedure which was practiced by some ignorant people, declaring it contrary to the institution of Jesus.⁴⁸ On the other hand, it was he who emphasized the symbolic sense of the commingling. Just as the wine receives the water

---

among the *Præcepta synodalia* of Bishop Odo, n, 28 (Mansi, XXII, 682 E) ; Synod of Clermont (1268), c. 6 (*ibid.*, XXIII, 1190 E). Cf. also Corblet, I, 200 f.— William de Waddington is quoted as saying "E le vin vermail ou blanc"; see *Robert of Brunne's Handlyng Synne*, F. J. Furnivall, ed. (EETS, OS, 119 [1901], 7301.—There can be no doubt that tradition has always required a grape wine *(vinum de vite)*.
⁴³ So the I Provincial Synod of Milan (1565), II, 5 (Hardouin, X, 650 f.) ; the synods of Ameria (1595) and Majorca (1639), in Corblet, I, 200.
⁴⁴ Hanssens, II, 217 f.—The Council of Winchester, 1076, under Lanfranc, took the precaution to legislate lest through ignorance priests should attempt to celebrate either with water alone, or with beer as a substitute for wine: *Quod sacrificium de cerevisia, vel sola aqua non fiat; sed solum modo aqua vino mixto* (Mansi, XX, 459).
⁴⁵ Strack-Billerbeck, IV, 613 f.; cf. 61 f., 72; G. Beer, *Pesachim* (Giessen, 1912), 71 f., 106.—The dilution of wine with water is specially noted at the Passover supper, so there is no doubt that our Lord actually used a mixed chalice. Origen alone seems to deny this, for symbolic

reasons; *Hom. in Jerem.*, 12, 2 (PG, XIII, 380-381).—Although the Gospels do not expressly mention this mixing of water and wine, the oriental anaphoras in their account of the institution as a rule do; see *infra*.
⁴⁶ Justin, *Apol.*, I, 65; 67 *(supra, I, 22 f)*; Irenæus, *Adv. hær.*, V, 1; 2 (Harvey, II, 316; 319 f); Inscription of Abercius (Quasten, *Mon.*, 24) : κέρασμα διδοῦσα μετ' ἄρτου.
⁴⁷ The material is gathered in A. Harnack, *Brod und Wasser* (TU, 7, 2, [Leipzig, 1891], p. 115-144).—Among the heretical sects using only water were the Ebionites mentioned by Irenæus (see note 49 below) and the Aquarii mentioned by Augustine)PL, XLII, 42). A eucharist with water appears in the apocryphal Acts of the Apostles (2nd cent.), and still survives in certain monkish circles in the 5th century (Theodoret, *Hæreticarum fabularum comp.*, I, 20). For an answer to Harnack's thesis that in the early Church water and wine were both considered as equally licit, see C. Ruch, "Messe," II, 6: DThC, X, 947-955.
⁴⁸ Cyprian, *Ep.*, 63, ad Cæcilium (CSEL, 3, 701-717).

in itself, so has Christ taken to Himself us and our sins. Therefore, the mixing of the water with the wine symbolizes the intimate union of the faithful with Him to whom they have bound themselves in faith; and this union is so firm that nothing can sever it, just as the water can no longer be separated from the wine. From this, Cyprian concludes: "When someone offers only wine, then the blood of Christ begins to exist without us; but when it is only water, then the people begin to exist without Christ."[49] These words were often repeated and extended all through the Middle ages.[50] Along with this symbolism, another made an early appearance—the reference to the blood and water which flowed from Christ's side on Calvary.[51] But in the foreground was always the symbolism of Christ's union with His Church. This was intensified by the statement in the Apocalypse (17:15), that in the water the peoples are represented.[52] The jubilant nations, who are represented by the singers, offer it up. As a picture of the people who still need expiation, it is blessed, while the wine as a rule is not.[53] In the course of the Middle Ages the little ceremony was made the basis for theological reflections: the commingling of the water shows pointedly that in the Mass not only is Christ offered up, but the Church too; still this can be done only by the priest who is not separated from the Church.[54] Precisely because of this symbolism, wherein he perceived the handiwork of God being belittled by human admixture, Luther declared the commingling of the water unfitting inasmuch as it was indicative of our oneness with Christ.[55] Therefore the Council of Trent explicitly defended the practice and threatened its rejection with an anathema.[56]

In the Orient, too, there were some stubborn battles over the droplet of water. Behind the reference to the blood and water from Christ's side,

---

[49] *Ibid.*, n. 13 (CSEL, 3, 711). A symbolism tending in this direction is already hinted at in Irenæus, *Adv. hær.*, V, 3 (Harvey, II, 316): The Ebionites, who do not believe in Christ's divinity, "reject the mixture of the heavenly wine and prefer to be only earthly water, by not admitting God into the admixture with themselves."—Cf. also Clement of Alexandria, *Pæd.*, II, 2 (PG, VIII, 409 f.).

[50] See the references in F. Holböck, *Der eucharistische und der mystische Leib Christi*, 200 f.

[51] John 19: 35. This last connection is found already in Ambrose, *De sacr.*, V, 1, 4 (Quasten, *Mon.*, 164). Ambrose makes an additional reference to the water which came from the rock that was Christ (I Cor. 10. 4). Both concepts also in Eusebius Gallicanus (5th c.), *Hom.*, 16 (PL, LXVII, 1055 A; ascribed to Cæsa-

rius, but cf. ed. Morin, 925: *Magnitudo*). —Only the symbolism of blood and water is stressed in the Carolingian examination questions, *Ioca episcopi*, in Franz, 343, note 1; further references in Holböck, 201 f.

[52] According to various early scholastic authors the water which flowed along with the blood from Christ's side also refers to the people whom Christ had redeemed; Holböck, 202. — Cf. also the Council of Trent, sess. XXII, c. 7.

[53] For exceptions, see *infra*, p. 65 ff.

[54] Lepin, *L'idée du sacrifice de la messe*, 96 f., 142 f.

[55] M. Luther, *Formula missæ et communionis*, n. 16 (Kleine Texte, 36, p. 15).

[56] *Concilium Tridentinum*, sess. XXII, c. 7 (Denzinger-Umberg, n. 945); can. 9 (n. 956).

which was also the usual conception here, the Orientals found a theological symbolism that took a somewhat different turn. Matching the acuteness of the christological strife in the Orient, the wine and water were made to represent the divine and human natures in Christ. The Armenians, whose ranks were penetrated by a radical Monophysitism (which taught that after the Incarnation there could be question of only one nature in Christ, namely, the divine), eliminated the admixture of water as early as the sixth century, at any rate surely before 632. In spite of some waverings, they held to their position, even though, in their repeated efforts to unite with Byzantium and with Rome, this point always formed a block.[57]

The exclusion of leaven, too, was given a similar theological signification by the Armenians. "The Chalcedonian error of the two natures" and the practice of "tainting [the Sacrament] by the fermenting of the bread and by [the admixture of] water" are occasionally mentioned in Armenian sources in one and the same breath.[58] Because of this theological background the Catholic Armenians have taken up the use of water with the wine.

In the Roman liturgy of today the water that is added is only a small amount in comparison with the wine, but in the liturgies of the Orient it forms, and has formed, a goodly portion of the contents of the chalice.[59] Amongst the Syrian Jacobites it has been the practice from olden times to add an equal quantity of water to the wine,[60] and this practice corresponds to what was customary in the surroundings of the nascent Church.[61] But in the Occident, too, there is the instance of the synod of Tribur (895), which required that the chalice contain two-thirds wine and one-third water,[62] and even in the thirteenth century it was considered sufficient to insist that more wine be taken than water.[63] But after that there is a definite shrinking of the minimum required by the symbolism, and at the

[57] Hanssens, II, 250-271. Even as late as the 14th century, this Monophysite argument is much in evidence among the Armenians; Hanssens, II, 261. The Armenian use of undiluted wine was formally condemned at the Trullanum (692), can. 32 (Mansi, XI, 956 f.). The dissident Armenians are the only group of ancient Christians who do not use the "mixed chalice"; Catholics, of course, follow the Roman usage.

[58] So the Armenian historian Stephen Asoghik (ab. 1025), who thus describes the principal object of an Armenian synod of the year 726; Hanssens, II, 163.

[59] Hanssens, II, 242-250.

[60] Ibid., 244, 248.—This regulation, which already appears in a West-Syrian source

in 538, is repeated in a Nestorian ruling about 900; the latter, however, declares that even up to three-fourths water is still permissible; ibid., 248 f.

[61] Cf. Strack-Billerbeck, IV, 58; 614. With Sharon wine it was the rule to take one-third wine and two-thirds water.

[62] Can. 19 (Mansi, XVIII, 142). A similar rule was in force at Rouen even in 1700; de Moléon, 366.

[63] Durandus, IV, 30, 21. Still even William of Melitona (d. 1260), Opusc. super missam, ed. van Dijk (Eph. liturg., 1939), 328, following his somewhat earlier Franciscan model, demands that the water be added only in modica quantitate, because (he says) we are as nothing in comparison with Christ.

same time the spoon appears, to make it easier to avoid exceeding the minimum.[64]

4. Laying the Offerings on the Altar.
The Accompanying Prayers

When the offerings of bread and wine are ready as required, there is still the problem of fitting them into a richly developed liturgy, there is still the question of how and by whom they are to be deposited on the altar, how they are to be disposed there, and particularly whether and how, in these moments before the ancient traditional *Eucharistia*, they are to be drawn by word and gesture into the sacrificial action.

The older Roman liturgy provided only for the well-regulated external activity,[1] and for the single prayer, the *oratio super oblata*, which, however, was said in the name of the whole assembly in a loud voice. When transferred to Frankish territory the external action was soon modified in several ways (principally by being coupled with the offertory procession, which itself was altered through the years), and was enriched by other preparatory acts, like the incensation and the washing of the hands. In addition, each step of the activity was joined by a significant word, spoken by the *liturgus* not aloud, but only softly to himself. Even the prayer itself acquired further addition. This showed the same half-private character and tried especially to connect individual desires with the offering. Moreover, all this liturgical growth in the Frankish realm was not regulated from one appointed center, but emanated rather from different points and criss-crossed in the most diverse ways over all the lands of Christendom. As a result the Mass books of the later Middle Ages contain at the oblation a veritable jungle of new prayers and texts. The diversity and multiplicity of these formulas and their grouping is so great that a

---

[64] *Ordo Rom.* XV, n. 81 (PL, LXXVIII, 1325 D): *post aquæ benedictionem ponit cum cochleari tres guttas aquæ.* The *tres guttæ* were already required at the Synod of Brixen in 1318; see J. Baur, "Die Brixner von 1318" (in the *Festschrift zur Feier des 200 jährigen Bestandes des Haus- Hof- und Staatsarchivs*, Vienna, 1949). Cf. *Cod. Iur. Can.*, can. 814: *modicissima aqua.* This formulation appears first in the Decretum pro Armenis (Denzinger-Umberg, n. 698).—The little spoon *(cochlear)*—and with it obviously the idea of a small amount of water, which underlies its use—appears towards the end of the 13th century in northern France; Braun, *Des christliche Altargarät,* 446 f.

The spoon is not mentioned in the Roman missal, but its use was approved by the SRC, Feb. 6, 1858 (n. 3064 ad 4). It is commonly used in Spain and Ireland; but elsewhere, e.g., Italy, is even at present entirely unknown.

[1] *Supra,* I, 71-2.—For a better understanding of this chapter, it is necessary to distinguish two purposes in the offertory ceremonials: (1) the provision of the elements of bread and wine, and (2) a ritual presentation of these elements at the sacrifice, arranging them on the altar and commending them to God. Cf. Alan Clark, "The Function of the Offertory Rite in the Mass," *Eph. liturg.,* 64 (1950), 309-344.

classification appears well-nigh impossible.² Nevertheless, if we want to get a closer understanding of the form of the oblation rite as it appears in the Roman Missal—comparatively scant though it be—we may not by-pass this jungle entirely.

The point of view which prevails today, in which the worth and importance of the *Eucharistia* is once more discovered and which is swayed but little by the novel medieval customs, makes it appear that the *offertorium* grew out of the fact that the offertory procession had vanished in the course of the Middle Ages and the vacancy which thus arose had to be filled out by these ceremonies and prayers. Besides, according to this conception, these prayers are ascribed in the first instance to the private Masses which were then coming to the fore, and which seemed to be especially adapted to such an enrichment. These are the two assertions that are repeated even by great authorities;³ but these opinions are in urgent need of investigation. We shall therefore try to follow, in rough outline at least, the development of the forms from their beginnings.

The first thing we notice—right within the framework of the old Roman oblation scheme—is the quiet praying of the celebrant, even before he says the *secreta*. The eighth-century Frankish recensions of the *ordo* of John the Arch-chanter prescribe that at a solemn high Mass, after the offerings of the faithful and the clergy have been arranged on the altar, the celebrant take his own offering in hand and lifts hands and eyes to God in silent prayer.⁴ This is also indicated in the other Roman *ordines*. The fact that the celebrant turned to the surrounding clergy to ask for their prayers is also mentioned here.⁵

The first brief wording of such an offering prayer is presented in the Sacramentary of Amiens. The heart of this prayer appears to be the humble offering of the gifts already prepared, which are designated as offerings of the faithful⁶ and therefore presuppose an offertory procession.

---

² Eisenhofer, II, 141.

³ Eisenhofer, II, 139. The derivation from private Mass, in Batiffol, *Leçons*, 21; 144. The void left by the disappearance of the procession, in Fortescue, 305.

⁴ *Capitulare eccl. ord.* (Silva-Tarouca, 198): *Ipse vero pontifex novissime suas proprias duas [oblationes] accipiens in manus sua[s], elevans [read: elevatis] oculis et manibus cum ipsis ad cœlum, orat ad Deum secrete, et completa oratione ponit eas super altare.* Thereupon the archdeacon arranges the chalice, and the bishop, bowing low, pronounces the *oratio super oblata.*—Similarly the parallel monastic text of the *Breviarium* (ibid.), where the same rite is repeated with the chalice: *similiter offerat et vinum.*

⁵ *Breviarium* (loc. cit.) : *Tunc vero sacerdos dextera lævaque aliis sacerdotibus postulat pro se orare.*—As the bad Latin reveals, these sources bring us back before the Carolingian reform, in the middle of the 8th century (Silva-Tarouca, 180 f.; but see M. Andrieu's new study, which dates the *Breviarium* and the *Capitulare* towards the end of the 8th century).

⁶ The two-part prayer reads: *Hanc oblationem, quæsumus, omnipotens Deus, placatus accipe, et omnium offerentium et eorum, pro quibus tibi offertur, peccata indulge. Et in spiritu humilitatis . . . Domine Deus* (Dan. 3 : 39 f., nearly as at present). Leroquais, *Les sacramentaires*, I, 39 f. The whole Mass-*ordo* edited by the same author, *Eph: liturg.*, 1927, 441.—The

The next thing we specially note in these more ancient oblation prayers and the practices connected with them, is that about the year 1000 they have grown tremendously, and that they are especially extended at the start of the oblation, before the chalice is brought to the altar. They have an essentially intercessory character; the offering is done "for" *(pro)* certain specified purposes and persons. This is evidently the consequence of recollections of the Gallican liturgy.[7] The trend can be traced even in Amalar. In his explanation of the *offerenda* he cites Old Testament requirements and then names a series of requests *pro quibus offerre debeamus sacrificia*:[8] for the fulfillment of vows which were made in affliction, for the expiation of our sins, for the royal house, for the ecclesiastical estates, for peace. His younger contemporary, Walafrid Strabo (d. 849), feels compelled to combat the opinion that a special offering and a special petition must be made for each intention, and that it was not possible to beg *una petitione pro multis*.[9] Along with this another factor, reverence for certain mysteries of faith, found expression both in the prayers themselves [10] and in the manner in which the oblations were distributed on the altar. Indeed we encounter this trend about the same time in the East as well as in the West. While in the older Roman *ordines* little importance was attached to the manner of composing the oblations on the altar,[11] in the Carolingian territory we hear of two crosses which the priest is to build *de oblata* and place next to the chalice.[12] Even as late as 1100 some missals from the orbit of Monte Cassino demand that the oblations be arranged *in modum crucis*.[13] In Spain, around 845, a Bishop Ildefons gives even more detailed directions: whereas on ordinary days only one bread is laid out, on Sundays five breads are to be taken and arranged crosswise; on Christmas and some other feast days seventeen breads, of which five are to form a cross, the other twelve a circle around the chalice; on Easter and Whitsunday forty-five breads, for which a combined cross-

---

first formula *(Hanc . . . indulge. Per.)* is also found later similarly employed: Leroquais, I, 126; 155, 211; II, 25; 34 f.

[7] Cf. the texts below for the Memento of the Living.

[8] Amalar, *De eccl. off.*, III, 19 (PL, CV, 1127).

[9] Walafrid Strabo, *De exord. et increm.*, c. 22 (PL, CXIV, 948). Regino of Prüm, *De synod. causis*, I, inquis. 73 (PL, CXXXII, 190), also insists that only one *oblata* be offered for all intentions.

[10] See *infra*, p. 46 ff.

[11] The*Ordo Rom.* I, n. 14) PL, LXXVIII, 944), merely says of the archdeacon: *componit altare.* Only the *Ordo of St. Amand* directs him to take the *oblatæ* and

form three or five *ordines* on the altar (Duchesne, *Christian Worship*, 460).—In the mosaic of San Vitale in Ravenna two breads are placed symmetrically to the right and left of the chalice; Braun, *Der christliche Altar*, I, plate 6. Likewise in the mosaic of Sant' Apollinare, where Melchisedech, represented as the celebrant, holds a third bread in his hands; Dölger, *Antike u. Christentum.* 1 (1929), table 10.

[12] Rabanus Maurus, *De inst. cler.*, I, 33, additio (PL, CVII, 324 D). Illustrations in the Stuttgarter Bilder-Psalter (Stuttgart illuminated psalter) of the 9th century; Fiala, 190.

[13] Ebner, 309; Fiala, 203. Clearly there is question here of hosts for the Communion of the monks.

form is sketched.[14] Even in the eleventh century the Trier *Liber officiorum* takes a stand against those who insist that, for the sake of the number three, three *oblatæ* are always to be consecrated.[15] Besides a regard for the Communion of the faithful, such efforts indicate also the tendency to give symbolical expression to certain offertory-motifs or at least to give prominence to symbolic numbers.[16]

If we turn our glance to the contemporaneous development of the Byzantine Mass, we find that it has gone even a step farther in the same direction. In its arrangement of the bread-oblation there are at work not only the effort to indicate symbolically certain mysteries of faith, but also the most important petitions. While the other oriental liturgies have no further prescriptions in this matter, and even on Communion days merely use and consecrate a correspondingly larger bread,[17] in the Byzantine Mass it has gradually become a rule since about the year 1000 that in the *proskomide* five breads are to be laid out, of which, however, only certain particles are to be selected for the altar and there to be arranged in a fixed manner. From the first bread the "Lamb" is cut; from the second, a particle (the "All-holy") in honor of the Blessed Virgin; from the third nine particles in honor of specified saints who are named; from the fourth, an arbitrary number for the living who are to be recommended

---

[14] Ildefons, *Revelatio* (PL, CVI, 883-890; also in Martène, 1, 4, 6, 10 [I, 389]). Similar directions in Irish sources, but apparently only since the 11th century; see the references in K. Burdach, *Der Gral* (Stuttgart, 1938), 206.—This formation of certain figures is also found in the Old Spanish Mass (as we will see later) at the *fractio*, even at an earlier date.

[15] Franz, 374.—This use of the number three is traditional; cf. the mosaic of Sant' Apollinare (*supra,* note 11). According to *Ordo Rom.* I, n. 48 (PL, LXXVIII, 958), the archdeacon hands *oblatas tres* to each of the cardinal priests who concelebrate with the pope on great feasts.—Since the late Middle Ages it has been the practice at solemn papal Mass to bring three hosts to the altar, of which two, however, are immediately consumed by the *episcopus sacrista*, just as he also tastes the wine and water; *facit probam,* as the *Ordo Rom.* XV (about 1400), n. 81 (PL, LXXVIII, 1325 D), puts it; cf. Martène, 1, 4, XXXVII (I, 681 E). This is what we today call the *prægustatio*, a survival from those perilous days when poison played a part in public life. Cf. Martène, 1, 4, 6, 14 (I, 391 f.); Brink-

trine, *Die feierliche Papstmesse,* 19 f. Details regarding this darksome background in Corblet, I, 381.—Provision is still made for the *prægustatio* in the *Cæremoniale episc.,* II, 8, 60 f.; cf. II, 8, 11; I, 11. In Narbonne, about 1700, it was still observed day after day; de Moléon, 255.

[16] At any rate, odd numbers still play a role (cf. *supra,* I, 387). According to the *Canones Basilii,* c. 99 (Riedel, 277), there should be one bread or three; according to the Ordo of the Lateran basilica (Fischer, 81), one or three or five. At Cluny there were, as a rule, three or five *oblatæ;* in making the prescribed crosses, etc., the priest was to use the center one; Udalricus, *Consuet. Clun.,* II, 30 (PL, CIL, 718 B); cf. I, 6, 8 (652 f.); III, 12 (755 f.).

[17] Hanssens, II, 185. It is only among the Armenians, the Maronites and the Malabar Christians that special smaller breads are added for the Communion of the faithful.—In former years there were many discussions in the various rites regarding the number of the host-breads, and different odd numbers were decided upon. But the practical viewpoint proved an obstacle. One West Syrian bishop in early times

to God; and from the fifth, similarly, a number for the dead.[18] These all
have their proper position and arrangement on the *discos,* the large paten
on which they are carried to the altar and on which they remain lying to
the left of the chalice. The portions cut from the first three breads form a

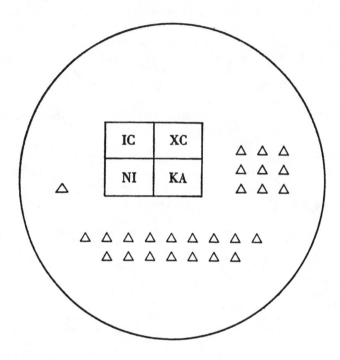

row in the middle of which lies the "Lamb," the portions for the living
form a second row, those for the dead a third.[19]

Amongst the Russians it is—or was—possible for the faithful also to
contribute a particle to the second or third row, a portion of the bread

directed the deacon to add one loaf for
every ten communicants. Hanssens, II,
196-200.

[18] Brightman, 356-359; Hanssens, II, 182-
185; *ibid.,* 185-196, the historical presentation of the practice. The typikon of the
Empress Irene (about 1100) orders that
seven breads are to be used; of these the
fourth is offered for the emperor, the fifth
for the deceased monks, the sixth for the
dead of the imperial family, the seventh
for the living of that family. Hanssens, II,
188 f.

[19] This sketch patterned after Mercenier-
Paris, *La prière des églises de rite byzantin,* I, 216.—In the dissident churches
these particles are not consecrated with
the "Lamb," but as a rule are put into the
chalice before the Communion of the people and, thus moistened with the Precious
Blood, are removed by means of the little
spoon and given in Communion; Hanssens,
II, 200-206. The particles of host-breads
that remain are dispensed to the faithful
after Mass as *antidoron.* Among the uniate
Ruthenians the regulations regarding the

they had presented before Mass being used for this purpose; thus they would be drawn closer to the sacrifice.

In the Occident such a symbolic commemoration for stipulated intentions was never carried through. But for that very reason these latter have stretched to greater proportions in the prayers. Around the same year 1000 we see the bishop at a solemn high Mass stepping to the altar after the offertory procession of the people and clerics, and pronouncing a whole series, more or less long, of offertory prayers in which the most important requests are set forth. And all are formed according to one scheme that plainly displays Gallican features, though previously there were some tentative efforts to model them more or less strictly on the pattern of prayer in the Roman canon.[20] They begin with the phrase *Suscipe sancta Trinitas hanc oblationem quam tibi offero pro . . .*; then the request is named and continued with an *ut*-clause; the conclusion can be either Gallican or Roman.[21] The formula is met as early as the ninth century in Northern France, either as a single prayer[22] or as a series of prayers in multiple variation.[23] In the Mass *ordines* of the succeeding years it appears in use for the most diverse purposes; for the celebrant himself, for the congregation and its benefactors, for the King and the Christian people,

particles have more recently been greatly modified; *ibid.*, 183 f.

[20] See *supra*, note 6, the formula *Hanc oblationem*. It is obviously modeled on the *Hanc igitur oblationem* of the canon, which is meant for the naming of intentions. The same formula in the 11th century in the sacramentaries of Limoges (Leroquais, I, 155) and Moissac (Martène, 1, 4, VIII [I, 539 A]); in Limoges still as principal oblation prayer in the Missal of 1438: Martène, 1, 4, 6, 16 (I, 393 D). The formula is also in the Mozarabic *Missale mixtum* (PL, LXXXV, 536 C). — Other echoes of the canon formularies are to be seen in the terms of address, e.g., *clementissime Pater*: Sacramentary of Angers (10th c.): Leroquais, I, 71.—For the present-day *Suscipe sancte Pater*, see *infra*, p. 57.

[21] Besides the Roman *Per Christum* the Gallican *Qui vivis* is often found, and occasionally also *Per te Jesu Christe* (thus in a Dominican missal of the 13th century: Sölch, 77, note 152) and *Quod ipse præstare dignetur* (missal of Fécamp: Martène, 1, 4, XXVI f. [I, 637; 640]). For the Gallican origin of these closing formulas, see Jungmann, *Die Stellung Christi*, 84 f., 88, 105, note, 43 f.):—The address, *sancta Trinitas*, is also Gallic. It

is totally unknown in the older Roman liturgy. *Ibid.*, 80, 91, 109; cf. 193 ff.

[22] As a *memoria Imperatoris* in the Sacramentary of Sens (L. Delisle, *Mémoire sur d'anciens sacramentaires* [Paris, 1886], 107): *Suscipe, sancta Trinitas, hanc oblationem quam tibi offerimus pro Imperatore nostro illo et sua venerabili prole et statu regni Francorum, pro omni populo christiano et pro elemosinariis nostris et pro his qui nostri memoriam in suis continuis orationibus habent, ut hic veniam recipiant peccatorum et in futuro præmia consequi mereantur æterna.*—In the Prayerbook of Charles the Bald (ed. Felican Ninguarda, Ingolstadt, 1583, p. 112 f.) it is turned, with only tiny modifications, into a prayer for laymen, *Oratio quando offertis ad missam pro propriis peccatis et pro animabus amicorum.* It begins: *Suscipe, sancta Trinitas atque indivisa unitas, hanc oblationem quam tibi offero per manus sacerdotis tui, pro me . . . ut . . .*; then follows Psalm 115: 12 f., slightly altered, and the continuation as a prayer for the dead.—Further examples in sacramentaries of the 9th and 10th centuries in Leroquais, *Les sacramentaires*, I, 52; 59; 63; 71; 76.

[23] Two sacramentaries of S. Thierry near Reims (second half of the 9th and end of the 10th century; see Leroquais, I, 21 f.,

for various persons amongst the living, for the sick, for the dead. At the top is usually the formula which has been retained till now and which, in imitation of the canon of the Mass, presents as the first intention of the offertory the remembrance of the mystery of redemption,[24] with which is linked the commemoration of the saints.[25]

In some Mass books since the eleventh century as many as thirteen formulas of this type are found one after the other.[26] They were appointed to be said by the celebrant when, after the offertory procession,[27] the

---

91 f.) agree in having the present-day formula *(in memoriam)* along with three others: for the king, for the priest himself, and for the dead; Martène, 1, 4, IX; X (I, 545; 548 f.). So, too, the Sacramentary of S. Amand (end of the 9th c.): Leroquais, I, 56; similarly that of Corbie (without the formula for the priest): *ibid.*, 27.— The Sacramentary of Amiens, which originated in the second half of the 9th century, contains the prayer cited in note 6 above, followed by *Suscipe sancta Trinitas,* with five divergent clauses (the four already mentioned, plus a formula for the Christian people); Leroquais (*Eph. liturg.,* 1927), 441 f.—Various later versions are brought together in F. Cabrol, "Diptyques: XII," *DACL,* IV, 1081-1083.

[24] Sometimes a phrase is added that implies a kind of apology for having included so many intentions: *Suscipe, sancte Trinitas, hanc oblationem quam offero imprimis, ut iustum est, in memoriam . . .* Thus, e.g., in the Mass-*ordo* of Séez (PL, LXXVIII, 248 B).

[25] Related in content to this formula is the last oblation formula which is found in the Stowe missal (ed. Werner [HBS, 32], 9), inserted by Moelcaich (9th cent.) immediately before the *Sursum corda.* It reads: *Grata sit tibi hæc oblatio plebis tuæ, quam tibi offerimus in honorem Domini nostri Jesu Christi et in commemorationem beatorum apostolorum tuorum ac martyrum tuorum et confessorum, quorum hic reliquias specialiter recolimus n. et eorum quorum festivitas hodie celebratur et pro animabus . . . et pœnitentium nostrorum, cunctis proficiant ad salutem. P. D.*

[26] Thirteen formulas in the Missa Illyrica: Martène, 1, 4, IV (I, 509 f.),—The missal of St. Lawrence in Liége (Martène, 1, 4, XV [I, 590 f.]) has seven; the Mass-

ordo of Gregorienmünster (*ibid.,* XVI |I, 598 f.]) has six; an 11th century missal from S. Denis (*ibid.,* V [I, 524 f.]) has four; likewise the missal of Troyes (*ibid.,* VI [I, 533]) of the same period, and the Mass formulary originating in Séez (PL, LXXVII, 248).—For the most part, therefore, these are all Mass books from the so-called Séez group (*supra,* I, 93 f.).— Italian examples from the 11th century in Ebner, 171; 304 f., 337 f. Several formulas having the same content but with a different form of address in a Milanese Mass-*ordo* of the 11th century: *Codex sacramentorum Bergomensis* (Solesmes, 1900), p. 91, note 1.

[27] A series of Mass-*ordos,* all of this period but of different provenience, plainly indicates that there was an offertory procession in which at least the clergy participated; thus in the Missa Illyrica (Martène, 1, 4, IV [I, 508 B]) a rubric precedes: *Tunc convertat se suscipere oblationes presbyterorum aliorumque.* After receiving the offering of bread properly so called, he recites this series of oblation prayers.—Similarly (but without *aliorumque*) the Mass formulary of Séez: PL, LXXVIII, 248 A; missal of Monte Cassino (11-12th c.): Ebner, 309, cf. *ibid.,* 346; missal of St. Lambrecht (1336): Köck, 120.—Bernold of Constance, *Micrologus,* c. 10 f. (PL, CLI, 983 f.) is equally clear; he mentions first the procession, then the arrangement of the gifts on the altar, then the prayers *Veni sanctificator* and *Suscipe sancta Trinitas* which are to be said *composita autem oblatione in altari.*—It is possible that the older arrangement was for the celebrant to say these prayers when the altar was being readied after the procession of the people and before he received the gifts of the clerics; cf. *Ordo*

bread-oblation had been arranged on the altar by the deacon,[28] and very likely after his own oblation was added,[29] but before the chalice was brought to the altar.

But soon other influences began to be felt, influences that resulted from the transformation of the offertory procession. The offertory procession survived above all at the great feast day high Masses which the rubrics of the Mass books usually spoke of, but the offerings made at it were no longer brought to the altar. The bread-oblation consisted mostly of just the thin host which the priest himself offered as his own gift. Therefore, before starting these prayers the celebrant had to await this gift. And in view of its smallness, it is quite understandable that he would also wait till the chalice was prepared; this, as we shall see in a moment, was usually handed to the celebrant along with the paten. The series of offertory prayers therefore moves back to a later position. In fact there must even have been some question whether the prayers were not actually to be postponed till after all the other preparatory activities, which had meanwhile often gained a place in this spot—the hand-washing, the incensation—and so inserted immediately before the petition for prayer (Orate fratres) which had long since found a secure place; it would thus serve as the last personal concurrence in the official priestly act, the sacrificial work of the canon of the Mass, which was then usually thought of as starting with the secreta.[30]

About the same time another trend was to be noticed, a trend towards limiting the number of these prayers. Bernold of Constance (d. 1100) appears as advocate for this limitation, praising, as he does, those who were content with a single formula in which they commended to God both living and dead.[31] The formula which he means, and which he suggests the priest should say inclinatus ante altare, follows the traditional type:

Rom. II, n. 9 (PL, LXXVIII, 973 B): orat . . . et suscipit oblatas de manu presbyterorum.

[28] Mass formulary of Séez (PL, LXXVIII, 248 C): Tunc puro corde offerat Domino oblatas altari superpositas dicens.

[29] In the Missa Illyrica the rubric before this series of prayers states that these are to be spoken cum oblationes offeruntur; however, the whole series is introduced between the first and the second formulas with which the bishop offers up the oblation which he holds in his hands: Martène, 1, 4, IV (I, 508 E-510 E). Both the Mass-ordo of Troyes and that of Gregorienmünster presupposes that at least at the start the celebrant holds in his hands and lifts up his own bread oblation: ibid., i, 4, VI, XVI (I, 532 C; 598 B). Cf. supra, note 26. Elsewhere a bow was prescribed,

and this implies that the celebrant's gift already lay on the altar.

[30] See infra, p. 82 f. — Jungmann, Gewordene Liturgie, 105 ff.—An indication that a certain need was felt for preparatory prayers is the fact that here and there we come across the prayer Aperi Domine os meum which at present is found, slightly modified, at the beginning of the breviary. Sacramentary of S. Denis (11th c.): Martène, 1, 4, V (I, 526 B); Spanish missals of the 15th century: Ferreres, 130.

[31] Bernold of Constance, Micrologus, c. 11 (PL, CLI, 984): Quæ utique oratio a diligentioribus ordinis et comprobatæ consuetudinis observatoribus tam pro defunctis quam pro vivis sola frequentatur.— Amalar, too, had already taken a stand against the multiplication of prayers; see supra, I, 385.

Suscipe sancta Trinitas. It is the prayer we still recite with bowed head just before the *Orate fratres,*[32] therefore at the later spot as indicated above; formerly this prayer was found at the very top of the list of formulas.

In this place, just before the *Orate fratres,* and said by itself in this bowed attitude,[33] the prayer is to be found even in an earlier period,[34] and in Italy itself,[35] as a component part of the Roman offertory plan there developing.[36] Not till later does it appear at the same place in various countries outside Italy.[37]

In contrast to the present-day wording, the formula regularly showed two expansions, particularly in the older texts. The list of redemptive mysteries commemorated—a list transferred from the canon: Passion, Resurrection, Ascension—was usually enlarged to read: *in memoriam in-*

---

[32] Bernold, *loc. cit.,* quotes merely the introductory words (and preceding them, the *Veni sanctificator,* which was not presented as an offertory prayer). But he gives the full text later, c. 23 (PL, CLI, 992 f.) : *Suscipe, sancta Trinitas, hanc oblationem, quam tibi offerimus in memoriam passionis, resurrectionis, ascensionis Domini nostri Jesu Christi et in honorem sanctæ Dei genitricis Mariæ, sancti Petri et sancti Pauli et istorum atque omnium sanctorum tuorum, ut illis proficiat ad honorem, nobis autem ad salutem, et illi pro nobis dignentur intercedere, quorum memoriam agimus in terris. Per Christum.* William of Hirsau (d. 1091), Const., I, 86 (PL, CL, 1017), also suggests that the same invariable formula, *Suscipe sancta Trinitas,* be always used. The inclusion of the dead, as Bernold recommends, was expressly inserted, among others, in the version which was used in the ancient Cistercian rite : ... *ut eam acceptare digneris pro nobis peccatoribus et pro animabus omnium fidelium defunctorum.* Bona, II, 9, 2 (710 f.). Cf. also *infra,* note 42.

[33] The parallel formula for the dead remained connected with it the longest. Thus it is found before the *Orate fratres* in the Sacramentary of Modena (after 1174): Muratori, I, 92; in a missal from lower Italy about 1200: Ebner, 322; in two Hungarian Mass books, one about 1195, the other the 13th century: Radó, 43 (n. 17) ; 62.—Both formulas are found in their original place before the offering of the chalice in the Sacramentary of Limoges (11th c.) : Leroquais, I, 155. This pair of formulas

is still found in Franciscan Mass books in the 15th century: Martène, i, 4, XXVI ff. (I, 637; 640; 644) ; cf. *ibid.,* 1, 4, 6, 16 (I, 393 A). Still it seems that the second formula was used only in Masses for the dead.—A third formula for the living survived in a Salzburg missal about 1200: Köck, 124.—The Milan oblation rite has retained to the present day two formulas of our *Suscipe sancta Trinitas* type for ordinary days, and three for Sundays and feasts; they are recited with arms outstretched. Preceding these is another formula of the same kind, but with a modified form of address; this prayer is said bowed and follows at once after the double offering. *Missale Ambrosianum* (1902), 168.

[34] The oldest example appears to be the "ninth or tenth century" supplement in the St. Gall. MS. 348 of the Frankish *Sacramentarium Gelasianum,* ed. Mohlberg, p. 247; cf. XCIX.

[35] Examples from the 11-13th century in Italian books, especially in the region of Monte Cassino, in Ebner, 298; 301; 310; 322; 326; 337; Fiala, 205 f. Here, it seems, we have an innovation which spread from the North, following the Cluniac reform; cf., for the bowing, the sacramentary from the Cluniac monastery of Moissac (11th c.) : Martène, 1, 4, VIII (I, 539 A).

[36] Innocent III, *De s. alt. mysterio,* II, 60 (PL, CCXVII, 834 C) does not cite the formula, but notes that the priest says a prayer with bowed head.

[37] For Lyons, see Ebner, 326 (Cod. XII, 2) ; Martène, 1, 4, XXXIII (I, 659). For south Germany, Köck, 119 ff.; Beck, 328;

carnationis, nativitatis, passionis, resurrectionis, ascensionis D. n. J. C. The mention of saints was made, as a rule, according to the formula: *et in honore* [38] *sanctorum tuorum, qui tibi placuerunt ab initio mundi, et eorum quorum hodie festivitas celebratur et quorum nomina hic et reliquiæ habentur.* [39] In one group of texts, however, the first expansion was soon dropped. In the second expansion, other additions were made; here and there even in the eleventh century the name of the Blessed Virgin was added; a little later, and at first outside Rome, the names of the Princes of the Apostles were inserted; [40] lastly, the Baptist. In place of this comprehensive expansion, however, a simple *istorum* was inserted, especially in the later Mass books. [41]

As for the other contents of the formula, there seems to have been but little concern over the *ut*-clause in which the prayer is continued, and this corresponds exactly with its origin as a formula of commemoration. The clause appears to have been appended only to round out the form: May the sacrifice bring honor to the saints, and to us salvation

---

308; Hoeynck, 373 f.; cf. Martène, 1, 4, XXXII (I, 656).

[38] Lebrun, *Explication,* I, 315-317, points out that most medieval texts and even the older editions of the Missal of Pius V have the reading *in honore* in our formula: "in honoring," "on the day when we honor" (similar in meaning to the *in veneratione B.V.M.* of the Marian preface); not *in honorem,* "in honor," "to honor," because in conjunction with the phrase that follows, *ut illis proficiat ad honorem,* such a wording would be essentially tautological. In some churches, in fact, the oration was said only on feast days: *ibid.,* 317. However the Congregation of Rites, on May 25, 1877, decided in favor of *in honorem: Decreta auth. SRC,* n. 3421, 3.

[39] Both amplifications already in the oldest texts: Sacramentary of S. Thierry (9-10th cent.): Martène, 1, 4, IX; X (I, 545 B; 548 E).—The present-day wording (without *Johannes Baptista*) appears in Bernold, *Micrologus,* c. 23 (note 32 *supra*).—Material from many manuscripts is assembled and studied in P. Salmon, O. S. B., "Le 'Suscipe sancta Trinitas' dans l'Ordinaire de la messe," *Cours et Conférences,* VI (Louvain, 1928), 217-227.

[40] Mass-*ordo* of Gregorienmünster: Martène, 1, 4, XVI (I, 598 C). Further references in Salmon, 222; but the *Micro-*logus (see previous note) is not taken into account.—Some few Mass-books contain a special formula of the *Suscipe sancta Trinitas* in honor of all the saints, with corresponding expansions: Sacramentary of S. Denis (11th c.): Martène, 1, 4, V (I, 524 f.).

[41] *Supra,* note 32; Salmon, 223. This *istorum* is also found in the Ordo of the papal chapel about 1290; ed. Brinktrine (*Eph. liturg.,* 1937), 203.—Probably the original idea of this *istorum* was to indicate that the priest should insert saints' names of his own choosing—like the later "N." Cf. the enumeration of various saints in the second part of the *Confiteor* in the Augsburg *Ordinarium,* as found in the commentary "Messe singen oder lesen," which was printed several times since 1481; here we read: . . . *s. Katharinam, istos sanctos et omnes electos Dei,* and the commentator advises what names are to be included. Franz, 751. In cases like this, the older Roman liturgy generally used the word *ille;* see *Ordo Rom.* I, n. 7 (PL, LXXVIII, 940 C), and *infra,* the discussion of the Memento formulas.—In Salmon, *loc. cit.,* a discussion of some purely linguistic variants of the *Suscipe sancta Trinitas.*—In place of the present *offerimus* the more ancient texts have mostly *offero.* So also the Dominican rite; see Bonniwell, *A History of the Dominican Liturgy* (New York, 1944), 186.

and the efficacy of their intercession. The function of the formula as a substitute for all other versions and as an epitome of all other offertory intentions is thus only imperfectly expressed.[42]

Elsewhere an oration of the same type, *Suscipe sancta Trinitas*, continued to be connected with the presentations of the offerings, while before the *Orate fratres* another prayer appeared, spoken likewise in the bowed posture of these oblation prayers; the prayer is that of Azarias (Dan. 3:39 f.): *In spiritu humilitatis*. This formula appeared quite early as a rival to formulas of the *Suscipe sancta Trinitas* type.[43] In the Norman-English liturgy it actually won out and appears there as the concluding oblation prayer just before *Orate fratres*.[44] This is true likewise in the liturgies of many religious orders,[45] whereas in the Roman-Italian plan it is found very early, to be sure, but usually it appears as in today's design, immediately after the offering of the chalice.[46] Thus we have in our present-day arrangement two prayers which, even by the bodily posture

---

[42] Here and there attempts were made to render the formula complete. Thus the Regensburg missal of 1485 inserts: (. . . *ad salutem*) *et omnibus fidelibus defunctis ad requiem* (Beck, 238); similarly the Freising missal of 1520 (Beck, 308) and the Missal of Upsala of 1513 (Yelverton, 15). In the present-day arrangement of the offertory prayers the mention of the dead already occurs in the first oblation prayer. And so Batiffol, *Leçons*, 23, had grounds for thinking the Missal of Pope Pius V could just as well have omitted our formula.

[43] See *supra*, p. 42, note 6. Further sources, presumably from the 9th to the 11th centuries, in Lebrun, *Explication*, I, 284. That northern France is the point of origin and spread is confirmed by the Sacramentary of S. Denis (middle of the 11th c.); here, too, there is the rubric: *inclinatus ante altare dicat;* Martène, 1, 4, V (I, 526 C).

[44] For Normandy see examples in Martène, 1, 4, XXXVI f. (I, 673 C, 678 A); Legg, *Tracts*, 42; 60. For England examples in Legg, *Tracts*, 5; 221; Maskell, 94 f. For Sweden see Yelverton, 15. Likewise in Spain; see Ebner, 342; Ferreres, 130 (n. 520).

[45] For the Cistercians, see Franz, 587. For the Carthusians, see Legg, *Tracts*, 101; *Ordinarium Cart.* (1932), c. 26, 20. For the Dominicans, Sölch, *Hugo*, 82; Bonni-

well, *op. cit.*, 186. Also in the widespread Benedictine *Liber ordinarius* of Liége: Volk, 92.

[46] A third formula, of like import and purpose, originally destined (to judge from its wording) to be said right after the preparation of the chalice, disappeared in the course of time. It read as follows: *Domine Jesu Christe, qui in cruce passionis tuæ de latere tuo sanguinem et aquam, unde tibi Ecclesiam consecrares, manare voluisti, suscipe hoc sacrificium altari superpositum et concede, clementissime, ut pro redemptione nostra et etiam totius mundi in conspectum divinæ maiestatis tuæ cum odore suavitatis ascendat. Qui vivis.* In the Missa Illyrica it follows immediately after the chalice is set on the altar: Martène, 1, 4, IV (I, 511 B); so, too, in the Mass-*ordo* of Séez (PL, LXXVIII, 249 A) and in central Italian Mass formularies of the 11th-12th centuries (Ebner, 298; 313; Fiala, 204; Muratori, I, 90 f); also in a Missal of 1336 from St. Lambrecht (Köck, 121). In the Missal of St. Lawrence in Liége it accompanies the raising of the chalice: Martène, 1, 4, XV (I, 591 D). But at the same time in some central Italian formularies of the 11th-12th centuries it appears immediately before the *Orate fratres*, in one instance marked as exchangeable with the formula *Suscipe sancta Trinitas* (Ebner, 301) and with the rubric: *Tunc inclinet se sacerdos ante altare et dicat* (*ibid.*, cf. Ebner, 296; 341).

with which they are said, give an indication that they are meant to anticipate the oblation prayers of the canon.[47]

Another point to remark in this connection is that even in the more recent texts where these prayers are employed as accompaniment to the external act of offering, yet the endeavor is made to join the bowed posture with the gesture of offering. With a demeanor that is quite courteous—forms of social intercourse do recur often enough in divine worship—the gifts are presented to the Almighty while *In spiritu humilitatis* [48] or *Suscipe sancta Trinitas* is said.[49]

Not much later in origin is a second rank of text elements, but these are much more intimately connected with the external rite and essentially directed to the purpose of explaining the visible activity.[50] We can therefore understand them best if we combine our study of them with an exposition of the outer activity itself.

First of all, the altar has to be readied. At a high Mass even today, immediately before the offertory—or during the *Credo* if there is one—the corporal enclosed in the burse is carried by the deacon to the altar and there spread out, while otherwise the priest carries it to the altar when he comes in, and spreads it out before Mass. This corporal is nowadays reduced to a very modest size; only at a solemn papal Mass does it cover the entire width of the altar, and in this case it is laid out over the altar by a (Cardinal) deacon and the subdeacon at the start of the offering of gifts.[51] This was the practice already in the Roman services of the

---

[47] Both formulas as at present in the Mass formulary of the 11th century from Monte Cassino: Ebner, 340 (Cod. C 32); cf. 309 f. But generally the use of both formulas is infrequent in Italy till the *Missale Romanæ Curiæ* became common and the Franciscans put in their appearance (cf. Ebner, 314). However, cf. for Lyons, starting only in the 13th century: Ebner, 316; Martène, 1, 4, XXXIII (I, 659); for the south German area, Beck, 237 f.; Köck, 122.

[48] The commentary of William de Gouda which first appeared in 1486, *Expositio mysteriorum missæ*, has this to say: *Elevato igitur calice, parum suspiciens, devote affectans, humili corde* pronus, *genibus parum flexis, ut ille dignissimus dignetur aspicere: In spiritu humilitatis.* Quoted in M. Smits van Waesberghe, "Die Misverklaring van Meester Simon van Wenlo" (*Ons geestelijk Erf*, 1941), 303. This refers to the double offering of chalice and paten, as it occurred according to Netherland formularies; cf. *ibid.*, 325-327.

[49] Camaldolese Sacramentary of the 13th century: *patenam cum oblatis accipit et inclinans se ad altare suppliciter dicit hanc orationem: Suscipe sancta Trinitas;* Ebner, 355.—Similar was the custom in England about the same period: The priest picks up the chalice and the paten, *et inclinato parum elevet calicem, utraque manu offerens Domino sacrificium . . .: Suscipe sancta Trinitas;* Frere, *The Use of Sarum,* 75. As late as 1617 the Cistercian missal orders: *elevatis patena cum pane et calice et genuflectens dicat;* Schneider (Cist.-Chr., 1926), 349.

[50] The principle that every action should be embellished by an accompanying statement is noticeable, for example, in the penitential discipline as early as the 9th century and becomes more and more operative with time; Jungmann, *Die lateinischen Buszriten,* 91 ff., 212 f. The formulas of absolution have their origin here.

[51] Brinktrine, *Die feierliche Papstmesse,* 18.—In the Roman stational Masses of the 7th century (see *supra*, I, 71) two deacons

eighth century.[53] In the Middle Ages this action was frequently accompanied with prayer.[58]

When the altar is ready, the gifts can be brought to the altar and properly arranged. For this, too, there was a well-balanced plan in the Roman stational services: the archdeacon, assisted by the subdeacons, selects the oblation from amongst the gifts offered by the people and disposes it on the altar; the pope puts the bread-offering of the clerics and his own next to it; the archdeacon then places the chalice beside the bread offering of the pope.[54] All this without a word being spoken. But such silence was intolerable to the Frankish liturgical concept. In the rite as we find it in the North about the year 1000, a rite developed upon the groundwork of the Roman arrangement as adapted in the Frankish realm, we see how fully this supposed deficiency was provided for. The greatest wealth is supplied in the so-called *Missa Illyrica*,[55] even if we take no account of the overgrowth of apologiæ which we here encounter both at the start of the offering and again in the course of it.[56]

stretched the long corporal over the altar from end to end. The deacon's ritual spreading of the corporal at the *Credo* must be viewed as a trace of that more ample ceremony of the early Middle Ages; see Lebbe, *The Mass: A Historical Commentary* (Westminster, 1949), 54-55.

[52] *Ordo Rom.* I, n. 12 (PL, LXXVIII, 943); *Ordo Rom.* II, n. 9 PL, LXXVIII, 972 C). Whereas in the early centuries only the altar coverings made of precious stuffs—from which our antependium derives—remained on the altar outside divine service, by the 7th century it was customary to leave cloths made of linen on the altar continually. A trace of the more ancient practice is to be seen even today on Good Friday when the altar cloths are put on the altar only at the start of service. Among these was the *palla corporalis* (so called because it came into contact with the body of Christ), our present-day corporal; it was so folded that after the host-breads and the chalice were set on the altar it could be used as a covering over them. But since the later Middle Ages a special pall for the chalice was prepared. Braun, *Die liturgischen Paramente*, 184-192; 205-212; Eisenhofer, I, 353-360. In some countries two corporals were—and are—employed, Ferreres, 126, n. 499 f. Even today the Carthusians still use only a corporal folded over the chalice; *Ordinarium Cart.* (1932), c. 26, 20.

[53] Central Italian Mass books of the 12th century order the priest to say Ps. 67: 29 f. *(Confirma hoc . . . munera)* and to add: *In tuo conspectu Domine hæc munera nostra sit placita, ut nos tibi placere valeamus. Per.* Ebner, 333; cf. 337, 340; Fiala, 203. Another formula *(Per hoc sacrificium salutare)* in a Florentine missal of the 11th century; Ebner, 300.—The formula *In tuo conspectu* also in the Mass-ordo of the papal chapel about 1290; ed. Brinktrine *(Eph. liturg., 1937)*, 201; and with the rubric: *Ad corporalia displicanda*, in Spanish Mass-books even of the 15th-16th centuries, Ferreres, 126.

[54] *Supra*, I, 71-72.—The practice of placing the chalice to the right, the host to the left continued into the later Middle Ages. However, according to the Mass rubrics of the Dominicans proposed by Humbert in 1256 the host was placed in front of the chalice, as is done now in the Roman Mass. See Wm. Bonniwell, *A History of the Dominican Liturgy* (N.Y., 1944), 125 and note 5.

[55] Cf. *supra*, I, 79; 94.

[56] Martène, 1, 4, IV (I, 508-512); the *apologiæ*, pp. 506 ff., 509 CD).—*Apologiæ* were also inserted at the hand-washing: *ibid.*, i, 4, V (I, 525 f.).—A prayer in the *apologia* style is already mentioned for this location by Amalar, *De eccl. off.*, III (PL, CV, 1130 C), when he says that the priest, before receiving the gifts of the clergy,

Even at the presentation of the gifts during the offertory procession, each of the donors is to pronounce a little phrase, the recipient responding each time with a counter-phrase.[57] Then when the deacon accepts from the subdeacon the bread-oblation intended for the celebrating bishop, this act is to be accompanied by a blessing: *Acceptum sit omnipotenti Deo et omnibus sanctis eius sacrificium tuum.*[58] When he hands it to the bishop, the latter receives it with a similar blessing, and the deacon meanwhile in his turn pronounces a blessing, and with it offers up the gift to God.[59] Then the bishop himself offers up the gift to God, either with a similar blessing, which comprises approximately the first half of our present-day *Suscipe sancte Pater,*[60] or with some other suitable formula;[61] and then follows the long series of oblation prayers which were spoken of in a previous paragraph.

Similar is the procedure when this series of prayers is finished and the chalice is brought over to the celebrant.[62] As a rule this is a chalice already filled, at least with wine.[63] The deacon hands it to the celebrant with a

---

prays *pro suis propriis delictis remissionem, ut dignus sit accedere ad altare et ad tactum oblatarum.* [57] *Supra,* n. 18.

[58] Later also in amplified form. A Spanish missal of the 15th century appoints for the deacon *ad hostiam ponendam* the prayer: *Grata sit tibi hæc oblatio, quam tibi offerimus pro nostris delictis et Ecclesia tua sancta catholica.* After J. Serra di Vilaro: *JL,* 10 (1930), 392.—Cf. Ferreres, p. LX, LXIX, LXXX, CV, CXI, 126, where, however, it is no longer appropriated to the deacon.

[59] *Suscipe, Domine, sancte Pater, hanc oblationem et hoc sacrificium laudis in honorem nominis tui, ut cum suavitate ascendat ad aures pietatis tuæ. Per. L. c.,* 508 D.

[60] The bread is therefore reckoned as the oblation of all through whose hands it passed: subdeacon, deacon, bishop. The formula with which the celebrant makes his offering to God is only a personal prayer, not a priestly one; this is plain from the fact that the formula is used, practically unchanged, for the lay people when they make their offering. Thus in a sacramentary from upper Italy, 12th century (Ebner, 306) :*Tibi Domino creatori meo;* cf. *supra,* p. 18, note 99. The deacon, too, often uses this formula when he hands the priest the paten with the host; thus in an Italian pontifical of the 11-12th century: Ebner, 312; in the Sacramentary of Modena (before 1174) : Muratori, I, 90.

[61] In the Italian pontifical just cited the priest is told to recite Ps. 19: 2-4; see Ebner, 312.

[62] As a rule, only one chalice was brought to the altar. But there were exceptions, as was to be expected in view of the Communion of the people *sub utraque specie.* Thus at Monte Cassino even in the 11th century there were seven chalices; Martène, 1, 4, 6, 11 (I, 390). St. Boniface asked Rome concerning this, but received the answer that it was not seemly *duos vel tres calices in altario ponere*: Gregory II to Boniface (726) (MGH, Ep. Merow. et Karol. ævi, I, 276).—In the Eastern liturgies, too, several chalices on the altar are mentioned: *Const. Ap.,* VIII, 12, 3 (Quasten, *Mon.,* 212, 1. 21) ; Greek liturgy of St. James (Brightman, 62, 1. 17 ; 28) ; East Syrian liturgy (*ibid.,* 295, 1. 18; Greek liturgy of St. Mark (*ibid.,* 124, 1. 8; 134, 1. 10). Cf. Andrieu, *Immixtio et consecratio,* 240-243.

[63] It is the deacon who sees to the pouring of the wine; thus, e.g., in the Missal of Troyes (about 050) : *Diaconus vergens libamen in calicem dicat: Acceptum sit omnipotenti Deo sacrificium istud*; Martène, 1, 4, VI (I, 532 D). Elsewhere the deacon recites the same phrase when he sets the chalice upon the altar; central Italian Mass books of the 11-12th century in Ebner, 328, 337; Fiala, 204; Sacramentary of Besançon (11th c.) :Leroquais, I, 139.

prayer composed of several combined psalm verses.[64] Thereupon the celebrant offers it up with the oblation prayer that is customary today, *Offerimus*,[65] or with some like formula. Still, even here there are early examples where the celebrant simply accepts the chalice with a psalm verse[66] or even—as a parallel to the host—with a blessing as a response.[67]

Later on, the procedure was compressed more tightly or more plainly coordinated. After the bread-oblation began to consist mostly of the thin host of the priest (a change which is matched by the change in the size of the paten—now small and flattened), it became more and more the custom for the deacon to bring over the entire offering as a unit:[68] the chalice with the wine, and lying upon it the paten with the host.[69] In this more recent, more developed rite, the deacon addresses the celebrant with the psalm verse (49:14): *Immola Deo sacrificium laudis et redde Altissimo vota tua*. The celebrant answers him with a different psalm verse (115:4 [13]): *Calicem salutaris accipiam et nomen Domini invocabo*.[70] However,

---

[61] *Immola Deo sacrificium laudis et redde Altissimo vota. Sit Dominus adiutor tuus, mundum te faciat, et dum oraveris ad eum exaudiat te* (Pss. 49: 14, 27: 7; 90: 15). Missa Illyrica: Martène, 1, 4, IV (I, 511 A); Mass-*ordo* of Séez (PL, LXXVIII, 249 A) and certain related Mass arrangements (among others Ebner, 301, 309; Fiala, 203).

[63] Missa Illyrica, *loc. cit.*

[64] With Ps. 115: 3 (12) f. *(Quid retribuam)*, which is placed before the *Immola* of the previous note; both Sacramentaries of S. Thierry (9 and 10th c.): Martène, 1, 4, IX f. (I, 545 D, 549 B); Mass-*ordo* of Gregorienmünster (11th c.), *ibid.*, XVI (I, 599 B).—With Ps. 115: 4 (13) *(Calicem salutaris)*: Mass-arrangement of St. Peter's (beginning of 12th c.), Ebner, 333.

[67] Mass-arrangement of St. Peter's (previous note): *Acceptum sit omnipotenti Deo sacrificium istud*. Cf. *supra*, note 63.

[68] Otherwise in the Missal of St. Vincent-on-Volturno, wherein (about 1100) the Communion of the whole convent is still presupposed; here the subdeacon carries the chalice in his left hand, and in his right *patenam cum oblatis;* Fiala, 203, 216.— Since about the year 1000 the paten has been the small circular plate it now is, slightly depressed to fit the *cuppa* of the chalice; Braun, *Das christliche Altargerät*, 211. Regarding this gradual reduction of the size of the paten, see *infra*, p. 306 ff.

[69] Among the Cluniacs at a private Mass

this carrying of both chalice and paten (with host) was customary already in the 11th century. William of Hirsau, *Const.*, I, 86 (PL, CL, 1015 D; cf. Udalricus, *Consuet. Clun.*, II, 30 (PL, CIL, 724 B). Medieval allegory, taking up and expanding certain Greek suggestions, looked upon the chalice as a symbol of Christ's tomb, the paten as the stone. Upon it lay the host with the folded corporal—Christ's body and the burial cloths. A popular verse incorporating these ideas is found in Sicard, *Mitrale*, III, 9 (PL, CCXIII, 146). Here too we might mention the designation of the corporal as *sindon* (Ebner, 328; Fiala, 204).—In the Regensburg missal about 1500 (Beck, 267; cf. 266) the pall is described as the gravestone: *Accipe lapidem et pone super calicem*. Likewise in a Brixen missal printed in 1493, p. 130v: *Hic ponitur lapis super calicem*.—According to the Mass-*ordo* of Liége (16th c.), the priest should say, while covering the chalice: *In pace factus est locus eius . . .* Smits van Waesberghe (*Ons geestelijk Erf*, 1941), 326. The same phrase in a similar connection in a Hungarian missal of the 14th century: Radó, 68. The same reference to the repose of the grave in the missal of Riga (15th c.): v. Bruiningk, 81.

[70] *Ordinarium O.P.* of 1256 (Guerrini, 239); cf. Bonniwell, *A History of the Dominican Liturgy* (New York, 1944), 124; Legg, *Tracts*, 78. This is still done in the present-day Dominican rite, but

other formulas were also in use.[71] Then the priest lifts chalice and paten just as they were handed to him and pronounces a brief oblation for both together. In the Dominican liturgy it is a version of the *Suscipe sancta Trinitas*, short but enriched as to contents;[72] similarly for the most part in England,[73] often also in France, where the same oblation rite had a wide influence.[74]

now the priest's response begins with *Quid retribuam: Missale O.P.* (1889), 18, 27; the deacon's phrase is dropped at a simple Mass; *ibid.*, 18. Similarly in Tongern about 1413; de Coswarem, 126.—According to the Benedictine *Liber ordinarius* of Liége, the deacon's phrase is transferred to the priest, who continues with *Quid retribuam* (Volk, 92). Likewise in a Sacramentary of the 12th century from Camaldoli (Ebner, 296). Consistently, then, the priest says: *Immolo . . . et reddam;* thus in the Rhenish missal (13th c.) described by F. Rödel (*JL*, 1924, 84); cf. missal of Riga: v. Bruiningk, 81.—Without the deacon's phrase frequently in many later Mass arrangements: Martène, 1, 4, 6, 16 (I, 393, B.D.); *ibid.*, 1, 4, XVII; XXXIII (I, 600 E; 659 B); Legg, *Tracts*, 41; 59. —A Premonstratensian missal of 1539 has expanded the formula with reference to the paten: *Panem cœlestem et calicem salutaris accipiam;* Waefelghem, 60, note 1.—According to the Cologne *Ordo celebrandi* of the 14th century (and likewise as late as 1514) the priest started the offertory with *In nomine Patris . . . Quid retribuam;* then the oblation prayers followed; Binterim, IV, 3, p. 222; cf. *ibid.*, 227. Similarly in the Cistercian rite of the 15th century (Franz, 587) and in the rite of St. Pol-de Léon (Martène, 1, 4, XXXIV [I, 662 E]).

[71] Bernold of Constance, *Micrologus*, c. 23 (PL, CLI, 992): *Cum sacerdos accipit oblationem, dicit: Acceptabile sit omnipotenti Deo sacrificium nostrum.* Likewise the Missal of Fécamp (about 1400): Martène, 1, 4, XXVII (I, 640 B); Augsburg missal of 1386 (Hoeynck, 373); cf. the Styrian missals: Köck, 119; 122; 125. Also in Riga: v. Bruiningk, 81.—According to a Pontifical of the 11-12th century in Naples (Ebner, 312), the priest responds to the *Immola* with the Roman penitential oration: *Præveniat.*—An early collection of short oblation formulas in

the Hungarian Sacramentary of Boldau (about 1195): Radó, 43 (pertinent here especially n. 8; 10, 13, 14).
[72] *Missale O.P.* (1889), 18 f.; *Suscipe sancte Trinitas hanc oblationem, quam tibi offero in memoriam passionis Domini nostri Jesu Christi, et præsta ut in conspectu tuo tibi placens ascendat et meam et omnium fidelium salutem operetur æternam.* Likewise in the Dominican liturgy of the 13th century: Legg, *Tracts*, 78; Sölch, *Hugo*, 77 f. with note 152; this Dominican *Suscipe* is identical with that of the rite of Hereford; cf. Bonniwell (*supra*, note 70), 187. The Premonstratensians also followed a similar *ritus* till 1622; Sölch, 78; Waefelghem, 63, note 1.—The shorter form of the *Suscipe sancta Trinitas* which we saw used for receiving the offerings of the faithful (*supra*, p. 54, note 59), is also employed for this single offering: Martène, 1, 4, XXXI (I, 650 f.); cf. Ebner, 326.
[73] Sarum Ordinary (13th c.; Legg, *Tracts*, 220): *Suscipe, sancta Trinitas, hanc oblationem, quam ego miser et indignus offero in honore tuo et beatæ Mariæ perpetuæ virginis et omnium sanctorum tuorum pro peccatis meis et pro salute vivorum et requie omnium fidelium defunctorum. Qui vivis.* Cf. Martène, 1, 4, XXXV (I, 667 A); Maskell, 82 f.; Simmons, *The Lay Folks Mass Book*, 98 f.—The Westminster missal (about 1380), ed. Legg (HBS, 5), 500, has a different formula: *Offerimus tibi, Domine, calicem et hostiam salutaris tuam clementiam deprecantes . . . ascendant. In nomine Patris.*
[74] *Ordinarium* of Coutances: Legg, *Tracts*, 59; cf. the *Alphabetum sacerdotum*, oftprinted in France (*ibid.*, 41).—The same ritus, but with other oblation prayers, in missals of the 15-16th century in Tours and Limoges: Martène, 1. 4, 6, 16 (I, 393).—The Carthusians retain this single offering rite to this day, but employ as the prayer the words: *In spiritu humilitatis;*

But in other places the oblation rite was soon broken up further. At first, indeed, the paten and host were regularly laid on the chalice. Sometimes a blessing was pronounced over them.[75] Then, however, the priest took first the paten[76] and, with an accompanying prayer, offered up the host; only then did he offer up the chalice, unless this was still committed to the deacon to do.[77]

For such a double oblation there were already a number of precedents in the earlier stage of the offertory rite, when the chalice was still handed to the celebrant separately. In the *Missa Illyrica* there is even the beginning of the late Roman formula for the offering of the paten: *Suscipe sancte Pater*,[78] and the complete formula for the chalice: *Offerimus*,[79] both enchased by other texts.[80] Still, even this double accompaniment did not seem to have had the import of a real prayer, at least not that of a priestly oration.[81] Especially with the chalice a simple and brief blessing was frequently thought sufficient.[82] But little by little the details of the later

---

Martène, 1, 4, XXV (I, 632 D); Legg, *Tracts*, 100 f.; *Ordinarium Cart.* (1932), c. 26, 20; cf. for the ritus, *ibid.*, c. 29, 5-12.
[75] According to the Pontifical of Durandus, the priest who celebrates Mass in the presence of a bishop, should not only ask the bishop to bless the water, but afterwards should also hold out the chalice and the paten towards him, likewise for a blessing (see *infra*, note 127). Cf. the *Statuta antiqua* of the Carthusians (13th c.): Martène, 1, 4, XXV (I, 632 D).
[76] An intermediate form, e.g., in the *Alphabetum sacerdotum*: First an oblation of both elements together, then a short prayer over the paten (Legg, *Tracts*, 41); likewise the *Ordinarium* of Coutances (*ibid.*, 59). Similarly in the Cologne *Ordo celebrandi* of the 14th century (Binterim, IV, 3, p. 222 f.).
[77] The transition is plainly to be seen in a comparison of the older Sarum rite (13th c.; Legg, *Tracts*, 220 f.) with the later one (14th c.; *ibid.*, 4 f.; even at the start of the 14th century: Legg, *The Sarum Missal*, 218, note 8): the separate oblation is found in the latter. However, the change was not effected everywhere in England.—On the other hand, it is found mostly in the later south German arrangements (Beck, 237 f., 307f.; Hoeynck, 373; Köck, 119-125).—In Italy the double offering is the rule already in the 11th century; Ebner, 300 f., 306, 309, 328, etc.
[78] For the offering of the bread: *Suscipe, sancta Pater omnipotens æterne Deus, hanc*

immaculatam hostiam, quam ego indignus famulus tuus tibi offero Deo meo vivo et vero, quia te pro æterna salute cunctæ Ecclesiæ tuæ suppliciter exoro. Per. Martène, 1, 4, IV (I, 508 E). The same short formula in corrupt form in a Mass-*ordo* from Lower Italy: Ebner, 346.
[79] The formula appears first as a "9th or 10th century" supplement to the St. Gall Sacramentary MS. 348 under the heading *Offertorium sacri calicis post oblationes oblatarum.* Mohlberg, *Das fränkische Sacramentarium Gelasianum*, p. 247; cf. XCIX. Here and in other early sources the words *pro nostra et totius mundi salute* are wanting; cf. Lebrun, *Explication*, I, 279.
[80] Martène, 1, 4, IV (I, 508 E, 511 A); between the two formulas are found the offertory prayers beginning *Suscipe sancta Trinitas* mentioned above.
[81] This would explain why, for example, Innocent III, *De s. alt. mysterio*, II, 58 (PL, CCXVII, 833 f.), does not make mention of them in his description of the offertory rite, even though the central Italian Mass-plans of the 11th and 12th centuries all present a full series of offertory prayers. They are mostly formulas which in other cases the deacon or even the laity recite; cf. examples *supra*, p. 54.
[82] Sackau missal about 1170 (Köck, 120): *Acceptabile sit* . . . Likewise certain English Mass plans: York, about 1425: Simmons, 100; cf. Sarum: Martène, 1, 4, XXXV (I, 667 B); Maskell, 82.

Roman offertory plan, already present in essentials in the *Missa Illyrica,*
became more evident, particularly in Italian Mass *ordines* from the
eleventh and twelfth centuries on. The psalm verses that accompanied the
handling of the chalice disappear. Alongside a short oblation passage which
was often used alone,[83] the otherwise infrequent *Suscipe sancte Pater* (in
its full form) now appears for the offering of the host.[84] After the admixture of the water there follows the offering of the chalice with the formula
Offerimus.[85] But for a long time it was not a general rule that the celebrant
raise paten and chalice above the altar,[86] although in some scattered in-

---

[83] It is the formula *Tibi, Domine, creatori
meo hostiam offero pro remissione omnium peccatorum meorum et cunctorum fidelium tuorum,* which is also recited by the
laity (*supra,* p. 18, note 99), or by the
deacon or the subdeacon when handing
over the chalice (Ebner, 298, 300, 312).
Thus in Italy: Ebner, 337; cf. 296, 306,
340; also in southern Germany: Hoeynck,
373; Beck, 266, 307; Köck, 119 to 123;
Salzburg printed missals (Hain, 11420 f.).
[84] Cf. Ebner, 13, 328, 340. The last citation
would be the oldest instance (11th century, vicinity of Monte Cassino), but
Ebner's annotation ("as now") is true
only of the first half of the prayer, up to
vivo et vero, as an examination of the MS
(Rome, Bibl. Vallic. C 32) revealed. The
prayer continues: *qua te pro te [!] eterna
salute cuncte ecclesie tue suppliciter exoro.* Cf. *supra,* note 78. Otherwise the
formula appears but infrequently in Italy
till the Minorite missal. But 13th century
commentaries on the Mass presuppose it:
William of Melitona, *Opusc. super missam,* ed. by Dijk (*Eph. liturg.,* 1939), 327;
Durandus, IV, 30, 17.—Eisenhofer, II,
141, reproduces an error when he states
that the formula is already found in the
Prayerbook of Charles the Bald; cf.
supra, note 22.—The opening phrases in
a missal of the 10-11th century from Bobbio (Ebner, 81) reads: *Accipe, quæsumus
Domine s. P. o. æ. D., hanc immaculatam
hostiam, quam tibi suppliciter offero Deo
vivo et vero . . .* Cf. note 78. Echoes *(quam
ego indignus famulus tuus offero)* in
Frankish sacramentaries of the 10th century. Leroquais, I, 69, 71, 76. The phrases
of the second half of the prayer recur
often in *apologiæ,* e.g., in an *oratio ante
altare* of a 9th century sacramentary from
S. Thierry (also in the sacramentary from

Monte Cassino just mentioned: Ebner,
339): *Deus qui de indignis dignos facis
. . . concede propitius ut . . . hostias acceptabiles . . . offeram pietati tuæ pro
peccatis et offensionibus meis et innumeris
quotidianis excessibus . . . et omnibus circumstantibus . . . cunctisque simul fidelibus christianis . . .* Martène, 1, 4, IX (I,
547 B).—To the closing words cf. the conclusion of a *Suscipe* formula in the Sacramentary of S. Denis (middle of the
11th c.): Martène, 1, 4, V (I, 525 A):
*. . . pro peccatis omnium christianorum
tam vivorum quam defunctorum, ut vivis
hic ad salutem et remissionem peccatorum
et defunctis proficiat ad requiem sempiternam et vitam sempiternam.* The present
formula must have originated in France in
the early 11th century.
[85] In most Italian Mass-plans: Ebner, 301,
306, 322, etc. The form prevalent also in
Southern Germany, where the *Suscipe sancte Pater* was unknown: Hoeynck, 373;
Beck, 238, 267, 307 f.; Köck, 120, 122,
124.—Whereas for the most part only
slight variants are to be found, there is a
noteworthy prolepsis in a Hamburg missal of the 11th century (Ebner, 200):
*Offerimus tibi Domine sanguinem Filii tui
deprecantes . . .*
[86] Until far in the 13th century Italian
Mass-plans simply introduce the pertinent
oblation prayer with the rubric: *Quando
panem et vinum super altare ponit* (Ebner,
326); *Quando offert hostiam super altare;
Quando ponitur calix super altare* (the
papal chapel about 1290; *ibid.,* 347; cf. 296,
306, 322, 328, 337). Cf. Innocent III, *De
s. altaris myst.,* II, 58 (PL, 217: 833).—
Other Mass-arrangements state: *Cum
oblatum accipit,* etc. (Ebner, 340; cf. 298,
300), but in one case a later hand inserted
the explanation: *Tenens patenam in mani-*

stances this had been done even in very early times.[87] Add to these, besides, the invocation of the *sanctificator*, the two prayers, *In spiritu humilitatis* and *Suscipe sancta Trinitas*, which were to be said bowed, and were thus somewhat independent.[88]

It is not entirely an accident that the formula for the paten retains the singular number which predominates in these medieval oblation texts, while the formula for the chalice, *Offerimus*, is couched in the plural. For the latter is found not only put in the mouth of the priest,[89] but instead in that of the deacon, who places the chalice on the altar and accompanies this with these words, which he would then be saying in the celebrant's name.[90] Soon, however, there is an insistence on the fact that the deacon keeps the chalice with wine, which he has carried to the altar, and offers it up, and then arranges it on the altar, but the conclusion is drawn precisely from the *Offerimus*, that in reality the priest is acting through the deacon and that the priest must therefore pronounce the *Offerimus*[91] or at least say it with the deacon.[92] This latter arrangement has in a sense persisted, with the deacon touching the chalice and supporting the priest's arm, and pronouncing the words with the priest,[93] but it is the priest, and not the deacon, who is now considered the chief offerer of the chalice. Thus, in the present-day solemn Mass, there is still a vestige of that older order in which the deacon was entrusted with the chalice,[94] that older relationship which is given utterance in the legend where St. Lawrence says to Pope Xystus: *Nunquam sacrificium sine ministro offerre consueveras . . . cui commisisti Dominici sanguinis dispensationem.*[95]

A change which was to be found quite early in the rite of the Roman curia, and was then confirmed by the reform of Pius V, consisted in this, that the preparation of the chalice, or in the first instance at least, the

---

bus (ibid., 340, note regarding Cod. Vall. F 4), a direction which had already appeared in a Benedictine Mass-book of the 11-12th century *(ibid.,* 309) and similarly in one of the 11th century *(ibid.,* 340: Cod. Vall. C 32).

[87] *Supra,* p. 42, note 4.

[88] Among the earliest witnesses to the Roman offertory arrangement, including the *Orate fratres*, are a Minorite missal of the 13th century in Naples (Ebner, 314) and the Mass-*ordo* of the papal chapel about 1290 *(Ibid.,* 347 f.; ed. Brinktrine, *Eph. liturg.,* 1937, 201-203). Further references in P. Salmon, "Les prières et les rites de l'Offertoire de la messe dans la liturgie romaine au XIII° et au XIV° siècle," *Eph. liturg.,* 43 (1929) 508-519.

[89] Cf. *supra,* note 79.

[90] Italian Mass-plans of the 11-12th century in Ebner, 309, 328; Fiala, 203 f.—By

way of exception the prayer is found in the singular, to be said by the priest alone: *Offero tibi*: Central Italian sacramentary of the 12th century (Ebner, 340) ; Zips missal of the 14th century (Radó, 71).

[91] *Ordo Rom.* XIV, n. 53 (PL, LXXVIII, 1164 A).—Likewise a Pressburg Missal of the 15th c.: Jávor, 115.

[92] Durandus, IV, 30, 17. That Durandus also had in mind the ceremony of priest and deacon together holding up the chalice is excluded by the context.

[93] Rit. serv. VIII, 9.—For the first time in 1485 in the Roman pontifical of Patrizio Piccolomini; see de Puniet, *Das römische Pontificale,* I, 185.—The rite is modeled on that at the closing doxology of the canon; see *infra,* p. 267 ff.

[94] *Supra,* I, 71, 73.

[95] Ambrose, De off., I, 41 (PL, XVI, 84 f.)'.

admixture of the water, was transferred to the altar and was thus incorporated into the oblation rite. According to the customs prevalent outside Italy this was all taken care of, as a rule, at some earlier moment, after the Epistle,[96] or already at the beginning of Mass,[97] even in Masses celebrated without levites.[98] But according to the rule that was henceforth followed, the subdeacon at a high Mass, after the *Oremus*, brings up the paten with the host, but along with it only an empty chalice or a chalice containing wine alone,[99] hands these to the deacon, and then, without special formality, pours (wine and) water into the chalice. The act of conveying the gifts to the altar—an act of some liturgical significance—thus suffers a certain impoverishment, even at a high Mass where, after the disappearance of the offertory procession, it might still have been continued.

The attempt had been made, time and again, to keep, at least at high Mass, the symbolism inherent in the impressive transfer of the gifts. Durandus still mentions the practice of having a subdeacon bring to the altar the paten and chalice along with the corporal, to be followed by two singers, one carrying the host in a little cloth, and a cruet of wine; the other, a cruet of water which the subdeacon uses for mingling with the wine.[100] The usage did not take root. Still, there is an expression of great reverence in the very way chalice and paten have been handled these many centuries. When the gifts were to be carried over to the altar, the cleric whose duty it was to see to this, following an ancient ordinance,

[96] *Supra*, I, 278, 441 f.—In the use of Sarum, which was common in England before the Reformation, the chalice was prepared between the epistle and the gospel; see J.W. Legg, *Ecclesiological Essays* (London, 1905), 171.

[97] Before putting on the vestments, e.g., in two Mass-plans from Normandy: Martène, 1, 4, XXVI, XXXVI (I, 635 D, 671 D). Before the *Confiteor* in Cologne Mass-arrangements: Smits van Waesberghe, 299. At Paris, and in France generally, the host and chalice were readied at the altar before a low Mass; at a solemn Mass the deacon spread the corporal during the epistle, and the subdeacon prepared the chalice during the gradual and sequence; Legg, *op. cit.*, 106-146. There is a special study of the whole subject: "A Comparative Study of the Time in the Christian Liturgy at Which the Elements Are Prepared and Set on the Holy Table," *Transactions of the St. Paul's Ecclesiological Society*, 1895, vol. III, p. 78; see Legg, *Tracts*, 239.—In many Mass-arrangements no mention at all is made of this preparation of the elements, perhaps because it was regarded as outside the bounds of the liturgy proper; thus, e.g., in the otherwise very detailed Mass-*ordo* of S. Denis (11th c.): Martène, 1, 4, V (I, 518 ff.); also in most English Mass-books.

[99] According to the Bavarian Benedictine, Bernhard von Waging (d. 1472), some priests poured wine and water into the chalice before Mass, others after the *Confiteor*, still others after the epistle; but he himself recommends doing it right before the offering. Franz, 575. The practice first mentioned is still customary in today's Dominican rite; as soon as the priest reaches the altar, ready for Mass, he uncovers the chalice, pours wine into it and, with a blessing, water, and covers it again. The offertory itself begins with the oblatory lifting of chalice and paten. *Missale O.P.* (1889), 17 f.; cf. *supra*, note 72.

[80] So, e.g., in the *Ordo* of the Lateran basilica (about 1140): Fischer, 81, 1. 15; 82 f.

[100] Durandus, IV, 30, 25.—Cf. Ordinarium of Laon (about 1300): Martène, 1, 4, XX

threw a veil around his shoulders, and touched the sacred vessels only through this medium.[101]

Another practice on the increase was one prescribing that the deacon, too, when handing the chalice and paten to the priest, do this *mediante mappula*.[102] Even in the most ancient Roman *ordines* when the deacon put the chalice in its place, and likewise when he lifted it aloft at the end of the canon, he used a special cloth for this, the *offertorium*;[103] and the paten, too, was held by the cleric entrusted with it, by means of a veil— called by such names as *sindo, linteum*—until he handed it back before the *fractio*.[104] This concealing of the paten was then transferred to the non-solemn Mass.[105]

(I, 608 B).—A faint attempt to render visible the transfer of both elements is found also in the Liber ordinarius of the capitular church of Essen (14th c.); here the subdeacon handed the deacon not only the cruets for the chalice but also a pyx with the host for the paten. Arens, 16. In the present-day Dominican rite for high Mass, too, the transfer of the gifts (made during the *Gloria*) is still made in a somewhat visible manner; H. L. Verwilst, *Die Dominikanische Messe* (Düsseldorf, (1948), 13; cf. 15.

[101] J. Braun, *Die liturgischen Paramente* (2nd ed., Freiburg, 1924), 230 f.—The chalice and the paten, too, as soon as they held the wine and the host, were covered with a cloth, out of which grew our present chalice veil; *ibid.*, 213-215. In the late medieval Cistercian rite the deacon removed the *offertorium* which was spread over the chalice, covered his hands with it, and so carried the paten with the host and the chalice with the wine to the altar; Schneider (*Cist.-Chr.*, 1926), 349.

[102] *Ordo Rom.* XIV, n. 53 (PL, LXXVIII, 1163 C). In some Mass-arrangements we find *manipulus* instead of *mappula*: Martène, 1, 4, XXIV, XXXVI (I, 628 C, 681 C D); cf. Durandus, IV, 30, 16.— This manner of handling chalice and paten, although so dignified and suitable, does not seem to have had much vogue. Burchard of Strassburg, in his Mass-*ordo*, directs the Mass-server to handle the cruet *manu dextera nuda;* Legg, *Tracts,* 150.— It is interesting to note that the maniple (which is likewise often called a *mappula*), when thus used, was actually reviving its original function.

[103] *Ordo Rom.* I, n. 15 f. (PL, LXXVIII, 944 f); *Ordo Rom.* II, n. 9 f. (PL, LXXVIII, 973 f.).—Cf. Amalar, *De eccl. off.*, præfatio altera (PL, CV, 992 B).

[104] *Ordo Rom.* I, n. 17 (PL, LXXVIII, 945 B); *Ordo* of Johannes Archicantor (Silva-Tarouca, 206, 1. 23). This latter work, done by Frankish clerics in an effort to fit together Roman and Gallican customs, presupposes a ceremonial in which the paten serves to bring the bread-oblation to the altar, somewhat in the manner of the Gallic offertory procession. But in the tradition of the city of Rome, incorporated in *Ordo Rom.* I, the paten was not used till the fraction of the species, although it was brought forward already at the start of the canon.—Batiffol, *Leçons,* 88, explains the veneration shown the paten by supposing that it bore a consecrated particle (the *sancta*) which was dropped into the chalice before the Communion. But this assumption is not really necessary.

[105] At present, rubrics demand that the paten be slipped part way under the corporal and covered with the purificator. We find this practice of shoving the paten under the corporal mentioned already by Bernold of Constance, *Micrologus*, c. 10 (PL, CLI, 983 D), and explained, as above, as a vestige of the practice at solemn Mass. But then allegorizing takes over, and the practice is interpreted as representing the disciples of Christ hiding themselves at the beginning of His passion; Innocent III, *De s. alt. mysterio*, II, 59 (PL, CCXVII, 834). The realization that not all were unfaithful then seems to have led to the practice of only partially concealing the paten,

There is also an early mention of the kissing of the hand when paten and chalice are handed to the celebrant.[108] The sign of the Cross over the altar, which the celebrant makes with both the paten and the chalice after the oblation is somewhat more recent,[107] but it had its forerunners even in early times.[108]

After the preparation of the chalice was thus transferred once more to the altar, texts to accompany this action also begin to come to our notice. It stood to reason, for instance, that in the Roman liturgy as accommodated to Frankish tradition, the admixture of water, whose symbolism had so early and so generally become the object of profound consideration, would not long remain without accompanying words. That type of oblation rite which we first encounter in various scattered points along the northern border of the Carolingian realm, and then in the eleventh century in the Italian sphere affected by the Cluniac movement,[109] presents a definite form for this, one which has been retained more or less in the Roman Mass of the present day. This form is as follows: the water is put into the chalice at the altar itself, either before[110] or even after the offering of the chalice;[111] and meanwhile is said the oration, *Deus qui*

---

a practice mentioned since the 13th century; Durandus, IV, 30, 29; Frere, *The Use of Sarum*, I, 75. But even at the end of the Middle Ages the practice was not universal; according to the *Ordinarium* of Coutance (1557) the priest places the paten *sub corporalibus aut super altare*: Legg, *Tracts*, 59.

[108] Missal at Monte Cassino (11-12th c.): Ebner, 309.—*Ordo Eccl. Lateran.* (about 1140; Fischer, 82, l. 33, 38), and here also when handling the water cruet.—*Ordo Rom.* XIV, n. 53 (PL, LXXVIII, 1163 D).—According to *Ordo Rom.* I, n. 18 (PL, LXXVIII, 945 B) the archdeacon kisses the paten when he receives it after the *Pater noster*.

[107] Mentioned for the paten by Durandus, IV, 30, 17; for the chalice in *Ordo ecclesiæ Lateranensis*: Fischer, 83, l. 2. As a rite performed by the deacon with the chalice, in Benedictine missals of the 11-12th century: Ebner, 309; Fiala, 203.— Where paten and chalice were offered together under one ceremony, the cross was made with both together; Missal of Evreux (about 1400): Martène, 1, 4, XXVIII (I, 644 B); cf. a Cologne *Ordo celebrandi* of the 14th century: Binterim, IV, 3, p. 222.

[108] According to Innocent III, *De s. alt. mysterio*, II, 58 (PL, CCXVII, 833 f.), the priest makes a sign of the cross over the gifts previous to receiving the paten and the host, the water cruet and the chalice (and likewise the *thuribulum*).— There are isolated instances of a sign of the cross over the host-bread since the 4th century. Augustine, *In Joh. tract.*, 118, 5 (PL, XXXV, 1950); *Canones Basilii*, c. 99 (Riedel, 276).—In St. Ephraem's locality the Marcionites marked a cross with red wine over the eucharistic bread: Dölger, *Antike u. Christentum*, 1 (1929), 30 ff.—This signing with the cross was not customary in the older Roman liturgy; nevertheless *Ordo Rom.* I, n. 14 (PL, LXXVIII, 944 B), says of the deacon who is to pour the wine into the chalice: *infundit faciens crucem in calice*—he forms a cross as he pours. Cf. *Ordo Rom.* II, n. 9 (PL, LXXVII, 973 B).

[109] *Supra*, p. 47, note 26 ff.; p. 53 ff.

[110] Missa Illyrica: Martène, 1, 4, IV (I, 510 f.); central Italian Mass-books since the eleventh century: Ebner 300, 347.

[111] Mass-plan of Séez: (PL, LXXVIII, 249 B); Benedictine Mass-*ordo* of the 11-12th century: Ebner, 309.

humanæ substantiæ,[112] an ancient Roman Christmas oration[113] amplified by a reference *per huius aquæ et vini mysterium* and by the solemn invocation of Christ's name before the concluding formula.

Thus the Christmas thought, which hardly ever came under discussion in this connection in the literature of the foregoing centuries, the thought of man's participation in the divinity through the Incarnation of the Son of God,[114] suddenly comes into prominence. It is a concept which presupposes and, to some extent, comprises both the oriental interpretation of the admixture rite, the human and divine natures of Christ, and the western interpretation, our own union with Christ.[115]

Much oftener, however, we come across a very different formula, even in Italian Mass *ordines*. This formula derives from the symbolism of the water-and-blood,[116] and outside of Italy it appears, along with the mixing rite connected with it, not in the offertory itself (though there are exceptions,[117] but rather right after the Epistle,[118] or even at the start of Mass, where it is said by the deacon.[119] The reference to the blood and water from

---

[112] In some of the cases mentioned above (note 110, 111), a second formula is introduced.—Noteworthy is the way the commingling formula is accentuated by means of preliminary versicles (*Ostende, Domine exaudi, . . .*), as in Hungarian Mass-books: Radó, 24, 43, 76, 123.

[113] Leonianum (Muratori, I, 467); Gelasianum (Wilson, 5); Gregorianum (Lietzmann, n. 9, 6).

[114] F. Holböck, *Der eucharistische und der mystische Leib Christi,* 203, traces the concept of this oration among early scholastic writers only in Honorius Augustod., *Gemma an.,* I, 158 (PL, CLXXII, 593 B).

[115] See *supra,* p. 39.

[116] Central Italian Mass-books since the 11th century (Ebner, 298, 300, et al.): *Ex latere Christi sanguis et aqua exisse perhibetur et ideo pariter commiscemus, ut misericors Deus utrumque ad medelam animarum nostrarum sanctificare dignetur. Per.* Also in the Sacramentary of S. Gatien in Tours (9th c.): Martène, 1, 4, VII (I, 535 D). With the variant, *ut tu pius et misericors utrumque sanctificare et benedicere digneris,* about 1290 in the papal chapel: Brinktrine (*Eph. liturg.,* 1937), 202. Similarly since the 14th century in Hungary *ut Dominus utrumque dignetur benedicere* (Jávor, 114, Radó, 24, 96, 118, 123 et al.): *ut Dominus utrumque dignetur benedicere et in odorem suavitatis accipere.* Still another

modification in the Sacramentary of Boldau about 1195; Radó, 43.—Besides this formula there are also others which, however, regularly have the starting phrases in common with it: *De latere D. n. J. C. exivit sanguis et aqua pariter in remissionem peccatorum.* Martène, 1, 4, XXVI (I, 635 D). Or the same with the extension: *sanguis ut redimeret, aqua ut emundaret; ibid.,* XXXVI (I, 671 D). Or else a simple quotation from John 19: 34 b-35 a; *ibid.,* (I, 677 D). Or the same with several amplifications: Ebner, 326, and similarly, but with the opening *In nomine D. n. J. C.* (Lyons, 11th c.): Leroquais, I, 126. Further developed as a petition for a worthy celebration *(et aqua quem pretiosissimum liquorem . . . influi peto in cor meum . . .)* in use in Holland in the 15th century; s. P. Schlager, "Uber die Messerklärung des Franziskaners Wilhelm von Gouda," *Franziskan. Studien,* 6 (1919), 328. Note that only a few typical examples of the numerous variations are reported here.

[117] Thus, in the Mass-plan of the Carthusians, where it follows the handing-over of chalice and paten: Martène, 1, 4, XXV (I, 632 D); Legg, *Tracts,* 100; *Ordinarium Cart.* (1932), c. 26, 20.

[118] See *supra,* I, 441.

[119] See the Mass-plans from Normandy and Cologne cited in note 97 above.

the side of Christ must have been very much a favorite; it did, of course, come within the compass of the ordinary allegorism which explained the Mass in terms of Christ's Passion. The notion was kept alive also by a widely-used oblation formula which was spoken over the chalice instead of one of the other formulas mentioned earlier;[120] but more especially by the regulation that the chalice was to stand on the altar to the right of the host *quasi sanguinem Domini suscepturus,*[121] an interpretation which is indeed more recent than the custom upon which it is founded,[122] but which recurs, along with the regulation itself, in nearly all the commentaries on the Mass of the later Middle Ages,[123] and was not generally discarded, until the basis for it was removed by the Missal of Pius V.

If the symbolism of the water was thus to be emphasized, at the same time the water was also to be blessed. This is done at the present time by a sign of the Cross which is coupled with the words *per huius aquæ et vini mysterium,* and which is omitted at a Requiem Mass because all formal blessings therein are bestowed only on the dead. In the oldest Roman *ordines,* as we have already seen, the act of pouring the water into the chalice was done in the form of a cross.[124] In medieval missals this blessing was not infrequently accented even more forcefully. Perhaps it was as much for the sake of this blessing as for a greater emphasis on the symbolism that the addition of the water was reserved to the priest;[125] at any

---

[120] See note 46.

[121] Bernold of Constance, *Micrologus,* c. 10 (PL, CLI, 983 D).

[122] *Ordo Rom.* I, n. 15 (PL, LXXVII, 944 C) : the chalice stands *iuxta oblatam pontificis a dextris.*

[123] Durandus, IV, 30, 22 f., makes mention of both arrangements; likewise Radulph de Rivo, *De canonum observ.,* prop. 23 (Mohlberg, I, 143). According to the latter the arrangement followed at present was then observed by the *Gallicani.* Actually even Amalar, *De eccl. off.,* præfatio altera (PL, CV, 992 B), notes as a diverging Roman custom: *Calix in latere oblatæ in altari componitur, non post tergum.* The Gallican practice was adopted by several religious orders (see note 24 *supra*) and in 1485 also by Rome; Lebrun, *Explication,* I, 278. — According to the *Directorium div. off.* of Ciconiolanus (1539) the priest was to place the chalice *ad sinistram hostiæ;* Legg, *Tracts,* 207.

[124] *Supra,* note 108.

[125] The practice of the celebrant himself adding the water is found, among others, in Bonizo of Sutri (d. about 1095), *De vita christiana,* II, 51 (ed. Perels [Berlin,

1930[, 59) ; in the *Ordo ecclesiæ Lateranensis* (middle 12th c.), ed. Fischer, 82 f.; Innocent III, *De s. alt. mysterio,* II, 58 (PL, CCXVII, 833) ; Durandus, IV, 30, 18; *Ordo Rom.* XIV, n. 53 (PL, LXXVIII, 1163 f.). As an argument to justify the usage Innocent III remarks that Christ had shed His own blood for the nations (represented by the water). —A Graz missal from the 15th century expressly declares that the deacon may, indeed, put the wine into the chalice, but not the water; this only the *sacerdos celebrans* is permitted to pour in; Köck, 126 (here also the rubric which also appears elsewhere in isolated instances: *prius effundi debet parum super terram ex ampullis de vino et aqua).* This marked underscoring of the priestly privilege is obviously done in view of an opposite practice, still in use. According to the Benedictine *Liber ordinarius* of Liége (Volk, 100) it was the Mass-server's duty, even at a low Mass, to put wine and water into the chalice, provided only that he be *in sacris.* According to a Mass-plan of English Carthusians about 1500 (Legg, *Tracts,* 100) it was enough if he was a cleric. This is

rate the mixing of the water had to take place at the altar, with the result that the pouring of the wine was likewise transferred to the altar.[126]

For the blessing itself various formulas were handed down. According to the Pontifical of Durandus, the bishop spoke as follows when he blessed the water at the Mass of his chaplain: *Ab illo benedicatur, cuius spiritus super eam ante mundi exordium ferebatur.*[127] According to English Mass books, the celebrant said the following over the water: *Ab eo sit benedicta de cuius latere exivit sanguis et aqua. In nomine Patris. . . .*[128] Elsewhere the priest used words analogous to those used at the commingling of the species before Communion: *Fiat commixtio et consecratio vini et aquæ in nomine D. n. J. C., de cuius latere exivit sanguis et aqua,*[129] or: *Fiat commixtio vini et aquæ pariter in nomine Patris et Filii et Spiritus Sancti,*[130] or simply—apparently the original way—*In nomine Patris et Filii et Spiritus Sancti.*[131] Most often such a blessing, coupled with the sign of the Cross, was appended to the formula which was designed to explain the commixture, or it was even combined with it into a single formula.[132]

The later Middle Ages were a thriving era for blessings. All the products of nature and all the objects of human use were recipients of the Church's benedictions. No wonder, then, that a blessing was bestowed here at the oblation not only on the water, but also on all the other gifts which were destined for so exalted a purpose. Thus we come to a final layer of texts that were built up in the medieval oblation rite, a series of benediction formulas of which one, the *Veni sanctificator,* has secured a permanent place in the Roman Missal. Since for the most part these blessings take the form of an invocation, calling down God's blessing, the power

matched by the present-day arrangement of having the subdeacon at high Mass see to the pouring of the water.

[126] Only by way of exception was a special formula composed to accompany the pouring of the water. In Spanish Mass-books of the 15th century there is the excerpt from the Psalm (74: 8 f.), *Hunc humiliat . . .,* but it does not appear very apropos. Ferreres, 127 f. (n. 503, 506).

[127] Martène, 1, 4, XXIII (I, 619 D); Andrieu, III, 645. Still another blessing follows, according to the Pontifical cited; the priest lays the paten with the host on the chalice and turns once again to the bishop with a *Benedicite;* the latter says: *Benedictionis et consecrationis angelus virtute sanctæ Trinitatis descendat super hoc munus.*

[128] Frere, *The Use of Sarum,* I, 71; cf. Ferreres, 132f. Likewise in the Cologne rite of the 14th century: Binterim, IV, 3, p. 222.

[129] A 13th century missal from Schlägl (in the diocese of Linz, Austria) : Waefelghem, 59, note 3. Likewise in a 14th century missal from Zips (in Slovakia) and in a Breslau missal of 1476: Radó, 71; 163.

[130] A Seckau missal about 1330 (Köck, 121); the Cologne *Ordo celebrandi* of the 14th century (Binterim, IV, 3, p. 222); Statutes of Tongern, 1413 (de Corswarem, 125 f.); Hungarian missals of the 15th century (Jávor, 114; Sawicki, 148).— Likewise the Augsburg Mass-plan of the close of the 15th century (Franz, 752); the Regensburg missal about 1500 (Beck, 265); a Mass-*ordo* of the 14-15th century from Toul (Martène, 1, 4, XXXI [I, 650 E]); a Mass-*ordo* from Rouen (*ibid.,* XXXVII [I, 677 D]).

[131] Missal of the 12th century from St. Peter: Ebner, 333; missal of 1417 from Valencia: Ferreres, 127 (n. 503; cf. n. 505).

[132] E.g., missal from Toul (note 130

of the divine Spirit, or simply the Holy Ghost, we can also talk of epikletic formulas.[133]

The simplest form [134] is the one mentioned in a previous paragraph: the name of the triune God is mentioned at the preparatory action. In the Carthusian rite the priest sets the chalice (with the paten resting upon it) on the altar with the words: *In nomine Patris . . . Amen.*[135] Or the same trinitarian formula stands at the start of the whole oblation rite,[136] or is correlated to the various parts of the action;[137] or, above all, it is tied in with other epikletic formulas,[138] where, however, as an introductory it is

supra) ; cf. also the petition for a blessing at the end of the formula *Ex latere : supra*, note 116. Multiple blessings by way of sign of the cross were customary among the ancient Irish monks; cf. Andrieu, *Les ordines*, III, 21; 212 f.; 218 f.

[133] However, it would be misleading to talk here precisely of the epiklesis, as Gihr, 569 ff., does, for the formularies are not within the canon, and the blessing is only preparatory in character.

[134] Insofar as there is question of a text and not of a simple unaccompanied crossing, as was the case about 1100 in the missal of St. Vincent (Fiala, 203).

[135] So according to the *Statuta antiqua* (13th c.) : Martène, 1, 4, XXV (I, 632 D) ; cf. Legg, *Tracts*, 101; *Ordinarium Cart.* (1932), c. 26, 20. So also Frere, *The Use of Sarum*, I, 78; Maskell, 98. In these cases the words follow *In spiritu humilitatis* and thus correspond exactly to the Roman *Veni sanctificator.*—A similarly independent *In nomine Patris* between *Suscipe sancta Trinitas* and *Orate* in the Lyons monastic missal of 1531: Martène, 1, 4, XXXIII (I, 659 D).—In the Mozarabic Mass the priest recites the same trinitarian formula when putting down the paten and the chalice (PL, LXXXV, 536 B C) ; the recitation of the formula is labeled a *sanctificare* (ibid.).

[136] Breviary of Rouen: Martène, 1, 4, XXXVIII (I, 678 A) ; Cistercian rite of the 15th century: Franz, 587; Netherlands Mass-plans of the 15-16th century: Smits van Waesberghe (*Ons geestelijk Erf*, 1941), 325, 327.

[137] In the *Alphabetum sacerdotum* the oblation prayer with which the chalice is raised aloft closes with *in nomine Patris*,

and also the formula with which the host is laid on the altar. Legg, *Tracts*, 41.—In the Cologne missal of 1498 the trinitarian formula is found also at the beginning, before the *Quid retribuam;* Smits van Waesberghe, 327; the development was not so far advanced yet in the 14th century. *Ordo celebrandi;* Binterim, IV, 3, p. 223.— Likewise in the Mass-*ordo* of S. Pol-de-Léon: Martène, 1, 4, XXXIV (I, 662 f.), where the trinitarian formula also follows the *Veni sanctificator*—therefore it appears four times in all. It also appears four times in the *Ordinarium* of Coutance of 1559: Legg, *Tracts*, 59 ff.—It is also found in four places in the offertory according to the Mass-arrangement at Augsburg in the 15th century, if the blessing of the wine is included: *Benedictio Dei Patris . . . descendat super hanc creaturam* (Franz, 752) ; in the Augsburg missal of 1386 (Hoeynck, 373) this formula is still absolutely wanting. In a Salzburg missal of the 15th century the trinitarian blessing is found three times during the preliminary arrangement and preparation of chalice and host, and four times during the offertory; Radó, 141.—Cf. also the *In nomine Patris* at the start of the incensation in the Roman oblation-plan of the 13-14th century, in Salmon (*Eph. liturg.*, 1929), 512 f.

[138] In particular the formula *Sit signatum* (or *Sit benedictum;* see below, note 144) often begins with *In nomine Patris.* Thus already in the Missa Illyrica: Martène, 1, 4, IV (I, 511 C), and in a Central Italian sacramentary of the 11th century: Ebner, 298; cf. 327.—Similarly in the Liége missal of the 16th century: Smits van Waesberghe, 325; cf. *Liber ordinarius* of Liége: Volk, 92.—The *Veni sanctificator* sometimes concludes with *in nomine Patris;*

often replaced—especially in earlier times—by the formula *In nomine Domini nostri Jesu Christi.*[189] After the year 1000 a double formula frequently appears, a double petition for a blessing connected with the action of depositing the bread-oblation and the chalice: *Sanctifica, Domine, hanc oblationem, ut nobis unigeniti Filii tui D. n. J. C. corpus fiat. Qui tecum . . .*, and in relation to the chalice: *Oblatum tibi, Domine, calicem sanctifica, ut nobis Unigeniti tui D. n. J. C. sanguis fiat. Qui tecum . . .*[140] In South-German Mass *ordines* they often appear in a form where the second formula is fashioned more closely on the first: *Sanctifica quæsumus Domine hunc calicem, ut nobis Unigeniti tui sanguis fiat.*[141]

As a sort of condensation of this double formula there follows in many cases a further formula which often occurs by itself; it begs that the double earthly offering might be exalted into the single holy one: *In nomine Domini nostri Jesu Christi sit sacrificium istud immaculatum et a te Deo vivo et vero adunatum et benedictum.* Like the formulas already mentioned, this, too, appears first along the northern rim of the former Carolingian domain,[142] then later chiefly in Italy,[143] where still another

---

see English and North-French Mass-plans in Legg, *Tracts*, 5, 42, 60 f., 221.

[189] Mass-*ordo* of Séez (PL, LXXVII, 248 B) ; Central Italian Mass-arrangements since the 11th century : Ebner, 296, 301, 310, 313, 333. The *Ordinarium* of Toul (14-15th c.) combines both formulas : *in nomine Jesu Christi fiat hoc sacrificium a te Deo vivo et vero coadunatum et benedictum in nomine P. et F. et Sp. S.*: Martène, 1, 4, XXXI (I, 651 A).

[140] Missa Illyrica: Martène, 1, 4, IV (I, 510 f.). The second formula, *Oblatum . . . fiat*, is found as a supplement of the 9th or 10th century in the Frankish Sacramentarium Gelesianum, ed., Mohlberg, p. 244, where it follows immediately after the *Offerimus* (see *supra*, note 79).—In Central Italian Mass-plans since the 11th century, these formulas, in the versions given, appear only in isolated cases : Ebner, 301 ; cf. 296 ; in other instances they are found modified (*ibid.*, 326 B.), or combined into one formula (*ibid.*, 298). Mostly they have disappeared.—In German Mass-plans the two formulas appear more frequently : Mainz (about 1170) : Martène, 1, 4, XVII (I, 600 f.) ; Gregorienmünster (14-15th c.) : *ibid.*, XXXII (I, 656) : Augsburg Missal of 1386 : Hoeynck, 373 ; Augsburg Mass-plan of the end of the 15th century Franz, 752 ; Salzburg incunabula of

1492 and 1498 : Hain, 11420 f. Cf. the statement of Bernhard of Waging (d. 1472), in Franz, 575.

[141] Sacramentary presumably from Regensburg (11th c.) : Ebner 7.—Beck, 237 f., 266 f., 307 ; Köck, 120 f., 125 ; Radó, 141. —But thus also in the Sacramentary of Modena : Muratori, I, 91, and in a Sacramentary of the 12th century from Camaldoli : Ebner, 296 ; likewise a Sacramentary from Fonte Avellana (before 1325) : PL, CLI, 887.—A different paralleling of the two formulas in the *Missale Ambrosianum* (1902), 168 : *Suscipe, clementissime Pater, hunc panem sanctum, ut fiat Unigeniti tui corpus, in nomine Patris . . . Suscipe, clementissime Pater, hunc calicem, vinum aqua mixtum, ut fiat Unigeniti tui sanguis in nomine Patris. . . .* It is not till the added prayers that the special intentions are expressed.

[142] Mass-*ordo* of Séez: PL, LXXVIII, 249 B) ; in France only here and there : Martène, 1, 4, XXXI f. (I, 651 A, 656 C). Nor is it frequent in German countries : Mass-*ordo* of Gregorienmünster : Martène, 1, 4, XVI (I, 599 C) ; *Liber ordinarius* of Liége, about 1285 : Volk, 92 ; Liége missals of 1486 and 1499 : Smits van Waesberghe, 325 ; Styrian Mass-books : Köck, 121, 124.

[148] Ebner, 20, 296, 298, 301, 310, 313, 333.

parallel formula is found as an alternative.[144] Even here, however, neither of the formulas held their ground, but on the contrary were supplanted by a third, which had put in an appearance early in the ninth century in the Irish Stowe Missal[145] and which is still found in the present day *Missale Romanum*, namely, the prayer *Veni sanctificator*, which was but sparsely spread in Italy before the appearance of the *Missale Romanæ Curiæ*.[146] Whereas in Italian Mass *ordines* it usually stands in the same spot it occupies at present and amid similar surroundings,[147] in German *ordines* it regularly followed the two *Sanctifica* formulas as a sort of recapitulation,[148] thus accentuating its significance as a blessing.[149] But it was also used in these ways. In some few Mass *ordines* the *Veni Sanctificator* introduces the offertory.[150] According to an *ordo* which circulated widely on both sides of the English Channel, it concluded the entire rite, coming

[144] Again it is the formula which makes its initial appearance in the Missa Illyrica [*In nomine P. et F. et Sp. S.*] *sit signatum, ordinatum, sanctificatum et benedictum hoc sacrificium novum;* Martène, 1, 4, IV (I, 511 C). For Italy (11-12th c.) cf. Ebner, 14, 328. In two Central Italian Mass-books of the 11th century (Ebner, 301; cf. 298) the formula is doubled: *bene-dictum hoc corpus,* for the host; *benedic-tum hoc sanctum sacrificium,* for the chalice; whereupon there follows *In nomi-ne D. n. J. C. sit sacrificium istud,* to merge the two.—From this arose, in later Italian Mass-plans (12-13th c.; Ebner, 327, 341), another combination formula: [*In nomine Patris . . .*] *sit signatum et benedictum et consecratum hoc corpus et hoc sacrificium.* By *sacrificium,* therefore, the chalice was meant.—In the Freising missal of 1520 this formula is spoken only over the chalice *(Sanctificatum sit hoc liba-men)*: Beck, 308, 1. 3; cf. the Salzburg missal of 1200: Köck, 123.—Further modi-fications of the formula: Mass-*ordo* of York about 1425: Simmons, 100; missal of Liége, 16th century, where it forms the opening of the offertory: Smits van Waes-berghe, 325.

[145] Warner (HBS, 32), 7: At the unveil-ing of the chalice (before the gospel) the invocation *Veni, Domine, sanctificator omnipotens, et benedic hoc sacrificium præparatum tibi. Amen.* is recited three times. In the sacramentary of S. Thierry, end of the 10th century: Martène, 1, 4, X (I, 548 E), the prayer *Veni, sanctificator, omnipotens æterne Deus, benedic hoc sac-*

rificium præparatum tibi is said after the first of the oblation prayers. In the Missa Illyrica, about 1030: *ibid.,* IV (I, 511), after the incensing . . . *hoc sacrificium tibi præparatum. Qui vivis.*

[146] Ebner, 306, 327, 333, 340, 348.—Some-times a much expanded version is found, *Veni, sanctificator omnium, Sancte Spiri-tus, et sanctifica hoc præsens sacrificium ab indignis manibus præparatum et descen-de in hanc hostiam invisibiliter, sicut in pa-trum hostias visibiliter descendisti.* Missal at Monte Cassino of the 11-12th century: Ebner, 310; cf. *ibid.,* 328. Missal of St. Vincent-on-Volturno: Fiala, 205. Likewise in a Minorite missal: Ebner, 314; also in the missal of the chapter church of St. Lambrecht, 1336: Köck, 121.—The second half of the prayer goes back to a prayer for the incensation of the gifts in the Missa Illyrica (Martène, 511 D), where the con-nection with the epiklesis of the canon is patent: *Memores . . . petimus . . . ut ascen-dant preces . . . et descendat . . .* Obviously some Gallican schema is here belatedly at work; cf. *Missale Gothicum*: Muratori, II, 654; cf. *ibid.,* 548, 699 f., 705; Lietzmann, *Messe und Herrenmahl,* 93 ff.

[147] Akin, too, is the position it occupies in most of the Netherlands Mass-plans: Smits van Waesberghe, 326 f.; cf. 301.

[148] The sources as above, note 141. Like-wise in the German Mass-plans enume-rated in note 140.

[149] The 13th century missal of Schlägl (Waefelghem, 61, note 0) entitles the for-mula: *Benedictio panis et calicis.*

[150] *Liber ordinarius* of Liége (Volk, 92);

in just before the *Orate fratres*.[151] On the other hand, other formulations of the invocation of heaven's power and grace seldom proved even relatively permanent.[152]

In the territory just indicated, another phenomenon should be recorded because it throws some light on the frame of mind in which this epikletic formula was spoken. Towards the end of the Middle Ages both in Normandy and England—and elsewhere, too—we encounter not only one of the invocation formulas mentioned above, but also the hymn *Veni Creator*.[153] The wording of the formula *Veni sanctificator* does not neces-

---

also in the Liége missals of 1486 and 1499: Smits van Waesberghe, 325; Missal of Upsala (1513): Yelverton, 14; Missal of Fécamp (14-15th c.): Martène, 1, 4, XXVII (I, 640 B).—In the *Ordo Rom.* VI, n. 10 (PL, LXXVIII, 993), it is the only prayer mentioned for the offertory.

[151] Sacramentary of S. Denis (11th c.): Martène, 1, 4, V (I, 526 D); *Ordinarium* of Toul: *ibid.*, XXXI (I, 651); 13th century *Ordinarium* of Sarum: Legg, *Tracts*, 221; cf. *ibid.*, 5, 42, 60 f.; Legg, *The Sarum Missal*, 219.—In the York Mass-plan (Simmons, 100) exactly the same position is occupied by the formula *Sit signatum*, which is therefore regarded as equipollent. Cf. the missal of 1336 of St. Lambrecht, where the *Veni sanctificator* is declared as interchangeable with [*In nomine Patris* ...] *sit hoc sacrificium* (cf. *supra*, p. 67); Köck, 121.

[152] A formula, *Descendat* [*hic sanctus*] *angelus benedictionis et consecrationis super hoc munus*, appears since the 11th century in the French oblation arrangements: Sacramentary of Limoges: Leroquais, I, 155; cf. *ibid.*, 211; Sacramentary of Moissac: Martène, 1, 4, VIII (I, 539 C); *ibid.* also an expanded *Descendat* formula. A three-member *Descendat* formula, which serves as an *epiklesis* in the *Missale Gothicum vetus* of the 7th century (Muratori, II, 699 f.; cf. Lietzmann, *Messe und Herrenmahl*, 94 f.), appears in this location since the 11th century: Leroquais, I, 164; II, 25; III, 126.—Cf. the formula for blessing in the *Pontificale* of Durandus, *supra*, note 127; the continuation of the *Veni sanctificator*, *supra*, note 146; the formulas in Martène, 1, 4, 6, 3 (I, 395 D). An 11th century sacramentary of Monza (Ebner,

106) says more simply: *Benedictio Dei P. et F. et Sp. S. descendat super hanc nostram oblationem*. Three *Descendat* (*descende*) formulas are contained in the oblation rite of the Sacramentary of Boldau; Radó, 43.—In Spanish missals an oration for the consecration of an altar, from the Gregorianum (Lietzmann, n. 196), beginning with the word *Descendat*, is placed after the answer to *Orate fratres*, being recited, according to varying forms, either before or after the other *secreta* prayers. Ferreres, 132 f.—In Spain there often appears, instead of *Veni sanctificator*, the formula: *Dextera Dei Patris omnipotentis benedicat hæc dona sua*. Ferreres, 129 (n. 513); Ebner, 342.—In the same position the Milanese Mass presents the formula: *Benedictio Dei omnipotentis Patris . . . descendat super hanc nostram oblationem . . .*; Missale Ambrosianum (1902), 169. The Augsburg Mass-plan at the end of the 15th century starts the offertory with the invocation of God's blessing upon the wine: *Benedictio Dei Patris . . . descendat super hanc creaturam vini*. Further on, there are two *Veni* formulas. Franz, 752 f.—A missal of the 12th century from Tortosa has a continuation of the *Suscipe sancte Pater* after the first phrase, as follows: *. . . offero, et mittere digneris sanctum angelum tuum de cœlis, qui sanctificet corpus et sanguinem istud;* Ferreres, 129 (n. 512). —The Cologne *Ordo celebrandi* of the 14th century has one *Benedicat* formula each for the bread, the wine and the water; Binterim, IV, 3, p. 222.

[153] For England: *Ordinarium* of Sarum, 14th century (Legg, *Tracts*, 5; not found, however, in MSS. of the 13th or start of the 14th century: Legg, *The Sarum Missal*, 219); Mass- *ordo* of York, about 1425 (Simmons, 100).—Mass-arrangements of

sarily force us to refer the invocation to the Holy Spirit,[154] and thus to include in the series of offertory prayers and of the Mass prayers in general a form of address alien to them. Still, in view of the fact just noticed, there can hardly be any doubt that the invocation was often so understood in the Middle Ages. In fact, in some instances the address to the Holy Ghost is explicitly included in the *Veni sanctificator*.[155] Notice, finally, that the various texts that accompany the oblation ritual—exclusive of the oblation prayers themselves—do not pretend to have the character or the import of orations and are therefore couched in the freer forms of simple invocations and blessings.

5. The Incensation

After the gifts have been deposited on the altar, there follows at high Mass[1] yet another ceremony, the incensation. Today, and already in the *Missale Romanæ Curiæ*, it has been so thoroughly incorporated into the course of the offertory, that, besides the washing of hands, there is still another oblation act to follow, whereas in other places, and according to the original plan, it formed the conclusion, coming immediately before the

---

Normandy: Legg, *Tracts,* 59 f.; Martène, 1, 4, XXVI, XXVIII, XXXVI, f. (I, 637 E, note b; 644 C; 673 B; 677 E). For sources elsewhere cf. Lebrun, *Explication,* I, 288, note a.—The hymn is inserted generally after the gifts are laid on the altar. Then is added *In spiritu humilitatis* (cf. *supra,* p. 51 f.) and the further epikletic formulas, mostly *Veni sanctificator.*—In a similar role the antiphon *Veni Sancte Spiritus, reple* appears here and there in the 15-16th century; *Alphabetum sacerdotum:* Legg, *Tracts,* 42; Liége missal of the 16th century: Smits van Waesberghe, 326; a Breslau missal of the year 1476: Radó, 163; the Lyons monastic missal of the year 1531: Martène, 1, 4, XXIII (I, 659 C); cf. the missal of S. Pol de Léon: *ibid.,* XXXIV (I, 663 B), where *Kyrie eleison, Christe eleison, Kyrie eleison, Pater noster* and *Ave Maria* precede the *Veni Sancte Spiritus.*—In the Westminster missal (about 1380), ed. Legg (HBS, 5), 500 f., *Veni Creator* is followed by the antiphon *Veni Sancte Spiritus, reple* with the versicle and the oration, *Deus cui omne cor patet.*—Similar invocations are found in the same area at the beginning of Mass; see *supra,* I, 274, 280, 296 f., in the notes.
[154] Batiffol, *Leçons,* 27 f., rightly stresses this point.—In some few instances an ad-

dress to the Holy Spirit is even excluded by the wording of the text; thus, in two Norman texts we find: *Omnipotens Pater, benedic . . . hoc sacrificium;* Martène, 1, 4, XXXVI (I, 673 C); *Domine Deus omnipotens, benedic et sanctifica;* Martène, XXXVI (I, 637 f.).
[155] Two Italian missals of the 11-12th century (Ebner, 310; 328; cf. *supra,* note 146): *Veni sanctificator omnium, Sancte Spiritus.* Another from St. Peter (*ibid.,* 333) has: *Veni Spiritus sanctificator omnium.*—A Sarum ordinarium of the 13th century (Legg, *Tracts,* 221) has: *Veni Sancte Spiritus, benedic . . .*—The Mozarabic *Missale mixtum* (PL, LXXXV, 113 A) also has: *Veni, Sancte Spiritus sanctificator.* The Augsburg missal of 1386 contains an obvious borrowing from the beginning of the hymn: *Veni creator et sanctificator;* Hoeynck, 373; cf. the somewhat varied formula in the Augsburg arrangement of the end of the 15th century: Franz, 752 f.—According to the commentary of Balthasar of Pforta, which appeared in 1494, it was customary at that time to recite either *Veni invisibilis sanctificator* or the antiphon *O rex gloriæ . . . [mitte promissum Patris in nos Spiritum veritatis].* Franz, 587.
[1] But cf. *supra,* I, 317, note 1.

Orate fratres.[2] The incensation at the conclusion of the offertory is first mentioned by Amalar;[3] but in a special preface to his work, written about 832 after his trip to Rome, he indicates that this custom of incensation was unknown in Rome.[4] For that reason it was long contested even in the North,[5] until the date when it at last found entry into Rome itself.[6] In Roman usage incense was burned in fixed braziers; in addition, incense was carried about at the entrance procession, at the procession with the Gospel book, and at the recession; but there was no real incensation.[7] Incensation is therefore a fruit of Carolingian liturgical development. In particular, the incensing at the offertory which we are talking about became far more prominent than the incensations at the beginning of Mass and at the Gospel.[8] And this prominence has been retained in our current liturgy, as is seen in the fact that it is richest in prayers and that the incensing of persons is most developed.

The outline of the present-day form is already encountered in the eleventh century. The Mass *ordo* of Séez has the incensation of the gifts, of the altar, and of those standing around, along with all the prayers that are customary today,[9] while several more recent Mass *ordines* are content with one or the other of these formulas.[10] We thus meet here first of all a prayer for the moment the incense is being put into the censer: *Per inter-*

---

[2] In this trifling detail of medieval liturgical evolution two separate groups are sharply differentiated. The first arrangement is followed in the Sacramentary of the Abbey of S. Denis (11th c.): Martène, 1, 4, V (I, 525 f.), and then in Central Italian abbatial churches: Ebner, 296, 301, 310, etc. Cf. also the Benedictine Mass-plans in Köck, 120, 121.—The other arrangement, with the incensation immediately before the *Orate fratres*, is found in the 10th century Sacramentary of S. Thierry: Martène, 1, 4, X (I, 549 C); Missa Illyrica: *ibid.*, IV (I, 511); Mass-*ordo* of Séez (PL, LXXVIII, 249). Also later outside of Italy, e.g., in Salzburg: Köck, 124 f.

[3] Amalar, *De eccl. off.*, III, 19, 26 (Hanssens, II, 319)—Cf. Hincmar of Reims, *Capitula* (852), c. 6 (PL, CXXV, 774); *Ordo sec. Rom.*, n. 9 (Andrieu, II, 220; PL, LXXVIII, 973 C).

[4] Amalar, *op. cit.*, præfatio altera (PL, CV, 992 B); *Post evangelium non offerunt incensum super altare.*

[5] As late as the 11th century, by Bernold of Constance, *Micrologus*, c. 9 (PL, CLI, 983 B).

[6] The incensation puts in an appearance since the 11th century in Central Italian abbey churches (note 2, *supra*); at the beginning of the 12th century also in Rome, in St. Peter's (Ebner, 333); is then mentioned by Innocent III, *De s. alt. mysterio*, II, 57 f. (PL, CCXVII, 832-834).

[7] Cf. *supra*, I, 68, 71.

[8] The *Ordo "Postquam"* for an episcopal Mass, which originated in Germany in the 10th century, puts the incensation of the altar after the offertory: *offerat illud [incensum] altari*, while it mentions a similar action after the Introit as the practice only of some few churches (Andrieu, II, 354; 360; PL, LXXVIII, 990; 993). Regarding the transient development of the incensation after the gospel, see *supra*, I, 451 f.—For the development of these rites see Batiffol, *Leçons*, 153-158. Numerous details regarding the incensation at the offertory in Atchley, *A History of the Use of Incense*, 247-264.

[9] PL, LXXVIII, 249. Also in the Missa Illyrica: Martène, 1, 4, IV (I, 511), where the anamnesis-type prayer *Memores* cited above, p. 68, note 146, is added.

[10] Cf., e.g., two sacramentaries of the 13th century in Ebner, 326, 342, both of which have only the *Dirigatur*.

cessionem beati Gabrielis archangeli,[11] with a petition to bless the incense and to receive it "for a sweet savor"; a further prayer accompanying the incensation: *Incensum istud*, which continues with the psalm verse, *Dirigatur oratio mea sicut incensum in conspectu tuo, Domine*;[12] and finally the formula which is now spoken by the celebrant when he puts the censer back into the hands of the deacon:[13] *Accendat in nobis Dominus ignem sui amoris et flammam æternæ caritatis*, a prayer which the Mass *ordines* of the eleventh and twelfth centuries appointed to be said by each individual who received the incensation.[14]

These words give us a clue to the meaning then attributed to this incensation, a significance similar to what we saw on earlier occasions:[15] the incense is something dedicated to God, something holy, in which, by a sort of communion, we want to be associated. The glowing coal and the smoke arising from it draw the mind to the very highest thing that we can beg of God as answer to our gift-offerings—the fire of divine love. This

---

[11] The allusion to Michael in the present-day version seems somewhat curious. This name does not appear often, and then only in later texts (e.g., Ebner, 327: 13th c.). It is apparently a deliberate substitution for the Gabriel that is found in most medieval texts. Even as late as Sept. 25, 1705, the Congregation of Rites had to insist on using Michael: Martinucci, *Manuale decretorum SRC*, p. 139. It was perhaps Michael's office as defender of the Church that brought about the abandonment of the clear scriptural reference to Gabriel (Luke 1: 11, 18 f.). There is a certain justification for handling the matter so freely in the fact that the angel in the Apoc. 8: 3-4, who stands beside the heavenly altar with the censer of gold in his hand, is without a name and could therefore as well be Michael as anyone else. But cf. the discussion in Gavanti-Merati, *Thesaurus*, II, 7, 10 (I, 274 f.); U. Holzmeister, *Eph. liturg.*, 59 (1945), 300 f.—The text cited (*Stetit angelus*; cf. the offertory for Sept. 29) is added to the *Dirigatur* in the Pontifical of Christian I of Mainz (1167-1183; cf. Leroquais, *Les pontificaux*, LL, 25): Martène, 1, 4, XVII (I, 601 B).

[12] Already in the 9th-10th century the psalm verse is spoken by the priest: Remigius of Auxerre, *Expositio* (PL, CI, 1252).—In medieval texts as a rule only the one verse, Ps. 140: 2, or even only the half-verse just quoted, is indicated.

This is still the case in the Carthusian rite: *Ordinarium Cart.* (1932), c. 26, 21; and was true till the 13th century of some of the immediate predecessors of the *Missale Romanum* in Central Italy: Ebner, 310, 333, 342. The full text, Ps. 140: 2-4, in Ebner, 327 (13th c.) likewise in the Ordo of Stefaneschi (about 1311), n. 53 (PL, LXXVIII, 1164 C), where, however, the initial verse, *Dirigatur*, is said three times during the triple crossing of the gifts.— The addition of verses 3 and 4 was made not for the sake of the contents but merely as a continuation of the psalm. Nevertheless the celebrating priest had good reason to ask that his lips be hallowed: Gihr, 578 f.

[13] Thus, already in a Central Italian sacramentary of the 13th century in which the texts at the incensation coincide exactly with the present-day ones: Ebner, 327; cf. 314.

[14] This formula, which is often missing, is preceded in the 11th century by the rubric: *Quando odor incensi porrigitur sacerdoti et fratribus, dicat unusquisque eorum: Accendat*. Missa Illyrica: Martène, 1, 4, IV (I, 511 E); Mass-*ordo* of Séez: PL, LXXVIII, 249 C; Camaldolese sacramentary: Ebner, 301 (cf. also 298, 322, where the words appear to be assigned to the incensing cleric). With other formulation also in the Mainz pontifical about 1170 (*supra*, note 11): Martène, 1, 4, XVII (I, 601 B): *Cum redolet incensum*.

[15] *Supra*, I, 318, 451-2.

symbolism we may still apply today to the incensing of the participants. The liturgical texts under consideration avoid using the concept of offering, *sacrificium, oblatio,* in express reference to the incense. The only thing asked for is that the incense might ascend to God and God's mercy might descend to us. The verses of Psalm 140 present the soaring clouds of incense as an illustration of the prayer which we send up to God. The incense is never designated as a formal sacrifice, not even a simple gift. In earlier times, however, even in the West, less care was expended to stay within such strict limits. Amalar calls the activity an *offerre incensum super altare* and manifestly puts it parallel to the Old Testament offering of incense.[16] Already a century earlier the same thought appears in a letter which announces to St. Boniface a shipment of some incense.[17] In the liturgy itself the idea found expression in the prayers accompanying the incensation in the Sacramentary of St. Denis about the middle of the eleventh century;[18] these prayers, which differ sharply from the usual tradition, beg that God may accept this incense as he accepted the gift of the holy men of the Old Covenant. These are the prayers whose Eastern origin, namely, in the Greek liturgy of St. James, has been recognized for some time.[19] In this Eastern sphere both the use and the religious evaluation of incense were strongly developed very early.[20] In the West-Syrian Liturgy mention was made of a three-fold sacrifice completed at each holy Mass— the sacrifice of Melchisedech in the presentation of the bread and wine at the beginning of the celebration, the sacrifice of Aaron in the incensation, and the sacrifice of Christ.[21]

As a matter of fact there is little to reproach in the use of such language as soon as we establish the plain dogma that in the New Testament the one essential sacrifice for the worship of the Church—uniquely essential because God has so ordained it—is the Eucharist.[22] We can symbolize our

---

[16] Lev. 2: 1 f., 15 f. *Supra,* note 4.

[17] Letter of a Roman deacon (742) to Boniface (MGH, Ep. Merow, et Karol. ævi, I, 308): the writer sends him *aliquantum cotzumbri, quod* incensum Domino offeratis *temporibus matutinis et vespertinis, sive dum missarum celebratis sollemnia, miri odoris atque fragrantiæ.*

[18] Martène, 1, 4, V (I, 525 f.).—Cf. also the paraphrase added to Ps. 140: 2 in the missal of St. Vincent (about 1100) : . . . *et elevatio manuum nostrarum cum oblatione huius incensi sit tibi in sacrificium laudis.* Fiala, 205.

[19] Brightman, p. LIV, 1, 10 ff., indicates the model in the Greek liturgy of St. James (Brightman, 32, 36) for three of the six formulas (namely : *Domine D. n. qui suscepisti; Omnipotens s. D. qui es in sanctis;*

Omnipotens s. D. qui es repletus. Also a fourth prayer, *Suscipe quæsumus Domine* —which reappears in the missal of Troyes : Martène, 1, 4, VI (I, 532 E)—is a translation from the same source, being the second half of the incense prayer after the Great Entrance (Brightman, 41, 1. 16: καὶ πρὸςδεξαι).

[20] Cf. E. Fehrenbach, "Encens," DACL, V, 6-11; Atchley, *A History of the Use of Incense,* 117-130. Here in the Orient there are evidences of the use of incense at the start of Mass, at the Gospel and at the climax of the Mass proper, since the fourth century.

[21] M. Jugie, "La messe en Orient," DThC, X, 1331. But cf. in a somewhat different sense Raes, *Introductio,* 66 ff.

[22] Cf. the pertinent discussions in Brink-

abasement before God both by word and by signs, even by gifts of our own selection, and few gifts are so expressive as the incense which is consumed in the charcoal, and then rises skyward in fragrant clouds. In the West, however, incense prayers of this kind were soon dislodged.[23] Obviously the singleness of the Christian sacrifice—which was not diminished by extending the concept of offering to the bread and wine—ought not to be unnecessarily obscured in the prayer-language of the liturgy.[24] Even the symbolic action of lifting the incense up towards God[25] before the incensation of the gifts was dropped.[26] The use of incense even within the offertory was thus only a complement, not an independent gift to almighty God. Wherefore the first swings of the censer are for the gifts of bread and wine which are incensed three times cross-wise, three times in a circle. It is the fullest expression of blessing and consecration and in this way really a re-enforcement of the *Veni sanctificator*.[27] The incense here,

---

trine, *Die hl. Messe*, 143 ff.; Eisenhofer, II, 148 f.; J. Kramp, *Die Opferanschauungen der römischen Meszliturgie*, (2nd. ed.; Regensburg, 1924), 253 note.
[23] The first of the incense prayers in the sacramentary of S. Denis—a prayer originating in the East—with the start: *Domine, Deus noster, qui suscepisti munera pueri tui Abel, Noe, Aaron et omnium sanctorum tuorum*, appears also in the sacramentary of Amiens (*supra*, I, 78); further in the sacramentary of Abbot Ratoldus (d. 986) of Corbie (PL, LXXVIII, 243 A), in the sacramentary of Moissac (11th c.) : Martène, 1, 4, VIII (I, 538 E) ; in the missal of Troyes (about 1050) : *ibid.*, VI (I, 532 D) ; in two Benedictine missals of the 11th, *resp.* 11-12th century from Fonte Avellana: PL, CLI, 934 C, as well as in a ritual of Soissons (not dated) : Martène, 1, 4, XXII (I, 611 f.). Two sources of the 11th century also in Leroquais, I, 139, 161. I have not been able to locate any later examples. (An exception is the missal of Chalons-sur-Marne, printed 1543, in Martène, 1, 4, 7, 1 [I, 394 E]).
—The other borrowings from the liturgy of St. James which Brightman, p. LIV, notes, belong to the same monastic range, from the 10th (not 9th) and 11th century on.
[24] In the *Exultet* of Holy Saturday the Roman liturgy also displays an exception to the stylistic law of liturgical language: *Suscipe, sancte Pater, incensi huius sacrificium vespertinum quod tibi in hac cerei oblatione . . . reddit Ecclesia.* By *incen-*

sum is here meant the ("lighted") candle.
[25] Such a rite is mentioned in the Ordo of Card. Stefaneschi (about 1311), n. 53 (PL, LXXVIII, 1164 C) : *elevet paulisper in altum.*
[26] Akin to this ceremony, although differing in kind, is the use to which the incense is today most frequently put, the incensation of the Eucharist, whereby the censer is swung towards the Blessed Sacrament. But the idea behind the action is not so much to pay homage as to show and symbolize veneration, as is done otherwise in incensing objects and persons. The same is true of the incensation of the cross which follows right after that of the gifts.
[27] Even in the oldest rubrics the incensation is arranged in this fashion; e.g., in the Missa Illyrica: . . . *Thuribulum super panem et calicem circumducitur*, then: *Circumiens autem altare cum incenso;* and lastly: *odor incensi porrigitur . . .*; Martène, 1, 4, IV (I, 511). The crosses made with the incense over the gifts are also expressly mentioned since the 11th century, either a single cross (Ebner, 298) or a triple cross (*ibid.*, 310, 327, 333). At Cluny about 1080 the ceremony included three crosses and a circle; Udalricus, *Consuet. Clun.*, II, 30 (PL, CIL, 717 D.) Innocent III, *De s. alt. mysterio*, II, 57 (PL, CCXVII, 832), like other older sources, mentions only the (threefold) encircling of the gifts. Durandus, IV, 31, 1, who here for the most part copies Innocent III, makes note of a threefold crossing and a threefold encircling of the chalice, but

just as the further incensing of the altar and the congregation, is intended to envelop the gifts in the holy atmosphere of prayer which "ascends to Thy countenance like incense clouds"; thus it is intended to symbolically represent and to fortify the primary action at the altar.

In the manner of performing the incensation only a few variations need be mentioned. In some cases the celebrant himself performs only the incensation of the sacrificial gifts and perhaps the altar front, leaving the rest to the deacon, who circles the altar.[28] Otherwise, the encircling of the altar is also accented.[29] But although it remained as at least a liturgical norm at the consecration of the altar,[30] at the offertory it gave way before the actualities of Gothic altar-building, so that as a rule it is now omitted even where structural conditions would allow it.[31] However, even in the present-day manner of incensing the altar, the original conception is still plainly to be recognized. According to current custom, the incensation of the altar is always followed by the incensation of the celebrant,[32] and at the offertory also by the incensation of the choir by the deacon,[33] the manner and exact seriation of which, especially for the various circumstances of a great cathedral, are determined by numerous decrees of the

also acknowledges that some are content with a single circle and a single cross; *ibid.,* 31, 3. For further details see Atchley, 249-254.—During this censing of the gifts sometimes only *In nomine Patris* . . . is recited; Mass plan of the Carthusians (which also contains a peculiar arrangement for the censing of the altar): Martène, 1, 4, XXV (I, 632 E); *Ordinarium Cart.* (1932), c. 26, 21. Cf. missal of Fécamp (about 1400): Martène, XXVII (I, 640 C), and *supra* p. 66, note 137 (near the end).

[28] John of Avranches, *De off. eccl.* (PL, CXLVII, 35 C); Missal of St. Vincent (Fiala, 205; cf. 199); *Ordo eccl. Lateran.* (Fischer, 83); Mass-*ordo* of the Carthusians: Martène, 1, 4, XXV (I, 632 f.); *Ordinarium Cart.* (1932), c. 26, 21. Cf. a missal of the 11-12th century in Ebner, 310. According to the *Rituale* of Soissons: Martène, 1, 4, XXII (I, 612 A), the deacon incenses the priest, the *cornua altaris,* the Eucharist hanging (in a Dove) over the altar, then the other altars, the crucifix and the rood altar, finally the *succentor.* While doing so he recites Psalm 140 from the beginning: *Domine clamavi.* The choir is incensed by the *clericulus.*— A detailed norm for the incensation of the choir (by the thurifer) is given in the

Sarum Missal: Martène, 1, 4, XXXV (I, 667); cf. the Sarum Customary (13th c.); Frere, *The Use of Sarum,* I, 76 f.

[29] Cf. *supra,* note 27; Missa Illyrica: Martène, 1, 4, IV (I, 511 E); Mass-*ordo* of Séez: *ibid.,* XIII (I, 578 B); PL, LXXVIII, 249 C.

[30] *Pontificale Romanum,* II, *De altaris consecratione.*

[31] However, a contrary custom was admitted by the Congregation of Rites on Feb. 3, 1877: *Decreta auth. SRC,* n. 3413.

[32] A peculiar usage is offered by the *Liber ordinarius* of the Premonstratensians (12th c.; Lefèvre, 10; Waefelghem, 66 f.): the deacon, after meanwhile incensing the altar, incenses the celebrant when the latter turns for the *Orate.* Likewise later, besides other Benedictine sources (Waefelghem, 67, note 1) the *Liber ordinarius* of Liége (Volk, 93) and even at present the Carthusian rite: Martène, 1, 4, XXV (I, 633 A); *Ordinarium Cart.* (1932), c. 29, 13.

[33] According to the English usage of the late Middle Ages the incensation of the choir was provided only on days with a *Credo,* that is, on days of greater rank; Frere, *The Use of Sarum,* I, 77; Sarum Missal: Martène, 1, 4, XXXV (I, 667 E).

Congregation of Sacred Rites;[84] and finally by the incensation of the deacon, of the lower assistants, and of the people by the thurifer.[85]

6. The Washing of the Hands

After the sacrificial gifts are laid ready on the altar, and after the incensation, if there is any, there follows the washing of the hands. Its meaning today in the spot it occupies is no longer plainly to be seen. Evidently the action, which now consists of nothing more than wetting the fingertips, has some symbolic significance. But even so we would like to know why it takes place just here and now.

It is natural that we handle precious things only with hands that are clean. Or to put it more generally, a person approaches a festive or sacred activity only after he has cleansed himself from the grime of the workday and besides has donned festive attire. Thus we find in the liturgy, besides the vesting in liturgical garments, also a washing of hands. In Christian antiquity there is repeated evidence of the established custom of washing the hands before giving oneself to prayer.[1] Domestic devotion was also ruled by this law. We are, therefore, not surprised to find a washing of hands expressly mentioned in the liturgy at a very early date. At Jerusalem in the fourth century, the Mass of the Faithful began with the deacon's administering the water to the celebrant and the surrounding presbyters,[2] and from the very start the symbolic meaning of the act was stressed. Similar was the custom in the Antiochene church.[3] We gen-

---

[84] Gavanti-Merati, *Thesaurus*, II, 7, 10 (I, 274-282). The *gubernator civitatis* is censed, as well as the *baro dominus in ecclesia parochiali*. Yet even for a large choir no second censer is permitted (281). And both of these rubricists are agreed that scope should be given for any *rationabilis consuetudo*, alleging as a reason: *ad pacem et concordiam tum cleri tum laicorum conservandam* (274, 282). This last remark was prompted by some very unhappy experiences. The acts of the Council of Trent (*Concilium Trid.*, ed. Gœrres, IX, 591 f.) tell of a *magna contentio* that occurred at high Mass on June 29, 1563, between the Spanish and French delegates *in dando thure et pace.*—A detailed arrangement for the choir often even in the Middle Ages, e.g., in the *Ordinarium O.P.* of 1256 (Guerrini, 234, 239 f.) ; here and in other cases it embraces also the giving of the *pax* and the *aspersio.*

[85] Already in the *Ordo eccl. Lateran.* (Fischer, 83) the arrangement is much like the present, only that the *mansionarius* un-

dertakes the incensation also of the choir: *Mansionarius itaque accipiens thuribulum de manu diaconi ei incensum odorandum præbet. Quod postquam fecerit, dat incensum fratribus per chorum, postea dat et populo.* For this *odorare* cf. *supra,* I, 452, note 68.

---

[1] Hippolytus, *Trad. Ap.* (Dix, 65; Hauler, 119) ; *Canones Basilii,* c. 28 (Riedel, 246). —Tertullian, *De or.,* c. 13 (CSEL, 20, 188 f.), combats the notion that this washing of the hands was necessary. Cf. for this Elfers, *Die Kirchenordnung Hippolyts,* 38-42.

[2] Cyril of Jerusalem, *Catech. myst.,* V, 2 (Quasten, *Mon.,* 97 f.).

[3] *Const. Ap.,* VIII, 11, 12 (Quasten, *Mon.,* 211) : a subdeacon hands all the priests the ἀπόρρυψις χειρῶν after the kiss of peace. The same arrangement in Theodore of Mopsuestia, *Sermones catech.,* V (Rücker, 25).—In Ps.-Dionysius, *De eccl. hierarchia,* III, 2; 3, 10 (Quasten, *Mon.,* 295; 308 f.), the washing of the hands is

erally come upon this same washing of the hands likewise in the oriental liturgies of the following era. As a rule it comes right after the gifts have been carried over to the altar.[4] The rite received a notable extension in the Ethiopian Mass: after the priest has unveiled the gifts on the altar, he washes his hands but does not dry them at once; instead he turns and sprinkles the water clinging to his fingers towards the people with a threatening word of warning to those unworthy ones who might want to draw nigh to the Lord's table.[5]

There were attempts, too, to extend to the people either the washing itself or at least some token of it that referred admonishingly to the purity of the interior man. In the atrium of the ancient Christian basilica stood the fount or well[6] which was understood precisely in this sense, and even at the entrance of our own churches there is the holy-water stoup for the people to sprinkle themselves. But since Carolingian times the parish high Mass on Sundays begins with the sprinkling of holy water over the assembled congregation, a custom explained by the very words which are linked with it: *Asperges me Domine hyssopo et mundabor.* The symbolism of purity and purification has obviously been from the very start the guiding factor for the ablutions in the liturgy. This is made clear in the oriental liturgies where the washing of the hands at the prescribed time was never, or hardly anywhere, based on the fact that the offerings were received just previously, for this was done before the beginning of Mass.[7] It is simply an act of reverence after the Great Entrance, connected with the actual entrance into the sanctuary.

It is significant that even in the Western Mass we find the washing of the hands precisely in that place where the holy circle is entered; and because it is a multiple circle, we encounter this hand-washing at divers points: first when we penetrate the outermost circle, and last when we stand at the very threshold of the innermost sanctuary. Even in the earlier medieval sources a hand-washing before vesting is found as a constituent

---

placed somewhat later, after the reading of the diptychs; the fact that only the fingertips are washed is enough to indicate the state of perfect purity which is here required.

[4] Brightman, 82, 62, 1. 32; 226; 271, 1. 13; 432, 1. 29.—This washing of the hands is missing in the Byzantine liturgy. Here there is only a hand-washing before Mass, as in most of the other liturgies. In the East-Syrian Mass of the Nestorians a threefold hand-washing is customary; the third takes place before the fraction. Hanssens, III, 7-11. Cf. also the surveys in Raes, *Introductio,* 72 f., 84 f. In the East-Syrian custom cited by Raes, 97 f., a *thurificatio digitorum* appears to have taken

over the function of the hand-washing before the fraction.

[5] "If there be any who is pure let him receive of the host, and whoso is not pure let him not receive, that he be not consumed in the fire of the Godhead, whoso hath revenge in his heart and hath an alien mind by reason of unchastity. I am pure from the blood of you and from your sacrilege against the body and blood of Christ: I have nought to do with your reception thereof: I am pure of your error, and your sin will return upon your own head if ye receive not in purity." Liturgy of the Abyssinian Jacobites (Brightman, 226).

[6] Beissel, *Bilder,* 254 f.

[7] *Supra,* p. 4.

of the Mass pattern,[8] and even today it is still presupposed, though with mitigated importance, in the hand-washing in the sacristy.

However, we come upon some isolated instances of hand-washing immediately before the consecration.[9] The ring encircling the consecration is the canon. Since the canon has been considered as beginning with the *Te igitur*, there are to be found some cases of a hand-washing just before the *Te igitur*. Originally it was the deacon who washed his hands here,[10] since he would assist in the elevation of the chalice at the end of the canon, or else it was the deacons[11] who had to help with the fraction; but towards the end of the Middle Ages this hand-washing had to a great extent become the priest's, especially in German territory.[12]

But the hand-washing that came into special prominence was the more ancient one at the beginning of the sacrifice-Mass in connection with the offertory. This, too, bears first of all a symbolic character. According to the oldest sources, the pope at the Roman stational service first washed his hands right after the *Oremus*.[13] Then he received the gifts of the nobility. Returning to his throne, he again washed his hands, and only then did he go to the altar and receive the gifts of the clerics.[14] In other

---

[8] *Supra*, I, 277 f.

[9] In the Milanese Mass: *Missale Ambrosianum* (1902), 177. The custom is naturally of a later date. Nevertheless it is found in the missal of 1560: Martène, 1, 4, III (I, 484 f.). In the older Milanese rite there was only a hand-washing at the beginning of Mass. Originally, it seems, this hand-washing at the vesting was the only one found in the Gallic liturgies. Fortescue, *The Mass*, 311.

[10] Ordinarium of Bayeux (13-14th century): Martène, 1, 4, XXIV (I, 629 B).— Elsewhere this washing of hands takes place only after the *Supplices;* thus at Cluny in the 11th century: Udalricus, *Consuet. Clun.*, II, 30 (PL, CIL, 719). Durandus, too, knows of this hand-washing of the deacon in this spot as a custom *in nonnullis ecclesiis:* Durandus, IV, 44, 5. Among these churches was that of Sarum, where the subdeacon participated in the hand-washing: Frere, *The Use of Sarum*, I, 79; 82. This last is true also of one Cistercian arrangement, where the hand-washing was placed right after the *Orate fratres;* de Moléon, 233.

[11] *Ordo "Postquam"* for a bishop's Mass (10th c.), n. 11 (Andrieu, II, 360; PL, LXXVIII, 993 B): After the *Sanctus* three acolytes appear with water for the deacons. Even in Amalar, *De eccl. off.*, III,

25 (PL, CV, 1143 A), this hand-washing of the deacon is mentioned near the close of the canon, and an allegorical reason— the purifying action of the Passion of Christ—is given for it. In the sacramentary of Ratoldus (10th c.) it appears after the secreta (PL, LXXVIII, 243 B; cf. Netzer, 229). This appears to be an ancient Gallic usage.

[12] Franz, 106; 550, 575; 753; Binterim, IV, 3, p. 224; Beck, 268; Köck, 62; Gerbert, *Vetus liturgia Alemannica*, I, 330.— This hand-washing, too, took place on the epistle side; Beck, 268.—According to the Cologne *Ordo celebrandi*, the action was accompanied by the words: *Dele Domine omnes iniquitates meas, ut tua mysteria digne possim tractare;* Binterim, *loc. cit.*— This hand-washing already in a 14th century missal from upper Hungary, where the accompanying words were Is. 53: 7 and the secreta for Maundy Thursday, *Ipse;* Radó, 68.

[13] Ordo of Johannes Archicantor (Silva-Tarouca, 197 f.); Ordo of S. Amand (Duchesne, 459).

[14] Ordo of Johannes Archicantor *(loc. cit.)*. In the Ordo of S. Amand this second washing is for the deacon, not the celebrant. If we follow Andrieu's study of the sources *(Les Ordines Romani)* we must conclude that the first of these hand-washings is

accounts this second washing alone is mentioned,[15] but it takes place before the reception of the clerical oblation and is therefore governed not so much by practical motives, but rather by symbolical ones. It is an expression of reverence at the threshold of the Holy of Holies.[16] The same arrangement is to be found in various localities throughout the entire Middle Ages, insofar as a hand-washing is provided for in the course of the Mass. It is found at the start of the offertory, fixed in such a way that any preoccupation with the gift-offerings can hardly come into consideration as a basis of explanation.[17] This is particularly plain in the rite of the Franciscans, who generally did not permit the oblations of the faithful at Mass;[18] they, too, began the offertory with the washing of the hands.[19]

At the same time, however, there also appear various arrangements of the Mass in which the hand-washing is set to follow the offertory procession of the faithful; without detracting from any other symbolic interpretation, they establish the principle that by this hand-washing the priest must cleanse his hands *a tactu communium manuum atque terreno*

Gallican in origin, the second Roman.

[15] *Ordo Rom.* I, n. 14 (PL, LXXVIII, 944) ; *Ordo Rom.* II, n. 9 (PL, LXXVIII, 973). Also in the Gregorian Sacramentary of Ratoldus (10th c., PL, LXXVIII, 243 A), which adapted to Frankish conditions, and which likewise has a hand-washing at the vesting before Mass, with a prayer accompaniment (*ibid.*, 241 A).— Cf. *Ordo eccl. Lateran.* (Fischer, 82, 1. 25).

[16] Cf. Cod. Ratoldi *(loc. cit.)*: *lavetque manus et sic ingrediatur propitiatorium, et omnis processio offerant sibi oblationem.* —In the East Syrian (Chaldean and Syro-Malabarese rite the symbols of reverence have been developed with special luxuriance. Here, after washing his hands, the priest leaves the bema (sanctuary) and pausing three times he re-enters the sanctuary, praying the while and making several bows; then he genuflects three times and kisses the altar first in the middle, then at the right and left, and again in the middle. Raes, *Introductio*, 83; cf. Brightman, 271-274.—Cf. the kissing of the altar in this place also in the ancient Roman liturgy, *supra*, I, 71; 314, note 20.

[17] Missa Illyrica: Martène, 1, 4, IV (I, 505 E) ; Sacramentary of S. Denis: *ibid.*, V (I, 523 C) ; Missal of St. Vincent: Fiala, 202 f. ; Italian Mass-books of the 12-

14th century: Ebner, 312, 314, 347; *Liber ordinarius O. Præm.* (Waefelghem, 59; cf. 57 with note 2). In the Scandinavian province of Lund the ablution took place at the start of the offertory, in the province of Nidaros (Trondheim) and of Upsala, before the oration *In spiritu humilitatis*: Eric Segelberg, "De ordine Missæ secundum ritum scandinavicum medii ævi," *Eph. liturg.*, 65 (1951), 256.—The symbolical meaning of the ablution was given emphatic expression at Klosterneuburg even as late as the 15th century, for at a high Mass the subdeacon washed his hands before touching the chalice, the deacon before he spread the corporal, and lastly the priest before he took the paten; Schabes, 63.—The deacon's ablution is also mentioned in St. Vincent: Fiala, 202.—Lebrun, *Explication*, I, 304, note a, cites a Mass-ordo printed at Antwerp as late as 1570, where the ablution of the hands is placed right at the start of a low Mass. The same peculiarity is found in the commentary of William of Gouda (15th c.; P. Schlager, *Franziskan. Studien*, 6 [1919], 332) and in the Cologne missal of 1506 (Freisen, *Manuale Lincopense*, p. LVIII, note).

[18] *Supra*, p. 24, note 134.

[19] William of Melitona, *Opusc. super missam*, ed. van Dijk (*Eph. liturg.*, 1939), 328 f., and the further references of the

pane.[20] Sometimes it still precedes the arranging of the gifts on the altar,[21] and in some instances even the incensing is designed to follow.[22]

It is easy to understand how the next step would be taken; the incensation would be made to precede, and this would be done *ad maiorem munditiam*.[23] According to one monastic instruction, the priest should now take care not to grasp anything with the fingers that would touch the Body of the Lord.[24] This hand-washing often stands side by side with the first more ancient one which is done before the offertory,[25] as is still the case in the present-day pontifical rite.[26] But in the following years the older one was dropped, and only the more recent one remained.[27] In the rite of the Carthusians, however, the hand-washing has retained its position in the more ancient spot.

Since the Frankish era the fundamental symbolic thought of the hand-washing is regularly expressed in the words which accompany it. The *Lavabo*, which is literally a protestation of the Psalmist's innocence, and which becomes in our mouth an expression of a longing for purity and a worthy service at the altar, was associated with this hand-washing at quite an early period, but its earliest association was with the washing done at the vesting. Usually the only portion used was the one verse, Psalm 25:6, or the two verses 6 and 7. Later, the rest of the psalm was

---

editor (*ibid.*, note 182).—Cf. Ebner, 177, 314.

[20] Amalar, *De eccl. off.*, III, 19 (PL, CV, 1130 B). Cf. Rabanus Maurus, *De inst. cler.*, I, 33, additio (PL, CVII, 324 D); *Ordo Rom.* VI (10th c.), n. 9 (PL, LXXVIII, 992 D).—In some few Italian Mass-books the ablution follows immediately after the offertory procession: Ebner, 309; 340 (Vall. C 32); cf. Bonizo of Sutri (d. about 1095), *De vita christiana*, II, 51 (ed. Perels, 59). Likewise to all appearances in the Netherlands Mass-plans and in the Cologne Mass at the end of the Middle Ages: Smits van Waesberghe, 300; cf. 325 ff.; Binterim, IV, 3, p. 227.

[21] Thus, *inter alia*, French Mass-plans of the late Middle Ages: Martène, 1, 4, XXVI, XXXI, XXXIII, f. (I, 637 D, 651 A, 659 C, 663 B); likewise English Mass-plans: Legg, *Tracts*, 5, 221; Cistercian Mass-plan of the 15th century: Franz, 587. But also earlier the order for the private Mass at Cluny: Bernardus, *Ordo Clun.*, I, 72 (Herrgott, 264).

[22] Sacramentary of the 13th century of Lyons: Ebner, 326; Benedictine missal of the 11-12th century from Central Italy: *ibid.*, 337.

[23] *Ordo Rom.* XIV, n. 53 (PL, LXXVIII, 1165 A).

[24] Udalricus, *Consuet. Clun.*, II, 30 (PL, CIL, 717 B); William of Hirsau, *Const.*, I, 84 (PL, CL, 1012 A). The same rule in Durandus, IV, 31, 4, who adds that the priest should close his fingers after the ablution.

[25] *Ordo Rom.* XIV, n. 53 (PL, LXXVIII, 1163 B); the second is mentioned as tolerated, but otherwise not customary *in Ecclesia Romana* (1165 A); cf. *Ordo Rom.* XIV, n. 71 (PL, LXXVIII, 1186 f.), and the Mass-*ordo* of the papal court chapel about 1290 (Brinktrine: *Eph. liturg.*, 1937, 201 f.), where in both cases only the first ablution is found. This is still true at Tongern as late as 1413; de Corswarem, 126.—Both ablutions also in the *Statuta antiqua* of the Carthusians: Martène, 1, 4, XXV (I, 632 C E).—Pontifical of Durandus, *ibid.*, XXIII (I, 617 C, d); Andrieu, III, 640. Here is the remark that at the second ablution the celebrant washes only *summitates digitorum et labia*. Obviously this goes beyond mere symbolism.—Durandus, V, 28, 1; cf. Sölch, *Hugo*, 80.

[26] *Cæremoniale episc.*, I, 11, 11.

[27] Thus already in the rite of the Carmel-

appended, but this was done without any special consideration of the contents, which have no intimate relation to the washing.[28] Medieval arrangements of the Mass often added more appropriate texts to the verses mentioned, both for the hand-washing at the start of Mass[29] and for this one here. In the ambit of Monte Cassino, in the eleventh and twelfth centuries, there was added to the *Lavabo* an oration, *Concede mihi, omnipotens Deus, ita manum lavare ut puro corde et corpore possim dominicum corpus et sanguinem tractare.*[30] Late Mass *ordines* in northern France supplement the *Lavabo* with a three-fold *Kyrie eleison* and *Pater noster.*[31] Often, too, some such complementary oration appears as the only accompanying text.[32] All the elements that go to make up a well-arranged ceremonial are thus brought together.[33]

How strongly the symbolic sense of the hand-washing is emphasized can be seen in a monastic Mass-*ordo* of Rouen; according to this, the cele-

ites, of the Dominicans (except in the earliest period: Sölch, 81) and formerly of the Cistercians; see the references in Sölch, 80. Only the later ablution, following the model of the *Ordinarium O.P.* of 1256 (Guerrini, 240), in the Benedictine *Liber ordinarius* of Liége: Volk, 93.—Late medieval Mass-arrangements in Martène, 1, 4, XX, XXII, XXIV (I, 608 D, 612 B, 629 A). In the later Mass-*ordo* of Gregorienmünster: *ibid.*, XXXII (I, 656 E), the ablution does not occur till after the *Orate.*
[28] Spanish Mass-books of the late Middle Ages use verses 2-4 for the ablution (Ferreres, 129); similarly also the present-day *Ordinarium Cartusiense* (1932), c. 26, 18. The Mass-plan of York about 1425 uses only one verse (Simmons, 100). The Dominican missal of 1256 indicated only the first verse; see Bonniwell, *A History of the Dominican Liturgy* (New York, 1944), 125; the present Dominican rite still has only one verse (*Missale O.P.*, 1889, 181).—The complete section as at present was very rare in the Middle Ages; but see the text above. [29] *Supra*, I, 277.
[30] Ebner, 309, 340; Fiala, 202. Later in the missal of Toul (14-15th c.) this oration is the sole accompaniment of the ablution at this place; Martène, 1, 4, XXXI (I, 651A).
[31] Missal of Evreux: Martène, 1, 4, XXVIII (I, 644 C); *Alphabetum sacerdotum*: Legg, *Tracts*, 41 f.; *Ordinarium* of Coutance: *ibid.*, 60.
[34] Missa Illyrica (cf. *supra*, note 17): *Largire sensibus nostris, omnipotens Pater, ut sicut hic exterius abluuntur inquina-*

menta manuum, sic a te mundentur interius pollutiones mentium et crescat in nobis sanctarum augmentum virtutum. Per.; Martène, 1, 4, IV (I, 505 E). Likewise in the sacramentary of S. Denis: *ibid.*, V (I, 523 C), and in Central Italian Mass-plans: Ebner, 337, 347, 356; cf. Ferreres, 129.— Gerhoh of Reichersberg (d. 1169) introduces the oration in his explanation of Psalm 25: 6 (PL, 193, 1165 B). The Pontifical of Durandus (Andrieu, 640) uses the oration *Largire* at the ablution before the offertory and the *Lavabo* after the incensation when the bishop washes *summitates digitorum et labia.* — An Italian pontifical of the 11-12th century (Ebner, 312) offers the prayer: *Omnipotens sempiterne Deus, ablue cor nostrum et manus a cunctis sordibus peccatorum, ut templum Spiritus Sancti effici mereamur. Per.* — According to the late medieval order of Sarum, in Martène, 1, 4, XXXV (I, 667 E), the celebrant says: *Munda me Domine ab omni inquinamento cordis et corporis nostri, ut possim mundus implere opus sanctum Domini.* Cf. Ferreres, 133 (n. 531); Frere, *The Use of Sarum*, I, 77; Maskell, 92.—According to the commentary of William of Gouda (15th c.) the priest prays: *Amplius lava me sanguine tuo sicut puer in baptismo ...*; P. Schlager, *Franziskan. Studien*, 6 (1919), 332.
[33] In the Regensburg missal of 1500 (Beck, 261), the priest at the ablution before vesting recites the verse *Lavabo* first as an antiphon, then Psalm 25 in its entirety, again the antiphon, *Kyrie eleison*, etc.,

brants's *Lavabo* is answered by the abbot with the *Misereatur*.[34] Thus the hand-washing is turned into a formal act of absolution.

However, the hand-washing is occasionally found even at a later time without any formula,[35] and oftener still there is no mention of it whatever in the course of the Mass.[36] In the case of late medieval arrangements of non-solemn Mass, the explanation for this lack is to be found in the practical motivation of the hand-washing, since there would be no question of it when there was neither offertory procession nor incensation. In the Missal of Pius V, however, the hand-washing was retained for every Mass, high or low. This shows that the symbolic meaning of the rite still remained in the foreground; only the position it occupies in the Mass is reminiscent of the other and later concept of its purpose as a precaution before handling the sacred Host and chalice during the canon.

7. *Orate Fratres*

One of the few fixed points which recur unchanged in all the medieval oblation rites is a petition found near the end of the rite, a petition by the priest for the prayer of the bystanders. According to the eighth century Roman pontifical rite as adapted to Frankish circumstances, such a ceremony occurred right after the celebrant had added his own gift to the oblation of the faithful and the clergy; he then turned around and, stretching out his arms, asked the other priests to pray for him.[1] No response is indicated. As is the case today, *oratio super oblata* followed, and it is significant that this prayer was here spoken for the first time in a hushed voice, so that it appears to form some sort of unit with the canon.

The petition for prayer thus occurs at the moment when the presentation and arrangement of the gifts is completed, and the priest at the head of the congregation and in its name is about to draw near to God with those gifts. The ceremony has its parallel,[2] perhaps even its model, in the

Pater noster, Ave, some versicles and the oration *Largire.* Cf. above, I, 277, note 9.
[34] Martène, 1, 4, XXXVII (I, 677 f.).
[35] Thus in a Minorite missal, in Ebner, 314.—Elsewhere at the ablution the priest recites the *Veni Creator* (cf. *supra,* I, 274, note 15; 280, note 28): Mass-*ordo* of Bec: Martène, 1, 4, XXXVI (I, 673 B); Westminster missal (about 1380), ed. Legg (HBS, 5), 500; cf. Maskell, 92 f. In Hereford (1502) he adds thereto the oration *Ure igne S. Spiritus:* Maskell, 93. — In German Mass-arrangements at the close of the Middle Ages the hand-washing appears after the *Sanctus* without any accompanying prayer: Franz, 753; Bec. 268.
[36] Thus in many Italian Mass-plans; see

Ebner, 296, 298 f., 300 f., etc. Also in South German Mass-books: Beck, 307 f.; Köck, 119-ff.
[1] *Breviarium eccl. ord.* (Silva-Tarouca, 198) : *Tunc vero sacerdos dextera lævaque aliis sacerdotibus postulat pro se orare.* Probably this passage is not Roman in origin, for the parallel text in John the Arch-chanter's *Capitulare* (*ibid.*) has no such sentence.
[2] In the Greek liturgy of St. Mark we find, in a similar connection, the priest's greeting and then the deacon's summons: Προςεύξασθε ὑπὲρ τῶν προςφερόντων; thereupon an oblation prayer of the priest and the introduction to the anaphora: Brightman, 124.

Eastern liturgies.[3] Here, too, the original meaning seems to be the same. For the Western rite we have the early opinion of Amalar to the same effect. It anticipates the *Sursum corda* and endeavors to summon, so to say, all the forces of prayer; for this reason let the priest turn to the people *et precatur ut orent pro illo, quatenus dignus sit universæ plebis oblationem offerre Domino*.[4] The priest feels very strongly that he is exalted above the people—a matter the early medieval Church was fully conscious of—and even in his sacrificial prayer he realizes he stands alone before God as the people's mediator.[5]

The same idea may be gleaned from the fact that even in the earliest examples where the wording is included—and thence throughout the Middle Ages—the petition for prayer almost always retains a personal character *Orate pro me*.[6] Instances where this *pro me* is wanting do appear in some of the oldest sources,[7] but on the other hand the personal note recurs in the most diverse forms: *pro me* or *pro me peccatore*,[8] also *pro me misero peccatore*,[9] and *pro me miserrimo peccatore*;[10] or the personal note is even stressed by the phrase: *Obsecro vos, fratres, orate pro me*,[11] or by the promise: *Orate pro me, fratres et sorores, et ego orabo pro vobis . . .*,[12]

---

[3] In the West Syrian (Brightman, 83, 1. 2) and in the East Syrian Mass (*ibid.*, 272 f.) there is a traditional custom, common to both and consequently quite ancient, which is closely allied to the western practice. In the first (the Syrian Jacobite) liturgy the priest says: "My brethren and my masters, pray for me that my sacrifice be accepted." In the second (the Nestorian) rite his prayer is longer: "Pray for me, my brethren and my beloved, that I be accounted worthy to offer before our Lord Jesus Christ this sacrifice living and holy for myself and for all the body of the holy Church by the grace of His compassion forever. Amen." And in this latter liturgy there is also a response somewhat similar to our *Suscipiat* (273).

[4] Amalar, *De eccl. off.*, III, 19 (PL, CV, 1132); cf. Remigius of Auxerre (d. about 908), *Expositio* (PL, CI, 1252): *ut iungant preces suas precibus eius et mereatur exaudiri pro salute eorum. Hoc autem dicendum est a sacerdote cum silentio.*

[5] Cf. *supra*, I, 82 f.

[6] Simply these words in *Ordo Rom.* VI, n. 10 (PL, LXXVIII, 993 B); with the present-day extension in the sacramentary of the papal chapel about 1290: Brinktrine (*Eph. liturg.*, 11937), 203; yet cf. *Ordo Rom.* XIV, n. 72 (PL, LXXVIII,

1194 A) against n. 53, 71 (1165 B, 1187 B).

[7] Sacramentary of Amiens (9th c.): *Orate fratres, ut...*, Leroquais (*Eph. liturg.*, 1937, 442. Likewise the two sacramentaries of S. Thierry (9th and 10th c.): Martène, 1, 4, IX; X (I, 446 E, 549 D); cf. *ibid.*, XV (I, 592 C). In *Ordo Rom.* II, n. 9 (PL, LXXVIII, 973 C) the priest says only: *Orate.*

[8] For the latter see Sacramentary of Lorsch (10th c.): Ebner, 247; Missa Illyrica: Martène, 1, 4, IV (I, 512 A). Also in Italian Mass orders since the 11th century: Ebner, 301, 306, 327. Likewise still in the *Ordinarium Cartusiense* (1932), c. 26, 21.

[9] Martène, 1, 4, XIII; XXVII (I, 578 C, 640 E); cf. *ibid.*, XXXII (I, 656 D).

[10] Missal of Fécamp: Martène, 1, 4, XXVI (I, 638 A); a Dominican missal of the 13th century: Sölch, 83, note 193.

[11] Sacramentary of Moissac: Martène, 1, 4, VIII (I, 539 D); further examples, *ibid.*, 1, 4, 7, 4 (I, 396); Ferreres, 131 f.; cf. Ebner, 323.—In the Mozarabic liturgy there is a further reinforcement: *Adiuvate me, fratres, in orationibus vestris et orate pro me ad Deum; Missale mixtum* (PL, LXXXV, 537 A).

[12] Missal from S. Pol de Léon: Martène,

or even, in one case, by a formal self-accusation;[13] or the humility of the petition is underlined by the bodily bearing, the priest crossing his hands over his breast.[14] At any rate the next clause, which is seldom missing,[15] stresses the idea that the aid of prayer is being asked for the priest's own sacrifice, which is likewise the sacrifice of the congregation, so that it might be acceptable. The usual version reads: *ut meum pariter et vestrum sacrificium acceptum sit Deo.*[16]

The original conception is finally abandoned when in England and in Normandy, in special formulas for Masses for the Dead, prayer is asked only for the dead.[17]

To whom is the petition directed? In the most ancient example cited above it is addressed to the priests standing around. The statements of the succeeding era, beginning with Amalar, mention the people without

1, 4, XXXIV (I, 663 C); similarly *ibid.*, 1, 4, 7, 4 (I, 396 A); 1, 4, XXVIII (I, 644 D); *Alphabetum sacerdotum*: Legg, *Tracts*, 42; Hugo of St. Cher, *Tractatus* (ed. Sölch, 23); Durandus, IV, 32, 3.

[13] Missal of Toul: Martène, 1, 4, XXXI (I, 651 C): *Orate fratres pro me peccatore, ut auferat Deus spiritum elationis et superbiæ a me, ut pro meis et pro cunctis vestris delictis exorare queam. Per.*

[14] According to a didactic poem on the Mass written in German towards the end of the 12th century: Leitzmann (Kleine Texte, 54), 18, 1. 18.

[15] It is missing in a few older Mass orders: *Ordo Rom.* II, n. 9 (*supra*, note 7); *Ordo Rom.* VI, n. 10 (PL, LXXVIII, 993 B: *Orate pro me*); Ebner, 329, 334. But it is also still wanting today in the Dominican and Carthusian uses.

[16] Thus already in Remigius of Auxerre, *Expositio* (PL, CI, 1252 B). Still the formula seldom recurs without some slight alteration: . . . *sit acceptum in conspectu Domini*: Martène, 1, 4, V (I, 526 D); cf. *ibid.*, XXVI, XXVIII (638 A, 644 D); *in conspectu D. n. J. C.*: Martène, IV (533 C); *sit acceptabile in conspectu divinæ pietatis*: Martène, XIII (I, 578 C); . . . *coram Deo acceptum sit sacrificium*: Martène, XXXIV (I, 663 C); *aptum sit Domino Deo nostro sacrificium*: Martène, XXXV (I, 668 A); etc.—The missal of St. Lawrence in Liége: Martène, 1, 4, XV (I, 592 C), offers a choice of this formula or two others, more freely composed: *ut me orantem pro vobis exaudiat Dominus,*

and: *Orate fratres pro me peccatore, ne mea peccata obsistant votis vestris.* A Mass-*ordo* of Bec: *ut digne valeam sacrificium offerre Deo*: Martène, XXXVI (I, 673 C); cf. Amalar's formulation, *supra*, p. 83. A Missale of Narbonne (1528) begs prayer *pro statu s. Dei Ecclesiæ et pro me misero peccatore, ut omnipotens et misericors Deus placide et benigne sacrificium nostrum humiliter dignetur suscipere.* Martène, 1, 4, 7, 4 (I, 396 A).—Or else there is added to *Orate* the words *ad Dominum* —either *ad Dominum Deum Patrem omnipotentem* (Beck, 268), or even: *ad Dominum Jesum Christum, ut . . . placabile fiat* (Ferreres, 131).—By way of exception we find mention only of *vestrum sacrificium*: Martène, 1, 4, XXXIII (I, 659 DE), or of *nostrum sacrificium*: XVII (I, 601 C). —Striking is the formula in the sacramentary of Amiens (9th c.): *ut vestrum pariter et nostrum sacrificium acceptabile fiat Deo;* Leroquais (*Eph. liturg.*, 1927), 442.

[17] Thus the use of Sarum: *Orate fratres* (later version: *et sorores*) *pro fidelibus defunctis;* Martène, 1, 4, XXXV (I, 668 B); Legg, *Tracts*, 5, 221; Legg, *The Sarum Missal*, 219. Somewhat expanded in the late medieval missals of Fécamp: Martène, 1, 4, XXVI (I, 638 A), and of Evreux: *ibid.*, XXVIII (I, 644 D). The response is correspondingly changed. The transformation appears to have emanated from Rouen; cf. Martène, 1, 4, XXXVII (I, 678 A): *Orate fratres carissimi, pro me peccatore, ut meum pariter ac vestrum in conspectu Domini acceptum sit sacrificium*

exception. In the second Roman *ordo* (a product of Frankish territory), the bishop first gives the *schola* a signal *ut sileant;* then it continues: *et convertet se ad populum dicens: Orate.*[18] He therefore addresses himself to the whole assembly in a distinctly audible voice. In some isolated instances provision is even made for the priest to prefix a *Dominus vobiscum.*[19] Little, therefore, is lacking to make this address match those addresses which the priest sings at the service. In fact, in the Mozarabic liturgy the corresponding *Adjuvate me fratres* is actually sung.[20] In the Roman liturgy, however, it never came to this. The *Dominus vobiscum* was merely spoken softly—the directions for this are remarkably discordant— but then disappeared again.

The further development adhered to the direction that the priest turn *ad populum;* in at least half the cases this is expressly stated.[21] Before this, he kisses the altar,[22] as became the rule later on for all such occasions when the priest turns to the people. But he speaks the words in a subdued voice, as is indicated at various times.[23]

The fact that the priest, in turning towards the people here, completes the turn—a procedure differing from that at the *Dominus vobiscum*—[24] might incline one to look upon this as a similar stressing of the address to the people, but in reality there is a different explanation.[25]

That the people, and not merely the clerics, are addressed seems evident from the very form of the address as found in those non-monastic documents of the Middle Ages, outside Italy and Spain, which connect an

apud Deum omnipotentem pro salute et requie tam vivorum quam mortuorum.

[18] *Ordo Rom.* II, n. 9 (PL, LXXVIII, 973 C).

[19] Durandus, IV, 32, 3 (cf. IV, 14, 10): *sub silentio* the priest should say *Dominus vobiscum,* then, *voce aliquantulum elevata,* the petition for prayers. Cf. John Beleth, *Explicatio,* c. 44 (PL, CCII, 52 B). Two 1417 missals from Valencia exactly as in Durandus: Ferreres, 131. In Germany, too, even as late as 1462, Bernard of Waging makes mention of the practice many have of inserting the *Domine exaudi orationem meam* or the *Dominus vobiscum* before the *Orate pro me fratres;* Franz, 575.

[20] *Missale mixtum:* PL, LXXV, 537 A.

[21] In Italian Mass orders this rubric often reads: *ad circumstantes*—which in this era would not necessarily mean the same thing; Ebner, 301, 306, 314, 334, 341, 346.

[22] Cf. *supra,* I, 316, 36.

[23] Remigius of Auxerre (*supra,* note 4); Statuta antiqua of the Carthusians: Martène, 1, 4, XXV (I, 633 A): *dicens in*

silentio; Hugo of St. Cher, *Tract. super missam* (ed. Sölch, 23): *secreto.*—The present-day rule that the first words be recited *voce aliquantulum elata* and the rest secreto (*Missale Rom. Ritus serv.,* VII, 7) appears for the first time in the *Ordo* of John Burchard (Legg, *Tracts,* 152). Further references in Sölch, *Hugo,* 83.

[24] Nevertheless this was not the practice in the ancient Cistercian rite; Schneider (*Cist.-Chr.,* 1927), 6.

[25] The real reason is probably that given by Gavanti, namely, that the priest turns to where the book is from which he is to read; cf. Lebrun, *Explication,* I, 326, with reference also to the fact that formerly the book frequently stood farther from the center of the altar than it does now. In fact, this is made clear, for instance by the *Ordinarium O.P.* of 1256 (Guerrini, 240); according to this order the priest during the secreta stands between the book and the chalice and not simply in the middle, and therefore here too the priest is expected to make a complete turn (cf. to the

explicit address to the formula; the words *fratres et sorores* appear quite consistently.[26] In earlier sources, it is true, the address is usually made to the *fratres* alone,[27] and it is quite possible that the word specifies not the entire community of the faithful, as it did in ancient times,[28] but only the clergy.

But the unrestricted addition of *sorores* corroborates the belief that the medieval liturgists were in agreement with us in extending the word to include everyone, men and women, in the same way that St. Paul did when he addressed the whole community with the title "brethren."

The present-day wording of the formula used by the priest first appears in Italian Mass *ordines* of the twelfth century and after.[29]

In the oldest witnesses to our petition for prayer,[30] no provision is made

contrary *Liber ordinarius* of Liége, ed. Volk, 93, 1. 19). It is the same already in the 12th century in the *Liber ordinarius* of the Premonstratensians (Lefevre, 11; cf. Waefelghem, 67 with note 2). Cf. also the *Liber usuum O. Cist.*, c. 53 (PL, CLXVI, 1424 D). Thus, we have the same situation as today before the last Gospel.—At the present time the rule just given suffers an apparent exception in the case of the *Dominus vobiscum* before the offertory; but here the reading of the offertory text is only secondary; Gavanti-Merati, II, 7, 7 (I, 265 f.). Durandus, IV, 14, 11; 32, 3, remarks that the priest in general turns back to the left. The same remark in the *Liber ordinarius* of Liége: Volk, 93, 1. 19; cf. 90, 1. 19; 97, 1. 14.— On the other hand, Fortescue, *The Mass*, 214, note, seems to regard the complete turn as the normal and natural one, and he explains the incomplete turn as the result of the priest's not wanting to turn his back on the deacon standing next to him at high Mass—a very questionable explanation, to say the least.

[29] Thus in the Missa Illyrica: Martène, 1, 4, IV (I, 512 A), and in the sacramentary of S. Denis: *ibid.*, V (I, 526 D). Common in the Netherlands Mass orders: Smits van Waesberghe, 325-327; also in those of Cologne; *ibid.*, 327; Binterim, IV, 3, p. 223; in the orders of Southern Germany: Beck, 238, 268, 308; Köck, 120, 121, 122, 125, 126; Hoeynck, 374; Franz, 753; in those of England: Martène, 1, 4, XXXV (I, 668 A, B); Legg, *Tracts*, 5; Legg, *The Sarum Missal*, 219, note 5

(only the oldest Sarum MS, of the 13th century, has only *fratres*); Simmons, 100; Maskell, 98 f.; in Sweden: Yelverton, 15; in Riga: v. Bruiningk, 81. The double address also in some French Mass-orders: Martène, 1, 4, 7, 4 (I, 396 B); *ibid.*, i, 4, V; XXVI; XXXIV (I, 526 D, 638 A, 663 C); *Alphabetum sacerdotum*: Legg, *Tracts*, 42. Exceptionally also in Italy: Sacramentary of Modena (before 1174; Muratori, I, 92); and in Hungary: Jávor, 121.

[27] Remigius of Auxerre (PL, CI, 1252): *Orate pro me fratres, ut.* Likewise in both sacramentaries of S. Thierry, 9th and 10th centuries: Martène, 1, 4, IX; X (I, 546 f.; 549 D); similarly in the Sacramentary of Ariens (*supra*, note 7).—Often they are addressed as *fratres carissimi*: Ebner, 299, 301; Martène, 1, 4, XXVII; XXXVII (I, 640 E, 678 A); also as *beatissimi fratres*: Ebner, 338. The *Ordinarium* of Coutance of 1557 (Legg, *Tracts*, 60) has: *Orate vos fratres mecum unanimes.*

[28] Cf., e.g., Minucius Felix, *Octavius*, c. 9, 2 (CSEL, 2, 12): the pagan objector is surprised that Christians love each other even before they know each other and call each other, without distinction, *fratres et sorores*. Then the Christian answers, c. 31, 8 (*ibid.*, 45): *nos, quod invidetis, fratres vocamus, ut unius Dei parentis homines, ut consortes fidei, ut spei coheredes.*—Cf. Tertullian, *Apologeticum*, c. 39, 8 ff. (CSEL, 69, 93).

[29] Ebner, 296, 313, 314, etc.

[30] *Supra*, p. 82.

for any answer. Even much later,[31] right down to the present,[32] there are isolated *ordines* where no response follows, just as in the present-day Roman service for Good Friday. The petition is interpreted simply as a request for the prayer of each individual. But already in the Carolingian period, answers of a kind were advised. Amalar heard it said that the people ought to pronounce three verses for the priest, namely vérses 3-5 from Psalm 19: *Mittat tibi Dominus auxilium de sancto et de Sion tueatur te. Memor sit omnis sacrificii tui et holocaustum tuum pingue fiat. Tribuat tibi secundum cor tuum et omne consilium tuum confirmet.*[33] These verses, or also the first three verses of the psalm,[34] or at least the one or other verse of the same psalm, recur nearly everywhere during the following centuries in the answer to the *Orate fratres*, seldom alone, however,[35] but usually in combination with other formulas of intercession, which in their turn often occur all by themselves.

Thus, according to Remigius of Auxerre (d. *c.* 908), the people can respond with Psalm 19:2-4, or else with the words: *Sit Dominus in corde tuo et in ore tuo et*—in this continuation we have the first evidence of a *Suscipiat*—*suscipiat sacrificium sibi acceptum de ore tuo et de manibus tuis pro nostra omniumque salute. Amen.*[36] The Prayerbook of Charles the Bald, written about 870, contains under the inscription *Quid orandum sit ad missam pro sacerdote, quando petit pro se orare,* the words of the angel in Luke 1:35 transformed into a blessing: *Spiritus Sanctus superveniat in te et virtus Altissimi obumbret te;*[37] then Psalm 19:4-5, and after that the further prayer: *Da Domine pro nostris peccatis acceptabile et susceptibile fieri sacrificium in conspectu tuo.*[38] For the prayer which each is to say,

---

[31] Mainz Pontifical, about 1170: Martène, 1, 4, XVII (I, 601 C); cf. *ibid.*, XXXII f, XXXVII (I, 656 D, 659 E, 678 A); Lebrun, I, 328, note d. Thus frequently in later German Mass orders: Beck, 238, 268, 308; Köck, 121, 126; Salzburg incunabula of 1492 and 1498 (Hain, 11420 f.); also in Netherlands Mass-orders: Smits van Waesberghe, 325-327; likewise in Swedish orders: Yelverton (HBS, 57), 15; Freisen, *Manuale Lincopense*, p. XXVI.
[32] Dominican rite: Sölch, 84.—Also the Carthusians: A. Degand, "Chartreux," DACL, III, 1056.
[33] Amalar, *De eccl. off.*, III, 19 (PL, CV, 1132).
[34] Remigius of Auxerre, *Expositio* (PL, CI, 1252 B). According to the Mass-order of York even as late as 1425 (Simmons, 100) and 1517 (Maskell, 100) the *chorus* responded with these verses, Ps. 19: 2-4.
[35] The three verses mentioned are found in the missal of Féca.np (14-15th c.): Mar-

tène, 1, 4, XXVII (I, 641 A); a second response is introduced by the word *sive*. Only one verse, Ps. 19: 4, in the missal of Toul: *ibid.*, XXXI (I, 651 C).—According to John Beleth, *Explicatio*, c. 44 (PL, CCII, 52 B), Pss. 19, 20 were said in full.
[36] Remigius, *Expositio* (PL, CI, 1252). The same double formula, with *Dominus sit* and *recipiat sacrificium*, in the contemporary Mass-*ordo* of Amiens, ed. Leroquais (*Eph. liturg.*, 1927), 442. It also appears later in Italian Mass-plans: Ebner, 310, 313, 346. Somewhat modified, in the later missal of Toulon (about 1400): Martène, 1, 4, 7, 4 (I, 396 B).
[37] These words form the response in the older missal of Fécamp: Martène, 1, 4, XXVI (I, 638 A); in Beauvais; *ibid.*, 1, 4, 7, 4 (I, 396 A); also in two Sarum MSS. of the 14th cent.: Legg, *The Sarum Missal*, 219, note 7.
[38] *Liber precationum quas Carolus Calvus . . . mandavit*, ed. Fel. Ninguarda, 115.

the Sacramentary of Séez has the initial words: *Orent pro te omnes sancti*,[39] and adds, after Psalm 19:4, the phrases: *Exaudiat te Dominus pro nobis orantem*[40] and *Misereatur tui omnipotens Deus, dimittat tibi omnia peccata tua*.[41] Elsewhere appears the psalm verse (49-14): *Immola Deo sacrificium laudis et redde Altissimo vota tua*,[42] or the benediction: *Sancti Spiritus gratia illuminet cor tuum et labia tua*.[43] Several Mass *ordines* present a number of these answers, to be chosen at will,[44] and often the prayer is taken up again after the *Sanctus*.[45]

Aside from the psalm verses, the most widespread were the *Suscipiat* formulas, but these appeared in various versions [46] and usually as the continuation of some other text which was conjoined.[47] The version familiar to us, which appeared but seldom outside Italy,[48] had become the only formula current in Italy since the eleventh century,[49] and thus reached the *Missale Romanum*.

[39] This formula alone forms the response in Italian Mass-books: Ebner, 329, 341. In other cases with various additions; see, e.g., the Rhenish missal described by F. Rödel: JL, 4 (1924), 84.

[40] Thus the response in some Mass-books of Italian monasteries of the 11-12th century: Ebner, 306, 310; cf. 14, 20, 323; Fiala, 206. In the Hungarian sacramentary of Boldau (but with Psalm 19: 3-5; Radó, 43) and in two Seckau missals: Köck, 120, 122. The same with the addition of Ps. 49: 14 (*Immola*) in the Augsburg missal of 1386: Hoeynck.

[41] PL, LXXVIII, 249 D.—Likewise with the addition of Luke 1: 35, Psalm 49: 14 and *Suscipiat* in the Mass-order of Gregorienmünster: Martène, 1, 4, XVI (I, 599 D).—Cf. the Missal of St. Lawrence in Liége: *ibid.*, XV (I, 592 C); sacramentary of Modena: Muratori, I, 92; sacramentary of Boldau: Radó, 43.

[42] These words are the beginning of the response as provided in the Pontifical of Durandus in the case when a bishop assists at the Mass of his chaplain: Martène, 1, 4, XXIII (I, 619 F); the bishop continues: *ipseque, tuus pius et misericors adiutor, exauditor existat;* Psalm 19: 3-4 and today's *Suscipiat* follows.—Psalm 49: 14 is also found within a long series of formulas in the Missa Illyrica: Martène, 1, 4, IV (I, 512 B), and in the Sacramentary of S. Denis: *ibid.*, V (I, 526 f.).

[43] With an added *Suscipiat* formula (*et accipiat ...*) in the use of Sarum: Legg, *The Sarum Missal*, 219; Martène, 1, 4, XXXV

(I, 668 A); cf. Ferreres, 133; Maskell, 100.

[44] Sacramentary of S. Denis (11th c.): Martène, 1, 4, V (I, 526 f.); William of Melitona, Opusc. *super missam,* ed. van Dijk (*Eph. liturg.*, 1939), 329; Durandus, IV, 32, 3.

[45] See *infra*.—The Sacramentary of Fonte Avellana (before 1325) has the priest himself recite the respective psalms, 24, 50, 89 and 90, after he receives the response to his *Orate fratres* (PL, CLI, 887 B).

[46] E.g., in the Sacramentary of S. Denis: Martène, 1, 4, V (I, 526 E): *Suscipiat Dominus sacrificium de manibus tuis ad tuam et nostrorum salutem omniumque circumadstantium et animarum omnium fidelium defunctorum.*—In Spain: *Suscipiat Dominus Jesus Christus sacrificium de manibus tuis et dimittat tibi omnia peccata;* Ferreres, p. CV; 131, 132; Ebner, 342. A Bobbio missal of the 10-11th century: *Accipiat Dominus Deus omnipotens sacrificium ... ad utilitatem totius sanctæ Dei Ecclesiæ;* Ebner, 81.—MSS of the 14th century from Gerona offer as the sole response a formula that is otherwise hardly ever found: *Oratio tua accepta sit in conspectu Altissimi et nos tecum pariter salvari mereamur in perpetuum;* Ferreres, 131 (n. 524); cf. *ibid.*, XXVIII; also in the Missal of Narbonne (1528): Martène, 1, 4, 7, 4 (I, 396 A).

[47] Cf. *supra*, p. 87.

[48] An example *supra,* note 42.

[49] Ebner, 299, 301, 323, 334, 338, 348, 356.

As is evident from the statements above, the answer is committed, time and again, to the people. This assignment to the people occurs in some individual instances right on to the end of the Middle Ages.[50] At least in those cases where *fratres* and *sorores* are addressed, it can hardly cause astonishment.[51] At other times, both in early and late texts, the *circumstantes* [52] or the *clerici* [53] or the *chorus* [54] are named. It is noteworthy that in a group of Mass-orders of the 11-12th century the answer should be given by each one (*a singulis*).[55] It is curious that the text is not to be said aloud, but is to be regarded as an aid to private prayer. Silent prayer by the individual was evidently presupposed from the very start wherever the books did not contain an answer; and even where texts were then presented, they were at first probably intended for a similar purpose.[56] The later rule [57] was probably that the answer be given by the choir of clerics in common, since its Latin form and considerable length was too much for the people to master.[58] There is one extreme case of an *ordo* of Sarum in England, where at a Mass for the Dead the special answer is united with the chant of the offertory. When the priest has softly spoken the *Orate fratres et sorores pro fidelibus defunctis*, the clergy

---

[50] Sacramentary of Barcelona (13th c.): Ebner, 342; Spanish missals of the 14th and 15th centuries: Ferreres, 131.—Missal of Fécamp about 1400: Martène, 1, 4, XXVII (I, 641 A): *Oratio populi pro sacerdote dicentis hos versus.*—Cf. Missal of Toul (about 1400): *ibid.,* XXXI (I, 651 C): *respondetur ei ab omnibus.*

[51] A Pontifical of Laon (13th c.) has even a rubric: *Et respondeant fratres et sorores: Suscipiat.* V. Leroquais, *Les Pontificaux,* I (Paris, 1937), 167.

[52] Ebner, 314, 323, 338; Martène, 1, 4, VI; XV (I, 533 C; 592 C). Thus also in the present-day Roman Missal: *Et responso a Ministro, vel a circumstantibus: Suscipiat* ...; Rit. serv., VII, 7.

[53] Martène, 1, 4, XVI; XXVI (I, 599; 638 A); Ferreres, 133.

[54] Martène, 1, 4, XXII (I, 612 C); York Mass order: Simmons, 100.

[55] Martène, 1, 4, IV; XIII (I, 512 A; 578 C); Ebner, 301, 334.

[56] This is the natural interpretation for the text in the Prayerbook of Charles the Bald, *supra,* p. 87.—Therefore also the stressing of silent prayer. Cf. John Beleth, *Explicatio* c. 44 (PL, CCII, 52 B): When we hear the priest saying the *Orate fratres,* we must pray quietly *(secreto);* and the author suggests Psalms 19 and 20. Similarly Durandus, IV, 32, 3: *populus debet similiter secrete orare respondens* ...

[57] But authentic examples are to be found already since the 11-12th century: Ebner, 338.—In the Custumarium of Sarum (13th c.) we find the following in the order for high Mass after the priest has said the *Orate fratres et sorores* softly *(tacita voce): Responsio clerici privatim: Sancti Spiritus* ... Frere, *The Use of Sarum,* I, 78.

[58] According to the English *Lay Folks Mass Book* (Simmons, 24; cf. *supra,* I, 243), a participation of the laity is urged on all: "Then he asks with quiet voice— For each man's prayers to God of heaven. Take good heed unto the priest.—When he turns knock on thy breast—And think then for thy sin—Thou art not worthy to pray for him . . . Answer the priest with this aloud ("on high"):—The Holy Ghost in thee light—And send His grace unto the right—To rule thy heart and thy speaking—To God's worship and His loving. (Modernized wording and spelling.) The rimed prayer over, the author continues, you might add a *Pater, Ave* and *Credo.*—In the same sense the Melk Commentary, written in 1366, introduces the three formulas for the response with the remark: *tunc astantes et literati dicent: Memor sit;* Franz, 510, note 3.

answer by singing the last verse of the offertory chant: *Requiem æternam
dona eis Domine et lux perpetua luceat eis, Quam olim Abrahæ promisisti
et semini eius.*[59]

8. The Secret

In the liturgy of the city of Rome in the early Middle Ages, the collect-
ing and depositing of the offertory gifts was not accompanied by any prayer
at all, but simply by the singing of the offertory. Not till the external
activity had come to an end did the celebrant once more take up the
phrases of the *oratio super oblata*, the present-day secret. Just as the
entrance procession was concluded with the collect, and the communion
with the post-communion, so the oblation was concluded with this oration
which appears, like the others, in all the Roman sacramentaries and, like
them, varies according to the Church year, and agrees with them in structure and design. Like them, it is spoken in the prayer posture of the
orantes,[1] and was likewise at one time (as is self-evident) pronounced in
a loud voice. Even today the final words *Per omnia sæcula sæculorum*,
like the *Oremus* at the start, which belongs to it,[2] are sung aloud. In the
Milanese Mass the practice has been retained even at present of saying
the whole *oratio super oblata* aloud.[3]

The first point to clear up is the puzzling problem of how the *oratio
super oblata*[4] came to be said silently. The earliest evidence of the quiet
recitation of this prayer appears in the middle of the eighth century in
Frankish territory, in the tradition of John the Arch-chanter.[5] We are
thus led to the opinion that the name *secreta* appeared in the North and
that it was here created to indicate that the pertinent oration was to be
spoken softly.[6] From then on, the quiet recitation of this prayer was taken

[59] Martène, 1, 4, XXXV (I, 668 B);
Frere, *The Use of Sarum*, I, 78; cf. *supra*,
p. 84. The same answer already in the
Ordinarium of the 13th century, but here
with the superscription: *responsio populi.*
Legg, *Tracts*, 221.

[1] The *Ordinarium* of Coutances (1557) has
a late deviation from this rule; according
to this order the secreta is said *manibus
super sacrificio extensis*: Legg, *Tracts*, 61.
[2] *Supra*, I, 483 f.
[3] *Missale Ambrosianum* (1902), p. V.
[4] This title is found in the *Sacramentarium
Gregorianum* (Lietzmann, n. 1). Here
even the individual formulas are headed:
Super oblata (Cod. Pad. D 47, ed. Mohlberg-Baumstark: *Super oblatam*); likewise in the later Gelasianum, ed. Mohlberg. The same designation is to be found
in the oldest *ordines*, insofar as they note

the subject; in the *Ordo Rom.* II, n. 10
(PL, LXXVIII 973 D): *dicta oratione
super oblationes secreta;* and in the *Ordo*
of Johannes Archicantor, *Capitulare* (see
following note).
[5] *Capitulare eccl. ordinis* (Silva-Tarouca,
198: *Tunc pontifex inclinato vultu in terram dicit orationem super oblationes ita ut
nullus præter Deum et ipsum audiat nisi
tantum Per omnia sæcula sæculorum.*
Similarly the adaptation in the *Breviarium*
(ibid.).
[6] This is the explanation given by Fortescue, *The Mass*, 312. Other explanations
of the name are pure hypotheses. Ever
since Bossuet it has come to be generally
accepted — without historical evidence —
that *secreta* = *oratio ad secretionem*, that
is, either at the "sorting out" of the sacrificial gifts (an action which as such had

for granted in the Frankish realm, and the custom became common. In fact, the practice was brought into line with this same *secreta*,[7] which was likewise commonly employed.[8] The name *secreta* does indeed appear as a heading even in one portion of the Roman tradition, the earliest evidence being the older Gelasian Sacramentary. But the question is whether its use is not to be traced entirely to the influx of the Gallic liturgy.[9] The cardinal argument for this is the manuscript evidence that at least fifty years before this first Roman witness to its use, it is found in a source of the Gallic liturgy, namely, the Missal of Bobbio, and with every indication of a non-Roman origin.[10] We then find we are forced to a second conclusion, that it was in Gallic territory that this low speaking was first employed for the Roman *Oratio super oblata,* just as was the case somewhat later in regard to the canon. For this low pronouncement of a liturgical text is as much in contradiction to ancient Roman usage as it is in harmony with the tendency of the Gallo-Frankish liturgy. Here, in fact, it is

no religious signification beyond this, but only a purely practical one; thus the secret is equivalently *oratio super secreta* [a merely conjectural form]; or else at the "sorting out," that is, the dismissal of the catechumens (there is nothing in the contents to show any connection with this act). —Batiffol, *Leçons,* 161 (cf. *ibid.,* 7th ed., p. XXI), proposed a derivation of *secreta* from *secernere* in the sense of *benedicere,* a meaning which is nowhere to be traced.— Brinktrine, *Die hl. Messe,* 171 f., regards *secreta* as equivalent to *mysteria,* which appears in Innocent I, *Ep.* 25 (PL, XX, 553 f.) as a designation of the prayers of the canon; the word, he thinks, then survived as the name of the introductory prayer. However, we are concerned not with *mysteria* but with *secreta,* and this is not found as the name of the canon from *Te igitur* on till the 9th century, and for the full canon including our oblation prayer not till the 12th century, so that its clinging to our prayer already in the 8th century remains unexplained. Cf. Jungmann, *Gewordene Liturgie,* 93 ff., 105 ff. Even what Th. Michels, *Liturg. Leben,* 3 (1936), 307 f., adduces in support of Brinktrine only proves that *secreta* = canon in the 11th century.

[7] Amalar, *Liber off.,* III, 20, 1 (Hanssens, II, 323): *Secreta ideo nominatur, quia secreto dicitur.* The same thing is implied by the designation *arcana* in Frankish sacramentaries, to which Martène, 1, 4, 7 5, (I, 396 D), refers.

[8] The older designation survived the longest in MSS. of the Gregorianum. But even here it was soon replaced by *secreta,* as e.g., partially in the MS. of Pamelius (Cologne, 1571).—A group of South French and Spanish MSS. since the 11th century uses the name *sacra,* which arose from a misunderstanding of the abbreviation *scr.* Cf. A. Wilmart, "Une curieuse expression pour designer l'oraison sécrète," *Bulletin de litt. ecclés.,* 1925, 94-103; cf. *JL,* (1925), 291 f. Examples of this also in Ferreres, 132, and *passim* in his introductory description of the MSS.

[9] Cf. Jungmann, *Gewordene Liturgie,* 93 ff.

[10] Here, too, the name *secreta* appears as a heading over the last formula that precedes the preface. Although the Bobbio missal displays a large degree of Roman liturgy, still among perhaps a dozen cases where the heading occurs there is one, if I mistake not, where the name indicates a Roman *oratio super oblata;* this is the oration *Munda nos Domine* (Sacramentary of Padua: Mohlberg-Baumstark, n. 706); see Lowe, *The Bobbio Missal* (HBS, 58), n. 514. As for the other instances, there are some few Roman collects, rather general in content, that are used as *secreta,* and mostly they are purely Gallic formulas. On the other hand, time and again Roman *super oblata* formulas appear under the Gallic captions *Post nomina* and *Ad pacem;* see Lowe, 6, 154, 260, et al. This shows conclusively that their designation

that all the silent prayers come to light which have since filled out the offertory.[11]

In the formation of the practice, reminiscences of the Gallic liturgy and, in the last analysis, some suggestions from the Orient must have been at work. The place of the Roman offertory was taken in the Gallican Mass by the offertory procession at which a holy silence was advised.[12] At any rate, silent prayer at this point is an ancient tradition in the sister-liturgy, the Mozarabic.[13] And silent prayer, especially in the form of *apologiæ*, as well as of incense prayers, and (by no means lastly) oblation prayers, must have become customary in the Gallican Mass, in connection with the offertory procession. Otherwise, the elements of this sort which had forced their way here into the Roman Mass as early as the ninth century, are not understandable.[14] We have already had occasion to ascertain that precisely at this point oriental models had an influence in the Frankish realm, where we have even encountered word-for-word borrowings from the Greek Liturgy of St. James, *i. e.*, from the liturgy of the center of pilgrimage, Jerusalem.[15] For here we also came upon the pictorial model: the solemn entrance of the Great King (proleptically honored in the gift-offerings) amid the resounding lines of the Cherubic hymn, which demands silence while the priest performs silent prayer.[16] The tendency to perform the prayer at the oblation softly must have been given even further force in the East, since in 565 Justinian felt compelled to issue a

here as *secreta* does not stem from the Roman source, much as the Bobbio missal otherwise shows only Gallic formula headings.—A more primitive interpretation of the word is found in the designation *Post secreta* (for which also *Post mysterium*) which is used in the *Missale Gothicum* and also in the *Missale Gothicum vetus* for the first prayer after the consecration; Muratori, II, 522, 534, 559, etc.; 699, 705.

[11] The main argument against this explanation is the fact already noted that the other Gelasianum, which in general presents us with the Roman liturgy of the 6th century, has the heading *secreta* throughout. But against this is to be observed that the only surviving manuscript of this sacramentary was not written till the 8th century, in Frankish territory, and displays many different Frankish additions Presumably the Roman orginal for this copy generally had no captions for the individual formulas, as is the case in the Leonianum. Otherwise it would be hard to understand how the later Gelasianum, which in general takes the formulas from the older one, substituted as a caption the

Gregorian *Super oblata.*

[12] *Expositio ant. lit. gallicanæ* (ed. Quasten, 17): *spiritaliter iubemur silentium facere.* Righetti, *Manuale*, III, 288, wrongly refers the *spiritaliter* to a mere "raccoglimento spirituale interiore." Naturally it does not exclude the singing of the *sonus.*

[13] After the *Adiuvate me fratres*, an apologia which goes back to Julian of Toledo (d. 690) is spoken quietly (*silentio*): *Missale mixtum* (PL, 85, 538 f.).

[14] Cf. *supra*, I, 78 f.; II, 5.

[15] *Supra*, p. 73.

[16] Brightman, 41: Σιγησάτω πᾶσα σάρξ. Immediately preceding is the incensation prayer used in S. Denis; see *supra*, p. 73. Cf. the Byzantine liturgy: Brightman, 377 f.—How much this silence at the Entrance with the sacrificial gifts was already stressed in the 5th century can be seen from the commentary on the liturgy in Theodore of Mopsuestia, *Sermones catech.* V (Rücker, *Ritus bapt. et missæ*, 22): all must look at the offering, when it is carried in by the deacons, *in silentio et timore et oratione tacita.* Likewise in the Apostolic Constitutions, VIII, 12, 44 (Quasten,

special ordinance against it.[17] It is quite possible that recollections from pagan antiquity were still operative here.[18]

That the *secreta*, as it is now usually called, possessed a greater importance in comparison with the other offertory prayers, somehow remained in the consciousness even in the new Frankish arrangement of the offertory. In a few isolated instances it was realized that the secret was conjoined to the foregoing *Oremus*,[19] or it was given a new introduction befitting an oration. The *Statuta antiqua* of the Carthusians stipulate that the priest repeats the *Oremus*, both before the first and before the second secret,[20] but they insist (obviously in opposition to a contrary practice then in process of forming) that no *Domine exaudi* be prefaced. As a matter of fact, this versicle too is found more than once since the thirteenth century prefixed to the secret.[21] Elsewhere the *Orate Fratres* was made equivalent of the *Oremus* and, as we saw, the *Dominus vobiscum* was consistently prefixed to it.[22] All these were attempts at remodeling in line with a late medieval conception of the canon, which was considered as starting with the secret, and in fact as forming a unit with it, a single *secreta*.[23]

Mon., 212), silent prayer is indicated for the celebrant at the same moment: εὐξάμενος οὖν καθ'ἑαυτὸν ὁ ἀρχιερεύς. Cf. also Jungmann, *Gewordene Liturgie*, 96-98.

[17] Novelle, 137, 6: *Iubemus omnes et episcopos et presbyteros non tacite, sed ea voce quæ a fideli populo exaudiatur, sacram oblationem . . . faciant.* Batiffol, *Leçons*, 210 f.

[18] Cf. O. Casel, *Die Liturgie als Mysterienfeier*, 3-5 ed. (Ecclesia Orans, 9; Freiburg, 1923), 135-157.

[19] Thus even Innocent III, *De s. alt. mysterio*, II, 55; 60 (PL, 217, 831; 834): At the *Oremus* the priest interrupted the prayer which he now resumes. Similarly Durandus, IV, 32, 3.

[20] Martène, 1, 4, XXV (I, 633 A).

[21] *Ordinarium O.P.* of 1256 (Guerrini, 240), and in the present-day *Missale O.P.* (1889), 19; *Liber ordinarius* of Liége: Volk, 93; Cologne *Ordo celebrandi* of the 14th century: Binterim, IV, 3, p. 223; *Ordinale* of the Carmelites of 1312 (Zimmerman, 80) and the present-day *Missale O. Carm.* (1935), 226.—Late medieval Mass orders from France: Martène, i, 4, XXXI; XXXIV (I, 651 C, 663 C); Lebrun, I, 331 note c; and from the Netherlands: Smits van Waesberghe, 325; 326; 327.—In some few cases the *Dominus vobiscum* precedes: *Alphabetum sacerdo-*

tum: Legg, *Tracts*, 42; *Ordinarium* of Coutances: *ibid.*, 61. In Iceland it was prescribed in 1345 at a synod: Segelberg, 256 f. Likewise in the Upsala Missale of 1513, which in addition puts the versicle *Domine Deus virtutum* at the start: Yelverton, 15. Cf. also Lebrun, I, 331.—Brinktrine, *Die hl. Messe*, 173, expresses the opinion that already in the oldest manuscript evidences of the Gelasian Sacramentary, which do not note a *Dominus vobiscum* before the *Sursum corda*, one is to be presupposed along with the *Oremus* before the secreta. This conjecture is bracketed with his conception of the secreta as a pre-formula for the preface, analogous to the pre-formula at the consecration of the chrism on Maundy Thursday (older Gelasianum, ed. Wilson, 70). Even if the idea of a pre-formula is not to be rejected absolutely—for the whole offertory is a fore-rite, a pre-consecration—yet the conclusion he draws goes too far, for in the period under consideration the coherence with the *Dominus vobiscum* and *Oremus* before the offertory was surely known and recognized.

[22] Cf. *supra*, p. 85.

[23] See *infra*, p. 104. In the Cod. 150 of St. Gall (9th c.) the presentation of the rubrics of the canon known as *Ordo "Qualiter quædam orationes"* begins with the secreta (Andrieu, II, 295).—As a matter of fact,

But if we want to find the real meaning of our oration, that is, the meaning consonant with its origin, we must look, as we have said, not forwards but backwards. The secret is the prayer which concludes the offering and depositing of the material gifts and which explains their significance by transmuting them into the language of prayer. The creation of such a prayer must be considered a natural result, if not a matter of course, once the material gift itself was regarded as an oblation to God and, by the inclusion of the people in it, its symbolic meaning was emphasized. Thus we find already in the oldest Roman sacramentary, the *Leonianum*, precisely those traits clearly marked which still, even at the present time, distinguish the secret. No matter how the formula varies, the same thought consistently recurs in different words: We offer God gifts, *dona, munera, oblationem;* less frequently—and then obviously only to diversify the expression—*hostias, sacrificium.* They are in the first instance earthly gifts, as is occasionally pointed out in due form: *Altaribus tuis, Domine, munera terrena gratanter offerimus, ut cœlestia consequamur, damus temporalia ut sumamus œterna. Per . . .*[24] Or: *Exercentes Domine gloriosa commercia offerimus quœ dedisti.*[25] Or, in one formula, which we still use today: *Domine Deus noster, qui in his potius creaturis, quas ad fragilitatis nostrœ prœsidium condidisti, tuo quoque nomini munera iussisti dicanda constitui . . .*[26] Or the attention is called with unconstrained assurance to the heap of gifts offered up: *Tua Domine muneribus altaria cumulamus . . .*[27] But the gifts represent no independent sacrifice; they are offered up only to be merged into the sacrifice of Christ. At times, even in the secret, the prayer touches upon this disposition of the gifts: *Sacrandum tibi, Domine, munus offerimus . . .*[28] Or: *Propitius, Domine quœsumus, hœc dona sanctifica.*[29] Or: *Remotis obumbrationibus carnalium victimarum spiritalem tibi, summe Pater, hostiam supplici servitute deferimus.*[30] Still, such an extension of the thought, although corresponding to a general law of development, is less frequent in the older texts, particularly in the *Leonianum*, than in later ones and those of the present time, just as on the other hand the complete absence of the thought of sacrifice has always, from the beginning until now, continued to be an exception.[31]

Brinktrine (cf. above, note 21) seeks to revive this concept of the canon; according to him the second main portion of the Mass, the "Eucharistic consecration," begins with the secreta (168 ff.).

[24] Muratori, I, 303.   [25] *Ibid.*

[26] Muratori, I, 415. Further sources in the oldest sacramentaries, see Mohlberg-Manz, n. 388.—*Missale Rom.,* Thursday of Passion week.

[27] Muratori, I, 324; Mohlberg-Manz, n. 930.—For the expression *altaria* cf. *supra,* p. 7.—For the idea that the secreta is intended first of all for the material gifts, see also Batiffol, *Leçons,* 162 ff.

[28] Muratori, I, 465; Mohlberg-Manz, n. 1368. *Missale Rom.* on Nov. 29.

[29] Muratori, I, 318; 320, Mohlberg-Manz, n. 823.

[30] Muratori, I, 327; Mohlberg-Manz, n. 846.

[31] Examples of such exceptions in the *Missale Rom.* on Dec. 31 and often on saints' feasts: *Sancti tui* (cf. the Frankish Gelasianum, ed. Mohlberg, n. 74; Mohlberg-Manz, n. 74) ; on March 25: *In mentibus*

However, the sacrificial oblation does indeed appear in divers modifications. Besides the *offerimus* and *immolamus* there stands the *suscipe, respice, ne despicias, intende placatus* or—often on feast days—the reference to the merits of the saints or to the redemptive mystery being celebrated, which may recommend our gifts to God: *Ecclesiæ tuæ, quæsumus, Domine, preces et hostias beati Petri Apostoli commendet oratio.*[32] Or prayer is said for the right disposition to offer the sacrifice worthily or, inversely, even for the fruit of the sacrifice already offered up, with the sacrifice itself being named only *in obliquo*. Sometimes we even get a momentary glimpse of the whole composite of sacrifice and sacrificial symbol, as in the wonderful secret on Pentecost Monday: *Propitius, Domine quæsumus, hæc dona sanctifica et hostiæ spiritalis oblatione suscepta nosmetipsos tibi perfice munus æternum. Per . . .*[33] Mostly, however, the petition that is linked with the oblation—the secret is indeed formulated as an *oratio*, that is, a prayer of petition—is kept very general: as our gift mounts up, so may God's blessing come down upon us. Thus there is frequent mention of the mystical exchange, of the *sacrosancta commercia*, of the *huius sacrificii veneranda commercia* which are consummated in the sacred celebration.

In the whole tradition of the Roman sacramentaries two points are strictly maintained; the secret is always formulated in the plural as a prayer of the congregation: *offerimus, immolamus, munera nostra, oblationes populi tui;* and it is directed to God and concluded with *Per Dominum*. Even the Missal of Pius V contains not one exception to this rule. As a matter of fact, if that ancient law: *Cum altari assistitur, semper ad Patrem dirigatur oratio,*[34] should have been maintained anywhere in liturgical prayer it was here where there was question not of receiving the sacrifice instituted by Christ, but of offering it up to the heavenly Father. Of course, it is still conformable to Catholic dogma to direct the oblation to Christ Himself.[35] The first exception of this sort in the *Missale Romanum* is found in the secret for the feast of St. Anthony of Padua, which was prescribed for the Church universal by Pope Sixtus V. Later on, a few other cases were added right down to most recent times.[36]

For a long time it has been the rule that at each Mass there should be

nostris (cf. Gregorianum, ed. Lietzmann, n. 31, 3).

[32] In cathedra s. Petri; cf. the Frankish Gelasianum, ed. Mohlberg, n. 218; Mohlberg-Manz, n. 218).

[33] Already also in the Leonianum (Muratori, I, 318; 320); Mohlberg-Manz, n. 823.

[34] *Supra*, I, 379 f.

[35] In the Byzantine Church during the 12th century, a controversy was waged regarding the dogmatic admissibility of offering to Christ; it was settled in 1156 by a synod at Constantinople, along the lines noted above. C. J. Hefele, *Conciliengeschichte*, V (2nd ed.; Freiburg, 1886), 567 f.—The decision would run differently, of course, if passed from the viewpoint not of dogma but of kerygma.

[36] More detailed references in Jungmann, *Die Stellung Christi* (1925), 103, 106 f.—And, since 1932, the Mass of St. Gabriel Possenti on Feb. 27 (28), where all three orations are addressed to Christ.

as many secrets—and then also post-communions—as there are collects.[37]
This rule is not entirely self-evident since in the formulas for the secret—
which revolves more strictly around its own theme and seldom adds a
relative predication to the word of address [38]—the content varies but little
and the influence of the Church year is slight, aside from the fact that on
saints' feasts the intercession of the saints is usually bracketed with the
oblation. Thus, the superaddition of several formulas at times simply
amounts to a repetition of the same thought. Still, the rule was inculcated
with increasing positiveness,[39] evidently because it conformed to a sense
of symmetry.

The concluding words of the last secret, *Per omnia sœcula sœculorum*,
are spoken in a loud voice.[40] That at least the words of a prayer destined
for public performance should be said aloud is a law which we see followed in other places too: at the conclusion of the canon and the final
words of the embolism. In both cases the same phrase is in question, *Per
omnia sœcula sœculorum*. The Our Father is also often handled in the
same way outside of Mass. In the oriental liturgies, the silent praying of
the priestly orations occupies a much larger space, especially owing to
the convergence of the priestly prayer with the alternate prayer of deacon
and people which used to precede it; as a result, the so-called ἐχφώνησις
plays a grand role.[41] It is generally more extensive than its occidental
counterpart, comprising as a rule a complete doxology, so that the people's
Amen retains a meaning as an affirmation of the latter. Our *Per omnia
sœcula sœculorum* demands a complement in the foregoing prayer of the
priest. This is not difficult, inasmuch as the course of the priestly prayers
remains essentially constant in all three instances. Looked upon formally,
this loud-spoken *Per omnia sœcula sœculorum* refers back once more to
the *Oremus* that stands at the beginning and draws all that comes in between into a unit. For what comes in between is actually an *orare*, with this
difference, that the words have been reinforced by the external symbol.
Remigius of Auxerre (d. *c.* 908) still had a vital sense of just this reality,
for he explains the seemingly isolated *Oremus* by claiming it to be an
invitation to the faithful to be mindful of the oblation by joining to it their
inmost offering so that their gift might be agreeable to the Lord.[42] In the
same sense a large number of ancient formulas of the secret speak expressly not only of the sacrificial gifts, but at the same time of the prayers
of the people: *Suscipe quæsumus Domine preces populi cum oblationibus*

---

[37] Cf. *supra*, I, 387.

[38] Cf. *supra*, I, 375.

[39] See, e.g. Durandus, IV, 15, 16.

[40] Cf. *supra*, p. 90, and likewise Amalar
Liber off., III, 19, 9 (Hanssens, II, 313 f.).
—Later MSS. of the Gregorianum (Lietzmann, n. 1) also add to the mention of the
oratio super oblata the direction: *qua com-*

*pleta dicit sacerdos excelsa voce: Per
omnia.*

[41] Technical expressions from the non-
Greek liturgies, see Brightman, 596. Fortescue, *The Mass*, 314, note 2, also presents several oriental terms. The Nestorians call it *kanuna*, from χανών.

[42] Remigius of Auxerre, *Expositio*, (PL,
101, 1251 C) : *Ita autem potest intelligi...*

hostiarum;[43] *Muneribus nostris, quæsumus Domine, precibusque susceptis;*[44] *Offerimus tibi, Domine, preces et munera.*[45] The repeated occurrence of such formulas in the Mass formularies that bear the stamp of greatest antiquity forces the conclusion that the mention of prayer refers basically to that prayer which the *Oremus* had ushered in.[46]

9. The Oblation Rites as a Unit

In view of the perplexing plenitude of forms and formulas which we have seen building up in the offertory during the course of centuries, there is ample ground for inquiring just how, in the light of what we have learned, are we to evaluate the completed structure. More particularly, how should we regard as a whole the series of texts which, as a result of the medieval development, now stand in our *Missale Romanum?*[1] And how can we give this whole its fullest significance in the course of our celebration of Mass?

There is, first of all, no denying that here we have an anticipation of the thought of the canon, and therefore a certain duplication. True, it was not till the late Middle Ages that the term "little (or lesser) canon" was applied to the offertory rites,[2] but the idea long stood unexpressed behind the new formation. In the liturgical thinking of the Middle Ages the wording of the Great Prayer of the Mass had only a small role to play. It was couched in a language whose Roman stamp continued to be strange and foreign to the newer nations, no matter how hard they tried to speak Latin and think Catholic. The canon, and this understood more and more

ut omnis populus oblationi insistere iubeatur, dum oblaturi intentionem suam offerunt, quatenus illorum oblatio accepta sit Domino. Cf. also Amalar, *Liber off.,* proœmium n. 13 (Hanssens, II, 16).

[43] The formulas from Holy Saturday to Easter Tuesday begin in this way, already in the Gregorianum (Lietzmann, n. 87 90).

[44] Commune martyrum, et al.; in the Gregorianum in six places (Lietzmann, p. 182). Cf. also Mohlberg-Manz, n. 69.

[45] Votive Mass of the Apostles. Cf. Mohlberg-Manz, n. 982, 1111, 1255. Already in the Leonianum (Muratori, I, 334; 335).

[46] Cf. *supra,* I, 483 f.

[1] With the present-day wording and in the present-day order (with two additions, and leaving aside the hand-washing which is still at the start of the series) already in the Mass order of the papal chapel about 1290, ed. Brinktrine (*Eph. liturg.,* 1937), 201-203; Ebner, 347. Cf. the Minorite missal of the 13th century; *ibid.,* 314.—Rome

did not share at all in the late medieval developments (*supra,* p. 65 ff.).

[2] This description of the offertory as a "canon in miniature" appears, e.g., in Hungary in the 15th century: Jávor, 120, Radó, 125; in two Regensburg missals of the 15-16th century: Beck, 237, 266; in Augsburg missals already since 1386: Hoeynck, 372 f. In the Mass-commentary "Messe singen oder lesen" (To sing or read Mass) of 1484, which likewise appeared in Augsburg, we even read that it does not behoove lay people to read the *canon minor,* which it calls "A lesser silent Mass": *Und hye hebt an Canon minor, das ist die minder Stillmesse, die dem leyen nit zymment zu lesen;* Franz, 713; cf.. 633. The rigorous interpretation expressed in these words was otherwise applied only to the text beginning with the secreta. That is to say, it was only with the start of the secreta that the concept of the *canon minor* was reduced to practice in dead earnest.

as starting with the *secreta* and continuing through its entire course, was taken as the hallowed consecration text, to be given out objectively and faithfully just as it was, but hardly appeared to be a medium for expressing one's own thought or one's own prayer needs.

So the opportunity was soon taken, in connection with the preparation of the gifts, to get these personal matters into the rite. Basically, however, it was the olden concepts that came to the fore: oblation, prayer for acceptance, intercession; even the wording was taken in great part from the Roman canon and the texts of the *oratio super oblata*. But some new points also put in an appearance. The oblation was made "for" certain intentions; today, however, these are to be found only in a few phrases. The oblation of the "spotless sacrifice" was raised out of the dusty shadows of personal sinfulness; this, too, in contrast to the frequency it had once upon a time amid a profusion of *apologiæ*, is now mentioned only in the first offertory prayer. Besides, the personal activity of the priest is now more to the fore. The priest speaks in the singular, a mode of expression consonant with the new position of the priest, who feels himself more sharply detached from the people. Still, in some passages the singular was again restricted.[3]

On the other hand, in the response to the *Orate fratres* provision was also made, at least in principle, for the prayer of the people, a prayer that represents intercession for the priest himself. There was also a break-up that took place in the formation of a separate oblation for each of the sacrificial elements. The tendency to coordinate the two oblations that had developed out of the original oblation phrases, and to arrange them together in marked symmetry did indeed make some headway, but never succeeded entirely. But if the oblation service was broadened out in extent, it also disintegrated in another way, for the presentation and offering was supplemented by the epikletic pleas for power from above. This double movement is well disclosed in the present-day ceremonial when, after the individual offering of the paten and the chalice, there follows first the humble petition for acceptance, *In spiritu humilitatis*, in which expression is given with biblical force[4] to the more profound meaning of all external oblation, the personal surrender of one's heart and the interior readiness for sacrifice; but then comes a cry for the sanctifying power from above, which can give our earthly gift its proper dedication.

Considered from the viewpoint of language and style, the Roman oration spoken at the commingling of the water with the wine stands in definite contrast to the remaining prayers, which are not formulated with such exactness and which, because of their close connection with the individual activity, manifest no rigorous line of thought. On the other

[3] See *supra,* p. 46 ff. with note 41, p. 50.
[4] See the fine biblico-liturgical exposition of the text in G. E. Closen, *Wege in die Hl. Schrift* (Regensburg, 1939), 148-156.

hand, a closer resemblance to the form of the prayer of the canon (such as might have existed had the prayers each ended with *Per Christum*[5] did not gain general acceptance.

All in all, the offertory prayers of our present-day *Ordo Missæ* can be considered a needless anticipation of the canon only if we pivot our attention on the *missa lecta* where the dominant and recessive elements of the service are all evened out, and if consequently we bestow on these prayers as much weight as on the pithy phrases of the canon. These prayers do not pretend to be an anticipation of the canon, but rather a suggestion of its various motives. Indeed they are generally not even "prayers" in the full sense, but predominantly accompanying phrases to match the external action. They were never intended—excepting in part the *Orate fratres*— to be recited publicly before the congregation, and thus make no pretense at furthering the dramatic performance of the Mass.

To some extent it is different with regard to the ancient *oratio super oblata*, which is, too, in its own way, actually an anticipation of the concept of sacrifice. From it, too, the proper arrangement of the medieval texts must derive. The *oratio super oblata* endeavors to underline the one step taken during the entire oblation rite: the provisional offering of the material gifts. Even these material gifts of bread and wine can be symbols of our interior surrender. So, just as they were brought to the altar by the faithful, in an external rite, they are now offered up to God by the Church in prayer, but at the same time the attention focuses on the veritable gift which will issue from the material ones. These latter, then, receive thereby a preliminary dedication, a "pre-consecration,"[6] similar to the preparatory consecration received by other requisites of divine worship, church and altar, chalice and paten, candles and altar-linens. There is no reason why we cannot include the more recent oblation prayers in this function of the secret; thus they will best fit into the course of the Mass.[7]

---

[5] In several late medieval Mass arrangements not only some but all the proper formulas were applied with this conclusion, including *In spiritu humilitatis* and *Veni sanctificator,* sometimes even *Orate fratres* and short accompanying phrases like *Acceptabile sit omnipotenti Deo sacrificium nostrum*; see, e.g., Martène, 1, 4, XXXI f. (I, 651; 656); Köck, 125 f.; likewise the Regensburg missal of the 15-16th century, according to which the priest was to say the *canon minor* with hands uplifted: *elevatis manibus in cœlum;* Beck, 266 f. The only prayers that could possibly be meant here are those which, according to prevailing medieval custom, were said bowed or with hands folded. The

formula *Suscipe sancte Pater* has the christological conclusion already in the Missa Illyrica: Martène, 1, 4, IV (I, 508 E).

[6] This idea is advanced especially by Batiffol, *Leçons,* 162-164. Following Suarez, he regards the secreta as *quædam dedicatio materiæ sacrificandæ per futuram consecrationem.* That the gifts are considered already dedicated is shown by the prescription of the *Missale Romanum* (*De defectibus,* X, 9), which directs that a host laid aside before the consecration as unsuitable, *si illius hostiæ iam erat facta oblatio,* is to be consumed after the ablution.

[7] See also Batiffol, *Leçons,* 26. Similarly C. Callewaert, "De offerenda et oblatione

If the first prayer includes a phrase, *hanc immaculatam hostiam,* in reference to the bread, this may have been intended by the medieval composer for the Holy Eucharist.[8] But objectively we can refer the phrase just as well to the simple earthly bread, and with the same right that we apply the words of the canon, *sanctum sacrificium, immaculatam hostiam* to the sacrifice of Melchisedech. Something like this holds true also for the words *calix salutaris* in the formula for the chalice. Even on this threshold of the sacrifice our chalice is at least as holy and wholesome as the thanksgiving cup of the singer in Psalm 115, from whom the words are borrowed.[9] Of course it is self-evident that when we say these prayers the higher destiny of our gifts is always kept in view.

Seen thus as a complete unit, we have no reason to deplore the development of the liturgical structure as we have it in the offertory, not at least if we are ready to acknowledge in the Mass not only an activity on God's part, but also an act of a human being who is called by God and who hastens with his earthly gifts to meet his Creator.

---

in Missa," *Periodica,* 32 (1944), 60-94, who takes a cue from certain expressions used in the secreta to stress even more emphatically the coherent line of the oblatory procedure, of which the offertory forms *aliqualis inchoatio.* A pertinent study is found in the chapter "The Meaning of the Offertory" in B. Cappelle, *A New Light on the Mass* (trans. by a monk of Glenstal, Dublin, 1952), 20-32, esp. 27.

[8] Even plainer examples of such a proleptic manner of speech from medieval Mass books in Eisenhofer, II, 144.

[9] In the literal sense of the original psalm this cup is one used to offer thanks for health attained, for being saved from danger. But here, when turned into a church prayer, it must naturally be interpreted in line with the context.—We note in passing that at the Council of Trent the expressions *immaculata hostia* and *calix salutaris* were listed among the grievances which the committee that composed the memorandum on the *abusus missæ* thought should be eliminated. *Concilium Tridentinum,* ed. Gœrres, VIII, 917.

II. The *Canon actionis*

1. The *Canon actionis* or the Eucharistic Prayer as a Whole

IN OUR STUDY OF THE HISTORY OF THE MASS WE HAVE COME TO recognize that the core of the Mass and the inner area within which Christ's institution is fulfilled is plainly and simply the *Eucharistia*. A thanksgiving prayer rises from the congregation and is borne up to God by the priest; it shifts into the words of consecration, and then into the oblation of the sacred gifts, and this oblation, in turn, concludes with a solemn word of praise. Although the fabric thus formed continues to survive unbroken in our present Mass, it is difficult for anyone not initiated into the history of the Mass to recognize the outlines of such a plan in the text of today. In the "preface," the prayer of thanksgiving is presented as an isolated unit, a preparatory item to be followed by the canon. The canon itself, however, with the exception of the words of consecration, appears to be nothing more than a loosely arranged succession of oblations, prayers of intercession and a reverential citation of apostles and martyrs of early Christianity. Still greater is the divergence from this plan when we turn our attention to the external presentation. At the *Sanctus* the audible performance breaks off, and all the rest is done in utter stillness, with only the altar boy's bell to give warning of the elevation of the sacred species, and again the silence resumes. At a high Mass this quiet is overlaid with the singing of the *Sanctus* and the *Benedictus*. Then the torchbearers appear in procession and range in front of the altar as for a grand reception; those assisting in choir fall on their knees; the *Hosanna* resounds in jubilant worship of Him who cometh in the name of the Lord. The God-ward movement of the great prayer of thanksgiving has been replaced by a reverse movement, turning upon the descent of the sacred mystery, and it is the impetus of this movement which has determined to a large extent the present pattern of the ancient *Eucharistia*.

It will therefore be our task to trace the various elements of this central portion of our Mass to their sources and to show more clearly the underlying ancient plan. We have already mentioned the decisive theological factor: the movement in the eucharistic teaching which led to a lessening regard for the oblation which we ourselves offer up and in which we offer ourselves as members of the Body of Christ, and a greater attention to the act of transubstantiation in which the divine omnipotence becomes operative in the midst of us, bringing Christ to us under the appearances of bread and wine.[1] This theological movement left its mark in various additions and appendages to the eucharistic prayer in the Roman Mass, and thus the work of recasting it was started. The most notable modification was the break at the *Te igitur* which led to splitting off the preface and to a new make-up of the canon that now followed.

In all the ancient liturgies the eucharistic prayer is composed as a unit and also titled as a unit. The original name (εὐχαριστία) was soon replaced by other designations, but these, too, kept the entire canon in view as a single whole. Nearly everywhere in the Orient the substitute for *eucharistia* was found in the word "anaphora," which brings to the fore the notion of sacrifice.[2] In the older Western liturgies, too, there were similar designations which emphasize the sacrifice:[3] *oratio oblationis, actio sacrificii.* But here in the West the names more widely distributed were others that referred immediately only to the accompanying prayer, and either named it in a very general way as a prayer: *oratio,*[4] *prex,*[5] or else, like the word εὐχαριστία designated its contents as divine praise, above all *prædicatio*[6]—terms which we can represent to a certain extent by "Great Prayer" and "Eucharistic Prayer." Another designation, the word *actio,* defined the section beginning here as a sacred activity;[7] *intra*

---

[1] Above I, 82 f., 118 ff.

[2] In every instance the anaphora embraces the Eucharistic prayer, but is extended in various ways in different rites, to include the prayers that precede and also the Communion portion of the Mass. Brightman, 569. Cfr. above I, 171. In the *Euchologion* of Serapion, n. 13 (Quasten, *Mon.,* 59) the Eucharistic prayer is captioned εὐχὴ προςφόρου.

[3] P. Cagin, "Les noms latins de la préface eucharistique": Rassegna Gregoriana 5 (1906) 321-358, especially 331 ff.

[4] Cyprian, *De dom. orat.,* c. 31 (CSEL, 3, 289 l. 14).

[5] Gregory the Great, *Ep.* IX, 12 (PL, 77, 956): the *Pater noster* is said *mox post precem.* Pope Vigilius, *Ep.* 2, 5 (PL, 69, 18 D); *canonica prex.*—Innocent I. *Ep.* 25 (PL, 20, 553).—Augustine, *De Trin.,* III, 4, 10 (PL, 42, 874); *prece mystica; Contra litt. Petil.* 2, 69 (CSEL, 52, 58 f): *precem sacerdotis;* cf. Batiffol, *Leçons,* 186 f. Fortescue, *The Mass,* 323, refers to the following passages in Cyprian, in which he sees in the word *prex* the name of the Great Eucharistic prayer: *Ep.* 15, 1 (PL, 4, 265); 60, 4(*ibid.,* 362); 66, 1

(*ibid.,* 398).—The word survived for a long time later as a designation for the Preface. It is used regularly as a title for the Preface in the Mass-book fragments of Zurich and Peterling of the 10th century ed. Dold (Beuron, 1934). In the Spanish Mass-book fragments of the 11th century also; see A. Dold, "Im Escorial gefundene Bruchstücke eines Plenarmissales in beneventanischer Schrift des 11. Jh. mit vorgregorianischem Gebetsgut und dem Præfationstitel *'prex'*": *Spanische Forschungen der Görresgesellschaft,* 5 (1935), 89-96.

[6] Cyprian, *Ep.* 75, 10 (CSEL, 3, 818), in the account of Firmilian of a woman who presumed [*non*] *sine sacramento solitæ prædicationis* to celebrate the Eucharist; cf. Batiffol, 186.—*Liber pont.* (Duchesne, I, 127): *Hic [Alexander I] passionem Domini miscuit in prædicatione sacerdotum quando missæ celebrantur.—Ibid.* (I, 312): *Hic [Gregory I] augmentavit in prædicationem canonis diesque nostros* . . . Cf. in regard to this the *benedicere et prædicare* mentioned in the introduction of the Preface of the Blessed Virgin.

[7] Cf. above I, 172 f.

actionem (says a sixth century source) the people should sing the *Sanctus* along with the priest.[8] This name is also found in several of the most ancient sacramentary manuscripts in the heading over the dialogue that introduces the preface: *Incipit canon actionis*.[9]—Here begins the canon of the action. The text beginning with the words *Sursum corda* is thus designated as the norm, the fixed groundwork for the sacred activity that follows. Later the word *canon* was used all by itself in the same sense.[10]

Even as late as the turn of the eighth century the preface was still included in the conception of the canon. Thus it is directed that the Easter candle should be consecrated *decantando quasi canonem*.[11] Even more plainly in a later writing we read that the subdeacon takes the paten *medio canone, id est cum dicitur Te igitur*.[12] Thus the unity of the Great Prayer was also preserved in the concept of "canon." The canon began with what we call the preface, and even the external ritual at the solemn pontifical functions signalized this spot as a beginning.[13]

Later on, however, a splitting of this original unity occurred, and preface and canon appear as separate parts thereof. This split proceeded from the Gallic liturgies. For here the eucharistic prayer, or rather all the praying in the course of the sacrifice-Mass, was from the start a series of individual prayers. The *oratio sexta*, to which Isidore assigns the consecration without further distinction, reached from the end of the *Sanctus*-chant to the *Pater noster*.[14] This scheme derived from Isidore was the one which Frankish commentators of the eighth and ninth centuries applied to the Roman liturgy. Here, too, the *oratio quinta* would have to conclude with the *Sanctus*, and the consecratory *oratio sexta* would begin at that point. What went ahead was the *præfatio*, that is, in the new language that evolved from the Gallic liturgy, the proem and introduction to the Great Prayer. In the Gregorian Sacramentary the word *præfatio* was to be seen as a heading for the *Vere dignum* formulas. Without hesitation its meaning was confined to the unit that preceded the *Sanctus*.

---

[8] *Liber pont.* (Duchesne, I, 128).

[9] So the older *Gelasianum* III, 16 (Wilson, 234).—Ebner, 395, n. 3; B. Botte, *Le canon de la messe romaine* (Mont César, 1935), 30 (in the Apparatus).

[10] In the Sacramentary of Angoulême (ed. Cagin, Angoulême, 1919, p. 117) the superscription mentioned already reads: *Incipit canon.* — Cf. Walafrid Strabo, *De exord. et increm.*, c. 22 (PL, 114, 950 A): *Canon vero eadem actio nominatur, quia in ea est legitima et regularis sacramentorum confectio.*

[11] *Ordo Rom.*, I, n. 39 (PL, 78, 955 C). The Sacramentary of Gellone, about the year 770-780, uses the same expression with regard to the delivery of the prayer used in the blessing of the baptismal water: Martène, 1, 1, 18, VI (I, 184 E).

[12] Amalar, *De eccl. off.*, III, 27 (PL, 105, 1146 D).

[13] This was done chiefly through the well-ordered and highly symmetrical arrangement of the assistants around the altar, provided for at this point. Cf. above I, 72. A trace of this arrangement is still retained in the Pope's Mass of today; cf. Brinktrine, *Die feierliche Papstmesse*, note 24.

[14] Cf. above I, 82.

And in consequence, the canon was understood as comprising what followed, namely, the prayer beginning with *Te igitur.*

Despite the prevailing opposition of the Roman books, this notion appeared to be corroborated by a remark in the first Roman *ordo* where, after the mention of the *Sanctus*-chant, the rubric continues: *Quem dum expleverint, surgit pontifex solus et intrat in canone;*[15] the canon (it seems to imply) is a sanctuary into which the priest enters alone.

The sanctity of this inner chamber, which must be kept closed to the people, is matched by the silence reigning in it. The canon becomes a prayer spoken by the priest in so low a tone that even the bystanders cannot hear it. The transition to this is to be noticed very evidently about the middle of the eighth century in the Frankish revision of the Roman *ordo* of John the Arch-chanter; here, after the *Sanctus*, we read: *Et incipit canere dissimili voce et melodia, ita ut a circumstantibus altare tantum audiatur*[16]—he starts to sing in a different tone and melody, so as to be heard only by those standing around the altar. At first the canon was said merely in a subdued tone, whereas the secret had become a completely silent prayer. But about the turn of the eighth century various authentic reports begin to make mention of an absolute silence also for the canon.[17] In the second Roman *ordo,* which represents a late Carolingian revision of the first, the rubric cited above is reworded as follows: *surgit solus pontifex et tacite intrat in canonem.*[18]

In the period that followed, the quiet recitation of the canon became the established rule, but this is not to say that before Pius V the rule was everywhere taken in the sense of a fully inaudible recitation.[19] That the canon, however, was a holy of holies which the priest alone could

---

[15] *Ordo Rom.,* I, n. 16 (PL, 78, 945); cf. Jungmann, *Gewordene Liturgie,* 100 ff., for textual criticism of the passage. The meaning of the words is only that the celebrant "enters into" that is, continues alone with the Canon after the singing in common of the *Sanctus;* cf. *ibid.,* 101 f.

[16] *Capitulare eccl. ord.* (Andrieu, III, 103). Andrieu is hardly right in doubting the originality of this reading (*ibid.,* note), found in the older recension (St. Gall 349) in favor of the later version (without *et melodia; canone* instead of *canire = canere*); in the latter the mention of the melody could have been quietly dropped if, about 800, the transition to complete silence had been accomplished.—Cf., also for the following, Jungmann, *Gewordene Liturgie,* 53-119: the study "Præfatio und stiller Kanon" (= *ZkTh,* 1929, 66-94; 247-271), especially p. 87 ff.—That the canon until then was said in a perceptible tone is pre-

supposed also in the *Ordo Rom.* I, n. 16 (Andrieu, II, 96; PL, 78, 945), for the statement is made, without further remark, that the subdeacons resume an erect position at the *Nobis quoque peccatoribus.Ordo sec. Rom.,* n. 10 (Andrieu, II, 222; PL, 78, 974), which already supposes the canon's being said in silence, quite logically directs that the bishop say these words *aperta clamans voce.* This is also attested by Amalar, *Liber off.* III, 26, 5; 14 f. (Hanssens, II, 345; 347 f.): *exaltat vocem, elevat vocem.*

[17] The commentary "Quotiens contra se": Martène, 1, 4, 11 (I, 455 D); Florus Diaconus, *De actione miss.,* n. 42 f. (PL, 119, 43); Remigius of Auxerre, *Expositio* (PL, 101, 1256 C); *Expositio,* "Introitus missæ quare," ed. Hanssens (*Eph. liturg.,* 1930) 45.

[18] *Ordo Romanus* II, n. 10 (PL, 78, 974 A).

[19] Such the warning issued by the Synod of

tread, was a concept that was continually developed and consolidated.[20] Other reasons for silently reciting the canon pointed in the same direction; the sacred words must not be profaned, lest we call down God's punishment upon our heads.[21] The same thought is put in a positive way when it is emphasized that the canon must be reserved to the priest alone: *specialiter ad sacerdotem pertinet.*[22]

The splitting-off of the preface was also marked out very plainly in the set-up of the Mass book. At the beginning of the eighth century, in *Cod. Reg.* 316, which gives us the older *Gelasianum*, the *Te igitur* follows right after the last *Hosanna* without a break, indeed without even starting a new line,[23] even though the manuscript is definitely an artistic one; other manuscripts, however, of the same century already show the break.

The cleavage was displayed in several ways. The "T" of *Te igitur* was expanded into an initial. Then the initial was revamped into a picture of the Crucified. At first this was done only in isolated instances,[24] but since the tenth century it became more and more the normal thing.[25] Since the twelfth century the picture was frequently separated from the text and became a special canon-plate; a new initial "T" was then introduced at the start of the text and this, in turn, was not seldom treated as a decorative figure.[26] Along with this there was another tradition of long standing, the artistic transfiguration of the start of the preface, the first words of which *(Vere dignum)* were displayed, as a rule, with two artistically

---

Sarum in England 1217, can. 36 (Mansi XXII, 1119); *ut verba canonis in missa rotunde et distincte dicantur;* see Hardouin, XI, 1335. According to the *Ordo Rom.* XIV, n. 53 (PL, 78, 1165) the Canon was to be said *submissa voce* by the priest, but in the same manner as the deacon and subdeacon together said the *Sanctus,* therefore in a loud tone of voice. The consecration of the Oil of the Sick before the *Per quem hæc omnia* on Maundy Thursday, spoken in a subdued tone *(voce demissa),* is a carry-over from this older practice.
[20] Cf. above, I, 82 f.
[21] Remigius of Auxerre, *Expositio* (PL, 101, 1256 D). Remigius introduces a story told originally by John Moschus (d. 619), *Pratum spirituale,* c. 196 (PL, 74, 225 f.; PG, 87, 3081 f.), a story repeated by many later commentators on the Mass, how shepherd boys were struck by lightning because they dared to sing the canon in the open field. The movement for the silent recitation of the canon in the Orient is even older, although it did assume different forms; cf. E. Bishop, *Silent Recitals in the Mass of the Faithful*: the Appendix to R. H. Connolly, *The Liturgical Homilies of Narsai,* 121-126.
[22] *Eclogæ* (10th cent.; PL, 105, 1326 C). Only since the 12th century do some interpreters call attention to the fatigue of the priest that is to be avoided by the silent prayer; see Eisenhofer, II, 154, who sees in it a possible supporting factor. We might agree with his opinion.
[23] See the facsimile, DACL, VI, 756-57.
[24] In the Sacramentary of Gellone (about 770); see pictures in Leroquais IV, Table II.
[25] Ebner, 445 f. Illustrations of the two methods, *ibid.,* 9; 16; 50; 130; 184; 444, and in the frontispiece; Leroquais, *Les Sacramentaires,* IV. Sometimes this cross-formed T stands as an abbreviation for the words *Te igitur* and the text then continues with *clementissime Pater.*
[26] For this purpose a favorite in the Middle Ages was the representation of the celebrant at the altar, or of the Pietà, or of the Brazen Serpent. Ebner, 447 f.

ornamented letters *V D*,[27] usually converted into the form ⊕. Since the ninth century the rounding of this figure was utilized more and more by miniaturists as a space for the *Maiestas Domini*.[28] But towards end of the Middle Ages the preface-symbol disappeared, and with it the special beginning of the Great Prayer.[29] The only picture our missal has, is one before the *Te igitur*, so that even the book-making art marks the beginning of the canon as something entirely new.[30] In the manuscripts the greatest care is often expended on the text of the canon. Not infrequently it is written in gold or silver lettering on purple parchment.[31] Even today the Mass books usually print this part in a large (48-point) type which typographers call "canon."

In the course of centuries, the close of the canon was set at various places. The conclusion at the doxology is still presupposed in the third Roman *ordo*,[32] and basically even in the present-day rubrics.[33] On the other hand, our missals extend the page heading *canon actionis* and the large print to the last Gospel. Since the ninth century the conclusion of the canon has varied, shifting between these two points, particularly in accord with the various theories regarding the consecration prayer and those rites by which the sacrifice is completed, or the representation of Christ's Passion is concluded. The end of the canon was set after the *Pater noster*, after the embolism, at the *Agnus Dei*,[34] or after the Communion. Other particulars of the external rite were also determined in accordance with these same theories, like the extent of the silence during the canon, the duration of the time assistants stayed on their knees, etc.[35] We will have occasion later to speak about these different regulations. But there can be no doubt that in the original construction of the Mass-liturgy the principal portion of the Mass ended at the *Amen* before the *Pater noster*.

The pre-Carolingian Roman liturgy had, as we have said, no thought at all of the division into preface and canon which we are considering. Not only was the entire eucharistic prayer comprised under the word *canon*,

[27] Ebner, 432 ff.; for illustrations see the list, p. XI. Individual MSS., like the Cod. Ottobon. 313 (beginning of the 9th cent.) which scarcely emphasizes the beginning of the canon, still have the elaborate symbol for the preface; Ebner, 233 f.

[28] Ebner, 438-441.

[29] Ebner, 434 f., 437.

[30] The Herder Missal of 1931, prepared by the Abbey of Maria Laach, is perhaps the first printed missal with a preface picture placed before the *præfatio communis*, which moreover is set in the large type usual for the canon.

[31] Ebner, 449; Martène, 1, 4, 8, 2 (I, 399). Older memories still exerted their

influence. A Sacramentary of Tours at the end of the 9th century has the *Præfatio communis* along with the canon in gold lettering upon a purple background; another of the 10th century from Trier has only this preface with the *Sanctus*. Leroquais, I, 53. 83.

[32] *Ordo Rom.* III (11th cent.), n. 16 (PL, 78, 981 C).

[33] *Missale Rom., Ritus serv.* VIII; IX.

[34] Ebner, 425.—In the last-mentioned instance the end of the canon was distinguished by a picture, the Lamb of God in a round medallion. Ebner, 448 f.

[35] Cf. Jungmann, *Gewordene Liturgie*, 133-135.

but even the word *præfatio* to all appearances had the same meaning.[36] It was the solemn prayer which ascended to God before the whole assembly. In this sense the word was already current in ancient sacral language,[37] and we find it being employed in a similar sense as a liturgical term in Christian usage.[38] Thus it became, by preference, the name for the Great Prayer of the Mass.

If, in arguing as we do, we are on the right track, then the name only confirms what we have been forced to conclude from other considerations, namely, that the whole prayer was said in a loud voice. If anywhere, then surely here, the solemn recitation must have become even at an early period a kind of speech-song.[39] Since the sixth century there are witnesses to the song-like performance of the Mass-prayers, and obviously these must be referred above all to the eucharistic prayer.[40] This does not mean, of course, that originally the whole eucharistic prayer was sung to the tune of the preface. A great deal of it, indeed, must have been chanted.[41] But we must conclude that after the *Sanctus* a mere recitative—the simple reading tone—predominated from time immemorial.[42] This, indeed, corresponded to the character of the prayer-text which no longer displayed the

---

[36] For the following see Jungmann, *Gewordene Liturgie,* 53-80, which also contains more detailed proofs. The word *præfatio* was used for the separate parts of the Eucharistic prayer, not only for the *Vere dignum,* but likewise also for the *Hanc igitur* and for the blessing formulas that were to be interpolated before the concluding doxology; thus in the Gregorianum (Lietzmann, n. 2, 9; 138, 3; cf. n. 77, 3 in the Apparatus). This presupposes an earlier application of the word for the entire Eucharistic prayer.

[37] There are phrases like *præfari divos* (Virgil), *præfari Vestam* (Ovid), *fausta vota præfari* (Apuleius); *præfatio* was precisely the prayer which was joined with the sacrifice (Suetonius). Even in common parlance the word was used in the sense of a public announcement, a proclamation. Further proofs in Jungmann, *Gewordene Liturgie,* 76-78. The same spatial significance is here attached to the *præ* as in the *prælectio, præsidium;* it designates an action that is performed *in the presence* of someone, and not one that precedes another in point of time.

[38] Council of Mileve (416), c. 12 (Mansi, IV, 330.—*Liber pont.* (Duchesne, I, 255): (Gelasius): *fecit etiam et sacramentorum præfationes.* When Cyprian, *De Dom. or.,* c. 31, calls the *sursum corda* a *præfatio,*

he has a different meaning in mind. Here *præfatio* does not mean the speech said in common before the people, but the speech said as a preliminary or preparation before the holy of holies. The word corresponds to the Greek πρόρρησις; cf. Dölger, *Sol salutis,* 288 ff. In the Gallican liturgy *præfatio* was used in the sense of a preparatory announcement for the invitation to prayer.

[39] Cf. above I, 377 f.

[40] The oldest testimony is probably to be found in the Leonianum (Muratori, I, 375): *Incipiunt preces diurnæ cum sensibus necessariis.* By the word *sensus* is meant the recitative melody; cf. above, I, 409, n. 36. The word is used for the melody of the Psalms in the *Liber Pont.* in a reference to Gregory III (d. 741) Duchesne, I, 415, 1. 3). Cf. also for the priest's chant in the Mass, the Synod of Cloveshoe, can. 12, cited *supra,* I, 377, note 17.

[41] That seems to be the sense of the expression mentioned above: *decantando quasi canonem.*

[42] This is indicated by the expression *dissimili voce et melodia* in the text cited above, p. 103 f., from the *Capitulare ecclesiastici ordinis.* At all events, in the Roman prayer for the blessing of the baptismal water on Holy Saturday, a prayer that parallels the Eucharistic prayer, we have

sublime accent to the hymn of thanksgiving, but rather the quiet current of petition, of oblation and the biblical account; but even here in each case it might be presumed that at least the closing doxology (and not merely the *Per omnia sæcula sæculorum*) returned once more to the solemn tone.

It was in the preface that the altar chant found its richest development as the years passed. The recitative here was not merely provided with proper cadences, but at the start and end of each sentence it took on psalmodic forms and evolved partially into a simple melody. But the step to a full song was never completed.[43] The very seriousness of the meeting with almighty God, who seems to be right before the priest during the Great Prayer, was without doubt what hindered this step.[44] On the other hand, the performance of the preface was never so strictly objective that all mood and emotion were excluded. Music history definitely proves that even the chants at the altar, and especially the preface, were caught up in the stream of Gregorian vitality.[45]

The unity and exclusiveness of the Great Prayer of the Roman Mass, made up of preface and canon together, is indeed none too great, even if we disregard its external delivery, its appearance in the book or its double name, and confine our attention solely to the contents. Besides the oblations, there are the intercessory prayers, which occupy a large space. In turn, these intercessory prayers are broken up into individual prayers, one part of them being placed before the consecration, the other part after. The original basic idea of the *eucharistia* is retained clear and distinct only in the initial prayer, the preface.

This breaking-up of the contents of the eucharistic prayer had already begun at a very early period, Aside from a few phrases, the whole text of today's canon is found already in the fifth century, and the notion which had much to do with producing this dissolution, namely, the recital within

already in the 7th century the rubric that to this day requires the transition to the *tonus lectionis* for the last part; in the older Gelasianum I, 44 (Wilson, 86): *hic sensum mutabis;* in the Sacramentary of Gellone (about 770): *hic mutas sensum quasi lectionem legas;* Martène, 1, 1, 18, VI (I, 184 E). Regarding the word *sensus,* see above, note 40. That a rubric so frequently used at Mass should not be transmitted can be explained by the fact that, unlike the blessing of the Easter water, it was sufficiently current by constant practice.

[43] That is shown in the fact that the melody of the preface was not written in notes, but was maintained merely with the help of certain reading signs; cf. above, I, 378.

[44] Concerning certain trends beyond these

bounds even in the 8th century, see above, I, 377, note 17.

[45] Ursprung, *Die kath. Kirchenmusik,* 58 f.; cf. 27 f. According to this study the first step in the development was the replacement of the subtonal "tuba" or recitation note, which made a full step down from b to a. About the 10th century we find in its stead a sub-semitonal tuba—a recitation note which made only a half step down (from c to b flat; our ferial preface tone). A further development, along with the elaboration of the initial and final phrases, was the introduction of a special accent tone above the tuba for certain syllables (cf. our festive *Pater noster*). And since the 12th century we have the development of a secondary tuba, the recitation moving along for a time on a note below the ordi-

the *mysteria,* and not before, of the names of those who had offered the gifts, is found even in Innocent I.[46] In the Orient, the intercessory prayers, in a very elaborate form, obtained an entrance into the inner circle of the Great Prayer as early as the fourth century.[47] The evolution seems to have followed this pattern: By degrees the viewpoint changed, and the celebration was no longer looked upon as an altogether spiritual *eucharistia;* over and above this there was the offering of the gifts, the ἀναφορά, the *oblatio* (according to the current designation),[48] and this, too, had to be clearly kept in view; naturally, then, there developed a provision for putting this oblation of gifts forward in an intercessory sense, a thing not easily done in a "thanksgiving prayer." Or, putting it a different way, there was a growing trend to relocate the intercessory prayers which had been said from time past right after the readings, linking them more closely with the gifts. This connection was certainly closest when the intercessory prayers were included in the very inner circle of the oblation prayers.

The driving force could well have been the closely related notion that our prayers would be all the more efficacious the nearer they were drawn to the Holy of Holies, thereby attracting to themselves the power of the Sacrament Itself. Even today, a person asking help is advised to place his needs before God at the consecration.[49] Thus the importunate friend could seek to gain access even into the sanctuary of the Great Prayer. In the Orient the damage done to the prayer by this insertion took place in only one spot, either after the consecration (as in the liturgies of the Syrian and Byzantine domains), or before the consecration, in fact before the *Sanctus* (as in the Egyptian liturgies). But in the West the effect was greater because the prayer of thanks had always been so much more terse (and when the *præfatio communis* became the normal text, it was actually reduced to a mere minimum), and because, on the other hand, the intercessory prayers were inserted finally in two different places, before the consecration and after.

---

nary recitation (our solemn preface tone). Lastly, about the same time, the introductory and final phrases on festive occasions were set with melismas of three or four notes, so that we have a really melodic form (our *tonus sollemnior* for the preface).

[46] Above I, 53 f.

[47] *Euchologion* of Serapion 13, 18 (above I, 34); *Const. Ap.,* VIII, 12, 40-49 (Quasten, *Mon.,* 224-227); Cyril of Jerusalem, *Cat. myst.,* V, 8-10 (Quasten, *Mon.,* 102 f).

[48] Above I, 171.

[49] This is a psychological parallel to the practice of recommending a great many intentions to a newly ordained priest for his first Mass, or to a child on the occasion of its First Communion; or, to take a case from olden times, to the practice Tertullian, *De Bapt.,* 20 (CSEL 20, 218), had of requesting the candidates for baptism instructed by him to remember him in the first prayer that they, as newly baptized, would say in church immediately after their baptism.

2. The Introductory Dialogue

Whereas generally the priestly prayer is preceded only by the customary greeting and the invitation *Oremus*, the Great Prayer displays its higher importance in the increased formality of its introduction. After the greeting there is an invitation not simply to a prayer, to an *oratio*, but to a prayer of thanks, an εὐχαριστία: *Gratias agamus Domino Deo nostro:* Εὐχαριστήσωμεν τῳ χυρίῳ. And this formal invitation is preceded by still another: *Sursum corda.* In both instances the people are not ignored, as they are with a mere *Oremus*, but are given a special concurrent response: *Habemus ad Dominum, Dignum et iustum est.*

In this introductory dialogue we have a most ancient Christian tradition.[1] Cyprian already comments on the *Sursum corda* and sees in these words the expression of the mood in which the Christian should properly begin every prayer: every fleshly and worldly thought should be suppressed, and the mind bent solely upon the Lord.[2] Augustine takes occasion, time after time, to speak of the *Sursum corda*. For him the words are the expression of a Christian attitude, much the same as St. Paul's admonition to those who have risen with Christ: *quæ sursum sunt quærite;*[3] our Head is in heaven, and therefore our hearts must also be with Him. It is through God's grace that they are with Him, and the gladsome consciousness of this, as expressed in the common response of the faithful, *Habemus ad Dominum,* is basically the factor which, according to St. Augustine, urges the priest on to the *Gratias agamus.*[4] Of course our thoughts cannot always be on God, but certainly they should be so—as another commentator insists—at least in this sublime hour.[5]

---

[1] Above I, 16; 29.

[2] Cyprian, *De dom. or.*, c. 31 (CSEL 3, 289): *Cogitatio omnis carnalis et sæcularis abscedat nec quicquam animus quam id solum cogitet quod precatur. Ideo et sacerdos ante orationem præfatione præmissa parat fratrum mentes dicendo: Sursum corda, dum respondet plebs: Habemus ad Dominum, admoneatur nihil aliud se quam Dominum cogitare debere.*

[3] Col., 3: 1.

[4] Augustine, *Serm.* 227 (PL, 38, 1100 f.). —Nine more pertinent passages are recorded by Rötzer, 118 f., to which he adds an *et cet.* The word *Dominus* here, just as in the *Dominus vobiscum*, is not always understood by Augustine to mean Christ, e.g., *Serm.* 6, 3 Denis (*Miscell. Aug.* I, 30 f.) : *Quid est Sursum cor? Spes in Deo, non in te. Tu enim deorsum es, Deus sursum est.* With the same emphasis as St. Augustine, Cæsarius of Arles explained

Sursum corda in his homilies; see *Sermones*, ed. Morin, in the Register, p. 999. He connects the *Sursum corda*, among others, with Phil. 3: 20; *Serm.* 22, 4 (Morin, 97).

[5] Cyril of Jerusalem, *Cat. myst.* V, 4 (Quasten, *Mon.*, 99 f.). The summons to be rid of βιωτιχαὶ φροντίδες that Cyril inserts in the "Ανω τὰς χαρδίας later comes to light in the oriental liturgy, in the hymn of the cherubim that accompanies the Great Entry (Brightman, 377). From a later age we might be permitted a reference to Henry Suso, who always sang these words in the Mass with special fervor. Asked what was his object, he answered that he was calling upon all creatures of heaven and earth and that he felt himself as their precentor in the praise of God; and, finally, that this song was for him a plea to all the tepid, who belong neither entirely to God, nor are yet entirely absorbed in

The precise origin of this preliminary *Sursum corda* is not known.[6] On the other hand, *Gratias agamus* is already found as an introduction to the prayer of thanks in the Jewish order of prayer.[7] Likewise the response to the invitation to prayer by a *Dignum et iustum est* was current there.[8] And in ancient culture too, acclamations of this kind played a grand role. It was considered the proper thing for the lawfully assembled people to endorse an important decision, an election, or the taking of office or λειτουργία, by means of an acclamation.[9] And there are evidences that besides the formula most used, ἄξιος, there were phrases like *Æquum est, iustum est;*[10] *Dignum est, iustum est.*[11]

An acclamation of this kind accorded well with the make-up of the Church and the nature of her worship. It is the ecclesiastical assembly that desires to praise God; but its organ, duly authorized from above, is the priest or bishop at its head. Only through him can and will she act, confirming this by her endorsement. But for his part, too, the priest does not wish to appear before God as an isolated petitioner, but rather only as speaker for the congregation.[12] Thus, by means of a dialogue at the great moment when the eucharistic prayer is to begin and the sacrifice is about to be performed, the well-ordered community that is at work secures an expressional outlet. At the same time there is a manifestation of how self-evident and becoming is the action which the Christian congregation has undertaken.[13]

Granted such a line of thought, it would appear to be obvious that the

creatures. *Vita* I, 9 (*Des Mystikers H. Seuse deutsche Schriften,* ed. N. Heller [Regensburg, 1926], p. 29 f.).

[6] Jno. 11: 41; Col. 3: 1 f.; especially Lament. 3: 41 are considered as possible biblical references. Cf. Gassner, 106. A. Baumstark "Wege zum Judentum des neutestamentlichen Zeitalters": *Bonner Zeitschrift f. Theologie u. Seelsorge,* 4 (1927), 33, calls attention to a formula in the Samaritan liturgy that requires the uplifting of hands before designated high points in prayer. Recently, however, he is more inclined to consider a Hellenistic origin and supposes that the greeting at the beginning of the prayer was somehow united sometimes with the *Gratias agamus,* sometimes with the *Sursum corda,* until at last both invocations were set side by side. Baumstark, *Liturgie comparée,* 97. A. Robinson, on the other hand, considers the expression *sursum corda habere* a naturally Latin one; see the note of R. H. Connolly, *The Journal of Theol. Studies,* 39 (1938), 355.—In Hippolytus, *Trad. Ap.* (Dix 50 f.) the thanksgiving prayer that

introduces the Agape, is preceded only by the *Dominus vobiscum* and the *Gratias agamus,* and the point is stressed that the *Sursum corda* should be said only at the Sacrifice. Hence it appears as a confirmation and enrichment of the invocation implied in the *Gratias agamus.*

[7] Above I, 15, note 40.

[8] As a confirmation equivalent to the *Amen* in the Schema of the morning prayer: *'emet wajazib;* I. Elbogen, *Der jüdische Gottesdienst,* 22 f., 25.

[9] E. Peterson, Εἷς θεός, 176-180; Th. Klauser, "Akklamation," *RAC,* I, 216-233.

[10] Thus at the election of the Emperor Gordian; *Scriptures hist. Aug.,* Gordian, c. 8 (ed. Didot 501) ; Peterson, 177.—Cf. the list of acclamations in Klauser, 227-231.

[11] Both at the election of the Bishop in Hippo; Augustine, *Ep.* 213 (CSEL, 57, 375 f.).

[12] Cf. Chrysostom, *In II Cor. hom.,* 18 (PG, 61, 527) : "It is not the priest alone who completes the thanksgiving, but the people with him."

[13] Peterson, *op. cit.,* 179, surmises that in

responses mentioned were actually spoken by the people. In fact, in the evidence already presented, this matter is made clear enough.[14]

One peculiarity in the ritual of this introductory dialogue is the fact that the priest does not turn to the people when greeting them, as he does otherwise. In the Roman Mass he continues to face the altar.[15] Here, too, we have an example of the more delicate sense of form which ancient culture possessed, for once the sacred action is inaugurated, once this God-ward activity has begun, it would be improper to turn away.[16] At any rate, on this depended the decision as to what precisely was considered the opening of the sacred action, whether at the beginning of the *Eucharistia* itself, as was evidently the case in the Byzantine liturgy,[17] or rather at the presentation of the gifts, as is apparently presupposed in our Mass. This ancient sense of form is also manifested in the accompanying gestures: the summons to lift up the heart is accompanied by the priest's lifting of his hands,[18] and they then remain outstretched in the attitude of the *orantes*, the prayer-attitude of the ancient Church.

proportion as in the Christian Eucharistia the idea of sacrifice was brought to the fore, this legal character and with it the need for confirmation of the act had to be stressed by the acclaim of the people. Elfers, 270, n. 84, referring to Clemens of Alexandria, *Strom.* VII, 6; Irenæus, *Adv. hær.* IV, 18, 4 (al. IV, 31, 4; Harvey II, 205) emphasizes the point that the celebration of the Eucharist was strongly regarded as an "act of duty and justice" toward God. Cf. the explanation of Ἄξιον καὶ δίκαιον given by Cyril of Jerusalem, *Cat. myst.* V, 5 (Quasten, *Mon.*, 100): "When we give thanks, we do what is fitting and just; but He acted not only justly, but beyond all justice, inasmuch as He accorded us all blessings and considered us worthy of His great benefits" (he had just finished considering the Redemption and the Sonship of God). The obligation of giving thanks is also stressed already in Thess. 1: 3 ff.

[14] Above, p. 110 f. Chrysostom, *De s. Pentec.* hom. 1, 4 (PG, 50, 458 f.). *De pœnit. hom.* 9 (PG, 49, 345; Brightman, 473 f.).—Cf. the word of encouragement to the somewhat timid newly baptized, with which St. Augustine accompanies his instruction on the *Sursum corda*, in *Sermo* Denis, 6, 2 (PL, 46, 835; Rötzer, 119): *hodie vobis exponitur, quod audistis et quod respondistis; aut forte, cum responderetur, tacuistis, sed quid respondendum esset hodie, heri didicistis.* Augustine testifies to the

general spread of this response in his *De vera religione,* c. 3, 5 (PL, 34, 125): mankind throughout the world answers daily in this phrase.

[15] It is otherwise in the Byzantine liturgy, where the salutation has the solemn form of II Cor. 13: 13 (see above in the text) and is also accompanied by a gesture of blessing; Brightman, 384. While saying this as well as the following Ἄνω σχῶμεν τὰς καρδίας he stands facing the people whom he is addressing; it is not till he intones the Εὐχαριστήσωμεν τῷ κυρίῳ that he turns "towards the East." Hornykewitsch, 76.

[16] Cf. Dölger, *Sol Salutis,* 322. Amalar, *De eccl. off.* III, 9 (PL, 105, 1116), also shows a clear perception of the meaning of this prescription, *Ibi jam occupati circa altare ... Nec debet arator, dignum opus exercens, vultum in sua terga referre.* That later times would no longer have hit upon such an idea is shown in the case of Lebrun, *Explication,* I, 335 f. He can only explain the execution by saying that at one time at this passage in the liturgy the altar was shut off from the view of the people by curtains and that consequently a turning towards them would have made no sense.

[17] Note 15 above.

[18] Cf. the Ἄνω σχῶμεν τὰς καρδίας in the Byzantine Rite, where the rubric is added: δεικνύων ἅμα τῇ χειρί; Brightman, 384.

In this section of the Roman Mass the heritage of the ancient Church has been preserved with special fidelity also in regard to the simple form of the text, which still retains the dialogue, almost word for word as found in Hippolytus.[19] There are none of those additions or expansions which in other liturgies partly disguise the concise exclamations. Here as elsewhere the greeting is confined to the words *Dominus vobiscum*. In the Orient, only Egypt shows a similar simple form of greeting for the opening of the dialogue: Ο κύριος μετὰ πάντων (ὑμῶν), while the other liturgies employ some modification and extension of the solemn triple blessing of the Apostle in II Cor. 13 : 13.[20] Even the *Sursum corda* has elsewhere undergone enlargements[21] and likewise, though less extensively, the *Gratias agamus* along with its response. In the latter case, where the exclamation announces the theme of the Great Prayer that follows, the changes that have been introduced here and there are all the more characteristic. The West Syrian liturgy of St. James emphasizes the motif of the awesome: "Let us say thanks to the Lord with fear, and adore Him with trembling".[22] The East Syrian Mass brings to the fore the notion of sacrifice which is concealed in the thanksgiving: "The sacrifice is offered up to God, the Lord of all," whereupon the usual answer follows: "It is meet and just." [23] The Mozarabic liturgy connects with this exclamation a trinitarian confession,[24] just as the Byzantine does with the response of the people.[25]

In most of the oriental liturgies the introductory dialogue is separated

[19] Above I, 29.

[20] H. Engberding, "Der Gruss des Priesters zu Beginn der Eucharistia in östlichen Liturgien," JL, 9 (1929) 138-143.—The most important development is that the part which pertains to God the Father is placed at the very front: Ἡ ἀγάπη τοῦ κυρίου καὶ πατρός, ἡ χάρις . . . This form spread from Jerusalem. The Mozarabic *Missale mixtum* has a similar version (PL, 85, 546 B).—Baumstark, *Liturgie comparée*, 89 f.

[21] In the Syrian-Antiochian sphere: Ἄνω σχῶμεν τὰς καρδίας ἡμῶν; Baumstark, 90 f. Alongside the *Sursum corda* there is the formula of the Apostolic Constitutions VIII, 12, 5 (Quasten, *Mon.*, 213): Ἄνω τὸν νοῦν. The Greek liturgy of St. James combines both: Ἄνω σχῶμεν τὸν νοῦν καὶ τὰς καρδίας. Brightman, 50; cf. 85; 473. The Mozarabic Mass inserts after the trinitarian plea for blessing, the invitation to the kiss of peace, to which the choir responds with a chant of several verses; next the words of the Psalm *Introibo ad altare Dei mei* which the choir again takes up with *Ad Deum qui lætificat*

juventutem meam; then the invocation *Aures ad Dominum,* to which the choir answers *Habemus ad Dominum.* Only then comes the *Sursum corda* with the alternate response from the choir *Levemus ad Dominum* and the invitation to give thanks, again in a peculiar formulation. *Missale mixtum* (PL, 85, 546 f.).

[22] Brightman, 85; cf. above I, 39.

[23] Brightman, 283. The same stress on the sacrificial character in this passage, though in more elaborate phraseology, in both the East Syrian anaphora of Theodore of Mopsuestia and that of Nestorius; Renaudot, *Liturgiarum orient. collectio*, II (1847), 611; 620 f.

[24] *Liber ordinum* (Ferotin, 236): *Deo ac Domino nostro, Patri et Filio et Spiritui Sancto, dignas laudes et gratias referamus.* In the *Missale mixtum* (PL, 85, 547) Christ is substituted in place of the Three Persons.

[25] Brightman, 384: Ἄξιον καὶ δίκαιόν ἐστιν προςκυνεῖν πατέρα υἱὸν καὶ ἅγιον πνεῦμα τριάδα ὁμοούσιον καὶ ἀχώριστον. In many texts the addition is missing.

from what precedes, and is given greater emphasis by an exclamation of the deacon, admonishing the people to assume a proper demeanor of reverence and attention in view of the Holy Sacrifice now to be offered up: Στῶμεν καλῶς, στῶμεν μετὰ φόβου, πρόςχωμεν τὴν ἁγίαν ἀναφορὰν ἐν εἰρήνῃ προςφέρειν: Let us stand upright, let us stand in fear, let us give our attention to offering the Holy Sacrifice in peace. The choir confirms his admonition by glorifying the oblation as a grace-laden pledge of peace and a sacrifice of praise: "Ελεον εἰρήνης, φὑσίαν αἰνέσεως.[26] In some churches of the West Syrian ambit, a monition of this sort was augmented as early as the fourth-fifth century by a whole series of warnings from the deacon to guard against the possibility of anyone unworthy remaining amongst the participants.[27] We have here the ancient πρόρρησις, the *præfatio* in the sense indicated by St. Cyprian.[28] The kiss of peace, too, which, in the oriental liturgies precedes the dialogue, *resp.*, the deacon's warnings, either immediately[29] or mediately, evidently had the same function of an assurance that all were ready for the sacred action.

The Roman liturgy has no such monitory pause at this juncture. The deacon's function is scarcely developed at all, and the kiss of peace is deferred to a different place. Conversely, the dialogue that introduces the prayer of thanks is today so closely interwoven with what precedes that there is no evident break-off. After his silent preparation of the gifts, the priest begins by saying aloud: *Per omnia sæcula sæculorum*, the concluding words of the *secreta* and therefore a part of the offertory. Thus the *Dominus vobiscum* does not sound at all like a start, but rather like a continuation. Such was the case already in the eighth century.[30] Still, at that

---

[26] Thus in the Byzantine Mass; Brightman, 383. In other liturgies within the Syrian sphere the same invocation underwent various revisions. It is considerably amplified in the East Syrian and Armenian Mass; Brightman, 282; 434 f. In the Egyptian it must have found partial acceptance only later, as is shown by the still prevailing Greek text of the Copts; *ibid.*, 164. The answer of the choir "Ελεον εἰρήνης, θυσίαν αἰνέσεως and its equivalent, as the translations show, seems not to have been understood any more. θυσία αἰνέσεως (from Ps. 115: 8, according to the Septuagint) can just about be rendered with λογικὴ θυσία ; a sacrifice consisting of praise. The revision cited above for ἔλεος εἰρήνης follows Mercenier-Paris, *La prière des églises de rite byzantin*, I, 238. The invitation that Theodore of Mopsuestia (d. 428) attests and explains in this passage, *Sermones catech.* V (Rücker, *Ritus bapt. et missæ*, 25 f.) forms the heart

of the deacon's cry: *Aspicite ad oblationem.*
[27] *Const. Ap.*, VIII, 12, 2 (Quasten, *Mon.*, 212). In the *Testamentum Domini*, I, 23 (Rahmani, 37 f.; Quasten, *Mon.*, 250) there is a series of thirteen outcries that begin with: *Si quis odium contra proximum habet, reconcilietur! Si quis in conscientia incredulitas versatur, confiteatur! Si quis mentem habet alienam a præceptis, discedat!*
[28] Note 2, above. Dölger, *Sol Salutis*, 290, refers to Livy, 45, 5: . . . *cum omnis præfatio sacrorum eos, quibus non sint puræ manus, sacris arceat.*
[29] Thus in the Coptic, Ethiopian, and in the East Syrian liturgy: Brightman, 162 f.; 227; 281 f.
[30] Gregorianum (Lietzmann, n. 1). The Cod. Otobon. 313, which goes back to the 9th century, inserts expressly: *qua* (sc. *oratione super oblata*) *completa dicit sacerdos excelsa voce: Per omnia (ibid.);*

time there was a conscious knowledge that the real beginning started with the *Dominus vobiscum,* several of the Carolingian commentaries commencing with these words.[31] Some of the oldest manuscripts which contain the canon leave out the *Dominus vobiscum*—taking it for granted—and introduce the canon with the words *Sursum corda.*[32] It is possible to admit that at least the solemn melody did not start till the *Dominus vobiscum.*[33]

3. The Preface

The prayer ushered in with the preface is *the* prayer of the Church, her Great Prayer.[1] It is an attempt to create with human words a worthy framework and more especially a fitting adit for the holy mystery which will be accomplished in our midst and which we are privileged to present to God. There are two ranges of ideas which here press for expression: first, the primitive consciousness that we owe God, our Creator and Lord, adoration and praise, the basic acts of all religion and worship; and second, the Christian acknowledgment that we who have been elected and honored by the wonderful vocation which is ours through Christ, can do nothing less than thank Him again and again. The only proper response to the εὐ-αγγέλιον is the εὐ-χαριστία.[2] For what we have here received is something far beyond anything that our human nature might expect from its Creator as a fitting endowment. Gratitude is also called for by the vision of earthly creation, the vision of all that nature provides for men. This gratitude for the benefits of the natural order is to be found remarkably amplified in a number of examples from the early Christian period, both within the

regarding the tradition of the text, see JL, 5 (1925) 70 f. In the *Ordo* of John Archicantor, the present texts of which (8th cent.) require the silent prayer in the Secreta, the priest raises his voice already for the *Per omnia sæcula sæculorum* (Silva-Tarouca, 198).

[31] Cf. Franz, 344, 349, 350, 395 f. Amalar also, *De eccl. off.,* III, 21 (PL, 105, 1133), has the *præfatio* considered here begin *a salutatione, quæ dicitur ante Sursum corda.*

[32] Cf. above, p. 103.

[33] The incongruity here considered was the topic of a note in *Les Questions Liturgiques,* 4 (1913-14), 244. The solution proposed was to sing the *Per omnia sæcula sæculorum* in a somewhat lower tone of voice with the understanding that the organist then play a transitional melody to the *Dominus vobiscum.* Cf. *Cours et conférences* VIII (Louvain, 1929), 143, note 8, where reference is also made to the custom prevalent among the Premonstraten-

sians and Trappists, to recite the *Per omnia* and begin the singing only with the *Dominus vobiscum.* The same condition is found at the end of the Canon, where the introduction to the *Pater noster* follows and again after the Embolism, where the *Pax Domini* follows.

[1] See above, regarding the use of the words *præfatio* and *prex* in the Roman liturgy. In the Gallican liturgy it is called *contestatio,* a solemn confession, a designation corresponding to the ἐξομολόγησις used for the preface in the *Canones Basilii* c. 97 (Riedel, 274). In the Gallican liturgical sphere designations appear that point to the sacrifice: *immolatio* (in the *Missale Gothicum*), *illatio* (in the Mozarabic liturgy). Cf. Jungmann, *Gewordene Liturgie,* 72 f.; 82 f.

[2] It is therefore not by accident that the gospel forms the high point of the fore-Mass.

eucharistic prayer and outside it.[3] Later, the theme is less common. It is particularly infrequent in the Roman liturgy, though even here it is not entirely absent.[4] But there is a new note and a new urgency in the gratitude with regard to the Christian economy of salvation. The Epistles of St. Paul, which almost invariably begin with a word of thanksgiving,[5] are the first manifestations of this.[6]

In this connection it is hard to decide whether the liturgical *eucharistia* in its pre-Greek beginnings (as they are to be found in the *Berachah*) possessed this evident preponderance of thanksgiving over the general expression of praise or of adoration.[7] This last objective has indeed always been an important factor in the eucharistic prayer, especially after the *Sanctus* was included; it is its expansion into the realm of the universal and metaphysical.[8] Petition, too, is included along with the thanksgiving, at first tentatively,[9] later even in a relatively developed form. But it is equally evident from the earliest sources that in principle, and aside from certain more recent marginal developments, the keynote of the *eucharistia* that now begins has always been thanksgiving.

Besides the character of the Christian dispensation, there was another element that helped bring this about. The Lord had given the Sacrament to his disciples with the command: "Do this for a memory of me." Accordingly, all the liturgies include this commemoration in some form or other in the *anamnesis* after the words of consecration. But in this place they all turn more or less hurriedly to the offering of the gifts just hallowed, as the very nature of the case demands. So the proper place for this concept, a place where it can expand, is not here after the transubstantiation, but rather *before* the words of consecration, for the consecration can be inserted suitably only in a space filled by the thankful remembrance of the Lord. And this concept is most adequately expressed when it is something

---

[3] Above I, 31-2, 35 f.

[4] Cf. in the Leonianum (Muratori 1, 303) : *VD. Quoniam licet immensa sint omnia quæ initiis humanæ sunt collata substantiæ, quod eam scilicet crearis ex nihilo, quod tui dederis cognitione pollere, quod cunctis animantibus summæ rationis participatione prætuleris, quod tota mundi possessione ditaris; longe tamen mirabiliora sunt* . . .

[5] According to the Hellenistic epistolary style a thanksgiving was certainly part of the beginning of a letter; see A. Deissmann, *Licht vom Osten*, 4. Aufl., Tübingen, 1923, 147, n. 3.

[6] Cf. E. Mócsy, "De gratiarum actione in epistolis Paulinis": *Verbum Domini*, 21 (1941), 193-201; 225-232.

[7] Cf. J. M. Nielen, *The Earliest Christian Liturgy*, 295-296. Nielen refers to M. J. Lagrange, *Evangile selon S. Luc.* (3d ed.; Paris, 1927), 544, who regards the biblical word εὐχαριστεῖν not simply as a translation of a Hebrew word of general meaning, and who, therefore, infers a tradition of the primitive Church, "que la prière de Jésus bénissant avant de distribuer le pain et le vin était une action de grâces."

[8] In the oriental liturgies, as a rule, the preface up the *Sanctus* is dedicated to the praise of God in general; in those outside of Egypt a christological prayer of thanksgiving follows upon the *Sanctus*, a prayer that, because of its closer connection with the account of the Institution, shows itself to be more original. Cf. Hanssens, III, 356.

[9] Cf. *Euchologion Serapions*, above I, 34.— With regard to Justin, *Apol.* I, 67 below p. 152, n. 3.

more than a thoughtful recalling of memories from the past, when it is rather enveloped in prayer before God. It then becomes an act of gratitude, a prayer of thanks for the great thing that has been given us in Christ. "To thank" is after all etymologically nothing less than "to think" about benefits received, and not thoughtlessly to ignore them.

As the central theme of his remembrance, St. Paul already mentions the death of our Lord, the work of redemption.[10] And this continued to be, far and wide, the cardinal object of the *eucharistia,* and as such was conscientiously retained.[11] We should remember what the action is really a remembrance of; we should remember what is represented in the action as a memorial. The Mass is not a sacrifice reposing on its own self; it is a sacrifice only insofar as it is at the same time a memorial of the sacrifice already consummated, which brought us redemption. Therefore, it is at the same time a thanksgiving, and demands of us such a thanksgiving.[12] When the fundamental mysteries of the Christian economy are focused in this way in a prayer of thanks that rises to God in the sight of the congregation, the prayer itself becomes a most effective expression of a consciousness of their faith and their acknowledgment of it. Thus, in the most ancient tradition the *eucharistia* appears at the same time as another more exalted form of the profession of faith.[13]

Gratitude for the advent of the Lord, for His Passion and death, for His Resurrection and Ascension, for all that He has done to procure our salvation—these are the themes that form the object of thanksgiving in the prefaces of the Roman liturgy as they range through the course of the year. It is a peculiarity of the occidental liturgies that their prayer, including the Great Prayer, varies with the progress of the year, and, in consequence, the mysteries of faith are kept in view only one portion at a time. Other

---

[10] I Cor. 11 : 26.

[11] The latter is very clearly the case, e.g., in the letter of James of Edessa (d. 708) to Thomas the Presbyter (Brightman, 492): "and whereas the priest and the people have meetly accounted it right to give thanks unto the Lord, he says, *It is meet and right to praise thee* and in a few words commemorates the whole scope of the grace of God as touching man and his first creation and his redemption thereafter and as touching the dispensation which Christ wrought in our behalf when He suffered for us in the flesh: for this is the whole *kurobho* that we should commemorate and declare the things which Christ wrought in our behalf." How close the formulas of the changing Roman preface could adhere to the anamnesis is shown in the Sunday preface after the feast of Ascension, which the Alcuin appendix

(Muratori, II, 319) presents: *VD. Per Christum Dominum nostrum. Qui generi humano nascendo subvenit, quum per mortem passionis mundum devicit, per gloriam resurrectionis vitæ æternæ aditum patefecit et per suam ascensionem ad cælos nobis spem ascendendi donavit. Per.*

[12] Both ideas are remarkably well expressed by Fulgentius, *De Fide,* n. 60 (PL, 65, 699): *In illis enim carnalibus victimis significatio fuit carnis Christi, quam . . . fuerat oblaturus . . . in isto autem sacrificio gratiarum actio atque commemoratio est carnis Christi, quam pro nobis obtulit,* Ep. 14, 44 (PL, 65, 432 C): *Ideo . . . a gratiarum actione incipimus, ut Christum non dandum, sed datum nobis in veritate monstremus.*

[13] Regarding the original connection between the Eucharistic prayer and the Symbolum cf. the reference *supra,* I, 473.

liturgies, especially the liturgies of the East (taken as a whole), do not have this variety. They do have variations in the formularies, often in great profusion; take the West Syrian liturgy, for example, or the Ethiopian.[14] But each formula of the anaphora surveys the whole field of the Christian economy in a new way. This was likewise the principle which governed the *eucharistia* of the early Church.[15] There was only one further rule, that the preface at a Sunday or a feast-day assembly should be longer and more solemn than at the celebration at the graves of the martyrs, since these latter celebrations naturally drew a smaller congregation and were not fully public in character.[16] In the course of centuries, however, the custom of constantly reshaping the prayer of thanks, along with the effort to say something new for each occasion, must have resulted in the formation of many a version that touched only the periphery of the theme peculiar to the prayer. Traces of such a tendency can be found even in the oldest examples.[17] And those centrifugal forces must have been all the more powerful when every festal ceremony not only gave occasion for a new version but seemed to demand a new theme, one more consonant with the feast itself. This was the case from the very start in the liturgies of the West, and especially in the Latin liturgy of Rome. The most ancient collection of Roman Mass formularies, the *Sacramentarium Leonianum*, has a proper preface for each Mass; thus, although it is quite incomplete, the sacramentary has 267 prefaces! Even the older *Gelasianum* still furnishes 54 prefaces,[18] the later *Gelasianum* in the St. Gall manuscript, 186.[19]

The lion's share of such prefaces fell to the feasts of martyrs. As a special theme on such days, the obvious one, was derived from the martyr's victory-in-death. When in the preface of martyrs only the fundamental concept of their bloody witness to Christ was emphasized, the result was a prayer of thanks that stayed pretty close to the basic theme of our salvation, as when, after the mention of Christ's name, the special text continued:

> *Qui ad maiorem triumphum de humani generis hoste capiendum præter illam gloriam singularem, qua ineffabilibus modis Domini virtute prostratus est, ut etiam a sanctis martyribus superaretur effecit, atque in membris quoque suis victoria sequeretur, quæ præcessit in capite. Per.*[20]

At other times the victorious struggle of the martyr or even his intercessory power after his victory stands as an independent theme of thanksgiving. Sometimes, however, a panegyric on the hero is developed in formal

---

[14] Above I, 41-42.

[15] Above I, 29; 34-37.

[16] *Canones Basilii*, c. 97 (Riedel, 274).

[17] To some extent the formulary in the *Euchologion* of Serapion probably belongs here, above I, 34.

[18] These figures according to Eisenhofer II, 157. His other enumerations for the Gregorianum are, however, incorrect.

[19] Mohlberg, *Das fränkische Sacramentarium Gelasianum*, after the index, p. 280-282.—Baumstark refers these prefaces of the later Gelasianum back to a primitive Gelasianum, in which almost every Mass formulary would have its own preface. Mohlberg-Baumstark, *Die älteste erreichbare Gestalt*, 128*.

[20] Leonianum (Muratori, I, 311 f.).

outline, and becomes at last a more or less expanded recounting of the history of the saint's suffering. It is not to be wondered at that among the five prefaces which the *Leonianum* contains for the feast of St. Cecilia, one or another should have succumbed to this last danger.[21] Rather is it astonishing to find that, of the twenty prefaces provided in the several Mass formularies for the feast of the apostles Peter and Paul, almost all are still concerned with the theological and Christological contents of the apostolic office.[22]

In this oldest of sacramentaries, even Mass-formularies lacking a distinctively festal character are sometimes found with a preface whose contents are far different from the original conception of a eucharistic prayer, for example when it is used as a tirade against objectionable adversaries or as an exhortation to lead a moral life.[23] Such curiosities as these must lead sooner or later to a reaction. Perhaps an advance along these very lines is to be discerned behind the narrative of the *Liber pontificalis* regarding Pope Alexander: *Hic* [Alexander] *passionem Domini miscuit in prædicatione sacerdotum, quando missæ celebrantur.*[24] Phenomena of the sort described must finally have induced that drastic reform which is revealed in the Gregorian Sacramentary. In the genuine portions of this sacramentary as remanded by Adrian I to Charlemagne,[25] there are only

---

[21] Muratori, I, 456-459.

[22] Muratori, I, 330-345.—A summary of the whole situation in Stuiber, *Libelli sacramentorum Romani* (Bonn, 1950), 67 f. This particular development was even stronger in the Gallic liturgies; cf., e.g., the preface for the feast of St. Maurice in the *Missale Gothicum* (Muratori, II, 634). The prefaces of the Mozarabic liturgy frequently present extended accounts of the lives and sufferings of the saints; cf., e.g., the story of the passion of St. Vincent in the *Missale mixtum* (PL, 85, 678-681).

[23] Muratori, I, 350 ff.; cf. *supra*, I, 61-62.

[24] Duchesne, *Lib. pont.*, I, 127. The fact that the report is found in the *Liber Pontificalis* leads one to surmise that at the time the account was written (about 530) the counter-movement had not yet run its full course. Among the prefaces that corresponded to this program would be, e.g., those cited below, p. 122 ff., which in general are surely pre-Gregorian. By *passio Domini* is evidently meant Christ's redemptive work, as is the case already with Cyprian.—The meaning that Th. Schermann, "Liturgische Neuerungen," (Festgabe A. Knöpfler zum 70. Geburtstag [Freiburg, 1917], 276-289), 277 ff., at-

tributed to the passage, namely that the formulary of the "General Church Order" (= Hippolytus) was introduced in Rome at the time of Alexander I (d. 116), is unacceptable for various reasons. Equally unacceptable is the opinion expressed by others, that there was question here of the *Unde et memores* (. . . *tam beatæ passionis*) or of the words *Qui pridie quam pateretur.* Cf. Fortescue, *The Mass*, 346; Botte, *Le canon*, 64.—Likewise Elfer's assumption in *Die Kirchenordnung Hippolyts*, 248-253, that what is meant here is the account of the institution linked with the *passio*, and that all that is affirmed is that it was Pope Alexander who first interpolated into the eucharistic prayer of thanksgiving the narrative of the institution to which had been joined a recital of our Lord's sufferings, is based on unsubstantiated and inadmissible premises; see *ZkTh*, 63 (1939), 236 f.

[25] It is strange that the Sacramentary of Fulda, which Baumstark edited, with a few slight excisions, as the "oldest obtainable form" of the Gregorianum, still contains 46 prefaces, and even if we subtract those elements that are evidently later (n. 387, 623, 654, 674), there yet remain 42.

fourteen prefaces[26] counting the *præfatio communis*. Of these, a number—those for extraordinary occasions and for the two saints' feasts which were still favored—were later discontinued in Frankish territory, so that the grand wealth of ancient Roman tradition was reduced to seven formulas. But this poverty was somewhat augmented in the centuries to follow, that same Frankish territory contributing the preface of the Holy Cross,[27] of the Holy Trinity,[28] and of Lent.[29] These ten prefaces—or rather, since the *præfatio communis* was not counted in, the total was usually reckoned as nine—were the only ones considered admissible in the Decretals first mentioned by Burchard of Worms,[30] and by him ascribed to Pelagius II (d. 590) ; from here they were incorporated in the *Corpus Iuris Canonici*.[31] Finally, to this sparse group was added the Marian preface, prescribed by Urban II at the Synod of Piacenza in 1095, although it is itself of an earlier date.[32]

Many medieval churches, however, were not content with this poverty. Even in the appendix which Alcuin attached to the Gregorian Sacramentary coming from Rome, there was included, among other things, a special section containing a large number of prefaces, stemming for the

---

For the most part the majority are martyr prefaces. Mohlberg-Baumstark, *Die älteste erreichbare Gestalt*, see in the index, p. 96 f. Does this mean that the final curtailment did not take place till after Gregory?

[26] Lietzman, see Register, p. 185. Besides the *præfatio communis,* they are the prefaces for Christmas, Easter, Epiphany, Ascension, Pentecost, and for the feasts of the Apostles. Besides these there is a preface *in natali Papæ,* for ordination, consecration of an altar, for the bridal Mass, for Andrew, two for Anastasia (one an extra preface for Christmas). The preference for these two Saints shows a Byzantine influence at work, as was the case with the introduction of St. Andrew into the embolism, see below.

[27] Of unknown origin. I could nowhere discover it in the sources of the 8th and 9th centuries. A preface of the Holy Cross with the antithesis of the two woods is found in the Alcuin appendix; Muratori, II, 318. This antithesis itself is surely an ancient one, since, among others, it is found in Irenæus, *Adv. hær.,* V, 17 3; see H. Rahner, *Antennæ crucis,* III, (ZkTh, 1943) 1, n. 1.

[28] It appeared first in the older Gelasianum I, 84 (Wilson, 129) on the Sunday after Pentecost, which later became Trinity

Sunday. It could have originated in Spain and thus be dated back to the 7th century ; cf. A. Klaus, *Ursprung und Verbreitung der Dreifaltigkeitsmesse* (Werl, 1938), 17 f.; 81-83.

[29] This appears in the later Gelasianum (Mohlberg, n. 254), but also in the oldest available form of the Gregorianum (Mohlberg-Baumstark, n. 161) ; hence it belongs to an older Roman tradition.

[30] Burchard of Worms (d. 1025), *Decretum* III, 69 (PL, 140, 687 f.). Capelle (see below, n. 32) expresses a well-founded suspicion that Burchard himself was the author of this Canon (47).

[31] *Decretum Gratiani,* III, 1, 71 (Friedberg, I, 1313). Cf. Durandus, IV, 33, 35.

[32] Some suggestions of it are found in the later Gelasianum.—With a minor variation *(huic mundo lumen æternum effudit)* and an introductory clause referring to Virgins in general, today's wording is the same as that found in about 850 in the Cod. Ottobon. 313 of the Gregorianum, ed. Wilson (HBS, 49), 283 f.; also in the Sacramentary of Eligius (PL, 78, 133) ; see B. Capelle, "Les origines de la préface romaine de la Vierge," *Revue d'histoire eccl.,* 38 (1942), 46-58. Cf. C. Mesini, "De auctore et loco compositionis præfationis B. M. V.", *Antonianum,* 10 (1935), 59-72

most part from old Roman tradition.[33] Up to the eleventh century and even beyond, the Mass books frequently preserved some heritage, large or small, of this tradition. The Leofric Missal (11th century), which originated in the Rhineland, still has a special preface for every Mass-formulary. Similarly, several sacramentaries from France.[34] But in the end the victory was won by the canon which was promoted by Burchard, and which after that was repeated by all commentators on the liturgy. Even in the Middle Ages, however, the victory was not an absolute one. For saints who were singularly venerated—John the Baptist, Augustine, Jerome, Francis, Roch, Christopher—special prefaces again came into use, but because of the unhistorical contents they provoked the antagonism of various reforming circles at the time of the Council of Trent, and so most of them had again to be dropped.[35] Only in certain orders and in the *proprium* of this or that diocese were special prefaces retained or even brought into use anew.[36] But not till most recent times did the Roman Missal itself experience an enrichment of this sort, after the canon of eleven prefaces had held firm for almost eight hundred years. And this enrichment actually involved, on the whole, a development of the central concept of the prayer of thanks. In 1919 the prefaces for the Requiem Mass[37] and for St. Joseph were introduced; in 1925 there followed the preface for the feast of Christ the King, in 1928 the preface for the Mass of the Sacred Heart.

A remarkable thing in the medieval canon of prefaces is the absence of any special preface for Sundays. In the older Roman sacramentary tradition such was not the case. Prefaces for Sunday appear in the newer *Gelasianum* and in the Alcuin appendix.[38] Within the festal cycles, in Advent, after Epiphany, during Lent, and after Easter, they adhere to the

---

[33] Muratori, II, 273-356.

[34] The Sacramentary of S. Armand (9th cent.) presents 283 prefaces, that of Chartres (10th cent.) 220, that of Angers (10th cent.) 243, that of Moissac (11th cent.) 342; Leroquais, *Les sacramentaires* I, 57; 76; 86; 100.—An example from upper Italy in the 10th century by Ebner, 29.

[35] Jedin, "Das Konzil von Trient und die Reform des Römischen Messbuches" (*Liturg. Leben,* 1939) 43, 46, 55, 60 f.

[36] In the liturgies of religious orders these include proper prefaces for Benedict, Augustine, Francis, Francis de Sales. Since 1919 others were added: Norbert, Dominic, John of the Cross, Teresa, Elias, Our Lady of Mt. Carmel. Many dioceses in France have their own proper preface, thus, e.g., Lyons has such not only for certain Saints, but also (from neo-Gallican

tradition) for Advent, Maundy Thursday, Corpus Christi, Consecration of a Church. B. Opfermann, "Die Sonderpräfationen des römishen Ritus," *Liturg. Leben,* 2 (1935), 240-248. A. Zak O. Praem., "Ueber die Präfationem": *Theol. prakt. Quartalschrift,* 58 (1905), 307-325.

[37] It is a revision of an originally Mozarabic preface (*Missale mixtum*: PL, 85, 1019 A) that came into the Mass-books of the Middle Ages by way of the Alcuin appendix (Muratori, II, 354 f.; 355 f.) and remained in use, among others, in the diocese of Besançon. The happy christological addition in the new text (*in quo nobis*) did not appear in this older version. J. Brinktrine, "Die neue Präfation in den Totenmessen": *Theologie u. Glaube,* 11 (1919), 242-245.

[38] The later Gelasianum here contains the genuine Roman tradition: see Baumstark's

theme suggested by the festal cycle. Thus, for the last Sunday of Advent [39] we have:

> VD. Sanctificator et conditor generis humani, qui Filio tuo tecum æterna claritate regnante, cum de nullis extantibus cuncta protulisses hominem limosi pulveris initiis inchoatum ad speciem tui decoris animasti, eumque credula persuasione deceptum reparare voluisti spiritalis gratiæ æterna suffragia mittendo nobis Jesum Christum Dominum nostrum. Per quem.[40]

A preface for the second Sunday after Epiphany reads as follows:

> VD. Semperque virtutes et laudes tuas labiis exultationis effari, qui nobis ad relevandos istius vitæ labores super diversa donorum tuorum solatia etiam munerum salutarium gaudia contulisti mittendo nobis Jesum Christum Filium tuum Dominum nostrum. Per quem.[41]

In the neutral period after Pentecost several formulas appear that depart from the character of the prayer of thanks and either take in the features of a prayer of petition after the manner of a collect [42] or are at least content with a very general theme of praise of God's goodness. Thus, on the Sunday of the autumn Embertide we have:

> VD. Quia cum laude nostra non egeas, grata tibi tamen est tuorum devotio famulorum nec te augent nostra præconia, sed nobis proficiunt ad salutem, quoniam sicut fontem vitæ præterire causa moriendi est, sic eodem iugiter redundare effectus est sine fine vivendi. Per Christum.[43]

At other times a beauteous universality of Christian gratitude is achieved, as on the fifteenth Sunday after Pentecost:

> VD. Qui nos de donis donorum temporalium ad perceptionem provehis æternorum et hæc tribuis et illa promittis, ut et mansuris iam incipiamus inseri et prætereuntibus non teneri; tuum est enim quod vivimus, quia licet peccati vulnere natura nostra sit vitiata, tui tamen est operis, ut terreni generati ad cœlestia renascamur. Per Christum.[44]

Several formulas, however, present very prominently the cardinal theme of the eucharistia, which we must expect above all on Sundays just as we expected it on Easter; a sample of this is found in the third Sunday after Pentecost:

> VD. Per Christum. Cuius hoc mirificum opus ac salutare mysterium fuit, ut perditi dudum atque prostrati a diabolo et mortis aculeo ad hanc gloriam vocaremur, qua nunc genus electum, sacerdotium regale ac populus adquisitionis et gens sancta vocemur. Agentes igitur indefessas gratias sanctamque munificentiam tuam prædicantes maiestati tuæ hæc sacra deferimus quæ nobis ipse salutis nostræ auctor Christus instituit. Per quem.[45]

---

proofs in Mohlberg-Baumstark, Die älteste erreichbare Gestalt, 128*.

[39] This assignment and the one that follows for certain Sundays are according to the Frankish Gelasianum of Mohlberg. They do not occur in the same form in all the MSS.

[40] Mohlberg, n. 1454. Cf. the further sources, ibid., p. 336 (=Mohlberg-Manz, n. 1454).

[41] Mohlberg, n. 124; further sources, ibid., p. 296.

[42] For example in the Alcuin appendix (Muratori, II, 285): VD. Et immensam bonitatis tuæ pietatem humiliter exorare . . .

[43] Mohlberg, n. 1203. Further sources, ibid., p. 328. Also already in the Leonianum.

[44] Mohlberg, n. 1135. Further sources, ibid., p. 326.

[45] Mohlberg, n. 873. Further sources, ibid., p. 318. Also already in the older Gelasianum, I, 65 (for the Sunday after Ascension).

Or on the seventh Sunday:

> *VD. Per Christum. Verum æternumque pontificem et solum sine peccati macula sacerdotem, cuius sanguine omnium fidelium corda mundantur, placatonis tibi hostias non solum pro delictis populi, sed etiam pro nostris offensionibus immolamus, ut omne peccatum quod carnis fragilitate contraximus summo pro nobis antistite interpellante salvetur. Per quem.*[46]

Or again concisely and to the point:

> *VD. Per Christum Dominum nostrum. Qui vicit diabolum et mundum hominemque paradiso restituit et vitæ ianuas credentibus patefecit. Per quem.*[47]

It may well be that the tenacious retention of the special Sunday concepts precisely in Frankish territory is a result of the fact that, even in the ninth century, the Sunday was here called *Dominicæ Resurrectionis dies*,[48] and was consciously celebrated as such. But in the eleventh century the prescription supposedly written by Pelagius II finally prevailed everywhere, and thus evidently the *præfatio communis* was at first used on Sundays, since it had already acquired this role at Rome perhaps as early as the sixth century, and generally took the lead among all the prefaces.[49] Since the thirteenth century, however, the Trinity preface began to be used for Sundays.[50] But it was not prescribed by Rome till 1759.[51]

Among the prefaces in use today, two appear to escape the ordinary scheme for prefaces: the Trinity preface (which presents a profession of belief in the mystery of the Trinity rather than a prayer of thanks) and

---

[46] Mohlberg, n. 979. Further sources, *ibid.*, p. 321.

[47] Text according to the Alcuin appendix: Muratori, II, 337.—Mohlberg, n. 1236. Further sources, *ibid.*, p. 329.—Further examples of Sunday prefaces of the kind mentioned: Mohlberg, n. 1296 *(VD. Maiestatem tuam)*; 1305 *(VD. Per Christum. Per quem sanctum)*; Alcuin appendix: Muratori, II, 323 *(VD. Quoniam illa festa)*. Some prefaces of Eastertide also come into consideration.

[48] Jungmann. *Gewordene Liturgie*, 214; cf. 223. Cf. also *Vita Alcuini*, c. 11 (MGH, Scriptores, 15, 1, p. 191, 1, 21): *Præter enim dies resurrectionis ac festivitatis jejunium protelabat . . .*

[49] This seems to be evident from the fact that they are connected with the oldest tradition of the Canon of the Mass. That it developed specifically into a Sunday preface, is shown by the fact that, e.g., in the older Gelasianum, III, 6 (Wilson, 234) the canon which begins with the *præfatio communis* comprises a series of sixteen

Sundays which do not have a proper preface. That it was still a Sunday preface in this or that place during the later Middle Ages, is shown, e.g., in the Mass-*ordo* for the first Sunday after Pentecost in the *Rituale* of Soissons: *Præfatio nulla dicatur nisi quotidiana;* Martène, 1, 4, XXII (I, 612 C).

[50] Thus in the *Missale* of Sarum, ed. Legg, p. 171. Radulph de Rivo (d. 1403), *De canonum observ.*, prop. 23 (Mohlberg, II, 146) knows it as a Sunday preface from the Feast of the Trinity until Advent. Without further detail Bernold of Constance (d. 1100), *Micrologus*, c. 60 (PL, 151, 1020 C), also testifies to the use of the Trinity preface on Sundays (*quam in diebus dominicis frequentamus*).

[51] *Decreta auth. SRC.*, n. 2449. The reason for this is based on the fact that it was on a Sunday that the creation of the world began, on a Sunday that the Resurrection and the Descent of the Holy Ghost took place. But, of course, this view of the mystery of the Trinity in the economy of sal-

the preface of the Apostles. There is, to be sure, no reason for supposing that this latter is addressed to Christ,[52] since there is no precedent for such a supposition in the whole Roman sacramentary tradition. But starting with the very introductory phrases, the thanksgiving in this preface is transformed into a prayer of petition, though it is possible to discover in the continuation echoes of the thanksgiving that was heralded by the *Gratias agamus*. We have here a distortion of the original text. The original is found in the *Leonianum* where the preface presupposes the entire normal introduction, starting with a word of thanks and concluding with *Per Christum* (thus obviously assuming the usual mode of address to God the Father): *Vere dignum . . . gratias agere . . . æterne Deus suppliciter exorantes ut gregem tuum, pastor æterne, non deseras . . . pastores, per (Christum Dominum nostrum, per quem).*[53] It might be added that even in the *Leonianum* the preface (aside from the introductory phrases) not infrequently takes on the features of a petition.[54]

The basic schema of the Roman preface is to be seen in the *præfatio communis*. Without descending to prosaic banality, it embraces only the barest outline of the prayer of thanks. The reason for giving thanks is no longer expounded, but is included in the fact that the thanksgiving is offered *per Christum Dominum nostrum*. The reason is thus presented in the fact that the vast distance separating man from God has been bridged, that we have the access and the trusty password "through Christ our Lord."[55] In the other prefaces this schema is either repeated word for word, as in the prefaces for Lent and Passiontide where, after the word *Deus*, the corresponding expansion is inserted and then the preface continues with *per Christum Dominum nostrum, per quem,*[56] and similarly

---

vation is not expressed in the text of the preface.

[52] Because of the word *pastor æterne;* thus, e.g., in Gihr, 616, note 55. Conforming to the spirit of ancient tradition, this title is used in the Oration for the Commune summorum pontificum (prescribed in 1942) in reference to God. Leonianum, ed. Muratori, 332.

[53] Feltoe, 506; Muratori, I, 345. Note *exorantes* instead of *exoramus*. Likewise in the older Gelasianum, II, 36 (Wilson, 186). The Sacramentary of Eligius (10th cent.; PL, 78, 124 CD) also gives the complete introduction and continues: *(gratias agere . . .) et te suppliciter exorare.* It is the same in the English missal MSS. of the 13th and 14th centuries (Legg, *The Sarum Missal*, 214) and also in the printed editions of the Sarum Missal of the 15-16th century (F. H. Dickinson, *Missale ad usum ecclesiæ Sarum*, [Burntisland, 1883],

605).—On the other hand, the Gregorian tradition as well as the later Gelasianum already has today's text, although there are fluctuations in the demarcation of the introductory phrase, betraying the secondary character of this version. The critical evaluation here made is also found in Jungmann, *Die Stellung Christi* (1925), 97 f. It has also been made elsewhere, as appears from a report of V. Oderisi, *Eph. liturg.*, 58 (1944), 307-309.

[54] There is even the case where a collect (with relative predication:*Deus qui*) serves as the center portion of the preface, e.g., Muratori, I, 334, in the sixth Mass of the Apostles, in which only the *præsta* is omitted from the *præsta ut* of the collect (*ibid.*, 339, XVII). Similar cases are frequent in the Milan liturgy; see P. Lejay, "Ambrosien (Rit.)", DACL, I, 1413.

[55] Cf. Eph. 3: 12; Rom. 5: 2.

[56] The *Per Christum* thereby acquires a dif-

in the prefaces for the Blessed Virgin and St. Joseph where the expansion begins with the words *per quem*. Or else the Christological expansion is included after the word *Deus*, but in such a way that the *Sanctus* is introduced at once with the phrase *Et ideo*, as in the prefaces for Christmas, Epiphany, the Sacred Heart, and Christ the King. In the Easter preface the introduction itself is also altered somewhat. Or again the expansion occurs only after the phrase *Per Christum Dominum nostrum*, as in the preface for Ascension, for Masses for the Dead and (with a freer conclusion) for Pentecost. In every instance the name of the Saviour comes in the middle. The original arrangement was, no doubt, the introduction of our Lord as a mediator of our prayer of thanks.[57] The delineation of the Christ-mystery in other versions would be taken as merely a variant or substitute. And so, the absence of the name of Christ in the Trinity preface and in the present version of the preface of Apostles is really a more recent and secondary phenomenon.[58]

It is necessary to consider more minutely certain details in this ever-recurring basic schema. Every Roman preface begins, and has for a long time begun, with a declaration of the propriety, we might even say the obligation, of giving thanks: *Vere dignum et iustum est, æquum et salutare.* This phrasing is not to be found in the *eucharistia* of Hippolytus. But it is the reiteration of the yet more ancient response to the priest's *Gratias agamus: Dignum et iustum est.* In nearly all the liturgies this or similar presumption of the people's acclamation has prevailed.[59] Thus the priest, too, declares that what the congregation offers up to God is simply a service ·due.[60] Regarding the content of this service, only the cardinal thought is expressed: it is gratitude, but gratitude which embraces all the powers of our soul, gratitude measured by that love we owe to God—with our whole heart and our whole soul and all our strength—gratitude that

ferent meaning; it is no longer our thanks through Christ, but God's acting through Christ. Cf. Jungmann, *Die Stellung Christi*, 156 f.

[57] Thus also in the Eucharistia of Hippolytus, above I, 29. An Arian of the 4-5th century in arguing against the ὁμοούσιος of the Catholic Christology, bases his reasoning on the Catholic custom of directing the thanksgiving prayer *in oblationibus* through Christ to God; there it says *Dignum et justum . . . neque est alius per quem ad te aditum habere, precem facere, sacrificationem tibi offerre possimus nisi per quem tu nobis misisti.* G. Mercati, *Antiche reliquie liturgiche* (Studi e Testi, 7; Rom., 1902), 52.

[58] A more exact classification of the entire Latin tradition with regard to the preface

is supplied by P. Cagin, *Te Deum ou illatio* (Solesmes, 1906), 356-371.

[59] In the Gallic liturgy the beginning reads *Dignum et justum* est, in the oriental either as at Rome Ἀληθῶς γὰρ ἄξιόν ἐστιν καὶ δίκαιον (Egyptian anaphora of St. Mark: Brightman, 125; cf. 164; Byzantine liturgy of St. Chrysostom: *ibid.*, 321 f.) or the expression is enriched with a certain emotional tone: Ὡς ἀληθῶς ἄξιόν ἐστι καὶ δίκαιον (West Syrian anaphora of St. James: Brightman, 50; cf. *Const. Ap.* VIII, 12: *ibid.*, 14).—The Byzantine liturgy of St. Basil has a solemn address to God preceding this introductory phrase: Ὁ ὢν δέσποτα κύριε θεὲ πάτερ παντοκράτορ προσκύνητε, ἄξιον ὡς ἀληθῶς. . . Brightman, 321 f.

[60] Cfr., above, p. 111.

must in essence be paid always and everywhere.[61] Other liturgies intensify the word "thanksgiving" by adding a long series of expressions all designating the praise and worship of God.[62]

The address to God which at present is divided as follows: *Domine sancte, Pater omnipotens, æterne Deus* [63] must originally have been arranged in this way: *Domine, sancte Pater, omnipotens æterne Deus.*[64] Both the *Domine* and the *omnipotens æterne Deus* are usual forms of address in the Roman liturgy. *Sancte Pater* evidently corresponds to the *clementissime Pater* which follows later. The solemnity of this address, grouping as it does various popular titles for God,[65] underlines once again the importance of the moment.

Our thanks and worship we do not bring to God directly as just any group of human petitioners; we offer it rather as a congregation of the redeemed, through Him who is our Redeemer and our Head, through Christ, our Lord. In the festal prefaces this step disappears in favor of a jubilant celebration of the festal theme; since this theme always has reference to a mystery of Christ, it is unnecessary to add that we praise God through Him.

Finally, our praise is joined to the praise of the heavenly choirs. In ancient Christendom a favorite way of representing the salvation which is ours in Christ was to show that it associates us with the blessed spirits of heaven and that by its means we are able to take the place of the fallen angels. "The scene of your approach now is mount Sion, is the heavenly

---

[61] Cf., I Thess. 5: 18; Col. 1: 12; 2: 7; 3: 15-17.

[62] This is true especially in regard to the liturgy of St. Basil. It is noteworthy in this connection that in all its versions, outside the Egyptian, the sacrificial character of the Eucharist is revealed along with the εὐχαριστεῖν and the accompanying phrases. The Byzantine liturgy continues (*loc. cit.*) ... σὲ αἰνεῖν, σὲ ὑμνεῖν, σὲ εὐλογεῖν, σὲ προςκυνεῖν, σοὶ εὐχαριςτεῖν, σὲ δοξάζειν τὸν μόνον ὄντως ὄντα θεὸν, καὶ σοὶ προςἐρφειν ... τὴν λογικὴν ταύτην λατρείαν ἡμῶν. The Armenian version is rendered: καὶ σοὶ προςφέρειν θυσίαν αἰνέσεως; Engberding, *Das eucharistische Hochgebet der Basileiosliturgie* (Münster, 1931), 2 f.

[63] Thus already about 800 the *Expositio* "*Quotiens contra se*" (PL, 96, 1489 B). Remigius of Auxerre, *Expositio* (PL, 101, 1253) also unites: *Domine sancte.*

[64] Brinktrine, *Die hl. Messe*, 168. He refers to the *Qui pridie* of Ambrose (above I, 52): *ad te, sancte Pater omnipotens æterne Deus,* and to our first offering

prayer at the Offertory: *Suscipe, sancte Pater* that could have its beginning in the 10-11th century. The General Chapter of the Cistercians in 1188 decided that a cæsura could be made only after the word *Pater;* Schneider (*Cist.-Chr.*, 1927), 8 f.— Cf. Baumstark, *Liturgie comparée, 72,* who sees in the arrangement of the single, double, and triple expression a mannerism of ancient rhetoric. See for further references A. Dold, *Bened. Monatsschrift*, 22 (1946), 143; 146. A summary of all the arguments for the suggested re-arrangement in Jean Juglar, "'Sancte Pater': Note sur la ponctuation de la formule d'invocation de la Preface," *Eph. liturg.,* 65 (1951), 101-104. — E. C.-V. "De Genuina Interpretatione Formulæ 'Domine Sancte Pater Omnipotens æterne Deus'," *Eph. liturg.,* 66 (1952), 77-80, upholds the customary pointing.

[65] This occurs with true oriental prolixity at the same place in some liturgies of the East; thus, e.g., note 59 above, and also I, 35 f.

Jerusalem, the city of the living God; here are gathered thousands upon thousands of angels, here is the assembly of those first-born sons whose names are written in heaven." [66] Thus even in this life, as children of the Jerusalem which is above,[67] and especially when we are assembled for the celebration of the New Covenant, we may join our voices to the songs of praise raised by the hosts of heaven.[68] At first the preface lets us listen, so to speak, to these songs of praise. One thing that surprises us here is that these songs, too—as the *præfatio communis* puts it— are offered up through Christ: *per quem maiestatem tuam laudant angeli* . . . But why should we be surprised? He is set "high above all princedoms and powers and virtues and dominations, and every name that is known, not in this world only, but in the world to come." [69] "All the angels and powers and princedoms [are] made subject under His feet." [70] In Christ "all that is in heaven, all that is on earth [are] summed up." [71] The concept is therefore thoroughly biblical, although the Scholastics were wont to add that the angels cannot bear the same relationship to Christ as do men who were redeemed by Him.[72] Thus even in the concise *præfatio communis* the second part is dominated by the Christ-theme: Christ appears before our gaze as the King of the triumphant Church.

The Bible also furnished the materials for the detailed description of the choirs of angels and their activity.[73] The *præfatio communis* presents the lengthiest enumeration of their names: *angeli, dominationes, potestates, cæli, cælorum virtutes, seraphim*. A shorter series is associated with the concluding formula *Et ideo*, but here two other groups are recorded, *archangeli* and *throni*. The Trinity preface, in spite of its terse arrangement, adds the *cherubim* to the list.[74] The Pentecost preface summarizes

[66] Hebr. 12: 22 f.; cf. also the conception of the parable of the Good Shepherd, (Luke 15: 4-7), which is almost universal among the Fathers. According to this, the Son of God left the ninety-nine sheep, the angels of heaven, to seek the one lost sheep, lost man, and to bring him back happily to the fold; see evidences from Irenæus, Origen, Methodius, Hilary, Cyril of Alexandria, Peter Chrysologus in Th. K. Kempf, *Christus der Hirt, Ursprung und Deutung einer altchristlichen Symbolgestalt* (Rome, 1942), 10-166. Gregory the Great, among others, takes the same view, *In Ev. hom.*, 34, 3 (PL, 76, 1247).

[67] Gal., 4: 26.

[68] Even the Old Testament frequently manifests this effort of joining the world of angels in the praise of God, especially the Psalms (102: 20 ff.; 148: 2 ff.; etc.).

[69] Eph. 1: 21 f.

[70] I Pet. 3: 22.

[71] Eph. 1: 10.

[72] That is true of Scholasticism, except Scotism. The latter proceeds from the assumption that it was in the designs of God to send the God-man regardless of the sin of Adam. Christ is considered from the very beginning as the crown of creation and the source of all graces, even of those that were given to the angels; cf. anent the matter J. Pohle-M. Gierens, *Lehrbuch der Dogmatik*, II (9th ed.; Paderborn, 1937), 136-139; 176-182.

[73] Eph. 1: 21; Col. 1: 16; I Pet. 3: 22; I Thess. 4: 15; Ez. 10, 1 ff.; Is. 6: 2, etc.

[74] Nine different names and classes of heavenly spirits appear. They do not coincide with the nine choirs as enumerated by Dionysius, *De cæl. hierarchia*, 6, 2 (PL, 3, 200 f.) because no *principatus* appears among them, although in their place are welcomed the *cæli*. The *cæli* (cf. Dan. 3:

the whole series in the phrase *supernæ virtutes atque angelicæ potestates*, much as the *Et ideo* formula mentions last of all *omnis militia cælestis exercitus*. All bow in reverence before God's majesty, they sing out their song *una voce*, they cry out *sine fine*—two phrases adapted from the earthly custom of the acclamation and applied to the description of the heavenly liturgy.[75]

It is in this heavenly liturgy, which is described with even greater emphasis in the texts of the oriental anaphora, that we are bidden to take part. Placing on our lips a humble plea, the *præfatio communis* has us enter the circle of the heavenly spirits: *cum quibus et nostris voces ut admitti iubeas deprecamur*, and intone with them the triple *Sanctus*.

4. *Sanctus* and *Benedictus*

The *Sanctus* is the continuation of the preface. So true is this that the oldest melody of the *Sanctus* [1] is simply a continuation of the ferial melody of the preface. But because the *Sanctus* is here more than a mere citation from the account of the Prophet Isaias, because it is intended to do more than recall to our mind that the seraphim sang this hymn,[2] but is rather a reminder that the earthly church should take part in the heavenly singing, the *Sanctus* takes on its own independent importance. All the people join in singing the *Sanctus*—that was taken for granted in ancient Christian times,[3] and to some extent still is in the Orient.[4]

59) are mostly treated by the commentators of the Middle Ages as equivalent to the *throni*, which are not mentioned in the respective series. The consideration of the *cæli* as an angelic choir became the occasion for using Ps. 18 (*Cæli enarrant*) in the Office of the Angels. Originally the *cæli* were thought of as spirits that stood in some relation to the stars of heaven.

[75] Th. Klauser, "Akklamation," RAC, I, 227; Peterson, Εἰς θεός, 192, n. 1. In the preface for Pentecost the *sine fine* is referred to the angels, in all other instances to us.

[1] In Mass XVIII of the Vatican edition of the *Graduale Romanum*, the Mass appointed for week-days in Advent and Lent, coincides with the melody for Requiem Mass.

[2] Thus Luther interpreted the *Sanctus*. Martin Luther's *Deutsche Messe* (1526) edited by H. Lietzmann (Kleine Texte, 37: Berlin, 1929), p. 14.

[3] *Const. Ap.* VIII, 12, 27 (*supra*, I, 36).—Gregory of Nyssa, *De Bapt.* (PG, 46, 421 C): join the holy people and learn hidden words, proclaim with us the same as the six-winged angels proclaim.—Cyril of Jerusalem, *Catech. myst.* V, 6 (Quasten, *Mon.*, 101).—Chrysostom often comes back to the subject, e.g., *In illud, "Vidi Dominum"* hom. I, 1 (PG, 56, 97 f.): "Above the Seraphim shout the thrice-holy hymn and below all mankind sends it aloft." Cf. *In Eph.* hom. 14, 4 (PG, 62, 104); *In II Cor.* hom. 18, 3 (PG, 61, 527). Chrysostom often extols the value of this community singing; see *In I Cor.* hom. 27, 5 (PG, 61, 232); *In Is.* hom. 6, 3 (PG, 56, 138). Cf. J. Gülden, "Liturgische Erneuerung und die Beteiligung des Volkes am Gottesdienst in der Väterpredigt, *StZ* 137 (1940, I), 178-186, especially 182.

[4] In the oriental liturgies, though the transitional words of the preface seldom mention it, the *Sanctus* as a rule is expressly given over to the people by a special rubric, as was already done in the Apostolic Constitutions VIII, 12, 27 (Quasten, *Mon.*, 220); in the West Syrian and Egyptian liturgies (Brightman, 50;

Even in the West as late as 530 the *Liber pontificalis* indicates that Pope Sixtus I ordered: *ut intra actionem, sacerdos incipiens, populo* [1. *-us*] *hymnum decantare* [*t*] *: Sanctus.*[5] Perhaps it was already necessary at that time to recall to memory the tradition which was to be found implicit in the text itself, for then as now it read: *cum quibus et nostras voces ut admitti iubeas deprecamur.* As a matter of fact the singing at Rome, as described in the Roman *ordines* for feast-day service, was transferred to a group of clerics.[6]

In the land of the Franks, however, provision continued to be made for the people to sing the *Sanctus* as of yore.[7] Thus the *ordo* of John the Archchanter still mentions the people.[8] In fact, the reform decrees of the Carolingian period did not have to insist that the people sing the Sanctus, but instead had to demand that the celebrating priest go along with the singing to its finish and only then continue with *Te igitur.*[9]

86; 132; 176; 231); also in the older Byzantine liturgy (*ibid.*, 385; 403; 436). Cf. Hanssens III, p. 392 f.; 400.

[5] Duchesne, *Liber pont.*, I, 128.—Cf. O. Casel, *JL*, 1, (1921), 151.

[6] *Ordo Rom.* I, n. 16 (PL, 78, 944 f.): *subdiaconi regionarii.* Cf. *Ordo Rom.* II, n. 10 (PL, 78, 973): *subdiaconi; Ordo Rom.* V, n. 9 (PL, 78, 988): *Subdiaconi itaque dum canitur Sanctus, post altare pergant stare,* and others also sing along. *Ordo Rom.* XI, n. 20 (PL, 78, 1033) has the *basilicarii*, that is, the clergy attached to the respective basilica, sing the *Sanctus*, as they do the *Credo;* cf. above, I, 473, n. 69. Therefore, even here the *Sanctus* is never left to the Schola cantorum. Quite probably the congregational singing of the *Sanctus* is considered as the ideal also in the *Ordo eccl. Later.* (ed. Fischer, 44). Still in the Pontifical Mass it is sung by the choir, *in choro*, (*ibid.*, 83, L. 38). Perhaps the exclusion of the people, as noted in the Roman *Ordines*, is also to be understood as holding only for the Pontifical Mass.

[7] *Capitulare eccl. ord.* (Silva-Tarouca, 199): *proclamantibus omnibus clericis vel* (mostly = *et*) *populo cum tremore et reverentia: Sanctus.* Cf. *Breviarium eccl. ord.* (*ibid.*, 198 f): *diaconi et clerus cum populo.* This is a Carolingian text, and cannot therefore be relied upon to show what is the Roman custom; but it does give evidence of the adaptation to Frankish conditions.

[8] Cæsarius of Arles, *Serm.*, 73, 3 (Morin, 294; PL, 39, 2277) says of those who leave before time: *qualiter cum tremore simul ct gaudio clamabunt: Sanctus, Sanctus, Sanctus. Benedictus qui venit in nomine Domini?* Cf. Gregory of Tours, *De mir. s. Martini*, II, 14 (PL, 71, 946 f.). —It is an error to quote can. 3 of the Synod of Vaison (529) as a proof that the *Sanctus* was not sung at the time, but rather reintroduced just then. Here there is question not of the *Sanctus*, but of the Trisagion (*Aius;* cf. above, I, 47). See the proof for this in Nickl, *Der Anteil des Volkes an der Messliturgie im Frankenreich*, 25-29.

[9] *Admonitio generalis* (789) n. 70 (MGH, Cap., I, 59): *Et ipse sacerdos cum sanctis angelis et populo Dei communi voce Sanctus, Sanctus, Sanctus decantet.* Herard of Tours (858) *Capitula*, n. 16 (PL, 121, 765): *ut secreta presbyteri non inchoent, antequam Sanctus finiatur, sed cum populo Sanctus cantent.* Amalar, *De eccl. off.* III, 21 (PL, 105, 1134 C) refers to the decree of Sixtus I mentioned above. With the rise of the Apologies these prescriptions were again transgressed; cf. further the Sacramentary of Amiens in the 9th cent. ed., Leroquais (*Eph. liturg.*, 1927), 442: *Quando tractim canitur Sanctus, idem sacerdos cursim decantet*, followed by an Apology. But towards the end of the 11th century the Missal of St. Vincent, for example, again has neums marked over the *Sanctus*, obviously for the priest to sing; Fiala, 192.

Being music for the people, the *Sanctus* retained its traditional simple melody, which hardly goes beyond a mere recitative. This explains why one Carolingian music writer about 830, in enumerating the songs of the Mass, makes no mention whatever of the *Sanctus*.[10] There is evidence that the *Sanctus* continued to be sung by priest and people together even in the twelfth century; it is so described in Hildebert[11] and Honorius.[12] An intermediate step before its complete disappearance as a people's chant was to be found in northern countries where it was assigned to the clergy assisting in choir.[13] There is a relic of this in the present-day prescription that at high Mass the deacon and the subdeacon[14] recite the *Sanctus* together with the celebrant. The transfer of the *Sanctus* from the people to the special singing choir goes hand in hand with the composition of the more recent *Sanctus* melodies and is finally complete when polyphonic music came into its own in the Gothic period. It is significant that the text of the *Sanctus*—basically little more than a simple outcry of praise, an acclamation[15]—was altered for a time to suit the newer settings, and like the other chants it was expanded by the addition of tropes.[16]

[10] Aurelian of Reaumé, *Musica disciplina*, c. 20 (Gerbert, *Scriptores de mus. sacra*, I, 60 f.). He discusses the Introit, *Kyrie, Gloria*, Gradual, Alleluja, Offertory, and Communion. Cf. Wagner, *Einführung*, I, 58 f. Evidently the melody under discussion is the melody mentioned above, n. 7, the only one that is in use among the Carthusians, even as late as the 18th century; Wagner, 114. It seems that more elaborate melodies for the *Sanctus* in general were not created till the 11-12th century, hence a century later than was the case with the *Kyrie* (Cf. below, n. 16).—This also fits in with the fact that the *Sanctus* was set to polyphonic melodies only at a later date. The oldest collection of two-voiced compositions, the Winchester Troper (HBS, 8) has twelve settings for the *Kyrie*, 8 for the *Gloria*, but none for the *Sanctus* (and likewise none for the *Agnus Dei*). Cf. Ursprung, 57; 119.

[11] Hildebert of Le Mans, *Versus de mysterio missæ* (PL, 171, 1182); *Hinc bene cum populo ter Sanctus . . . canit.*

[12] Honorius Augustod., *Gemma an.*, I, 42 (PL, 172, 556 D).

[13] A Sacramentary of the 9th century of Le Mans and likewise one of the 11th century from Echternach (Leroquais, I, 30 f.,122) *Quando clerus . . . Sanctus can-*

tat; cf. Leroquais, I, 59.—Robert Paululus (d. about 1184), *De cæremoniis*, II, 24 (PL, 177, 425 D) : *Hunc hymnum sacerdos cum choro dicere debet.*—Durandus, IV, 34, 1: *totus chorus . . . simul canit dictum evangelicum hymnum.* According to A. Gastoué, *L'église et la musique*, (Paris, 1936), 80, the *Sanctus* in many cathedrals was for a long time reserved to seven subdeacons, who formed a semicircle before the altar; cf. above I, 197, note 9. Even at the beginning of the 14th century rubricists were vividly aware that the *Sanctus* was to be said by the clergy present in choir, as is clear from the Ordo of Stefaneschi, n. 61 (PL, 78, 1176), where it states that when a cardinal is present at the chaplain's Mass, *dicta præfatione dicat sine nota Sanctus, etc., cum astantibus sibi.*

[14] Regarding the practice in Roman basilicas, where only the deacon does so, see Gavanti-Merati, II, 7, 11 (I, 282 f.).

[15] E. Peterson, *Das Buch von den Engeln* (Leipzig, 1935), 58; *idem.*, Εἷς θεός, 234; 325.

[16] Blume-Bannister, *Tropen des Missale*, I (Analecta hymnica, 47) p. 301-369 (n. 247-338). As the editors point out, a number of these originated in the 10th century.

Honorius also stresses the point that the organ—a very primitive instrument still—was joined to the chanting of people and clergy: *Unde solemus adhuc in officio sacrificii organis concrepare, clerus cantare, populus conclamare.*[17] The sound of the organ *in hoc concentu angelorum et hominum* is likewise emphasized by later commentators.[18] In the compendious liturgical manual of Durandus the *Sanctus* is the only place where any mention is made of the organ.[19] It therefore has here a more conspicuous function than the usual one of accompanying the singing. It has the same purpose as the Psalmist's sounding of many instruments—an expression of joy.[20] It is not unlikely that originally the ringing of the altar bell—a triple ring, to correspond to the triple *Sanctus*[21]—was also intended for the same purpose.[22]

[17] *Loc. cit.*

[18] Sicard of Cremona, *Mitrale*, III, 6 (PL, 213, 123 D).

[19] Durandus, *Rationale*, IV, 34, 10.

[20] Cf. Durandus, who, *loc. cit.*, remarks regarding the musical accompaniment of the *Sanctus*: David and Solomon introduced *hymnos in sacrificio Domini organis et aliis instrumentis musicis concrepari et laudes a populo conclamari.*

[21] According to our present *Missale Romanum*, even in the first edition of 1570, there are only two signals with the bell, one at *Sanctus* and one at the consecration. *Ritus serv.*, VII, 8; VIII, 6. The decree of the Congregation of Rites, Oct. 25, 1922, speaks of a signal with the bell shortly before the consecration, without actually demanding it; *Decreta auth. SRC*, n. 4377. Moreover, even these signals are not universally in use in the Roman basilicas. There is no mention of them in the *Cæremoniale Episc.*, I, 8, 67, 69. Cf. *Les Questions liturgiques*, 4 (1913-14), 164 f.

[22] The reports about the bell signal that begin to appear in the 13th century pertain almost exclusively to the elevation of the Sacred Species at the consecration, that was, of course, introduced at the time; cf. Braun, *Das christliche Altargerät*, 573-577. Nevertheless, even before the *Missale* of Pius V, testimony for a signal with the bell at the *Sanctus* is not entirely lacking. According to an endowment foundation made at Chartres, 1399, one of the bells suspended above the choir was to be rung *dum incipietur cantari Sanctus,* and the reason given is that the attention of the people might be called to the *levatio sacramenti;* Du Cange-Favre, VII, 259. The inventories of the English churches made under Edward VI (d. 1553) frequently record the Sanctus bells (santtes or saunce bell). F. C. Eeles, The Edwardian Inventories for Buckinghamshire (Alcuin Club Coll., 9) 3; 5. P. Browe, "Die Elevation" (*JL*, 1929), 39, who cites these passages, assumes (as the foundation mentioned above clearly indicates), that the signal of the bell at the *Sanctus* was only a preliminary warning of the approach of the consecration. That, however, need not have been its full purpose. While the little hand-bell may have been introduced to signal the consecration and was then extended also to the *Sanctus,* its primary purpose was not to give a signal, since the singing of the hymn itself was already sufficient for the purpose, but rather for much the same object we have in mind today, when at a solemn *Te Deum,* or, as was done for ages, at the *Gloria,* when it is resumed on Holy Saturday, every available instrument is sounded. The latter custom is attested in the *Ordo ecclesiæ Lateranensis* (middle of the 12th century; Fischer, 73) : . . . *Gloria in excelsis, et statim omnia signa pro gaudio tantæ sollemnitatis in classicum pulsentur.* According to Gavanti-Merati, II, 7, 11, (I, 282), one should ring the *campanas majores* at High Mass, and at private Mass the *campanula parva* (which could be dispensed with at High Mass, unless it is to be used as a signal for the ringing of the large bell). The custom of ringing the large bell at High Mass during the preface un-

The origins of the *Sanctus* in Christian liturgy are not fully clear. There is no *Sanctus* in the eucharistic prayer of Hippolytus of Rome.[23] On the other hand, even as early as the turn of the first century, it appears to have been part of the prayers of the Christian community right in Rome itself. For it is very surprising that Clement of Rome should not only cite the song itself from the vision of Isaias (Isaias 6:3) but also introduce it with the passage from Daniel 7:10, just as is done later in most of the liturgies of the Orient:

> *Let us consider the vast multitude of His angels, and see how they stand in readiness to minister to His will. For the Scripture says: "Ten thousand thousand stood ready before Him, and a thousand thousand ministered to Him, and cried out: Holy, Holy, Holy is the Lord of Hosts; the whole creation is replete with His splendor." And so we, too, being dutifully assembled with one accord, should as with one voice, cry out to Him earnestly, so that we may participate in His great and glorious promises.*[24]

The triple *Sanctus* is to be found likewise in all the other liturgies known to us, starting with the *Euchologion* of Serapion and the Clementine liturgy.[25] It is then but a step to assume that the *Sanctus* had been sung already in the primitive Church. Perhaps the synagogue served as a model and so concurred in some way in establishing its use.[26]

---

til the *Sanctus* is reported from the monastery of Hohenfurt in Czechoslovakia (about 1937); the ringing of the large bell at the *Sanctus* itself is still customary in the Weterwald (1947; Prof. B. Fischer).

[23] *Supra*, I, 29 f.—Note, however, that St. John quotes a triple "holy" from the mouths of the four-winged figures (cherubim) in Apoc. 4: 8; cf. Gassner, *The Canon*, 138 ff.

[24] Clement of Rome, *Ad Corinth.*, c. 34; see J. A. Kleist, *The Epistles of St. Clement of Rome and St. Ignatius of Antioch* (Ancient Christian Writers, 1; Westminster, 1946), 30. That this, however, is not clearly a reference to the Eucharistic prayer is shown by W. C. van Unnik, "I Clement 34 and the 'Sanctus'," *Vigiliæ christianæ*, 5 (1951), 204-248.—A similarly indefinite reference also in Tertullian, *De or.*, 3 (CSEL, 20, 182); cf. Dekkers, *Tertullianus*, 43 f. Somewhat plainer in Origen, *De princ.*, I, 3, 4; IV, 3, 14 (GGS, Orig., V, 52 f., 346); cf. G. Dix, "Primitive Consecration Prayer," *Theology*, 37 (1938), 261-283.

[25] Cf. *supra*, I, 34; 36. An exception is

perhaps the second of the Eucharistic prayers cited by an Arian author in the fragments published by G. Mercati, *Antiche reliquie liturgiche* (Studi et Testi, 7; Rome, 1902), 52 f. Cf. P. Alfonso, *L'eucologia romana antica* (Subiaco, 1931), 101-104.

[26] Regarding the supposition that the *Sanctus* is a heritage from the synagogue, see A. Baumstark, "Trishagion und Qeduscha," *JL*, 3 (1923), 18-32; Lietzmann, *Messe und Herrenmahl*, 128 ff., 258 f.; W. O. E. Oesterley, *The Jewish Background of the Christian Liturgy* (Oxford, 1925), 144-147. The *Sanctus*, says the *Jewish Encyclopedia*, VII, 463, "must have been borrowed by the Church from the Synagogue at an early date." This statement is at best highly doubtful. W. H. Frere, *The Anaphora or Great Eucharistic Prayer* (SPCK, 1938), is inclined to put the *Sanctus* after the time of Hippolytus. —The triple "holy" or Kedushshah used in various parts of the present synagogue service was surely introduced into that service by the second century A.D.; see C. W. Dugmore, *The Influence of the Synagogue upon the Divine Office* (Lon-

Be that as it may, this hymn, derived from the prophet's vision, so sparing in words, yet so powerful and weighty, fits best of all in the structure of the eucharistic prayer, especially in the setting mentioned. All of God's benefits and the manifestations of His favor, for which we must give thanks, are after all only revelations of His inmost being, which is all light and brilliance, inviolable and without stain, before which creation can only bow in deepest reverence—his holiness. Wherefore the first phrase taught us by our Lord in his own prayer is: *Sanctificetur nomen tuum.*[27] That the cry resounds three times must have but increased the joy the Christians had in this song, for even when a trinitarian meaning

---

don, 1945), 102-103, 108. This is a benediction and song of praise sung not only by the Seraphim among themselves, as in Is. 6:2, but by all the angels (all His servants) just as is presupposed as a rule in the Christian liturgies, although individual choirs are not marked out. See the Hebrew text in W. Stærk, *Altjüdische liturgische Gebete* (2nd ed.; Kleine Texte, 58; Berlin, 1930), 5.—Worthy of note is the fact that the triple "holy," treated as a song of praise sung by the entire host of angels, is found in Bk. VII of the *Apostolic Constitutions* within that very section (c. 33-38) which is evidently only a superficially christianized collection of Jewish prayers (VII, 35, 3; Funk, I, 430). And here is something to which Baumstark, *op. cit.*, 22 ff., attaches a great deal of importance: Ez. 3: 12: Εὐλογημένη ἡ δόξα κυρίου ἐκ τοῦ τόπου αὐτοῦ, is added as the response of the other choirs of angels; this is a benediction which is also found in later Jewish services as an accompaniment to the triple "holy," and which corresponds to the *Benedictus* which follows immediately after the triple "holy" in the Christian liturgies except that of Egypt. In the Clementine liturgy this *Benedictus* has the form: Εὐλογητὸς εἰς τοὺς αἰῶνας. 'Αμήν.·(*Const. Ap.* VIII, 12, 27; Funk, I, 506; Quasten, *Mon.*, 220). In the other liturgies it reads more or less like that of the Roman Mass; in other words, it is the shout of the crowd recorded in Matt. 21 : 9, with doubled *Hosanna.* This combination *Hosanna - Benedictus* must have been joined to the triple "holy" at a very early date, in Palestine itself, in conscious opposition to the narrowly national

Jewish formula (Baumstark, 23 ff.). — Against this assumption, which Baumstark in particular upholds, we have the fact that outside the short and rather irrelevant phrase in *Const. Ap.* VIII, 12, 27, there is no early evidence of this *Hosanna-Benedictus.* Even in the East it does not appear till the 8th century; on the contrary, the oldest Palestinian and Antiochene sources (Cyril of Jerusalem, Chrysostom, Theodore of Mopsuestia) do not mention it in this connection at all. (It does appear in *Peregrinatio Aetheriæ*, c. 31, but in an entirely different connection, as a responsorial processional chant sung by the people, and without *Hosanna*). Add to this the sharp dissimilarity of the *Tersanctus* itself, and especially of the sentences leading into it, where the Jewish version indicates the troops of angels only in a general way, while the Christian texts always mention various choirs. These are differences that cannot be accounted for as merely polemic antagonism. Hanssens, *Institutiones*, III (1932), 402 f., 404; E. Peterson, *Das Buch von den Engeln* (Leipzig, 1935), 115-117. — Baumstark, *Liturgie comparée* (1939), 55 f., 92 f., continues to hold to his thesis, without, however, adverting to the objections raised against it. Perhaps, as Hanssens, III, 404, remarks, the example of the Jews somehow did act as a stimulus for the Christians when they interpolated the *Sanctus* from Is. 6: 2 f., into their Eucharistic prayer.

[27] The parallel to the threefold "holy" here discussed was already noticed by Tertullian, *De or.*, 3 (CSEL, 20, 182). For this reason, so he argues, we say the *Sanctificetur* as *angelorum candidati.*

was not expressly attached to the triple "holy," still there was inherent in it an echo of this most profound of Christian mysteries.[28]

It is surprising, indeed, that the text of the *Tersanctus*, despite its brevity, shows some variations from the basic biblical text and also from that used in the synagogue. The basic text as found in the Vulgate reads as follows: *Sanctus, sanctus, sanctus Dominus Deus exercituum, plena est omnis terra gloria eius.* Even here the word *Deus* is an addition, already to be found in the Old Latin version.[29] The liturgical text leaves the word *sabaoth* untranslated. God is the Lord of "armies," of "hosts." This refers not only to the hosts of angels but to the "whole multitude" of beings which God had made in the six days of creation.[30] With this the appended clause agrees, for it makes the angels assert that the glory of God fills the whole earth. The liturgical text changes the cry into a form of address, *gloria tua*,[31] thus reinforcing its character as a prayer.

More important is the addition in the song of the word "heaven": *cœli et terra;* this is true of all the Christian liturgies,[32] and only of them.[33] This peculiarity is in line with the introduction to the *Sanctus* where all the Christian liturgies have likewise acquired a rather imposing augment.[34] No longer is it the Temple of Jerusalem that resounds with the triple *Sanctus*,

---

[28] The addition of a trinitarian meaning is already found in John 12: 41, when it is said of Isaias in reference to Christ that he had seen His glory. It plays a part in the struggle against Arianism; see, e.g., the confession of the Catholic Bishops in opposition to the Arians in Victor of Vita, *Hist. pers. Afric.*, II, 80, 100 (CSEL, 7, 59. 70 f.). In later times the West Syrian anaphoras regularly have the priest continue the prayer after the *Sanctus* with a trinitarian paraphrase of the *Sanctus* itself. In its simplest form it is already attested by Theodore of Mopsuestia, *Sermones catech.*, VI (ed. Rücker, *Ritus bapt. et missæ*, 30): *Sanctus Pater, sanctus quoque Filius, sanctus quoque Spiritus Sanctus.*—In the West, as the *Sanctus* melodies became richer, texts of trinitarian content were selected, for the most part, although not exclusively, for the tropes that were fitted to the notes; see Blume-Bannister, *Tropen*, n. 250 f., 253, 256 f., etc. The trinitarian meaning of the three-fold mention of *Sanctus* at the time is found regularly in the medieval interpreters of the liturgy and they add that the oneness of the divine essence is indicated in the *Dominus* or *Deus;* thus already Remigius of Auxerre, *Expositio* (PL, 101, 1255);

Sicard of Cremona, *Mitrale*, III, 6 (PL, 213, 123 B). Scholastic circles even stress the proper method of singing the chant, namely, according to Parisian custom, that the same half of the choir that sings the third *Sanctus*, should also add *Dominus Deus*, so that only one *trina prolatio* may result. A. Landgraf, "Scholastische Texte zur Liturgie des 12. Jh." (*Eph. liturgie.*, 1931), 213.

[29] P. Sabatier, *Bibliorum sacrorum latinæ versiones antiquæ*, II, (Rheims, 1743), 528; Baumstark, *Trishagion und Qeduscha*, 28. —Also in the Syrian liturgy; cf. Dix, *The Shape of the Liturgy*, 538; Dix is therefore inclined to trace the *Sanctus* to Syria.

[30] B. N. Wambacu, *L'épithète divine Jahvé Seba'ôt* (Paris, 1947), especially p. 199 ff., 277 ff.

[31] Thus, with few exceptions, in all Christian liturgies, and only in them, if we may include the christianized text of *Const. Ap.*, VIII, 35, 3; Baumstark, *Trishagion und Qeduscha*, 27 f.

[32] Baumstark, 28 f.; *Const. Ap.*, VII, 35, 3, herein also showed signs already of christianization.

[33] Peterson, *Das Buch von den Engeln*, 115 f.

[34] Peterson, 39-81; 113-133.

nor is it only the seraphim who cry out one to another; heaven has become the scene,[35] and all the choirs of heavenly spirits, the *militia cœlestis exercitus*, are united in the singing. *Socia exultatione* they sing their song of praise, and their cry is *sine fine*.

Even more impressive is the picture presented in this same spot by the oriental liturgies, like the Egyptian anaphora of St. Mark where the curtain is drawn aside to reveal a thousand times a thousand and ten thousand times ten thousand angels [36] and choirs of archangels standing in God's presence, and the six-winged cherubim calling to each other in this hymn of victory "with untiring mouth and never-ceasing praises of God" and "singing, calling, praising, sounding and speaking" the song "before Thy great glory." [37]

These changes cannot have been fortuitous,[38] even though they could hardly have resulted from any conscious plan. The enlargement of the picture corresponds to the breakdown of the national narrowness of Judaism and of its cult which was conjoined to the Temple. "The glory of the Lord" which had once dwelt in the Temple, had, in a manner new and unparalleled, pitched its tent on earth in the Incarnation of the Son of God (John 1:14). Now, however, no longer to be confined by the boundaries of one country, but to be a light to enlighten all people and—more completely after the Ascension—to be the Head beneath which earth and heaven should be conjoined. From this Head the Spirit should be poured cut over the entire world as a new revelation of divine grace and of divine glory.[39] Since the exaltation of the God-man therefore, the proper locale for the praise of God has been the heavenly Jerusalem where the earthly Church has its true home and towards which it makes its pilgrimage. Part of the value of the Church's liturgy is that it is already a participation in the never-ending song of praise of the City of God.[40]

---

[35] The threefold Holy of Apoc. 4:8, was a cue for this development.

[36] Dan. 7:10.

[37] Brightman, 131 f. Cf. also the examples of the 4th century, above, I, 34; 36. See the survey of the different transitions to the *Sanctus* in Cagin, *Te Deum ou illatio*, 65-72. The Gallican liturgies also show a great wealth of expression, *ibid.*, 83-95. Here in particular the saints are frequently drawn into the hymn of praise along with the angels.

[38] Peterson, 43 ff.

[39] In the Christian conception of the phrase the *Pleni sunt cœli et terra gloria tua* is enveloped in great part with the Pentecostal *Spiritus Domini replevit orbem terrarum*. The grace bestowed in the Holy Ghost is at the same time the beginning of heavenly glory for men and consequently the beginning of the conclusive revelation of divine glory. The interpretation of the δόξα in the *Sanctus* as the grace of the Holy Ghost is manifested also in the Egyptian liturgies, where after the πατήρης ὁ οὐρανός . . . they continue with the πλήρωσον = Epiklesis. Thus the *Euchologion* of Serapion (Quasten, *Mon.,* 61; above I, 34); cf. moreover Brightman, 132 and parallels (below, *l. c.*). Cf. M. Steinheimer, *Die δόξα τοῦ θεοῦ in der römischen Liturgie* (Munich, 1951), 95 f.

[40] Cf. Chrysostom, *In illud "Vidi Dominum" hom.*, 6, 3 (PG, 56, 138) "After Christ removed the wall between heaven and earth . . . He brought us this song of praise from heaven."

The New Testament motif that bursts forth in the angelic hymn has found even fuller expression in the appended *Benedictus*, with its two enclosing *Hosanna's*. Here, too, the praise resounds "to Him who sits on the throne, and to the Lamb" (Apoc. 5:13). It seems that it was in Gallic territory that the *Benedictus* was first annexed to the *Sanctus*.[41] At any rate the thought that must have been determining was this, that the glory of the Lord, which fills heaven and earth, did not begin to shine in its fullest splendor till the Son of God came to us in the form of flesh. Therefore, even in Bethlehem His coming was heralded by the *Gloria* of the angels' song, and therefore the crowds welcomed Him to Jerusalem in the phrase of the Psalm as He "who comes in the name of the Lord."[42]

In the basic text from the Gospel the words *qui venit* (ὁ ἐρχόμενος) must certainly be taken in the present tense: the people greeted one who was just coming. But one could well inquire whether the liturgical text is to be understood in the preterite (perfect) tense: *qui vēnit*. Naturally the question is independent of the position occupied by the *Benedictus*, whether before or after the consecration, for in either instance the praise must be referred to one who once came down to our midst in His Incarnation. Still, the change of meaning could be unnecessary. Christ is still always "coming." We still continue to pray for the coming of His kingdom, and even at Christmastide when we recall His *adventus* our mind turns as much to the

---

[41] While the *Benedictus* can be verified in the Orient only since the 8th century (cf. above, note 26), it must already have been customary in the Roman Mass at least in the 7th century. For it appears in most MSS. of the Roman Canon, though not in all; see Botte, *Le canon*, 30 Apparat. The earliest testimony for Gaul is presented by Cæsarius of Arles (d. 540), see note 8, above. The *Benedictus* is also a permanent part of the Gallican Mass. For it is presupposed in the *Post-Sanctus*, which frequently begins with *Vere sanctus, vere benedictus Dominus noster Jesus Christus;* Muratori, II, 518, 526; 534; etc. Also with preceding *Osanna in excelsis; ibid.*, II, 29, or with a repetition of the *Benedictus; ibid.*, 699. The same occurrence already in the Mone Masses, that probably originated in the 6th century, (PL, 138, 866 C., 875 B). In another place, namely, within the Communion portion of the Mass, the *Benedictus* (Mt. 21: 9 and Ps. 117: 26) was certainly used in answer to the Τὰ ἅγια τοῖς ἁγίοις; *Const. Ap.*, VIII, 13, 13 (Quasten, *Mon.*, 230).

[42] Matt. 21: 8, is probably the immediate prototype of the liturgical text, but with one divergence, that the first *Hosanna* of Matthew reads *Hosanna filio David*. In the liturgical text, however, the reading of the second *Hosanna* was inserted in its place, a reading, that, as a matter of fact, because it is a praise of God, results in a better transition. The form of the original text, Ps. 117, 25 f., may have had its part in bringing this about: *O Domine, salvum me fac . . . benedictus qui venit in nomine Domini.* These verses from the Psalm refer to the arrival of the festive procession to the Temple. In the meantime, however, the words "He who comes" without the addition "in the name of the Lord" had for a long time been turned into a term for the Messias, see Matt. 11, 3. Cf. J. Schneider, ἔρχομαι; *Theol. Wörterbuch z. N. Test.*, II, 664-672, especially 666 f. The hosa-nnah, which the Psalm still retains in its original meaning "help, we pray" assumed in the language of the people the meaning of a respectful invocation, "Hail," as is easily recognized in *Hosanna filio David* and as the addition *in excelsis* shows; cf. *Gloria in excelsis*. It is a hymn of praise to Him who dwells on High, praise in view of the manifestation of His

future as it does to the past.[43] Thus, too, His nearness in the Sacrament is a continuous coming which will attain its crown only on the last day.

Although in the *Missale Romanum* the *Sanctus* and the *Benedictus* appear together as a single song, the *Cæremoniale episcoporum* which appeared in 1600 presumes that the *Benedictus* will not be sung till after the consecration, *elevato sacramento*.[44] In recent times, this rule has been raised to a general directive.[45] This is obviously an attempt to accommodate to the canon a polyphonic style of song wherein the richer melody of the *Sanctus* (to which the first *Hosanna* is attached in a thoroughly acceptable manner) stretches out to the consecration, while the *Benedictus*, along with the second *Hosanna*, fills out the rest of the canon. In other words, the silence of the canon is completely surrendered in a Mass celebrated with singing, and space is given over not indeed to the loud praying of the priest, but to the singing of the choir, which thus does essentially little more than continue the dominant note of the Great Prayer—thanksgiving and praise—and unfolds it musically to the ear of the participant over the entire canon.

Suiting his action to the character of this double song—a song of adoration—and to the words *supplici confessione dicentes* in the usual introduction to it, the priest (and the two levites with him when the occasion demands) says the *Tersanctus* with head bowed. The practice is rather expected and certainly very ancient. According to old Roman tradition the assistants at a high Mass held this position—which they took, according to another rule, at the words *adorant dominationes*—till the end of

benevolence, just as is said of those who were witnesses of the miracles of Jesus," they extolled and praised God." Cf. in the Byzantine Mass the version in the second passage 'Ωσαννὰ ὁ ἐν τοῖς ὑψίστοις; Brightman, 385. When Brinktrine, *Die hl. Messe*, 173, states that *Hosanna* is tantamount to δόξα, *gloria*, we may let it pass. (The Armenian Mass actually substitutes a word with this meaning for the *Hosanna;* Hanssens, III, 394). But it is incorrect to place this (subjective and moreover unspoken) *gloria* on the same plane with the (objectively meant) *gloria* of the *Pleni sunt cæli* and so to see a connection between the two.

[43] It was clearly used in this predominantly future sense when the *Benedictus qui venit in nomine Domini* was employed as a memorial inscription, as in the Greek inscription on the portal of a Syrian mountain hypogeum; see C. M. Kaufmann, *Handbuch der christlichen Archæologie*, (3rd ed.; Paderborn, 1922), 148. For the rest, the oriental liturgies insert instead of the simple *qui venit* a double phrase that places past and future together: "he who has come and is to come." Hanssens, III, 394 f.

[44] *Cæremoniale episc.*, II, 8, 70 f.—In the Paris cathedral the same arrangement is found already in 1512; see below, p. 216. In the Mass that Luther, 1523, has in mind, the *Benedictus* was sung while the host and chalice were elevated, a method he wanted retained. M. Luther, *Formula missæ et communionis* (1523), n. 21 (Kleine Texte, 36, p. 16). A Gastoué, "Le Sanctus et le Benedictus," *Revue du chant gregorien*, 38 (1934), 12-17; 35-39, tries to prove from a musical standpoint that the *Benedictus* was forced into its place after the consecration, even earlier. (See *JL*, 14 (1938), 549 f.).

[45] Decree of Jan. 14, 1921, in which the rubric in the *Graduale Romanum* was changed at the same time; *Decreta auth. SRC*, n. 4364; this confirms an earlier decree of Dec. 16, 1906, n. 4243.

the canon.[46] Only the celebrant returned to an upright position when the song was finished, and continued the prayer. According to the present-day usage as laid down in the *Missale Romanum,* he stands erect as soon as he begins the *Benedictus.*[47] This is probably due to the fact that during the *Benedictus* he signs himself with the sign of the Cross, of which mention is made as early as the eleventh century.[48] A sign of the Cross and a blessing also accompany the song, in some fashion or other, in the oriental liturgies.[49]

5. Various Practices during the Canon

The *Tersanctus* finished, it was originally the custom in Rome for the celebrating priest to continue the performance of the Great Prayer in a loud voice but—we must presume [1]—as a simple recitation, without any melody. Once the Roman Mass was transplanted to Frankish territory, however, the picture was altered, and our present *ritus* is broadly stamped with the new customs that sprang up here. *Surgit solus pontifex et tacite intrat in canonem.* This phrase, which crystallizes the Carolingian revision of the older norm found in the first Roman *ordo,*[2] can be considered the basic pattern followed in transforming and reshaping the rite in the inmost part of the celebration of Mass.

The priest enters the sanctuary of the canon alone. Up till now the people have thronged around him, their songs at times accompanying him in the fore-Mass. But the songs have become less frequent, and after the steep ascent of the Great Prayer they have come to an end in the *Tersanctus.* A sacred stillness reigns; silence is a worthy preparation for God's approach. Like the High-priest of the Old Testament, who once a year was

---

[46] *Ordo Rom.* I, n. 16 (PL, 78, 945). Cf. Jungmann, *Gewordene Liturgie,* 126 ff.
[47] *Ritus serv.,* VII, 8.
[48] *Bernardi Ordo Clun.,* I, 72 (Herrgott, 264), according to which the priest makes the sign of the cross while still bowed and straightens up only at the *Te igitur.* Rule of the Canons of St. Victor in Paris, c. 67; Martène, *De ant. eccl. ritibus,* Appendix (III, 791). At the same time in Paris John Beleth, *Explicatio,* c. 45 (PL, 202, 53), gives evidence of the sign of the cross and alleges as a reason, because the *Benedictus* is taken from the Gospel.
[49] In the Egyptian liturgies, while the people sing the *Sanctus,* the priest makes the sign of the cross over himself, over the Mass servers, and over the people. The Armenian rite has a triple accompanying sign of the cross over the chalice and

paten. In the West Syrian rite the priest covers the chalice and paten with his hands during the *Sanctus,* and this, among the Maronites, is followed with the sign of the cross; Hanssens, III, 395 f. The basis for the sign of the cross is perhaps the idea touched upon above, n. 39, that the approaching glory of God signifies, or may signify, a blessing for the creature, and it is a blessing that must transform the gifts. In this sense Severian of Gabala (d. after 408), *De mundi creatione,* II, 6 (PG, 56, 446 f.), transfers to the Eucharist the sequence of actions in Is. 6. 3-7, where the angel first sings the *Sanctus* and only then takes the burning coal from the altar (burning coal = the host after the consecration); cf. above, note 41.
[1] Above, p. 104.
[2] Cf. above, p. 104.

permitted to enter the Holy of Holies with the blood of a sacrificial animal (Hebr. 9:7), the priest now separates from the people and makes his way before the all-holy God in order to offer up the sacrifice to Him.[3] In the early medieval Mass he did not do so without first acknowledging his unworthiness in a humble apology,[4] or begging prayerfully for God's help.[5] Sometimes a hand-washing was prescribed.[6] The whole assembly knelt down [7] or, when this was forbidden because of the Sunday or feast day, remained bowed.[8] In many churches of the eleventh and twelfth centuries the choir of clerics surrounding the altar, taking up the *Orate*-plea of the

---

[3] This allegorism was developed by the Carlovingian and post-Carlovingian interpreters to greater and greater lengths; Florus Diaconus, *De actione miss.*, n. 42 f. (PL, 119, 43) ; Remigius of Auxerre, *Expositio* (PL, 101, 1256) ; especially Ivo of Chartres, *De conven. vet. et novi sacrif.* (PL, 162, 554) who extends the parallel with Hebr. 9:7 (the priest enters the Holy of Holies with the Blood of Christ, i.e., with the memorial of His passion) ; Hildebert of Le Mans, *Versus de mysterio missæ* (PL, 171, 1183) ; Isaac of Stella, *Ep. de off. missæ* (PL, 194, 1889-1896) ; Robert Paululus, *De cæremoniis*, II, 23-30 (PL, 177, 425-430) ; Sicard of Cremona, *Mitrale*, III, 6 (PL, 213, 125 B) ; Durandus, IV, 36, 5.

[4] The Missa Illyrica, which is especially rich in apologiæ, inserts here three formulas with which the priest begins, even while the *Sanctus* is still being sung. The third one reads as follows : *Facturus memoriam salutaris hostiæ totius mundi, cum illius dignitatem et meam intueor fœditatem, conscientia torqueor peccatorum. Verum quia tu Deus multum misericors es, imploro ut digneris mihi dare spiritum contribulatum, qui tibi gratum sacrificium revelasti, ut eo purificatus vitali hostia pias manus admoveam, quæ omnia peccata mea aboleat et ea deinceps in perpetuum vitandi mihi tutelam infundat omnibusque fidelibus vivis et defunctis, pro quibus tibi offertur, præsentis vitæ et futuræ salutis commercia largiatur. Qui vivis.* Martène, 1, 4, IV (I, 512 E) ; further illustrations, *ibid.*, 1, 4, 7, 9 (I, 398). Cf. also Ebner, 396 f.

[5] At times, since the 11th century, the *Aperi* found in the present-day breviary appears in this place. Sacramentary of Moissac : Martène, 1, 4, VIII (I, 539 E).

Cf. also the statement in Leroquais, I, 158 and in the *Register* (III, 339 f.). Several evidences from Italy in Ebner, 396. *Ibid.*, 206 for Spain, and also Ferreres, p. XXVIII, XXXIII, XLVIII f. The *Munda cor meum* also appears here (XLIX : Gerona, 14th cent.).—In two Mass-ordos in Beneventan script, 11-12th centuries (Ebner, 149, 329), the invocation *Christe audi nos* follows three times upon the *Sanctus*, the second of which is joined with invocations, mostly biblical. Similar invocations of a later period mentioned by Bona II, 11, 1 (745). Cf. *Missale of Hereford* (about 1400). Maskel, II, 111.

[6] Above, p. 78.

[7] This kneeling posture may have been the incentive for interpolating here (*post offertorium et ante canonem*) a prayer for help against the Tartar danger ; this a Synod of Mainz, 1261 (Hartzheim, III, 611) does, commending Psalm 78, with a *Pater noster* and the oration for peace ; Franz, 205. f. The case seems to be an isolated one. Similar prayers in time of distress will be found inserted most frequently either before or after the embolism.

[8] Evidences since the 9th century ; Jungmann, *Gewordene Liturgie*, 126 ff. (cf. above I, 240).—Regarding the gradual change in the meaning of this practice from adoring reverence to God to veneration of the Blessed Sacrament, see Jungmann, *Gewordene Liturgie*, 127-131. A bowed attitude during the Canon is in accordance with an old tradition, see above I, 72.— Humble submission before God's majesty is most likely the original meaning of the custom that is reported today from many countries (among others, Poland, Portugal, Central America) where the faithful

priest, began to recite psalms for him in a loud voice.[9] A formal office of accompanying prayers of petition, akin to the oriental ἐκτενής, was for a time employed as an outward veil to cover the silent prayer of the celebrant.[10] No surprise, then, that there were even attempts to hide completely the visible activities of the priest from the congregation.[11]

On the other hand, more recent rules, still in force at the present, prescribe that at a pontifical function a procession of clerics should appear with burning tapers and range symmetrically in front of the altar.[12] The result of consecration practices which meantime came into being, this procession functions as a preparation for the reception of the great King. In some churches another practice was added: namely, two clerics to right and left of the altar continually swinging censers from this moment till the Communion.[13] Outside pontifical functions at least two wax tapers (torches) are to be lighted at a high Mass right after the preface.[14] In the same sense another custom grew in many places since the thirteenth cen-

strike their breasts three times at the *Sanctus;* Kramp, "Messgebräuche der Gläubigen in den ausserdeutschen Ländern" (*StZ,* 1927, II) 359; 362; 364; 366. Cf. also Kramp, "Messgebräuche der Gläubigen in der Neuzeit" (*StZ,* 1926, II) 215; 217.

[9] Cf. above, p. 87.—For this a definite arrangement was developed that is presented in its fullest form in the Missa Illyrica: Martène, 1, 4, IV (I, 513 A) : When the bishop begins the *Te igitur,* the *ministri* should pray Psalms 19, 24, 50, 89, 90, until the *Te igitur* (i.e., clearly, the Canon) is ended. A list of versicles follows, succeeded by an oration *pro sacerdote: Gaudeat Domine,* and another *communis* (elsewhere captioned *pro omnibus*) : *Precibus nostris.* The same arrangement occurs again, but in part only, inasmuch as Psalm 89, or 90, or the second oration, or the precise statement of the time, is missing, in the Sacramentary of Séez: PL, 78, 249 ; in the Mass arrangement of Liége and Gregorianmünster: Martène, 1, 4, XV, XVI (I, 592, 599 f.) ; in Italian Mass arrangements of the 11th until the beginning of the 13th century; Ebner, 306 f., 313, 323. In the Sacramentary of Modena written before 1174 (Muratori, I, 92), the Gradual Psalms (Pss. 119-133) are interpolated and before the versicles *Kyrie el., Christe el., Kyrie el., Pater noster* are interpolated. Here also we should cite the statement in *Ordo Rom.* VI (10th cent.),

n. 10 (PL, 78, 993 B) that the deacon and subdeacon should chant *quindecim grad.,* after the bishop has said *Orate pro me.*

[10] The cessation of the practice seems to coincide with the elaboration of the *Sanctus* melodies (cf. above, p. 130) ; then, too, with the elevating of the host that was coming more and more into vogue.

[11] In this sense Durandus, IV, 39, 1: *In quibusdam ecclesiis . . . quasi tegitur et velatur.* Still, even in these instances, clearly not many, it was a symbolical concealment *(quasi),* since a real concealment of the priest is excluded, at least since the 13th century, by the very fact that he held up the host to view. Even earlier there is evidence of various altar curtains, but they were hung rather on the sides and were for the sake of ornamentation, especially on altars covered with a ciborium or canopy, where the veils would be fastened between the pillars right and left. Braun, *Der christliche Altar,* II, 133-138; 166-171.

[12] *Cæremoniale episc.,* II, 8, 68: *Quattuor, sex aut ad summum octo ministri,* with the thurifer in the lead.

[13] *Ordinarium* of Laon (13-14th cent.) : Martène, 1, 4, XX (I, 608 D). Likewise in the late Middle Ages at Lyons; Bünner, 258. Also in Paris and in Liége the practice is verified; Atchley, *A History of the Use of Incense,* 265.

[14] *Missale Rom., Ritus serv.,* VIII, 8. Thus also in the *Ordinarium* of Laon (note 13)

tury, the custom of lighting the so-called *Sanctus* candle at every Mass.[15] This custom was elevated to a rubric in the *Missale Romanum*,[16] but by contrary custom the rule has lost its force.[17]

Through such rites, without doubt, there was awakened during the Mass in the later Middle Ages a lively reverence for the mystery that took place at the consecration like a new epiphany of the God-man. On the other hand, no one any longer thought of following the priest's prayers, which indeed were now only whispered quietly, and whose ideas turned in a very different direction. In fact, they were in essence for the priest exclusively, and were not supposed to be accessible to lay folk.[18]

The only part of the liturgy of the canon that was open to the faithful was the external action of the priest, and, until the elevation of the species became customary in the thirteenth century, this consisted in little more than the extension of the arms, bowing, kissing the altar, and making signs of the Cross over the gifts. We must therefore cast a glance at these external rites, inasmuch as they reappear several times in the course of the canon.

It is taken for granted that the basic attitude of the priest during this most ancient traditional prayer should continue to be the same as that of the preface, the traditional stance of the *orantes*. This same posture was originally taken also by the surrounding clergy, and perhaps also by the faithful,[19] until for them bowing or kneeling became the predominant rule. Only the priest continues to remain standing with arms extended. In the

---

for the Sunday Masses. See Eisenhofer, II, 163 in regard to the present practice.
[15] Plentiful material on this in Browe, "Die Elevation in der Messe" (*JL*, 1929), 40-43. Pictures from the 13th century in Ch. Rohault de Fleury, *La Messe*, I (Paris, 1883), Table XX; pictures from later times in F. Falk, *Die deutschen Messausslegungen von der Mitte des 15 Jh. bis zum Jahre* 1525 (Cologne, 1889), 28, 30, 33, 37, 46.
[16] *Rubr. gen.* XX; cf. *Ritus serv.*, VIII, 6.
[17] This contrary custom was recognized and approved by the Congregation of Rites, July 9, 1899: *Decreta auth. SRC*, n. 4029, 2.—But the sanctus candle still survives in many places. In Spain at the *Sanctus* the server lights a smaller candle (much like the bugie used by prelates) and places it close to the priest's right arm; it remains lighted till the Communion, when the server holds it over the paten while the priest collects any detached particles; then it is extinguished; Raphael M. Huber, "Unusual Spanish and Portuguese Litur-

gical Customs," *Homiletic & Pastoral Rev.*, 52 (1951), 323. The *Sanctus* candle is still in use also in Central America, in many parts of Switzerland, in a few parishes of the diocese of Rottenburg and Würzburg, and in the Freiburg cathedral; Kramp, "Meszgebräuche der Glaübigen in der Neuzeit," (*StZ*, 1926, II), 218; *idem.*, Meszgebräuche der Gläubigen in den ausserdeutschen Ländern," (*StZ*, 1927, II), 352, note 2; 364; Krömler, 58. In Vorarlberg the custom continued till World War I; L. Jochum, "Religiöses und kirchliches Brauchtum in Vorarlberg," *Montfort*, I (Bregenz, 1946), 280 f. The Carthusians have kept it: *Ordinarium Cart.* (1932), c. 29, 14; 32, 13. Likewise the Dominicans: G. Sölch, "Die Liturgie des Dominikanerordens" (*Angelicum*, 1950), 32.

[18] Cf. *supra*, I, 82 f.; 143 f.

[19] *Supra*, I, 239, Cf. the illustrations (9th-11th cent.) in Righetti, *Manuale* II, 357; 361; also the late remnant of the practice at the consecration, *infra*.

Middle Ages it was often customary for him to stretch his arms out wide in the form of a cross, at least after the consecration, as is still the practice with the Dominicans, amongst others. Then at the *Supplices te rogamus* it was usual to cross them in front of the breast.[20] Both these postures are evident references to the Crucified, whom an older Christendom was accustomed to see in the very attitude of the *orantes*,[21] although no special emphasis was laid on this.

The reverential bowing—the posture stipulated by the Roman *ordines* for the surrounding clergy all through the canon—was originally shared by the celebrant, as we have seen, only at the *Sanctus*. Then he also bowed after the consecration when he began the humble petition for acceptance, at the *Supra quæ*[22] or, as at present, at least at the *Supplices*,[23] and he held this pose to the end of the petition. The textual analogy of the introductory petition for acceptance in the *Te igitur* must have led to a similar bowing right after the *Sanctus*,[24] while pronouncing the words: *rogamus ac petimus, uti accepta habeas . . . hæc dona*. While this practice of bowing was stabilized already in the thirteenth century, the preparatory gestures of extending, lifting and joining the hands,[25] and in general also the concluding kiss of the altar were at this same period still unknown.[26]

When the priest straightens up from this first bow after the *Sanctus*, he makes three signs of the Cross over the sacrificial gifts. These are the first signs of the Cross within the canon, and likewise the oldest. First evidence

[20] *Infra* for proofs. The Carthusian rite prescribes outstretched arms also before the consecration; *Ordinarium Cart.* (1932), c. 27, 2.

[21] Cf. Dölger, *Sol salutis*, 318 with n. 4.

[22] *Ordo* of John Archicantor, Silva-Tarouca, 199).

[23] Cf. Amalar, *De eccl. off.*, III, 25 (PL, 105, 1142). Proofs from later times in Sölch, *Hugo*, 95.

[24] Missal of the Minorites of the 13th century: Ebner, 314; cf. *Ordinarium O.P.* of 1256 (Guerrini, 241); *Liber ordinarius* of Liége (Volk, 94).—Unless he maintained the position assumed at the *Sanctus; Liber usuum O. Cist.*, c. 53 (PL, 166, 1425); cf. Sölch, 88, note 20.—Because such a plea for acceptance is present also in the *Hanc igitur*, though in a special connection, we find the profound bow very much in use here too, in the later Middle Ages; see below.

[25] Here we clearly have the same idea as at the beginning of the *Gloria* and *Credo* and at the invitation to pray *Oremus* and *Gratias agamus*: namely, a gesture introductory to a proper prayer attitude at an important moment of the service, comparable to the melodious initium of the verses of a solemn psalmody. Before the *Te igitur* the gesture is in a certain sense an independent one and of itself forms, as it were, a silent invocation. Such is the case at least if we follow the usual understanding of the rubric; namely, that the gesture comes first, and only then the *Te igitur* is actually to begin in a bowed attitude. Cf Merati in Gavanti-Merati, *Thesaurus*, II, 8, 1 (I, 284 f.). The rubric (*Ritus serv.*, VIII, I) which was slightly altered in 1897, admits of more than one meaning; see J. B. Müller, *Zeremonienbüchlein*, (13th ed.; Freiburg, 1934), 63.

[26] Sölch, *Hugo*, 88 f. This first kissing of the altar is mentioned only by Sicard of Cremona, *Mitrale*, III, 6 (PL, 213, 125), whose note is repeated by Durandus, IV, 36, 6: *hic osculatur altare in reverentiam passionis*. It may be doubted if the last word indicates the original meaning of this kiss. Possibly it is a copy of the older kissing of the altar at the *supplices te ro-*

for them is found at the beginning of the eighth century.[27] Other crosses follow during the *Quam oblationem,* in the account of the institution, in the *Unde et memores,* in the *Per quem hœc omnia.* These, too, from indications in the manuscripts, came into use in the eighth century, and we are made aware of the headway they achieved when we read in a letter of Pope Zachary to St. Boniface, dated November 4, 751, that he had acceded to the latter's request to mark in the *rotulus* he had sent him through Lullus the passages in the canon where the crosses were to be made.[28] In the ninth century were added the crosses during the closing doxology. The second Roman *ordo,* in a detailed exposition, makes mention of these *sex ordines crucium.*[29] Aside from those in the concluding doxology, these crosses were, in general, in the same number as at present.[30] The only crosses that are of a somewhat later date are those in the *Supplices te rogamus*[31] and—in a later passage—at the *Pax Domini.*

The significance of these signs of the Cross in the canon formed since the tenth century one of the main themes in the medieval commentaries on the Mass.[32] It is plain that the sign of the Cross should point to the

---

gamus occasioned by the *supplices rogamus,* consequently a gesture of reverential pleading. The Mass-*ordo* of Cologne, 14th century (Binterim, IV, 3, p. 224), shows a further development of this kiss, inasmuch as it adds a kissing of the picture of the crucifixion and a prayer (paraphrasing Psalm 138, 16 a). The rubric of the Mass-*ordo* of Amiens in the 9th century, ed. Leroquais (*Eph. liturg.,* 1927), 442, is an entirely isolated one: *Postea osculetur altare et dicat:* Te igitur. This can only mean a greeting, a salute upon "going into" the canon; cf. the salutation of the altar at the offertory in the *Ordo Rom.* I, n. 15 (above, I, 314, note 20) and the parallel in the East Syrian Rite (above, II, 79, n. 16); here in the Syro-Malabar Rite the further parallel of the repeated kissing of the altar (twice in the center, then to the right and to the left) also during the *Sanctus;* Hanssens, III, 395 f.
[27] In the Cod. Reg., 316 of the older Gelasianum; here and in other individual MSS. a fourth sign of the cross at the *benedicas* appears along with the customary three. Cf. also in addition to the following references the excursus on the cross in the canon, in Brinktrine, *Die hl. Messe,* 295-303. Several other individual instances in Eisenhofer, II, 171 f.
[28] Zacharias, *Ep.,* 13 (PL, 89, 953 B). Cf. Botte, *Le canon,* 21.

[29] *Ordo Rom.* II, n. 10 (PL, 78, 974).

[30] That there was no complete uniformity in the 11th century is shown by the fact that Bernold of Constance, *Micrologus,* c. 14 (PL, 151, 986 f.) expressly appeals to the authority of Gregory VII in support of the method he advocates (among others, the uneven numbers).

[31] In individual cases today's customary signs of the cross appeared here already at an early date, as in the Sacramentary of Angoulême written about the year 800. However, they are still missing often enough in the 11th and 12th centuries; Brinktrine, 299.

[32] The *Expositio "Missa pro multis,"* ed. Hanssens (*Eph. liturg.,* 1930), 39, explains the *sex ordines crucium* in the appendix of the *Ordo Rom.* II by means of the relationship of the six eras of the world to the cross of Christ. Since the 11th century many an interpreter loved to ascribe some sort of symbolical meaning to every number of the signs of the cross; Franz, 415 f., 419. Others again, like Rupert of Deutz and Innocent III, connect them with some phase of Christ's passion (Franz, 418, 455, 662); or all these interpretations are jumbled together, as Honorius Augustod. (Franz, 424) does. Or, again, with Berthold of Regensburg, a special signification from the representation of Christ's passion

sacrifice of the Cross which is being made present sacramentally.[33] Nowadays it is taken for granted that the *signum crucis* also signifies a blessing; one meaning of "to bless" is to make the sign of the Cross. Although in the Church of the first thousand years the laying-on of hands was generally the form used for blessing, still this form seems to have been superseded more and more by the sign of the Cross, especially in Gallic territory.[34] In some passages, indeed, it is quite apparent that the cross is meant as a blessing, being linked with words that signify just that: the double *benedixit* at the consecration, the words *benedictam, adscriptam, ratam,* and *sanctificas, vivificas, benedicis.*

But it also appears in other passages. Brinktrine maintains that the sign of the Cross in the canon was intended from most ancient times not only to emphasize the notion of blessing and sanctifying, but also to underline certain significant words.[35] This latter intention (he holds) must be granted in the case of the two crosses that accompany the words *ut nobis corpus et sanguis fiat* just before the consecration, and likewise the five crosses right after the consecration, at *hostiam puram, hostiam sanctam, hostiam immaculatam, panem sanctum vitæ æternæ, calicem salutis perpetuæ.* To these would naturally be added at least the crosses over the consecrated gifts in the *Supplices,* at the words *corpus et sanguinem.* The use of the

is attributed to each one of the twenty-five signs of the cross, with the basic idea "short sign of the cross, quick torment; prolonged torment, big sign of the cross." (Franz, 656; cf. 695 f.), or with an imitator of his, who discovers in the 30 signs of the cross (inclusive of the three at the *Pax Domini* and two more in the canon, as they are, e.g., in the Freising Missal of 1520; see Beck, 308) the thirty miracles of the Redemption (662 f.). Cf. Franz, 733: "The explanation of these signs of the cross gained greater importance in proportion as the instruction of the people regarding the canon was restricted exclusively to these signs."
[33] St. Thomas, *Summa theol.,* III, q. 83, a. 5 ad 3, stresses this as the fundamental idea. The signs of the cross after the consecration are to be understood in this sense. Thus already Ivo of Chartres, *De conven. vet. et novi sacrif.* (PL, 162, 556 C) : *Quid est enim inter ipsa mysteria rebus sacratis vel sacrandis signum crucis superponere nisi mortem Domini commemorare?* He compares the signs of the cross over the offerings with the Old Testament sprinkling with sacrificial blood.
[34] The German word *"segnen,"* to "bless," is etymologically akin to *signare,* to sign. In Gaul the blessing was generally given

with a sign of the cross, for in a "miracle" of St. Martin of Tours it is recorded that the saint appeared in the apse window of the church dedicated to him, descended and blessed the sacrifice on the altar by extending his right hand *juxta morem catholicum signo crucis superposito.* Gregory of Tours (d. 594), *Vitæ Patrum,* 16, 2 (PL, 71, 1075). In a formulary of the Mozarabic Mass a prayer is said after the consecration *Hanc hostiam . . . per signum crucis sanctifices et benedicas;* Ferotin, *Le liber mozarabicus sacramentorum,* p. 321. But a singularly definite testimony is already presented by Augustine, *In Joh. tract.,* 118, 5 (PL, 35, 1950). *Quid est, quod omnes noverunt, signum Christi nisi crux Christi? Quod signum nisi adhibeatur sive frontibus credentium sive ipsi aquæ, ex qua regenerantur, sive oleo, quo chrismate unguntur, sive sacrificio, quo aluntur, nihil horum rite perficitur.* James of Edessa (d. 708), in describing the West Syrian liturgy speaks of eighteen signs of the cross that are made over the offerings; A. Rücker, "Die Kreuzzeichen in der westsyrischen Messliturgie," *Pisciculi F. J. Dölger dargeboten* (Münster, 1939), 245–251.
[35] Brinktrine, 303.

signs of the Cross over the consecrated gifts has often been commented on with some astonishment, because the first thought that strikes one is that these are blessings.[36] A blessing is obviously out of place here. Yet it may be questioned whether it is enough to explain them as underlining certain words. Why precisely are these words emphasized? They are certainly not the most sacred words that appear in the canon.

We must remind ourselves that the solemn prose style that dominates the Roman canon is the type of speech that was cultivated in the schools of rhetoric in the decadent Roman empire. The oratorical phrase implies also the oratorical gesture. The oratorical phrase that touches on some object in the view of the listener implies a gesture directing the attention to that object, a principle that governs every vital speech and therefore likewise the prayer which was naturally and originally eloquent. Although such things, because taken for granted, are seldom mentioned in liturgical works, still there are some examples, and not only in oriental liturgy,[37] but

---

[36] Thus, the commission on the removal of *abusus missæ* in the Council of Trent proposed abolishing the signs of the cross after the consecration; *Concilium Tridentinum,* ed. Görres, VIII, 917. R. Haungs, "Die Kreuzzeichen nach der Wandlung im römischen Messkanon" *Benediktin. Monatsschrift,* 21 (1939), 249-261, reviews the history of the interpretation of the signs. According to this study the Middle Ages attributed only commemorative significance to the sign of the cross, as we have just stated, whereas more modern times, with few exceptions (Maldonatus especially among them, see below) viewed them, with restrictions, as signs of blessing. The Syrian Narsai (d. about 502) already made the same assumption and had the same problem, but suggested, "He [the priest] signs now [after the epiklesis] not because the Mysteries have need of the signing, but to teach by the last sign [of the cross] that they are accomplished." Connolly, *The Liturgical Homilies of Narsai,* 22.

[37] In the Coptic Anaphora of St. Cyril the priest is required to point first to the bread and then to the chalice, when, after the words of the institution, he further adds the Pauline words (I Cor. 11: 26): "As often as you shall eat this bread and drink this chalice . . ." The same procedure already at the first offering of the gifts; Brightman, 148 l., 17 ff.; 177 l., 29 ff. Along with this, Kyrillos ibn Laklak (d.

1243) in his book of instructions (ed. Graf: *JL,* 4, 122) points out that the priest may no longer make the sign of the cross over the offerings after the consecration. In the Ethiopian anaphora of the Apostles the words of the institution are given as follows, "Take, eat: (pointing) this bread (bowing) is my body (pointing) . . ." and likewise with the chalice. In the anamnesis and offertory prayer that follows (which still preserves the Hippolytus text almost unchanged, see *supra* I, 29) we have the words "and [we] offer unto thee this bread (pointing to it) and this chalice, inasmuch as . . ." The same gesture is repeated immediately at the petition that God would send the Holy Ghost "upon this bread (pointing to it) and over this cup (pointing to it)," whereupon, nevertheless, follow some signs of the cross. Brightman, 232f.—The connection is still clearer in the Anaphora of St. Mark, ed. T. M. Semharay Selim (*Eph. liturg.,* 1928, 510-531), where regularly before, during, and after the consecration, the demonstrative pronoun, *hic (panis)* etc., is accompanied with the note *signum* (515 ff.).—In the Byzantine liturgy of St. Chrysostom the deacon takes over the duty of pointing at similar points. At the words of the institution over the bread, as well as those over the chalice, he points with the orarion: δειχνύει . . . τὸν ἅγιον δίσκον, *resp.* συνδεικνύει . . . τὸ ἅγιον ποτήριον. The same motion is made at the epiklesis over the species of bread

in the Roman as well.[38] We must conclude that these gestures were subsequently—that is, since the eighth century—stylized into a sign of the Cross.[39] For such a process of transformation there is no lack of examples and parallels.[40]

If, with this in mind, we con the text of the canon, we actually find that every time the gifts are mentioned the sign of the Cross is also indicated, with the exception of the *Hanc igitur oblationem,* where the hands are spread out over the gifts, and possibly the phrase *qui tibi offerunt hoc sacrificium laudis,* in which the sacrifice is mentioned in passing. In fact, we have a document, the *Admonitio synodalis* of the ninth century, that may perhaps permit us to see the transition very plainly.[41] The conclusion is thus forced upon us that the original gesture within the canon was a demonstrative one, and as such was not mentioned in the liturgical text. And this would hold not only for the three passages cited above, but also at least for the *Te igitur* where the petition for acceptance is mentioned for the first time in the canon: *uti accepta habeas et benedicas hæc dona,*

as well as over the chalice; Brightman, 386 f.

[38] In the orations of reconciliation for Maundy Thursday, presented in the Pontifical of Poitiers, written in the 9th century, and emanating from the Roman usage, the priests were obliged to touch with the right hand *vice pontificis* the prostrate penitents each time the bishop spoke the words *hos famulos tuos* in the orations; J. Morinus, *Commentarius historicus de disciplina in administratione sacramenti pœnitentiæ* (Antwerp, 1682), Appendix, p. 67. The touching here is in all likelihood also equivalent to the laying on of hands.

[39] The opinion that the sign of the cross here was not meant as a blessing, but simply as a sign, was upheld by J. Maldonat, S.J. (d. 1583), *De cæremoniis,* II, 21 (in F. A. Zaccaria, *Bibliotheca ritualis,* II, 2 [Rome, 1781], 142 f.; cf. 131 f.).

[40] Attention is especially to be called to the transformation of the laying on of hands as a form of blessing into the sign of the cross over the object to be blessed. Thus, in the *Indulgentiam* before the sacramental absolution we still have a trace of the imposition of hands, as it was formerly united with the formula, whereas outside of confession only the sign of the cross is conjoined to the formula; cf. Jungmann, *Die lateinischen Bussriten,* 263 f. But even otherwise the sign of the cross occasionally replaced a gesture of pointing; thus in the

Ordo Rom. I, n. 21 (PL, 78, 947) when the regional subdeacon gives the sign to the leader of the schola, at the end of the Communion of the people, to conclude the Communion Psalm with *Gloria Patri: aspicit ad primum scholæ, faciens crucem in fronte sua, annuit ei dicere Gloriam.* The signal has been stylized into the sign of the cross, just as the simple greeting addressed to the people developed into a conventional religious greeting *Dominus vobiscum.* There are, moreover, evidences at present of a parallel manifestation, where the sign of the cross is often substituted for punctuation marks in the artistic script in which religious texts are written.

[41] In the version of Ratherius of Verona (d. 974; PL, 136, 560 A) *Calicem et oblatam recta cruce signate, id est non in circulo et varicatione* (al. *variatione,* PL, 135, 1071 D; *vacillatione,* PL, 132, 459 A., 461 A) *digitorum, ut plurimi faciunt, sed stricte duobus digitis et pollice intus recluso.* The passage is missing in one portion of the traditional texts (see Leclercq, DACL, VI, 576-579), but was present at least in the 10th century. In the movement of free hand and finger which is here censured we might possibly have a vestige of the ancient oratorical gestures which are now supplanted by the sign of the cross; see Eisenhofer, I, 280 f. regarding the position of the fingers in the signs of blessing.

hæc munera, hæc sancta sacrificia illibata. The *benedicas* would then be
the occasion for a change, a transformation into the sign of the Cross,[42]
while in the other passages the pointing gesture would still be retained, and
as such would not be mentioned.

Looking yet more closely at the significance of this pointing gesture, we
are forced to remark the following: Since we are concerned with the offering up of gifts which we cannot transfer to an invisible God except by
means of interpretative words and gestures, the gesture of pointing would
become a gesture of oblation whenever it accompanied the plea for acceptance *(petimus uti accepta habeas ; offerimus præclaræ maiestati tuæ).* This
is not the only gesture used to give visible expression to the oblation. Mention has already been made of bowing which is tied in with the plea for
acceptance.[43] Extending the hands over the gifts embodies the same symbolism. Recall that we came upon a prescription in Hippolytus of Rome,
ordering the bishop to say the eucharistic prayer extending his hands over
the gifts.[44] This extension of hands, which represents the same thought,
but with greater emphasis, never became a permanent gesture or one that
accompanied the entire eucharistic prayer. Only at the *Hanc igitur* did it
remain until the present day, or rather once more come into use. It was
also used for a time at *Supra quæ propitio.*[45] For the rest, the hands were
left free for the ordinary posture of the *orantes,* signifying our striving
God-ward. Only when the phrase calls for it are the hands used to indicate
the gifts that should belong to God. Seen from this vantage point, it is not
at all unreasonable that the gesture of pointing—still always valid—should
be combined with a sign of the Cross, and thus our offering of Christ on
the Cross. These demonstrative signs of the Cross are therefore merely
another expression of our will humbly to offer up to God the gifts that lie
on the altar, and in this sense they rank with the laying of hands over
the gifts, the bowing that accompanies the petition for acceptance, and
the elevation of chalice and host connected with the closing doxology.

6. *Te igitur.* The Plea for Acceptance

The first prayer that we meet in the text of the canon after the *Sanctus*
is an offering of the gifts in the solemn yet suppliant form of a plea for
gracious acceptance. Such an offering, at least in this position, is not self-
explanatory. It is on the same footing as the offertory, or more precisely

---

[42] The fact that in the oldest occurrence of
these signs the *benedicas* also has a sign
of the cross, would be in accord with this;
see note 27 above.

[43] Cf.. above, p. 142. Cf. the exactly corresponding practices at the offertory, above,
p. 51.

[44] Above, I, 29. The same prescription also
in the *Testamentum Domini,* I, 23 (Quasten, *Mon.,* 249.

[45] Balthasar of Pforta, O. Cist., verifies it
as the practice of the secular clergy in
Germany towards the end of the 15th century, Franz, 587.

the *oratio super oblata,* the offering up even of the earthly gifts, which is distinctive of the Roman Mass. In other liturgies such an offering, as well as the insertion of the intercessions after the *Sanctus,* is unknown. Instead, they build a short span from the *Sanctus* to the words of institution, either by developing the Christological theme of the prayer of thanks, as in the West Syrian and the Byzantine formularies; [1] or by continuing in a free fashion the words of praise, as often happens in the *Post-Sanctus* of the Gallic liturgies [2]; or, finally, by attaching an epiklesis, to the *Pleni sunt cœli,* as the Egyptian liturgies do.[3]

The transition from the *Sanctus* to this offering in the *Te igitur* has been considered rather abrupt, and the word *igitur,* which seems to mark the connection externally, has been found unintelligible.[4] Even up to the very present the word has been given various and varied interpretations.[5] But obviously its only purpose is to link the action which is beginning to unfold in the plea for acceptance with the foregoing thanksgiving of the preface, by which it was, in substance, already set in motion.[6] It is the same *igitur* which forms the transition between the first section of the

---

[1] Cf. above I, 43. In the liturgy of St. Basil it is done very elaborately.

[2] In a short and typical manner, e.g., in the first Mass of the *Missale Gothicum*: *Vere sanctus, vere benedictus Dominus noster Jesus Christus Filius tuus, manens in cœlis, manifestatus in terris. Ipse enim pridie quam pateretur;* Muratori, II, 518. —It seems that in the Gallic Mass, too, the basic form of the *Post Sanctus* was a christological continuation of the thanksgiving prayer; Cagin, *Te Deum ou illatio,* 381-385.

[3] Thus in the anaphora of St. Mark (Brightman, 132): "Heaven and earth are truly full of Thy glory through the appearance of our Lord God and Savior Jesus Christ. Make this sacrifice also, O God, replete with Thy blessing through the descent of the Holy Ghost; for He, our Lord and God and all-king Jesus Christ in the night took . . ." cf. above, p. 135, n.39.

[4] Upon this foundation one portion of the canon theories cited above I, 50, n. 1, is built; cf. e.g., P. Drews, *Zur Entstehungsgeschichte des Kanons in der römischen Messe* (Tübingen, 1902; especially p. 23), who placed the three following prayers after the consecration, before the *Memento etiam.* Fortescue, 328 f., also complains of the incomprehensibility of the *igitur.*

[5] The question is, for what idea in the prayer now to begin is the *igitur* supposed to

supply a link with the motivation or explanation in the prayer which precedes? Among others, the address *clementissime Pater* is mentioned, since the address to the Father is also contained in the preface (J. de Puniet, *De liturgie der mis.* [Roermond, 1939], 196 f., and already F. X. Funk, *Kirchengeschichtliche Abhandlungen,* III, [Paderborn, 1907], 87 f.); the formula per *Jesum Christum* that is also in the preface (Brinktrine, *Die hl. Messe,* 175); the *supplices* of the invocation for acceptance, because it once again takes up the *supplici confessione dicentes* (Baumstark, "Das 'Problem' des römischen Messkanons" [*Eph. liturg.,* 1939], 241 f.); the trustful *rogare,* because the way of God is opened through the mediation of the angels (J. Bona, *De sacrificio missæ,* V. 8 (Bibliotheca ascetica, 7; Regensburg, 1913, 119]); the *rogamus ac petimus uti accepta habeas* in which the oblation prayer of the Secreta is again taken up (V. Thalhofer, *Handbuch der katholischen Liturgik,* II, [Freiburg, 1890], 199); finally the *benedicas,* because only holy gifts are due to the Holy God, whom we have thrice praised as holy (Eisenhofer, II, 173).

[6] Cf. in this sense Batiffol, *Leçons,* 237. Likewise already Odo of Cambrai (d. 1113), *Expositio in canonem missæ,* c. 1 (PL, 160, 1055 A).

Holy Saturday *Exultet,* the *laus cerei,* with the oblation that follows,[7] only in our case the juncture is even closer and more natural. We must try to remember how closely conjoined in ancient Christian thought were the concepts of thanksgiving and offering. What up to the third century was prevailingly styled a thanksgiving: εὐχαριστία, was thereafter usually called an offering, *oblatio.*[8] The Mass is a thanksgiving which culminates in the offering of a holy gift; it is an offering which is so spiritual that it appears to be only a thanksgiving. The expressions, *sacrificium laudis* and *oblatio rationabilis,* stress within the Roman canon itself this spirituality of the sacrifice. On the other hand, we must not see in the *Gratias agamus* simply an invitation to give thanks by word only. A Christian *gratias agere* is meant, a *eucharistia,* a thanksgiving which terminates sacrificially in the self-oblation of Christ. Therefore it was possible occasionally to enlarge the *Gratias agamus* in the sense of an oblation,[9] just as the expression of thanks within the preface was associated with paraphrases of the notion of sacrifice. This latter proceeding is to be found in extra-Roman liturgies [10] as well as in the Roman.[11] The intermixture of expressions of thanks and sacrifice is particularly noticeable in the second portion of a *eucharistia* cited among the Arian fragments, a piece bearing evident resemblances to the *Te igitur:*

> *Dignum et iustum est* . . . [a description of the work of redemption follows].
> *Cuius benignitatis agere gratias tuæ tantæ magnanimitati quibusque laudibus nec sufficere possumus, petentes de tua magna et flexibili pietate accepto ferre sacrificium istud, quod tibi offerimus stantes ante conspectum*

---

[7] *In huius igitur noctis gratia suscipe, sancte Pater, incensi huius sacrificium vespertinum.* The *præconium,* which is then resumed, is once more switched, by means of the equipollent *ergo* into the prayer of petition *Oramus ergo te Domine.*
[8] *Supra,* I, 23 ff.; 169 ff. In embryo the idea of an oblation was already presented in the Jewish *berachah; Dix, The Shape of the Liturgy,* 272; cf. *supra,* I, 21, note 63.
[9] *Supra,* p. 114.
[10] Cf. the liturgy of St. Basil in the fundamental form which must be considered pre-Basil, *supra,* p. 126, n. 62. In the anaphora of St. Mark the thanksgiving prayer in the fragments of the 4th century also switches over at once into an offering . . . Ἰησοῦ Χριστοῦ, δι' οὗ σοί . . . εὐχαριστοῦντες προσφέρομεν τὴν θυσίαν τὴν λογικήν, τὴν ἀναίμακτον λατρείαν ταύτην; Quasten, *Mon.,* 44 f.; cf. Brightman, 126; 165.— Within the Gallic liturgical sphere the idea of oblation is presented in two Sunday prefaces of the *Missale Gothicum*

(Muratori, II, 648 f., 652), a document in which the preface is generally designated as *immolatio,* just as in the Mozarabic it is captioned *illatio.*
[11] A Christmas preface found both in the Leonianum and in the Gelasian Sacramentary (Mohlberg, n. 27; cf. sources, p. 293) begins: *VD. Tuæ laudis hostiam immolantes,* whereupon Old Testament prototypes of the Christian sacrifice and their realization at Christmas are described. For more examples in the Leonianum see Muratori I, 303 (12, n. XXIV), 403; cf. also above, 122 f. Besides this the Leonianum presents a transitional formula to the *Sanctus* that is relevant here, it reads (on the feast of Martyrs: . . . *quorum gloriam hodierna die recolentes) hostias tibi laudis offerimus, cum angelis, etc.* (Muratori, I, 296; also I, 332; 392): or: . . . *hostias tibi laudis offerimus. Per.* (*ibid.,* 336, 391, 396, 397); or also: . . . *hostias tibi laudis offerimus, etc., (ibid.,* 318).

tuæ divinæ pietatis, Per Jesum Christum Dominum et Deum nostrum, per quem petimus et rogamus.[12]

In a word, the *Te igitur* and its plea for acceptance merely take up the thread of thought begun in the preface, putting it in a definite form, with an eye on the gifts.

In accord with this resumption of the thought after the slight pause in the *Sanctus*, both the term of address and the formula of mediation are repeated. The address, however, is no longer in the solemn, three-section form as found in the beginning of the preface, but merely a simple phrase, *clementissime Pater*, corresponding to the second section, *sancte Pater*. This confident term, otherwise scarcely to be met, is probably inspired by the nearness of the grace-laden mystery.[13] Regarding the formula of mediation, the remarkable thing here is that it appears not at the end of a prayer or of a segment of prayer, as it otherwise always does, but at the beginning. Here it is plainly a supplement to the *rogamus ac petimus*: we carry our petitions before God's throne through our advocate and mediator Jesus Christ. The union of the faithful with the exalted Christ is here so vividly clear that it enters into the prayer even without the impetus of a closing formula.

The plea for acceptance is a reverently reserved form of offering, as the word *supplices* and the deep bow that accompanies it likewise indicate. The gifts are not yet dedicated, but we realize that they must be accepted just as they must be dedicated or consecrated; hence the words: *uti accepta habeas et benedicas*. In this petition for a blessing, taken strictly, is contained a plea for the transformation. It is, then, the start of an *epiklesis*, much like those found in some *secreta* formulas,[14] or like the *Quam oblationem* where the epiklesis will appear more formally and extensively. It is significant that in the Georgian liturgy of St. Peter, which represents in its core a tenth-century translation of the Roman canon, a real epiklesis is inserted in this spot.[15] The gifts themselves are indicated by a threefold designation: *hæc dona, hæc munera, hæc sancta sacrificia*

---

[12] G. Mercati, *Antiche reliquie liturgiche,* (Rome, 1902), 52 f. Note especially the phrases *agere gratias* and *petentes de tua pietate, accepto ferre sacrificium istud.*

[13] Cf. *elevatis oculis in cœlum ad te, Deum Patrem suum omnipotentem* in the account of the institution. The name of Father is otherwise very rare, even in the older Roman liturgy. Some few instances appear in the Leonianum: Muratori, I, 304 f. 320, 447.

[14] *Supra* 95.—Cf. also *supra* 65 ff.

[15] H. W. Codrington, *The Liturgy of St. Peter* (LQF, 30; Münster, 1936), 158, in which the Georgian text is reproduced as follows: *nous nous prosternons et te*

prions de reçevoir et de bénir ces dons qui sont à toi et d'envoyer ton Esprit-Saint sur ces dons ici présents et sur ce sacrifice, pourque tu l'acceptes avec bienveillance, que nous t'offrons d'abord . . . The opinion of Baumstark (Mohlberg-Baumstark, *Die ältestete erreichbare Gestalt*, 33*) that this epiklesis is to be regarded as a piece of fundamental Roman text lost at an early date, is no longer tenable. It is, rather, as the crude form of the interpolation proves, a later additional insertion, which goes back to Egyptian influence and which, moreover, is missing in the traditional text of the liturgy of St. Peter; Codrington, 47 f., 182. An idea very like this, namely,

illibata. We cannot put too much store in this tri-membered expression.[16] In the formulas of the secret prayer all three terms are used to designate the same thing, namely the material gifts. In our passage they are merely juxtaposed in order to emphasize the expression, in accordance with a stylistic law that also operates elsewhere in the canon. A certain gradation, however, is plainly discernible; first the gifts are just called *dona,* gifts such as we are accustomed in some way or other to exchange from man to man; [17] as *munera* they appear a result of a more fixed arrangement, as a public service;[18] and finally as *sacrificia* they are labeled as the sacred tribute dedicated to God.[19]

It is not improbable that in the first version of the Roman canon, in the form it had till about the end of the fourth century, the plea for an acceptance of the gifts,[20] as here outlined, was followed at once by the *Quam*

that God might bless the gifts through the Holy Ghost (*ut hæc spiritu tuo benedicas*), is also read into the words of the Roman Canon by Florus Diaconus, *De actione miss.,* c. 44 (PL, 119, 44); Botte, *Le canon,* 52 f.

[16] Brinktrine, *Die hl. Messe,* 176, taking a hint from *Ordo Rom.* I, n. 48, would see in this a reference to the three separate hosts that were laid upon the separate corporals of the co-consecrating cardinals (this is not the only mention of the number three; cf. above, p. 44). A different interpretation is given by E. Peterson, Dona, munera, sacrificia: *Eph. liturg.,* 46 (1932) 75-77. Reference is made to a parallel in the liturgy of St. Mark (Brightman, 129, 1. 20 f. in which the prayer is said to accept the θυσίαι, προςφοραί, εὐχαριστήρια; accordingly εὐχαριστήρια (= *dona*) is taken to stand for offerings for the dead; προςφοραί (= *munera*) for the offerings for the living; and θυσίαι (= *sacrificia*) for the oblations that are to be consecrated.

[17] An indication of the sharp retrenchment which gradually took place in the consideration of the role of the Church in the sacrifice (cf. *supra,* I, 91) is the fact that already Innocent III, *De s. alt. mysterio,* III, 3 (PL, 217, 841 B), no longer understands *dona* to mean the gifts which we offer God but the gift that God makes to us in the person of His Son (corresponding then to the interpretation of *munera* and *sacrificia* as the actions of Judas and

of the Jews). This explanation is later repeated by others. But it is strange that Eisenhofer, II, 173, still considers *dona* as "gifts of God."

[18] For a treatment of *munera* as equivalent to λειτουργία, meaning a public work in both the profane and the religious sense, see O. Casel "λειτουργία—munus,"*Oriens christianus,* 3rd ser., 7 (1932), 289-302; H. Frank, "Zu λειτουργία — munus," JL, 13 (1935), 181-185.

[19] See above, p. 94, with regard to *sacrificium* as a designation for a material gift. Even the expression *sancta sacrificia illibata* no more requires the accomplished consecration than the addition of the words *sanctum sacrificium, immaculatam hostiam* in regard to the sacrifice of Melchisedech demanded for the latter a sacramental sanctification. *Illibata* refers to the natural lack of blemish that was always demanded in a sacrificial offering; cf. *Batiffol, Leçons,* 238. At all events the thought that the consecration would soon take place may well have been a contributing factor in bringing this notion of holiness to the fore; cf. perhaps Gihr, 634.

[20] Cfr. above I, 55, n. 21. One would then have to surmise that the petition for acceptance contained only the *accepta habeas,* because the petition for a blessing is especially stressed in the *Quam oblationem.* As a matter of fact, the *et benedicas* is missing in the Sacramentary of Gellone (Botte, 32, Apparatus), but this, of course, is rather a secondary matter.

oblationem and the consecration. This design was then disrupted by the interjection of the intercessory prayers.[21]

7. General Intercessory Prayers

About the end of the fourth century intercessory prayers began to be inserted into the Great Prayer even in Rome, just as had become customary in the Orient perhaps since the beginning of the same century.[1] As we have already seen in Justin's account, intercessory prayers were conjoined to the eucharistic celebration,[2] but they preceded the *eucharistia* and formed the conclusion of the service of prayer and reading.[3] It is in this very same place that we have located the "General Prayer of the Church," even down to the present time, although here a process of contraction set in quite early.[4] As a result the core of the intercessory prayer, in the Roman liturgy as well as in others, was transferred to the inner sanctuary of the eucharistic prayer. Only the Gallic liturgies withstood this development, so that to the last—and in the Mozarabic Mass right down to the present—the intercessions remained standing outside the gates of the eucharistic prayer, in the portion of the Mass given over to preparing the gifts. In the Roman Mass the intercessions, as we know them at the present, were remodeled in the course of the fifth century and built into the canon between the *Sanctus* and the prayer for the consecration in the *Quam oblationem,* and the corresponding remembrance of the dead was then added after the consecration.

If we may perceive in the *orationes sollemnes* of Good Friday the General Prayer of the Church as it appeared in the primitive Roman liturgy,[5] we are struck by the strong contrast between these ancient intercessions and the newer type constructed within the canon. In the latter, the formulation would, as a matter of course, have to be more brief. But only echoes of the former type that really recur are the prayer *pro ecclesia sancta Dei,*

[21] That something new is inaugurated with *in primis* was sensed even later on. Cf. e.g., Ebner, 16, the illustration of the beginning of the canon from Codex, 2247 of Cologne (11th cent.) ; *in primis* has an initial just the same as *Memento* and *Communicantes.* Hugo of S. Cher (d. 1263), *Tract. super missam* (ed., Sölch, 27) has the second of his eleven parts of the canon begin with *in primis.*

[1] Above I, 53 ff.

[2] Above I, 22 f. Petitions, together with the mentioning of names, must also have been made in the sacrifice that took place in the divine service of the Jewish temple; cf. I Macc. 12: 11.

[3] At any rate Justin, Apol., I, 67, 5, para-phrases the Eucharistic prayer as εὐχὰς ὁμοίως καὶ εὐχαριστίας. Herewith, however, in agreement with I, 65, 3, the εὐχαί are rather to be understood as coupling the αἶνος καὶ δόξα that are mentioned in the latter passage before the εὐχαριστία. Outside of that, Justin's *Eucharistia* must have included a prayer for an efficacious Communion; cf. above I, 35, 37. The view advocated by Baumstark among others, *JL*, 1 (1921), 6, that a prayer of petition is already to be assumed within the Eucharistia of Justin, is, in the face of further facts, not acceptable.

[4] Above I, 480 ff.

[5] Above I, 481 f.

the prayer *pro beatissimo papa nostro,* and the prayer *pro omnibus epis-copis,* etc.—and this last only in more recent texts—while the prayer for the Church in the canon accords with its model all the more plainly since in both petition is made for peace, protection, and unity for the Church *toto orbe terrarum.* The explanation lies in the fact that, as Innocent I tells us, the chief concern was the mention of the names within the canon, that therefore the main stress was on the *Memento;* and, on the other hand, the General Prayer for the Church still continued in use. Besides this, the prayer for the emperor appears to have actually had its place here in the fifth century.[6] The prayer for the catechumens, of whom there were but few, would naturally have been considered no longer so opportune as to require a place in the canon.[7] The prayer for heretics, Jews, and pagans, however, as it appeared in the *orationes sollemnes,* was somewhat of a specialty of Rome's, in comparison with the other liturgies; it therefore continued to be restricted to the *orationes sollemnes.* These *orationes sollemnes* seem not to have been excluded entirely from the ordinary service until a suitable substitute appeared in the *Kyrie* litany.[8] The *deprecatio Gelasii,* which we took as evidence for this inference, includes in its seventeen petitions all nine titles of the *orationes sollemnes.*[9]

In the canon the pertinent names ought to have been spoken simply with a brief accompanying phrase. The framework provided for this is the *Memento,* with the short preliminary piece beginning with the words *in primis.* Somewhat later the *Communicantes* sprouted from the same root, and lastly the *Hanc igitur* took its place alongside as an independent structure. If the rights of the individual should thus be acknowledged in the very sanctuary of the liturgy, then it is only right and proper that at the head of the list of names should appear the first name of the Christian community and the community itself. The sacrifice which we offer up humbly to God, and which should, in the first instance, be our thanks and our tribute to our Creator and Father, will also draw down upon us God's protection and grace precisely because it is a sacrifice and because it is this sacrifice. May it be of avail above all [10] for the whole Catholic Church!

---

[6] Above I, 53.

[7] However, we must certainly take into account the possibility that, like the mentioning of the emperor, it was dropped later on.

[8] Above I, 336 ff.

[9] The prayer to God *ut cunctis mundum purget erroribus,* etc., is also contained therein; cf. above I, 337, VIII; IX.

[10] The *in primis* is considered meaningless by P. Drews, *Zur Entstehungsgeschichte des Kanons in der römischen Messe* (Tübingen, 1902), 5, n. 1, "since various gifts were not offered." Likewise R. Buchwald,

Die Epiklese in der römischen Messe (Weidenauer Studien I, special printing; Vienna, 1907), 34 f. However, the *in primis* is not intended to introduce various offerings, but various recommendations united with the offering. The *in primis quæ* would, therefore, be rendered as "above all insofar as we . . ." Evidently, too, these words convey a quiet reason for their acceptance; we offer the gifts "for" the entire holy Church, for her benefit, and also as her humble representative here and now.

The prayer for the whole Church was a matter very close to the heart of the primitive Christians. Well known are the prayers of the *Didache* (9,4; 10,5). When Bishop Polycarp of Smyrna (d. 155-156), upon being arrested, begged for a little time to pray, he prayed aloud for all whom he had known and for the whole Catholic Church, spread over the world."[11] Another martyr-bishop, Fructuosus of Tarragona (d. 259), about to be burnt to death, answered a Christian who sought his prayer, saying in a firm voice: "I am bound to remember the whole Catholic Church from sunrise to sunset."[12]

Only two attributes are joined to the mention of the Church, but in them its entire greatness is made manifest. The Church is *holy;* it is the assembly of those who are sanctified in water and in the Holy Spirit. *Sancte* is the earliest of the adjectives customarily attached to the mention of the Church. And it is *Catholic;* according to God's plan of grace, the Church is appointed for all peoples, and at the time this word was inserted into the canon it could be said triumphantly that it was actually spread to all peoples, *toto orbe terrarum*—an expression that merely serves to underscore the *Catholica*.[13] What we petition for the Church is peace (*pacificare*), or putting it negatively, defense from every threat of danger (*custodire*), so that she might bring forth rich fruit, so that the leaven of the divine power within her might penetrate every level of human society. For the Church internally we follow the example of the Master Himself (John 17:21) by asking above all for unity: that she might continue to be guarded against division and error, that she might be held together through love, the bond of the one family of God (*adunare*), and that the Spirit of God Himself might lead and govern her (*regere*).[14]

This leads on to the mention of those through whom the Spirit of God wills to direct the Church and hold it together as a visible society. In other rites, too, since earliest times, we find that at the start of the intercessory prayer the mention of the Church is followed at once by that name which visibly represents the leadership of the Church.[15] Often the

---

[11] *Martyrium Polycarpi*, c. 8, 1; cf. 5, 1.
[12] Ruinart, *Acta Martyrum* (Regensburg, 1859; 266).
[13] The formula is already verified in liturgical practice in the 11th century by Optatus of Mileve, *Contra Parmen.*, II, 12 (CSEL, 26, 47): *offerre vos dicitis Deo pro una Ecclesia, quæ sit in toto terrarum orbe diffusa.* In this reference Optatus presumes that the Donatists had retained this prayer since their break with the Church in 312. It is possible that the phrase in the canon is linked with the fact that since the 4th century the original meaning of *catholica* was weakened more

and more to a mere antithesis to heresy. Botte, *Le canon*, 54.
[14] Regarding this petition Pope Vigilius (d. 555), *Ep. ad Justin*, c. 2 (SCEL, 35, 348) has given direct testimony: *omnes pontifices antiqua in offerendo sacrificio traditione deposcimus, exorantes, ut catholicam fidem adunare, regere Dominus et custodire toto orbe dignetur.*
[15] At Antioch in the 4th century the celebrant (who is presumably the Patriarch himself) mentions his own person immediately after the invocation for the whole Church, *Const. Ap.*, VIII, 12, 41 (Quasten, *Mon.*, 225): Ἔτι παρακαλοῦμέν σε καὶ

view does not extend beyond the bishop. In the Roman canon the words in this passage that represent the traditional basic text are the words *una cum famulo tuo papa nostro illo*,[16] whereupon the *Memento* follows at once. But outside of Rome these words were soon expanded in various ways. In the Frankish realm during the sixth century the title *papa* could, for example, mean any bishop;[17] therefore we find various clarifying additions that univocally designate the Roman pontiff.[18] More and more since the sixth century the naming of the pope in the intercessory prayer became a fixed rule in the churches of the West. In Milan and Ravenna the custom existed already about 500.[19] In the year 519 two bishops from an episcopal city of Epirus tell about it.[20] In the year 529, at the urgent insistence of St. Cæsarius of Arles, the practice was prescribed by the Council of Vaison for that section.[21] Pope Pelagius (d. 561) desired the Bishops of Tuscany to mention his name at Mass: *quomodo vos ab universi orbis communione separatos esse non creditis, si mei inter sacra mysteria secundum consuetudinem nominis memoriam reticetis.*[22] At Constantinople, too, during the sixth century the name of the pope was mentioned in the diptychs, and since the time of Justinian it was put in the first place.[23]

In Italian manuscripts especially, up to the eleventh century, the pope is often named alone.[24] But outside of Rome the name of the bishop could not long be omitted. That name appears with increasing regularity, usually

---

ὑπὲρ τῆς ἐμῆς τοῦ προςφέροντός σοι οὐδενίας καὶ ὑπὲρ παντὸς τοῦ πρεσβυτερίου. In the 7th century anaphora of St. James "our patriarchs N. N." are mentioned by name in this place; Rücker, 214 f.; cf. Brightman, 89 f. The correspondence of these intercessions (namely by the incorporation of the diaconal litany) with the Roman formula under consideration was used by P. Drews for all it was worth in his theory of the canon; cf. Fortescue, 157 f.; 329.

[16] Botte, *Le canon*, 33. Several of the oldest manuscripts have *beatissimo famulo tuo*. This is possibly the primitive reading. Cf. Brinktrine, 178.—Dix, *The Shape of the Liturgy*, 501, seeks to associate the expression under consideration with the *Memento* of the living: *Una cum famulo tuo . . . memento, Domine.* Aside from the fact that it is difficult to approve this assumption on stylistic grounds and that it has no support in tradition, the point against it is that in this way the naming of the Pope would have to be considered as a mere side issue.

[17] Gregory of Tours, *Hist. Franc.*, II, 27

(PL, 71, 223 A). On the other hand, *papa* for the naming of the Pope was used already in the year 400 at the Council of Toledo. P. Batiffol, "Papa, sedes apostolica, apostolatus," *Revista di Archeologia Cristiana*, 2 (1925), 99-116, especially 102; idem., *Leçons*, 241 f. Cf. H. Leclerq, "Papa": DACL, XIII (1937) 1097-1111.

[18] Thus, in the Irish Stowe Missal (about 800): *sedis apostolicæ episcopo.* Ebner, 398.

[19] Ennodius, *Libellus de synodo*, c. 77 (CSEL, 6, 311); E. Bishop, "The diptychs" (Appendix to Connolly, *The Liturgical Homilies of Narsai*), 113, n. 2.

[20] Hormisdas, *Ep.*, 59, 2 (CSEL, 35, 672): *nullius nomen obnoxium religionis est recitatum nisi tantum beatitudinis vestræ.*

[21] Can. 4 (Mansi, VIII, 727): *Et hoc nobis justum visum est, ut nomen domini papæ, quicumque sedis apostolicæ præfuerit in nostris ecclesiis recitetur.*

[22] Pelagius I., *Ep.*, 5 (PL, 69, 398 C).

[23] Bishop, *op. cit.*, 111; 104, n. 1.

[24] Ebner, 398.

with the wording: *et antistite nostro illo.*[25] The further supplement: *et omnibus orthodoxis atque catholicæ et apostolicæ fidei cultoribus,* is also found first outside Rome, in Gallic territory,[26] and this at a surprisingly early date.[27]

Who are meant by the *orthodoxi?* The word could designate simply those who were sound and solid in doctrine, the Catholic Christians.[28] The same meaning is conveyed by the complementary phrase, *catholicæ et apostolicæ fidei cultores,* a phrase appended in conformity with a stylistic law of the canon which prefers twin-type expressions. The only difference is that the latter phrase designates in the first place those who esteem the Catholic and apostolic faith [29] and who consciously profess it.[30] The first-named *cultores fidei* are obviously, then, the shepherds of the Church, the bishops. A confirmatory argument to show that they, and not simply the faithful, are meant by the double expression, is found in the construction *una cum,* which would otherwise be meaningless; may God, we say, protect the Church (which is composed of the faithful as a unit), along with the pope and all those who, as faithful pastors, have a part in her governance.[31] But in more recent times, when the tautology that arose in connection with *Ecclesia tua* was no longer sensed, the expression was taken to refer to all the faithful; it was opposed as superflu-

---

[25] Thus already some of the oldest MSS. The MS. of the older Gelasianum (1st half of the 8th cent.) has *et antistite nostro illo episcopo;* Botte, 32. The naming of the abbot also occurs; see examples in Ebner, 100, 163, 302; Martène, 1, 4, 8, 7, (I, 403 D).—The celebrating bishop, *resp.* the pope, substitutes in place of the usual formula *me indigno famulo tuo.* Eisenhofer, II, 175.

[26] Bishop, *Liturgica historica,* 82.

[27] In the Bobbio Missal (about 700) the entire addition has the following form: *una cum devotissimo famulo tuo ill. papa nostro sedis apostolicæ et antistite nostro et omnibus orthodoxis atque catholicæ fidei cultoribus.* Lowe, *The ·Bobbio Missal* (HBS, 58), n. 11; Muratori, II, 777. Cf. also the study of B. Capelle, "Et omnibus orthodoxis atque catholicæ fidei cultoribus," *Miscellanea hist. Alb. de Mayer,* I (Louvain, 1946), 137-150. Capelle advocates the assumption that the supplement belonged to the original text of the canon, but that it was deleted by Gregory the Great. See *Eph. liturg.,* 61 (1947), 281 f.

[28] *Orthodoxus* in opposition to *hæreticus,* e.g., in Jerome, *Ep.,* 17, 2.

[29] The expression was current in the 5th century. Gelasius, *Ep.,* 43 (Thiel, 472); the pope designates himself *minister catholicæ et apostolicæ fidei.*

[30] Cyprian, *Ep.,* 67, 6 (CSEL, 3, 740, 1. 11): *fidei cultor ac defensor veritatis* (regarding a bishop). There is an undertone of conscious pride in the inscription *Quis tantas Christo venerandas condidit ædes, Si quæris: cultor Pammachius fidei,* at the entrance to the Basilica of John and Paul. Here the expression certainly does not designate a bishop.—Brinktrine, *Die hl. Messe,* 176, refers to the parallel *cultor Dei,* II Macc. 1 : 19; John 9 : 31. He therefore clings to the interpretation of this phrase as referring to all the faithful.—A. Mauretanian inscription of the 3rd century designates the Christian as *cultor verbi;* C. M. Kaufmann, *Handbuch der altchristlichen Epigraphik* (Freiburg, 1917), 127.

[31] Cf. Capelle, *loc. cit.,* who stresses the tautology that would otherwise ensue. Moreover, mentioning the names of bishops of leading metropolises must have been customary in the 5th century in Rome as well as elsewhere; this is obviously to be deduced from a writing of Leo the

ous, for example, by Micrologus, adducing the rather poor argument, among others, that the *Memento* followed.[32]

The civil authorities, for whom St. Paul, even in the time of Nero, earnestly desired the prayer of the faithful community (1 Tim. 2:2), get no mention in the Mass of the city of Rome. This is understandable, considering the time from which the oldest extant manuscripts derive, for then the pope was, in point of fact at least, the civil lord of the "Papal" State. Hardly a shadow of the eastern Roman empire was any longer noticeable.[33] In the preceding centuries, on the contrary, prayer for the emperor was decidedly a part of the canon.[34] In the Milanese form of the Roman canon, representing a text taken over from Rome perhaps already before Gregory the Great,[35] the prayer for the ruler is still to be found,[36] and this is true also in other isolated instances.[37] When the Roman Empire was revived in the year 800, the mention of the emperor occurs at first

Great to the Patriarch of Constantinople, *Ep.*, 80, 3 (PL, 54, 914 f.). Cf. Kennedy, *The Saints*, 24; Duchesne, *Christian Worship*, 179 f. In the 11th century there are again reports regarding attempts to introduce the practice; see Martène, 1, 4, 8 (I, 403 E). The Missa Illyrica, which belongs to this period, seems to have so construed our formula, when it gives its version: *et pro omnibus orthodoxis atque catholicæ fidei cultoribus, pontificibus et abbatibus, gubernatoribus et rectoribus Ecclesiæ sanctæ Dei, et pro omni populo sancto Dei*: Martène, 1, 4, IV (I, 513 C).

[32] Bernold of Constance, *Micrologus*, c. 13 (PL, 151, 985). Bernold's reasoning is not pertinent, because in the *Memento* the prayer is said only for the offerants and those present, whereas we are considering prayers for the faithful of the whole Church in general; thus also H. Ménard, PL, 78, 275 B—The *Sacramentarium Rossianum* (10th cent.; ed. Brinktrine [Freiburg, 1930], p. 74) has the specific addition *ominum videlicet catholicorum* joined to *famularumque tuarum*.

[33] But for the mention of the Byzantine emperor in the Roman liturgy of the 8-9th century, cf. J. Biehl, *Das liturgische Gebet für Kaiser u. Reich*, 54, 55 f.

[34] Cf. *supra*, I, 53, 54.—Tertullian, *Apol.*, c. 39, 3 (Floril. patr., 6, 110), is witness to common prayer *pro imperatoribus*. Cf. J.Lortz, *Tertullian als Apologet* (Münster, 1927), 292 f.; Archbp. J. Beran, "De ordine missæ sec. Tertulliani Apologeti-

cum" (*Miscellanea Mohlberg*, II, 7-32), 12 ff.

[35] Cf. P. Lejay, "*Ambrosien* (Rit.)": DACL, I, 1421.

[36] In the Sacramentary of Biasca (9-10th cent.) the addition reads: *cum famulo tuo et sacerdote tuo pontifice nostro illo et famulo tuo imperatore illo regibusque nostris cum conjugibus et prolis, sed omnibus orthodoxis.* Ebner, 77; A. Ratti-M. Magistretti, *Missale Ambrosianum duplex* (Milan, 1913), 415. Cf. a similar formulary in the MS. edited by J. Pamelius, *Liturgica Latina*, (Cologne, 1571), 301: *et famulo tuo N. imperatore sed et regibus.* The plural specifically recalls the prayer in the Mass *pro regibus*, as verified in Milan by the Ambrosianum (above I, 53). Therefore, it is not necessary to suggest a reference to the rulers of the Carlovingian provinces since the division of the empire in 843, as Biehl, 57 does. An Ambrosian MS. adduced by Muratori, I, 131, merely presents *et famulo tuo (illo) imperatore.* The simple naming of the emperor is still found in the Milan Missal of 1751, but quite naturally no longer in that of 1902; Ratti-Magistretti, 240.—The view that in the naming of the emperor at Milan we have a residue of an even older Roman custom, is held by Kennedy, *The Saints*, 21, 48, 189.—Batiffol, *Leçons*, 243, n. 2, shows, with a reference to the Leonianum, how strongly the prayer for the Roman empire corresponded to the attitude of the Roman Church at the end of the ancient era. [37] Biehl, 37 f.

only in some few examples.[38] A more frequent occurrence is not noticed till the eleventh century [39] and by this time, because of the trouble arising over investiture, it was again challenged, as erasures and deletions in the text of the canon frequently show.[40] In general, however, it was retained. Commentators on the Mass since the twelfth century refer to it without question.[41] The formula is either: *et imperatore nostro,* or (at first with the same meaning): *et rege nostro.*[42] Later, both emperor and king are mentioned together or—an indication of the growing sense of territorialism—the *rege nostro* is understood of the king alone as the ruler of the land.[43]

The *Missale secundum usum Romanæ Curiæ* of the thirteenth century, which originated in an atmosphere of ecclesiastico-political strife, mentions only pope and bishop.[44] Because of its general acceptance, and because of the Missal of Pius V which was founded on it, mention of the civil ruler was generally discontinued.[45] It was only by way of privilege that the monarch was mentioned in the canon; this custom prevailed in Spain in former times,[46] and since 1761 in Austria,[47] with the latter custom continuing till 1918.[48] In the framework of the formula *una cum,* which can comprise only the heads of Catholic Christendom, the naming of the

[38] As his correspondence with Byzantium shows (MGH, Ep. Karol. Aevi, V, 387), Emperor Louis II seems to have presumed that his name was mentioned *inter sacra mysteria, inter sancta sacrificia,* but hardly only in the Greek Church; cf. Biehl, 55 f. If the name of the emperor does appear in the Sacramentaries before the 10th century, as in the Cod. Eligii (PL, 78, 26: *et rege nostro ill.*), it is each time only by way of exception. Among the commentators of the Mass until Bonizo of Sutri (d. about 1095) there is no mention of it at all; Biehl, 48 ff.

[39] Ebner, 398.

[40] Ebner, 399; Biehl, 60 f.

[41] Biehl, 49-53; Sölch, *Hugo,* 89 f. Cf. also William of Melitona, *Opusc. super missam,* ed. van Dijk (*Eph. liturg.,* 1939), 333.

[42] As Egeling of Brunswick (d. 1481) later explains, by the word *rex* was to be understood the *constitutus in suprema dignitate laicali.* Franz, 548.

[43] Thus frequently, though not universally, among the German Mass commentators at the end of the Middle Ages; Biehl, 51 f., 58. Regarding countries outside of Germany, cf. Biehl, 58 f.; for Spain, Ferreres, 146 f.

[44] That deference to the Pope as secular

ruler of the Papal States was the deciding factor in this case, as, among others, Sölch, 90, surmises, is difficult to accept; for the emperor's name was mentioned elsewhere outside his territory. Innocent III, *De s. alt. mysterio,* III, 5, (PL, 217, 844), indeed notes that only outside Rome is the prayer also said for the bishop, but with an appeal to I Tim. 2: 2, he requires the prayer for the secular ruler without any restriction.

[45] That holds for all rites influenced by this Missal. Even at present the Dominican Missal has the addition *et rege nostro;* cf. regarding it, Sölch, 91.

[46] Guéranger, *Institutions liturgiques,* I, 454 f. For France see *ibid.,* 471 f.

[47] Biehl, 62 f. The privilege was approved in Austria by a decree of the Congregation of Rites, Feb. 10, 1860, reproduced in Biehl, 170-173.

[48] But elsewhere, too, the sovereign was frequently named. Different moralists, e.g., even P. Scavini (d. 1869), speak of a *consuetudo* that became a matter of law; see Kössing, *Liturgische Vorlesungen,* 471, n. 244.—*Ibid.,* 468-471, Kössing objects to the thesis of A. J. Binterim, *Uber das Gebet für die Könige und Fürsten in der Katholischen Liturgie* (reprint from the

ruler is possible only in a Christian state.[49] For the rest, the great needs of the political order are expressed in the preceding *pacificare*, which necessarily implies a condition of ecclesiastical life tranquil and undisturbed.

8. The *Memento* of the Living

The decisive factor which brought about in the Roman Mass the division of the Great Prayer and the insertion of the intercessions was, as we learn from the letter of Pope Innocent I, the desire to mention *inter sacra mysteria* the names of those offering. The precise setting for this mention of names is the prayer that follows, *Memento Domine*, along with the *Communicantes*.[1] In the intercessory prayer of oriental liturgies the same words Μνήσθητι κύριε are used to introduce a whole series of petitions commending to God various groups of the faithful; these were at one time closely linked with the names from the diptychs.[2] In ecclesiastical life, especially in oriental Christendom, the diptychs have played a major role since the fourth century.[3]

Most prominent there were the diptychs of the dead, but besides these there were also special diptychs of the living, at least in Constantinople. Seemingly as early as the start of the sixth century, both were read out in a loud voice within the intercessory prayer that followed the con-

---

Memoirs, IV, 2; Mainz, 1827), according to which a special rubric to the effect that outside the Papal States the sovereign should be named, was omitted only because the mention of the name was taken for granted. In a decree of March 20, 1862, the Congregation of Rites expressly stated that the Catholic sovereign may be mentioned only by special indult to that effect; Gihr, 640, n. 26 (not contained in the authentic collections). — The recurrent movement is manifested even in the present years of Pius XII, in the insertion in the Austrian *Exsultet* of a petition for those *qui nos in potestate regunt;* cf. *Acta Ap. Sedis,* 43 (1951), 133 f.
[49] However, in this case other forms were chosen. The Sacramentary of the 10th century published by U. Chevalier, *Sacramentaire et Martyrologe de l'abbaye de S.-Remy* (Bibliothèque liturg., 2; Paris, 1900) continues after naming the bishop: *Memento, Domine, famulo tuo rege nostro ill. Memento Domine famulorum famularumque tuarum . . .*(344).—The same method is also found already about the year 800 in a Sacramentary of Angoulême

and, as a later supplement, in the Vat. Reg., 316; Botte, *Le canon,* 32, Apparatus. An example from the 11th century in Ebner, 163.
[1] The interrelation of the two formulas will occupy our attention again later on. That they belong together seems clear from the fact that the *Per Christum* comes only at the end of the second formula. On the other hand, there does not seem to be sufficient reason to take the *Te igitur,* which likewise lacks the concluding formula, into the same close relationship. For here the *Per Jesum Christum* is already woven into the beginning of the formula.
[2] Liturgy of St. James: Brightman, 55 ff.; liturgy of St. Mark: *ibid.,* 129 f.; Byzantine liturgy of St. Basil: *ibid.,* 336 (cf. 409). In the passages cited the τὰ δίπτυχα that the deacon is to read off, are explicitly named by the rubric. Examples of oriental diptych texts from the 12th, 15th, and 19th centuries in Brightman, 501-503, 551 f.
[3] E. Bishop, "The Diptychs," in the appendix to Connolly, *The Liturgical Homilies of Narsai,* 97-117; F. Cabrol, "Diptyques":

secration.[4] Regarding the δίπτυχα τῶν κεκοιμημένων, we know that they contained the names of prominent personages, above all in ecclesiastical life, but also in civil life, arranged in specified series starting with those of former bishops of the imperial city.[5] The insertion or omission of a name could thus at times cause a popular uproar, as happened at the beginning of the fifth century in the case of the name of St. John Chrysostom,[6] for the inclusion of a name in the diptychs indicated the attitude of the ecclesiastical community towards the person involved and its acknowledgment of his orthodoxy. Therefore, in oriental diptychs since the sixth century, we sometimes find at the top of the list, along with the "patriarchs, prophets, apostles and martyrs,"[7] mention of the fathers of the first councils, above all the "318 orthodox fathers" of Nicea.[8]

In the West, and particularly in the Roman liturgy, the listing of the names of the living takes the lead. Regarding the dead there is, as we shall see, no mention at this moment in public worship. This fits in with what we have already pointed to as the starting-point of the list, namely the offering of the sacrificial gifts of the faithful. Their offerings were to be commended to God by a special prayer, which is precisely what happened in the *oratio super oblata*. Besides this, there was within the canon an additional plea that God might be mindful of those *qui tibi*

DACL, IV, 1045-1094. δίπτυχον = twofold, double tablet. In ancient times they served as a sort of announcement book, which, because of their beautiful design, were presented as gifts by aristocratic people. In Church circles they were used for a list of names, even if, as was often the case, they were of purely secular origin. The covers were often inlaid on the outside with plates of precious metal or ivory and adorned with sculptured ornaments. Many of these precious ecclesical diptych tablets, among them some that date back to the Roman Consuls, were later used as covers for liturgical books and were thus preserved.
[4] Bishop, 109 ff. Elsewhere, as was frequently the case in the Syrian sphere, the diptychs were read while the people exchanged the kiss of peace; Bishop, 108, 111 f. In the East Syrian Rite the reading of the diptychs, the comprehensive "book of the living and the dead," is still done today by the deacon, at this place, on Sundays and feast days. The names of one's own community are included in these lists and they are no longer written on special tablets. In the Byzantine Mass mentioning the deceased by name is done silently by the priest, as happens in our *Memento*; Brightman, 388, 23.

[5] Cf. the arrangement in the diptychs according to the Armenian liturgy of today; Brightman, 441 f. Dix, *The Shape of the Liturgy*, 502-504, establishes the fact that the diptychs at least in Constantinople lost their original "parochial" character and finally also the character as a list of names noted down for the purpose of intercession.
[6] Bishop, 102 ff.
[7] Thus, already Cyril of Jerusalem, *Catech. myst.*, V, 9 (Quasten, *Mon.*, 102). Here there is no question of reading the names, though it is the case with Serapion; cf. *supra*, I, 35. In the East Syrian Mass the list that comprises several hundred begins with "Adam and Abel and Seth"; Brightman, 276 ff. Towards the end of the ancient era acceptance into the diptychs corresponded more or less to our canonization in the Church, just as a cancellation was equivalent to excommunication.
[8] Thus, in the East Syrian Mass: Brightman, 277, 1. 3; *in the Ethiopian anaphora* of the Apostles: *ibid.*, 229, 1. 2. The Monophysite West Syrians mention the "three pious and holy and ecumenical Synods": *ibid.*, 94, 1. 3. The "four holy synods" were named by the deacon in the reading of the diptych at the Synod of Con-

offerunt hoc sacrificium laudis. In this connection the names of the officers were read aloud. This much information can be gleaned from the exposition of Pope Innocent I,[9] but the account is so sketchy that we are left without any details of how it was done. There were probably only selected names, for obviously it was neither feasible nor reasonable to publish the names of all those who participated in the Sunday service.[10] On the other hand, it stood to reason that where the Mass was celebrated for the benefit of such and such group, as was the case in votive Masses for certain needs or certain occasions, the names involved would be read out.[11] In some instances this would be carried over to public service. The older *Gelasianum* presents an illustrative example on the third Sunday of Lent, on the occasion of the first *scrutinium electorum.* It reads as follows:

> *Infra canonem ubi dicit: Memento Domine famulorum famularumque tuarum, qui electos tuos suscepturi sunt ad sanctam gratiam baptismi tui, et omnium circumadstantium. Et taces. Et recitantur nomina virorum et mulierum, qui ipsos infantes suscepturi sunt. Et intras: Quorum tibi fides cognita.*[12]

While the priest is silent, another cleric reads aloud the names of the godparents or sponsors. At the ordinary service the only names mentioned

stantinople under Mennas (544). Cf. the references in Martène, 1, 4, 8, 11 (I, 405 B; I looked in vain for this in the acts of the council).—Elsewhere, too, a close watch was kept regarding the true faith of those whose names were read off in the canon. According to the *Pœnitentiale Theodori* (England, end of the 7th cent.) a priest, at whose Mass any names of heretics happened to be read off with the rest, was obliged to do penance for a week. H. J. Schmitz, *Die Bussbücher und die Bussdisziplin der Kirche,* (Mainz, 1883), 529; Finsterwalder, *Canones Theodori,* 258.

[9] Above I, 54.—Already a century earlier a similar custom must have existed in Spain, as appears from can. 29 of Elvira (Mansi, II, 10); regarding an *energumenus* the canon stipulates *neque ad altare cum oblatione esse recipiendum.* Cf. Bishop, 98 f. Cyprian, *Ep., 62, 5 (CSEL, 3, 700 f.),* is also worthy of note. When sending money to the Numidian bishops, Cyprian also transmits the names of those who gave it: *in mente habeatis orationibus vestris et eis vicem boni operis in sacrificiis et precibus repræsentetis.* See *Ep., 16, 2 (CSEL, 3, 519),* where he states accusingly with regard to the *lapsi: offertur nomine eorum.* What is alleged against this by Augustine refers only to the naming of the deceased; Kennedy, *The Saints, 27 f.;* Srawley, 137.

[10] Cf. *Capitulare eccl. ord.* (Silva-Tarouca, 205). No names of the deceased are permitted to be read off on Sundays, *sed tantum vivorum nomina regum vel principium seu et sacerdotum, vel pro omni populo christiano oblationes vel vota redduntur.*

[11] *Ordo "Qualiter quædam orationes"* = *Ordo Rom.* IV (Hittorp, 588; cf. PL, 78, 1380 B; Botte, 32, Apparatus): *Hic nomina vivorum memorentur si volueris, sed non dominica die nisi ceteris diebus.* Thus also the *Sacramentarium Rossianum* (Botte, 32, Apparatus) and Bernold of Constance, *Micrologus,* c. 23 (PL, 151, 985).

[12] I, 26 (Wilson, 34). It is self-evident that the names of the candidates for baptism could not be mentioned here, because the *qui tibi offerunt* could not be said of them. Their names, however, appear in the *Hanc igitur,* in which the purpose of the prayer was to be mentioned. The Roman expression *electi* for the candidates for baptism shows that the rubric originated in Rome and not in the Gallic territory where the MS. comes from. Consequently, we may take this as 6th century evidence.

would probably have been those which merited marked prominence for having given a special oblation over and above the liturgical offering of bread and wine.[13] This can be gathered from a somewhat testy remark of the hermit of Bethlehem, who had probably heard about the new practice at Rome: *ut . . . glorientur publiceque diaconus in ecclesiis recitet offerentium nomina: tantum offert illa, tantum ille pollicitus est, placentque sibi ad plausum populi.*[14]

A reading similar to that at Rome is evidenced beyond doubt in the domain of the Gallic liturgy, and here it is the offerers who are expressly named. The Gallican Mass of the seventh century—and likewise the Mozarabic—includes a special priestly oration *Post nomina* after the offertory procession and the introductory prayer. The wording of this oration is often linked to the reading of the names that just took place, then launches into a prayer of intercession for living and dead. An example is the prayer on the feast of the Circumcision: *Auditis nominibus offerentum, fratres dilectissimi, Christum Dominum deprecemur* [a reference to the feast follows] *. . . præstante pietate sua, ut hæc sacrificia sic viventibus proficiant ad emendationem, ut defunctis opitulentur ad requiem. Per Dominum.*[15] The reading itself, however, includes under the notion of *offerentes* not only those present, above all the clergy assembled here, but also all whose society is valued while the sacrifice is being offered up. Even the dead are embodied in this circle of offerers, either because those offering the sacrifice do so "for" them, that is, as their representatives, or that they "remember" them in the oblation. In the Mozarabic Mass this reading, which precedes the oration *Post nomina*, has been retained to the present.

> The priest [formerly it was perhaps the deacon] begins: *Offerunt Deo Domino oblationem sacerdotes nostri, papa Romensis et reliqui pro se et pro omni clero et plebibus ecclesiæ sibimet consignatis vel pro universa fraternitate. Item offerunt universi presbyteri, diaconi, clerici ac populi circumadstantes in honorem sanctorum pro se et suis.*
> R. [the choir corroborating]: *Offerunt pro se et pro universa fraternitate.*
> The priest: *Facientes commemorationem beatissimorum apostolorum et martyrum.*[16] [Names follow.]

---

[13] Cf. *supra*, p. 11.

[14] Jerome, *Comm. in Ezech.* (of the year 411), c. 18 (PL, 25, 175).—Cf. Jerome, *Comm. in Jerem.* (of the year 420): *At nunc publice recitantur offerentium nomina et redemptio peccatorum mutatur in laudem.* The practice was therefore considered an innovation. That Jerome is referring to a Western practice is clear also from this, that in oriental liturgy the names of the *offerentes*, as far as present information goes, never played such a part.

[15] *Missale Gothicum*, Muratori, II, 553; cf. 542 f., 554, etc. Such a Gallican *Post-*

nomina formula is still found in today's Roman Mass, in the Secreta that is supposed to be said in Lent: *Deus cui soli cognitus est numerus electorum in superna felicitate locandus.* Cf. Cabrol, *La messe en occident*, 120. A 6th century testimony for the reading of the names from an ivory diptych in Venantius Fortunatus, *Carm.*, X, 7 (MGH, Auct. ant., IV, 1, 240): *cui hodie in templo diptychus edit ebur.* He is referring to the names of King Childebert and his mother Brunehild. Cf. Bishop, 100, n. 1.

[16] This formula *Facientes* with a long list

R. *Et omnium martyrum.*
The priest: *Item pro spiritibus pausantium.* [A long roll of sainted confessors is listed: *Hilarii, Athanasii . . .*]
R. *Et omnium pausantium.*[17]

It is noteworthy that not till the second sentence is the word *offerunt* applied to those present, while in the first sentence it is ascribed in honorary fashion to the representatives of the grand ecclesiastical communion. It is probably to be presumed that originally the names of the persons in office—the leading bishops in Spain and the *papa Romensis*—were pronounced.[18] In the course of time this mention of names was omitted in favor of the bare formula, either because it was deemed unimportant or because it was found too bothersome.

Something like this must also have occurred in the Roman canon where the oldest extant manuscripts in general no longer have any indication whatever of an explicit listing of names after the words: *Memento Domine famulorum famularumque tuarum.*[19] But since the formula obviously implies it, the indication for such an insert was later restored, some way or other, even soon after the Roman Mass was transplanted to Frankish soil. In his *Admonitio Generalis* of 789 Charlemagne decreed: The names should not be publicly read at some earlier part of the Mass (as in the Gallican rite), but during the canon.[20] The express direction is then found variously in the Mass books.[21]

of names that followed is preserved on a diptychon that dates back to the Roman Consul Anastasius of the year 517 and that was in ecclesiastical use in Northern France. Cf. Leclerq, "Diptyques": DACL, IV, 1119 f.; Kennedy, *The Saints*, 65-67. [17] *Missale mixtum* (PL, 85, 542 ff.). *Pausantes* are those who "rest" (from worldly cares). It is to be noted here, however, that a summons on the part of the priest precedes this diptych formula, though it is separated from it (probably as a later and secondary intrusion) by an oration: *Ecclesiam sanctam catholicam in orationibus in mente habeamus ut eam Dominus . . . Omnes lapsos, captivos, infirmos atque peregrinos in mente habeamus, ut eos Dominus . . . (loc. cit., 540).* Another diptych formula is given in the Stowe Missal, where it is inserted in the *Memento* of the Dead of the Roman Mass; it begins: *Cum omnibus in toto mundo offerentibus sacrificium spiritale . . . sacerdotibus offert senior noster N. presbyter pro se et pro suis et pro totius Ecclesiæ coetu catholicæ et pro commemorando anathletico gradu . . .* Then comes a lengthy list of saints of

the Old and then of the New Testament, martyrs, hermits, bishops, priests, and the conclusion: *et omnium pausantium qui nos in dominica pace præcesserunt ab Adam usque in hodiernum diem, quorum Deus nomina . . . novit.* Warner (HBS, 32), 14-16; cf. Duchesne, 222 f. The rule of the Order of St. Aurelian (d. 551) ends with a like formula; (PL, 68, 395-398).
[18] Thus A. Lesley, PL, 85, 542 C D. Cf. also preceding note.
[19] The Stowe Missal, which notes before the words, *Hic recitantur nomina vivorum,* forms an exception. Botte, 32; Warner (HBS), 32), 11.
[20] C. 54 (MGH Capit., I, 57). Cf. also can. 51 of the Council of Frankfurt (754): *De non recitandis nominibus antequam oblatio offertur. (ibid., 78).*
[21] The Sacramentary of Rotaldus (10th cent.) speaks of the subdeacons who shortly before, facing the altar, *memoriam vel nomina vivorum et mortuorum nominaverunt* (PL, 78, 244 A). A note, *Hic nominentur nomina vivorum,* appears again in a Central Italian Missal of the 11th century; (Ebner, 163) and thence frequently

Since the canon began to be said in a low tone, this reading of names could no longer be loud and public. According to one eleventh century account, the names were whispered into the priest's ear on those occasions when he had assistants around him.[22] In another instance the names were pronounced by the priest himself. Many Mass books, therefore, even indicate certain names right in the text of the canon, at least as a marginal notation,[23] perhaps by reason of foundations. Or a corresponding general formula was inserted, embracing those names that had a right to be mentioned.[24] Sometimes the register of names was laid on the altar and merely a reference introduced into the *Memento*,[25] a practice similar to one still in use at present in the West Syrian rite.[26]

in this or similar form until well into the 5th century (Ebner, 146, 157, 194, 204, 280, 334 f.) also as a later addition (*ibid.*, 27) ; see also Martène, 1, 4, XVII (I, 601). Nevertheless the corresponding remark regarding the deceased is more frequent.

[22] In this way the Bishop at Rheims recalled the names of his predecessors in the Mass for the Dead; Fulkwin, *Gesta abbatum Lobiensium*, c. 7 (d'Achery, *Spicilegium*, 2 ed., II, 733). Cf. Martène, 1, 4, 8, 13 (I, 405 f.).

[23] A Sacramentary of the 11th century from Fulda (Ebner, 208) mentions names from the Byzantine Imperial Court. Heading the list is *Constantini Monomachi imperatoris* (d. 1054). More examples, Leroquais, I, 14, 33 (9th cent.; see moreover in the Register, III, 389) ; Ebner, 7; 94 ("margins covered over with names, 10th c.") ; 149; 196; 249; Martène, 1, 4, 8, 10 (I, 404 f.). In a deed of gift from Vendôme in the year 1073 the benefactors of the church stipulated that their names will be mentioned in the Canon of the Mass both during life and after death. Merk, *Abriss*, 87, n. 11; here also further data.

[24] Thus, a 10th century marginal gloss in the famous Cod. Paduanus reads : *omnium Christianorum, omnium qui mihi peccatori propter tuo timore confessi sunt et suas elemosynas ... donaverunt et omnium parentorum meorum vel qui se in meis orationibus commendaverunt, tam vivis quam et defunctis.* Ebner, 128; Mohlberg-Baumstark, n. 877. Formulas according to this scheme then appear in ever widening circles; see Martène, 1, 4, IV; VI; XXXVI

(I, 513C., 533 E., 673 f.) ; Bona, II, 11, 5 (756 f.) ; Leroquais, I, 103, etc.; Ebner, 402 f.; cf. the notices in the description of the MSS., *ibid.*, 17, 53, etc. A formula that appears at Seckau in the 15th century (Köck, 62), and in 1539 at Rome in Ciconiolanus (Legg, *Tracts*, 208), begins : *mei peccatoris cui tantam gratiam concedere digneris, ut assidue tuæ maiestati placeam, illius pro quo ...*

[25] So, too, a marginal gloss already in the Sacramentary in J. Pamelius, *Liturgica Latina*, II (Cologne, 1571), 180: (*Memento Domine famulorum famularumque tuarum*) *et eorum quorum nomina ad memorandum conscripsimus ac super sanctum altare tuum scripta adesse videntur.* More examples in Martène, 1, 4, 8, 15 (I, 406) ; Ebner, 403; cf. 94; PL, 78, 26, note g (from a 9th cent. MS. of Rheims). Such references were occasioned, among others, by the *libri vitæ* that were introduced in monasteries on the basis of prayer affiliations; cf. A. Ebner, *Die klösterlichen Gebetsverbrüderungen bis zum Ausgang des karolingischen Zeitalters* (Regensburg, 1890), 97 ff., 121 ff. But reference is made to such registers without their having been placed on the altar; see the entry of the 11th century in a Sacramentary of Bobbio: *et quorum vel quarum nomina apud me scripta retinentur;* Ebner, 81; Ferreres, 147.

[26] In the West Syrian Mass the names of such families as requested prayers for their deceased members during a specific period of the ecclesiastical year were inscribed upon a tablet that was laid upon the altar. At the Memento of the Dead the priest lays his hand upon the host and then makes a

Since the eleventh century these insert formulas, bearing a general character and often joined to the reference mentioned, grew transiently to memorable proportions, encompassing not only the *Memento* itself, but also the preceding intercessory plea for pope and bishop.[27] Often, too, a self-recommendation was added at the start: *Mihi quoque indignissimo famulo tuo propitius esse digneris et ab omnibus me peccatorum offensionibus emundare,*[28] or less frequently: *Memento mei quæso,* with various continuations.[29]

But very early a contrary tendency arose, leading in the course of the centuries to a complete suppression of all such additions.[30] Only names were allowed to be inserted,[31] or generally only a silent commemoration was permitted at this moment,[32] and in this the faithful were probably invited to take part.[33]

In the Missal of Pius V the indication of a mention of names and the corresponding pause have been retained.[34] But no rule is prescribed regarding the choice of names: *orat aliquantulum pro quibus orare intendit.* It is in line with the original intent and with the context that at a Mass

---

threefold sign of the cross over the tablet. S. Salaville in R. Aigrin, *Liturgia* (Paris, 1935), 915 f., note; cf. Hanssens, III, 473 f.

[27] Cf. e.g., *Adiuncta Pauli Diaconi intra canonem quando volueris* in Ebner, 302.

[28] Ebner, 401; see also the description of the MSS. *ibid.,* passim. Cf. also Martène, 1, 4, 8, 15 (I, 406 f.).

[29] Ebner, 247; Leroquais, I, 40; 84; Ferreres, p. C; cf. Martène, 1, 4, 8, 15 (I, 406 b). A formula of this kind frequently precedes the *Memento* of the Dead; see *infra.* The case of the Valencia Missal (1492) may be exceptional, inasmuch as a whole list of invocations from the litany precedes the *Memento: Per mysterium sanctæ incarnationis tuæ nos exaudire digneris, te rogamus audi nos,* etc. Ferreres, P. XCI. Cf. *ibid.,* p. LXXXVIII, the *deprecatio* before the *Memento.* Often a Memento of the Dead is here appended at the same time.

[30] Nevertheless even Merati (d. 1744) still proposes a lengthy interpolated prayer that the priest could here pray secretly; Gavanti-Merati, II, 8, 3 (I, 289).

[31] Bernold of Constance (d. 1100), *Micrologus,* c. 13 (PL, 151, 985) opposes those who interpolate *suas orationes* here. The chapter is captioned: *Quid superfluum sit in canone.* John Beleth (d. about 1165),

Explicatio, c. 46 (PL, 202, 54 B): *addemus nulli hic* [in the canon] *concessum esse aliquid vel detrahere vel addere, nisi quandoque nomen illorum, pro quibus specialiter aut nominatim offertur sacrificium.*

[32] Hints regarding the matter are often given in the Mass commentaries of the Middle Ages. Thus, Hugo of S. Cher, *Tract. super missam* (ed. Sölch, 27) advises to proceed *juxta ordinem caritatis* and to pray first for parents and relatives, then *pro spiritualibus parentibus,* next for those who have recommended themselves to our prayers (*commendaverunt;* this phrase is the first mention of the *offerentes* in the traditional sense of those who offered a stipend and the like, see above, p. 130), then for those present, and finally for all the people. The Missal of Regensburg about 1500 lists eight groups in another way: Beck, 273.

[33] The *Liber ordinarius* of Liége (Volk, 69, 1. 4) requires, that if any one is ill, a sign be given after the *Sanctus, ut fratres in suis orationibus infirmi recordentur et dicant psalmum Miserere.*

[34] Along with the *ill.,* as a sign for the name to be inserted, the *N.* of today was already used at an early date; thus, in fact, the Stowe Missal about the year 800; Warner (HBS, 32), 11; cf. 6, 10, 14, 19 ff.

said for a stipend the one who in this way became an *offerens* should be especially remembered here.[35]

But in the text of the *Memento* itself the circle is broadened. Into it are drawn all those present, since they did come to church in order to honor God by this communal oblation.[36] They are called *circumstantes* or, in the more ancient texts, *circum adstantes*.[37] During the first thousand years, standing was the principal posture even during the canon.[38] Note, however, that the *circum* is not to be construed as though the faithful had ever completely surrounded the altar. Rather the picture intended is what is suggested by the structure of the old Roman basilicas, where the altar stood between the presbytery and the nave, so that the faithful—especially if there was a transept—could form a semi-circle or "open ring" [39] around the altar.

About those mentioned by name and about the group of *circum adstantes*, a two-membered clause originally had two things to say. One phrase regarded their general state of soul, namely: their faith and their devotion[40] is well known to Thee.[41] The other phrase took notice of their activity: they offer up to Thee a sacrifice of praise; this is further described and defined. The original text, like the text of the first prayer after the consecration, ascribes to the faithful the offering of the sacrifice, without any special restriction: *qui tibi offerunt hoc sacrificium laudis.*[42]

[35] Cf. above, p. 24. Thus also Benedict XIV, *De s. sacrificio missæ*, II, 13, 9 (Schneider, 167). Florus Diaconus (d. about 860), *De actione miss.*, c. 51 (PL, 119, 47 B) and Remigius of Auxerre (d. about 908), *Expositio* (PL, 101, 1258 B), were emphatic about the liberty to insert other names in the place where from time immemorial the names of the *offerentium* were used *(quos desideravit particulariter nominare).*

[36] Spanish Mass books of the 12th century also add: *(circumstantium) atque omnium fidelium christianorum (quorum tibi)*; Ferreres, P. XXXI, LXX ff., CVIII; cf. XXIV, XXVI, XLVI, XLIX, LII, CXII. This last extension in reference to the *qui tibi offerunt* to include those who are absent is in line with the Spanish tradition; see above, p. 162.

[37] Ebner, 405; Ménard, PL, 78, 275 BC.

[38] Above I, 239 ff.

[39] Cf. Schwarz, *Von Bau der Kirche* (Würzburg, 1938, where the inherent correctness of this plan is made clear. The opening of the ring, where the altar stands, indicates the movement by which the congregation, led by the priest, strive towards God; cf. also above I, 256.

[40] Cf. A. Daniels, "Devotio," *JL*, I (1921) 40-60. The word *devotio*, which otherwise frequently signifies in some form or other the very actions of divine service, here refers to the disposition of heart. *Fides* is the basic attitude by which one's whole life is erected upon God's word and promises; *devotio* the readiness faithfully to regulate one's conduct accordingly without reservation. The two expressions are similarly united by Nicetas of Remesiana (d. after 414), *De psalmodiæ bono*, c. 3 (PL, 68, 373; Daniels, 47): *nullus debet ambigere hoc vigiliarum sanctarum ministerium, si digna fide et devotione vera celebretur, angelis esse conjunctum.*

[41] F. Rütten, "Philologisches zum Canon missæ" (*StZ*, 1938, I) 43 f., has claimed a deeper meaning for the word *(fides) cognita*: tried, proven. But it seems rather that we have here only a doubling of the expression *nota* in conformity with a rule of style applied in the canon; cf. above, I, p. 56. The *tibi* ahead makes it necessary to abide by this interpretation.

[42] Regarding the biblical expression *sacrificium laudis*, cf. above I, 24 f.; II, p. 114, n. 26.—The word brings out the spiritual

They are not idle spectators, even less a profane crowd; rather they are all together sharers in that sacred action with which we stand before Thee, O God. But in more recent times, when by reason of language and spatial arrangement the celebration of the priest is markedly withdrawn from the people, who can follow the service only at a certain distance, this unrestricted expression apparently looked too bold, and so the words, *pro quibus tibi offerimus vel* were prefixed. This insertion made its first appearance in several manuscripts of the Gregorian Sacramentary prepared by Alcuin,[43] and after the tenth century speedily became almost universal, not, however, without encountering some opposition.[44] The point made by this phrase was that the priest at the altar (surrounded by his assistants) was primarily the one who offered the sacrifice. It is possible that a contributing factor was to be found in the consideration that in this period, when foundations and stipends were gaining headway, those whose names were to be recalled at the *Memento* were often not present at the Mass, so that the priest was also their representative even in a narrower sense.[45] Still, as a rule the original concept continued to stand unimpaired.[46]

The sacrificial activity of the faithful is next more clearly defined according to its purpose. They offer up the sacrifice for themselves and for their dear ones; the bonds of family have a rightful place in prayer. They offer their sacrifice that thus they might "redeem (purchase) their souls."[47] According to Christ's own words, no price can be high enough

character of the Christian sacrifice and its primary purpose, the glorification of God.
[43] Cod. Ottobon, 313 (first half of the 9th cent.), also in the Cod. of Pamelius; cf. Lietzmann, n. 1, 20.
[44] Bernold of Constance, *Micrologus*, c. 13 (PL, 151, 985 C).—Lebrun, I, 369, note *a*, mentions among others, a Cistercian Missal of 1512, in which the insertion is still missing. The omission of this insertion was a common peculiarity of the Cistercian rite until 1618; Schneider (*Cist.-Chr.,* 1927), 9 f.
[45] V. Thalhofer, *Handbuch d. kath. Liturgik*, II (Freiburg, 1890), 204, and with him Ebner, 404, would consider the gradual cessation of the oblation on the part of the faithful as the main reason for the interpolation mentioned above, but without justification. The oblation was still in full force at this time. Cf. above.
[46] Only in exceptional cases did anyone go so far as to eliminate the words *qui tibi offerunt*. They are erased in an 11th century Sacramentary of Salzburg (Ebner, 278). The words were left out at first in

the St. Gall MS. 340 (10-11th cent.) and not supplied until later; Ebner, 404 f. Ebner, 128, mentions also the famous Padua MS. D. 47, but this is a mistake; cf. Mohlberg-Baumstark, n. 877. The traditional *vel* does not necessarily denote a reduction of the *qui tibi offerunt* to a mere outside possibility since at that time it was used in the sense of *et;* cf. H. Ménard, PL, 78, 275 D. The primitive idea is also given a strong prominence in the formula as expanded by Peter Damien, *Opusc. "Dominis vobiscum,"* c. 8 (PL, 145, 237 f): *In quibus verbis patenter ostenditur, quod a cunctis fidelibus, non solum viris, sed et mulieribus sacrificium illud laudis offertur, licet ab uno specialiter offerri sacerdote videatur: quia quod ille Deo offerendo manibus tractat, hoc multitudo fidelium intenta mentium devotione commendat.*
[47] Here there is clearly an allusion to Ps. 48; 8 f.: *non dabit Deo . . . pretium redemptionis animæ suæ,* i.e., no one can ransom his soul from death. Cf. Mt. 16: 26; Mk. 8; 37. The supposition is, therefore, that the soul is in danger, but by a

to make such a purchase, and yet this will surely do. They want to redeem their souls, that is they want to gain the welfare and health that
they as Christians may dare to hope for—as the clarifying clause puts it—
pro spe salutis et incolumitatis suæ. In this phrase the word *salus* can
be taken for the salvation of the soul, as Christian usage employs the word,
while *incolumitas* at least includes the notion of bodily health and
security.[48]

The *Memento* closes with the words *tibique reddunt vota sua æterno
Deo vivo et vero,* thus tacking a second phrase to the words *qui tibi
offerunt hoc sacrificium laudis.* One might possibly expect to find in this
a continuation of the thought, but this is rather hard to establish. Although
vota can have other meanings, *reddere vota* is without doubt either the
dutiful gift of something commended to God (as is the case in many
passages in the Latin rendering of the Old Testament), or it is, as here,
simply the giving of a gift to God, taking into account a previous obligation; it is the offering up of a sacrifice, but with a sharp underscoring of
the thought inherent in every sacrifice, that the work is one that is due.[49]

In the clause doubled in this way we have a clear imitation of Psalm
49:14: *Immola Deo sacrificium laudis et redde Altissimo vota tua.* The
only addition is the solemn invocation of God's name, likewise formed
on a scriptural quotation,[50] and emphasized by prefacing the word *æterno.*
It dawns on one's consciousness that in the sacrifice one is face to face
with the eternal, living, true God.

All in all, however there seems to be something very curious in the
twin phrase in this passage, for the poetic parallelism of the two members,
as it is found in the quotation from the Psalm, is not to be found here.
We are tempted to conclude that the detailed description of the sacrifice
of the faithful as outlined here was inserted only belatedly, and that the
original text ran as follows: *Memento Domine famulorum famularumque
tuarum, qui tibi offerunt hoc sacrificium laudis et tibi reddunt vota sua
æterno Deo vivo et vero.* This conclusion is corroborated by the Mozarabic
citation from the Roman canon already referred to.[51] But how is it possible
that the first member should have been supplemented as we find it today,

---

bold twisting of our Lord's words, like
those used for the Canaanite woman,
(Matt. 15: 27), the great *sacrificium laudis* is set in opposition to that danger; cf.
Ambrose, *De Elia et jej.,* c. 22 (PL, 32,
2, 463 f.) : in baptism the *redemptio animæ*
is granted us. It is therefore hard to justify
interpreting the word as an indication of
the material performance, as we often find
in medieval charters, and as Gihr, 645-646,
tries to render it.

[48] Proofs from ecclesiastical language for
both meanings of *incolumitas* in Batiffol,

Leçons, 246 f. Nor will it do to try to narrow down the meaning of *salus;* the same
double expression sometimes has a simple
temporal meaning, as in the *Hanc igitur* of
the Gelasianum, I, 40 (Wilson, 70) : *ut
per multa curricula annorum salvi et in-
columes munera . . . mereantur offerre.*

[49] For *votum* = sacrifice, cf. Batiffol,
Leçons, 247.

[50] I Thess. 1: 9. The expression here is
explained by its antithesis to the dead gods,
from whom the faithful turned away.

[51] *Supra* I, 55, n. 20.

while the second member, widely separated from it, should have remained unaltered?

This first surprise is joined by a second. In all the oldest texts of the Roman canon, without exception, the suffix—*que* is missing at the beginning of the second member; invariably it reads: . . . *incolumitatis suæ tibi reddunt vota sua . . .*[52] Grammatical carelessness of this type, copied century after century, must indeed be serious cause for wonder, particularly in a text of the Roman canon which, taken all in all, is otherwise smooth.

Both problems are solved at one blow if we put a period after the words *incolumitatis suæ,* and then begin with a new sentence: *Tibi reddunt vota sua æterno Deo vivo et vero communicantes . . .*[53] that is to say, these words take up the *tibi offerunt sacrificium laudis* with a different wording in order to append to it the idea of the grand Communion.[54] Thus, communion with the saints was originally claimed principally for the faithful, just as the offering of the sacrifice was, but then, influenced by the different atmosphere of the Frankish church, both claims were at the same time not indeed voided but at least obscured, not, however, to such an extent that even at the present the ancient thought should not be offered as the most natural interpretation of the text. In other words, we feel justified in considering and explaining the phrase *tibi reddunt,* etc., as a part of the *Communicantes* text.

[52] Botte, *Le canon,* 34. Of the 19 pertinent texts that begin about 700 there is but a single one, according to Botte, that presents *tibique* at first hand; it is the one in the *Cod. Pad.* D 47, written during the time of King Lothar I (d. 855) in the neighborhood of Liége. But, as the printed edition of this MS. shows (Mohlberg-Baumstark, *Die älteste erreichbare Gestalt,* n. 877), the -*que* here too is in reality an addition by a second hand. The -*que* is still missing in the *Cod. Eligii* (10th cent., PL, 78, 26 B) and also in the Sacramentary of the Papal court chapel about 1290; Brinktrine (*Eph. liturg.,* 1937), 204. Ebner, 405, refers to this peculiarity, but without attempting an explanation.

[53] The old MSS., as is known, have either no punctuation at all, or very little, and seemingly, as a rule, no paragraphs (sections) within the canon. The latter is also the case in the Cod. S. Gall, 348 (ed.

Mohlberg, n. 1551), but it does make use of red initial letters in three places within the *Communicantes;* the word *communicantes* itself, however, is connected with the preceding without any such distinguishing mark (n. 1552). Unambiguous, too, as Botte, 55, also notes, is the uninterrupted union of *Deo vivo et vero communicantes* in two of the most important texts of the Roman Canon; in the Bobbio missal, ed. Lowe, I (HBS, 58), n. 11, see Facsimile (HBS, 31), fol. 25. Cf. moreover, a like construction in a *Hanc igitur* formula of the Gelasianum, III, 37 (Wilson, 254); *pro hoc reddo tibi vota mea Deo vero et vivo maiestatem tuam suppliciter implorans.*

[54] Grammatically independent sentences begin within the canon also in other places: in the two *Mementos,* in the *Supplices,* and in the *Nobis quoque.*

9. *Communicantes*

The *Communicantes* that follows is not, as it now stands, a grammatically complete sentence. The first question therefore regarding it naturally is: what is it connected with? Other links have been propounded,[1] but the one that appears most natural is that suggested to us by the text just studied, a proposal that was already made years ago.[2] Just as by origin the *Communicantes* is a continuation of the *Memento*, so also its content is a reinforcement of the plea in that *Memento*: Remember all of them, for the congregation which now stands before Thee with its sacrifice does not stand solitary, since it belongs to the great nation of the redeemed, whose foremost ranks have already entered into Thy glory. Once again is made manifest that bond with the Church Triumphant which had already been vividly recalled in a different way by the singing of the *Sanctus*.

The emphasis here is on the word *communicantes*, on the comradeship with the saints whose names are about to be mentioned.[3] At the same time, however we become aware of the distance that separates us and so, by the subsequent words, *et memoriam venerantes*, this comradeship is altered into a look of awe and respect.[4] It is this second phrase that governs the following grammatical construction, which would otherwise have run as follows: *communicantes in primis cum*. But this in no way weakens

[1] Juncture with a verb of the *Te igitur*, either *supplices rogamus ac petimus* (Batiffol, *Leçons*, 248) or *in primis quæ tibi offerimus*, or (an evidently impossible solution) with the naming of the Pope *cum famulo tuo papa nostro illo communicantes* (Schuster, *The Sacramentary*, I, 274-277). Against all of these solutions it must be noted that the *Communicantes* was never immediately connected with the *Te igitur*, because it is later than the *Memento*; cf. *supra*, I, 54 f. Others abandon the idea of a grammatical relation with anything preceding and complete the word with *sumus* or *offerimus* or *offerunt* (thus, among others Brinktrine, 180; 218) or explain the *communicantes et memoriam venerantes* as equivalent to *communicamus et memoriam veneramur* (thus Fortescue, *The Mass*, 332). But in both these cases the result is an unnatural isolation of the prayer and the ideas it contains.

[2] This was already advocated by Suarez, *De Sacramentis*, I, 83, 2, 7, *Opp.*, ed. Berton, 21, 874) . . . *ita ut sensus sit: Tibi reddunt vota sua æterno Deo vivo et vero communicantes, vel inter se tamquam corporis tui vel cum sanctis tuis* . . .

[3] The assumption that *communicare* here is meant in the absolute canonico-legal sense (= *c. ecclesia catholicæ*), "to have a place in the (ecclesiastical) community" (cf. Batiffol, *Leçons*, 248, with reference to Cyprian, *De dom. or.*, c. 18 and Optatus, VII, 3, 6), is hard to justify in the setting this prayer has. It would be more plausible to think directly of the Church as *communio sanctorum* in this way; they present Thee their gifts as members of the holy community and, inasmuch as they honor the memory . . . .Cf. Gihr, 649. At all events, we shall have to accord some meaning to the word in those cases in the feast-day formulas where the connection with what follows is interrupted: *Communicantes et diem sacratissimum celebrantes . . . et memoriam venerantes;* cf. Botte, 55 f.; cf. below.

[4] The fuller meaning of *memoria*: memorial monument, (martyr's) grave, that has been suggested, is out of the question in this connection. Cf. Botte, 56 f.; also Th. Klauser, *JL*, 15 (1914), 464.

the basic idea of stressing the communion. We have already seen [5] how in the oriental liturgies the reading of the diptychs was correlated since the fifth century with the concept of ecclesiastical communion, and how this thought was logically developed into a consciousness of communion with the saints in heaven. But communion is not mentioned in a direct form; the mention of those who "from the beginning have been pleasing to God" is simply appended to the listing of other names or groups of those who have departed from the earthly congregation. Often the same formula is used to frame both the sections.[6] "We offer up this sacrifice also for . . ."[7] or ". . . in pious memory of,"[8] or "Remember also . . .," "Deign to remember . . .[9]. In fact at one stage, when theological thinking was less clarified, we even find the formal petition that God may give them "peace" applied also to the saints.[10]

But in all these instances the main stress is laid on emphasizing the communion. Thus, too, the *memoriam venerantes* is to be construed.[11] That we are correct in drawing on the oriental diptych practice to illustrate this portion of the ecclesiastical prayer is confirmed not only by the fact that the *Communicantes* must have been introduced into the canon about the same time that this practice was in full flower in the East, when Roman popes were corresponding with the Orient regarding questions of the diptychs,[12] but even more immediately by the wording of the *Communicantes* itself, wherein a model from the area of the Syrian liturgy was evidently of some influence. The formula with which the list of saints begins: *in primis gloriosæ semper Virginis Mariæ Genitricis Dei et Domini nostri Jesu Christi*, has a counterpart—to mention but one— in the Antiochene anaphora of St. James: ἐξαιρέτως τῆς παναγίας ἀχράντου ὑπερευλογημένης δεσποίνης ἡμῶν θεοτόκου καὶ ἀειπαρθένου Μαρίας.[13] For the

---

[5] Page 159.

[6] However, as a rule, in such manner that the Saints are clearly distinct from other deceased persons. It is only in the East Syrian anaphoras that we find an exception. Hanssens, III, 471 f.

[7] *Const. Ap.* VIII, 12, 43 (Quasten, *Mon.*, 225 f.) : Ἔτι προσφέρομεν σοι καὶ ὑπέρ πάντων τῶν ἀπ' αἰῶνος εὐαρεστησάντων σοι ἀγίων, πατριαρχῶν, προφητῶν, δικαίων, ἀποστόλων, μαρτύρων . . . (cf. also Quasten's notes). Similarly also in today's Byzantine liturgy of St. Chrysostom; Brightman, 387 f. Cf. also the East Syrian fragment from the 6th century; *ibid.*, 516, 1. 21 ff [The *Missale Romanum* also speaks on June 15 of *munera pro sanctis oblata*. In regard to the indefinite meaning of ὑπέρ, *pro*, "for" as here used, see Jungmann, *Die Stellung Christi*, 234-238.

[8] East Syrian anaphora of Theodorus: Renaudot, II, (1847), 614.

[9] Anaphora of St. James: Brightman, 56, 1. 20. Ἔτι μνησθῆναι καταξίωσον τῶν ἀπ'αἰωνός σοι εὐαρεστησάντων; cf. *ibid.*, 57, 1. 13; 92 f. Similar formulas also in the Armenian liturgy (Brightman, 440, 1. 13), in Egypt (Brightman, 128, 1. 23 ; 169, 1. 7), and also among the East Syrians; Brightman, 440, 1. 1.

[10] Armenian liturgy; Brightman, 440, 1. 1.

[11] Cf. also the Mozarabic *facientes commemorationem, supra*, p. 162.

[12] Leo the Great, *Ep.*, 80, 3 ; 85, 2 (PL, 54, 914 f., 923 f.) ; John II of Constantinople to Hormisdas (d. 523) (CSEL, 35, 592).

[13] Brightman, 56. In addition the word ἐνδόξου is inserted in the Byzantine formulas of the present; Brightman, 388. Further parallels in Kennedy, *The Saints*, 36. In

closing formula: *et omnium sanctorum, quorum meritis precibusque concedas, ut in omnibus protectionis tuœ muniamur auxilio*, there is likewise
a corresponding phrase in the same anaphora of St. James [14] and an even
more faithful trace in the Byzantine liturgy: χαὶ πάντων τῶν ἀγίων σου, ὧν
ταῖς ἱκεσίαις ἐπίσκεψαι ἡμᾶς ὁ θεός. [15]

Thus, for all the insistence on the concept of communion, the beginning
and the end in both instances present a slight anomaly. For the one
singled out to head the list of saints is one who had the incomparable
dignity of being Mother of God and ever virgin. And at the end of the
list the relation we bear to the saints in general is indicated with greater
exactness by the humble prayer that their intercession might avail us. By
such clarifying phrases the ancient formula, accidentally left unchanged,
the formula of an offering "for" all of them, was rectified along the lines
of the principle already expounded by St. Augustine for the naming of
the saints *ad altare Dei*, namely: *Iniuria est enim pro martyre orare, cuius
nos debemus orationibus commendari.* [16]

The list of names in the present-day Roman canon here consists of two
well-balanced groups of twelve names, twelve apostles and twelve martyrs,
led by the Queen of all saints; similarly, the second list in the *Nobis
quoque peccatoribus* comprises twin groups of that other sacred number,
the number seven: seven male martyrs and seven female, led by him
whom the Lord himself had termed the greatest of those born of woman
(Matthew 11:11). Thus a double choir of saints is arrayed, much in the
same way as Christian art had sought to represent it. [17] The venerable
antiquity of the lists is clearly manifested by the fact that, besides the
biblical names, only those saints are included who were honored at Rome
as martyrs; the cult of confessors, whose beginnings are surely to be
found in the fourth century, has not yet left a mark here. The honor
of being mentioned in the Great Prayer of the sacrifice is reserved to
those heroes of the faith who had faced the struggle of suffering along
with Christ.

Upon closer scrutiny the *Communicantes* list reveals a well-planned
arrangement. The twelve martyrs are aligned in hierarchical order. First
come six bishops, five of them popes, and then a non-Roman, Cyprian,

---

this and also in the Byzantine liturgy, as
compared with the sober and retiring Roman, the memory of the Mother of God
is given striking emphasis not only by
highly ornate, not to say showy formulas,
but by other devices also. In the anaphora of
St. James an *Ave Maria*, combining Luke
1: 28; 42 as we know it, is inserted by
the priest immediately before this phrase.
In the Byzantine liturgy, after the priest
has in a loud tone of voice commemorated
the Mother of God, while incensing the

altar, the choir intones a special hymn of
Mary, one in conformity with the season
of the year: the μεγαλυνάριον, so called because of the word μεγαλύνει (Magnificat)
that occurs in it; Brightman, 388; 600.

[14] Brightman, 48; cf. 94.

[15] Brightman, 331 f, 388, 406 f.; Kennedy,
37 f.

[16] Augustine, *Sermo* 159, 1 (PL, 38, 868);
cf. *In Joh. tract.*, 84, 1 (PL, 35, 1847).

[17] Cf. Raffaele's "Disputa."

contemporary of St. Cornelius (who is therefore the only one taken out of chronological order so as to be set side by side with Cyprian). Among the other six martyrs, the first two are clerics. Lawrence and Chrysogonus; [18] then follow the laymen, John and Paul, Cosmas and Damian. Clearly we have here the work of a systematic hand. In the sacred precincts of the Great Prayer, so to say, a properly chosen representation from the choirs of martyrs ought to appear. This is the one conception that we can make our own even at the present; the one thought that can reconcile us with the catalogue of saints in the canon, in spite of its weaknesses, even though two thousand years of Church history and the extension of the horizon beyond that of a city-liturgy into a world-liturgy has presented us with numberless other names to choose from. To this double series of twelve names from the early ages of Christianity and from the life of the Roman Mother-Church we are pleased to grant the privilege to be named at the altar as representatives of the Church Triumphant.

It is obvious, no doubt, that the list of saints in the *Communicantes*—and something similar must be said later about the second list—is not a first draft. In some oriental anaphoras the list of saints named in the prayer of intercession has been kept at a minimum.[19] In the Roman canon as it was when transferred to Milan, perhaps in the sixth century, some names found in our present-day list are missing, namely, those of Popes Linus and Cletus, and the names included are not yet presented in the nice order they now possess.[20]

The original list must have comprised those saints who enjoyed a special cult at Rome at the time of the introduction of the *Communicantes*. Around the turn of the fifth century these were: Mary, Peter and Paul, Xystus and Lawrence, Cornelius and Cyprian.[21] Soon after the Council of Ephesus devotion to the Blessed Virgin in the Eternal City had acquired

---

[18] At any rate, Chrysogonus is always described as a cleric in the legend; J. P. Kirsch, "Chrysogonus"; *LThK*, II, 949 f.

[19] Baumstark, *Das Communicantes*, 11 ff. The formula of the Apostolic Constitutions, VIII, 12, 43 (see note 7 above) did not present any names at all.

[20] The Ambrosian Mass has the following list after the twelve Apostles: *Xysti, Laurentii, Hippolyti, Vincentii, Cornelii, Cypriani, Clementis, Chrysogoni, Johannis et Pauli, Cosmæ et Damiani*, and then follows a lengthy list of Milanese names. The basis for this order of names seems to be the succession in the development of the veneration of the martyrs at Rome, whose beginnings are somewhere in the 3rd century. F. Savio, *I dittici del Canone Ambro-*

siano e del Canone Romano (special printing of the *Miscellanea di storia italiana*, III, 11; Turin, 1905), 4 f.; Kennedy, 60-64; 191. Kennedy, 195 f., assumes that Hippolytus and Vincent were named in individual Roman churches, but not in the papal liturgy. Likewise the two last named must have been taken over from Rome as an afterthought.

[21] Kennedy, *The Saints of the Canon of the Mass* (1938), 189 ff. The following presentation is based essentially on Kennedy's fundamental research. Akin to these are the assertion of Lietzmann, *Petrus und Paulus in Rom,* (2nd ed.; Berlin, 1927), 82-93, who considers the list of saints together with their sequence to have been taken over from the Roman calendar of

a magnificent center through the consecration of the renovated Liberian basilica in her honor, S. Maria Maggiore, under Sixtus III (432-440). The development of the cultus of the Princes of the Apostles, Peter and Paul, is attested not only by the most ancient sacramentaries with their Mass formularies for their feasts, but above all by the graves of the apostles, which had acquired beautiful buildings already in Constantine's time. Pope Xystus (or, as his name was later spelled, Sixtus), the second of that name, was seized in the cemetery of Callistus in 258, during the persecution of Valerian, and summarily executed. He was followed in martyrdom a few days later by his deacon, Lawrence. The memorial days for both of them, which were celebrated yearly on the sixth and tenth of August, belong to the oldest Martyr feasts of Rome. Pope Cornelius, of an old Roman family, died in exile after a short reign (251-253); his remains were shortly after returned to Rome. His grave is the first of the papal tombs to bear a Latin inscription: *Cornelius Martyr ep.* Bishop Cyprian of Carthage, who had corresponded with Cornelius, was one of the great figures of the third Christian century; he suffered martyrdom a few years later (258). His memorial day was celebrated at Rome already in the fourth century, and the oldest sacramentaries present Cornelius and Cyprian together on the fourteenth of September.[22]

The twelve apostles as a group were venerated at Rome as early as the fifth century.[23] Still the full listing of their names cannot have been included in the canon till later. For this list displays a very curious dissimilarity to both the biblical list and to all other known catalogues. It is closest to that in Matthew 10:2-4, but is distinguished from it (aside from the insertion of St. Paul and the reversal of the last two names, as found likewise in Luke and the Acts of the Apostles) by the fact that the sons of Zebedee are followed at once by Thomas, James and Philip, of whom the last two take the ninth and the fifth place in all the biblical catalogues. A special cult of the Apostle Thomas is attested since the days of Pope Symmachus (498-514), who had erected an *oratorium Sancti Thomæ*. A similar *cultus* for Philip and James is found since the time of Pelagius I and John III (556-574), when the great Basilica of the Apostles was built in their honor.[24] Of the preceding names in the list, the apostles John and Andrew had their sanctuaries in Rome already in the fifth century. James the Greater appears originally to have been celebrated at Rome along with his brother John on the feast of December 27, for which

---

saints in the 4-5th century. This assumption (contra Kennedy, 195, n. 3) is also held by H Frank, "Beobachtungen zur Geschichte des Messkanons," *Archiv f. Liturgiewiss.,* I (1950), 111 f.

[22] More detailed accounts in E. Hosp, *Die Heiligen im Canon Missæ* (Graz, 1926). —See also P. Van Doren, "Les saints du

canon de la messe," *Questions liturgiques et paroissiales,* 16 (1931), 57-70; C. L. Russmann, "Die Heiligen des Meszopfer Kanons," *Theol.-prakt. Quartalschrift,* 101 (1953), 1-15; 101-113.

[23] Kennedy, 109 f.

[24] Kennedy, 102-111.

there is evidence a bit later.[25] But evidence for a *cultus* of the other apostles that follow is wanting. So it is probable that the list of apostles in the canon consisted at first of the names of Peter, Paul, Andrew, (James?) and John, and that in the course of the sixth century Thomas, James and Philip were added, and finally the remainder, until the number' twelve was filled out.[26] Something like that must also have occurred in the list of martyrs.

In the course of the same century there was an increase of devotion to Pope Clement, who was being glorified by an extensive literature; to Chrysogonus, the martyr whose history is interwoven with legend and who was identified with a like-named founder of one of the Roman titular churches;[27] for John and Paul, whom one legend assumed to have been Roman martyrs of the time of Julian the Apostate; for the two physicians and martyrs so highly venerated in the Orient, Cosmas and Damian, who were invoked as liberal helpers in cases of sickness. Thus the list must have grown during the sixth century more or less of itself. The redactor who put the list in the order we have today, to fill out the number twelve for the martyrs as for the apostles must have inserted the two first successors of St. Peter, Linus and Cletus, who are otherwise seldom mentioned.[28] This redactor, whose work must have been done about the turn of the sixth century, can have been no other than Pope Gregory the Great. Due to the circumstance that the Roman Church in the period of the persecutions, unlike the Church in North Africa, kept no acts of the Martyrs, and so gave ample play for the development of legend, there is considerable doubt about the last five names in the series of martyrs, so that from the viewpoint of historical truth little more can be established than the names.[29]

In the centuries following there was no feeling that the list as found in the Roman canon was closed once and for all. While keeping the twice twelve saints, there was nothing to hinder the addition of names of other prominent figures, in keeping with the altering features of ecclesiastical life. Thus the oldest Frankish manuscripts tack on not only the two great saints of Gaul, Hilary and Martin, but also the Doctors of the Church then already in high honor: (Ambrose), Augustine, Gregory, Jerome, along with the father of Western monasticism, Benedict.[30]

[25] Lietzmann, *Petrus und Paulus in Rom.*, 140, with n. 2; Baumstark, *Das Communicantes*, 23.

[26] Cf. Kennedy, 105, 110 f. (without St. James).

[27] Behind the legend the martyr-bishop Chrysogonus of Aquileja (beginning of the 3d cent.) appears to loom as the historic figure. J. P. Kirsch, *Die römischen Titelkirchen im Altertum*, (Paderborn, 1918), 108-113; Kennedy, 128-130; H. Delehaye,

Etudes sur le légendier Romain (Brussels, 1938), 151-162.

[28] Kennedy, 111-117; 128-140.

[29] Cf. the presentation in Hosp, 110 ff., 222 ff., 38 ff., and Kennedy, 128-140. The judgment regarding these names was substantially less skeptical a few decades ago than it is today after the important work by H. Delehaye, P. Franchi de' Cavalieri and others.

[30] Botte, 34. Ambrose appears in only two

Sometimes additions were made of regional saints or of patrons of the particular diocese or church. Thus, in the environs of Fulda, Boniface was attached to the list of martyrs.[31] The names thus added in many manuscripts have become important indexes in establishing their provenience. Often enough the number of additional names became unbearably long; thus in one eleventh-century manuscript of Rouen twenty-three names are annexed.[32]

One expedient for satisfying local requirements without lengthening the list unduly was intimated by Pope Gregory III (731-741) when he prescribed for the monks of an oratory of St. Peter's endowed with a wealth of relics an addition to the *Communicantes* as follows: *sed et diem natalitium celebrantes sanctorum tuorum martyrum ac confessorum, perfectorum iustorum, quorum sollemnitas hodie in conspectu gloriæ tuæ celebratur, quorum meritis precibusque . . .*[33] As a matter of fact, this or a similar additament is found in numerous medieval Mass books, mostly (it is true) as a further enrichment of the already longish formula, especially as a means of including the special saints of the day.[34] But in the meantime there arose a determined opposition to the unnatural distension of the *Communicantes* formula,[35] until at last all such accretions disappeared altogether.[36]

A different type of addition, however, has continued down to our own day, the most ancient addition to the *Communicantes* that we know of, namely the announcement of the day's mystery on Christmas, Epiphany, Maundy Thursday, Easter, Ascension and Pentecost. The addition on

---

of the MSS. recorded by Botte.—These names recur in numerous MSS. until late in the Middle Ages; Ebner, 407 f.

[31] Ebner, 408. Cf. Martène, 1, 4, 8, 16 (I, 407 f.).

[32] Ebner, 409. Cf. the compilation from the French MSS. in Leroquais, *Les sacramentaires,* III, 353.

[33] Duchesne, *Liber Pont.,* I, 422. Walafried Strabo, *De exord. et increm.,* c. 22 (PL, 114, 950 A), cites these words with the amplification: . . . *celebratur, Domine Deus noster, toto in orbe terrarum.* The formula in the Mass books of the later Middle Ages frequently reads: *quorum hodie in conspectu tuo celebratur triumphus,* or something similar; see Ferreres, p. 150-152. On the other hand, the Bobbio Missal (Muratori, II, 777; Lowe, I [HBS, 58], n. 11) adds to the original text, after the *omnium sanctorum tuorum,* the following: *qui per universo mundo passi sunt propter nomen tuum, Domine, seu confes-*

soribus tuis.

[34] Cf. *Ordo Rom.* IV (PL, 78, 1380 B): (after *Cosmæ et Damiani) si fuerit natale sanctorum, hic dicat: Sed et diem natalitii beati ill. vel beatorum ill. celebrantes et omnium sanctorum.* Ebner, 409 f.

[35] Bernold of Constance, *Micrologus,* c. 13 (PL, 151, 985 f.): *Aliorum vero sanctorum nomina* [except the names at the *Memento*] *annumerare non debemus, nisi quos in canone invenimus antiquitus descriptos.* But it is to be noted that Bernold then makes the restriction: *excepto post Pater noster in illa oratione ubi juxta ordinem quorumlibet sanctorum nomina internumerare possumus.* The addition of names in the canon is bitterly attacked in a Stuttgart MS. that originated in 1435; Franz, 612.

[36] Still, Hilary and Martin retained their places until the present time in French dioceses; Duchesne, *Christian Worship,* 180, n. 2.

these six days is provided consistently in the old sacramentaries.[37] Besides, the pre-Gregorian sacramentaries have an extra formula for the vigil of Pentecost,[38] and the *Leonianum* has a further formula for two of the days mentioned that differs from the one in use at present.[39] These additions were therefore in existence by the middle of the sixth century. It was just about this time that they appear to be cited in a message addressed to Bishop Profuturus of Braga by Pope Vigilius, in which the pontiff stresses the fact that the Roman eucharistic prayer is otherwise unchangeable.[40]

But in spite of their venerable age, and in spite of the masterly commentary on the festal mystery which they supply, we are unable to account these formulas as organic continuations of the text of the canon. They jumble still further the word *communicantes* (already disjointed by the words *memoriam venerantes* and formed into a sort of anacoluthon), and separate it entirely from the names of the saints to which it naturally belongs. Viewed in their relationships to other forms, these inserts are of a piece with the prefaces of the *Leonianum*, which, after becoming a plaything for composers of novelties, departed consciously or unconsciously from the basic concept of the eucharistic prayer and therefore earnestly invited reform.[41] If these festal inserts in the *Communicantes* escaped such

---

[37] Gregorianum, ed. Lietzmann, n. 6, 4; 17, 4; 77, 3; 88, 4; (87, 4); 108, 4; 112, 4; (111, 4).—The same formulas in the Gelasian Sacramentaries. Noteworthy variations are present only at Epiphany and the Ascension; in the former: *quo Unigenitus tuus . . . natus Magis de longinquo venientibus visibilis et corporalis apparuit;* Vat. Reg., I, 12 (Wilson, 11 f.); S. Gall. (Mohlberg, n. 99). On the feast of the Ascension the remarkably antique mode of expression :*. . . unitum sibi hominem nostræ substantiæ in gloriæ tuæ dextera collocavit;* Vat. Reg., I, 63 (Wilson, 107) and also in the Leonianum (Muratori, I, 316).

[38] *Communicantes et diem ss. Pentecostes prævenientes, quo Spiritus Sanctus apostolos plebemque credentium præsentia suæ maiestatis implevit, sed et;* Vat. Reg., I, (Wilson, 120); S. Gall. (Mohlberg, n. 803); Leonianum (Muratori, I, 318).

[39] Namely, a second formula on the feast of the Ascension (Muratori, I, 314) and a divergent one for Pentecost (*ibid.*, I, 321). The Leonianum, which starts only after Easter, naturally has only the four formulas mentioned.

[40] PL, 69, 18: *Ordinem quoque precum in celebritate missarum nullo nos tempore,*

nulla festivitate significamus habere diversum, sed semper eodem tenore oblata Deo munera consecrare. Quoties vero Paschalis aut Ascensionis Domini vel Pentecostes et Epiphaniæ sanctorumque Dei fuerit agenda festivitas, singula capitula diebus apta subiungimus, quibus commemorationem sanctæ sollemnitatis aut eorum facimus, quorum natalitia celebramus; cetera vero ordine consueto prosequimur. Quapropter et ipsius canonicæ precis textum direximus subter adiectum, quem Deo propitio ex apostolica traditione suscepimus. Et ut caritas tua cognoscat, quibus locis aliqua festivitatibus apta connectes, paschalis diei preces similiter adiecimus. It is impossible, however, that the *capitula diebus apta* meant exclusively our *Communicantes* formulas, or the other insertions in the canon; rather the preface, too, must be included, since it forms a complete unit with the canon. For, what Vigilius has to say about the consideration given to the feasts of saints within the limits of the eucharistic prayer was true even at that time only of the preface, as the Leonianum clearly shows.

[41] P. Borella, "S. Leone Magno e il Communicantes," *Eph. liturg.*, 60 (1946), 93-

reform, it is probably because they go back in substance to the very basic concept of all eucharistic solemnity and also, perhaps, because we have grown accustomed to giving the word *communicantes* a broader meaning, so that the line of thought on these days might be paraphrased somewhat in this fashion.

They render Thee their gifts as members of the sacred congregation, in remembrance of the mystery of redemption which we recall this day, and in respectful regard for these saints. The insert would thus have become a sort of anamnesis.

In reference to these inserts, the words *Infra actionem* have been left in the Roman Missal within the canon, just before the *Communicantes*, the same words which, in accord with their strict meaning, are to be found as a heading above the text of the insert formula where this is usually located, namely, after the prefaces. These words signify that the text is to be inserted "within the action." This title, *Infra actionem*, derives from the Gelasian Sacramentaries, where it generally stands just before the *Communicantes* formulas to be inserted, and also before the *Hanc igitur* formulas. Many of the manuscripts of this group of sacramentaries likewise disclose a special caption just before the *Sursum corda*, namely: *Incipit canon actionis.*[42]

The *Communicantes* brings to a close the first section of the intercessory prayer. Externally this is manifested by the concluding formula, *Per Christum Dominum nostrum*, which thus appears for the first time in the canon. Our intercessory prayers and commendations, like all our prayers, should be offered up only "through Christ our Lord." This it is we are conscious of in this preliminary conclusion of our pleading. The same *Per Christum Dominum nostrum* then reappears after the *Hanc igitur*, after the *Supplices*, after the *Memento etiam* and after the *Nobis quoque.*[43] Like a sign-post marking the line of our prayer, the formula is found today after successive stages all through the canon. While in all these places the formula is part and parcel of the oldest canon text to come down to us (although, it is true, only in the train of a secondary augmentation of this text), its first appearance is in the preface: ... *gratias agere per Christum Dominum nostrum*. Here it strikes no definitely conclusive note, but rather, like the close of the *Nobis quoque*, it is at once expanded by means of a rela-

---

101, attempts to prove that the set formula and the feast-day insertions must have originated with Leo the Great. Similarly C. Callewaert, "S. Leon le Communicantes et le Nobis quoque peccatoribus," *Sacris erudiri*, I (1948), 123-164. The Leonine derivation of at least three of the insert formulas is acknowledged by H. Frank, "Beobachtungen zur Geschichte des Messkanons," *Archiv f. Liturgiewiss.*, I (1950), 114-119. Therefore the normal text, *Com-*

municantes et memoriam venerantes, must have been regarded even then as strictly formal.

[42] See above, p. 103.

[43] Remigius of Auxerre, *Expositio* (PL, 101, 1258), wanted even the first prayer of the canon after *fidei cultoribus* concluded with the *Per Christum Dominum nostrum*. But he seems to have had little success in his attempt, and rightly so; cf. above, p. 159.

tive clause. In the remaining four passages, where this expansion is omitted, the post-Carolingian Middle Ages seemed more and more to expect that the *Per Christum Dominum nostrum* must be followed by an *Amen*. In the manuscripts this *Amen* appears for the first time in the ninth century,[44] and after that with ever-increasing frequency, till by the twelfth century its insertion in all these passages became the prevailing rule, although even at the close of the Middle Ages there were some outstanding exceptions.[45] Since the *Amen* at the close of the canon—the only place where of old it was spoken by all the people—had lost its uniqueness, it became merely an indispensable sign of the end of the prayer and thus had to be added to the Christological formula.

Later on, in the neo-Gallican movement, this *Amen* which had passed into the Missal of Pius V played a new role. In some dioceses the faithful had to recite it in a loud voice.[46] It was thought that doing so revived a custom of the ancient Church.

10. *Hanc igitur*

By the closing formula *Per Christum Dominum nostrum*, the *Hanc igitur* also labels itself as an independent prayer that did not belong to the original draft of the canon but was inserted only later on. The meaning of the words appears, at first sight, obvious and unequivocal, leaving little to be explained. The only problem that seems to require further elucidation is why this prayer, in its present form, should have been inserted just here. Is the prayer nothing more than a plea for the acceptance of the sacrificial gifts, as it is captioned in some translations?[1] But such a plea has already been made and is here simply repeated in different words. One would scarcely have inserted an independent prayer just for this purpose. Or maybe the stress is on the contents of the petitions appended? But then why are these petitions included precisely in this place? It is around this prayer that the various theories regarding the canon have been de-

---

[44] Sacramentary of S. Thierry; Leroquais, I, 22.

[45] P. Salmon, "Les 'Amen' du canon de la messe," *Eph. liturg.*, 42 (1928), 496-506. *Ibid.*, 501, n. 4, the author mentions the printed missals of the 1518 and 1523 in which no *Amen* was interpolated.— G. Ellard, "Interpolated Amen's in the Canon of the Mass," *Theological Studies*, 6 (1945), 380-391. According to this there are traces of the *Amen* in the 13th century even in Rome (386 ff.). The medieval commentators who expressed themselves as opposed to the interpolation, alleged as a

reason that the angels here spoke the *Amen*. Thus, also, though along with other attempts for a reasonable explanation, Durandus, IV, 38, 7; 46, 8. In individual instances the *Amen* was added also at the end of the *Nobis quoque*. Salmon, 499; 501. —Cf. also Sölch, *Hugo*, 91-93.

[46] Salmon, 503-505. Cf. above.

[1] Thus Schott, *Das Messbuch der heiligen Kirche*, (37th ed.; Freiburg, 1934), 403. Likewise Brinktrine, *Die feierliche Papstmesse*, 27.

veloped, and a summary consideration has forced the conclusion that in this prayer we have "perhaps the most difficult prayer in the Mass."[2]

As regards its history, it is known, first of all, that the *Hanc igitur* (which all textual evidence shows to have belonged to the traditional wording of the Roman canon) did not acquire its present-day form before Gregory the Great, who (as the *Liber pontificalis* recounts) added the last words.[3] Even the earlier form of the prayer is not merely a matter of hypothesis. True, it is nowhere found, as we might be led to expect from this account, in a form which merely omits the Gregorian addition: *Hanc igitur oblationem . . . quæsumus Domine ut placatus accipias*. But in the pre-Gregorian sacramentaries there are certainly a considerable number of formulas in which these or similar initial words are connected to a lengthy complementary clause and fitted to the respective Mass-formularies in much the same way as the present-day basic formula is provided with special supplements for certain occasions like Holy Saturday, Easter, Pentecost, and the consecration of a bishop. Incidentally we thus discover that the account in the *Liber pontificalis* is not quite exact, since the additional phrase of Gregory proves to be not entirely new, and, on the other hand, in the most ancient texts the preceding initial phrases do not recur at all with the same wording, so that here, too, a crystallizing process must have occurred.[4] Thus the *Hanc igitur* in the *Leonianum* for (Easter and) Pentecost reads as follows:

> *Hanc igitur oblationem, quam tibi offerimus pro his quos ex aqua et Spiritu Sancto regenerare dignatus es, tribuens eis remissionem omnium peccatorum, quæsumus, placatus accipias eorumque nomina adscribi iubeas in libro viventium. Per.*[5]

In general, the formula shows great variability, both in the subordinate clause and in the main clause. Only the first few words, *Hanc igitur oblationem*, commonly remain unaltered. But in most cases the oblation was in some way more exactly defined in the subordinate clause, the determination having in view those who offer it up. As a rule, it was defined as an oblation which "we" offer up for someone; but it was also described as the oblatio of one person which we, in turn, offer up for a second

---

[2] Fortescue, *The Mass*, 333.

[3] Duchesne, *Liber pont.*, I, 312: *Hic augmentavit in prædicationem canonis; diesque nostros in tua pace dispone, et cetera.* The same account in Beda, *Hist. eccl.*, II, 1 (PL, 95, 80).

[4] In the older examples, as a rule, the qualification in the introductory words is missing: *servitutis nostræ sed et cunctæ familiæ tuæ*. The continuation *quæsumus Domine ut placatus accipias* is found only in a part of the old texts. There is at least a kinship between the Gregorian phrase and the clause in the *Hanc igitur* in the Leonianum for the anniversary of the bishop's consecration (Muratori, I, 426): *diesque meos clementissima gubernatione disponas. Per.* V. L. Kennedy, "The Pre-Gregorian Hanc igitur," *Eph. liturg.*, 50 (1936), 349-358; Th. Michels, "Woher nahm Gregor d. Gr. die Kanonbitte: Diesque nostros in tua pace disponas?" *JL*, 13 (1935), 188-190.

[5] Muratori, I, 318.

person, or as the oblation of one person which he offers up for a second, or even as an oblation which the priest offers up.[6]

Even more pronounced was the variation in the main clause, which was regularly annexed. It appears that generally there was no basic scheme, but that one of the alternate texts was chosen at random and inserted, these texts being augmented at pleasure. In this main clause mention was made of the special intention which was connected with the particular celebration. Such an intention did not come into consideration for every Mass. The Mass on Sundays and feast days, for example, is not, and never was, for a special intention, but was simply the Mass of the congregation. This tallies with the fact that in pre-Gregorian sacramentaries the *Hanc igitur* does not appertain to the Sunday Mass or feast-day Mass as such, but to the Mass for special occasions and to the Votive Mass, as is especially plain from the evidence of the older *Gelasianum*,[7] and is also confirmed by the *Leonianum*.[8]

This also tallies with the form the *Hanc igitur* takes, and more particularly with the manner in which certain persons or groups of persons are introduced in it. These, whether named or not, appear either as offerers themselves or—and this especially often—as those for whom the Mass is offered; or else mention is made of persons for both functions. An offering *for* someone turns out to be plainly a characteristic of the *Hanc igitur* formula. It finds expression in the formulas for the Masses for the Dead

---

[6] The data in Kennedy, *loc. cit.*, 353 f.

[7] This Sacramentary of the 6th century is divided into three books: (1) Proprium de tempore; (2) Proprium sanctorum; (3) Masses for different purposes and occasions. In the whole Sacramentary there are 41 *Hanc igitur* formulas, and yet the formula is missing entirely in the second book. In the first book it is generally missing, e.g., on all days of Lent, and appears only, outside of Maundy Thursday, on such days when within the festal celebration a particular group of the faithful come forward and thus provide a special motive: those to be baptized (n. 26, 45), those who commemorate the anniversary of baptism (*pascha annotina*) (54), the newly ordained deacons or priests, the newly consecrated bishop, the anniversary of their ordination or consecration (97, 98, 100, 101; cf. 102) and likewise the consecrated virgins and their anniversaries (105, 106), the dedication of a church or baptistry (89, 90, 94), the commemoration of the deceased founder of the church (92). In the third book this list is continued. Not all, but

many, votive Masses have a *Hanc igitur* formula: the Mass for the anniversary of a priest's ordination (37), for the wedding itself and its anniversary (52), for one who undertakes a journey (24), for one who arranges an agape (49), the Mass for the childless (54), the birthday Mass (53), the Mass for the king (62), and for the monastery (50), the Mass *pro salute vivorum* (106), and, finally (with one exception), the whole list of Masses for the deceased (92-96; 98-106).—In the later Gelasianum the MS. of Rheinau appears to present a similar picture; Ebner, 413.—Cf. also Mohlberg, *Das fränkische Sacramentarium Gelasianum*, p. LVII, LXVIII.

[8] Of the ten *Hanc igitur* formulas of this Sacramentary there is one each for those who are to be baptized on Pentecost eve (Muratori, I, 318), for the consecration of a virgin (331), the consecration of a bishop (421), a bridal Mass (446), two for the anniversary of the consecration of a bishop (426, 434), and four for Masses for the departed (451-454).

and in the Mass of the scrutinies of candidates for Baptism, both cases
where those involved cannot themselves make the offering. Certain Votive
Masses, too, from the very nature of the case, fit in here.[9] But neophytes
also, although possessing all the rights of full Christians, do not appear
as offerers themselves, and the same is true of newly-ordained deacons and
priests,[10] and of the bride at a Nuptial Mass.[11] We discover here a fine
piece of ancient Christian etiquette. It must have been accounted an honor
to relieve those concerned of their duty of offering on this their great day,
and to make the offering "for" them, in their stead and for their benefit.[12]

Further investigation finally brings to light the fact that the mention
of those for whom the offering is made is missing in the *Hanc igitur* only
where these persons are the same as the offerers, the sacrifice being offered
for oneself and one's own intentions.[13] It is only in such cases that the

[9] Of the two *Hanc igitur* formulas in the
Mass *Ad proficiscendum in itinere* in the
older Gelasianum (III, 24), the former has
the traveler himself as the offerant and the
second already supposes a substitute, who
offers in his stead: *Hanc igitur oblationem.
Domine, famuli tui illius, quam tibi offert
pro salute famuli tui illius.* The Mass *pro
sterilitate mulierum* (III, 54) does not permit the one to whom it pertains to be the
offerant, probably to save her from embarrassment *(pro famula tua illa).*

[10] I, 24: *Hanc igitur oblationem, quam tibi
offerimus pro famulis tuis, quos ad presby-
terii vel diaconatus gradus promovere dignatus es . . .* Therefore, at that time the
newly ordained did not concelebrate in
their ordination Mass, or at any rate they
did not co-consecrate. On the other hand,
a Mass is provided for a newly consecrated
bishop (I, 100): *quam pro se episcopus die
ordinationis suæ cantat.* Hence the corresponding formula begins with: *Hanc
quoque oblationem quam offero ego tuus
famulus et sacerdos ob diem in quo dignatus es . . .*

[11] The pertinent *Hanc igitur* is found in the
Gelasianum, III, 52, as well as in the Leonianum (Muratori, I, 446), and in another version also in the Gregorianum
(Lietzmann, n. 200, 4). In the Leonianum
it reads: *Hanc igitur oblationem famulæ
tuæ ill., quam tibi offerimus pro famula
tua illa, quæsumus Domine, placatus aspi-
cias, pro qua maiestatem tuam supplices
exoramus, ut sicut eam ad ætatem nuptiis
congruentem pervenire tribuisti, sic con-
sortio maritali tuo munere copulatam de-*
*siderata sobole gaudere perficias atque ad
optatam seriem cum suo conjuge provehas
benignus annorum. Per.*

[12] This is clear in the Bridal Mass of the
Gelasianum, III, 52, where evidently the
female relatives assumed the duty. Likewise (with a single female offerant) in the
Leonianum (previous note). Ambrose, *In
Ps.* 118, prol., 2 (CSEL, 62, 4), already
testifies to the custom of having the newly
baptized, beginning with the eighth day,
themselves make the oblation. The reason
seems to be that they first had to learn
the rite by an active participation during
Easter week: *tunc demum suum munus
sacris altaribus offerat, cum cœperit esse
instructior, ne offerentis inscitia contami-
nat oblationis mysterium.* One would think
that the offertory procession was no more
difficult than the Communion procession of
that period. The reason, however, may
have been intended as an allegorical one;
one becomes *instructior* through the mystery of the "eighth day" (eighth day =
Sunday = day of resurrection), hence not
by experience, but simply by waiting for
this day.

[13] Thus, e.g., in the first *Hanc igitur* in the
Mass for a successful journey: *Hanc igitur
oblationem, Domine, famuli tui illius, quam
tibi offert . . . commendans tibi Deus iter
suum . . .* Gelasianum, III, 24 (Wilson,
245). So, too, for the anniversary of baptism, ordination, and consecration. The
bishop on the anniversary of his consecration even prays in the first person: *Hanc
quoque oblationem, quam offero ego tuus*

offerer alone is mentioned, and even then he is mentioned not as such, but rather as one expecting the fruits of the sacrifice. Especially instructive is the case of the Mass of the scrutinies already cited, where the candidates for Baptism are, in the main, the only ones mentioned in the *Hanc igitur*. As already pointed out regarding this Mass,[14] at the *Memento* for the living the names of the sponsors were read out, and these could, of course, be offerers. Now at the *Hanc igitur* there follow the names of the children who are ready for Baptism, for whom the sacrifice is offered up.[15] Even if in other cases there is no evidence of such a distribution of names, and even if time and again in the *Hanc igitur* itself those who offer and those for whom the offering is made are both mentioned one after the other,[16] still this case makes it plain enough that the accent of the *Hanc igitur* is placed on naming the ones for whom Mass is offered and on the special intentions. Thus there exists a certain external parallel to the *Memento* for the living,[17] insofar as in either instance definite persons are mentioned and names are read out.[18] But there is more here than simply a doubling of the framework for such a listing of names.[19] The real matter is a determination of the aim of our action, the intention of the particular

famulus et sacerdos ob diem in quo me . . . Gelasianum, I, 100 (Wilson, 154).

[14] *Supra,* p. 161.

[15] Gelasianum, I, 26 (Wilson, 34) : *Hanc igitur oblationem, Domine, ut propitius suscipias deprecamur, quam tibi offerimus pro famulis et famulabus tuis, quos ad æternam vitam . . . vocare dignatus es. Per Christum. Et recitantur nomina electorum. Postquam recensita fuerint dicis: Hos, Domine, fonte baptismate innovandos Spiritus tui munere ad sacramentorum tuorum plenitudinem poscimus præparari. Per.*

[16] It is easily possible that in such instances, at least in the votive Masses, where other offerants did not come into consideration, the *Memento* concerning the offerants was omitted. There is a *Hanc igitur* formula in a Mass in the Leonianum (Muratori, I, 454) with the caption *sancti Silvestri* that is still treated as a Mass of the Dead *(in famuli tui Silvestri depositione)* this points to the great antiquity of the *Hanc igitur*.

[17] The parallel to the *Memento* of the dead would be even closer. Actually in two rather late MSS. of the liturgy of St. Peter, which incorporates a Greek translation of the Roman Canon, the *Hanc igitur* is frankly treated as a *Memento* of the dead; the rubric that is added reads: Ἐνταῦθα ἀναφέρει τοὺς κοιμηθέντας. Cod-

rington, *The Liturgy of Saint Peter,* 141.

[18] The reading of the names is omitted, *inter alia,* where an exclusive group of the congregation has been singled out by an earlier listing of names, as at the Baptismal Mass on the eve of Easter and Pentecost, at an ordination, and, of course, in the case where the Mass is offered for oneself. No rigid rule, however, is apparent. In the Leonianum a reading of the names within the *Hanc igitur* is provided for in eight out of ten cases; in the older Gelasianum in something more than half of the 41 instances.

[19] The hypothesis proposed by Botte, *Le canon,* 59 that the *Memento* and *Hanc igitur* had served for the naming of the offerants in one and the same way and that they were possibly distinguished only inasmuch as the deacon read off the former and the priest the latter is therefore without foundation. The deacon could have read the names in both instances whenever there was a longer list; cfr. above, n. 15. It is contrary to the spirit of the Roman liturgy that the deacon should have said the *Memento,* because such prominence was not accorded to the deacon. In all Sacramentary MSS. that have survived, the *Memento* of the living belongs to the prayer text of the priest.

celebration, mention of which is aptly included here. It was a very thoughtful plan, one that lies close to the human heart, to use this climactic moment of the sacred action not only to join the little congregation with the large society of the earthly and heavenly Church (as had been done in the preceding prayers), but to add thereto a list of names and petitions to be specially recommended to the divine favor and thus to "join" a personal offering to that which would soon be made on the altar.[20]

In view of the marked distinctiveness and almost unlimited changeableness of the *Hanc igitur* formula, it must not always have been easy for the celebrant to find a satisfactory form to include the names of all the offerers and all those for whose benefit the offering was made, or to define all the various intentions. Interested ears would be cocked to catch every word, and woe if he missed something. The difficulty grew with the ever-increasing development of the Votive Masses which we discover in the *Gelasianum* in the sixth century. The desire of the faithful to have their earthly intentions—often all too earthly—included in the sacred sacrifice must not infrequently have become a source of deep embarrassment. It is the same difficulty encountered everywhere by present-day pastors trying to incorporate all the intentions that have been recommended to their prayers, from ailing pets to menacing school exams. So it is not hard to understand why Gregory the Great put an end to all this variety by one unswerving direction. Henceforth, at the altar only a broad and general recommendation would be made, by substituting for the diverse offerers and recipients the great Christian community consisting of both clergy and people, in which every special group is comprehended: *Hanc igitur oblationem servitutis nostræ,*[21] *sed et cunctæ familiæ tuæ.*[22] All offer for all. And in place of the variety of individual petitions, the enduring and common interests of the community, in which all particular requests are included: the universal plea for a peaceful life on earth:

---

[20] This salient mode of expression is clearly to be discerned in the caption that introduces the *Hanc igitur* of the consecration of virgins in the Leonianum (Muratori, I, 331): *Coniunctio oblationis virginum sacratarum.* For another kindred explanation concerning the *coniunctio* cf. A. Dold, *Eph. liturg.,* 50 (1936), 372 f. In the Leonianum there is a *Hanc igitur* on the day of a bishop's consecration, (Muratori, I, 434) titled *Pro episcopo offerendum;* the designation *offerendum* is there, because the formula answers the question *pro quo est offerendum?*

[21] *Servitus nostra = nos servi.* Botte, *Le canon,* 37, refers to the Gelasianum, I, 98, in which the priest prays on the day of his ordination: *ut tibi servitus nostra com-*

placeat. The *servitus* here is taken in an abstract sense; our menial service, our servitude. The expression presupposes the not infrequent use of *servus* for those invested with the priesthood; cf. *ZkTh,* 56 (1932), 603 f. In Leo the Great, *Ep.,* 108, 2 (PL, 54, 1012 A), we find in due form *per servitutem nostram* in the sense of *per nos.* This is, therefore, merely the same Latin usage of substituting an appellation for a person that we find in such expressions as "Your Holiness," "Your Grace," "Your Lordship."

[22] God's people is here conceived as a domestic group with God as its *pater familias;* cf. Rütten, "Philologisches zum Canon missæ" (*StZ,* 1938, I) 45; Batiffol, *Leçons,* 250.

dies nostros in tua pace [23] *disponas;* and the all-conclusive plea for our eternal welfare: *atque ab æterna damnatione nos eripi et in electorum tuorum iubeas grege numerari.* And in this form—as we are forced to assume as a further direction of Gregory's—the prayer was to be said at every Mass.

Only in a very few Mass formularies was the right to a special formula subsequently permitted to remain. In the missal of today it is only in the two baptismal Masses of Easter and Pentecost, and (surprisingly) in the Mass of Maundy Thursday.[24] Besides these, the *Pontificale Romanum* retains a special *Hanc igitur* for the consecration of a bishop. The Gregorian Sacramentary of Hadrian I still exhibits additional formulas—traditional ones—for the ordination of a priest, for the Nuptial Mass and for the burial of bishops.[25]

The *Hanc igitur* formulas still in use are so constructed that the basic Gregorian form is retained even on these special days, a supplementary phrase derived from the ancient wording being incorporated into it.[26] On the other hand, Gregory the Great himself appears to have retained for these special formulas only the conclusion of his common text, not utilizing the continuation of the introductory words in all cases.[27]

Furthermore, outside of Rome not only did a certain amount of the older *Hanc igitur* formulas survive for a time, due to Alcuin's supplement to Gregory's Sacramentary,[28] but actually in the milieu of the Gallic liturgies there was a whole new growth of formulas, as we can see from examples in Gallican and Irish Sacramentaries,[29] and from the formation

[23] The peace that God gives comprises also, though not exclusively, the peace of nations. The constant troubles caused by the Lombards may have been the motive for introducing a request that has been fervently re-echoed in every war-ravaged age; cf. Duchesne, *Liber pont.,* I, 312.

[24] Perhaps the "law of retaining the ancient in seasons of high liturgical worth" (Baumstark) was especially effective here as in so many instances during the Holy Week liturgy. Still, the formula may originally have been intended for the penitents, who were permitted to offer their gifts again for the first time. In the Gelasianum the formula reads, . . . *ut (familia tua) per multa curricula annorum salva et incolumis munera sua tibi Domine mereatur offerre;* Gelasianum, I, 39 (Wilson, 67, 70).

[25] Lietzmann, n. 199, 4; 200, 4; 224, 3.

[26] Compare the present-day text in the neophytes' Mass with the original, *supra,* p. 180.

The intention for the newly baptized and for the newly consecrated bishop, which in the pre-Gregorian texts as a rule was the only intention mentioned—Leonianum (Muratori, I, 318; 421); Gelasianum, I, 100 (Wilson, 154); cf. *supra,* note 13—now occupies only a secondary position: *pro his quoque; etiam pro hoc famulo tuo.*

[27] The amplification *servitutis nostræ sed et cunctæ familiæ tuæ* is missing in the ordination and bridal Mass, and at least the second part in the formula for a deceased bishop. Lietzmann, *loc. cit.*

[28] Muratori, II, 188; 193; 195; 200; 219-223.

[29] Here the subordinate clause was amplified in a manner entirely contrary to the sense of the original formula, into formulations that express the offering in honor of the saints (mentioning their names) and also in honor of Christ and of God. Examples in Kennedy, 354-357; Botte, 36, Apparatus.

of new formulas even in the Carolingian period.[30] But the Roman Church adhered to Gregory's reform. The formulation of the particular intention for each celebration was excluded, thus to an extent shunting the formula away from its original and proper intent. But the loss was more than compensated for by the fact that the perpetual intentions of all Christendom— which are likewise those of every individual Christian—were firmly fixed therein, above all the decisive request for endless glory, a grace of which it is said that we can gain only by persevering prayer, and for which we therefore humbly beg, day after day, right before the sacred moment of consecration.

There was but one further change in the *Hanc igitur,* namely in the contours of the external rite. Because the sacrificial note was emphasized in the prayer, it was quite natural to employ the same bowed posture that was attached in other places to prayers of offering. For this bow there are various evidences throughout the course of the Middle Ages.[31] But since the close of the Middle Ages the present-day rubric of holding the hands outstretched over the offerings gradually prevailed, unless (as happened) objection was taken to every sort of accompanying rite.[32] The present rite was originally a pointing gesture, occasioned by the word *hanc.*[33] Thus the gesture indicates the gifts we wish to offer God, and insofar is an oblation rite, a very natural one at that, one we have come upon more than once in other connections.[34] But the meaning of the offering is not thereby more distinctly defined. In the Old Testament the same rite of laying the hands over the sacrificial victim is prescribed for various types of offering—for burnt offering and peace offering,[35] and more par-

---

[30] A comprehensive formula dating back to the Patriarch Paulinus of Aquileja (d. 802) which mentions in the form of a prayer of intercession a long list of requests, is discussed more in detail by Ebner, 415-417; cf. *ibid.,* 23. In its original version it is also found in a Missal of Tortosa (11th cent.) : Ferreres, 360. In the Sacramentary of S. Thierry, 9-10th cent.), Martène, 1, 4, X (I, 552-562), there are five formulas of a like nature within the compass of as many votive formularies, which in each instance include, along with the oration, a proper Preface and *Hanc igitur.* The Missa Illyrica has a *Hanc igitur* formula for the case of a lawsuit; *ibid.,* IV (I, 513 E). Further examples *ibid.,* 1, 4, 8, 17 (I, 408).

[31] *Ordo "Qualiter quædam"* (Andrieu, II, 298; PL, 78, 1380 C) : *Hic inclinat se usque ad altare.* Bernold of Constance, *Micrologus,* c. 88 (PL, 986 D) ; Honorius Augustod., *Sacramentarium,* c. 88 (PL,

172, 793 B) ; *Liber ordinarius O. Præm.* (Waefelghem, 71 f.) ; *Liber ordinarius* of Liége (Volk, 94). Durandus, IV, 39, 1, testifies to the profound bow *in quibusdam ecclesiis.* According to Eisenhofer, II, 180, also in "countless" Mass books until the 15th century. Cf. also Lebrun, I, 384.

[32] This is the case, e.g., in the Ordo of Cardinal Stefaneschi (about 1311), n. 53 (PL, 78, 1166 A), also in the Dominican Rite of today : *Missale O.P.* (1889), 19.

[33] The Mass-*ordo* of York (about 1425) has the rubric: *parum tangat calicem dicens: Hanc.* Simmons, *The Lay Folks Mass Book,* p. 106. The laying on of the hands appears in Mass books of the 14th century; Leroquais, II, 210; III, 41, 60, 82. Numerous examples of the 15th and 16th centuries, Lebrun, I, 384 f. Eisenhofer, II, 180.

[34] Above I, 29; II, p. 147, nn. 44, 45.

[35] Lev. 1: 4; 3: 2, 8, 13; 8: 18, 22.

ticularly for a sacrifice with propitiatory character,[36] pre-eminently the sacrifice of the scape-goat on the great Day of Atonement.[37] Still there is no real reason to interpret the gesture precisely in this last sense, as long as the accompanying text gives no hint of it.[38]

11. *Quam oblationem*

The last prayer before the account of the institution forms with it a grammatical unit. It is like an up-beat before the full measure, a final swell in human words before the introduction of the imposing phrases of the sacred account, which are attached by means of a simple relative pronoun. For this introductory prayer of our canon we have the early testimony of St. Ambrose, both for the prayer itself and for its introductory character, since when he cites it his chief concern is with the words of Christ thus introduced by it.[1] In the *eucharistia* of Hippolytus a preliminary of this kind is still lacking. There the account of the institution simply follows the words of praise regarding the redemption in the course of the prayer of thanksgiving. But meditation on the work of the divine omnipotence and favor which is about to be performed must have induced the notion of prefacing it with a formal prayer, much in the same way as we pray for our daily bread before we sit down to eat it.

The prayer *Quam oblationem* is the plea for the final hallowing of the earthly gift and, in the last analysis, a plea "that it may become for us the Body and Blood of Thy most beloved Son, our Lord Jesus Christ." The main thought is clear, but the expression is not very sharply stamped. The present-day wording of the prayer is already to be found in the Sacramentary of Gregory the Great,[2] but it differs considerably from the earlier form presented by Ambrose. The old traditional formulations are not fitted together into the newer framework very smoothly.[3] In Ambrose we read: *fac nobis hanc oblationem adscriptam, ratam, rationabilem, acceptabilem, quod figura est corporis et sanguinis Domini nostri Jesu*

---

[36] Lev. 4: 4, 15, 24, 29, 33; 8: 14.

[37] Lev. 16: 20 f.

[38] A reference to the sacrifice of the cross is included in such cases as when a Missal of Auxerre (14th cent) prescribes that the hands be imposed in the form of a cross; Leroquais, II, 262. The rite does not seem to have gained any extensive vogue. Regarding the warning bell rung at either the *Hanc igitur* or the *quam oblationem* see infra, chapter 13, n. 50.

[1] *Supra*, I, 52.

[2] With the exception that in the present-day text the word *(Domini) Dei (nostri Jesu Christi)* is lacking: Botte, 38. But it is also wanting in one Vatican MS. of the Greg. Sacramentary, Codex Ottobonianus, 313; cf. E. Bishop, "Table of Early Texts of the Roman Canon," *Journal of Theological Studies*, 1903, 555-578.

[3] Cf. the complaints in G. Rietschel, *Lehrbuch der Liturgik* (Berlin, 1900), 382, who declares the prayer "unintelligible." Suarez, too, thinks: *obscurior est reliquis;* De sacramentis, I, 83, 2, 9 (*Opp.*, ed. Berton, 21, 875).

Christi. Here the meaning is quite plain; an appeal[4] is made that God may turn the gift into a perfect offering, which[5] is the representation[6] of Christ's Body and Blood.[7] The expressions *adscripta*, etc., here describe the sacrificial gift in its already altered state.

It is not impossible to explain the present-day text in a similar sense. In the introductory phrase only the *fac* has been changed to *facere digneris* and the word *benedictam* added, in no way altering the meaning. The four-member expression has been changed into five, thus giving still greater force to the guarded legal terminology of the Romans which is here in evidence.[8] In the second clause a noteworthy addition, evoked doubtlessly by the nearness of the great, grace-filled event, is the emotional word joined to the mention of our Saviour, the word *dilectissimi*,[9] all the more remarkable because of the contrast to the legal language of the preceding phrase. Of greater importance, however, is the fact that, after the ambiguous *figura* was dropped, the *quod est* should be turned into *ut fiat*. Thus, according to the grammatical formulation now presented, the change into the Body and Blood of Christ is no longer contained amongst the properties of the sacrificial gift expected from God, but appears instead as the result of it (or as a goal to which that divine operation is ordered.) Still it is possible to consider this result as provided in that exaltation itself, so that only in concept would it be detached there-

[4] Ambrose, *De sacra.*, IV, 5, 21 (*supra*, I, 52). The amended text as edited by B. Botte (Sources chrétiennes, 25; 1950), 84, reads: *oblationem scriptam, rationabilem* (without *ratam*).

[5] The *quod* may be the Latin for *quæ*; O. Casel, "Quam oblationem" (*JL*, 2, (1922) 98-101) 100.

[6] *Figura* does not exclude the reality as does our word for "picture," but leaves room for it; in translation this is perhaps best expressed as "representation." A like mode of expression is known to occur frequently until into the 5th century. Cf. the parallels in Quasten, *Mon.*, 160, n. 1. Cf. also the equivalent expression in the *Liber ordinum* (Férotin, 322; *supra* I, 55, n. 20). Cf. W. Dürig, "Imago" (*Münchener Theol. Studien*, II, 5; Munich, 1952), 91 f.

[7] This explanation, which Casel adopted, *loc. cit.*, was later quietly toned down by him quite noticeably (*JL*, [for 1931] 1-19) 12 f.; now he stresses the point that the primitive meaning of the prayer was not "a petition for the consecration, but a prayer of sacrifice in the form of a petition for acceptance." The Church pleads for the acceptance of its sacrifice as something fully valid and agreeable, "because it is really identical with the sacrifice of Christ." At the same time he strikes out from the Ambrosian text above the word *rationabilem* (10 f.), which is not easy to connect with *fac*. Still he treats the *fac* as well as the *facere digneris* of today, as though *habe, habere digneris* were in its place; cf. the proposed translation, *ibid.*, 17, note 30: "Look upon (or regard) this offering . . . as blessed . . ." In reality it is still a matter of God's action. We are compelled to say that even with Ambrose the prayer had a twofold character, inasfar as expressions of an attitude of agreement are united with a petition for action; in other words, the prayer is conceived as though the consecration had already taken place, but we are once again praying for it.

[8] Cf. Baumstark, *Vom geschichtlichen Werden der Liturgie*, 84. The dying dedication of the Decians in Livy, VIII, 9, 6-8, presents a pre-Christian example of such a legal-sacral combination of terms.

[9] According to Matth. 3: 17; 17: 5 and parallels.

from as the sought-for consequence. Make this gift (we seem to say) into a perfect oblation in such a way that it becomes the Body and Blood of our Lord.

The attempt to wrest the ancient meaning out of the later wording is given special impetus by one expression which has survived in the first clause. Along with the other qualifications, our oblation gift should be *rationabilis*. Even in the Vulgate the word *rationabile* corresponds to the Greek λογικόν: spiritual, spiritualized, immaterial.[10] *Oblatio rationabilis* = λογική θυσία is an exact description of the spiritual sacrifice proper to Christianity, a sacrifice lifted high above the realm of matter.[11] In the Roman canon as quoted by Ambrose the same word reappears after the the consecration begged for a divinely effected exaltation and spiritualizing the sense just indicated: *offerimus tibi hanc immaculatam hostiam, rationabilem hostiam, incruentam hostiam.*[12] Thus, too, the prayer before the consecration begged for a divinely effected exaltation and spiritualizing of our sacrifice, beyond blood and earthly taint, and the other terms from the Roman legal language merely attempted to define this plea more exactly within the given context. *Adscriptam*, for instance, applied to citizens and soldiers, indicated that they were entered in the lists, and so here, too, it means recognized and accepted.[13] Still, it is precisely the meaning of the word *rationabilis* in our prayer which underwent a profound change between Ambrose's time and Gregory the Great. Already in the usage of Leo the Great, and definitely in Gregory's, *rationabilis* lost the shade of meaning it had in Christian cult and signified merely what was suited to reason or the nature of things.[14] So too in our *Quam oblationem*, where it is encircled by Roman legal terms, it reverts to the simple Roman signification, at least as far as it was understood in that era. Thus an opportunity was presented to see in what was petitioned by the *fac* or *facere digneris* not the completed transubstantiation but rather a preparation for that change, the condition by which the gift was made "serviceable" or "right." Furthermore, by means of the *ut*-clause, this latter was

---

[10] Rom. 12: 1; I Peter 2: 2.

[11] O. Casel, "Oblatio rationabilis," *Theol. Quartalschrift*, 99 (1917-18), 429 to 437; ibid., "λογική θυσία der antiken Mystik in christlich-Ziturgischer Umdeutung," *JL*, 4 (1924), 37-47.—Cf. *supra*, I, 24 f.

[12] Ambrose, *De sacr.*, IV, 6, 27.

[13] Cf. Casel, *Quam oblationem*, 100. Contrariwise Batiffol, *Leçons*, 251, n. 1, would rather take it in the sense of "accredited," with reference to the Leonianum (Muratori, I, 361): *Omnipotens sempiterne Deus, qui offerenda tuo nomini tribuis et oblata devotioni nostræ servitutis adscribis.* Perhaps it is best, however, to take the word to mean "consecrated, dedicated,"

considering *ascribere* as equivalent to *attribuere;* cf. *Thesaurus Linguæ Latinæ*, II, 772-776.

[14] But perhaps we ought rather to follow the argument of Botte, "Traduction du Canon de la Messe," *La Maison-Dieu*, 23 (1950), 41, 47-49, and take the word *rationabilem* in its older meaning even here in our present Roman Canon; after all, in the language of religion certain expressions do keep a more ancient significance even when in every-day use the meaning changes. Cf. Chr. Mohrmann, "Rationabilis-λογικός, *Revue internat. des Droits de l'Antiquité*, 5 (1950), 225-234.

defined as the proper goal,[15] but it is now spoken of not as the immediate object of the petition, but only as a consequence or intention. Once again the matter kept in view is a preparatory step to the consecration itself, with the latter mentioned only in the background. The train of thought is then the same as that which is manifested more than once in the *secreta*, the thought which is given full expression, for instance, in one of the secret prayers of the *Gregorianum: Munera, Domine, oblata sanctifica, ut tui nobis Unigeniti corpus et sanguis fiant. Per.*[16] But if one is unwilling to take the new version of the *Quam oblationem* in the original sense, even in the sense as thus half-buried,[17] it will then be necessary to accept a very weakened interpretation of the text, formulated somewhat as follows: Let this gift, O God, be in all blessed, approved, valid, right and acceptable, so that it (may) become for us the Body and Blood of Thy well-beloved Son, our Lord Jesus Christ.[18]

The goal of our petition is still the consecration, or more exactly the transformation of our sacrificial gift,[19] even though it is modestly pushed to the background in favor of the preparatory step. The formula thus represents the plea for consecration or—viewing the matter technically—the epiklesis of the Roman Mass. This is therefore the proper place to make a comparative study of what is generally called in other liturgies an epiklesis.

At two points in the Mass the sacramental world intrudes into the liturgical activity of the Church: at the consecration and at the Communion. God Himself is operative, giving us invisible grace by means of visible sacramental signs. Man can do nothing here except place the signs and —early reflection had soon deemed this proper—beg for the divine

---

[15] Preceding the change to the *ut* clause, there seems to have been a form with *quæ* and the subjunctive, one that is still presented in the Irish and Milanese tradition: *quæ nobis corpus et sanguis fiat;* Casel, 12; Botte, 38. The *ut* could not have come into its place until towards the end of the 6th century. A version with *quæ,* and even with the indicative in two texts of the Mozarabic liturgy; Botte, 37; see above I, 55, n. 20.

[16] Cf. *supra,* note 10.

[17] The older interpretation of *rationabilem* also in E. Bishop, "The Moment of Consecration" (appendix to Connolly, *The Liturgical Homilies of Narsai,* 126-163), 150 f. and in the earlier Middle Ages; also in Florus Diaconus (d. about 860), *De actione miss.,* c. 59 (PL, 119, 51), and in Remigius of Auxerre, *Expositio* (PL, 101, 1260). In fact the word *rationabilis* is here clearly understood in the older meaning:

ille quidem panis et illud vinum per se irrationabile est, sed orat sacerdos ut . . . rationabilis fiat transeundo in corpus Filii ejus.

[18] Thus Botte in the article mentioned in note 14.—For the combination of *rationablis acceptabilemque* proposed by Botte, cf. I Peter 2: 5: *spirituales hostias, acceptabiles Deo per J. Chr.*

[19] This *nobis* which appears already in the Ambrosian text is not without meaning. It is inserted to point out that the object is not merely Christ's presence as such, something that might have been sufficient for a later form of piety, but His presence as our sacrificial offering, in which our sacrifice is completed and into which He desires that we ourselves be finally taken up. Cf. P. de Puniet, "La consecration" (*Cours et Conférences,* VII; Louvain, 1929; 193-208), 198 f., 201 ff.

operation. Just how this appeal will be worded depends on the mode of theological thought, whether to call upon God in a formal request for this operation, or (more in line with pre-Christian forms of expression) to implore the assistance of divine power. Both of these modes of approach were designated in Christian antiquity as ἐπικαλεῖσθαι, ἐπίκλησις, because in both cases God's name is invoked and God's power is elicited.[20] The earliest record of an epiklesis is found in reference to Baptism, in the consecration of the baptismal water,[21] but there is also early mention of it in reference to the Eucharist.[22]

Coming now to particulars, it could be sufficient simply and bluntly to implore God for the hallowing of the gift and for its salutary and fruitful enjoyment, as actually happens in the Roman Mass at the *Quam oblationem* and the *Supplices*. Or one could attempt to define and designate the divine power by name. Christian terms which could be considered include: the Spirit of God, the power or the grace of God or His blessing, the Wisdom or the Word of God, the Holy Ghost; one could even think of an angel of God.[23] In the early Christian era there was no hard and fast rule in this regard. In Greek, where λόγος and πνεῦμα appear with the meaning "spirit," where, besides, in the theological consideration of the matter, a major role was taken by the idea that God had created and accomplished everything through the Logos, it was natural that mention should be made oftener of the Logos as the power by which the gift is sanctified.[24] In the *Mystagogic Catecheses,* with which (according to the prevailing opinion) Cyril of Jerusalem concluded his baptismal instructions in the year 348, we find the earliest record of the basic form of that epiklesis which became typical of the oriental liturgies: "Then . . . we call on the good God to send the Holy Ghost upon the gifts, so that He might change the bread into the Body of Christ and the wine into the Blood of Christ."[25] This epiklesis, taken in the narrow sense as a plea to God

---

[20] Cf. O. Casel, "Zur Epiklese"; *JL,* 3 (1923), 100-102; *ibid.,* "Neue Beiträge zur Epiklesenfrage," *JL,* 4 (1924), 169-178: see also the entire question of the epiklesis in Gassner, *The Canon of the Mass,* 324-339.

[21] Tertullian, De bapt., c. 4 (CSEL, 20, 204).

[22] In the broader sense the Eucharistia, like every prayer of dedication, is an ἐπίκλησις, namely, an invocation of the divine Name over the material elements. It is in this sense that Irenæus, *Adv. hær.,* IV, 31, 4 (al., IV, 18, 5; Harvey, II, 205 f.), speaks of the bread that receives τὴν ἐπίκλησιν τοῦ θεοῦ and is no longer ordinary bread. Cf. Casel, *Neue Beiträge,* 173 f.

[23] Cf. the problem below regarding *Supplices te rogamus.*

[24] *Euchologion* of Serapion, 13, 15 (Quasten, *Mon.,* 62 f.): ᾿Επιδημησάτω θεὲ τῆς ἀληθείας, ὁ ἅγιός σου λόγος ἐπὶ τὸν ἄρτον τοῦτον, ἵνα γένηται ὁ ἄρτος σῶμα τοῦ λόγου . . . Further data in Quasten, *Mon.,* 62, n. 5. *Ibid.,* 18, n. 1, the literature concerning the much discussed passage in Justin, *Apol.,* I, 66: the bread becomes the body of Christ δι' εὐχῆς λόγου τοῦ παρ' αὐτοῦ. See also the materials in Bishop, *The Moment of Consecration,* 155-163.

[25] Cyril of Jerusalem, *Catech. myst.,* V, 7 (Quasten, *Mon.,* 101). Cf. Bishop, *The Moment of Consecration,* 126-150. The Holy Ghost epiklesis after the consecration is not again clearly certified until

to send the Holy Spirit, thereafter appears first in the liturgies in the region of Syria; when it does appear it is found (as we might already gather from the passage cited above) *after* the words of institution and the anamnesis and oblation prayer that follow, and the object of the formula is that the Holy Ghost might "make" the gifts into Christ's Body and Blood (ποιήση: Liturgy of St. James) or "manifest" them as such (ἀποφήνη: *Apostolic Constitutions VIII;* ἀναδεῖξαι: Byzantine Liturgy of St. Basil) and that thus they might have a salutary effect on the recipients.[26] In the last sense, as a plea to the Holy Ghost to let the Communion strengthen the recipients in their faith, an epiklesis is to be found at the same point even in the *eucharistia* of Hippolytus. But there is no reference here to the transformation of the gifts.[27] The oriental liturgies, too, must have had originally in place of the epiklesis only a petition for the salutary effects of Communion,[28] from which a more general plea for blessing, with special reference to the transubstantiation, could easily have developed.[29]

Besides this consecratory epiklesis, which emerged from Syria, an

---

Theodore of Mopsuestia, *Sermones catech.,* VI (Rücker, 32 f). Bishop calls attention to the fact that in the conflict with the Macedonians (condemned in 381) regarding the divinity of the Holy Ghost, the Eucharistic consecration as the work of the Holy Ghost was not stressed by the Catholics (140 f.). In view of the pronounced isolation of the testimony mentioned (although one must take into consideration the passage to which M. de la Taille, *The Mystery of Faith,* II [London & New York, 1950], 412-413, notes 6 and 1, refers), we may again call attention to the question whether John of Jerusalem (d. 417) was the real author of the Catecheses rather than Cyril; cf. Quasten, *Mon.,* 70. That mystogogical catecheses were announced in the 18th catechesis and that a back reference is made to previous catecheses in the mystagogical one, proves little fundamentally, since these mystagogical catecheses generally followed after the catecheses of the symbol. In the meanwhile the question has been re-examined from the historical viewpoint by W. J. Swaans, "A propos des Catéchèses Mystagogiques," *Le Muséon* 55 (Louvain, 1942), 1-43; the results do not favor Cyril.

[26] Critical survey of the relevant texts and an analysis of them in Lietzmann, *Messe*

und Herrenmahl, 68-81; cf. G. Rauschen, *Eucharistie und Busszsakrament* (2nd ed.; Freiburg, 1910), 110-130; Hanssens, *Institutiones,* III, 454-463. A comprehensive summary of the theological problem in Th. Spacil, *Doctrina theologiæ Orientis separati de ss. Eucharistia,* II (Orientalia christiana, 14, 1; Rome, 1929), 1-114.

[27] *Supra* I, 29.

[28] A Baumstark, *Le liturgie orientali e le preghiere 'Supra quæ' e 'Supplices' del canone romano"* (Grottaferrata, 1913), especially p. 33; *idem,* "Zu den Problemen der Epiklese des römischen Messkanons," *Theol. Revue,* 15 (1916), 337-350, especially 341. Similarly Hanssens, III, 354 f.

[29] It is to be noted that in the Antiochene-Byzantine group of liturgies the space before the words of the institution was monopolized by the (mostly Christological) continuation of the thanksgiving prayer. And thus, the only possibility for a prayer of blessing was after the words of institution and oblation. The more vividly the process of the consecration was conceived as an effect of the bestowal of the divine blessing and Spirit, the more did the need of a consecration epiklesis obtrude itself. Cf. J. Brinktrine, "Zur Entstehung der morgenländischen Epiklese," *ZkTh,* 42 (1918), 301-326; 483-518.

epiklesis pronounced *after* the words of consecration, there was another in the Church of Egypt—originally, it is evident, the only one [30]—which *preceded* the words of consecration. The basic form of this reads as follows: Heaven and earth are full of Thy glory; fill this gift, too, with Thy blessing.[31] It was not till later that the Egyptian Liturgy of St. Mark also adopted the Syro-Byzantine epiklesis.

Thus the consecratory epiklesis following the words of institution became, by degrees, a distinctive feature of the entire Eastern Church, and in the dissident churches was given a theological interpretation consonant with the wording of the prayer.[32] But viewed in the light of tradition it represents the fourth century custom of only one of the three great patriarchates, namely, that of Antioch, while in the other two, Alexandria and Rome, the traditional practice, going back at least to the same early period, involved an invocation of the divine power *before* the words of institution.[33] The fact that more and more emphasis was given to the invocation of the Holy Ghost coincides with a basic trend of oriental theology, a trend noticed at a very early stage; for Eastern theologians are wont to consider the Holy Ghost as "the executor and accomplisher of every divine work," [34] and in general their theological thinking is built more strongly on the mystery of the Trinity.[35]

However, there is no solid and unimpeachable evidence in the original sources of the Roman liturgy that the Roman Mass also at one time had an epiklesis of the Holy Ghost as a plea for the consecration.[36] The pertinent remark in a letter of Pope Gelasius I is indeed striking but not un-

---

[30] Cf. Lietzmann, 76; Baumstark, *Liturgie comparée*, 7 f.—Hanssens, III, 462, expresses skepticism.

[31] *Supra*, p. 148. It is found in Serapion and in the Egyptian Mass liturgy, and besides also in the liturgical papyrus of Dêr-Balyzeh (Quasten, *Mon.*, 40; a more complete text in C. H. Roberts-B. Capelle, *An early Euchologium* [Louvain, 1949], 24 f.; cf. 44 f.), and in a Coptic anaphora of the 6th century discovered by L. Th. Lefort in 1940 (Roberts-Capelle, 25, 44 f.).

[32] That the epiklesis was necessary for the consecration along with the words of institution was maintained by oriental theologians already at an early date; that it alone was necessary, was not generally advocated until the 17th century. Cf. Pohl-M. Gierens, *Lehrbuch der Dogmatik*, III, (9th ed.; Paderborn, 1937), 278; see *ibid.*, 282-286, regarding the dogmatic judgment of the question.

[33] In this sense O. Heiming, *JL*, 15 (1941), 445-447.

[34] Thus the oriental theologian B. Ghius, *JL*, 15 (1941), 338 f.

[35] It must be granted that the basic notion is found in primitive Christianity. This is plain from the fact that in the Apostles' Creed the Holy Ghost appears at the head of the list of the gifts of salvation and as their source. A priori, therefore, one could expect a similar Trinitarian composition would have asserted itself at an early date in the Eucharistic prayer, as a prayer rising to God the Father, with thanks for the work of the Son, and with the petition for the fulfillment of the same through the Holy Ghost. Cf. *supra*, I, 32, n. 17. The Eucharistia of Hippolytus in fact shows this plan, for which the Anglican liturgist W. H. Frere has again pleaded at the present time (see *ibid.*).

[36] Regarding the testimony of the Georgian liturgy of St. Peter so often mentioned before, cf. above, p. 150, n. 15.

equivocal.[37] At any rate, an epiklesis of this sort did not belong to the older tradition in Rome, and later the simple ancient form of the plea for the blessing of the gift before the consecration remained as decisive as the plea after the consecration for the fulfillment of the blessing in all who received the gift of the altar.

This blessing was given further outward expression by means of the gestures, the first three of the five attributes of the sacrificial gifts being each accompanied by a sign of the Cross, to which were added two demonstrative signs of the Cross at the mention of the Body and Blood of our Lord.[38]

12. The Consecration: The Account of Institution

In all the known liturgies the core of the *eucharistia*, and therefore of the Mass, is formed by the narrative of institution and the words of consecration.[1] Our very first observation in this regard is the remarkable fact

---

[37] Gelasius I, *Ep. fragm.*, 7 (Thiel, I, 486) : *quomodo ad divini mysterii consecrationem cœlestis spiritus invocatus adveniet, si sacerdos (et) qui eum adesse deprecatur, criminosis plenus actionibus reprobetur?* For an explanation of the passage cf. Casel, *Neue Beiträge*, 175-177; Geiselmann, *Die Abendmahlslehre*, 217-222; J. Brinktrine, "Der Vollzieher der Eucharistie nach Gelasius," *Miscellanea Mohlberg*, II (1949), 61-69.—Taking the words at their obvious meaning, they certainly seem to include an express invocation of the Holy Ghost, which, as Eisenhofer, II, 169, assumes, could have existed in a transient extension of the *Quam oblationem*, e.g., *Quam oblationem . . . acceptabilemque facere eique virtutem Sancti Spiritus infundere digneris, ut nobis.* Or, with C. Callewaert, "Histoire positive du Canon romain" (*Sacris erudiri,* 1949), 95-97, we might see here a reference to other prayers, such as the several secret prayers of the Leonianum which invoke the Holy Ghost. Still, Gelasius, who places the consecration on a parallel with the effects of the Holy Ghost in the Incarnation, could conceive the calling down of the Holy Ghost as being presented throughout the canon with its many petitions for blessing, without any express invocation of the third Divine Person. Cf. Botte, *Le canon*, 60 f.; idem. *Bulletin de théol, anc. et méd.*, 6 (1951), 226.

[38] Cf. above, p. 143. It may seem strange that all five of the attributes were not accompanied with an individual sign of the cross. Bernold of Constance, *Micrologus*, c. 14 (PL, 151, 987), gives the answer : *ut quinarium numerum non excederemus et quintam crucem super calicem quasi quinti vulneris indicem . . . faceremus.*

[1] The East Syrian anaphora of the Apostles forms an exception here, inasmuch as the account of the institution is omitted in the MSS. of that liturgy. The same thing seems to be the case in a Syrian anaphora fragment originating in the 6th century (Brightman, 511-518), though this contains a short paraphrase. The instance is so strange that Lietzmann, *Messe und Herrenmahl,* 33, himself thinks the only motive could have been a reverential awe lest they profane the sacred words. A. Raes, S.J., "Le recit de l'institution eucharistique dans l'anaphore chaldéene et malabare des Apôtres" : *Orientalia Christiana Periodica,* 10 (1944), 216-226, thinks otherwise. He considers the possibility that the account of the institution was dropped after the defection of the Nestorians (431), at a time, therefore, when in Syrian lands there grew up an exaggerated esteem of the epiklesis (cf. above, p. 191 f.). Similarly B. Botte, "L'anaphore chaldéene des Apôtres," *ibid.,* 15 (1949), 259-276; however, Botte places the origin of the anaphora itself in the 3rd century, but at the same time

that the texts of the account of institution, among them in particular the most ancient (whether as handed down or as reconstructed by comparative studies), are never simply a Scripture text restated.[2] They go back to pre-biblical tradition. Here we face an outgrowth of the fact that the Eucharist was celebrated long before the evangelists and St. Paul set out to record the Gospel story.[3] Even the glaring discrepancies in the biblical texts themselves regarding this very point are explained by this fact.[4] For in them we evidently find segments from the liturgical life of the first generation of Christians.

Later on, because liturgical texts were still very fluid, the account of the institution was developed along three different lines.[5] First of all, the two sections on the bread and the chalice were refashioned to gain greater symmetry. Such a symmetrical conformation, undoubtedly introduced in the interest of a well-balanced audible performance, is seen already in the phrases of the rather simple account of the institution as recorded by Hippolytus: *Hoc est corpus meum quod pro vobis confringetur—Hic est sanguis meus qui pro vobis effunditur.*[6] The parallelism was even more advanced in a liturgy a good hundred years after, namely, the Liturgy of Serapion, where the single account has been broken up into two independent parallel accounts separated by a prayer.[7] The trend reached a crest before the middle of the fifth century in the basic form of the main oriental liturgies, the anaphoras of St. Mark, St. James and St. Basil. Here, for example, in both passages we find εὐχαριστήσας, εὐλογήσας, ἁγιάσας; and the additional phrase from Matthew 26:28 regarding the chalice, εἰς ἄφεσιν ἁμαρτιῶν, is transferred also to the bread.[8] Then came the second phase, wherein symmetry was abandoned in favor of a word-for-word dependence on the biblical accounts, some expressions from the Scriptures being interwoven bit by bit with the traditional text. And finally, along with these, a third phenomenon appeared, the effort to refit the

draws attention to various indications that the account of the institution was part of the primitive text. In modern times the Nestorians add an account of the institution from some other source to the anaphora of the Apostles (cf. Brightman 285); this was done in the Syro-Malabar rite since the 16th century. Concerning the manner of the insertion, or rather annexation, see Raes, S.J., *Introductio*, 91; 98 f.

[2] See the textual criticism and the historical research of F. Hamm *Die liturgischen Einsetzungsberichte im Sinne vergleichender Liturgieforschung untersucht* (LQF, 23; Münster, 1928). A good review of the interrelationship of the texts in P. Cagin, *L'Eucharistie canon primitif de la messe*, (Paris, 1912), where, pages 225-244, the

four biblical and the 76 liturgical accounts of the institution are printed side by side in 80 columns; in this way 79 distinct textual parts in the account are differentiated. —An earlier work on the symmetrical development of the consecration formula in K. J. Merk, *Der Konsekrationstext der römishen Messe* (Rottenburg a. N., (1915).

[3] Cf. also Hanssens, III, 440.
[4] Cf. above I, 8.
[5] Hamm, 33 f.
[6] Above I, 29.
[7] Above I, 34 f.; Hamm, 94.
[8] Hamm, 16 f., 21 f., 95. Further examples in comparative juxtaposition in Hanssens, III, 417 f.

phrases in decorative fashion, to underscore certain theological concepts,[9] and to make more room for a reverential participation. In addition, elements of local table etiquette,[10] or elements from the customs of worship [11] were frequently re-projected into the biblical account.

Viewed against such a background, the account of the institution in our Roman Mass [12] displays a relatively ancient character. The trend towards parallelism and biblicism has made great progress, but further transformation has remained within modest limits. The parallelism is manifested in the double occurrence of the ornamental phrase, *in sanctas ac venerabiles manus suas;* further, in the words, *tibi gratias agens benedixit deditque discipulis suis dicens: accipite,* of which only *gratias agens, dedit, dicens* are biblical, and only *dedit, dicens* are found in parallel in the scriptural text (of Matthew and Mark) ; and lastly in the words, *ex hoc omnes* and *enim,* both found in Matthew 26:28, but with reference only to the chalice.

The inclusion of the biblical wording is almost complete. Of the entire stock in the various biblical accounts, only one text-phrase is missing in our canon, aside from the command to "do this in remembrance of me" which is found in Paul-Luke right after the institution of the bread, and the remark in Mark 14:23, *et biberunt ex illo omnes.* However, this missing phrase, namely the words added to *Hoc est corpus meum* in the Paul-Luke report: *quod pro vobis datur,* is an amazingly significant omission. Its absence is all the more remarkable because it already appeared (in the form: *quod pro vobis* [resp. *pro multis*] *confringetur)* in both of the older texts of the Roman tradition. So it must have been expunged some time between the fourth and the seventh century, for a reason unknown to us.[13] On the other hand, in the oldest known text of the Roman Mass, the one in Hippolytus, almost half the biblical text is wanting.[14] In refer-

---

[9] Of this type are the terms found in oriental liturgies where, besides the intention "for the forgiveness of sins," we find other paraphrases of the purpose of Christ's gift, "as an atonement of transgressions," "for eternal life," "for the life of the world," "for those who believe in me." Cagin, 231 ff., 235 ff. Also the attributes given to the hands of Our Lord, and the word ἁγιάσας = *consecrans* are the result of theological reflection.

[10] Oriental liturgies often mention the mingling (χεράσας) and also the tasting (γευσάμενος, πίων). The idea that the Lord as host drank from the chalice first of all was already advanced by Irenæus; that He also partook of the bread was frequently mentioned by the Syrians; Hanssens, III, 444; Hamm, 51; 59.

[11] In this category are included the raising of the eyes and the making of the sign of the cross *(benedixit)* over the gift-offerings.

[12] The present-day text is the same as that of the oldest sacramentary tradition with this difference, that in three places the verbs are often joined without a conjunctive word; they were amplified: *et (elevatis oculis)* and twice *(dedit)que;* in place of *postquam* we find *posteaquam* in the sacramentaries. Other departures are found only in isolated MSS.; see Botte, 38-40.

[13] Botte, 61, conjectures that the suppression is connected with the simplification of the rite of the fraction. The likelihood of this is slim.

[14] Cf. *supra* I, 29.

ence to the bread, the words *benedixit, fregit, deditque discipulis suis* are missing. In reference to the chalice, the words *postquam cœnavit, gratias agens, bibite ex hoc omnes* are omitted, as well as the words *enim* and *multis* from Matthew, the expressions *calix, novum testamentum* and *in remissionem peccatorum*. About midway between the text of Hippolytus and our present canon is the text recorded by Ambrose, insofar as it still shows none of the additions regarding the chalice.[15]

Another surprising thing in our Roman canon is the beginning of the words over the chalice: *Hic est enim calix sanguinis mei novi (et æterni) testamenti*. To the simple formula of the older Roman tradition, *Hic est sanguis meus*, the *calix* of Paul-Luke has been added. And following the model of Matthew-Mark, the notion of a covenant has been included.[16]

Even though these additions make the formula somewhat cumbersome from the viewpoint of grammar,[17] still there is a double reward, for the mention of the chalice directly characterizes the Blood of our Lord as a drink, and the mention of the covenant opens up a broader vista of the work of redemption, accomplished (in fulfillment of the Old Testament figure) by the Blood of our Lord. Furthermore, it is a *testamentum*, a "covenant," a new divine economy binding heaven and earth together.[18]

The further transformation of our Roman text of the institution was very limited. The time is given in the words, *pridie quam pateretur*. This manner of chronicling the time is as characteristic of the occidental texts as the Pauline expression, "On the night when He was betrayed," is, in general, of the oriental ones. In the interest of theological precision, the latter text is often augmented by a reference[19] to the voluntariness of the

---

[15] *Supra* I, 52. However, as Hamm, 95, emphasizes, the Ambrosian text and our canon text simply are not in the same line of development. In some points the former is even further developed than our canon text; namely, in the twice-repeated *ad te sancte Pater omnipotens æterne Deus* and *apostolis et discipulis suis*. Besides, it has the *fregit fractumque* and the *quod pro multis confringetur*.

[16] The same combination also in the Syrian texts: Hamm, 74, n. 145.

[17] The realization of this is probably the reason why the words *sanguinis mei* are in individual instances missing: Sacramentary of the 13th century of the Cod. Barberini, XI, 179 (Ebner, 417); Missale of Riga about 1400 (see Bruiningk, 85, n. 1).

[18] In view of the marked difference at this point between the tradition of Paul-Luke on the one hand and of Mark-Matthew on

the other, the question arises, what was the exact wording as spoken by Our Lord. The decision of the exegetes leans towards Mark 14: 24: Τοῦτό ἐστιν τὸ αἷμά μου τῆς διαθήκης τὸ εκχυννόμενον ὑπὲρ πολλῶν, because of its agreement with Ex. 24: 8, which Our Lord probably had in mind. The revamping in Paul seems to have been done with the view of bringing the spiritual consideration into greater prominence. Arnold, *Der Ursprung des christlichen Abendmahls,* 176 f. For the rendering of διαθήκη *testamentum,* "alliance," as "divine economy," see *ibid.,* 181 f.—In favor of the form in Luke 22: 20, there is a late study by H. Schuermann, "Die Semitismen im Einsetzungsbericht bei Markus und bei Lukas," *ZkTh,* 73, (1951), 72-77.

[19] In the later text of the liturgy of St. Chrysostom and the anaphora of St. James: τῇ νυκτὶ ᾗ παρεδίδοτο, μᾶλλον δὲ

Passion. Similarly there is in the occidental text a special addition which emphasizes the redemptive quality of Christ's Passion: *qui pridie quam pro nostra omniumque salute pateretur*. This addition is used at present only on Maundy Thursday, but in Gallic texts it is also employed on other occasions.[20]

In all probability it was formerly a part of the everyday text, and may originally have been incorporated to underscore the all-embracing character of the redemption as a protest against the gloomy predestinationism rampant in the fifth and sixth centuries.[21]

An opening for the expression of reverence and awe was found by augmenting the word *accepit* with *in sanctas ac venerabiles manus suas*. The same motif appeared even earlier in oriental texts, and especially in Egypt reached even richer expanses,[22] but as a rule this occurred only in reference to the bread because with it was to be joined an offering gesture which suited the bread: The Lord (it reads) takes the bread *upon* His holy hands, *looks up* (ἀναβλέψας) to His heavenly Father, or *shows* it to Him (ἀναδείξας σοὶ τῷ θεῷ καὶ πατρί).[23]

Our Roman text also makes mention of looking up: *elevatis oculis*, and the reason for its introduction here is probably the same, the idea of oblation.[24] It does not derive from the biblical account of the Last Supper, but is borrowed, as in some of the liturgies of the Orient, from other passages of the New Testament.[25] Moreover, the attitude of prayer, which also dominates the account and gives it the note of worship, is emphasized by

ἑαυτὸυ παρεδίδου; Brightman, 51, 1. 24; 285, 1. 23. Cf. Hamm, 39-42.

[20] Hamm, 38 f.; Botte, 61 f.

[21] Thus G. Morin, "Une particularité inaperçue du 'Qui pridie' de la messe romaine aux environs de l'an DC," *Revue Béned.*, 27 (1910), 513-515.

[22] The Egyptian anaphora of St. Mark: ἄρτον λαβὼν ἐπὶ τῶν ἀγίων καὶ ἀχράντων καὶ ἀμώμων (the Monophysite text adds besides καὶ μακαρίων καὶ ζωοποιῶν) αὐτοῦ χειρῶν; Hamm, 16; 69 f. The normal Armenian anaphora has "in his holy, divine, immortal, immaculate, and creative hands": Brightman, 436 f. The accumulation of these distinguishing attributes corresponds to the Monophysite efforts to accentuate the divinity of Christ as strongly as possible.

[23] Thus, above all, in the Syrian tradition, also already in the basic text of the anaphoras of St. James and St. Basil; Hamm, 21; 25; 66 ff. In this connection we must mention also the much-discussed passage in

Basil, *De Spiritu Sancto*, c. 27 (PG, 32, 187 B), about the words of invocation at the ἀνάδειξις of the bread and the chalice. The West Syrian anaphora of Dioskurus of Gazarta paraphrases the idea presented by the words ἐπὶ χειρῶν more exactly with *accepit panem et super manus suas sanctas in conspectu turbæ et societatis discipulorum suorum posuit* (Hamm, 67, n. 124). Cf. E. Peterson,"Die Bedeutung von ἀναδείκνυμι in den griechischen Liturgien": *Festgabe Deissmann*, (Tübingen, 1927), 320-326; cf. in this regard *JL*, (1927), 273 f., 357. In the present-day West Syrian rite the priest first places the host in the flat of his left hand, makes the sign of the cross three times over it, and then takes hold of it with both hands; Hanssens, III, 422.

[24] Cf. Hamm, 67 f.

[25] Matth. 14: 19; John 11: 41; 17: 1. Besides, such an upward glance towards heaven was a part of the prayerful posture of Christians in Christian antiquity. Dölger, *Sol Salutis*, 301 ff.

the form regarding the heavenly Father—not a mere mention of Him, but a formal address: *ad te Deum Patrem suum omnipotentem.*

The solemn wording of this mention of God [26] somehow re-echoes the solemn address at the beginning of the preface. Then, in mentioning the chalice, the pathos hitherto suppressed breaks through in a single word: *accipiens et hunc præclarum calicem.* That expression, *præclarus calix,* is plucked from Psalm 22:5. And again it is quite natural to make mention of the venerable hands, since the meal ritual included raising the cup on high. [27]

The chief liturgies of the East also mention here the rite of admixture, usually balancing the commingling of the chalice against the taking of the bread: Ὁμοίως καὶ τὸ ποτήριον κεράσας ἐξ οἴνου καὶ ὕδατος, εὐλογήσας.... [28]

The blessing of the chalice, which is commonly expressed by the word ἁγιάσας, as in the case of bread, is given greater emphasis in one portion of the Greek texts after the Ecumenical Council of 381, the words πλήσας πνεύματος ἁγίου [29] being added. This practice parallels the development of the Holy Ghost epiklesis.

The most striking phenomenon in the Roman text is the augmentation of the words of consecration said over the chalice. The mention of the New Testament is turned into an acknowledgment of its everlasting duration: *novi et æterni testamenti.* [30] And then, in the middle of the sacred text, stand the enigmatic words so frequently discussed: *mysterium fidei.* Unfortunately the popular explanation (that the words were originally spoken by the deacon to reveal to the congregation what had been performed at the altar, which was screened from view by curtains) is poetry, not history. [31] The phrase is found inserted in the earliest texts of the sacra-

---

[26] The mode of expression in the Apostles' Creed has exerted its influence. The address in the Ambrosian text is even richer; above I, 52; cf. Hamm, 57.

[27] Above I, 21, n. 63. The critical remarks in Hamm, 68, may not be pertinent.

[28] Hamm, 28; 52-55. It is significant that the mention of water, καὶ ὕδατος, was suppressed in the version of the anaphora of St. James used by the strictly Monophysite Armenians; cf. above, p. 40.

[29] Hamm, 52.

[30] The *testamentum æternum* is frequently repeated in the Old Testament: Ps. 110, 9; Ecclus. 17: 10; 45: 8. 19. Further discussion in Gassner, 249-250.

[31] The idea goes back to A. de Waal, "Archæologische Erörterungen zu einigen Stücken im Kanon der hl. Messe, 3. Die Worte 'mysterium fidei'," *Der Katholik,*

76 (1896), 392-395; regarding this see Braun, *Der christliche Altar,* II, 169, n. 11a. Older attempts at an explanation are recorded by K. J. Merk, *Der Konsekrationstext der römischen Messe* (Rottenburg, 1915), 5-25. The explanation advanced by Merk himself, *ibid.,* 147-151, according to which the words are intended to exclude the epiklesis and accentuate the fact that the consecration was already completed by the preceding words, is without foundation. The explanation given by Th. Schermann, "Liturgische Neuerungen" (Festgabe A. Knöpfler zum 70 Geburtstag [Freiburg, 1917], 276-289), is no better; according to this the *mysterium fidei* originally belonged only to the Mass of Baptism, inserted to call the attention of the newly baptzed to an action that was entirely strange to them.

mentaries, and mentioned even in the seventh century.[32] It is missing only in some later sources.[33]

Regarding the meaning of the words *mysterium fidei*, there is absolutely no agreement. A distant parallel is to be found in the *Apostolic Constitutions*, where our Lord is made to say at the consecration of the bread: "This is the mystery of the New Testament, take of it, eat, it is My Body." [34] Just as here the *mysterium* is referred to the bread in the form of a predicate, so in the canon of our Mass it is referred to the chalice in the form of an apposition. It has been proposed [35] that the words be taken as relating more closely to what precedes, so that in our text we should read: *novi (et æterni) testamenti mysterium (fidei)*. But such a rendering can hardly be upheld,[36] particularly because of the word *fidei* that follows,[37] but also because the whole phrase dependent on the word *mysterium* would then become a man-made insertion into the consecrating words of our Lord. *Mysterium fidei* is an independent expansion, superadded to the whole self-sufficient complex that precedes.[38]

What is meant by the words *mysterium fidei?* Christian antiquity would

[32] As the *Expositio* of the Gallican Mass (ed. Quasten, 18) shows, it was already contained in the 7th century chalice formula, which was taken over from the Roman into the Gallican liturgy. Such a general diffusion can be explained only by postulating a Roman origin; cf. also Wilmart, DACL, VI, 1086.

[33] In the Milanese Sacramentary of Biasca (9-10th cent.) ; in the *Ordo Rom. Antiquus* of Maundy Thursday, at least in the 11th century MS. edited by M. Hittorp (Cologne, 1586, p. 57; the other MSS. described by M. Andrieu, *Les Ordines Romani* I, 27, etc., have still to be examined). The entire passage *novi et æterni testamenti mysterium fidei* is missing in the *Sacramentarium Rossianum* (10th cent.) ; Brinktrine, *Die hl. Messe*, 194.

[34] *Const. Ap.*, VIII, 12, 36 (Quasten, *Mon.*, 222) : Τοῦτο τό μυστήριον τᾶς χαινῆς διαθήχης. Some few Ethiopian anaphora have similar elaborations for the same passage: *admirabile prodigium*, or *potus vitæ verus.* Cagin, 231 ff., div. 27, 33, 35.

[35] Hamm, 75 f.

[36] Despite all studies of philological possibilities, it still remains difficult to conceive the genitive *novi et æterni testamenti* as dependent upon the *mysterium* immediately following, which is already associated with a genitive *(fidei); whereas Paul-*

Luke combine the words *sanguis (meus novi) testamenti* into a unit, at least as to sense, and Matthew-Mark do so even in form. Nevertheless the idea gains some support from the curious fact that it is precisely this group of words that is missing in the *Sacramentarium Rossianum* (above, n. 33).

[37] As a matter of fact, Hamm, 76, n. 147, also finds the *fidei* troublesome.

[38] The intrusion of such an addition into the very core of the words of consecration could be more easily explained, if, like the *æterni (testamenti)* they were of Scriptural origin. The expression is in fact found in I Tim. 3: 9, where the deacons are admonished to preserve the mystery of faith in a pure conscience: *habentes mysterium fidei in conscientia pura*. Of course, something quite different is here meant, namely, the Christian teaching, and thus it becomes quite difficult to understand how the phrase was seized upon in this connection. Brinktrine, "Mysterium Fidei," *Eph. liturg.*, 44 (1930), 493-500, tries to establish points of contact; the passage at times was understood in a Eucharistic sense, and the naming of the deacons, to whom the chalice pertained, could have led to this chalice formula. See also Gassner, 278-288. Florus Diaconus, *De actione miss.*, c. 62 (PL, 119, 54), had already drawn I Tim. 3: 9 into the exposition of this passage.

not have referred them so much to the obscurity of what is here hidden from the senses, but accessible (in part) only to (subjective) faith.[39] Rather it would have taken them as a reference to the grace-laden *sacramentum* in which the entire (objective) faith, the whole divine order of salvation is comprised.[40] The chalice of the New Testament is the life-giving symbol of truth, the sanctuary of our belief.[41]

How or when or why this insertion was made, or what external event occasioned it, cannot readily be ascertained.[42]

The sacred account concludes with the command to repeat what Christ had done. The text is taken basically from St. Paul; however, the entire Roman tradition, from Hippolytus on, has substituted for the Pauline phrase "whenever you drink it," the phrase "whenever you do this." In some form or other our Lord's injunction is mentioned in almost all the liturgical formularies.[43] Where it is missing, it is presupposed. It is in the very nature of the Christian liturgy of the Mass that the account of the institution of the Blessed Sacrament should not be recited as a merely historical record, as are other portions of the Gospels. Indeed, the words of the account are spoken over the bread and a chalice, and, in accord with our Lord's word, are uttered precisely in order to repeat Christ's action. This repetition, is, in fact, accomplished in all its essentials by rehearsing the words of the account of the institution.

---

[39] This interpretation, which is generally supported today, is found already in Durandus, IV, 42, 20 and in Florus, *loc. cit.*

[40] That the identification of *mysterium* and *sacramentum* is justified for the time that comes under consideration is clear from the fact that the series of catechetical instructions handling this matter is called in one case by Ambrose *De mysteriis* and then again *De sacramentis*. Opinions will differ, however, with regard to a narrower limitation of the idea *mysterium*. O. Casel, who in *JL*, 10 (1931), 311, agrees with Hamm, prefers in *JL*, 15 (1941) 302 f., to take the "mystery of the faith" as the new *mysterium* in opposition to the *mysterium* of the Gnosis. But it is still questionable whether the Gnosis is to be taken into account for this interpolation in the period under consideration.

[41] Cf. Binterim, II, 1 (1825), 132-137. The natural Englishing, "mystery of (the) faith," unfortunately suggests only the intellectual side and so seems to interrupt the train of thought.

[42] Th. Michels, "Mysterium fidei" im Einsetzungsbericht der römischen Liturgie," *Catholica*, 6 (1937), 81-88, refers to Leo the Great, *Sermo* 4, de Quadr. (PL, 54, 279 f.) ; the pope points out that at that time the Manicheans here and there partook of the body of Our Lord, but shunned "to drink the blood of our Redemption." He supposes that in opposition to them Leo wanted to accentuate the chalice by adding the words *mysterium fidei*.

[43] Hamm, 87 f.—In the Roman liturgy, until the Missal of Pius V, some indecision is apparent, whether the words *Hæc quotiescumque* are to be said over the chalice, or else during or after the elevation. Lebrun, I, 423 f.

13. The Consecration:
The Accompanying Actions

A rehearsal of the sacred narrative is included in the Lord's injunction
to do what He had done—that comes clearly to light in the actions
accompanying the words as they are said at Mass.

As the priest mentions the Lord's actions, one after the other, he suits
his own actions to the words in dramatic fashion. He speaks the words at
a table on which bread and wine stand ready. He takes the bread into his
hands, as also the chalice; the gesture of presentation that seems to lie
hid in this "taking"[1] was and is made even plainer by thus acting it
out.[2] Praying, he lifts his eyes to heaven, "unto Thee, God, His almighty
Father." At the words *gratias agens* he bows, just as he had done in
reverence at the *gratias agimus* and *gratias agamus* that he himself had
spoken earlier in the Mass. At the *benedixit*, by way of giving to an older
biblical expression a more modern interpretation, he makes the sign of
the Cross.[3] The West Syrians and the Copts go even further, and acting
out the *fregit*, crack the host without however separating the parts.[4] This
imitating of the actions, which expresses as clearly as possible the priest's
desire of fulfilling here and now the Lord's commission to do as He had
done, is lacking in the East only in the Byzantine rite, and even there it
would seem to have existed at one time.[5]

---

[1] It is likely that in the ἀναδείξας mentioned
above and in the gesture of raising the
bread aloft connected with it in the oriental
liturgies, we have a survival of a Palestinian table custom, a custom the Lord
Himself observed. Likewise the taking and
raising of the cup must have been done as
one movement; cf. above I, 21, n. 63. Cf.
Jungmann, "Accepit panem," *Zeitschrift f.
Assese u. Mystik*, 18 = *ZkTh*, 67 (1943),
162-165.

[2] In the Roman liturgy, too, before the
elevating of the consecrated host came into
vogue as a means of presenting it to the
view of the people, the taking and raising
at this point was understood as an oblation; see Honorius Augustod., *Sacramentarium*, c. 88 (PL, 172, 793 D): *Exemplo
Domini accipit sacerdos oblatam et calicem
in manus et elevat, ut sit Deo acceptum
sicut sacrificium Abel* . . .

[3] In the biblical text (in Matt. and Mark)
we find εὐλογήσας without *gratias agens*.
It indicates the short blessing formula
that was said over the bread. Likewise

in place of the customary lengthy table
prayer we have the εὐχαριστήσας without
benedixit over the chalice; cf. above I, 9.

[4] Hanssens, III, 422, 424; cf. Brightman,
177, l. 1; 232, l. 20. A hint of the breaking is found also among the Maronites;
Hanssens, III, 423. Moses bar Kepha (d.
903) in his Mass explanations, *ibid.*, 447,
already testifies to this breaking among the
Jacobite West Syrians. The same practice
can be proven to have existed within the
Roman liturgy since the 13th century,
chiefly in England and France, where different Mass books present the rubric: *Hic
facit signum fractionis* or *fingat frangere*,
or at least: *Hic tangat hostiam;* see anent
this the excursus in Legg, *Tracts*, 259-
261. Also in the *Ordinale* of the Carmelites
(about 1312), ed. Zimmermann, 81; and
still in the *Missale O. Carm.* (1935), p.
XXX.

[5] Hanssens, III, 446, expresses the opinion
that all this was removed in order to stress
the exclusive consecratory power of the
epiklesis. Similarly the signs of the cross

As the *dedit discipulis suis* is realized fully only in the Communion, and the *fregit* is usually carried out only at the fraction before Communion, so the *gratias agens* in its wider sense has already been anticipated,[6] and the *accepit* has been already portrayed in an earlier passage. But the heart of the process is renewed at this very instant. The narrative of what once took place passes into the actuality of the present happening. There is a wonderful identification of Christ and the priest. In the person of the priest, Christ Himself stands at the altar, and picks up the bread, and lifts up "this goodly chalice" (Psalm 22:5), *hunc præclarum calicem.*[7] Through this mode of speech clear expression is given to the fact that it is Christ Himself who is now active, and that it is by virtue of power deriving from Him [8] that the transubstantiation which follows takes place.[9]

---

for the blessing at the εὐχαριστήσας, εὐλογήσας, ἀγιάσας are missing only in the Byzantine Rite, *ibid.*, 447. Still the Byzantine Mass has the practice, that the deacon point with his orarion to the diskos, *resp.* the chalice, while the priest says the Λάβετε, φάγετε, *resp.* Πίετε ἐξ αὐτοῦ πάντες. The priest also takes part in this rite of "showing"; cf. J. Doens, *De hl. Liturgie van H. V. J. Chrysostomus*, (3rd ed.; Chevetogne, 1950), p. XIV f. The obvious meaning of these gestures is denied, however, in a note attached to these orthodox texts; Brightman, 386.—The purpose behind this dramatic copying of Our Savior's actions is perhaps best described by the term suggested in a recent study: *intention applicatrice,* applied intent, which plainly establishes the function of the words of institution; A. Chavasse, "L'épiclèse eucharistique dans les anciennes liturgies orientales. Une hypothèse d'interprétation," *Mélanges de science religieuse*, 1946, 197-206.

[6] Above, p. 115 ff.—Hanssens, III, 353 ff., 425 ff., espouses the opinion that from the beginning only the words of Christ spoken over the bread and wine at the time of the institution were considered as the fulfillment of Christ's mandate; that the prayer of thanks is not a copying of the εὐλογία, εὐχαριστία uttered by Christ; that the prayer said by Him over the chalice survives rather in the thanksgiving prayers after Communion. There may be a certain amount of justification for such a consideration if one has in mind only the ex-

ternal order in which the prayers follow one upon the other, but hardly when one considers the meaning and purpose of each separate part. Justin, e.g., attaches no significance to the prayer of thanks after Communion. On the other hand, it is hardly conceivable that the *eucharistia* in Justin, which in fact was underscored even before him and in the entire tradition after him, should have arisen without any relation whatever to the prayer of thanks spoken by Our Lord. Through the fusion of the two consecrations required by the circumstances and by the anticipation of the prayer of thanksgiving, the essence of the latter is not thereby changed; cf. above I, 16 f. The rather late and secondary origin of the prayer assumed by Hanssens, III, 355 f., is excluded not only by such considerations, but by the *Gratias agamus* which, in all likelihood, originated already in the primitive community.

[7] The same idea in the Ethiopian anaphora of Gregory of Alexandria (Cagin, 233, div. 35): *Similiter respexit super hunc calicem, aquam vitæ cum vino, gratias agens . . .* Cf. the pointing gestures in the Ethiopian liturgy with the same meaning, *supra*, p. 145, n. 37.

[8] Brinktrine, *Die hl. Messe* 191, sees therein more definitely an indication "that the sacred words spoken by Christ at the Last Supper extend their efficacy to all Masses that would be celebrated in the future."

[9] In the West it is Ambrose especially, who with complete clarity utters the conviction that the consecration takes place by repeat-

Numerous usages in oriental rites are understandable only from this same viewpoint. Thus, for example, the fact that the whole eucharistic prayer (aside from the *Sanctus,* which is sung in common) is spoken softly by the priest up to this passage, and then the words "take and eat, this is My body," and the corresponding words over the chalice are spoken in a loud voice; in fact, they are chanted in a solemn melody. And this is done over the bread held in the hands, and over the chalice grasped by the hands.[10] In the West-Syrian anaphora of St. James the people answer *Amen* both times the priest says the words of consecration.[11] This was already an established custom in the ninth century, when Moses bar Kepha was vainly tilting against it, for he rightly saw in the custom an acknowledgment of the completed transubstantiation, for which he contended the epiklesis was still requisite.[12] This *Amen* is found also in the Byzantine and the Armenian Masses.[13] In the present-day Ethiopian liturgy the *Amen* is repeated three times on each occasion, and followed by acts of faith.[14] In the Coptic liturgy the dramatic element is heightened by inserting the *Amens* between the phrases of the introductory words of the priest: "He took bread . . . and gave thanks"—*Amen;* "blessed it"—*Amen;* "consecrated it"—*Amen.* And after the words of consecration in each instance comes a profession of faith: Πιστεύομεν καὶ ὁμολογοῦμεν καὶ

---

ing the words of Christ; see above I, 52. Cf. Ambrose, *De mysteriis,* 9, 52; *In Ps.* 38 *enarr.,* c. 25 (PL, 14, 1052): *etsi nunc Christus non videtur offerre, tamen ipse offertur in terris, quando Christi corpus offertur; immo ipse offerre manifestatur in nobis, cuius sermo sanctificat sacrifiicium quod offertur.* In general Christian antiquity, even until way into the Middle Ages, manifested no particular interest regarding the determination of the precise moment of the consecration. Often reference was made merely to the entire Eucharistic prayer. It is Florus Diaconus, *De actione miss.,* c. 60 (PL, 119, 52 f.), in the Carolingian period, who with particular stress brought out the significance of the words of consecration; *ille in suis sacerdotibus quotidie loquitur.*
[10] Greek anaphora of St. James; Brightman, 51 f. The loud singing of these words is likewise found in the Byzantine liturgy already in the 9th century; *ibid.,* 328.
[11] Brightman, 52; cf. Hanssens, III, 420 f.
[12] Thus, according to the account of Dionysius bar Salibi, ed. Labourt (Corpus script. christ. orient., 93), 62; 77; O. Heiming, *Orientalia christ.,* 16 (1950), 195, published a palimpsest fragment of the 8th

century with an anaphora text used even prior to the 8th century, which likewise displays the *Amen.*
[13] Said by the choir, *resp.* the clerics; Brightman, 385 f., 437. The *Amen* must have come into the Mozarabic Mass from the Syrian-Byzantine sphere. Here the *Amen* of the choir is said three times, after the command to do this that follows upon the words over the bread and those over the chalice, and again after the Pauline *Quotiescumque manducaveritis* that is added at the end; *Missale mixtum* (PL, 85, 552 f.). This appropriation must have taken place before the middle of the 7th century, i.e., before the Arabs rendered commerce over the Mediterranean impossible; this circumstance is significant for the antiquity of the practice in the Orient; cf. H. Pirenne, *Geburt des Abendlandes* (1939), 160 ff. The *Amen* to which Augustine testifies, *Serm.,* VI, 3 Denis, and which Roetzer, 124, refers to this instance, belongs to the conclusion of the canon.
[14] Brightman, 232 f. After the words over the bread "Amen, Amen, Amen: we believe and confess: we praise thee, our Lord and our God. This is true; we believe." After the chalice: "Amen, Amen, Amen."

δοξάζομεν—in Greek, and therefore a tradition from as early as the sixth century at least.[15]

In comparison with these we must confess that the Roman liturgy of the first millenary lacked the impulse to direct the attention at once to the completion of the sacramental process, or to draw ritual deductions from it.[16] Only in the eleventh century do we begin to find, hand in hand with an increased care for everything connected with the Sacrament,[17] the first signs of a new attitude. According to the Cluniac Customary, written about 1068 by the monk Bernhard, the priest at the consecration should hold the host *quattuor primis digitis ad hoc ipsum ablutis.*[18] After the consecration, even when praying with outstretched arms, some priests began to hold those fingers which had "touched" the Lord's Body, pressed together,[19] others even began this at the ablution of the fingers at the offertory.[20] In one form or another the idea soon became a general rule.[21]

---

[15] Brightman, 176 f.; cf. Hanssens, III, 421. Further details in Spácil (see above n. 26), 108-111.

[16] There must have been a very lively sentiment in the Irish-Celtic tradition for the definitive meaning of the words of the institution. The Stowe Missal, ed. Warner (HBS, 32), 37; 40, stresses the fact that when the priest begins: *accepit Jesus panem,* nothing is to distract or divert him; for that reason it is called the *oratio periculosa.* The *Pænitentiale Cummeani* fixed three days of double fasting, according to another version even *quinquaginta plagas,* as a penance for a priest who was guilty of a mistake in any passage *ubi periculum adnotatur; Jungmann, Gewordene Liturgie,* 94 f.; 117, n. 232. A reminiscence of this is still retained in the *Pontificale Romanum* in the warning given to the newly ordained to learn carefully the rite of the Mass *(hostiæ consecrationem ac fractionem et communionem);* this warning begins: *Quia res, quam tractaturi estis, satis periculosa est.* Cf. *Pontificale* of Durandus (Andrieu, III, 372 f.); Durandus, *Rationale,* IV, 42, 19. In view of this awe regarding the words of consecration it is strange that it was apparently not until the 14-15th century that it became the practice to make the consecration prayers more prominent by means of special lettering. P. de Puniet, "La consécration," *Cours et Conférences,* VII, (Louvain, 1929), 193.

[17] Cf. The rite regarding the preparation of the hosts, above, p. 35.

[18] I, 72 (Herrgott, *Vetus disciplina monastica,* 264).

[19] Bernold of Constance, *Micrologus,* c. 16 (PL, 151, 987 C), opposes this: *Non ergo digiti sunt contrahendi semper, ut quidam præ nimia cautela faciunt . . . hoc tamen observato, ne quid digitis tangamus præter Domini corpus.* A fresco in the lower church of S. Clemente in Rome that presents a priest at the altar at the end of the canon shows him without this *nimia cautela.* Illustration in O. Ursprung, *Die kath. Kirchenmusik,* 27.

[20] Udalricus, *Consuet. Clun.,* II, 30 (PL, 149, 717 ff.); William of Hirsau, *Const.,* I, 84, 86 (PL, 150, 1012 f.; 1017).

[21] Thus in the 13th century Durandus, IV, 31, 4; IV, 43, 5, enjoins that thumb and forefinger may be parted after the consecration only *quando oportet hostiam tangi vel signa* (signs of the cross) *fieri.* The *Ordo* of Stefaneschi (1311), n. 53 (PL, 78, 1166 B), has the same rule. So, too, in the *Liber ordinarius* of Liége and also in the Dominican source of the same, dated about 1256 (Volk, 95, 1. 5); in both passages it is also required from after the *Lavabo* on: *Cum digitis, quibus sacrum corpus tractandum est, folia non vertat nec aliud tangat* (Volk, 93, 1. 22). According to the *Missale Rom., Rit. serv.* VIII, 5, even the *signa* no longer form an exception; the fingers simply remain closed. In the oriental liturgy similar prescriptions seem to exist only in the uniate communities; see Hanssens, III, 424 f.

Even in the twelfth century, however, the special takens of honor towards the Sacrament which began to appear were at first found not in this precise connection but rather in other parts of the Mass.[22]

Now, however, the people entered to dominate the scene. A religious movement swept over the faithful, prompting them, now that they hardly presumed to receive Communion, at least to look at the sacred species with their bodily eyes.[23] This impulse to see fastened upon the precise moment when the priest picked up the host and blessed it, as he was about to pronounce over it the words of consecration. The presentation of the Host by elevating it a little, which we find more clearly expressed in the oriental rites, had also become more pronounced in the Roman Mass.[24] Towards the end of the twelfth century[25] stories were in circulation of visions imparted at this very moment: the Host shone like the sun;[26] a tiny child appeared in the priest's hands as he was about to bless the host.[27]

In some places the priest was accustomed to replace the host upon the altar after making the sign of the Cross over it, and only then to recite the words of consecration; in other places, on the contrary, he would hold it aloft as he spoke these words.[28] Thus the people were not to be blamed if, without making any further distinction, they reverenced the host as soon as they were able to see it.

---

[22] The Cistercian Herbert of Sassari, *De miraculis*, III, 23 (PL, 185, 1371), about 1178, tells of a prescribed bow before the Blessed Sacrament after the breaking: *Et Agnus Dei iam dicto, cum iuxta illius ordinus consuetudinem super patenam corpus Domini posuit et coram ipso modice inclinando caput humiliasset* . . . Regarding Herbert's work, cf. now B. Griesser, "Herbert von Clairvaux und sein Liber miraculorum," *Cist.-Chr.*, 54 (1947), 21-39; 118-148.

[23] Regarding the ramifications of this movement see above, I, 120 ff. The history of the elevation was finally presented by E. Dumoutet, *Le désir de voir l'hostie*, Paris, 1926; P. Browe, *Die Verehrung der Eucharistie im Mittelalter*, (Munich, 1933, 26-69; = 2 Kap.: "Die Elevation," first published, *JL*, 9 (1929), 20-66). Cf. also Franz, *Die Messe im deutschen Mittelalter*, 32 f., 100-105.

[24] This elevation was developed in the 12th century to such an extent that Radulphus Ardens d. 1215), *Homil.*, 47 (PL, 155, 1836 B), already regarded it as a representation of Christ's elevation on the cross. Further data in Browe, *Die Verehrung*,

29 f.; cf. Dumoutet, 47.

[25] An example cited among others by Dumoutet, 46 f., from Wibert of Nogent (d. about 1124), *De pignoribus sanctorum*, I, 2, 1 (PL, 156, 616), can also refer to the elevation at the end of the canon.

[26] Cæsarius of Heisterbach, *Dialogus miraculorum* (written about 1230), IX, 33 (Dumoutet, 42, n. 3): vision of the nun Richmudis. In vouching for the story, he adds the remarkable note: *necdum puto factam fuisse transubstantiationem.*

[27] *Magna vita Hugonis Lincolnesis*, V, 3 (Dumoutet, 42, n. 2): This occurred at a Mass of the bishop, who died in 1200. The life was written by his chaplain.

[28] For the latter method see Hildebert of Le Mans (d. 1133), *Versus* (PL, 171, 1186); Stephan of Baugé (d. about 1140), *De sacris. altaris*, c. 13 (PL, 172, 1292 D). Browe, *Die Verehrung*, 30. As numerous Mass-books testify, the practice continued for a long time: until into the 15th century: Dumoutet, 42 f. But, along with this practice, that of today was also followed; cf. Mass-*ordo* of York (about 1425; Simmons, 106): the *Qui pridie* is said *inclinato capite super linteamina.*

To forestall this impropriety, the bishop of Paris in 1210 ordered that the priests should hold the host breast-high, before the consecration, and only *after* the consecration should they lift it high enough to be seen by all.[29] This is the first authentic instance of that elevation of the Host which is so familiar to us.[30]

The custom spread rapidly. A regulation of the year 1210 appears to have prescribed it for the Cistercians; for the Carthusians it was ordered in 1222.[31] From then until the middle of the century it was mentioned in various synods as a usage already in vogue.[32] At the same time, and on till the fourteenth and fifteenth centuries, other synods continued in various ways to oppose any elevation before the consecration, "lest" (as a London synod of 1215 put it) "a creature be adored instead of the Creator."[33] The great theologians of Scholasticism speak of the elevation of the Host as a general practice of the Church.[34]

But that does not mean that there was a similar elevation of the chalice. The elevation of the chalice is found, indeed, even as early as the thirteenth century, but the usage was rare and exceptional.[35] However, it forced its way through, but only slowly, especially outside of France.[36] Even the

---

[29] Among the Præcepta synodalia of Bishop Odo (d. 1208), c. 28 (Mansi, XXII, 628): *Præcipitur presbyteris ut cum in canone missæ inceperint: Qui pridie, tenentes hostiam, ne elevent eam statim nimis alte, ita quod possit ab omnibus videri a populo, sed quasi ante pectus detineant, donec dixerint: Hoc est corpus meum, et tunc elevent eam, ut possit ab omnibus videri.* Cf. regarding this, V. L. Kennedy, "The Date of the Parisian Decree on the Elevation of the Host," *Medieval Studies,* 8 (Toronto, 1946), 87-96. Dumoutet, 37 ff. and Browe, 31 ff. espouse the explanation given above regarding this measure against Thurston, who in several publications referred to the teachings of Peter Comestor (d. 1178) and Peter Cantor (d. 1197), according to whom the transubstantiation of the bread actually occurs only after the words over the chalice have also been said. To counteract this teaching, the elevation of the host is supposed to have been ordered immediately after the words of consecration had been said over it. As is shown with great thoroughness by V. L. Kennedy, "The Moment of Consecration and the Elevation of the Host," *Medieval Studies* 6 (1944), 121-150, the controversy can have influenced the decree only insofar as, in accordance

with the opposing teaching, which gradually gained the ascendency, the elevation, already sought for other reasons, was prescribed right after the words over the bread.

[30] It is possible that the practice was in vogue already elsewhere before 1200. In the year 1201 Cardinal Guido, O. Cist., came to Germany as Papal Legate and promulgated in Cologne the order: *Ut ad elevationem hostiæ omnis populus in ecclesia ad sonitum nolæ veniam peteret.* It seems that all the Cardinal did here was to re-establish the genuflection and perhaps also the signal with the bell. Cæsarius of Heisterbach, *Dialogus miraculorum,* IX, 51; cf. Browe, *Die Verehrung,* 35; Franz, 678.

[31] Browe, *Die Verehrung,* 34 f.

[32] Browe, 35, 37.

[33] Browe, 38.

[34] Browe, 36.—Still the Papal chapel knows nothing of the practice even in 1290; instead the oblatory elevation before the words of consecration is still clearly stressed: *levet eam* [s. *hostiam*], *levet calicem;* Brinktrine (*Eph. liturg.,* 1937), 204 f.

[35] Durandus, IV, 41, 52, recognizes it.

[36] The history of this advance in Browe, 41-46.

printed Roman Missals of 1500, 1507, and 1526 make no mention of it. Various difficulties stood in the way of a rapid spread of the rite, especially the danger of spilling the contents of the chalice. Then there was the fact that the chalice used to be covered with the back part of the corporal folded up over it.[37] But particularly cogent was the objection that in seeing the chalice one does not "see" the Precious Blood.[38] For this last reason, even where the elevation of the chalice took place, it was little more than a mere suggestion: the chalice was merely lifted up to about the level of the eyes.[39] Not till the Missal of Pius V was the second elevation made to correspond with that of the Host.

The desire of gazing upon the Lord's Body was the driving force which, since the twelfth century, brought about this intrusion of a very notable innovation into the canon which for ages had been regarded as an inviolable sanctuary. The oblatory elevation before the words of consecration lost its importance,[40] and the displaying of the Host after the words, instead became the new pivot and center of the canon of the Mass. From the intrusion of this new element a further development had to follow. It was at bottom only a pious idea to regard seeing the Host, "contacting" the species with the organs of sight, as a participation in the Sacrament and its streams of grace, and even to value it as a sort of Communion. But it was a logical conclusion that, the moment the consecration took place, all honor and reverence are owing to the Lord's Body and Blood. This conclusion, as we have seen, was actually realized in oriental rites.[41] So any further regulation of the new usage had to be directed to keeping

[37] Thus, a second corporal, or the pall that later developed from it, was required to be able to elevate the covered chalice; cf. Braun, *Die liturgischen Paramente*, 210 f. Still, Durandus already recognizes the elevation of the uncovered chalice in his *Const. synodales* (ed. Berthelé, 69); Browe, 40. Both methods were still in existence in the 14-15th century; Browe, 47.
[38] Durandus, IV, 41, 52.
[39] Browe, 47; cf. Franz, 105, n. 1. To this day the Carthusians recognize only this restricted elevation; *Ordinarium Cart.* (1932), c. 27, 16. However, the chalice was frequently held aloft until the *Unde et memores*. Thus according to Italian Mass-books of the 13th century: Ebner, 315; 329; 349.
[40] Strictly speaking, there is still an oblatory elevation at the consecration, since the priest "takes" the host in his hands. In fact, this original idea is not excluded even in the elevation for the view of others; now the oblatory elevation takes

place with the consecrated gift in place of the unconsecrated one, and is performed in such a way that it might be seen by more people. But this idea has not generally been fostered since the 12th century. However, traces of this older conception are still found even in modern times. Thus, among the Reformers, Karlstadt not only insisted that the elevation be dropped, but considered it an expression of oblation and therefore abominable and sinful; L. Fendt, *Der lutherische Gottesdienst des 16 Jh.* (Munich, 1923), 95; cf. also Berthold of Chiemsee, *Keligpuchel*, (Munich, 1535), c. 20, 7: "Wenn der Priester eleviert, d.i. die Hostie . . . sacramentlich opffert . . ." Similarly also Martin von Cochem, *Medulla missæ germanicæ*, c. 29 (3d ed., Cologne, 1724; 441): "Oh, what an excellent gift the priest presents to the all-holy Trinity when he lifts the divine Host on high!"
[41] Above, 203 f.

this desire to gaze on the Host within proper limits [42] and to working out suitable terms for honoring It .This, then, was substantially what was done.

The longing to look at the Host soon received ecclesiastical approval and support in several ways. This we see not only in the ruling that the Body of our Lord should be lifted high enough to enable the faithful to see It—to "show" It to the people, as our present-day rubric puts it: *ostendit populo*. There was even a tendency to emphasize this "showing" by lingering a moment while elevating the Host, or by turning to right and left. But a stop was soon put to such efforts, since they involved too large a break in the course of the action.[43] But then we hear of another custom, especially in French and English churches, the custom of drawing a dark curtain behind the altar in order to make the white Host stand out clearly against the background.[44] The consecration candle, from which in many places the *Sanctus* candle developed, was originally intended to be lighted and lifted aloft by the deacon or the Mass-server at the early Mass, when it was still dark, *ut corpus Christi . . . possit videri*.[45] We hear of admonitions directed to the thurifer not to let the clouds of incense obscure the view of the species.[46] In monastic churches the doors of the choir, which were ordinarily kept closed, were opened at the consecration.[47] The signal of the bell at the elevation was likewise introduced for similar reasons. The first evidence for such a practice comes from churches in Cologne as

---

[42] Here we make mention only of those things which are of importance for the development of today's practice. Regarding other usages and customs elsewhere, see above I, 119 ff.

[43] *Ordinarium O.P.* of 1256 (Guerrini, 242) : *Ipsam* [sc. *hostiam*]*vero non circumferat nec diu teneat elevatam.* Thus also in the *Liber ordinarius* of Liége (Volk, 94 f.). Further data in Browe, *Die Verehrung,* 63. It is only in the Papal Mass that the turning to the right and left at the elevation has been retained until the present time; Brinktrine, *Die feierliche Papstmesse,* 27.

[44] The practice was still retained in Chartres, Rouen, and other French cathedrals around 1700; de Moléon, 226 f., 367 f., 433, 435; Dumoutet, 58-60. In Spain it existed in some single instances even in the 19th century; Legg, *Tracts,* 234 f.

[45] Such was the arrangement of the Carthusians about the middle of the 13th century; DACL, III, 1057. According to the Mass-*ordo* of John Burchard (1502) the candle was to be lit at the *Hanc igitur* and extinguished after the elevation of the

chalice; Legg, *Tracts,* 155; 157; cf. Dumoutet, 57; Swiss church books of the 15-17th century mention "hebkertzen" and "kertzen der ufhebung" (elevation candles); Krömler, *Der Kult der Eucharistie in Sprache und Volkstum der deutschen Schweiz* (Basle, 1949), 57. Elsewhere it was lit sooner, or also extinguished only after Communion. Hence it turned into an expression of veneration for the Blessed Sacrament; for this development see H. L. Verwilst, *Die Dominikanische Messe* (Düsseldorf, 1948), 25 f. Concerning the history of this consecration candle, see P. Browe, *Die Elevation in der Messe (JL,* 9 [1929], 20-66), 40-43.

[46] The Carmelite Ordinal of 1312 (Zimmermann, 81 f.). Cf. Browe, *Die Verehrung,* 56. The incensing of the Blessed Sacrament at the consecration on feast days is already provided for in the *Ordinarium O.P.* of 1256 (Guerrini, 241 f.). However, for a long time, it was not customary; see more details in Atchley, *A History of the Use of Incense,* 264-266.

[47] Browe, *Die Verehrung,* 55 f.

early as 1201.[48] It makes its appearance first as a signal accompanying the elevation of the Host, and then the corresponding elevation of the chalice.[49] Soon we hear of the signal's being anticipated, when the priest makes the sign of the Cross over the Host and the chalice.[50] Further, the bell was used not only to direct the attention to the moment of the "showing," but also to call the people in to worship the Sacrament. So by the end of the thirteenth century the signal with the little bell [51] was augmented by a signal from the large church bell,[52] so that those who were absent, busy at home or in the field, might pause at this moment, turn towards the church and adore our Lord in the Blessed Sacrament.

It was self-evident from the start that honor should be paid to the Sacrament when It was elevated, all the more so when heresy had made an assault on faith in the Eucharist.[53] Clergy and faithful were to kneel down—this was the admonition of the first decrees and synods that dealt with the new consecration practices.[54] Or at least a humble bow was ordered, as in a regulation of Honorius III in the year 1219,[55] and in several later decrees.[56] Especially canons in various cathedral churches continued

[48] Cf. above, p. 207, n. 30. Cf. Braun, *Das christliche Altargerät*, 573-575.

[49] Durandus, IV, 41, 53. In England this was called the "sacring bell."

[50] *Liber ordinarius* of Liége (Volk, 94, 1. 29). Cf. H(erbert) T(hurston) "The 'Cross Bell' in the Mass," *The Month*, 172 (1938), 451-454. More details regarding the ringing of the bell at the consecration in Browe, *Die Elevation* (*JL*, 9), 37-40. According to many a report it would seem the ringing of the bell at the *Sanctus* was to serve the same purpose, *ut populus valeat levationis sacramenti . . . habere notitiam*, as is recorded in a foundation established in 1399 at Chartres for the ringing of the *Sanctus;* Du Cange-Favre, VII, 259. Cf. above, p. 131, n. 22.

[51] Such a bell was, as a rule, fastened to the wall of the choir. Small hand bells, that the server used at the altar, are generally in evidence only since the 16th century. And only since then, so it would seem, was the signal given with these bells also in private Masses. Braun, *Das christliche Altargerät*, 573-580, especially 576.

[52] Pertinent stipulations of 13-15th century synods in Browe, *Die Elevation*, 39 f.; Krömler, *op. cit.*, 33 f. gives examples of present-day customs in Switzerland.—The Holy See grants an indulgence of 300 days to all, wherever they may be, who adore the Blessed Sacrament at the sound of the

elevation bell. *Enchiridion Indulgentiarum* (Rome, 1950), n. 142.

[53] *Supra* I, 119.

[54] The oldest report is the disposition made by Cardinal Guido in the year 1201; above, p. 207, n. 30. Further reports in Browe, *Die Verehrung*, 34-39 in the notes. However, there is evidence as early as 1208 for kneeling down sooner, at *accepit panem;* see Kennedy, *The Moment of Consecration*, 149.

[55] Gregory IX, *Decretales*, III, 41, 10 (Friedberg, II, 642); cf. Browe, *Die Verehrung*, 37.

[56] P. Browe, "L'atteggiamento del corpo durante la messa" (*Eph. liturg.*, 50 [1936], 402-414), 408 f. As a minimum requirement it was expected that those who, according to the custom of the time were squatted on the floor, would, as a mark of respect, at least stand up. Still in many a place the Beghards and Beguines refused even this, a condition that induced the Council of Vienne (1311-12) to take a hand in the matter; Denzinger-Umberg, *Enchiridion*, n. 478. Likewise, according to a report from Flanders in the year 1349, the Flagellants refused to remove their head covering at the consecration; Browe, *loc. cit.*, 403; cf. 411. On the other hand again, a complete *prostratio* often became customary, especially in monasteries; see, e.g., the Statutes of the Car-

for a long time to follow their age-old practice of bowing: at Chartres this was done as late as the eighteenth century.[57] Here and there, too, the wish was expressed or even insisted on, that while kneeling the arms be stretched out and the hands raised.[58] But merely kneeling was the general rule. According to the thirteenth Roman *ordo*, which was written under Gregory X (d. 1276), the choir of clerics was to remain stretched out on the floor *quousque sacerdos corpus et sanguinem sumat* (unless, because of a feast day or a festal season, standing was prescribed).[59] According to the choir rules now in effect, where the influence of the ancient custom of standing bowed during the canon is at work alongside the newer attitude of special honor for the Blessed Sacrament, the choir usually kneels down at the *Te igitur*. Among the people, too, the idea of looking at the Sacrament was in many ways curbed, so that they knelt not only during the consecration but, where possible, from the *Sanctus* on, and remained

thusians: Martène, 1, 4, XXV (I, 633 C). Cf. also the illustration from S. Marco in Venice in Ch. Rohault de Fleury, *La Messe*, I (Paris, 1883), Tablet XVIII.
[57]Browe, "L'atteggiamento," 409 f. In the diocese of Basle in 1581 the Canons of St. Ursitz could be forced to kneel at the consecration only when threatened with ecclesiastical penalties (*ibid.*). Concerning French cathedrals cf. Cl. de Vert, *Explication simple*, I (Paris, 1706), 238 ff.; Martène, 1, 4, 8, 22 (I, 414 D); de Moléon, 230. This conservative retention of the older custom is explained by the recollection that from time immemorial the act of kneeling accompanied only prayers of petition and penance; cf. above I, 240. Even Durandus, VI, 86, 17, stresses the fact that one genuflected before the Blessed Sacrament only on Sundays and feast days and during the Pentecost season.
[58]Constitutions of the Camaldolese of 1233, c. 2, in Browe, *Die Verehrung*, 53, n. 160. In France about 1220 the poet of the "Queste del saint Graal" has the hero cry out, as he extends his hands towards the priest, who holds the Body of the Lord up to view: "Biaus douz pères, ne m'oubliez mie de me rente!" Dumoutet, 45, n. 1. In England the Christian of the 13th century was instructed to "hold up bothe thi handes" at the consecration; *The Lay Folks Mass Book*, ed. Simmons, 38. The canon picture in a Sacramentary of the 14th century from St. Peter's in Rome, in Ebner, 191, portrays the priest at the consecration

and "four figures seated, and one kneeling at the right, with their arms uplifted toward the altar." The same gesture of raising the hands is also seen in a miniature of Cod. 82 (14th cent.) in the Heidelberg University Library, fol. 158. Gabriel Biel, *Canonis expositio*, lect. 50, recommends *manus suas in cœlum tendere*, as a mark of reverence at the consecration. Sixtus IV, in 1480, granted an indulgence for saying five Our Fathers and Hail Marys *flexis genibus et elevatis manibus* at the consecration; Browe, *Die Verehrung*, 55. It is not clear, however, whether in all these instances the arms were held *outstretched;* it could mean a gesture that implied taking part in the oblation; cf. Balth. Fischer, "Liturgiegeschichte' und Verkündigung" (*Die Messe in der Glaubensverkündigung*, 1-13, 12, note 14, where O. Reinaldus, *Annales eccl.*, XIV (Cologne, 1694), 204, is cited for a practice of the English King Henry I (d. 1272), who was wont at the consecration *manum sacerdotis tenere*. The extending of the arms after the consecration (in the manner described below, p. 220, n. 15) is still customary in the monasteries of the Capuchins. The extension of the arms, when looking at the host, is also reported as a present-day custom in a southern Slavic country; Kramp, "Messgebräuche der Gläubigen in den ausserdeutschen Ländern" (*StZ*, 1927, II), 360.
[59]*Cæremoniale* of Gregory X (d. 1276), n. 19 (PL, 78, 1116).

on their knees till the Communion.[60] After the close of the Middle Ages the desire to honor the Sacrament, which led to this kneeling, had gained the ascendancy over the desire to see,[61] so far, indeed, that by the beginning of the twentieth century it even became customary in almost all countries to bow the head while kneeling at the consecration. Even at the elevation hardly a thought was given to looking up at the Host,[62] and this was not changed until Pius X, in 1907, gave a new incentive by granting an indulgence to those who, while contemplating the sacred Host, recited the prayer "My Lord and my God." [63]

It would be quite natural to expect the celebrant also to participate in giving these signs of reverence to the Blessed Sacrament. Yet for a long time the only token thus given was a slight bow made to our Lord's Body after the words of consecration, just before elevating It.[64] Here and there the practice grew of kissing the Host; [65] this was during the thirteenth century, the time which witnessed the multiplication of the altar kisses.[66] But these well-intentioned efforts were countered at once by various prohibitions,[67] subsequently repeated.[68] Our form of genuflection—falling on one knee and then rising at once—was not at that time recognized as a religious practice, and therefore was not used at this moment.[69] To kneel on both knees during the consecration was demanded early of deacon and subdeacon, but appears to have been impracticable for the priest,

---

[60] This view apparently was far more generally accepted in countries outside of Germany than in any German territory; cf. Kramp, "Messgebräuche der Gläubigen in den ausserdeutschen Ländern, 356 f. Here, 413 f., the reference to attempts to introduce among the people the complete *prostratio* after the consecration, cf. above note 56.

[61] Dumoutet, 73 f.

[62] Kramp, "Messgebräuche der Gläubigen in der Neuzeit" (*StZ.*, 1926, II), 215 f. "Messgebräuche der Gläubigen in den ausserdeutschen Ländern" (*ibid.*, 1927, II), 356.

[63] Browe, *Die Verehrung*, 68 f.

[64] *Liber ordinarius* of Liége (Volk, 94, 1. 31): *aliquantulum inclinans;* likewise in the Dominican copy of the work done in 1256 (Guerrini, 242). The Ordo of Stefaneschi, which originated about 1311, also has the priest venerate the host *inclinato capite* just before the elevation, and likewise *inclinato paululum capite* before the elevation of the chalice. Numerous other proofs from the 13th century until about the 16th century in Browe, *Die Elevation*, 44-47.

[65] Missale of Evreux-Jumièges (14-15th cent.) : Martène, 1, 4, XXVIII (I, 644 E). More examples in Browe, *Die Verehrung*, 65. Cf. also below, n. 67.

[66] Above I, 316. In several places it became customary to kiss both the host and the chalice before the respective words of consecration; Browe, *Die Verehrung, 65.* The Pontifical of Laon, Leroquais, *Les Pontificaux,* (I, Paris, 1937), 167, notes a kissing of the chalice before the words *Accipite et bibite.*

[67] Synod of Sarum, 1217, can. 37 f. (Mansi, XXII, 1119 f.) ; Bonaventura, *Speculum disciplinæ ad novitios,* I, 17 (Opp. ed. Peltier, XII [Paris, 1868], 467). Browe, *Die Verehrung,* 65 f.

[68] Examples until into the 17th century in Browe, 65 f.

[69] On the other hand, it was customary as a mark of respect before lay persons of rank. Berthold of Regensburg (d. 1272), in a sermon, stresses this distinction and urges a double genuflection before the Blessed Sacrament; Berthold of Regensburg, *Predigten,* ed. Pfeiffer, I (1862), 457.

although the insertion of a lengthy prayer—as was sometimes done after the *Pater noster*—seems to have been thought desirable.[70] The first evidence of a short genuflection made by the priest at the consecration is found in Henry of Hesse (d. 1397), who was teaching theology at Vienna.[71] Still, even in the fifteenth century the simple bow was still prevalent, and provision is made for it even in some of the Mass ordinaries of the sixteenth century.[72] In Roman Mass books the genuflection appears from 1498 on, and from the start the arrangement is the one we have today, with a genuflection before and after the elevation of the species.[73] It was made definitive in 1570 by the Missal of Pius V.

While the priest genuflects, the Mass-server grasps the edge of the chasuble. Because of the shape which the chasuble has commonly assumed since the close of the Middle Ages, the precise sense of this little ceremony is no longer evident. Nowadays it gives the general impression of being a gesture of readiness, not at all out of keeping with the sacredness of the moment. The explanation usually offered is that the chasuble is lifted so the celebrant might not be impeded when genuflecting,[74] and this might be understandable on the supposition that—as was the case in the last years of the Middle Ages—the chasuble used to reach in back down to the heels.[75] But at that time this reason was not actually given,[76] but instead a very different one, the same reason still found in the Roman Missal. According to this, the server should take hold of the edge of the *planeta*, *ne ipsum Celebrantem impediat in elevatione brachiorum.*[77] This explanation, it must be granted, is even less obvious today than the other. But that it is the true one can be deduced from the fact that the same gesture had already been prescribed for the deacon long before there was any thought of a genuflection.[78] And in the thirteenth century it was definitely

---

[70] Browe, *Die Elevation*, 47 f.

[71] Browe, 48 f.

[72] Thus, among others, in the *Ordinarium* of Coutances of 1557; in a Mass arrangement of the Cistercians in 1589; see Browe, *Die Elevation*, 46 f., 50. The Carthusians have retained only the bow to this day. *Ordinarium Carth.* (1932), c. 27, 5 f.; 9 f.; 12.

[73] Browe, 49 f. In several places, however, it was customary to elevate the host during the genuflection. Browe, *Die Verehrung*, 63. Cf. the Miniature of the *Legenda aurea* of Brussels in Braun, *Der christliche Altar*, II, Tablet 144.

[74] Cf. Ph. Hartmann, *Repertorium rituum* (11th ed.; Paderborn, 1908), 773. In Tyrol it is customary to explain this action of holding the chasuble as a symbol of popular participation.

[75] Cf. Braun, *Die liturgischen Paramente*,

110, who records the average length about the year 1400 as 1,40m (about 4'6") and about the year 1600, 1,25m (about 4'2").

[76] Nevertheless at the end of the Middle Ages representations are found in which the server raises the chasuble as the priest genuflects; cf. the miniature cited above; a further representation in Dumoutet, *Le Christ selon la chair et la vie liturgique au moyen-âge*, (Paris, 1932), p. 108-109.

[77] *Ritus serv.*, VIII, 6. Likewise in A. Castellani, *Sacerdotale Romanum* (appeared first in 1523; Venice, 1588), 68.

[78] *Liber ordinarius* of Liége (about 1285; Volk, 94, 1. 25): *diaconus retro sacerdotem levans eius casulam. Liber ordinarius* of the cathedral church of Essen (2nd half of the 14th century; Arens, 19): *levabit casulam presbyteri aliquantulum, ut eo facilius levet sacramentum.* Illustrations

in order. For then they still commonly used the bell-shaped chasuble, and when the arms were raised, the back part, being pulled away by the uplifted arms, presented a very ugly picture unless there was a helping hand to hold it neat. With the return of the ample chasuble the old ceremony is again regaining its full meaning, so that it is once more intelligible.

There remains yet another question: Should our worship of the Blessed Sacrament be manifested by prayers and songs? Prayers spoken aloud and songs during the consecration are not things that would explain themselves. The rule of silence during the canon had indeed been violated often enough in the thirteenth century, but it had not yet lost all its force. At all events, the celebrating priest was permitted to say special prayers, but only in a subdued tone.[79] Such an action was not at all strange in medieval times. True, the *apologiæ* which had cropped out everywhere between the various prayers had for the most part disappeared from the Mass books by the thirteenth century, and the injunctions, like those of Bernold of Constance, forbidding any and all insertions into the canon,[80] did not remain ineffective. But a short ejaculatory prayer right after the consecration still appeared admissible and was actually recommended and practiced by many,[81] although others again absolutely prohibited any such interpolation,[82] even before the appearance of the Missal of Pius V.[83]

But the faithful, at any rate, were admonished to pray, at first using prayers which they would recite quietly to themselves. About 1215 William of Auxerre, in his *Summa aurea*, mentions such prayers and asserts: *Multorum petitiones exaudiuntur in ipsa visione corporis Christi.*[84] According to Berthold of Regensburg, the faithful ought at this moment to pray for three things: for forgivenss of sin, for a contrite reception of the last

from a French Missal of the 14th century in Leroquais, IV, Tablet LXVII, 1.
[79] Regarding the attempts in the 15th and 16th centuries to have the priest say prayers in a loud tone of voice in the presence of the people, see Browe, *Die Verehrung*, 54.
[80] Cf. above, p. 165, n. 31.
[81] William of Melitona, *Opusc. super missam*, ed. van Dijk (*Eph. liturg.*, 1939), 338, even as his predecessor, Alexander of Hales, has the priest saying: *Adoro te Domine Jesu Christe Salvator, qui per mortem tuam redemisti mundum, quem credo esse sub hac specie quam video.* Durandus also as bishop in his *Constitutiones synodales* recommends prayers of this kind to his priests; Browe, *Die Verehrung*, 40; 53. A list of similar prayers in a Mass book of Valencia before 1411 (Ferreres, 154f.). Cf. Dumoutet, *Le Christ selon la chair*, 170-173. It is said of St. Francis Xavier

that he was accustomed to insert a prayer for the conversion of the heathens after the consecration; G. Schurhammer, *Der hl. Franz Xaver*, (Freiburg, 1925), 151.
[82] A commentary on the Mass in a 15th century MS. of Stuttgart (in Franz, 611) threatens those priests with excommunication who interpolate prayers at the elevation of the sacred Host, e.g.: *Deus propitius esto mihi peccatori*, or *Propitius esto peccatis nostris propter nomen tuum Domine*, or *O vere digna hostia.*
[83] Even Ph. Hartmann, *Repertorium rituum*, (11th ed.; Paderborn, 1908), 380 f., directs the celebrant at the elevation of the sacred host (and of the chalice): "let him then pray: *Dominus meus et Deus meus.*" But a decree of the Congregation of Rites, Nov. 6, 1925, expressly forbids any such additions henceforth: *Acta Ap. Sed.*, 18 (1926), 22 f.
[84] Dumoutet, *Le désir de voir l'hostie*, 18.

sacraments, and for eternal beatitude.[85] As outward expression of their prayer, the faithful might strike their breast or sign themselves with the sign of the Cross.[86] The only vocal prayers commonly recommended were the usual formulas,[87] or else a simple greeting or invocation. One such salutation which recurs in various versions, both Latin and vernacular, in many prayer books towards the end of the medieval era is the formula: *Ave salus mundi, verbum Patris, hostia vera.*[88] Another is the formula: *Te adoro, te verum corpus Christi confiteor.*[89] Other more elaborate formulas were probably products of the monasteries. Take, for instance, the fourteen-part invocation which starts with the verse: *Ave principium nostræ creationis, ave pretium nostræ redemptionis, ave viaticum nostræ peregrinationis.*[90] Such pieces as *Adoro te devote,*[91] *Anima*

---

[85] Berthold of Regensburg, *Predigten,* ed. Pfeiffer, II, 685 (Franz, 656) : cf. I, 459, where he even gives the wording of a prayer. Berthold of Chiemsee, *Keligpuchel* (Munich, 1535), c. 20, 7, 8, presents comprehensive prayers for the oblation and the memory of the Passion.

[86] Gabriel Biel, *Canonis expositio,* lect. 50, among other marks of reverence, recommends *pectora tundere.* Durandus (d. 1296) in his Pontifical (Andrieu, 646; Martène, 1, 4, XXIII [I, 620 A]), prescribed a comprehensive ritual of external marks of reverence for a bishop while present at the Mass of a priest. When the Body of the Lord is elevated, he should kneel upon the floor before his prie-dieu and having raised his eyes in adoration, he should strike his breast three times and then kiss either the floor or the prie-dieu. At the elevation of the chalice, after having raised his eyes, he should make the sign of the cross and strike his breast once. Here one recognizes the beginnings of that unnatural accumulation of pious antics so common today at the consecration.

[87] Indulgences are granted if an Our Father and Hail Mary, or five Our Father's and Hail Mary's are said during the consecration. Browe, *L'atteggiamento,* 411 f. Cf. above, p. 211, n. 58. The English *Lay Folks Mass Book* recommends the devout person of the 13th century to say a *Pater* and *Credo* (Simmons, 40) ; a prayer in rhyme is also supplied. Even the *Te Deum* is mentioned; see reference, *JL,* 3 (1923), 206 (according to M. Frost).

[88] Dumoutet, *Le Christ selon la chair,* 151-

154; already verified at 1212 in V. L. Kennedy, "The Handbook of Master Peter, Chancellor of Chartres," *Medieval Studies,* 5 (1943), 8. Cf. also Wilmart, *Auteurs spirituels,* 24. In Germany this invocation is certified in the 15th century in the form of a distichon: *Salve lux mundi, verbum Patris, hostia vera, viva caro, deitas integra, verus homo;* Franz, 22; German also *ibid.,* 703. A prayer at the consecration beginning with *Salve lux mundi,* also in England in the meditations of Longforde (15th cent.) ; Legg, *Tracts,* 24. A German ryhmed prayer in 12 verses beginning with "Got, vatir allir cristenheit" in a 13th century MS. of Weingarten in Franz, 23, n. 1. Cf. also the call of Parsifal in "Queste del saint Graal," note 58, above.

[89] Dumoutet, *Le Christ selon la chair,* 166 f., with parallel French formulas of the 14-15th century.

[90] Evidenced at the beginning of the 13th century in an English rule for nuns (Browe, *Die Verehrung,* 19; cf. also 53, n. 160) and in Peter the Chancellor of Chartres (Kennedy, *op. cit.,* 9). Cf. also Wilmart, *Auteurs spirituels,* 22 f.

[91] F. J. Mone, *Lateinische Hymnen des Mittelalters,* I, Freiburg, 1853, 275 f. The hymn appears for the first time in the 14th century, and precisely as a prayer at the consecration. The authorship of St. Thomas Aquinas is uncertain; see Wilmart, *Auteurs spirituels,* 361-414, especially 399 ff., and also the reference in *Bulletin Thomiste,* 7 (1943-46), n. 122 f. The last strophes *(Pie pelicane)* were at times combined with the elevation of the

Christi,[92] and *Ave verum corpus* [93] also served to salute the Blessed Sacrament at the elevation.[94]

Well-shaped texts of this sort were naturally an open invitation for common recitation and singing, even if they were not intended for this from the start. By the end of the Middle Ages a solemn salutation of the Blessed Sacrament at the elevation formed part of the ceremony of high Mass. According to a Strassburg statute of 1450, the antiphon *O sacrum convivium*, with versicle and oration, was to be sung on certain occasions *in elevatione immediate post Benedictus.*[95] A decree issued in 1512 by Louis XII of France ordained that at the daily high Mass in Notre Dame in Paris the *O salutaris hostia* was to be sung *in elevatione corporis Christi* between the *Sanctus* and *Benedictus*. A Paris foundation of 1521 presupposes the *Ave verum.*[96] Other songs, too, are mentioned for the same occasion.[97] We must admit that these songs are all, in general, truly artistic works which fit into the setting with theological propriety. The break in the God-ward motion of the prayer and oblation made by the ceremony of elevating the sacred species and showing them to the people is intelligently shaped and filled out by these hymnic salutations, the product reminding one of a similar creation on Maundy Thursday where, after the holy oils are blessed, a greeting of veneration is likewise offered them.

Soon after the expiration of the Middle Ages, and with them, of the Gothic spirit, there was a rapid decline in the simple desire to contemplate the sacred Host at the moment of the consecration.[98] That meant the disappearance, too, of the hymns which had been sung in honor of the Blessed Sacrament.[99] The elevation ceremony was maintained, but was conducted in utter silence. Often even the organ was silenced, although

chalice; Dumoutet, *Le Christ selon le chair,* 165-169, especially 168, note.

[92] Dumoutet, *op. cit.,* 160-165; P. Schepens, "Pour l'histoire de la prière Anima Christi," *Nouvelle Revue théol.,* 62 (1935), 699-710. Further references and data in Balth. Fischer, "Das Trierer Anima Christi," *Trierer Theol. Zeitschrift,* 60 (1951), 189-196; Fischer edits a Middle High German text of the early 14th century which probably represents the original. Cf. also H. Thurston, *Familiar Prayers* (Westminster, 1953), 38-52.

[93] Dumoutet, *op. cit.,* 169 f. The title in the MSS. commonly reads *In elevatione corporis Christi*. Mone, *op. cit.,* I, 280. Other hymns to the Blessed Sacrament with similar assignment *(In elevatione Corporis, Quando elevatur calix)*, *ibid.,* 271 f., 281-293.

[94] More data in Browe, *Die Verehrung,* 53. Dumoutet, *Le Christ selon la chair,* 164,

speaks of more than 50 prayers at the elevation, that are handed down from the Middle Ages. Short invocations of the Body and Blood of Christ were common even at an earlier date before the Communion of the priest (see below). Some of these were then transferred to the elevation; *ibid.,* 158 f.

[95] Browe, *Die Verehrung,* 53, n. 161.

[96] Dumoutet, *Le désir de voir l'hostie,* 60-62. Both hymns, as a matter of choice among the Cistercians; so also according to a prescription even as late as 1584; see J. Hau, "Statuten aus einem niederdeutschen Zisterzienserinnenkloster" (*Cist.-Chr.,* 1935), 132.

[97] *Gaudete flores*: Dumoutet, *Le désir,* 61. The *Benedictus* was also entoned with the same intent, above, p. 137, note 44.

[98] Dumoutet, *Le désir de voir l'hostie,* 72-74.

[99] The Synods of Augsburg, 1548 and 1567,

the decrees still in force would permit a soft playing of the instrument. The only perceptible sound was the server's little bell. The faithful venerated the sacred species, but did so in silent prayer.[100] Still there were some countries which maintained the old practice of saying certain designated prayers aloud. Thus in Spanish churches the following salutations are customary: "My Lord and my God, we adore Thee, Body of our Lord Jesus Christ, because by Thy holy Cross Thou hast redeemed the world.— My Lord and my God, we adore Thee, sacred Blood of our Lord Jesus Christ, which was shed on the Cross for the salvation of the world." [101] So nicely suited are such prayers as these that they emerge, now here, now there, in other countries also, at least outside of high Mass.[102]

already speak of *altissimum silentium* (Hartzheim, VI, 369), of an *altum sanctumque silentium* (ibid., VII, 172), that was not to be interrupted by hymns without reason. Elsewhere, though, they remained in use for a longer period. In the *Voyage liturgique* of de Moléon, which appeared in 1718, it is remarked as a peculiarity that in individual French cathedrals nothing is sung at the elevation of the host, but that it is adored in silence (117, 142, 147). Among the Premonstratensians the prescription of such a hymn *(O salutaris hostia)* was first incorporated in the *Liber ordinarius* in 1628 and again in 1739, where it still is found; Waefelghem, 122, n. 2. Even according to Roman directions hymns during the elevation were at first permitted. The question, *An in elevatione ss. sacramenti in missis sollemnibus cani possit, Tantum ergo, etc., vel aliqua antiphona tanti sacramenti propria*, was answered in the affirmative, April 14, 1753; *Decreta auth. SRC*, n. 2424 ad 6. A later decision of May 5, 1894, permits such hymns only *peracta ultima elevatione*, as soon as the *Benedictus* has been sung; *Decreta auth. SRC*, n. 3827 ad 3.

[100] The official *Enchiridion Indulgentiarum* (Vatican City, 1950), has a prayerful address in three parts, "Hail, saving victim offered upon the cross . . . (n. 132) and again the prayer which captivated St. Pius X, "My lord and my God" (n. 133). Cf. also *ibid.*, n. 142.

[101] Kramp, "Messopfergebräuche der Gläubigen in den ausserdeutschen Ländern" *(StZ*, 1927, II), 361. In Portugal the prayer reads: "Here is the body, blood, and divinity of our Lord Jesus Christ, as true

and complete as in heaven"; "Here is the blood, body, soul, and divinity . . . ; *ibid.*, 362. In Colombia the prayer "My Lord and my God" is commonly said; *ibid.*, 365. B. Lebbe, *The Mass: A Historical Commentary* (Westminster, 1949), 81-82, lists several ejaculations traditional with the people of Eire, among them a curious expression: "All praise to thee, Lord Jesus, white and red."

[102] Cf. Egyptian liturgies above, p. 204. A similar greeting as in Spain, only more carefully devised from a theological standpoint, is contained in the present German catechism, beginnng with "My Lord and my God! Hail, true body of Christ that was offered for me on the cross." It was taken up, e.g., in the diocese of St.Pölten and also in the diocesan hymnal (*Heiliges Volk*, [2nd ed.; St. Pölten, 1936] 67 f.) and was used in congregational Mass devotions. Noteworthy discussions have taken place in Germany in the last years from the viewpoint of the children's Mass, among others in the *Katechetischen Blättern*, 40 (1939) and 41 (1940). The discussion turned partly on the assumption that the idea of sacrifice, perhaps even with an address to God the Father, should be plainly expressed, but they inclined to the solution indicated above. However, Victor Schurr, C.SS.R., in *Paulus*, 23 (1951), 65, suggests prayers of offering like those at the offertory. With the regulating of the prayers at the elevation must be joined the arrangement of external signs of respect. As a general rule it may be stated that besides the raising of the eyes to the Blessed Sacrament, a sign of the cross at most would be proper.

14. *Unde et memores*

In reciting the account of the institution, the priest simply relates what then took place, and only the actions which are coupled with the words, and the veneration which follows upon them, make it clear that the scene is being re-enacted. But once the Great Prayer is resumed after the consecration, the very first thing done is to interpret the mystery thus accomplished. The link with the preceding account is made by the word *Unde*, harking back to our Saviour's injunction which closes the account.[1] Now what is it we are doing at the altar in conformity with this injunction?

In almost all the liturgies two ideas are used to define the mystery, the two being placed side by side and contrasted in various ways. The mystery is a *commemoration* or *anamnesis;* and it is an *oblation*, a sacrifice.[2] In some few instances the oblation is mentioned first, as in the Armenian Mass, where, after pronouncing the words of institution, the priest pursues and expands the thought of the command to do what Christ had done; he takes the gifts in his hands and says: *Et nos igitur, Domine, secundum illud mandatum, offerimus istud salutiferum sacramentum corporis et sanguinis Unigeniti tui, commemoramus salutares eius pro nobis passiones . . .*[3] As a rule, however, the remembrance is mentioned first, but in participial form, so that, though it is first, yet the main stress will be on the oblation, expressed by means of a verb like *offerimus*, προςφέρομεν.[4]

For both ideas the connection with the command of our Lord is the same: we come before Thee, O God—that is the basic thought—with a grateful memorial of the redemptive work of Christ and offer up to Thee His Body and Blood. And both ideas contain an objective element as

---

[1] A similar link *(igitur, ergo)* in the oldest Roman formularies; above I, 29, 52; and mostly (τοίνυν, οὖν), though not without exception, in the oriental formularies; Lietzmann, *Messe und Herrenmahl*, 50-55. The conjunction is missing for the most part in the Gallic texts, though they nevertheless establish, not infrequently, a close connection by the manner in which they take up the last word of Christ's injunction (. . . *facietis*, or something similar) : *Hæc facimus, Hoc agentes* and the like; *ibid.*, 60-68.

[2] By way of exception, a definite enunciation of the anamnesis character of the celebration (frequently itself called anamnesis for short) is missing; thus, in the *Euchologium* of Serapion, 3, 13 (Quasten, *Mon.*, 62; see above I, 34-35), whereas the offering is announced twice therein, once after the consecration of the host and again after

the consecration of the chalice. In any event, the sacrifice in the first instance is designated at the same time as a Memento of the Dead: διὰ τοῦτο καὶ ἡμεῖς τὸ ὁμοίωμα τοῦ θανάτου ποιοῦντες τὸν ἄρτον προσηνέγκαμεν; cf. O. Casel, *JL*, 6 (1926), 116 f. On the other hand, either the anamnesis or the offering has been frequently omitted in Gallican formularies; cf. e.g., Missale Gothicum: Muratori, II, 518, 522, 526, 544, 548, etc.

[3] Text according to Chosroe, *Explicatio precum missæ* (about 950) ed. Vetter (Freiburg, 1880), 32 f. For today's text see Brightman, 437: "We therefore, O Lord, presenting unto thee . . ., do remember the saving sufferings" . . .—For the accompanying rite see Hanssens, III, 452.

[4] The more ancient Byzantine liturgy (Brightman, 328 f.) has also the offering in the grammatical form of a participle:

well as a subjective one. What we hold here in our hands is a memorial [5] and an oblation. But memorial as well as oblation must be realized within ourselves as our own remembrance and our offering. Then, and only then, can a "worship in spirit and truth" in the fullest sense arise to God from our hands.

The *memorial* is usually referred to here in just a short phrase. This is only natural, for the whole Prayer of Thanksgiving is, in substance, a memorial prayer, particularly the Christological portion.[6] In fact, even the readings in the fore-Mass, especially the Gospel, have as their aim to revive the memory of our Lord, His word and His work.[7] The whole purpose of the yearly round of Church feasts is, at bottom, nothing other than an enlargement of that recollection, making room for an ever-increasing store of memories. The basic theme of the Church year, too, is precisely the *passio Domini*, the redemption accomplished by Christ's death and Resurrection. In the anamnesis this theme is treated very briefly, but its contents are not analyzed as a subjective memory, since it is taken for granted that the soul is already alive to everything contained therein. All that is stated here is that in the sacramental operation the divine charge to do this "in

---

Μεμνημένοι οὖν . . . τὰ σά ἐκ τῶν σῶν σοὶ προςφέροντες, σὲ (the people) : σὲ ὑμνοῦμεν. Apparently the celebrant joined in with the people's phrase.

[5] O. Casel, "Das Mysteriengedächtnis der Messliturgie im Lichte der Tradition," *JL*, 6 (1926), 113-204, has collected the testimonies for the real character of the commemoration from both liturgical and extra-liturgical sources, though Casel's interpretation of the real commemoration is still an object of controversy; cf. above I, 183 f. However, individual liturgical formularies clearly bring out the fact that an objective commemoration is in some way present. Thus we read in the East Syrian anaphora of Nestorius, just before the words of the institution : *Et reliquit nobis commemorationem salutis nostrœ, mysterium hoc, quod offerimus coram te;* Renaudot, II, 623. Cf. also the *Euchologion* of Serapion, above I, 34 f. Furthermore, many expressions of the Fathers are quite plain. Thus Chrysostom, *In Hebr. hom.*, 17, 3 (PG, 63, 131), says : We offer every day, inasmuch as we consummate the memory of His death, (ἀνάμνησιν ποιούμενοι τοῦ θανάτου αὐτοῦ); or Theodoret of Cyrus, *In Hebr.*, 8, 4 (PG, 82, 736) : It is clear that we offer no other sacrifice (than that which Christ offered), but celebrate the sole and sancti-

fying memory of it (μνήμην ἐπιτελοῦμεν). In the 9th century Florus Diaconus, *De actione miss.*, c. 63 (PL, 119, 54 D) : *Illius ergo panis et calicis oblatio mortis Christi est commemoratio et annuntiatio, quæ non tam verbis quam mysteriis ipsis agitur.*

[6] Cf. above, p. 116. In this respect it is significant that in the *Apostolic Constitutions,* VIII, 12, 35, the description of the redemptive Passion, which precedes the account of the institution, is summed up by means of μεμνημένοι οὖν εὐχαριστοῦμέν σοι, as the true anamnesis that begins after the institution : μεμνημένοι τοίνυν (προςφέρομέν σοι). Cf. above I, 36 f. In the Armenian normal anaphora, the prayer of thanksgiving which was prolonged before the account of the institution to include the Passion of Christ, is brought to a close after it by a reference to the descent into hell and the destruction of its gates (a favorite way the Orient has of representing the Easter victory) ; Brightman, 437.

[7] Cf. also R. Guardini, *Besinnung vor der Feier der hl. Messe,* II (Mainz, 1939), 111 f. For a study of the interpretation of the anamnesis in the preaching and services of ancient Christendom, cf. N. A. Dahl, "Anamnesis," *Studia Theologica* I (Lund, 1948), 69-95.

remembrance of Me" (Luke 22:19; 1 Cor. 11:24 f.) is being fulfilled, and that, moreover, we are thus doing what Paul had demanded in more detail, namely, to "proclaim the death of the Lord" (1 Cor. 11.26). Nevertheless, the concept of Christ's sacrificial death does undergo a certain development, for related—or shall we say component—concepts are disclosed in much the same way as in the ancient professions of faith.[8] The death of the Lord is His victory, it is His triumph over death. The Gallic Mass appears to have mentioned originally only the Passion.[9] Even in Hippolytus the Resurrection is already added: *Memores igitur mortis et resurrectionis eius.*[10] In Ambrose's text of the canon there is the further addition of the Ascension, and the *passio*—or rather, the triplet beginning with it—is characterized by the word *gloriosissima.*[11]

The text of our present-day anamnesis follows the same lines.[12] The adjective *gloriosa* has been transferred to the Ascension, while the *passio* has acquired the attribute *tam beata;* we surely have reason for hailing the Passion as blessed, since it is the root of our salvation.[13] The later Middle Ages sought to emphasize the memory of the Cross also in the outward gesture, by reciting the anamnesis prayer, and sometimes also the *Supra quæ,*[14] with outstretched arms.[15]

---

[8] Lietzmann, *Messe und Herrenmahl*, 50 ff.
[9] Lietzmann, 61 f. Cf. the first Mass in the Gothic Missal (Muratori, II, 518): *Hæc facimus Domine ... commemorantes et celebrantes passionem unici Filii tui Jesu Christi Domini nostri, qui tecum.* So, too, several Mozarabic Masses; Lietzmann, 63. For the rest it is precisely the anamnesis of the Gallic liturgies, where they did not disappear entirely, that show the most advanced deterioration; Lietzmann, 62 f. There is merely a general mention of the mysteries of our Redemption in the East Syrian anaphora of Theodorus; Renaudot, II (1847), 613.
[10] Above I, 29.
[11] Above I, 52. For Mozarabic parallels see Lietzmann, 63.
[12] The wording, as it appears in the Sacramentaries, shows only insignificant variations; after *Unde et memores* there is an insertion of *sumus.* But that disturbs the construction. It is, moreover, missing in Hippolytus and Ambrose and was later crossed out, probably by Alcuin (Lietzmann, 59). Some of the old witnesses have inserted *Dei (nostri J. C.)* after *Domini,* The *eiusdem (Christi F. t.)* that still precedes today was first put in by the Humanists of the 16th century; Botte, 40 Ap-

paratus. The *eiusdem,* however, is still missing in the *Missale Romanum* of 1474; ed. Lippe, HBS, 17), 207. Neither is it noted in the later editions; see Lippe (HBS, 33), 111.
[13] Because, of course, the term *passio* includes the death of Christ; see Chr. Mohrmann, *Vigiliæ christianæ,* 4 (1950), n. 21. The *tam* has been subjected to textual criticism, as if *quam* must have been omitted or lost. The criticisms, however, are not sound; see Botte, 63. It merely supplies an emotional re-enforcement in much the same manner as in the oriental anaphoras at the beginning of the preface: Ὡς (ἀληθῶς ἄξιον); see above, p. 125, n. 59. A Mozarabic anamnesis presents something similar with *Habentes ante oculos . . . tantæ passionis triumphos;* Férotin, *Le liber mozarabicus sacramentorum,* p. 250.
[14] A *Missale Ursinense* cited by Gerbert, *Vetus liturgia Alemannica* I, 363, puts before *Supra quæ* the notation: *Hic extende brachia quantumcumque potes.*
[15] End of the 12th century among the Premonstratensians (Waefelghem, 78); *Ordinarium, O.P.* of 1256 (Guerrini, 242); *Liber ordinarius* of Liége (Volk, 95). From then on the practice spread

In most of the oriental formulas the anamnesis underwent an extended evolution, but in the chief liturgies this did not go beyond a development of the theme of redemption. The three steps, Passion, Resurrection and Ascension, continue as the permanent threesome around which every added thing is marshalled. Thus to the Passion is added, for example, "the life-giving Cross and the three-days' stay in the tomb" (in the Byzantine Liturgy of St. James). And after the Ascension, is added in both these cases—and similarly in most of the others—the sitting at the right hand of the Father and "the glorious and awesome second coming."[16] It is the description of the second coming which bursts the limitations of the anamnesis as such, particularly in West-Syrian formulas, as (for instance) in the fourth-century addition: "when He comes with glory and power to judge the living and the dead and to reward everyone according to his deeds,"[17] a description which grows ever richer and more fearsome[18] and which, in the Greek anaphora of St. James, is supplemented by a plea for mercy.[19] Later West-Syrian formulas even tacked on other events in Christ's life.[20] Similarly, His birth is mentioned also in the Occident, but this is not found till long after, in late Carolingian Mass books.[21]

widely; cf. Franz, 612; Sölch, *Hugo*, 93 f.; Leroquais, I, 315; II, 182, 262, etc. St. Thomas Aquinas defends it, *Summa theol.*, III, 83, 5 ad 5. The first leaning towards this practice is found in Bernold of Constance, *Micrologus*, c. 16 (PL, 151, 987); Cf. Luykx (*Anal. Præm.*, 1946-1947), 68 f, 89. Dominicans, Carmelites, and Carthusians still do it. Contrary to the statements copied by Lebrun I, 428, it must have prevailed for a long time also at Rome; the strange mode of expression in the *Ordo* of Stefaneschi (about 1311), c. 71 (PL, 78, 1189 A), that certainly goes beyond n. 53 (1166 D): *Hic ampliet manus et brachia*, proves it, even as the Roman rubric of 1534 cited by Lebrun himself, *loc. cit.*: *extensis manibus ante pectus more consueto*, which is almost equivalent to a suppression.—Regarding the attempt to pantomine the resurrection and ascension, see above I, 107.

[16] Lietzmann, 50-57. The form in the *Apostolic Constitutions* is somewhat simpler; see above I, 37. The decorative adjectives in the Syrian formularies are worthy of note, e.g., in the anaphora of St. James (Brightman, 52 f.): Μεμνημένοι . . . τῶν ζωοποιῶν αὐτοῦ παθημάτων, τοῦ σωτηρίου σταυροῦ, . . . τῆς δευτέρας ἐνδόξου καὶ φοβεροῦ αὐτοῦ παρουσίας.

[17] *Const. Ap.*, VIII, 12, 38 (Quasten, *Mon.*, 223).

[18] In some of the West Syrian anaphoras of later origin the terrors of the second advent are depicted in glaring colors. The description at times is spread over half, in fact over an entire printed page. Renaudot, II (1847), 147, 165, 190 f., 205, 216, etc.

[19] Brightman, 53, 1. 3 : . . . κατὰ τὰ ἔργα αὐτοῦ φεῖσαι ἡμῶν, κύριε ὁ θεὸς ἡμῶν. A like petition from the people follows: see below, n. 31.

[20] The anaphora of St. Ignatius mentions birth and baptism (Renaudot, II, 216), the anaphora of St. Mark the conception, birth, and baptism (*ibid.*, II, 178), the anaphora of Maruthas the birth, the lying in the manger, baptism fasting, and temptation, as well as various phases of the history of the Passion (*ibid.*, 263).

[21] Botte, 40, Apparatus: *admirabilis nativitatis*. The adjectives vary. The *nativitas* was already read into the text by Amalar, *De eccl. off.*, III, 25 (PL, 105, 1141 B). But Bernold of Constance (d. 1100), *Micrologus*, c. 13 (PL, 151, 985 C) fights against this expansion. Nevertheless it survived until the late Middle Ages; see Leroquais, III, 420; Ebner, 418. Regarding the question whether a citation by

The mention of various phases in the work of redemption which are to be kept in remembrance is often matched in oriental liturgies by a well-rounded expansion of the words incorporating Christ's injunction to do as He had done. At first only the words of St. Paul are put on Christ's lips.[22] But then the addition is made of the Resurrection,[23] or of the Resurrection and Ascension, especially in Egyptian liturgies: "As often as you eat this bread . . . you shall manifest My death and profess My Resurrection and Ascension, until I come."[24] Similar formations made their way into the area of the Gallic liturgies;[25] thus a Milanese formula reads as follows: *Hæc quotiescumque feceritis, in meam commemorationem facietis, mortem meam prædicabitis, resurrectionem meam annuntiabitis, adventum meum sperabitis, donec iterum de cœlis veniam ad vos.*[26]

The remembrance should be realized not only in and by the priest, but also in and by the entire congregation assembled. In the Roman Mass this is brought out by the fact that the subject of the anamnesis is defined as *nos servi tui, sed et plebs tua sancta*. In Egypt, at an early date, it was revealed even more vividly; a solemn outcry of the people, corresponding to the expanded phrases of our Lord's injunction to do as He had done, followed immediately after it as a sort of response to it, and was then followed by the priest's prayer. Even today the Coptic Mass retains this anamnesis cry of the people, and since it still employs the Greek tongue it is evidently a heritage of at least the sixth century. Τὸν θάνατόν σου, κύριε, καὶ αγγέλλομεν καὶ τὴν ἀγίαν σου ἀνάστασιν καὶ ἀνάλημψιν ὁμολογοῦμεν.[27] In Egypt the anamnesis of the priest has likewise acquired its own special pattern by the use of the Pauline formulation. The main Egyptian liturgies not only begin with a *Memores*, Μεμνημένοι, but in addition use a rather expanded schema for what follows by announcing (καταγγέλλοντες)

Arnobius the Younger (about 460), *In Ps. 110* (PL, 53, 497 B; Botte, 41), presupposes the addition in the Roman Mass, see Botte, 63 f. The probability is slight. More likely it was in some Gallic Masses (for Arnobius is generally regarded as a Gaul) that the birth was already then named. In any case, it is found in substance in the Gothic Missal of the 7th century (Muratori, II, 522): *Credimus, Domine, adventum tuum, recolimus passionem tuam*. Mozarabic examples stress the *venisse, incarnatum fuisse*, Lietzmann, 65 f. The *incarnatio* also appears here and there in Roman Mass books of the Middle Ages, e.g., in the Missal of Lagny (11th cent.; Leroquais, I, 171): *incarnationis, nativitatis*.
[22] Thus *Const. Ap.*, VIII, 12, 37 (Quasten, *Mon.*, 223): . . . τὸν θάνατον τὸν ἐμὸν καταγγέλλετε, ἄχρις ἂν ἔλθω. More refer-

ence and detailed analysis also for that which follows in Hamm, 90 f.
[23] The anaphora of St. James (Brightman, 52); Byzantine liturgy of St. Basil (*ibid.*, 328); Papyrus of Dêr-Balyzeh (Quasten, *Mon.*, 42).
[24] Egyptian anaphora of St. Mark (Brightman, 133).
[25] Hamm, 91 f.
[26] Hamm, 91.
[27] Brightman, 177. Cf. also in the Ethiopian liturgy: *ibid.*, 232 f. In a somewhat more original form (κύριε, ἀγίαν σου and καὶ ἀνάλημψιν are missing) in the papyrus of Dêr-Balyzeh (Quasten, *Mon.*, 42). It is clear from the address to Christ that we have here a passage said by the people. The continuation after ὁμολογοῦμεν, which reads καὶ δεόμεθα is to be compared with the cry of the people in the Ethiopian Mass (Brightman, 233, l. 1).

His death, by confessing (ὁμολογοῦντες), His Resurrection . . . by awaiting (ἀπεχδεχόμενοι) His second coming, we offer up to Thee . . .[28]

The second point that is expressed in the *Unde et memores* and then taken up and developed in the following prayers, is the *oblation* or offering. Here we have the central sacrificial prayer of the entire Mass, the foremost liturgical expression of the fact that the Mass is actually a sacrifice. In this connection it is to be noted that there is reference here exclusively to a sacrifice offered up by the Church. Christ, the high-priest, remains wholly in the background. It is only in the ceremonies of the consecration, when the priest all at once starts to present our Lord's actions step by step, acting as Christ's mouthpiece in reciting the words of transubstantiation—only here is the veil momentarily withdrawn from the profound depths of this mystery. But now it is once more the Church, the attendant congregation, that speaks and acts. And it is the Church *in concreto,* manifest plainly in its membership; it is the congregation composed of the "servants" of God and the "holy people," which has already appeared as the subject of the remembrance in the anamnesis. To show how aware the Church is of what she is, we must point to the significant words here used, *plebs sancta,* words which bring to the fore the sacerdotal dignity of the people of God in the sense implied by 1 Peter 2:5, 9.[29]

In oriental liturgies the priest's prayer does not contain any equivalent expression which so clearly states that priest and people alike are subjects of the remembrance and the oblation. But instead, both for the remembrance and the oblation, they have exclamations by which the people ratify the action of the priest—and these in addition to the primitive and universal *Amen* at the end of the canon. In the Byzantine Mass the priest utters the words of remembrance and oblation in the form of participles: Μεμνημένοι . . . προσφέροντες; the people complete the sentence with the cry: σὲ ὑμνοῦμεν, σὲ εὐλογοῦμεν, σοὶ εὐχαριστοῦμεν, κύριε, καὶ δεόμεθά σου, ὁ θεὸς ἡμῶν.[30] It is an oblation of praise, of thanksgiving, of petition.

---

[28] Brightman, 133; 178.—Related formularies appear also in the Gallican and especially in the Mozarabic liturgy, where the anamneses begin with *nuntiamus, prœdicamus,* or with *credimus, confitemur,* respectively with *(venturum) prœstolamur.* Lietzmann, 60-67.

[29] The phrase *ordo et plebs* for clerics and people, in Tertullian, *De exhort. cast.,* c. 7 (CSEL, 70, 138, l. 18); cf. Rütten, "Philologisches zum Canon missæ" (*StZ,* 1938, I) 44 f. For *plebs sancta,* cf. St. Augustine's address to the people, *sanctitas vestra,* or also the designations *sacrata plebs, populus sanctus Dei,* in other passages of the Roman liturgy. See also the data in

Botte, 64 f. The clergy's designation of themselves as *servi* finds its justification in Scripture, especially in the Old Testament: *servi Domini* for the Levites (e.g., Ps. 133: 1), perhaps even in the Lord's parable of the *fidelis servus.* The plural *servi* is in accord not only with the conditions of the Roman stational services, but also with the rule that the priest must celebrate at least with a deacon; cf. above I, 208.

[30] Thus already in the text of the 9th century: Brightman, 329 (as a cry of the people); cf. 386 (now given to the choir). The phrase was also taken up by the remaining liturgies of the Orient.

In the West-Syrian Mass, too, the people add a cry of petition after the oblation;[31] this recurs in all West-Syrian anaphoras.

In the Roman Mass just a few impressive words are used for the oblation. In Hippolytus the terseness here as well as in the anamnesis borders on the extreme: *Memores igitur mortis et resurrectionis eius offerimus tibi panem et calicem.* In the present Roman canon the expression has hardly blossomed out beyond this, and it is not till the concluding words, the five-part description of the sacrificial gifts, that the phrasing is caught up in the enveloping praise: *offerimus præclaræ maiestati tuæ de tuis donis ac datis hostiam puram, hostiam sanctam . . .* By the use of the words *maiestas tua* (which we encountered already in the preface) as a term of address, we are brought face to face with the divine greatness before which man crumbles into nothingness. In accordance with this consideration, the gifts which we undertake to present to Him must be regarded as already His own; they are *de tuis donis ac datis.* This is a biblical concept (1 Paral. 29:14) that reappears time and again in different forms on foundation inscriptions of Christian antiquity. Where the pagan founder of a sanctuary or a memorial, conscious of his own largess, has the words *de suo fecit* carved on the stone, the Christian benefactor humbly acknowledges that all he has given was granted him by God; his gift is *ex donis Dei.*[32] Thus, too, every sacrificial gift which we can proffer to God is already "a gift and a present" which He had loaned us. And this is surely true in an eminent way of the gift on our altars. Another concept that might be a contributing factor here is the one proposed by Irenæus in his opposition to Gnosticism; with regard to the material components of our sacrifice, he argues that we do not offer up an uncreated being, but rather we sacrifice to the Lord of creation something that He himself has created.[33]

Similar thoughts are given solemn utterance in the Byzantine Mass, where the priest, after softly finishing the anamnesis, continues in a loud voice: τὰ σὰ ἐκ τῶν σῶν σοὶ προςφέροντες κατὰ πάντα καὶ διὰ πάντα; this is followed by the exclamation of the people already referred to.[34] The phrase is probably as old as the Roman *de tuis donis ac datis.* It even occurs, without any change whatever, on inscriptions. For instance, it

---

[31] The priest: "We offer this fearful and unbloody sacrifice that Thou deal not with us after our sins . . . for Thy people and Thy church (ὁ γὰρ λαός σου καὶ ἡ ἐκκλησία σου, and καὶ ἡ κληρονομία σου) entreat Thee . . ." And the people answer "Have mercy upon us, O God, the Father almighty!" Brightman, 53; 88; Rücker, *Die syrische Jakobusanaphora,* 18 f.

[32] Thus an evangeliary at Monza bears the inscription: *Ex donis Dei dedit Theo-*

delenda reg [ina] *in basilica quam fundavit.* More examples in H. Leclercq, "Donis Dei (de)": DACL, IV, 1507-1510.

[33] Irenæus, *Adv. hær.,* IV, 18, 5 (Quasten, *Mon.,* 347): προςφέρομεν αὐτῷ τὰ ἴδια. Cf. above I, 23 f.

[34] Brightman, 329. From the Byzantine liturgy the phrase passed over into the Egyptian and the Armenian: *ibid.,* 133, 1. 30; 178, 1. 15; 438, 1. 9.

decorates a silver chalice of the sixth century, discovered at Orontes. Later, it was to be found on the altar of the Hagia Sophia at Constantinople.[35] In either case, the words were meant to convey not only our acknowledgement that all we can offer God, whether it be celestial or terrestrial, comes from Him, but even more our proud satisfaction in being able to secure from this world of ours the visible garb for the sacred gifts that lie upon the altar.[36]

Next the gifts themselves are given mention, just as they are found in our hands, and the mention turns into a short hymn on the Blessed Sacrament. First, the sacrament is described in three phrases which stress the spotless purity and holiness of the sacrifice: *hostiam puram, hostiam sanctam, hostiam immaculatam.*[37] Our sacrifice is not like that of the heathens or even that of the Jews, who could offer God only a material and bloody sacrifice; ours is spiritualized and therefore clean. Its positive content is next suggested, first of all by the word *hostia*, which originally implied a living being. The subsequent words also continue the same line of thought,[38] for they are a two-part expression (corresponding to the double form of the sacrificial gifts) proclaiming the preciousness of these gifts, pointing to the results of partaking of them, the everlasting life towards which they tend:[39] *panem sanctum vitæ æternæ et calicem salutis perpetuæ.*[40]

---

[35] References in Rücker, *Die syrische Jakobusanaphora,* 19 apparatus.

[36] Cf. Gihr, 689. The same also in Benedict XIV, *De s. sacrificio missæ,* II. 16, 1 (Schneider 203 f.). Similar expressions in the secreta formulas of the Leonianum: *Deus . . . accipe propitius quæ de tuis donis tibi nos offerre voluisti* (Muratori, I, 386); *Offerimus tibi, Domine, munera quæ dedisti (ibid.,* 370). It is therefore at least highly improbable that, as most interpreters declare, only the consecration gifts are meant by the *de tuis donis ac datis.*

[37] Less euphonious but theologically more precise is the terminology in the Armenian text of the canon (see above I, 52), where the Christian sacrifice is characterized as *immaculatam hostiam, rationabilem hostiam, incruentam hostiam.* The word *rationabilis* describes the spirituality of the sacrifice (cf. above I, 24 f.); this same quality is indicated negatively in *incruenta* (ἀναίμαχτος), an adjective also favored for the first word of the group; Casel, "Ein orientalisches Kultwort" (*JL,* 11, 1931), 2 f.

[38] H. Elfers, *Theologie und Glaube,* 33

(1941), 352 f., makes the whole expression refer to the gifts yet to be "transubstantiated," but this is an assumption without foundation in the text and against which Ambrose—here surely a reliable witness—firmly protests (cf. above I, 52). The oriental liturgies also are content in this prayer to designate the sacrifice as "clean," "unbloody," "fruitful"; cf. Hanssens, III, 451, who calls this mode of expression *vaga et obscura.* Is it not rather in substance a reverential reserve that prompted this mode of expression?

[39] Cf. John 6: 51 ff.

[40] This double expression, but in simpler form, is also in Ambrose's text of the canon; see above I, 52. Perhaps the text presented at this particular place in the fifth Sunday Mass of the Gothic Missal is the more original (Muratori, II, 654) . . . *offerimus tibi, Domine, hanc immaculatam hostiam, rationalem hostiam, incruentam hostiam, hunc panem sanctum et calicem salutarem.* The designation of the chalice here according to Ps. 115: 13; it is evidently also the basis for the Roman text. Cf. Casel, *op. cit.,* 13 with n. 26.

In the *eucharistia* of Hippolytus the awareness that the possibility of offering such gifts is the greatest grace suggested the inclusion of a word of thanks at the close of the oblation: *gratias tibi agentes quia nos dignos habuisti adstare coram te et tibi ministrare.*[41] Some formularies in the East also contain a thanksgiving in the same position.[42] And either then, or else right after the oblation, they make a transition to the epiklesis. The Roman Mass, on the contrary, lingers on the main theme, the oblation, without going into these subsidiary ideas.

15. *Supra quæ* and *Supplices*

For man—and even for the ecclesiastical congregation—to offer God gifts, no matter how holy these might be, is certainly the utmost daring. For this reason the oblation is expressed in yet another manner, in words that endeavor to show that it is nothing less than a grace of God to expect the acceptance of the gifts from our hands.

All we can do is make the offering; *offerimus*. It is up to God to cast a favorable glance[1] upon our offering *(respicere)* and to consider it with approval *(accepta habere)*. Continuing in this figurative language, we add that it also pertains to God to have our gifts carried up to His heavenly altar of sacrifice.[2] The line of thinking manifested in these words follows easily and naturally from what precedes,[3] and it therefore belongs to the

---

[41] Cf. above I, 29, also retained in Greek in *Const. Ap.*, VIII, 12, 38 (Quasten, *Mon.*, 223): ἐφ' οἷς κατηξίωσας ἡμᾶς ἐστάναι ἐνώπιόν σου καὶ ἱερατεύειν σοι. The word ἱερατεύειν naturally signifies priestly service. But there is nothing here to prove that this word ἱερατεύειν refers only to the bishop and his priests, who with him spread their hands over the gift offerings (above I, 29), and still less, as Elfers, *Die Kirchenordnung Hippolyts*, 303 f., further argues, that the *offerimus* and lastly the prayer of thanksgiving in general is the function of the clerics only. If so, why, then, is the *Gratias agamus* addressed to all and answered by all? The ἱερατεύειν is the service of the ἱερεῖς. And under this term of ἱερεῖς not only Justin, but with special emphasis Origen, who is so close to Hippolytus, comprise the whole of God's people. Cf. E. Niebecker, *Das allemeine Priestertum der Gläubigen* (Paderborn, 1936), 18-27; St. v. Dunin Borkowski, "Die Kirche als Stiftung Jesu" (*Religion, Christentum, Kirche*, edited by Esser and Mausbach, II; Kempten, 1913), 55-70.

[42] Besides the *Const. Ap.*, VIII, 12, 38 (foregoing note), the Byzantine liturgy of St. Basil (Brightman, 329, 1. 14) and the Armenian liturgy (*ibid.*, 438, 1. 16). In these last texts it is clearly the thanks of the official priests who thus in prayer distinguish themselves from the general community.

[1] *Propitio ac sereno vultu*: with inclined (eager) and joyful countenance. The same picture in Ps. 30: 17: *illustra faciem tuam;* Ps. 66: 2: *illuminet vultum suum.*

[2] In Ambrose's text of the canon only the latter of the two ideas is expressed; see above I, 52. It is, therefore, the more original.

[3] A certain roughness of grammatical expression that was exploited by critics of the canon (Fortescue, *The Mass*, 153; cf. 348) does not really contradict this. It should, of course, read: *Supra quæ . . . respicere et quæ accepta habere digneris,* still this "more correct" sentence formation would be too draggy. A similar abbreviation of expression we found also at the beginning of the *Communicantes*.

most ancient portion of even the non-Roman liturgy.[4] And yet it gives occasion for more than one problem.

The first thing that strikes us is the fact that these prayers linger wholly over the external performance of the sacrifice, tracing each step of it prayerfully. They are concerned that the symbol be properly executed and also acknowledged by God. But regarding what is symbolized, that sacrificial sentiment from which our action must proceed, that spirit of sacrifice which rightly plays so great a role (perhaps not yet sufficiently stressed) in our present-day religious thinking and in our pastoral monitions regarding attendance at Holy Mass, the wholehearted subjection of the creature to the Creator, the ever-growing conformity of our will with that of almighty God, the resolute surge of our mind towards that mind "which was in Christ Jesus"—all this is here given no special consideration. But this should in no way astonish us. After all, in view of the sacrificial activity of the community, such a state of mind in the individual is taken for granted; it is presupposed, if not as something already acquired, then surely as something to be sought. Expression must be given not to the subjective striving (which varies from soul to soul), but to the objective act which is valid for all.

A further surprise is the fact that even after the gifts have been consecrated and changed there should still be a plea for acceptance. For there is question here really of the most sacred gifts, of the sacrificial oblation which Christ Himself makes *ministerio sacerdotum*. Certainly there can be no thought of pleading for its acceptance, since it is antecedently valid in full. On the contrary, all the sacrifices which are cited from the Old Testament, those of Abel and Abraham and Melchisedech, are only earthly shadows of its heavenly grandeur.

As a matter of fact, the Reformers who raised their voices against the Mass and canon also pounced on this point, that the priest undertook to play the part of mediator between Christ and God. Right down to our own day, therefore, modern commentaries on the Mass have assumed a tone of apology when explaining this passage.[5] But if we reflect for a moment that the sacrifice of the New Law, being an act of official worship,

---

[4] Cf. *Const. Ap.*, VIII, 12, 39 (Quasten, *Mon.*, 223) : here, too, the προσφέρομεν is expanded: καὶ ἀξιοῦμέν σε ὅπως εὐμενῶς ἐπιβλέψῃς. Cf. above I, 37.

[5] See the summary presentation in Benedict XIV, *De s. sacrificio missæ*, II, 16, 10-22 (ed. Schneider, 208-216). The learned Pope refers, among others, to Bellarmine, *Controv.*, II, 6, 24 (= *De sacrif. missæ*, II, 24; ed. Rom. 1838: III, 802), who states: In the *Supra quæ* we do not pray *pro reconciliatione Christi ad Patrem*, but for our own weakness; *etsi enim oblatio*

consecrata ex parte rei quæ offertur et ex parte Christi principalis offerentis semper Deo placeat, tamen ex parte ministri vel populi adstantis, qui simul etiam offerunt, potest non placere. Similar views expressed by Gihr, 691-696. The attack against the reality of the sacrifice of the Mass in the controversy with the Reformers served to bring the Sacrifice of Christ to the fore. But a consideration of the liturgical texts leads back to the sacrifice of the Church. Cf. above I, 180 ff.

is essentially placed in the hands of the Church, which in turn relies on the sacrifice of Christ, then it becomes clear at once that we possess therein, despite the solemnity of its essential core, only an external symbol by which the Church—or more immediately, the congregation—honors God. And God can really receive it from her hands as a gift of homage only when at least the lowest degree of an internal will to give on the part of the participants accompanies and quickens the external offering. In this sense, then, it would be quite understandable that the harsh words of the prophets, in which God rejects the purely external and soulless offerings of His people,[6] would refer with equal weight to the sacrifice of the New Law, were it offered by unworthy sacerdotal hands. Besides, in such a case little more would remain of this holiest of sacrifices than a new *hic et nunc* of Christ's sacrifice long since accomplished, a *hic et nunc* which is without its complete salvific meaning, since, contrary to its purpose, it is no longer the expression of a willing Christian mind, no longer has its roots in the earth, but hovers aimlessly in the air.[7]

Since corruptible and sinful man can never be sufficiently worthy of the great and holy God this humble plea for God's gracious glance is in any case well-grounded. Joined to it is a confident reference to the illustrative figures of the Old Testament, whose sacrifice had won God's pleasure. The outstanding types from the Old Dispensation are reviewed to encourage the soul, and a certain pride takes possession of our hearts as we link our action with the action of these biblical saints. Three figures are selected: innocent Abel,[8] who made a sacrifice of the firstlings of his flock (Genesis: 4:4) and himself succumbed to his brother's hate—our gift is "the Lamb of God," the first-born of all creation,[9] who turned His death, suffered at the hands of His own people, into a sacrifice of redemption. Next, Abraham who, as ancestor of all "who are of faith,"[10] is called "our patriarch," the hero of obedience to God, ready to make a sacrifice of his very son, but receiving him back alive (cf. Hebrews, 11:19)—our sacrifice, too, the most perfect expression of obedience unto death, has risen again and returned to life. Finally, Melchisedech who, as priest of the most high God,[11] offers up bread and wine[12]—our oblation also is taken

---

[6] Is. 1: 11; Jer. 6: 20; Amos 5: 21-23; Mal. 1: 10.

[7] This extreme case is, however, not entirely present even in an unworthy celebration of the priest, not so long as at least one participant takes part with proper dispositions.

[8] The adjective *justus* is applied to Abel by Christ Himself, Matt. 23: 35; cf. Herb. 11: 4. *Pueri tui* = of your servant, but as with παῖς, implying also a father-child relationship. In this sense the word is also applied to Israel in Luke 1: 54. Cf. also

J. Hennig, "Abel's Place in the Liturgy," *Theological Studies,* 7 (1946), 126-141.

[9] Cf. Hebr. 1: 6; Col. 1: 18; Romans 8: 29.

[10] Gal. 3: 7; cf. Leo the Great, *Sermo,* 53, 3 (PL, 54, 318) · *::os spiritale semen Abrahæ.* Batiffol, *Leçons,* 268.

[11] The canon calls him High Priest. Regarding the hypothesis which Baumstark builds upon this appellation, cf. I, 51, note 6.

[12] The biblical text of Gen 14: 18 speaks directly only of a "producing" or "bringing forward" by Melchisedech (Vulgate also:

from bread and wine.[13] May God (such is our prayer) look down upon our oblation with the same pleasure as He looked upon the oblation of these men; *respexit Dominus ad Abel et ad munera ejus,* as we read concerning the first of them:[14] on Abel, and on his offering, the Lord looked with favor. That prayer of ours will be fulfilled if the oblation proceeds from an intention pure as theirs, and if the temper of our own hearts accords in some measure with the incomparable holiness of our sacrifice.[15]

This comparative view of the Christian sacrifice in conjunction with the sacrifices of the Old Law, and in particular with those specially mentioned, was not alien to Christian antiquity. In fact, this consideration of the Old Testament as the antecedent shadow of the New was as self-evident to primitive Christianity as was the concept of the continuity of the history of grace. Abraham's sacrifice was one of the favorite subjects of ancient Christian iconography, and at least since the fourth century it appears predominantly as a type of the sacrifice of the Cross, and therefore, mediately at least, as a type of the eucharistic sacrifice.[16] But there is immediate reference to the Eucharist in the representation of the three types mentioned in the canon found in the two large mosaics in the choir of San Vitale in Ravenna. One of these shows Abel and Melchisedech, the former bringing a lamb, the latter bread and wine to the altar. The other pictures Abraham in two different scenes, in one case at the point of sacrificing his son, in the other as host to the three mysterious strangers.[17]

---

proferens). Still the reference to the priesthood gives reason and substance to the supposition that his deed involved a sacrificial action. Cf. the excursus on this question in P. Heinisch, *Das Buch Genesis* (Bonn, 1930), 222, and J. E. Coleran, "The Sacrifice of Melchisedech," *Theological Studies,* I (1940), 27-36. There is probably a similar relationship between the offering to God and the feeding of the assembled people as in the Jewish meal rites; cf. above I, 21, n. 63; II, p. 202, n. 1.

[13] The identity of the gift offering, which, as is known, is not mentioned in the Epistle to the Hebrews in the comparison of Christ with Melchisedech, is brought to the fore over and over again in Christian antiquity; thus Cyprian, *Ep.,* 63, 3; Ambrose, *De myst.,* VIII, 45 f.; Augustine, *De civ. Dei,* XVI, 22. Cf. also G. Wuttke, "Melchisedech der Priesterkönig von Salem. Eine Studie zur Geschichte der Exegese" (*Beihefte z. Zietschrift f. d. neutest. Wiss.,* 5; Giessen, 1927), 46 f.; J. Danielou, *La catéchèse eucharistique chez les*

Pères de l'Eglise (Lex orandi, 7; Paris, 1947), 33-72, especially 45 f.; idem, *Bible et Liturgie* (Lex orandi, 11, Paris, 1951), 196-201).

[14] Gen. 4: 4; cf. Deut. 26: 15. The expression is of course very common in the oratons: *Respice quæsumus Domine,* etc.

[15] It is worthy of note that in the prophecy of Malachy regarding the cult of the future the announcement of a purified priesthood should find its place alongside the announcement of a new, clean oblation, through which the name of the Lord God should be great among all nations (1: 11); "and he will purify the sons of Levi and shall refine them as gold and as silver, and they shall offer sacrifice to the Lord in justice. And the sacrifice of Juda and Jerusalem shall once more please the Lord . . ." (3: 3 f.). Cf. Gihr, 693 f.

[16] Cf. Th. Klauser, "Abraham": RAC, I, 18-27, especially 25.

[17] Cf. Beissel, *Bilder,* 170 f., 178; cf. *ibid.,* 189, regarding the related representation in S. Apollinare in Classe.

It may be that the wording of the Roman canon itself gave an impetus to these portrayals at Ravenna,[18] but the mention of Abel and Abraham (to whom Melchisedech was perhaps joined originally[19]) in an Egyptian offertory prayer brings us back to a much earlier period when Rome and Egypt had a liturgical practice in common.[20]

In the Roman canon the name of Melchisedech is followed by a further clarifying phrase: *sanctum sacrificium, immaculatam hostiam*. This is an addition which the *Liber pontificalis* attributes to Leo the Great: *Hic constituit ut intra actionem sacrificii dicetur: sanctum sacrificium et cetera*.[21] Older commentators frequently understood this addition as an attribute of the Christian sacrifice, as though meant in apposition to *(Supra quæ*, with the words in between, *sicuti . . . Melchisedech*, construed as parenthetical.[22]) but the purport of the words demands rather a connection with the sacrifice of Melchisedech. For this reason there is no accompanying sign of the Cross.[23] True, to us nowadays such an addition might appear superfluous. But it was otherwise in the fifth century, when anti-materialist heresies were still causing trouble, when in particular the use of wine was still exposed to Manichean attacks,[24] and the

---

[18] A parallel to this is offered in S. Apollinare nuovo at Ravenna, in the representation of a row of saints, that reproduce the list of the *Communicantes* as it was in the first half of the 6th century: Kennedy, 197. Prayer formulas with the names of Abel, Abraham, and Melchisedech, that derive from the Roman canon, are presented also in the Mozarabic *Liber sacramentorum* (Férotin, p. 262) and in the Leonianum (Muratori, I, 470) ; see Botte, *Le canon*, 43.

[19] Baumstark, *Das Problem*, 230 f. Rather loosely linked with the idea of sacrifice, although always called ἀρχιερεὺς σῆς λατρείας, Melchisedech appears in *Const. Ap.*, VIII, 12, 21-23 (Quasten, *Mon.*, 218), along with others named in the primitive biblical history, such as Abel, Noe, and Abraham. In the Byzantine liturgy of St. Basil there is also a petition of acceptance which refers, among others, to Abel, Noe, and Abraham (Brightman, 319 f.) ; so, too, in the anaphora of St. James (*ibid.*, 41 ; cf. 32 ; 48). The pertinent prayers are still found before the consecration. Cf. the survey in Lietzmann, *Messe und Herrenmahl*, 81-93 ; Fortescue, 349 f.

[20] Brightman, 129. The prayer is now included within the prayer of intercession and accompanies an incensation. As in Am-

brose's text of the canon, (above I, 52), so here, too, the names are combined with the petition that the gifts be placed upon the heavenly altar. Cf. Baumstark, *Le liturgie orientali e le preghiere "Supra quæ" e "Supplices" del canone romano* (2nd ed.; Grottaferrata, 1913), 4 ff.; *idem.*, "Das 'Problem' des römischen Messkanons (*Eph. liturg.*, 1939), 229-231.

[21] Duchesne, *Liber pont.*, I, 239. That the words are an addition is clear from the use of the *Supra quæ* in the Mozarabic liturgy, where precisely these words are missing; Férotin, *Le liber mozarabicus sacramentorum*, p. 262; *Missale mixtum* (PL, 85, 491 B).

[22] More details about this in Benedict XIV, *De s. sacrificio missæ*, II, 16, 16 f., 21 f. (Ed. Schneider, 211 f., 214 f.), who himself inclines to this explanation.

[23] Only in isolated instances is a (double) sign of the cross added: thus in the Sacramentary of the 10th century from Trier; Leroquais, I, 84.

[24] Duchesne, *loc. cit.*, thinks the supplement was directed against the Manicheans, to whom even an Augustine shortly before had given his adherence. The Manicheans, among other things, condemned the use of wine. The phrase, therefore, is on the same level as the *de tuis donis ac datis* of the

disuse of the chalice at Communion roused a suspicion of Manichean sentiment.[25]

The oblation is set forth in a third way, in the *Supplices*. A gift is fully accepted not when it has drawn to itself a friendly glance, but when it is actually taken into the recipient's possession. In a daring illustration this final phase of human gift-giving is transferred to our sacrificial gift and to God to whom we offer it. The Apocalypse, 8:3-5, tells of an altar in heaven on which the angel deposits incense and the prayers of the saints: "And there was given to him [the angel] much incense, that he should offer of the prayers of all the saints, upon the golden altar which is before the throne of God."[26] This is but a figure of spiritual activity, just as it is only a figure to speak of the throne of God. But the figure serves as a device in the third prayer, where the offering of our sacrifice is now to be set forth as a petition for its final acceptance.

The wording of the older version in Ambrose shows clearly that we are dealing with a plea for acceptance: *Petimus et precamur, ut hanc oblationem suscipias in sublimi altari tuo per manus angelorum tuorum, sicut suscipere dignatus es . . .*[27] In our current text the figure, as against the reality, is even more sharply delineated. The prayer begs for the sending of a holy angel [28] to carry the gifts [29] to the heavenly altar which is erected before the face of the divine majesty.[30] Such a mode of expression, speaking of the heavenly altar, is to be found in various places in the Eastern liturgies since early times.[31]

---

preceding prayer, as a new proof of the earthbound character of the Christian sacrifice.

[25] Leo the Great, *Sermo* 4 *de Quadr.* (PL, 54, 279 f.) ; Gelasius I, *Ep.* 37, 2 (Thiel, 451 f.).

[26] The heavenly altar also in Is. 6: 6. It appears likewise in Hermas, *Pastor*, Mand., X, 3, 2 f.; Irenæus, *Adv. hær.*, IV, 31, 5 (al. IV, 19, 1; Harvey, II, 210). Further passages in Righetti, *Manuale*, III, 336. The picture in the Apocalypse has nothing to do with the theological question whether there is a sacrifice in heaven. For avowedly in the biblical passage it is not a question of visible gifts but of prayer offered by the faithful that is symbolically represented as incense rising from the altar.

[27] Ambrose, *De sacramentis*, IV, 6 (above I, 52).

[28] The adjective *sancti (angeli)*, it is true, appears already in the early Irish tradition of the Roman canon, but is missing in the rest of the older texts. Botte, 42.

[29] These are simply designated by *hæc*. But that is more striking than the *(Supra) quæ* of the preceding prayer, which surely can be considered as combining *panem sanctum*, etc. This vagueness and mere hinting is apparently a manifestation of the reverent reserve which reappears throughout the history of religions in so many shapes and forms and which, in fact, is one of the sources of the discipline of the arcana; cf. W. Havers, *Neuere Literatur zum Sprachtabu* (Sitzungsber. d. Akademie d. Wiss. in Wien, Phil. hist. Kl., 223, 5). The isolated reading *jube hoc* appears in the late Middle Ages, wherein the *hoc* is understood to mean the Church on earth; Sölch, *Hugo*, 94 f.

[30] Thus according to the text of today. In the same passage some few MSS. have *in conspectum*. Moreover, the phrase is missing not only in Ambrose, but also in the Cod. Rossianus; consequently it is a later addition; see Brinktrine, *Die hl. Messe*, 204 f.

[31] *Const. Ap.*, VIII, 13, 3 (Quasten, *Mon.*,

In the Roman liturgy, where the *Supplices* in the canon is the only instance of the use of this figure, medieval commentators ascribed a very wide significance to the heavenly altar in the performance of the sacrifice. This is correlated for the most part with the incomplete sacramental theology of the time. Remigius of Auxerre considered that after the Body and Blood of Christ were made present by the words of institution, a second act was necessary by which the Body of Christ on earth, sacramentally present in many different places, was drawn into unity with the glorified *corpus Domini* in heaven. This action was petitioned and consumated in the *Supplices*.[32] The Cistercian abbot, Isaac of Stella, writing in 1165, also viewed the *Supplices* as completing our sacrifice, but in a different way. In the first step, which he likened to the altar of holocausts in the ancient Temple, we have offered up, with contrite hearts, bread and wine as tokens of our own lives; in the second step, which was compared to the golden altar of incense, we have offered up the Body and Blood of the Lord; in the third step, which corresponded to the Holy of Holies, our sacrifice was borne up by angel hands to be united to the glorified Christ in heaven, and thus was completed.[33] Just as the clouds of incense—another commentator takes up the theme—in which the highpriest stepped before the Ark of the Covenant on the great Day of Atonement, obscured his vision, so the earthly eyes of the priest can no longer at this point recognize anything; all that is left is to beg the angels to bear the sacrifice up before God's countenance.[34] Other theologians of this period also found that in this transfer of the gifts to the heavenly altar a real activity is connoted, in which the sacrifice attains its completion.[35]

228) : At the beginning of the preparation for Communion there is a summons to prayer, to the effect that God may accept (προςδέξηται) the gift, εἰς τὸ ἐπουράνιον αὐτοῦ θυσιαστήριον. The Greek liturgy of St. James repeats the expression a number of times; (Brightman, 36, 41, 47, 58 f.), so, too, the liturgy of St. Mark (*ibid.*, 115, 118, 122, 123 f.) and the Byzantine liturgy (*ibid.*, 309, 319, 359). In the non-Greek liturgies the expression is less frequent. It is found in the West Syrian anaphoras of Timothy and of Severus (*Anaphoræ Syricæ* [Rome, 1934-44], 23, 71), but they were originally likewise Greek. In several cases the ὑπερουράνιον θυσιαστήριον has reference to the offering of incense. But it is pushing things too far when Lietzmann, *Messe und Herrenmahl*, 92 f., connects the origin of the expression regarding the admission of the gift upon the heavenly altar with the introduction of incense into the Christian liturgy of the Orient (which he dates about 360). For the expression appears already around 300, not only in the Orient, but also in the West in Ambrose's text of the canon, a text which, after all, was not Ambrose's creation.

[32] Remigius of Auxerre, *Expositio* (PL, 101, 1262 f.) ; regarding this see, Geiselmann, *Die Abendmahlslehre*, 108-111. Geiselmann, 99 f., finds a cognate version in the commentary on the Mass "Quotiens contra se," (about 800).

[33] Isaac of Stella, *Ep. de off. missæ* (PL, 194, 1889-1896).

[34] Robertus Paululus, *De ceremoniis*, II, 28 (PL, 177, 429 D) ; Franz, *Die Messe*, 440-442.

[35] Paschasius Radbertus (d. 856), *De corp. et sang. Domini*, VIII, 1-6 (PL, 120, 1286-1292), Odo of Cambria (d. 1113), *Expositio in canonem missæ*, c. 3 (PL, 160, 1067 A). Cf. A. Gaudel, "Messe, III" : DThC, X, 1034 f., 1041.

By the *Supplices* this activity is petitioned. Thus, under the influence, no doubt, of the Gallic liturgy, the prayer became a sort of epiklesis;[36] and actually there is a plea that the power of God might touch our sacrificial gift, but in reverse order, not by the descent of the Spirit, but by the ascent of the gift.[37]

Closely allied to this in some way is the belief that in the "angel" something more is to be seen than just a created angel. It is Christ Himself who, as *magni consilii angelus*,[38] takes our sacrifice and bears it away to the altar celestial. This idea was repeated by several commentators, especially around the twelfth century,[39] and even in our own time it has been broached in the thesis which postulates a heavenly sacrifice into which our earthly sacrifice is merged.[40] Finally, taking the view that the *Supplices* is a consecratory epiklesis, as would appear by an external comparison with oriental and Gallic Mass formulas, the angel carrying the sacrifice aloft has been identified as the Holy Ghost.[41]

---

[36] Botte, 'L'ange du sacrifice et l'épiclèse de la messe romaine au moyen âge": *Recherches de théologie ancienne et médiévale*, 1 (1929), 285-308. On the part of the Orient the attempt was already made at the Council of Florence to find in our *Supplices* a real epiklesis with which the consecration would be completed. F. Cabrol, "Anamnèse" : DACL, I, 1892.

[37] Cf. Duchesne, *Christian Worship*, 182.

[38] Is. 9 ; 6, in the text form of the Introit of the third Christmas Mass.

[39] It appears first in Ivo of Chartres (d. 1116), *De conven. vet. et novi sacrif.* (PL, 162, 557 C) and the interpretation indeed becomes understandable here because of its connection. Ivo sees in the canon the renewal of the customs of the great day of atonement (cf. above I, 110), among them the scapegoat, laden with the sins of the people and driven out into the solitude of the desert; thus Christ, laden with our sins, returns to heaven. The reference to Christ, also held by Honorius Augustodunensis, Alger of Liége, Sicard of Cremona and others; see Botte, "L'ange du sacrifice et l' épiclèse," 301-308.

[40] M. de la Taille, *The Mystery of Faith and Human Opinion* (London, 1934), 59-79; report of an allied discussion, see *JL*, 4 (1924), 233 f. According to de la Taille, Christ is in heaven in the condition of a sacrifice; by the word *perferri* we are to understand the transubstantiation in which our sacrifice on the altar converts into a heavenly sacrifice. Under these two suppositions, poorly substantiated it must be granted, the reference to Christ is self-evident. In view of a hypothetical primitive form of the prayer, J. Barbel, "Der Engel des 'Supplices'," *Pastor bonus,* 53, (1942), 87-91, is also inclined to make the "angel" refer to Christ. He supposes that the plural form, as testified by Ambrose *(per manus angelorum tuorum)*, was preceded by a singular form, in which the *angelus*, according to the paleo-Christian fashion, was as a matter of fact understood to refer to Christ, until the Arian misconstruction occasioned the change to a plural form and so the reference of the word to the whole world of angels. Cf. also J. Barbel, *Christos Angelos, Die Anschauung von Christus als Engel und Bote in der gelehrten und volkstümlichen Literatur des christlichen Altertums* (Bonn, 1941). But if we do not follow de la Taille in linking the *perferri* to the consecration, then there is naturally no occasion for this special interpretation, for ample expression is given to the idea that we offer our prayer for acceptance through Christ (and therefore hope that our sacrifice will be offered through Him) when we end the prayer with *Per Christum Dominum nostrum.*

[41] L. A. Hoppe, *Die Epiklesis der griechischen und orientalischen Liturgien und der römische Consekrationskanon* (Schaffhausen, 1864), 167-191; P. Cagin, "L'an-

Since all these meanings are founded on certain assumptions which, to say the least, are very questionable, there is no good reason for departing from the natural sense of the word, which is supported by the reading in Ambrose *(angelorum)* and by parallel passages in oriental liturgies;[42] as the prayers of the faithful are deposited on the heavenly altar by the angel of the Apocalypse, so may the same be done by the holy angel with our sacrifice.[43] Without doubt this means that there is some participation of the angelic world in our oblation. But that can no longer be surprising, after the *Sanctus* that was sung by earth and heaven conjointly. Well known are Chrysostom's descriptions of the "awesome mystery," with the altar surrounded by angels. Gregory the Great pictures the hour of the sacrifice, with the heavens opening and choirs of angels coming down.[44] It is also in accord with the solidarity of the Christian order of salvation that the angels who (of course) have a very different relationship to man's redemption, should yet in some way take part in the sacrifice of redemption. But to try to define this participation in more detail or to single out the participating angels by name would be unbecoming curiosity.[45]

The second half of the *Supplices* takes a new turn; bringing our sacrifice up to the heavenly altar should give rise to a *fruitful reception* of the holy gift by the assembled congregation—such is the prayer we take up. Our view thus turns away to the concluding act in the celebration of the Eucharist, the Communion. Criticism in the past generation saw in this re-orientation a break in the thought which offered an opportunity for bold theorizing.[46] Actually, however, although there is progress in the

---

tiphonaire ambrosien" (*Paleographie musicale*, 5 [1896]), 83-92; cf. Cagin, *Te Deum ou illatio*, 221. As a basis for regarding the *Supplices* as an epiklesis Hoppe looks essentially to the fact that it occupies the same place as the epiklesis in the Orient. Hoppe was not in a position to know that the Holy Ghost epiklesis, even in the Orient, was of a relatively late date; see above, p. .—Cagin directs atention to the Gallican angel epikleses. But here the thing to be kept in mind is that even a pre-theological conception need not necessarily have had the Holy Ghost in view under the term of "Angel"; cf. above, p. 69, note 151, and below note 43.

[42] In the anaphora of St. Mark the transfer of the gifts to the heavenly altar is prayerfully requested διὰ τῆς ἀρχαγγελικῆς σου λειτουργίας. Brightman, 129.

[43] B. Botte, "L'ange du sacrifice," *Cours et Conferences*, VII (Louvain, 1929), 209-221. Here, p. 219 f., also examples from

Latin liturgy in which the intervention of the angel, who is obviously thought of as a created being, is requested at the sacrifice. More illustrations in Lietzmann, *Messe und Herrenmahl*, 103. See references also in Batiffol, *Leçons* (1927), p. XXIX f.

[44] Gregory the Great, *Dial.*, IV, 58 (PL, 77, 425 f.).

[45] Suggestive considerations on this subject in Gihr, 697-699.

[46] R. Buchwald, *Die Epiklese in der römischen Messe* (Weidenauer Studien I, special printing; Vienna, 1907), 34 f.; cf. 352. According to Buchwald a consecratory epiklesis must have had a place here, one that would then be concluded with a petition for a Communion replete with graces. He refers, among others, to the expression *ex hac altaris participatione*, which has something strange about it, because of its allusion to a temporal altar, where at the present moment we are deal-

thought, it is a thoroughly natural and uninterrupted transition, as we can see by comparison with the *eucharistia* of Hippolytus, where the oblation likewise turns shortly to a Communion plea.[47] Besides, we could regard this prayer in either case, both in Hippolytus and in the present Roman canon, as an epiklesis. But it is not a consecration but a *communion epiklesis* and so (to look at the heart of the matter) there is nothing significant about the fact that the invocation of the Holy Ghost is missing in our *Supplices*, though found in Hippolytus.[48] The Communion is the second great event which the celebration of the Eucharist comprises, the second intervention of God in the activity of the Church. The Christian sacrifice is so constituted that, from the very beginning, the congregation making the oblation is invited to the sacrificial meal. As soon, then, as the oblation is completed, the expectant gaze is turned without further ado to the sacrificial repast, and it is quite seemly that this expectation should become a humble prayer.

Next, the idea that all who wish can receive the Body and Blood of the Lord is introduced as something taken for granted. We receive this double gift *ex hac altaris participatione*, from this sharing at the altar. If the gifts of today's sacrifice, our very own, are carried up to the heavenly altar, *i.e.*, are accepted by God, then this sharing, the association thus established in God's heavenly table upon which our gifts rest, grants us the possibility of receiving the Body and Blood of the Lord truly as God's table guests,[49] and thus procuring not only the external appearance of the

---

ing with the heavenly altar. We shall presently return to the expression. A similar trend of thought already in F. Probst, *Die abendländische Messe vom 5. biss zum 8. Jh.* (Münster, 1896), 177-180. In favor of the idea that here a consecratory epiklesis was dropped, it is pointed out that the gifts are only now designated as the "Body and Blood" of the Son of God; still, as Batiffol, *Leçons*, 270, correctly notes, the consecration and transubstantiation is clearly enough supposed in the words *panem sanctum* of the first prayer.

[47] Above I, 29. That the consecratory epiklesis of the oriental liturgy is a later interpolation is plainly seen by comparing this basic text with the *Const. Ap.*, VIII, 12, 39 (Quasten, *Mon.*, 223 f.), as well as the Ethiopian anaphora of the Apostles (Brightman, 233); cf. the tables in Cagin, *L'eucharistia*, p. 148-149.

[48] Above, p. 191 f.—J. Brinktrine, "Zur Entstehung der morgenländischen Epiklese," *ZkTh*, 42 (1918), 301-326; 483-518, has attempted to show that the *Supplices* has

the character of an epiklesis by a comparison with the Gallic *Post pridie* and *Post secreta* prayers, which clearly occupy the place of an epiklesis and which, moreover, plead for an acceptance of the gifts (as the *Supplices* does) and again for their consecration. That this acceptance and consecration should guarantee a beneficial result is, according to Brinktrine, a part of the concept of every epiklesis, which he thinks grew out of older prayers of blessing, like those said over various foods (489 f.). It may be worth while to distinguish between the consecration and communion epiklesis in the sense developed above.

[49] Batiffol, *Leçons*, 271, also emphasizes the fact that the wording in the text of today's canon refers to the altar of heaven. True, the passages he cites for the *participatio altaris*, I Cor. 9: 13; Hebr. 13: 10, form only distant parallels. In this connection cf. also Lebrun, I, 446 f.; Hellriegel, *The Holy Sacrifice of the Mass* (St. Louis, 1945), 56.

mystery, but also its inmost power.[50] More simple was the thought as transmitted in the text of the Irish and Milanese canons, where we read: *ex hoc altari sanctificationis*,[51] thus signifying the earthly altar on which the gifts were hallowed. Still the greater simplicity of the thought is no guarantee of its originality. It is not likely that the word "altar" would be used in one and the same breath to signify first the heavenly and then the earthly altar. Rather it must be said that in the metaphorical language of our prayer the earthly altar wholly disappears from view and is absorbed, so to say, in the heavenly one which alone has validity.

What we ask for is that the reception may be for our good, so that we may be filled with every heavenly blessing and every grace. The "heavenly blessing" again corresponds to the heavenly altar. In the restrained enthusiasm of expression there are echoes of phrases from the introductory paragraph of the Epistle to the Ephesians (1:3).

Whereas the preceding prayers had but few ceremonial accompaniments —at present simply the crosses at *hostiam puram*, etc.—the *Supplices* once more brings movement into the bodily bearing of the priest. Bowing the body, which (according to olden custom) was usually linked with the humble oblation and therefore was at one time begun here at the *Supra quæ*,[52] is at present required at *Supplices te rogamus*. Here it is a practice of long standing.[53] To the profound bow is added a kiss of the altar. This

---

[50] Cf. possibly the Postcommunio of the feast of the Ascension: *ut quæ visibilibus mysteriis sumenda percepimus, invisibili consequamur effectu.*

[51] Botte, 42; Kennedy, 52. The Bobbio Missal of about 700 shows a mixture of the two readings: *ex hoc altari participationis.* The Sacramentary of Rocarosa (about 1200) has the simplified reading: *ex hac participatione;* Ferreres, p. CXII.

[52] Above, p. 142. Later there is mention of a raising of the eyes on the part of the priest at the *Supra quæ* (Benevent. MS. of the 11-12th cent.: Ebner, 330). According to Balthasar of Pforta it was the practice of the priest in 15th century Germany to spread the hands over the host at the *Supra quæ;* Franz, 587. Such also the direction in the Missal of Toul: Martène, 1, 4, XXXI (I, 651 D) and in Premonstratensian sources since the 14th century: Waefelghem, 79, n. 1.

[53] Above, p. 142. In the later Middle Ages frequently a bow was made here *cancellatis manibus ante pectus; Liber ordinarius O. Præm.* (Waefelghem, 79); a Paris Missal of the first half of the 13th century: Leroquais, II, 66; cf. 163, 232, etc.; *Ordi-*

narium O. P. of 1256 (Guerrini, 242) and *Liber ordinarius* of Liége (Volk, 95); for Cologne, see Peters, *Beiträge*, 78; for England, Frere, *The Use of Sarum*, I, 81; Maskell, 146 f.; also already in the Sarum Missal of the 13th cent. (Legg, *The Sarum Missal*, 232). The usage also found entrance in Rome: *Ordo* of Stefaneschi, n. 71 (PL, 78, 1189 B). It is generally in connection with the extension of the arms in the form of a cross at the *Unde et memores;* cf. above.—In Paris the *cancellatio* remained in use until 1615 (Lebrun, I, 442); cf. also de Moléon, 288. It is still found in the Dominican, Carthusian, and Carmelite rites of today. The fundamental idea of the practice was the representation of the Crucified. A Lyons Missal of 1531 explains the *manibus cancellatis* in the same terms as for the extending of the arms after the consecration: *quasi de seipso crucem faciens:* Martène, 1, 4, XXXIII (I, 660 BC); cf. Durandus, III, 44, 4.—The direction in the Pontifical of Christian of Mainz (1167-1183), is noteworthy: *Hic* [at the *Supplices*] *inclinet se ad dextram;* Martène, 1, 4, XVII (I, 601 E). So, too, in the Missale Ursi-

kiss is probably sunggested by the *Supplices,* as an expression of deep, reverent petition.[54] The mention of the holy gifts that follows again occasions the demonstrative gesture, added here in the form of two crosses at *corpus et sanguinem.* There are indications of this gesture here and there even in Carolingian texts, but it spread only very slowly and is still missing even in manuscripts of the thirteenth century.[55] In like manner, the priest's signing himself at *omni benedictione cœlesti*—a gesture that conveyed even by action the notion of pleading for heavenly blessing— did not become prevalent till towards the end of the Middle Ages.[56] Therefore, to consider the crossing of the gifts as a manifestation of our hope to transfer the blessing from them to ourselves is only a secondary interpretation, although not inadmissible.[57]

After the oblation has been completed and the Communion plea has been pronounced, at once, according to the most ancient pattern, the conclusion of the *eucharistia* follows, with a solemn doxology and the *Amen* of the people.[58] In our Roman Mass however, we find here only an anticipated *Per Christum Dominum nostrum,* which is repeated again after each of the two insertions that follow. Our prayer rises aloft to God through our high-priest when His servant at the altar, as His representative, has spoken the words of consecration.

16. The *Memento* of the Dead

The first of three inserts which precede the doxology in the present Roman canon is the *Memento* of the dead. That this is an insertion of a

nense of the 13th century in Gerbert, *Vetus liturgia Alemannica,* I, 363: *inclina te ad dextrum cornu altaris.* The latter document gives the explanation at the *Te igitur* (*op. cit.,* 341): *Hic deoscula angulum corporalis et patenam illi suppositum simul.*

[54] In ancient times they seem to have recognized a double gesture of homage in the bowing and the kissing; cf. Mohlberg, *Theol. Revue,* 26 (1927), 63. This kissing of the altar appears first (and still without a similar kiss at the *Te igitur;* cf. above in the Cod. Casanat., 614 (11-12th cent.): Ebner, 330, and in a 12th century Sacramentary of the city of Rome: *ibid.,* 335; see, moreover, Innocent III, *De s. alt. mysterio,* V, 4 (PL, 217, 890 C), and so, too, for the 12th-13th cent. Martène, 1, 4, XVII XXV (I, 601, 633). Since the 13th century (if we except the isolated instance in the *Ordo Cluniacensis*

of Bernard; see above, I, 316, n. 36), both kissings of the altar appear in the canon; see Ebner, 314 f., 349 f. Cf. Sölch, *Hugo,* 89; 95. It is, of course, conceivable that the mentioning of the altar provided the first occasion for the kissing of the altar.

[55] Brinktrine, *Die hl. Messe,* 299. This restraint is perhaps explained by the fact that there is no demonstrative pronoun here with the words.

[56] A note regarding this appeared already in 12th century MSS. (See Ebner, 330; 335), but is often missing even at a much later date. From the commentary on the Mass by Balthasar of Pforta, which appeared in 1494, we learn that in Germany at least the practice was not uniform. Franz, *Die Messe,* 587.

[57] This interpretation, among others, in Brinktrine, 205 f.

[58] Above I, 23; 29.

later date is evident on several grounds. First of all, there is nothing corresponding to it in the *eucharistia* of the primitive age.[1] Secondly, it is missing in a considerable portion of older manuscripts, *e.g.*, in the sacramentary which Pope Hadrian I had sent to Charlemagne;[2] indeed it is wanting in some text-sources here and there as late as the eleventh century.[3] And even where it appears, it is sometimes wedged into other spots than its present location.[4] This sporadic appearance of the remembrance of the dead can hardly be explained on the supposition that at one time it was placed on a special tablet, the *diptychon*,[5] for if that were the case similar vestiges would be found in the *Memento* of the living. Rather the explanation is to be sought in a fact which is sustained by several accounts of the Mass, namely, that the *Memento* of the dead for a long time had no place in the Mass on Sundays and feasts, that is to say, in public service properly so called. Since the turn of the fifth century a general remembrance of the dead had a place in the *Kyrie* litany.[6] But a special mention within the canon itself was probably regarded as a peculiarity of the Mass which was offered in some way for the dead; it was looked upon as something concerning only the group of relatives rather than the full community.[7] Its standing was similar to that of the pre-Gregorian *Hanc igitur*, which in many cases, in fact, was revamped and inserted for the

[1] The first examples of a Memento for the Dead in the Mass appear in the 4th century *Euchologion* of Serapion (see below) *Const. Ap.*, VIII, 13, 6. Accounts also in Cyril of Jerusalem, *Cat. myst.*, V, 9, and in Chrysostom, *In Phil. hom.*, 3, 4 (PG, 62, 204), who certainly sees in the Memento for the Dead an apostolic practice. Regarding Augustine see Rötzer, 125 f.; cf. below.—Botte, 45. Without a particular formulation within the Eucharistic prayer the offering for the deceased is certainly attested already in much earlier times; see above I, 217 f.

[2] Botte, *Le canon*, 44. The *Memento etiam* accepted into the version supervised by Alcuin; Lietzmann, 1, 28 Apparatus.

[3] Ebner, 7; 247; 421; Leroquais, *Les sacramentaires* (see List III, 389); Ménard (PL, 78, 280, n. 70); also in two sources published by A. Dold: the Palimpsest Sacramentary of Mainz (*Texte u. Arb.*, I, 5, p. 40) and the Zurich and Peterling fragments of a Mass-book (*ibid.*, I, 25, p. 16); also in the Greek liturgy of St. Peter, which rests upon a Latin basis of the 9-10th cent. (Codrington, 109, 125, etc.).

[4] Attached to the *Memento* for the Living (examples from the 8th and 10th centuries in Ebner, 421 f.), after the *Nobis quoque* (an instance from the 10th cent., *ibid.*, 43, 423).

[5] Thus L. Delisle, *Memoir sur d'anciens sacramentaires* (Paris, 1886), 174; Duchesnes, *Christian Worship*, 182, n. 1; H. Lietzmann, 'Auf dem Wege zum Urgregorianum" (*JL*, 9, 1929), 136.

[6] Above I, 337, n. XIV.

[7] In the *Capitulare eccl. ord.* (Andrieu III, 121 f.) the following is given as the practice of the Roman Church: *In diebus autem septimanæ, de secunda feria quod est usque in die sabbato, celebrantur missa vel nomina eorum commemorant. Die autem dominica non celebrantur agendas mortuorum nec nomina eorum ad missas recitantur, sed tantum vivorum nomina regum vel principum seu et sacerdotum ...* If, however, a burial service is necessary on Sunday, the priest should fast *cum parentibus ipsius defuncti usque ad horam nonam* and then hold the *oblatio* and burial. Cf. on this matter Bishop, *Liturgica historica*, 96 ff., especially 99: M. Andrieu, L'insertion du Memento des morts au canon romain de la messe," *Revue des sciences relig.*, 1 (1921), 151-154.

dead.[8] In some documents which introduced the *Memento* of the dead into the canon there is a definite rubric limiting it to weekdays only [9] and barring it on Sundays and feasts.[10] This old rule had not entirely vanished from memory even as late as the fourteenth century. The Mass commentary of Melk, from the year 1366, testifies to the practice of some priests of omitting the *Memento* of the dead on Sunday; even the author himself is inclined to give his approval, although he is unable to allege any authentic decisions in its favor.[11]

On the other hand, the oldest extant texts of our Mass book do contain the *Memento* for the dead. The Irish tradition of the canon, including the Bobbio Missal which was written about 700, contains it. In the case of the Bobbio Missal the presence of this *Memento* is not surprising, at least in the light of what was just explained above. For the Bobbio Missal is one of the first Mass books in which the needs of the private monastic Masses were given prime consideration. In this book the Roman canon is found within a Mass formula captioned *missa Romensis cottidiana,* hence one not intended for Sunday.[12] Therefore, in Rome even at an early period the *Memento* must have formed part of the *missa cotidiana,* which even then was most frequently devoted to the dead.[13]

But there remains one striking fact, namely, that the remembrance of

---

[8] In the Worms Missal of the 10th century the canon of which has no *Memento* for the Dead, a proper *Hanc igitur* is provided for the Mass of the Dead; Leroquais, I, 62 f.

[9] *Ordo Rom.,* IV (PL, 78, 983) = Ordo *"Qualiter quædam orationes"* [see Andrieu, *Les Ordines Romani,* I, 6) notes with regard to the *Memento* for the Dead: *Hæ orationes duæ dicuntur, una super dipticios, altera post lectionem nominum, et hoc quotidianis vel in agendis tantummodo diebus.* That the first part is to be said *super dipticia* and the second *post lectionem* is also stated in the Gregorianum at the place where the *Memento etiam* appears, namely in the Mass for a deceased bishop; Lietzmann, n. 224, 4; 5. The same superscriptions in part still in the Sacramentary MSS. of the 10-11th century; Ebner, 105; 213; 214; 289. The Gregorian Sacramentary of Padua has indeed taken up the *Memento* for the Dead into the canon, but prefaces it with the rubric: *Si fuerint nomina defunctorum, recitentur dicente diacono: Memento.* Mohlberg-Baumstark, n. 885.

[10] A Florentine Sacramentary of the 11th century has this rubric before the *Memen*-to: *Hæc non dicit in dominicis diebus nec in aliis festivitatibus maioribus;* Ebner, 34, who mistakenly refers the rubric to the preceding prayer (418). The Anglo-Saxon Canones Theodori (7-8th cent.; Finsterwalder, 273, cf. 265) affirms: *Secundum Romanos die dominica non recitantur nomina mortuorum ad missam.*

[11] Franz, *Die Messe,* 510. As a reason those priests allege the Sunday repose that is already granted to the souls in Purgatory anyway. Concerning this popular medieval belief see Franz, 147; 452. The same reason is given by Sicard of Cremona, *Mitrale,* III, 6 (PL, 213, 132), why the priest is to mention no names at the *Memento* for the Dead on Sunday, while he may do so on week days. A note from the 13th century in a central Italian Sacramentary MS. (Ebner, 204) corresponds to this: *Hic recitentur nomina defunctorum non dominico die.*

[12] Cf. in this same sense Batiffol, *Leçons,* 225. In the *Missale Gallicanum vetus,* which also comes into being about 700, the *Memento etiam* is already wrought into the Gallican Post nomina formula; Muratori, II, 702.

[13] Cf. above I, n. 217 ff. The linguistic for-

the dead was inserted here and not in connection with the intercessory'
prayers before the consecration, where it might have been yoked with the
remembrance of the living or with the recollection of the saints in heaven,[14]
or where a permanent *Hanc igitur* formula might have performed the
same function. This is all the more true if we are to regard the *Nobis
quoque* not as a part of the intercessory prayer, but as a special independent prayer, so that the *Memento* must be looked upon as isolated,
as a segregated part of that block of prayers which were inserted before
the consecration.

It is true that in the Orient—except Egypt—the memorial of the dead
is not only actually linked with the other intercessions after the consecration, but its location in this spot is emphasized and justified by
argument. Thus we read in the *Mystagogic Catecheses* of Jerusalem:
"Then we remember also those who have fallen asleep, first the patriarchs and prophets . . . and in general all who have fallen asleep amongst
us, because we believe it is of the greatest value for the souls for whom
the prayer is offered while the holy and tremendous sacrifice lies before
us." [15] The same idea appears in Chrysostom: "When . . . that awe-
inspiring sacrifice lies displayed on the altar, how shall we not prevail
with God by our entreaties for them [the dead]?"[16] Preceding the
Memento both in the Liturgy of St. James at Jerusalem and in the Byzan-
tine liturgy, we have the petition for a fruitful reception ($\mu\epsilon\tau\acute{\epsilon}\chi\epsilon\iota\nu$,
$\mu\epsilon\tau\alpha\lambda\alpha\mu\beta\acute{\alpha}\nu\epsilon\iota\nu$) of the Eucharist by the congregation.[17] Perhaps we have
to suppose that the thought of the Sacrament of union more or less con-
sciously concurred in placing the remembrance of the dead right here; the
sacramental proof of their membership in the communion of saints is no
longer theirs to have,[18] but a substitute for it would be offered if the living would remember them at this moment. It is this idea precisely which
Augustine suggests when he remarks that the dead are remembered at
the altar *in communicatione corporis Christi,* because they are certainly
not separated from the Church.[19]

---

mulation also points to ancient Christian
Rome; see the research of E. Bishop in
the appendix to A. B. Kuypers, *The Book
of Cerne,* Cambridge, 1902, 266-275.

[14] Cf. the striking considerations in Kennedy, 28 f., 35 f., 189 f.

[15] Cyrillus of Jerusalem, *Cat. myst.,* V, 9
(Quasten, *Mon.,* 102).

[16] Chrysostom, *In Phil. hom.,* 3, 4 (PG,
62, 204).

[17] Brightman, 54, l. 14; 330, l. 13. In the
Byzantine Mass, both in the liturgy of St.
Chrysostom and that of St. Basil the
Memento of those (saints and all) who
have passed away (332, l. 3) follows im-

mediately upon the petition for Communion which concluded the epiklesis.
[18] The notion that the departed themselves
yearn for the Sacrament seems to have
been particularly fostered among the Syrians; cf. the bold version of it in James
of Batna (d. 521), *Poem about the Mass
for the Dead* (BKV, 6, p. 312): the departed are called forth by the priest, "and
at the resurrection, which the body of the
Son of God causes to shed forth, the deceased breathe in life day after day and are
thus purified."
[19] Augustine, *De civ. Dei,* XX, 9 (CSEL,
40, 2, p. 451, l. 15). Likewise serm. 172,
2, 2 (PL, 38, 936): It is an old practice in

A corroboration of this opinion worth noting is to be found in the oldest Egyptian formulary, that of Serapion. Although the main traditional liturgies of Egypt generally place the intercession before the consecration, this most ancient text commemorates the dead likewise after the consecration,[20] attaching this commemoration immediately to a somewhat expanded petition for a fruitful communion, as follows:

> ... and grant that all who participate' (κοινωνοῦντες) might receive a medicine of life for curing every sickness and for strengthening every forward step and every virtue, not unto damnation, O God of truth, and not unto denunciation and shame. For we have called upon Thee, the uncreated, through Thy only-begotten in the Holy Ghost, that this people might find mercy and might be granted improvement; may angels be sent to assist the people to annihilate the evil one and to fortify the Church. We also cry out (Παρακαλοῦμεν δὲ καὶ) for all who have fallen asleep, who are also remembered. [Then, after the reading of the names:] Sanctify these souls, for thou knowest them all. Sanctify all who have died in the Lord, and number them among Thy holy troops and give them place and dwelling in Thy kingdom.[21]

Although the phrasing is quite different, yet there is a close kinship in the structure and in the train of ideas between this commemoration of the dead and the Roman *Memento*. In both cases there is the immediate attachment to the petition for Communion, the division of the remembrance into two parts, the reading of the names between these two parts, whereupon the prayer turns towards *omnibus in Christo quiescentibus* and closes with a picture of the life to come, conceived in local terms. This is not mere coincidence, but the result of a common tradition, as we can gather from those closer relationships between Egyptian and Roman liturgy which were established above.[22] But whereas in Egypt the *Memento* of the dead later on disappeared from this position,[23] at Rome it was retained except at Sunday service, and then later on it became general.

In regard to the wording, the word *etiam* in the introduction immediately arrests our attention. Usually this *etiam* is regarded as a coupling which establishes the connection with the *Memento* of the living, which is supposed at one time to have followed immediately.[24] The Egyptian parallel just quoted shows that this supposition is unnecessary. The line of ideas is rather as follows: When we are being filled "with every

---

the Church universal *ut pro eis, qui in corporis et sanguinis Christi communione defuncti sunt, cum ad ipsum sacrificium loco suo commemorantur, oretur ac pro illis quoque id offerri commemoretur.* Cf. Rötzer, 125 f. These observations of Augustine permit one to argue that the remembrance of the dead occupied a place similar to that in the Roman Mass, at the end of the offering, where mention is made of the *communicatio (participatio).*

[20] The same exception, moreover, in the

Arabic *Testamentum Domini* that originated in Egypt; ed. Baumstark (Oriens christ., I [1901], 1-45), 21.

[21] *Euchologion* of Serapion, 13, 15 (Quasten, *Mon.*, 63).

[22] Above I, 55 f.

[23] Nevertheless also in the form (perhaps 4th cent.) of the anaphora of St. Mark of the papyrus fragments, where prayers are said for the deceased already before the *Sanctus* (Quasten, *Mon.*, 46).

[24] Fortescue, *The Mass*, 354 f.

heavenly blessing" through the power of the Sacrament, we think also of those who can no longer have a part in the Sacrament. And the idea is extended: Even if they can no longer eat the hallowed bread, yet they have gone into the beyond with the seal of faith, *præcesserunt cum signo fidei.*

This *signum fidei,* σφραγὶς τῆς πίστεως, is not just a "sign of faith" in an indefinite and general sense; it is the seal which in Baptism is impressed upon the profession of faith;[25] thus it is Baptism itself.[26] Baptism is the completion, the sacramental authentication or "sealing" of faith. At the same time it is the mark with which Christ has stamped those who are His own, and it is therefore both a guarantee against the perils of darkness and a proud badge of the Christian confessor.[27] The *signum fidei* gives assurance of entrance into life everlasting provided that it is preserved inviolate.[28] In any case, those for whom we petition have not disowned their Baptism; the seal of Christ is shining on their souls.[29] It is indeed for this reason that the burial places of Christians in the catacombs and the primitive Christian sarcophagi are decorated with the allegorical symbols of Baptism.[30] In that age of adult baptism the reference to this

---

[25] Cf. the rite of questioning at baptism; Dekkers, *Tertullianus,* 189 ff.

[26] F. J. Dölger, *Sphragis. Eine altchristliche Taufbezeichnung* (Paderborn, 1911), especially 99-104; K. Prümm, *Der christliche Glaube und die altheidnische Welt,* II (Leipzig, 1935), 401-405. Taken very precisely baptism is a seal (cf. Hermas, *Pastor,* Sim., IX, 16, 4: "The seal therefore is water") and being baptized is the print of the seal, the imprinted χαρακτήρ. In the dismissal formula at the end of the liturgy of St. James of the Syrian Jacobites the faithful are designated as "stamped with the sign of holy baptism"; Brightman, 106, l. 15. The *signum fidei* could be rendered by "the baptismal character," if it were understood that the latter word included the grace of baptism. Since the 3rd century *(con)signare,* σφραγίζειν was predominantly understood to pertain to Confirmation, (Dölger, 179-183). But in the combination *signum fidei* the older meaning evidently survives.

[27] The word σφραγίς or *signum* (the word *sigillum* more common with us is only a diminutive of *signum*), *signaculum* has its complete meaning from the part that the *signatio* (a sealing) played in the contemporaneous profane culture. Not only the animals of a herd, slaves, but in particular the soldiers that belonged to a certain troop, were distinguished by a mark of recognition; the latter, for example, had the insignia of the emperor impressed upon their hands or forearms, or even on their foreheads (Dölger, 18-37), a circumstance that without much ado could have been transferred over to Christ, since it was customary to regard Christian life as a *militia Christi.* Above all else baptism was compared to the impression made by a seal upon wax or sphragide, which then was attached to an endangered object to preserve it from harm *(ibid.,* 7-14; 109-111). To the seal impress were then added qualifying words that properly belonged to the ornamental seal-ring; thus Bishop Abericus on his tomb inscription calls the congregation of Rome "the people with the radiant seal" *(ibid.,* 80-88).

[28] Hence Irenæus already, *Epideixis,* c. 3 (BKV, 4, 585), calls Baptism "Seal of eternal life"; cf. Dölger, 141-148.

[29] In the East Syrian Mass also the departed faithful are designated as those "that have been signed with the living sign of holy baptism"; Brightman, 287, l. 13. On the other hand, Chrysostom, *In Phil. hom.,* 3, 4 (PG, 62, 203), remarks that those of the dead must be mourned who passed away χωρὶς σφραγῖδος.

[30] Here we must cite the representations of

sacrament on the Christian grave was as natural an expression of Christian hope as in our own day the reception of the last sacraments is. It is quite in keeping with our changed circumstances to regard those sacraments in general by whose reception the preservation of our Baptism is made manifest, as the sacramental seal of faith, the *signum fidei* with which our brethren have departed this life.

The intercession here made for the dead is primarily for those who have departed this life as Christians. This coincides with the practice of the Church, which even from oldest times has offered the sacrifice only for those who have remained in communion with her, and who thus have a right to her treasuries of grace. Only those, at any rate, can be mentioned by name. But then the circle is widened: *et omnibus in Christo quiescentibus,* so that all are included who are waiting their final purification, since there is none among them who could have attained his salvation except *"in Christo."*

In this short sentence the other phrases, too, echo the first Christian centuries as closely as do the words *signum fidei.* Thus *præcessit in pace* or *præcessit nos in pace* is an expression which also occurs in the grave inscriptions.[31] Following our Lord's example,[32] the Church of old was wont to call the death of the just, from which they would arise after a short while, a sleep.[33] And it is a sleep of peace, not only because the struggle and strife of earthly life are past, but also because only in death is that peace which Christ willed to bring finally secured. *Et dormiunt in somno pacis.*[34] Countless are the inscriptions which employ the word peace: *requiescit in pace,*[35] *in somno pacis,*[36] *præcessit in somno pacis.*[37] An inscription from the year 397, at St. Praxedes' in Rome, begins: *Dulcis et innoces hic dormit Severianus XP in somno pacis. Qui vixit annos p.m.L, cuius spiritus in luce Domini susceptus est.*[38]

The deceased faithful are *in Christo quiescentes* in the same sense that

---

Noe, Moses at the spring, Susanna, the baptism of Jesus, the healing of the blind man, and the one afflicted with the gout (pardon of sins). The controversy regarding the meaning of Christian art is today gradually coming to recognize its symbolical meaning; cf. perhaps J. P. Kirsch, "Der Indeengehalt der ältesten sepulkralen Darstellungen in den römischen Katakomben," *Röm. Quartalschrift,* 36 (1928), 1-20. In passing we might say that baptism deserves more consideration in this connection than is accorded it.

[31] E. Diehl, *Lateinische altchristliche Inschriften,* 2 ed. (Kleine Texte 26-28; Bonn, 1913). n. 14; 71; cf. 20.

[32] Matt. 9: 24 and parallel.; John 11: 11.

[33] In the word *cœmeterium* (χοιμητήριον) the expression survives to this day. But we will not examine here to what extent the picture of sleep exerted its influence upon the representation that was commonly made in Chrstian antiquity regarding the condition of those who passed away.

[34] That the *pax* is to be understood as peace with the Church in opposition to heresy and excommunication, as Gihr, 709-10, assumes, is excluded by its original meaning and has absolutely no foundation in the wording here.

[35] Diehl, n. 2, 37, 41, 43, etc.

[36] Diehl, n. 34, 42, 81, 116, 173.

[37] Diehl, n. 96 (from Spoleto about 400).

[38] Diehl, n. 166.

Holy Writ speaks of *mortui qui in Christo sunt* (1 Thess. 4:17) and of those *qui in Domino moriuntur* (Apoc. 14:13). They are forever joined to Christ's Body, forever inspired by His life. But those for whom we pray have not yet attained the consummation. The dust of their earthly pilgrimage still clings to their feet. They have not yet been allowed to enter *in locum refrigerii lucis et pacis*. In the torrid lands of the South the word *refrigerium* was early employed as a designation of the state of those blessed who have been granted "coolness."[39] The word light, which is universally regarded as the epitome of joy, is given still greater prominence by the images used in the Apocalypse 21:23 f.; 22:5.[40]

The mention of personal names in the commemoration of the dead, as in that of the living, is also an ancient practice. An evidence of this is found in the text which the Irish tradition of the Roman canon presents: *Memento etiam Domine et eorum nomina qui nos præcesserunt . . .*[41] The celebrating priest at a Mass for certain deceased persons would therefore insert their names in place of the word *nomina* or else after *in somno pacis*. But the other textual form, with *famulorum famularumque*, as we have it in the tradition of the Roman canon[42] outside the Irish, had no such indication for the insertion of names. The first case of the use of *ill. et ill.* (equivalent to the present *N. et N.*) is presented in the group of sacramentaries which goes back to Alcuin, who had inserted the remembrance of the dead into the Hadrianic Sacramentary as a permanent part.[43] It was about this time that the custom began of saying the canon half-aloud or even silently; hence no surprise would be caused by such a

[39] A Parrott, *Le 'refrigerium' dans l'au-delà* (Paris, 1937). Originally the expression *refrigerium* referred to the libation by which, it was believed, the deceased obtained coolness (170). From this is derived the use of the word in the sense of a meal, a funeral feast. Cf. *supra* I, 218. Gassner, *The Canon*, refers also to Scripture allusions, e.g., Luke 11: 23 f.; Apoc. 7: 16 f.

[40] Obviously we cannot presuppose as a background for this prayer the clear representation of a soul mounting from place of purgation to the blissful vision of God. Rather we are concerned with a much less definite notion that in general the redeemed have not reached their final goal. Cf. A. Michel, "Purgatoire" (*DThC*, XIII, 1163-1326), 1212 ff.; B. Bernard, "Ciel" (*DThC*, III, 2474-2511), 2483 ff.; J. de Vuippens, *Le paradis terrestre au troisième ciel* (Fribourg, 1925), 17 ff.

[41] Botte, 44. The word *nomina*, that is missing in the *Sacramentarium Rossianum*

must originally have been a rubric. It is equivalent to the later *N. et N.* That becomes clear in the Stowe Missal, ed. Warner (HBS, 32), 14, where the word *nomina* likewise appears here, whereas the singular is regularly designated by *N.;* cf. above n. 19. In the printed edition of the *Missale Francorum* in Muratori, II, 694, the word *nomina* is enclosed in brackets.—The same version of the text also in later testimonies; *Ordo Rom.*, IV (PL, 78, 983 C); Bernold of Constance, *Micrologus*, c. 23 (PL, 151, 994). Several examples in Gerbert, *Vetus liturgia Alemannica*, I, 367 f.

[42] Kennedy, 52.

[43] Strangely Botte, 44, has inserted this *ill. et ill.* in his critical text, although only Cod. Ottobon. (the one MS. that presents Alcuin's version) is the sole witness to the reading of all the 19 textual witnesses, once we have discounted all the lacunæ and variants (Cod. Pad., also has the Irish version). Lebrun, I, 453, note b, names

cataloging of names, if it actually occurred," " or by the appearance of the *Memento* itself on Sundays and feasts.

Nevertheless there is evidence, even in the pre-Carolingian Roman liturgy, of the custom of formally reciting the names of the dead with the aid of diptychs (except on Sundays and feast days). The reading was done by the deacon," and in this case as a rule not in the place where the *N. et N.* now stands, but between the two sentences of the prayer, in the same place where today silent prayer is suggested."

Until late in the Middle Ages we not infrequently find the rubric here: *Hic recitentur nomina defunctorum.*" Less often we find the heading *Super diptycia* placed above the *Memento etiam.*" Insofar as this recitation of names found a place in public services, it must have been occupied, like its counterpart, the reading of the diptychs in the Orient, with the names of outstanding personalities and special benefactors." The deacon's role

---

French Missals of 1702 and 1709 that do not have the *N. N.* in the text.
" For the present time Gihr, 706, n. 5, notes that the priest should recall to mind particular dead not after the *N. et N.*, but after the *in somno pacis.* Cf. Fortescue, 355.
⁴⁵ Sacramentary of Padua (Mohlberg-Baumstark, n. 885): *Si fuerint nomina defunctorum, recitentur dicente diacono.* This rubric which was preferred to the *Memento etiam* probably goes back to the 7th century. We cannot conclude from this that the *Memento etiam* was also assigned to the deacon as Baumstark, "Das 'Problem' (*Eph. liturg.*, 1939), 237, n. 51 (likewise *Liturgie comparée,* 53, n. 4), assumes; this is not necessarily contained in the text and would be entirely contrary to Rome's well-known attitude towards the office of the deacon. In a Sacramentary of the 9-10th century from Tours, about which Martène, 1, 4, 8, 23 (I, 415 B), reports, the rubric appears in the form: *Si fuerint nomina defunctorum, recitentur; dicat sacerdos: Memento.* Cf. Leroquais, I, 49. Likewise (instead of *dicat: dicet*) in a Sacramentary of the 10th century from Lorsch: Ebner, 248. There is an outward resemblance, but nothing more in the case of the Bishop of Amiens, 1574, who states in his last will, that after his departure from this life, the deacon should address the celebrant *Memento Domine animarum servorum tuorum Johannis et Antonii de Crequy.* Elsewhere the choir boy had the

same task; Martène, 1, 4, 8, 24 (I, 415). Cf. de Moléon, 195; 374.
⁴⁶ The Missal of Bobbio already has the note at the place: *commemoratio defunctorum;* Botte, 44. As a practice of the Roman Church at the time (in contrast to the Frankish) the reading of the names *ex diptychis* is mentioned here by Florus Diaconus (d. about 860), *De actione miss.,* c. 70 (PL, 119, 62 C). Remigius of Auxerre, *Expositio* (PL, 101, 1264 A), repeats the same.
⁴⁷ Examples since the 9th century in Leroquais, I, 44; 84. Examples from the 10-15th centuries from Italy in Ebner, 17, 27, 109, 137, 149, 163, 204, 280, 292, 330, 335. The same notice in the *Ordo Rom.,* IV (PL, 78, 983 C; cf. note 9 above): *Et recitentur nomina. Deinde, postquam recitata fuerint, dicat: Ipsis.* Likewise, Bernold of Constance, *Micrologus,* c. 23 (PL, 151, 994). The formal entry of the name in a Sacramentary at the *Memento* of the Dead was sometimes stipulated in pious bequests of the Middle Ages; Martène, 1, 4, 8, 24 (I, 416 D). Names actually often inserted as annotations in the manuscripts. Examples from 9-10th century in Ehrensberger, *Libri liturgici Bibliothecæ Apost. Vaticanæ* (Freiburg, 1897), 394, 401, 409, 412, 451. Cf. also above, p. 164 f.
⁴⁸ See above, p. 239, n. 9.
⁴⁹ Martène, 1, 4, 8, 23 (I, 415 D) mentions a MS. that adds after *ill. et ill.* of the canon text: *episcoporum præsentis ecclesiæ.* Ibid., 24 (I, 415 f.) reports from

in this could not have lasted very long. Soon interpolated formulas, more or less comprehensive, were developed, so that the priest himself could combine them with the recitation of the names,[59] or could even substitute them for the latter,[51] unless perhaps a detailed catalogue or recitation of names of the dead with a similar formula was already joined to the remembrance of the living.[52] Finally, instead of all these interpolations, there remained a personal recollection by the priest according to his own judgment,[53] just as at the *Memento* of the living,[54] but for this, in turn—as in the case of the other *Memento*, too—special formulas to be used were worked out.[55]

Just as the *Memento* for the living became a basis for all sorts of additions, so the *Memento* for the dead, too, served as the groundwork to which a variety of interpolations could be affixed. For example, an *apologia* was widely used in this connection, inserted generally before the *Memento*.[56] Insertions of this type had already appeared within the

the 9-12th century and the text of a diptychon of the dead from Amiens of the year 1120. Insertion of a list of Bishops of Rheims (until about 1100) in Andrieu, *Les Ordines Romani*, I, 147. Cf. also the example from Arezzo in the following note.

[59] An 11th century Sacramentary of Arezzo inserts after the *in somno pacis* the words: *illorum et omnium fidelium catholicorum qui tibi placuerunt, quorum commemorationem agimus, quorum numerum et nomina tu solus, Domine, cognoscis et quorum nomina recensemus ante sanctum altare tuum.* Before the *Memento* we find over an erasure an apologia (in place of an older list of names?) and then 19 names of the cathedral clergy of Arezzo; Ebner, 225; 419; 421. Here we should also mention the fourth Memento formula of the Missa Illyrica; Martène, 1, 4, IV (I, 514 D). Numerous other examples in Leroquais, See Register, III, 389).—An interpolation of this period in the Mass-*ordo* of Amiens, ed. Leroquais (*Eph. liturg.*, 1927), 443, shows that in the 10th century the priest himself made such insertions; after the naming of some bishops and spiritual communities there follows *patris mei et matris*, etc.

[51] Mass orders from the region of Montecassino insert (in place of the *N. et N.*) *quorum vel quarum nomina scripta habemus et quorum vel quarum elemosinas accepimus, et eorum qui nos præcesserunt.* Ebner, 203; 421. Fiala, 211. A sacramen-

tary of the 11th century from Echternach names the benefactors of the church and those *quorum corpora in hoc loco requiescunt at in circuitu ecclesiæ istius;* Leroquais, I, 123. More examples, *ibid.* (see Register, III, 389 f.); Ebner, 420. Cf. also the second formula in the Missa Illyrica·. Martène, 1, 4, IV (I, 514 B). A lengthy insertion, but one that turns into a Gallican intercessory prayer, also in the Stowe Missal; see above, p. 163, n. 17; Botte, 44, Apparatus.

[52] Ebner, 401-403; 421 f.; cf. above, p. 164, n. 24.

[53] Thus in the Mass arrangement of Bec in the late Middle Ages: Martène, 1, 4, XXXVI (I, 674 B).

[54] Thus expressly Hugo of St. Cher, *Tract. super missam* (ed. Sölch, 40); cf. above, p. 165.

[55] The 1539 *Directorium divinorum officiorum* of Ciconiolanus has the formula: *Memento etiam, Domine, famulorum famularumque tuarum illius vel illorum vel illarum, pro quo vel qua vel quibus specialiter orare teneor, parentum, propinquorum, amicorum, benefactorum, et omnium fidelium defunctorum, quibus æternam requiem donare digneris. Qui nos præcesserunt.* Legg· *Tracts*, 211. A more detailed designation in the Regensburg Missal about 1500: Beck, 273.

[56] It is entered in the margin of the Cod. Ottobon. of the Gregorianum in its original form (Lietzmann, n. 1, 28, Apparatus):

preceding *Supplices*,[57] or even in front of it.[58] Ancient and widespread was a rubric which enjoined a pause after the words *Supplices te rogamus;* the rubric reads: *Hic orat apud se quod voluerit, deinde dicit: iube . . .*[59] The obtrusion of personal intentions had thus been inaugurated very early.

The conclusion of the remembrance of the dead is also *Per Christum Dominum nostrum.*[60] In this instance, the phrase is accompanied by a bow on the part of the priest. That is unusual. Many explanations have been offered.[61] Some suggest that the bow is meant for the preceding *deprecamur*, or for the humble self-accusation of the following *Nobis quoque peccatoribus*, or else that it is intended for the word *Christus*. The last postulate can appeal to several parallels since the fifteenth century.[62] But why, then, is this the only place that the bow is prescribed?[63] We should rather seek our explanation in the allegorical treatment of the Mass-liturgy, the same sort of thinking that led the later Middle Ages to give a symbolic representation of the Crucified by means of the outstretched arms after the consecration, and the crossed hands at the

Memento mei quæso, Domine, et miserere, et licet hæc sacrificia indignis manibus meis tibi offeruntur, qui nec invocare dignus sum nomen sanctum tuum, quæso iam quia in honore gloriosi Filii tui Domini Dei nostri tibi offeruntur, sicut incensum in conspectu divinæ maiestatis tuæ cum odore suavitatis accendantur. Also in the Sacramentary of Metz (9th cent.): Leroquais, I, 17, and already in garbled form about 800 in the Sacramentary of Angoulême (ed. Cagin [Angoulême], 1919], p. 118; Botte, 44, Apparatus). More sources since the 9th century in Leroquais, I, 48 f., 54, 63, etc. (see Register, III, 390); sources of the 10-12th century besides discussion of the same in Ebner, 419 (with n. 1-3); also Ferreres, 155 f.; Gerbert, *Vetus liturgia Alemannica*, I, 364; Martène, 1, 4, 8, 24 (I, 416 E) and *ibid.*, IV, V, IX (I, 514 C, 527 C, 547 E). In the Missa Illyrica a second *Memento*-apology: *ibid.*, IV (I, 514 A). In Ebner, 420, also another formula that belongs here, half apology, half offering of the type of the *Suscipe* formulas described above, beginning here with *Omnipotens s. D. dignare suscipere*; the same formula less garbled in Bona, II, 14, 1 (788 f.). A shorter expression of the same idea is presented in a Sacramentary of the 12th century from lower Italy; before the *Memento etiam* the priest prays three times: *Deus omnipotens, propitius esto mihi peccatori;* Ebner, 149, 420. Here we

see the influence of the Byzantine Mass; see Brightman, 354, 1. 41; 356, 1. 17; 378, 1. 26; 393, 1. 7. By the 12th century these apology insertions have disappeared; Durandus, III, 45, 1, knows of the formula *Memento mei quæso* only *in antiquis codicibus.*
[57] An example with intercession in Ebner, 418 f.
[58] A Missal from Lower Italy in the 12th century has the priest make a bow and repeat three times: *Deus omnipotens, propitius esto mihi peccatori;* Ebner, 149, 418. Cf. above, n. 56.
[59] *Ordo "Qualiter quædam"* (Andrieu, II, 300; PL, 78, 983 C). Further data, see Brinktrine, *Die hl. Messe*, 204; Gerbert, *Vetus liturgia Alemannica*, I, 363 f.
[60] Since the age of the Humanists: *Per eumdem Chr. D. n.;* see Botte, 44.
[61] L. Brou, "L'inclination de la tête au 'Per eumdem Christum' du Memento des Morts," *Miscellanea Mohlberg*, I, (1948), 1-31; eleven different explanations are cited p. 3-9.
[62] The Missal of the Bursfeld Congregation and the Mass-order of Burchard both have a bow of the head at the *Per Christum D. n.* in the preface; The Dominican Missal since 1705 similarly has such a bow after the *Communicantes;* Brou, 9-13.
[63] It appears for the first time in the Missal of Pius V, in the Antwerp edition of 1571; Brou, 2 f.; 28 f.

Supplices. Towards the end of the canon some externalization had to be made of the moment when the dying Redeemer bowed His head.[64]

17. *Nobis quoque*

In the present-day text of the Roman canon, the *Nobis quoque*, the last of the large prayers of the canon, is appended to the remembrance of the dead without giving the least impression of a skip or break. After we have prayed for the dead, that they may attain the place of light and peace, we pray also for ourselves, that we may obtain a part with the saints of heaven. But simple and natural though this thought transition appears at first, still upon closer study we encounter several problems. Why is this prayer put here at all? Has not its main theme already been expressed in the *Supplices,* with the appeal for "every heavenly blessing?" The problem grows even more vexing when we turn our attention to the history of the text, for we discover that the remembrance of the dead did not even belong to the permanent parts of the canon, whereas the *Nobis quoque* is found in all our text sources and must therefore have followed immediately after the *Supplices.*

The most obvious conclusion would then be that our prayer arose as a continuation of the *Supplices* and is to be explained as such, and this opinion, despite the difficulties already hinted at, has been maintained even in most recent times.[1] There is indeed a forward step in the thought of the second prayer, since the petition is not only for blessing and grace from heaven, but for eternal bliss itself in the company of apostles and martyrs. Besides, it is possible to point to oriental parallels which likewise extend the plea for the fruits of Communion into a plea for heavenly happiness,[2] and thus pursue the biblical concept of a bond between the Eucharist and heavenly life (John 6: 48-51) In one case, in fact, the wording reminds one of the phrases of our *Nobis quoque.*[3]

---

[64] This explanation in Gihr, 710. The leading commentators of the Middle Ages quite remarkably say nothing further about the little ceremony. Still Amalar, *De eccl. off.,* III, 25 (PL, 105, 1142 C) and later Bernold of Constance, *Micrologus,* c. 16 (PL, 151, 987 D) look for a liturgical expression in the fact that Christ, *inclinato capite,* gave up the ghost and find it probable because of the absence of any other ceremony of like nature, in the bow at the *Supplices.* Likewise Honorius Augustod. *Gemma an.,* I, 46 (PL, 172, 558). Durandus, IV, 7, 6 f., links the 13 *inclinationes,* established by him with the corresponding actions in the life and passion of the Lord, and among them also, that He rendered His soul to God. Still he mentions no special bow for it. Cf. further statements below.

[1] By Baumstark, "Das 'Problem' des römischen Meszkanons" (*Eph liturg.,* 1939), 238 f.

[2] Baumstark, *op. cit.,* 239. Baumstark stresses particularly the turn of expression in the liturgy of St. Mark (Brightman, 134) : may the Communion redound to the recipients εἰς κοινωνίαν μακαριότητος ζωῆς αἰωνίου, which he compares with the *societas* of the Roman text.

[3] In the Egyptian anaphora of St. Basil (Renaudot, I, 1847, 68), the words follow immediately after the epiklesis: Make us

On the other hand, it is certainly very surprising that an imposing construction like the *Nobis quoque,* an independent sentence, well-rounded in its phrases, should be set up for the simple continuation of a thought which was already expressed in substance, when it would have been more than sufficient to follow up the words *omni benedictione cœlesti et gratia repleamur* with a phrase like *et vitam æternam consequamur.* That this should have been the original pattern seems almost excluded by the fact that the *Supplices,* unlike the prayers that precede it, has the concluding formula *Per Christum Dominum nostrum.* Add to this the puzzling *quoque,* which is understandable on the supposition that the remembrance of the dead precedes, and a prayer is included "also" for us as for the dead; but remove the remembrance of the dead and the word *quoque* loses its point of reference, since "we" have already been named as recipients of the favor petitioned in the *Supplices.*[4]

But it is possible—and perhaps necessary—to take a different view, in which the *quoque* receives a satisfactory meaning. Is it so sure that the same group of persons is referred to in both the *Supplices* and the *Nobis quoque?* The terms *nos peccatores,* or more correctly *nos peccatores famuli tui,*[5] "us, thy sinful servants," could *per se* designate the whole congregation assembled, as many commentators suppose either by their silence or even expressly.[6] But amongst all the designations for the congregation represented by the priest in prayer—we possess thousands of examples in the sacramentaries—this would be the only case of the kind.[7] On the contrary, *peccator* had been used as a term of self-designation, especially as the self-designation of the clergy. At the close of his work on

---

worthy to partake in thy mysteries, ἵνα . . . εὔρωμεν μέρος καὶ κλῆρον ἔχειν μετὰ πάντων τῶν ἀγίων.

[4] P. Leo Eizenhöfer, a letter of Sept. 5, 1943, calls attention to the possibility that the *quoque* was equivalent in late Latin to a mere *-que,* and refers confirmation to Stolz-Schmalz, *Lateinische Grammatik* (5th ed., by Leumann-Hofmann; Munich, 1928), 662. This would solve the difficulty of the "also," but an appended *-que* seems to be excluded by the foregoing conclusion formula, *Per Christum Dominum nostrum,* which is found in all the texts, the Stowe missal excepted (Botte, 42), and which can therefore hardly be considered as a later addition.—Baumstark, 239 f., among others, interprets the *quoque* in such a way as to anticipate the list of apostles and martyrs mentioned near the end of the prayer, after several intervening phrases: we pray God may vouchsafe us a part along with them. However, there

is nothing in the text to warrant such a dislocation of the thought.

[5] Rütten, "Philologisches zum Canon missæ" (*StZ,* 1938, I), 46, pointing out that to this day the missal has no comma before the *famulis.* A very similar adjectival use of *peccatores* is found e.g., in Augustine, *Sermo,* 215, 4 (PL, 38, 1074): God became man *pro reis et peccatoribus servis,* and again, *ibid., pro peccatoribus servis.* It is also to be discovered in the Leonianum (Muratori, I, 329): *famuli peccatores.*

[6] Duchesne, *Christian Worship,* 182; Baumstark, "Das 'Problem'," 238 f.; also Brinktrine, *Die hl. Messe,* 222, with the rather weak argument that the *Sacramentarium Rossianum* (11th c.) has the addition: *(famulis) et famulabus*—an absolutely solitary reading; see Botte, 44.

[7] This impression is confirmed when, e.g., one examines the cases recorded in the word register of the Gregorian sacramentary of Lietzmann, p. 159, s. v. *peccator.*

Baptism, Tertullian begs *ut cum petitis, etiam Tertulliani peccatoris memineritis.*[8] For centuries, it was the practice in clerical circles to add the word *peccator* to one's signature.[9] Therefore here, too, the clergy must be meant by the *peccatores famuli*—the celebrating priest and his assistants.[10] If this be true, then the addition of a *quoque,* even right after the *Supplices,* takes on an acceptable meaning; *quoque* then signifies something like "and especially." To the prayer for all, we priests now add a particular appeal for ourselves, poor sinners.

Such a recommendation of self, pleading for one's own person, combined at the same time with the acknowledgment of one's own unworthiness, was part of the intercessory prayer already in the fourth century, at least in the Orient.[11] In the Syrian Liturgy of St. James it is inserted at the very beginning,[12] while in Egypt it appears near the end of the intercessions.[13] In the Alexandrian Greek Liturgy of St. Mark it consists of two members: "Remember, O Lord, in grace and mercy also us, thy sinful and unworthy servants (καὶ ἡμῶν τῶν ἀμαρτωλῶν καὶ ἀναξίων δούλων σου), and blot out our sins, good and loving God; remember, Lord, also me, thy lowly and sinful and unworthy servant . . ."[14] The similarity of expression is astonishing. In view of the connection—already verified more than once—between Egypt especially and Rome, this similarity can hardly be accidental. Thus we are forced to accept in the Roman Mass too, the meaning which is unequivocally given in the oriental text, the meaning of self-recommendation. Moreover, this was the meaning given the *Nobis quoque* by medieval commentators.[15]

In this way we make room for the possibility that the *Nobis quoque*

---

[8] Tertullian, *De baptismo,* c. 20 (CSEL, 20, 218).

[9] See, e.g., the signatures from the 6th century in Mansi, IX, 867 ff.—In Greek documents the word τ(απεινὸς), abbreviated, was sometimes added in the same sense; this is the word from which, as we know, was derived the cross that bishops and abbots place before their signatures.—Cf. also the *peccator* formulas (which are, however, much later in date) in the *Orate fratres,* above, p. 83.

[10] From the word *famuli,* however, we cannot draw the same conclusion, as P. Maranget, "La grande prière d'intercession," *Cours et conférences,* VII (Louvain, 1929), 188, note 19, attempts to do. For *famuli tui* is not equivalent to *servi tui, servitus tua,* which are found in two earlier passages of the canon; cf. above, pp. 184, 222.

[11] *Const. Ap.,* VIII, 12, 41 (Quasten, *Mon.,* 225): καὶ ὑπὲρ τῆς ἐμῆς τοῦ προσφέροντος οὐδενίας.

[12] Brightman, 55: Μνήσθητι, κύριε, κατὰ τὸ πλῆθος τοῦ ἐλέους σου καὶ τῶν οἰκτιρμῶν σου καὶ ἐμοῦ τοῦ ταπεινοῦ καὶ ἀρχείου δούλου σου . . .; cf. *ibid.,* 90. Regarding the numerous variants, see Rücker, *Die Jakobusanaphora,* 27.

[13] Brightman, 130. Likewise in the Byzantine liturgy of St. Basil, while the Byzantine liturgy of St. Chrysostom does not contain the petition.

[14] Brightman, 130.—The Coptic text is expanded in a different way, *ibid.,* 173.—Cf. also the related reading in the Egyptian Mass from the Arabian Testamentum Domini edited by Baumstark, *Oriens christ.,* 1 (1901), 23; Quasten *Mon.,* 256 note. Here the notice is given that the priest says the petition *secreto.*

[15] Thomas Aquinas, *Summa theol.,* III, 83, 4. A reference to this still in Gihr, 711, note 2.

was originally attached to the *Supplices*. But the fact is not therefore assured—not at all. It would be certainly very surprising to find this solitary instance where, in order to admit this recommendation of self, the oblation prayers would be concluded before the close of the canon and another special prayer would be introduced at once.[16] Such a fresh start might be brought about more easily if the remembrance of the dead were inserted first and if then the *Nobis quoque* followed as "a kind of embolism." [17] Thus, the order of the prayers as we have them at present would be nothing but a return to the original situation. To be sure, we would then be forced to admit that both prayers were at first alien to the Sunday and feast-day Mass. Then, about the turn of the sixth century, when the original number of the saints' names in the *Nobis quoque* began to be expanded into the present well-ordered double series and the list set consciously side by side with the series in the *Communicantes*, this parallel would have furnished a reason for including the *Nobis quoque* in the canon as a permanent part.

Related evidences in Egypt also lend a color of probability to such a connection with the remembrance of the dead. For it is worthy of note that there too a prayer which is remarkably reminiscent of the *partem* aliquam et societatem cum sanctis apostolis et martyribus* in our Roman formula is frequently [18] attached to the remembrance of the dead, not indeed as a self-recommendation on the part of the clergy, but as a petition for the congregation. This appears in the fourth century.

In the papyrus fragment of the anaphora of St. Mark which comes from this period, we read near the end of the intercession: "[1] Give peace to the souls of the deceased, [2] remember those [for whom] we keep a memorial on this day, [3] and those whose names we speak and whose names we do not speak, [4] [above all] our very faithful fathers and bishops everywhere, [5] and permit us to take part and lot (μερίδα καὶ κλῆρον ἔχειν), [6] with [the assembly] of the holy prophets, apostles, and martyrs."[19]

This wording recurs in later Egyptian texts, but with amplifications and several inversions.[20] We might mention in passing that as a matter

---

[16] The blessing of natural goods that then followed hardly ever became a fixed constituent of every Mass; see below, p. 261 ff.
[17] Botte, 69.—Besides Botte we can cite for this opinion Kennedy, 34 f.; Fortescue, 160 f., 355; Eisenhofer, II, 190-192.
[18] This is not the case exclusively; see *supra*, note 3, where however the textual relationship to the *Nobis quoque* is not so close as with the reading to be cited directly.
[19] Quasten, *Mon.*, 46-49. Cf. the first publication by M. Andrieu and P. Collomp,

"Fragments sur papyrus de l'anaphore de S. Marc," *Revue des sciences réligieuses*, 8 (1928), 489-515, and the commentary of the editors on this passage, p. 511 f.
[20] In the textus receptus of the Greek anaphora of St. Mark four of the six members of the text cited are found again in the sequence 1, 2, 5, 4 (Brightman, 128-130). After No. 1—apparently as a substitute for No. 6—there is inserted: May God "be mindful of the forefathers from the beginning, the fathers, patriarchs, prophets .. " (1 a) ; after No. 2 the names

of fact the West-Syrian Mass is also familiar with similar expansions of the remembrance of the dead.[21] Thus it is not impossible that the prayers added to the *Memento* of the dead in the Roman canon simply began: *Nobis quoque partem et societatem donare digneris cum tuis sanctis apostolis et martyribus . . .*[22] However, on the evidence of the oriental parallels cited at the start, it is patent that contemporaneously a self-recommendation was added to the preceding intercessory prayer, and the plea itself was restricted to the narrower circle of the clergy by means of the words *peccatoribus famulis*.

With the prayer certain names were probably linked from the very beginning. It is a striking fact that the first two names in the Roman prayer, John and Stephen, also appear in Egypt, in the corresponding prayer of the Coptic Mass; although the precise point of insertion here is slightly different and the name of Mother of God precedes.[23] It is very probable

of St. Mark and the Mother of God are added, and then follow the "Diptychs of the Departed" and another petition for the bliss of heaven. Between No. 5, which has the simple form: δὸς ἡμῖν μερίδα καὶ κλῆρον ἔχειν μετὰ πάντων τῶν ἁγίων σου, and No. 4 there are oblation prayers and a petition for patriarchs and bishops.—The old element recurs in even more faithful fashion in the Coptic version (Brightman, 169 f.), where the sections follow in the order 1, 1a, 4, 5, 2, 3, and again 5, but with the insertion of numerous expansions. In No. 1a the names of Mary, John the Baptist, Stephen and a series of bishops and abbots have been added. The diptychs stand between No. 2 and No. 3. A still simpler form of the Coptic tradition in H. Hyvernat, "Fragmente der altcoptischen Liturgie," *Röm. Quartalschrift*, 1 (1887), 339 f., with the sections of the text in the order 1, 1a, 5, 4, 2, 3, 5.—Andrieu-Collomp, p. 512, are inclined to view sections N. 5 and 6 of the papyrus fragment (which are of special interest to us here) as the original text.

[21] In the anaphora of St. James the last of the priest's petitions beginning with Μνήσθητι κύριε which follow upon the reading of the diptychs in the intercessory prayer after the consecration pertains to the deceased "whom we have remembered and whom we have not forgotten," that God may grant them rest in His kingdom, where there is no pain; "but grant us," it continues, "a Christian, pleasing, and sinless death in peace, Lord Lord, and lead us together to the feet of Thy elect, when Thou wilt and as Thou wilt, only without abashment and without failure." Brightman, 57; sharply expanded in the Jacobite text, *ibid.*, 95 f.; in a different form in the later Jacobite anaphoras.

[22] The language echoes Biblical expressions: Col. 1: 12; Acts 20: 32. Some of the older sacramentary manuscripts have *partem aliquam societatis* (Botte, 46), which is perhaps an attempt to follow Col. 1: 12 even more closely.—Cf. moreover Polycarp, *Ad Phil.*, 12, 2 (Funk-Biehlmeyer, I, 119; Greek text not preserved) : *det vobis sortem et partem inter sanctos suos.*

[23] Here the wording of the portion of the prayer marked No. 1 and 1a in note 20 above is as follows: "To our fathers and our brethren who have fallen asleep, whose souls Thou hast taken, give rest, remembering all saints who have been well-pleasing to Thee since the world began: our holy fathers the patriarchs, the prophets, the apostles, the evangelists, the preachers, the martyrs, the confessors, all just spirits who have been made perfect in the faith, and most chiefly her that is holy glorious mother of God and ever virgin, the holy *theotokos* Mary, and St. John the forerunner and baptist and martyr, and St. Stephen the protodeacon and protomartyr, and St. Mark the apostle and evangelist and martyr, and the holy patriarch Severus and St. Cyril and St. Basil and St. Gregory, and our righteous father the great abba Antony . . ." The

that at an early period these two or three names were added to the wording as it appears in the papyrus fragment already quoted,[24] and that the remembrance of the dead, along with the appendage thus expanded, belonged to the ancient fund of prayers which the Roman and Alexandrian churches had in common as early as the fourth century.[25] The general designation, *cum tuis sanctis apostolis et martyribus*, is Roman and corresponds to the *beatorum apostolorum ac martyrum* in the *Communicantes*. But then, feeling that the very first of the names that followed was beyond the announced group of apostles and martyrs, a new start was made by inserting a preposition, *cum Joanne*, another indication that a series of special names had already been supplied beforehand.[26]

As long as the emphasis was put on the remembrance as such, only a few names could possibily be brought forward for mention with the holy apostles and martyrs. Even here the earliest saints to be considered were those who already enjoyed a devotion at Rome. But then, in the period when the veneration of martyrs flourished so vigorously, there was a rapid growth in the list here, just as there was in the *Communicantes*. Of the saints in the *Nobis quoque* list, besides the Baptist and Stephen, those who had such honor paid them around the end of the fifth century were the following Roman martyrs: Peter and Marcellinus, whose grave on the Via Lavicana had been decorated with verses by Pope Damasus, and whose feast on June 2 was contained in the sacramentaries; Agnes, over whose grave on the Via Nomentana a basilica had already been erected by Emperor Constantine's daughter Constantia; Cecilia, whose grave in the catacomb of Callistus had been honored at a very early date, but whose veneration at any rate reached a peak about the turn of the fourth century (this was when a new basilica was built and dedicated to her at the old Titulus Cæciliæ in Trastevere, and thus in the end foundress and martyr became identified); further, a Roman lady, Felicity, over whose grave Pope Boniface I (d. 422) had built an oratory, and whose feast was celebrated in the oldest sacramentaries—as it is at present—on

---

continuation (No. 4 and 5) here reads: "Remember, Lord, our holy and right-believing fathers and archbishops who have long ago passed away, who have justly administered the word of truth, and give us a share and lot with them." Brightman, 169.

[24] To No. 6 before the transposition by which No. 1a arose, and in a simpler form than that shown in the text cited in the previous note. For this derivation see also Kennedy, 144; 148.

[25] Cf. *supra*, I, 55 f.—Kennedy, 34 ff., 189 f., 197, thinks that the *Nobis quoque* (along with the remembrance of the dead)

was first inserted into the canon by Gelasius I (492-496) in the same way as the *Communicantes*. As far as the *Communicantes* is concerned his thesis has been disputed. It is also untenable for the *Nobis quoque*; for at so late a date there is little likelihood of any transfer from Egypt to Rome, and this is the matter to be considered, for an older text, without the names, is already to be found in Egypt.

[26] This assumption has more in its favor than the opinion of Baumstark, *Das "Problem,"* 218, who sees in this second start with *cum* an indication that the names were inserted in the Roman text only later.

November 23.[27] Here again as in the case of the *Communicantes*, the list of saints in the Milanese Mass offers a confirmation of what we have established. The Roman martyrs are there set down plainly in their historical sequence; they show the following succession: Peter, Marcellinus, Agnes, Cecilia, and Felicity; and only after that some other names follow.[28]

Of the rest of the names in the Roman *Nobis quoque*, an Alexander is mentioned at least three times in the fourth-century Roman lists of martyrs. For two who bore this name there is also an annual commemoration in the sacramentaries, although they enjoyed no other special veneration. The Alexander in the canon appears to be the Alexander of the group of seven martyrs, who for a long time have been commemorated on July 10, and whom later legends linked with St. Felicity, as seven brothers; since the sixth century, Alexander stood out in this group.[29] Of the two women martyrs of Sicily, Agatha and Lucy, the former was honored at Rome in the fifth century, when the Goth Ricimer built a church in her honor, and the latter about the sixth century; although both had surely been venerated previously in their native cities of Catania and Syracuse. The rich possessions of the Roman church in Sicily probably led to this transfer of cult.[30] To Felicity the name of Perpetua was added. Perhaps the name of the Roman martyr drew after itself the name of the great African lady whose *Passio*, one of the most precious documents in the history of the martyrs, was known even at Rome at quite an early date. But that the names in the list are not to be referred to both the African martyrs, Perpetua and her slave Felicity,[31] is clearly deduced from the way they are mentioned, for if they did they would certainly have been left in their usual order.[32] Anastasia is the martyr of Sirmium whose body was brought to Constantinople in 460, and whose veneration had probably received an impetus in Rome during the period of Byzantine domination.[33]

---

[27] Kennedy, *The Saints of the Canon*, 141-188; 197.—Especially for Cecilia and Felicitas see also J. B. Kirsch, *Der stadtrömische christliche Festkalender im Altertum* (LQ, 7-8; Münster, 1924), 89 f.

[28] Kennedy, 62. In the Milanese list the names that head the list are: *Johannes et Johannes, Stephanus, Andreas.* The names of Matthias, Barnabas, Ignatius and Alexander are missing in the Milan text.

[29] Kennedy, 151-158. This is the Alexander reputedly martyred on the Salarian way. Another Alexander, of Ficulea (a village north of Rome), from the group commemorated on May 4, certainly emerges more prominently about this same time, but only by reason of his identification (certainly false) in the legend as Pope Alexander I (d. 115), who was not a martyr and who cannot be intended in our list because, as bishop of Rome, he would certainly be placed ahead of Ignatius; *ibid.*, 155 f. For the same reason we consider unacceptable the supposition of Baumstark, *Das "Problem,"* 238, that *a priori* the pope was meant because the martyrdom of Ignatius, who is mentioned just before him, was probably erroneously dated in his reign.

[30] Kennedy, 169-173.

[31] This assumption also in Hosp, 189-205; see especially 204 f.; so also Gassner, 391.

[32] Kennedy, 161-164. In the sequence Perpetua and Felicitas, the two lady martyrs, are found at Rome in the *Depositio martyrum* drawn up about 336. But they received no special veneration.

[33] Kennedy, 183-185.

Regarding the two Sicilian martyrs, a trustworthy account expressly tells us that Gregory the Great placed their names in the canon.[34] Nor can the rest of the names in this later layer have come into the canon much earlier than this. Regarding Alexander and Agatha, we might think of Pope Symmachus (498-514), who had provided funds for the memorial places of both, as he had also done for Agnes and Felicity.[35] On the other hand, Matthias and Barnabas, who appear as representatives of the "holy apostles,"[36] evidently did not acquire this role until the twelve Apostles had all found a place in the *Communicantes* series. To these two saints no particular veneration was paid in the liturgy of the city of Rome during the first millenary,[37] and the same is true of Ignatius, martyr-bishop of Antioch, in spite of his connection with the city of Rome.[38] Still, in view of the manuscript evidence,[39] their insertion into the canon cannot have been substantially later. So everything points to Gregory the Great as having undertaken the final revision here as in the *Communicantes*.[40] Duplication of the names was avoided, but the same principles regarding the disposition of names held in both instances: at the top of the list an outstanding name, John the Baptist;[41] then a double column of seven (the scriptural number)—seven men and seven women; among the men the hierarchical order once more: first the apostles, then the martyr-bishop Ignatius, then Alexander, who is designated by the legend as a priest (or bishop); likewise the pair of martyrs who are otherwise generally named in this order, Peter and Marcellinus, but in line with the legend are reversed according to their hierarchical standing: Marcellinus the priest and Peter the exorcist. Amongst the women a certain territorial division is recognizable. In the first pair, the names of the two African women seem to have been decisive; then follow the two martyrs from Sicily, Agatha and Lucy, then the two Roman maidens, Agnes and Cecilia, and finally the oriental Anastasia.

---

[34] Aldhelm (d. 709), *De laud. virg.*, c. 42 (PL, 89, 142; Kennedy, 170): *Gregorius in canone . . . pariter copulasse [Agatham et Luciam] cognoscitur, hoc modo in catalogo martyrum ponens: Felicitate, Anastasia, Agatha, Lucia.*

[35] Batiffol, *Leçons*, 229.

[36] Along with Paul, Barnabas is also called an apostle in Acts 14: 4, 13.

[37] Their commemorative days first appear on Frankish ground, for Barnabas since the 11th century, for Matthias since the 12th; see Baumstark, *Missale Romanum*, 212, 219.

[38] Ignatius the Antiochene, known as ὁ θεοφόρος, was considered by early Christians a disciple of St. Peter, from whom he was believed to have received episcopal consecration (St. Chrysostom, *Hom. in S. Ign.*, IV, 587 [PG, 50, 58]). He was martyred at Rome. His body was translated to Antioch but brought back to Rome in the 7th century at the time of the first Moslem invasion, and was placed near St. Clement's. A feast-day was assigned to him as early as the 9th century; see Baumstark, *Missale Romanum*, 210.

[39] The manuscript tradition is rather uniform, aside from two witnesses of the Irish group, the Stowe missal and the Bobbio missal, which have grouped the names of the seven lady martyrs, but without any apparent principle. Botte, 46, Apparatus.

[40] Kennedy, 198.

[41] The identity of this John as the Baptist

As is already clear from what has been said, those named (with the exception of the biblical characters, of Ignatius, the bishop of Antioch and author of seven letters [d.*c.* 107], and of the African lady Perpetua [d. 202-3]) are all martyrs of whom little is known beyond their name, the place of their confession and—through the annual commemoration of their death—perhaps the day of their death; no year, no history of their suffering, no biographical details. Not till later did legend sketch out a picture.[42] These are properly the true representatives of the unknown heroes of the first Christian centuries who, because of their glorious death for Christ, continued to live on in the minds and hearts of men. But their death for Christ was likewise their triumph with Christ, and that is enough to have their names serve as symbols of that blessed lot which we beg God we, along with our own departed, might, to some extent at least, share.

As in the case of the *Communicantes,* the list of the *Nobis quoque* was enlarged during the Middle Ages by the addition of favorite medieval names, particularly at the end of the list. But as a rule these additions stayed within modest bounds.[43]

The parallelism with the *Communicantes* and its series of saints extends also to the general features of both prayers. In both cases the prayer represents a continuation of the *Memento,* in such wise that a certain connection with the saints in heaven is represented. But the connection is different in the two cases. After the *Memento* of the living, the assembled congregation, looking up humbly to the saints, offers up its

whom Christ Himself exalted above all others and whose name is attached to the cathedral of Rome (the Lateran basilica) is now little more than an academic problem. It is plainly indicated by the parallel to the Mother of God. Add to this the evident effort not to duplicate the *Communicantes* list, since not even Mary has been carried over from it, while the Baptist is plainly kept out of it. Further there is wanting any special reason for such an exceptional preference for one of Zebedee's sons. Last, but not least, there is the parallel with the Eastern liturgies, and not only that of Egypt with its combination of the Baptist and Stephen. Cf., e.g., the intercessory prayer in the liturgy of St. James, where the Greek text has the following series: Mary, John the Baptist, apostles, evangelists, Stephen (Brightman, 56 f.); the Syrian has: John, Stephen, Mary (*ibid.,* 93; Rücker, 35; the Armenian has: Mary, John, Stephen, apostles (Rücker, 35, Apparatus). Further data in Kennedy, 37 f.; cf. also Fortescue 356 f.— Medieval commentors for the most part saw in this John generally the evangelist; Durandus, IV, 46, 7. In more recent times Baumstark, *Liturgia Romana e liturgia dell' Esarcato* (Rome, 1904), 144 f., in line with his theory on the canon, declared for the evangelist, but later after abandoning his theory he dropped him in favor of the Baptist (*Das "Problem,"* 238). The Congregation of Rites, being asked about the matter because of the bow on the respective feast, spoke out in favor of the Baptist, March 27, 1824 (Martinucci, *Manuale decretorum SRC,* n. 485; 1166), but this decree was not retained in the collection of the *Decreta authentica* of 1898 ff.

[42] More detailed information in Hosp, *Die Heiligen im Canon Missœ,* 103 ff., 128 ff., 205 ff., 254 ff. See also the authors cited *supra,* p. 252, note 22.

[43] MSS. from Fulda mention St. Lioba. In

sacrifice in common with them; the only connection here is that already established by association in the one kingdom of God. After the *Memento* of the dead the concept is raised a degree and the plea is for a final participation in the blessedness of the elect. Being about to eat the bread of life everlasting, we have prayed for the dead that God might be mindful of them and vouchsafe them entry into the place of light and peace. And it is this place of light and peace, viewed as the home of the saints, that we beg also for ourselves, *nobis quoque peccatoribus famulis tuis.*

Regarding the rest of the wording of the prayer, the only thing to notice is that the note of modest retirement and humble self-accusation which was struck by the word *peccatores* sets the tone of the whole prayer. The petition is spoken only with the utmost trust in the fullness of divine mercy,[44] and the only object sought is that God may grant *partem aliquam,* and even this not as a reward of present merit, but solely because He is the giver of grace (cf. Psalm 129:3-4). All this is quite in keeping in a prayer spoken before the people for one's own person, whereas in a prayer said in the name of the congregation it would sound rather unusual.

The words *Nobis quoque peccatoribus* are lifted out of the quiet of the canon, for the priest says them audibly, meanwhile striking his breast. There is scattered evidence of this striking of the breast as early as the twelfth century, and soon thereafter it became a general practice.[45] In some places, since the thirteenth century, there is mention even of a triple striking of the breast.[46]

And the custom of saying the first words aloud goes back even further. We hear of it already in the ninth century,[47] and since that time it has

---

Italy we frequently find Eugenia and Euphemia. Ebner, 423 ff.; Botte, 46 Apparatus.—Several names are added in the Milanese text. Most numerous seem to be the additions in France. Here we find, among others, Denis, Martin, Genevieve; Martène, 1, 4, 8, 25 (I, 416 f.); Ménard: PL, 78, 28 note. Leroquais, *Les sacramentaires,* III, 394, manages to assemble a list of 36 different names from French Mass-books alone.—Spanish Mass-books of the 13th-15th century from Gerona have after *omnibus sanctis tuis* the addition: *vel quorum sollemnitas hodie in conspectu tuæ maiestatis celebratur, Domine Deus noster, toto in orbe terrarum;* Ferreres, 156. Likewise in two MSS. of the 11-12th century from Vich; *ibid.,* p. CCIII. —The Irish Stowe missal sets St. Patrick at the head of the list, with Peter and Paul; Kennedy, 62.

[44] The use of the Biblical wording *de multitudine miserationum tuarum* (Ps. 50: 3,

et al.) has its oriental correspondence in the self-commendation of the liturgy of St. James (*supra,* note 12) and in that of the Byzantine liturgy of St. Basil (Brightman, 336, 1. 14). For the concluding words *intra quorum nos consortium,* etc., see the parallel in Ps.-Jerome, *supra,* I, 52, note 9.

[45] Innocent III, *De s. alt. mysterio,* V, 15 (PL, 217, 897); a sacramentary of the 12th century from Rome in Ebner, 335. Data from the following period in Sölch, *Hugo,* 97 f.

[46] Sölch, 98.—On the other hand, we hear nothing of the bystanders striking their breast, although their participation in other movements of the priest, as at the gospel, is generally stressed. Is this because even in the Middle Ages the prayer was regarded only as a self-commendation of the priest?

[47] Amalar, *Liber off.,* III, 26, 14 (Hanssens, II, 347 f.).

become and remained an almost universal usage.[48] However, there is no account at all prior to this of such a practice, which would be explained on the assumption that the whole canon was said aloud, and thus the words were already perceptible. But why is it that precisely these words are given special prominence? What passes at present as the reason for emphasizing these words is of no importance.[49] The real and adequate reason must be sought in the circumstances of the past. The survival of the practice is a typical case of the great endurance of liturgical customs even when the basis for them has long since been removed—in fact, when that basis was in existence only a short time.

In the Roman *Ordines* of the seventh century the plan supposed that the subdeacons, who, at the start of the preface, had ranged themselves in a row opposite the celebrant on the other side of the free-standing altar, and who during the canon bowed profoundly, would straighten up at the *Nobis quoque* and go to their assigned places so that they might be ready to assist in the fraction of the bread as soon as the canon was over.[50] This rule, which naturally had no meaning except at the grand pontifical services, was retained even when, at the end of the eighth century, it became customary to recite the canon in a low tone. So, to give the subdeacons the signal when the time came, the celebrant had to say these words in an audible voice: *aperta clamans voce.*[51] This relationship between the two was still to be seen in the Roman *Ordines* at the end of the tenth century.[52] Once admitted, the custom stayed, even though, in accordance with the Romano-Frankish liturgy, the subdeacons usually did not have to change their places till after the closing doxology,[53] and even though later on, in consequence of the introduction of unleavened bread and lastly of the small particles, the fraction became unnecessary and the assistance of the subdeacons superfluous. Its survival was sustained by the allegorical interpretation which saw in it the confession of the centurion beneath the Cross,[54] and thus the practice was transferred not only to the simple high Mass celebrated without assistants, but even to the private Mass.

This also makes it easier to understand the striking of the breast. The

---

[48] Information regarding this practice and other exceptions (the Carthusians, for instance, continued the soft tone for these words too) in Sölch, 96 f.

[49] Eisenhofer, II, 191, considers the words at present as an "admonition to the bystanders to join themselves in sorrow to the prayer of the priest"—an idea that is hardly in keeping with the course and conduct of the canon.—In some places this serves as a signal for the Mass-servers to return from the place where they had been kneeling during the consecration.

[50] *Ordo Rom.,* I, n. 16 (Andrieu, II, 95 f.; PL, 78, 944 f.) ; *Capitulare eccl. ord.* (Andrieu, III, 103 f.).

[51] *Ordo sec. Rom.,* n. 10 (Andrieu, II, 222; PL, 78, 974 B).

[52] *Ordo sec. Rom.,* loc. cit.; cf. Ordo *"In primis"* for the episcopal Mass (Andrieu, II, 334; PL, 78, 988 C).

[53] Amalar, *Liber off.,* III, 26, 19 (Hanssens, II, 349 f.) ; *Ordo "Postquam"* for an episcopal Mass (Andrieu, II, 366; PL, 78, 993 C).

[54] Thus already Amalar, *Liber off.,* III, 26

medieval interpreters since the thirteenth century explicitly cited, along with the centurion's outcry, the statement in Luke 13:48 that all the people went home beating their breasts.[55] And finally this throws light on the puzzling bow of the head at the words just before this, in the conclusion of the *Memento*:[56] this becomes the moment when our Lord bowed His head and died.

18. Concluding Doxologies

The canon closes with two formulas, both of which give the impression of a summary and a conclusion, the second formula quite plainly, since it is a true doxology *(omnis honor et gloria)*, and even the first, with a wording *(hæc omnia)* that suggests a recapitulation. Neither of these formulas are prayers in the usual sense of petition or oblation, as were the foregoing formulas; rather they display the traits of a commendatory statement, a "predication": Thou workest, it is. Thus, even a superficial examination of the first formula reveals the same character of a doxology which is patent in the second. In its wording, however, the first presents a picture of God's gifts streaming down from heaven through Christ's mediatorship, while the second brings into relief how, through Him, all honor and glory surge from creation up to God. The *admirabile commercium* which has just been given reality once again on the altar, thus gains expression in the very words of the canon and gives them their worthy crowning.

If we turn now to study the first of these two formulas, *Per quem hæc omnia*, we are confronted with certain obscurities. We do not see at first glance just where the emphasis is placed. Nor is it clear what idea this word of praise is unravelling, whether the creative work and the blessing of God, or perhaps the activity of Christ (with which the nexus is made to the preceding *Nobis quoque*). In any case, the *Per Christum Dominum nostrum* is seized upon as the opportunity for appraising, in retrospect, the divine grace which has again come and is coming to us in this hour "through Christ." He is the invisible high-priest who has exercised His

---

(Hanssens, II, 344 f.; 347); Bernold of Constance, *Micrologus*, c. 17 (PL, 151, 988 A).—Later the interpretation is made to include the confession of the Good Thief; Durandus, IV, 46, 1; 2.—The position and the change of place of the subdeacons is likewise supported and maintained for a long time by the allegorical interpretation of their role as the pious women who gazed upon the crucified Redeemer until He bowed His head and died,

and who then again sought His body in the tomb (paten for the fraction). This interpretation likewise proposed by Amalar, *loc. cit.*, is still in evidence in John of Avranches, (d. 1079), *De off. eccl.* (PL, 147, 35 f.).

[55] John of Avranches, *loc. cit.* (36). But cf. also Amalar *loc. cit.* (345).—Durandus, IV, 46, 2. Further references in van Dijk (*Eph. liturg.*, 1939), 340, note 294.

[56] Cf. *supra*, p. 247.

office anew and is exercizing it; through Him, God has sanctified these gifts once more and is now ready to distribute them—for reference has already been made to receiving *ex hac altaris participatione*. Now it is our task to examine how these salient ideas, patent as they are, are to be expounded in detail.

In order to make clear the exact meaning of the words, we must first of all note the important fact that in the earlier stage of the Roman canon, and for that matter right on to the late Middle Ages and even after, a blessing of natural products was on occasion inserted in this spot.[1] In the oldest sacramentaries we find a blessing of water, milk and honey on the occasion of solemn Baptism,[2] and a blessing of fresh grapes on the feast of St. Xystus (Aug. 6)[3]; the latter blessing also appears as a formula *ad fruges novas benedicendas*[4] and as *benedictio omnis creaturæ pomorum*,[5] but in particular as a blessing of beans.[6] The "Easter lamb" was also blessed at this point on Easter Sunday.[7] In the declining Middle Ages the blessing of other gifts of nature, which was customary on certain occasions, was sometimes inserted here: the blessing of bread, wine, fruits, and seeds on the feast of St. Blase; of bread on the feast of St. Agatha; of fodder for cattle on St. Stephen's; of wine on the feast of St. John Evangelist.[8]

[1] The practice of a special blessing within the canon seems to have remained restricted to the Roman liturgy. The Egyptian Mass has a recommendation of the gifts offered by the faithful in a similar place, namely within the intercessory prayer, and also a petition for the donors, but no formal blessing of the gifts. Brightman, 129, 170 f., 229.

[2] In the baptismal Mass of Pentecost (likewise to be presupposed for Easter) in the Leonianum (Muratori, I, 318); as *benedictio lactis et mellis* also in the *Pontificale* of Egbert, ed. Greenwell (Surtees Society, 27; Durham, 1853), 129; thus also together with the blessing of meat, eggs, cheese, in a Hungarian Missal of the 11-12th century; Morin, *JL*, 6 (1906), 59, and likewise in a Missal of the 14th century from Zips; Radó, 72.

[3] Gregorianum, ed. Lietzmann, n. 138, 4. The custom of blessing grapes in this place must have insinuated itself early within the Carolingian sphere, since Amalar, *De eccl. off.*, I, 12 (PL, 105, 1013 A), explains the blessing of oil on Maundy Thursday with the words: *In eo loco ubi solemus uvas benedicere*. It is still, e.g., in the Missal of Regensburg of 1485 (Beck, 244). On this day new wine was also used for the consecration, Durandus, VII, 22,

2; or grape juice was actually mixed into the consecrated chalice, an abuse that Berthold of Chiemsee fought against in 1535. Franz, 726. A 14th century Styrian Missal requires the grapes to be placed upon the altar after the consecration and so close to the priest that he can make the sign of the cross over them. Köck, 48; cf. *ibid.*, 2, 47. Numerous peculiarities in France about 1700, in part yet surviving, in de Moléon, Register, p. 560, s. v. "raisin."

[4] The older Gelasianum, III, 63, 88 (Wilson, 107; 294).

[5] Missale of Bobbio (Muratori, II, 959). The text is changed considerably.

[6] On the feast of the Ascension in the older Gelasianum I, 63 (Wilson, 107).

[7] As *benedictio carnis* in the Sacramentary of Rotaldus (10th cent.; PL, 78, 243 D); cf. Missal of Bobbio (Muratori, II, 959); *Pontificale* of Egbert, ed. Greenwell (see note 2 above, 129. Walafried Strabo, *De exord. et increm.*, c. 18 (PL, 114, 938 f.), fought hard against the practice as a judaizing one.

[8] *Sacerdotale Romanum* of Castellani (first published in 1523), in the Venice edition of 1588, p. 158 ff. As Brinktrine, *Die hl. Messe*, 210, n. 1, remarks in reference to the *Rituale Warmiense*, 270, the so-called

To this day the consecration by the bishop of the oil for the sick on Holy Thursday has continued in this location.[9] In all these cases the prayer ends with the mention of Christ's name and then, without any concluding formula of its own, continues with our *Per quem hæc omnia*, which thus plainly forms a unit with the respective prayers of blessing.

The question, therefore, that presses for an answer is, whether the *Per quem hæc omnia* is nothing else than the unchanging conclusion of the more or less variable prayer of blessing, perhaps because the latter was part of the plan of the canon, perhaps because both formulas originally arose as occasional inserts. Recently the question has been answered in the affirmative, particularly by Duchesne,[10] who stresses the point that without such a prayer of blessing there would be a hiatus between our formula and what precedes it in the canon, and moreover that the word *omnia* in particular could hardly be understood simply of the consecrated sacrificial gifts.[11]

A further point in favor of such an opinion is presented in the *Church Order* of Hippolytus of Rome. Here, as we have already seen,[12] mention is made of that custom, then very vigorous and alive, of which the blessing of water, milk, and honey is only a later relic. But in addition, right after the text of the *Eucharistia*, we find a rubric which tells about the blessing of natural products: If someone brings oil, the bishop should pronounce a prayer of thanksgiving similar to that for bread and wine, with the proper changes, and the same if someone brings cheese or olives. For both cases a short prayer-text is offered, to suggest the spiritual meaning of the natural gift, and a Trinitarian doxology is presented to be used for the conclusion.[13] These blessings apparently were independent liturgical creations, having only an extrinsic connection with the Mass. But perhaps they had been attached thus to the Mass even at an early period. At any rate, in the Egyptian Mass they were incorporated into the canon.[14] At

Agatha bread and Agatha water are still to this day blessed at this place in the diocese of Ermland on the feast of St. Agatha. The practice seems to be widespread in Poland; see Thalhofer-Eisenhofer, *Handbuch der katholischen Liturgik*, II (Freiburg, 1912), 191.

[9] Already in the Gelasianum, I, 40 (Wilson, 70) and in the Gregorianum (Lietzmann, n. 77, 4 f.).

[10] Duchesne, *Christian Worship*, 182-183; cf. *Liber pont.*, ed. Duchesne, I, 159.

[11] C. Callewaert, "La finale du Canon de la Messe," *Revue d'histoire ecclés.*, 39 (1943), 5-21, especially p. 7 ff., without being fully convincing, disputes the presence of the hiatus. The *omnia* can be explained by the greater quantity of offer-

tory gifts at the time; with the *hæc* the *jube hæc perferri* was again resumed. The hiatus is narrowed, if we accept the conjecture advanced by J. Brinktrine, "Uber die Herkunft und die Bedeutung des Kanongebetes der römischen Messe 'Per quem hæc omnia," *Eph. liturg.*, 62 (1948), 365-369; he assumes that the formula once followed the *Supplices* immediately.

[12] Above I, 29.

[13] Dix, 10 f.; Hauler, 108.

[14] In the Ethiopian tradition of Hippolytus' Eucharistia, the pertinent rubric with blessing prayer follows immediately upon Hippolytus' concluding doxology, but then is added the conclusion with *Sicut erat* (cf. note 79 below). Brightman, 190; cf. 233, l. 23.

least in this case the same thing happened which (as we saw) occurred everywhere in regard to the intercessory prayers which were placed just before the Sacrifice-Mass and then later were drawn into it. The blessings, too, which followed after the Mass proper were at last brought into the narrower compass of the canon. The same process obviously occurred also in the Roman Mass. This is shown by the remarkable agreement, sometimes word for word, between the basic text in Hippolytus and that in the Latin liturgy of Rome for the blessing of oil,[15] and also for the blessing of grapes, resp., new fruits.[16] They represent a direct continuation of the practice found in Hippolytus.

Therefore, the evolution must actually have been such that first the blessings of produce were inserted before the end of the canon, then later our *Per quem hæc omnia* was developed. The insertion of the blessing took place at this precise point because of the desire to link the ecclesiastical blessings with the great blessing which Christ Himself had instituted and in which He (and God through Him) grants to earthly gifts the highest hallowing and fullness of grace. This interconnection is brought out strikingly by the closing phrase: *Per quem hæc omnia*—the Eucharistic gifts are thus included—*semper bona creas*. By taking up again the antithesis against Gnosticism and Manichæism, our retrospective meditation leads to a statement of praise, proclaiming that the gifts which lie before us, sanctified, are God-created, and that God always has done well in His creative labors, and continues to do so.[17] This He does through the Logos,

---

[15] Hippolytus, *Trad. Ap.* (Dix, 10): *Si quis oleum offert . . . gratias referat dicens: Ut oleum hoc sanctificans das, Deus, sanitatem utentibus et percipientibus, unde unxisti reges, sacerdotes et prophetas, sic . . .* In the blessing of the oil today's Roman Pontifical still reads: *Emitte quæsumus Domine, Spiritum Sanctum . . . ut tua sancta benedictione sit omni hoc unguento cælestis medicinæ peruncto tutamen . . . unde unxisti sacerdotes, reges, prophetas et martyres . . . in nomine Domini nostri Jesu Christi. Per quem.* The prayer also in the older Gelasianum, I, 40 (Wilson, 70) and in the Gregorianum (Lietzmann, n. 77, 5): —Regarding the way this prayer has been preserved cf. Jungmann, "Beobachtungen zum Fortleben von Hippolyts Apostolischer Uberlieferung": *ZkTh,* 53 (1929), 583-585.

[16] Near the end of the work, Hippolytus offers still another complete formula for thanksgiving he demands for fruits; it begins (Dix, 54): *Gratias tibi agimus, Deus, et offerimus tibi primitivas fructuum quos*

dedisti nobis ad percipiendum . . . The blessing of the grapes in the Gregorianum (Lietzmann, n. 138, 4) reads: *Benedic Domine et hos fructus novos uvæ* (in the Bobbio Missal: *et hos fructus novos ill.*) *quos tu Domine . . . ad maturitatem perducere dignatus es et dedisti ea ad usus nostros cum gratiarum actione percipere in nomine Domini nostri Jesu Christi. Per quem.*

[17] As against the usual rendering of *hæc bona* by "these goods," Rütten, "Philologisches zum Canon missæ" (*StZ*, 1938, I), 47, rightly emphasizes the words, "God has created these (gifts) as good." An elaborated version in the Mozarabic *Missale mixtum* (PL, 85, 554 A) confirms this: *quia tu hæc omnia nobis indignis servis tuis valde bona creas, sanctificas . . .* Cf. also Callewaert, *La finale,* 10 f. Augustine, *De civ. Dei,* XV, 22 (CSEL, 40, 2, p. 108) cites from a *laus cerei* which he himself had composed the words: *Hæc tua sunt, bona sunt, quia tu bonus ista creasti.*— However, the opposite conception must also have been combined with the text at an

through whom all things came into being,[18] and through Him who Himself became man and a member of our earthly cosmos, He also hallows all things. The Incarnation itself was the grand consecration of creation.[19] But a new wave of blessing pours out over creation whenever the Church makes use of the power of sanctification granted her by her founder. The words *vivificas*[20] and *benedicis* are probably thought of only as re-enforcing the *sanctificas*. Sanctification is a herald of that new and everlasting life in which earthly creation has a share; indeed, the consecration of bread and wine has filled these figures, these species, with the noblest, the highest life.[21] Lastly, the word *benedicis* receives the cardinal stress. It was a blessing that was inserted, and this word makes the tie-in with it. In the chief formulas this blessing takes the following shape: *Benedic et has tuas creaturas fontis . . .*[22] *Benedic Domine et hos fructus novos . . .*[23] In other words the preceding activity, the completion of the *Eucharistia*, was also such a blessing, only of an incomparably higher kind. Already in the *Te igitur* the petition had been made *uti accepta habeas et benedicas*, just as we find it in the *Quam oblationem* and not seldom even anticipated in the *Oratio super oblata*.[24] The finale is presented by the words *præstas nobis*,[25] with the suggestion that every hallowing and blessing which proceeds from Christ has but one aim, namely, to enrich us. Communion, for which we are now preparing ourselves, is only the most wondrous example of this.

So we see that the words of the *Per quem hæc omnia* got their full meaning in connection with the preceding prayer of blessing, and that they

---

early date; cf. the Post-Secreta formula of the *Missale Gothicum* (Muratori, II, 534; note 25 below), in which the *bona* is missing.

[18] John 1: 3; Hebr. 1: 2; 2: 10. The formulation that relates the creation to Christ, more plainly according to Col. 1: 16 f. Cf. Callewaert, 9 f.

[19] Cf. *Martyrologium* for Christmas Eve: *Mundum volens adventu suo piissimo consecrare*. The idea is already found in another form in I Cor. 8: 6; Col. I: 15 f.

[20] As Sicard of Cremona, *Mitrale*, III, 6 (PL, 213, 133 f.), reports, some priests inserted *mirificas* after the word *vivificas*.

[21] Cf. the expression *panem sanctum vitæ æternæ* in an earlier passage. In the Mozarabic Post-Pridie formularies the consecration is described as a restoration to life: *vivificet ea Spiritus tuus Sanctus*. *Missale mixtum* (PL, 85, 605 A; cf. 205 A, 277 D).

[22] Muratori, I, 318.

[23] *Supra*, note 16. Notice the word *et* in these phrases: "Bless *also . . .*"

[24] Cf. P. Alfonso, *L'Eucologia romana antica* (Subiaco, 1931), 83. It is therefore purely arbitrary to try to conclude from this *et* that a Roman epiklesis formerly preceded and then was omitted, one that must have begun with *Benedic Domine has creaturas panis et vini*. Thus R. Buchwald, *Die Epiklese in der römischen Messe* (Weidenaur Studien I, special printing, Vienna, 1907), 31.

[25] The Mass of Milan on Maundy Thursday has here as well as in the following final doxology of the canon a notable variant: *benedicis et nobis famulis tuis largiter præstas ad augmentum fidei et remissionem omnium peccatorum nostrorum*. *Missale Ambrosianum* (1902), 154. Cf. Muratori, I, 134. A Post-Secreta formula of the Gothic Missal (Muratori, II, 534) concludes with the following variation of the Roman text: . . . *Unigeniti tui, per quem omnia creas, creata benedicis, benedicta sanctificas et sanctificata largiris, Deus*.

obviously owe to it their origin in the form we have at present. On the other hand, taking into consideration what we have said so often, that because of the consecrated gifts the connection with earthly creation is never lost sight of, we could still leave the words in the text of the canon even without any such blessing preceding them,[26] regarding them merely as a glorification of our Redeemer. In this case, however, the word *omnia* would lose some of its significance, since only the species of bread and wine are before us. The words are the counterpart of the plea for the consecration in the *Quam oblationem;* they are a thanksgiving for the consecration, a "thank you" to God and to our high-priest through whom He does all and through whom He grants all.[27] They are a doxological acknowledgment that every grace comes to us through Christ, and thus they form a preliminary to the greater doxology that follows, wherein we acknowledge further that all praise and glory return to God through Christ our Lord.

It is an old rule of public prayer that such a prayer should close with praise of God and thus revert to the grand function of all prayer, in which the creature bows before his Creator. Even the prayers in the *Didache* have this structure, and in oriental liturgies there is scarcely one prayer of the priest to be found which does not end in a solemn doxology: "For Thou art a kind and loving God and we offer up praise to Thee, the Father and the Son and the Holy Ghost, now and always and unto all eternity"—thus we read in the Byzantine liturgy. In the Roman liturgy, as in the rest of Christendom, this has been the rule for a long time in regard to the Psalms, where the *Gloria Patri* regularly forms the final verse. The closing formula of the priestly prayer, on the contrary, is somewhat less rigid in construction, bringing the mediatorship of our Redeemer to the fore usually in such a way that a doxological reference to His eternal dominion is worked into the formula. Only the main prayer of all liturgy, the Great Prayer of the Mass, has retained a formula of praise in the Roman style, a formula where simplicity and grandeur are combined most felicitously. The present form is that already found in the earliest tradition of the canon. An indication of its antique structure is the fact

---

[26] The meaning of canon 23 of the Council of Hippo (cf. above, p. 10) is probably that at such a blessing of the gifts a clear line of demarcation was to be made from the Eucharistic offerings; cf. Botte, 49; 69. The gifts concerned were presented at the offertory procession. In regard to the one exception granted by this canon of Hippo— honey and milk at the Easter Mass—the canon mentions an *offerri* that actually occurs *in altari*, whereas in Rome special tables were prepared for the oblations of the people. The line of separation was then secured by providing a special blessing for the gifts.

[27] It is probably not necessary to follow C. Ruch (*Cours et Conférences,* VII [Louvain, 1929], 93) in supposing a new interpretation of the word *creas* after the dissociation of the formula from the prayer of blessing, i.e., inasfar as the act of consecration results in a kind of creation. For the word *omnia*, even after such a new interpretation, still retains a certain inflexibility.

that it not only includes a praise of God, but insists that this praise is offered through Christ, a turn of thought which was lost in most of the oriental liturgies in consequence of the Arian turmoil, lost not only in this passage, but generally in all prayer-endings.[28]

As a matter of fact, the closing doxology of the Roman canon is closely akin to that which marks the end of the *Eucharistia* in Hippolytus. The connection is made apparent by setting the two side by side (with a slight transposition in the present text of the canon).

Per ipsum et cum ipso et in ipso	*Per quem*
est tibi	*tibi*
omnis honor et gloria	*gloria et honor*
Deo Patri omnipotenti	*Patri et Filio cum Sancto Spiritu*
in unitate Spiritus Sancti	*in sancta Ecclesia tua*
per omnia sæcula sæculorum.	*et nunc et in sæcula sæculorum.*[29]

The chief difference is that the Trinitarian names, which in Hippolytus are grouped together in the address, in our present canon, in accordance with the Christian economy of salvation, are fitted stepwise into the very structure of the encomium itself. The "unity of the Holy Ghost" in the modern Mass is only another way of saying the "holy Church," as in the Hippolytan text. The Church is brought to unity and communion in the Holy Ghost: *Sancto Spiritu congregata,*[30] and is sanctified by His indwelling. She *is* the unity of the Holy Ghost.[31] From her arises all honor and glory to God the Father almighty.[32] And it arises "through Him," for Christ is the Head of redeemed mankind, yea, of all creation, which is summed up in Him (Eph. 1: 10). He is her high-priest, standing before the Father. Therefore, *per ipsum* is more clearly defined by *cum ipso* and *in ipso*. He is not standing before His Father as a lone petitioner, as He had been during His earthly pilgrimage when He spent quiet nights on the mountain praying alone; now His redeemed are around Him. They have learnt how they can, with Him, praise the Father who is in heaven. In truth they are in Him, taken up into the living union of His Body and therefore drawn into the fervent glow of His prayer, so that they are really

[28] Cf. Jungmann, *Die Stellung Christi im liturgischen Gebet,* especially p. 151 ff.
[29] Above I, 29. A remarkable expansion of the Roman version is presented by the Milan form of the concluding doxology of the canon (Kennedy, 53; Botte, 46, unaccountably omits it): *Et est tibi Deo Patri omnipotenti ex ipso et per ipsum et in ipso omnis honor virtus laus gloria imperium perpetuitas et potestas in unitate Spiritus Sancti per infinita sæcula sæculorum.*
[30] Oration on the Friday of Pentecost week.
[31] In contrast to the concluding formula of

the oration where the *unitas Spiritus Sancti* is limited by its association to the Church in heaven (above I, 383), the idea here attains its full breadth inasmuch as it embraces the Church on earth and in heaven. Cf. J. Pascher, *Eucharistia* (Münster, 1947) 146-152. To the objections raised by Botte, "In unitate Spiritus Sancti," *La Maison-Dieu,* 23 (1950, IV) 49-53, see my reply *ZkTh,* 72 (1950), 481-486.
[32] Cf. Eph. 3: 21. See the further development of the idea in the chapter, "In der Einheit des Heiligen Geistes" in Jungmann, *Gewordene Liturgie,* 190-205.

in a position to worship the Father "in spirit and in truth." *In ipso* and *in unitate Spiritus Sancti* therefore designate one and the same all-encompassing well-spring, whence arises the glorification of the Father, in one case viewed in relation to Christ, whose Mystic Body the redeemed form, in the other case viewed in relation to the Spirit, whose breath inspires them.[33]

It is not by chance that this encomium stands at the end of the Eucharistic prayer, nor is it by chance that it has the indicative form *(est)* instead of the subjunctive or "wishing" form.[34] Here, where the Church is gathered, right in front of the altar on which the Sacrament reposes, gathered indeed to offer the Body and Blood of Christ in reverence—here God does actually receive all honor and glory. In this moment the word of Malachias (1:11) is fulfilled: The name of the Lord is great among the peoples.

This connection is represented also in the rite. The priest grasps the chalice and Host and lifts them aloft. This is the so-called "little elevation" —little not because it is of less importance or because it is the remnant of a larger one, but because it does not, like its younger sister, the "big elevation," consist in showing the holy gifts to the people, but only in raising them up to God as an oblation.[35] By its very nature this elevation can be a symbolic one, as we have already found on various other occasions,[36] even though at the same time it must always be a visible one.

At present, this elevation occurs only during the words *omnis honor et gloria*. Here we have a certain contraction. Its history is a long one.

---

[33] Jungmann, *Die Stellung Christi*, 178-182. I would not wish to uphold the attempt made there, 181 f., to interpret the Milanese *ex ipso et per ipsum et in ipso* (note 29 above) as equivalent in meaning to the Roman version, since the Milan form is obviously secondary. In it the *cum ipso* has been lost. Regarded from the standpoint of the history of the doxologies, the explanation of the Roman concluding doxology as it is presented by Eisenhofer, II, 193, and similarly by Brinktrine, 211 f., is impossible; according to this exposition the *cum ipso* unites Father and Son and the *in ipso* should be understood to pertain to the Trinitarian perichoresis. While the *cum ipso* could indeed in and by itself unite not only the redeemed world with Christ, but just as well, as happens in the oriental doxologies, unite Father and Son, the sense of the *in ipso* (and consequently, by its association, the sense also of the *cum ipso*) is absolutely unequivocal, as is seen

by the comparison with the Milanese version and also with Eph. 3: 21. Besides, such an explanation falls to pieces when we consider that *in unitate Spiritus Sancti* implies more than *cum Spiritu Sancto,* therefore cannot signify a mere association of the Holy Ghost in receipt of glorification; cf. above I, 383, n. 37.

[34] Cf. above I, 328, n. 41; 351.

[35] Amalar, *Liber off.*, III, 26, 18 (Hanssens, II, 349) paraphrases the meaning of the rite that immediately follows the doxology: *Hoc ipsum volendo tibi omni nisu monstrare tota fide me ita tenere, elevo præsentia munera ad te.* The Cod. Ratoldi of the Gregorianum (10th cent.) says of the deacon: *sublevans calicem in conspectu Domini* (PL, 78, 244 A). Regarding the oblatory character of the rite cf. also Andrieu, *Les Ordines*, II, 147, who even derives from this the name *offertorium* for the cloth used by the deacon in this rite.

[36] Above I, 21, n. 63; II, 42, n. 4.

It is in the seventh-century liturgy of the city of Rome that we first find the original and full form of the rite in unimpaired clarity.[37] The assisting archdeacon, who at *Per quem hæc omnia* had raised himself erect from his bowed position, at the words *Per ipsum,*[38] with hands covered with a linen cloth, grasps the chalice,[39] and raises it up while the pope at the same time picks up the bread, that is, the two consecrated breads from his own oblation, and raises them to the height of the chalice brim, and while touching the latter with them, finishes the doxology.[40] But gradually the rite was obscured and interrupted by the intrusion of the sign of the Cross which gradually grew more prominent. At first, and until the eleventh century, only the three signs of the Cross are mentioned, those made over Host and chalice at the words *sanctificas, vivificas, benedicis,*[41] which do not yet disturb the procedure at the doxology. But then appear, here and there, the crosses made with the Host at *Per ipsum et cum ipso et in ipso,* and these became a more general practice after the year 1000. In the beginning, there were but two,[42] later on regularly three as now-

---

[37] In the life of the Gaulish Bp. Evurtius of Orleans (4th cent.) we find a report somewhat less clear in meaning, but which probably has some pertinence here : *in hora confractionis panis cœlestis, cum de more sacerdotali hostiam elevatis manibus tertio Deo benedicendum offerret, super caput eius velut nubes splendida apparuit.* F. Cabrol, "Elevation": DACL, IV, 2662, 2666. On the contrary, the elevation of the sacred species, as was done for ages in the oriental liturgy in conjunction with the call Τὰ ἅγια τοῖς ἁγίοις has no relationship here, as its entire sense discloses, despite Baumstark, *Liturgie comparée,* 147, since it is not directed as a doxology and offering to God, but as an invitation to the people for Holy Communion. It is evident, of course, that nothing in this is altered by the fact that in the later Middle Ages our Western rite was here and there, in passing, given a similar interpretation; see below, p. 291; closer is the relationship with the ὕψωσις τῆς παναγίας, to which Brinktrine, *Die hl. Messe,* 216, n. 1 refers.

[38] According to the *Ordo "Qualiter quædam"* (Andrieu, II, 302; PL, 78, 983 f.) the archdeacon raises the chalice already at the *Per quem hæc omnia* and, in fact, *contra domnum papam,* that is, he has his position on the opposite side of the open altar.

[39] Other Mass arrangements have the deacon wash his hands and then take hold of the chalice without a cloth; Durandus, IV, 44, 5. Cf. above, p. 77 f.

[40] *Ordo Rom.* I, n. 16 (Andrieu, II, 96, PL, 78, 945 A) : *Cum dixerit 'Per ipsum et cum ipso' levat [archidiaconus] cum offertorio calicem per ansas et tenens exaltat* [Stapper : *tenet exaltans*] *illum juxta pontificem. Pontifex autem tangit a latere calicem cum oblatis dicens, 'Per ipsum et cum ipso' usque 'Per omnia sæcula sæculorum. Amen.'* The same prescriptions, but in different words in the *Capitulare Eccl. ord.* (Andrieu, III, 104), whose later recension (*ibid.,* III, 182) says of the elevation of the chalice : *sublevans eum modice.* The two hosts (c. above, p. 7) are expressly mentioned in the *Ordo "Qualiter quædam"* (Andrieu, II, 302; PL, 78, 984 B) : *Hic levat domnus papa oblatas duas usque ad oram calicis et tangens eum . . .*

[41] *Ordo "Qualiter quædam"* (Andrieu, II, 302; PL, 18, 983 f.). The deacon, at the words, already holds the chalice elevated. —Brinktrine, *Die hl. Messe,* 300, names a number of Sacramentary MSS. that mention these signs of the cross. Further examples without the sign of the cross at the *Per ipsum* until into the 11th century in Leroquais, I, 62; 71; 97; 118; 123, also in a Sacramentary of the 11th century; *ibid.,* I, 209.

[42] Amalar, *Liber off.,* III, 26, 10 (Hanssens, II, 346), mentions altogether only

adays.[43] Finally, since the eleventh century, a fourth appears, and not much later a fifth came into general use, those, namely, which now are tied in with the words *Deo Patri* and *in unitate Spiritus Sancti.*[44]

While the meaning of the crosses that accompany the words of blessing is clear—they are not, of course, an exercise of the power of blessing, but they do illustrate the statement contained in *sanctificas, vivificas* and *benedicis*—there is no directly convincing explanation of those which are joined to the doxology, not even in the sphere of their origin. The circumstances do, to some small degree, explain the triple cross made at the thrice-repeated *ipse;* here we probably have a strengthening and stylizing of the demonstrative or "pointing" gesture which is inherent in the elevation itself, and thus receives added stress at the word *ipse.*[45]

More obscure, however, is the origin of the last crosses. They go back to certain symbolic considerations. Obviously, the starting point hinged on the old rubric which enjoined that the priest was to touch with the Host the chalice lifted by the deacon: *tangit a latere calicem.*[46] This puzzling action of touching the chalice with the Host, originally intended, no doubt, to express the connection between the two species, invited further elaborations. The chalice was touched in all four directions.[47] The resulting sign of the Cross signified that the Crucified is desirous of drawing mankind to Himself from all the four winds.[48] If we add this fourth cross to the three made at *Per ipsum,* we again have the number four— another representation of the four corners of the earth. This system of

these two signs of the cross, made *juxta calicem,* but does note the preceding three. In other cases these three are added to the other two: *Ordo sec. Rom.,* n. 10 (Andrieu, II, 222; PL, 78, 974 B); likewise in the Sacramentary of Angoulême (about 800) and in isolated later MSS.; see Brinktrine, *loc. cit. Ibid.,* 214, the supposition that the reason for this dual number was the number of hosts; see below, note 53. Amalar, *loc. cit.,* adduces only one symbolical reason; because Christ died for the Jews and the Gentiles.

[43] Brinktrine, 330. Examples of these three (without any other) signs of the cross in Leroquais, I, 84; 86; 96; 100; 103; 108; 120. In the rite of the Carthusians according to the *Statuta antiqua* (before 1259): Martène, 1, 4, XXV (I, 634 A), the host remains above the chalice during the following words until the *Per omnia,* when both chalice and host are elevated.

[44] Examples in Brinktrine, 330 f.; Sölch, Hugo, 99 f.

[45] Cf. above, p. 145 f. However the beginning of this twofold sign of the cross remains obscure. Perhaps they, too, were intended as an extension of the three signs of the cross at the *sanctificas* into a fivefold sign.

[46] *Supra,* n. 40. *Ordo sec. Rom.,* n. 10 (Andrieu, II, 222; PL. 78, 974): *tangit e latere calicem cum oblatis duas faciens cruces.*

[47] John of Avranches (d. 1079), *De off. eccl.* (PL, 147, 36 B): *Sacerdos 'Per ipsum' dicendo oblata quattuor partes calicis tangat.*

[48] Ivo of Chartres (d. 1116) *Eph.* 231 (PL, 162, 234): *quod vero cum hostia iam consecrata intra vel supra calicem signum crucis imprimitur a latere calicis orientali usque ad occidentale et a septentrionali usque ad australe, hoc figurari intelligimus, quod ante passionem Dominus discipulis suis prædixit: Cum exaltatus fuero a terra, omnia traham ad meipsum.*

four crosses was certainly widespread until the Missal of Pius V.[49] In the thirteenth century a four-part sentence from Augustine on God's infinity was linked with the ceremony [50] and given some circulation; in its turn, this had an influence on the rite of the four crosses.[51] In accord with the catch-words: *Deus infra omnia non depressus*, at least the fourth cross had to be made at the base of the chalice.

The rubric of touching the chalice is also the starting-point for a second explanation, which in turn led to the five crosses. The rubric enjoined touching the chalice *a latere*. At a time which was able to discover everywhere reminiscences of the Passion of Christ, particularly near the close of the canon, this phrase, *a latere*, must have been a reminder of the wound in our Lord's side, and consequently of the five wounds.[52] To complete the representation of the five wounds, two more crosses had to be added to the three already in use.[53] These two complementary crosses appear in the manuscripts since the end of the eleventh century.[54] It is

---

[49] Brinktrine, 301 (with n. 2), mentions for this MSS. of the 11-14th centuries. The fourth sign of the cross appears sometimes at the *Deo Patri*, sometimes at the *in unitate*. The number four also among the Cistercians of the 12th century and in the older Dominican rite; see Sölch, *Hugo*, 99 f., where a further reference is made to the *Ordinarium* of Coutances (not Constance) of 1577 (Legg, *Tracts*, 64).

[50] Hugo of S. Cher cites it as a reason for his localizing of the signs of the cross (see next note), in the form: *Deus est extra omnia non exclusus . . . super omnia non elatus . . . intra omnia non inclusus . . . infra omnia non depressus;* Sölch, 101 f. In a somewhat different version in William of Meltona, "Opusc. super missam," ed. van Dijk (*Eph. liturg.*, 1939), 341 f.; further citations and references to sources in Augustine, *De Gen. ad lit.*, 8, 26 (PL, 34, 391 f.); cf. *Ep.* 187, 4, 14, (PL, 33, 837). Here, then, we have very free renderings, or rather recastings of the words used by Augustine.

[51] In the older Dominican rite three or four signs of the cross are made over the chalice, each one somewhat lower than the preceding one, the third one within the chalice and the fourth in front of the chalice; Sölch, 100. This localization was still retained in the later Dominican rite (since 1256) when a fifth sign of the cross was added, one that was made at the foot of the chalice; Sölch, 101. The same rite in the

Liber ordinarius of Liége; Volk, 95. The first three signs of the cross made at different elevations were later referred to Christ, who was first elevated upon the cross, then was taken down, and finally placed in the tomb. Thus M. deCavaleriis, *Statera sacra missam iuxta ritum O.P. . . expendens* (Naples, 1686), 408, sees in this a glorification of Christ that compensates for the omission of the *elevatio;* Sölch, 106; cf. also Verwilst, 30 f. Elsewhere three signs of the cross were made at the same height over the chalice; Sölch, 100.

[52] Cf. *supra* I, 109, 32; et al.

[53] Where the three signs of the cross at the *Per ipsum* did not come into use, those at the *sanctificas*, etc., could be adduced. Probably this explains the twofold sign of the cross at the *Per ipsum*, of which there is frequent notice (note 42 above).

[54] The earliest certain example is the Cod. 614 of the Bibliotheca Casanatensis (11-12th cent.) : *Hic faciat duas cruces in latere calicis cum oblata tangens illum.* Ebner, 330. These signs of the cross are found more frequently in the 13th century; Brinktrine, 301. Perhaps, too, we should cite here Bernardus, *Ordo Clun.*, I, 72, which appeared about 1068 (Herrgott, 265, 1. 13 : *duas cruces imprimit,* instead of *dum crucem imprimit*). Noteworthy is the Pontifical of Christian of Mainz (about 1170) : Martène, 1, 4, XVII (I, 602 A) : three signs of the cross at different eleva-

precisely in this period that we come upon explicit witnesses to the explanation about the five wounds, and we hear of differences of opinion as to the manner of executing the last sign of the Cross in order to represent the wound in the side more closely.[55] Since, according to a widespread custom, the chalice stood to the right of the Host, there was a double reason for making at least the last cross at the side of the chalice.[56] Thus it was kept until finally the law of symmetry won the upper hand over the symbolism.

However, as early as the twelfth century, there arose still another explanation of the system of the five crosses.[57] In harmony with this, we find a corresponding change in form, in which the size of the crosses played a role.[58] In the course of this change the last two crosses(of which especially the latter had not been definitely placed in position) received not only their exact placement, but also their proper connection with the text. For it is clear from what we have said that at first no precise relation to the text was looked for.[59] But now this was remedied, even though

tions over the chalice, *alias duas in labro calicis dicens: Per ipsum . . . Spiritus Sancti. Hic tangat calicem cum hostia ad dexteram partem.*

[55] Bernold of Constance (d. 1100), *Micrologus,* c. 17 (PL, 151, 988 A) : *Postea cum corpore dominico quattuor cruces super calicem facimus dicendo: 'Per ipsum et cum ipso et in ipso,' et quintam in latere calicis, videlicet iterum vulnus Domini[ci] lateris significando.* The fact that the signs of the cross number five is an established matter with Bernold. He then continues disparagingly: *Multi tamen tres tantum cruces super calicem et duas in latere eius faciunt;* that it is incorrect; since Christ had only one wound in His side; besides Pope Gregory (VII, d. 1085), as he knew for certain, advocated the first method.

[56] Nevertheless the *Liber ordinarius O. Præm.* (12th cent.) gives a *quintam ante oram calicis;* Lefèvre, 12 ; Waefelghem, 80.

[57] Richard of Weddinghausen, O. Præm., *De canone mystici libaminis,* c. 8 (PL, 177, 465 f.) : the first sign of the cross signifies the eternity of the Son together with the Father, the second the equality, and the third the essential unity, the fourth the same *modus existendi,* the fifth the unity of the Holy Ghost with the Father and the Son. Regarding the question of authorship cf. Franz, 418 f.

[58] Richard of Weddinghausen, *loc. cit.,*

(466 A) : *Prima quidem crux ex utraque parte ultra calicem protenditur. Secunda calici cœquatur. Tertia infra calicem coarctatur. Quarta eadem est ac prima. Quinta ante calicem depingitur.* This rule, moreover, which the *Liber ordinarius O. Præm.* (last note but one) has not as yet heard of, became standard in England; Missale of Sarum, Legg, *Tracts,* 13 ; 225 ; 263 f.; Martène, 1, 4, XXXV (I, 669 B) ; cf. Maskell, 152 f. So in Sweden, Missal of Upsala, 1513 : Yelverton, 19. With a more exacting version of the rubric in the Missal D of Pressburg (15th cent.) : Jávor, 117. This arrangement of the signs of the cross still holds good in the rite of the Carmelites : *Missale O. Carm.* (1935), 311.

[59] This is clearly apparent in the Mass-*ordo* of the papal chapel about 1290, ed. Brinktrine (*Eph. Liturg.,* 1937), 206, where it merely says: *Hic cum ipsa hostia bis inter se et calicem signet,* without marking the usual sign of the cross in the text. The same thing occurs in the Sarum Ordinary of the 11th century (Legg, *Tracts,* 13), where a rubric before the *Per ipsum* gives only the direction for the five signs of the cross that follow without inserting in the text the signs generally used. In the somewhat later Sarum Missal in Martène, 1, 4, XXXV (I, 669) the signs of the cross are marked in the place where they are usually set at present. Robert Paululus (d. about 1184), *De Cæremoniis,* II, 37 (PL,

in other ways the theologico-trinitarian explanation did not become universal.[60] Thus, just as the three crosses were made at the mention of the Son in the word *ipse,* now the last two crosses were joined to the mention of the Father and the Holy Ghost.

All that we have said so far forces the conclusion that in the later Middle Ages the old rite which accompanied the closing doxology, a simple rite indeed, had been overwhelmed by this luxuriant growth of crosses.[61] There is some consolation in the fact that the number of crosses, now increased to five, in the last analysis serves to emphasize the naming of Christ *(ipse)* all the more by a reference to the mystery of the Cross in which finally "all honor and glory" mounts to God.

In the Middle Ages, however, the rite which originally accompanied the doxology was often entirely absorbed by the signs of the Cross.[62] Or else it was turned into a demonstrative rite[63] which then in many cases was ejected from its original position (for example, we will meet the old ceremony again at the *Pater noster*). When there was no deacon to help along, the elevation of the chalice had to be postponed until after the celebrant was through with the signs of the Cross, that is, until the closing words of the doxology. And soon even at high Mass the assistance of the deacon shrank into insignificance, until at last[64] he did no more than sup-

177, 434), connects the last two signs with the Father and the Holy Ghost and views this as the reason why these signs have to be made outside the chalice.

[60] Along with it the interpretations indicated earlier remained in force, as well as others, e.g., a reference to the Passion, as advocated by Innocent III, *De s. alt. mysterio,* V, 7 (PL, 217, 894) : the first two times the threefold sign of the cross is used to signify the crucifixion by the Jews and the heathens, the last two crosses indicate the separation of the soul from the body.

[61] At the time, we might add, not only was an excessive importance attached to the signs of the cross and their prescribed symbolical distribution, but the movements with the host were sometimes even increased, so that circular motions were added. One of those who battled this abuse was Louis Ciconiolanus in a special chapter of his *Directorium divinorum officiorum* that appeared at Rome in 1539 (Legg, *Tracts,* 210). But even Henry of Hessen (d. 1397) in his *Secreta Sacerdotum* raises his voice against those priests who made *cruces longas,* so that the people might see them, as well as against the prac-

tice of elevating the host at *omnis honor et gloria* as high as they do at the consecration. The ceremony in England was therefore called a "second sakering." The English Reformers gibed at the "dancing God" of the Roman Mass; see the excursus in Legg, *Tracts,* 263 f.

[62] The Dominican rite no longer had this elevation since the middle of the 13th century. It is likewise missing in the rite of Sarum; Sölch, *Hugo,* 105; Legg, *Tracts,* 225, 262-264; Legg, *The Sarum Missal,* 224. Cf. also Volk, 95.

[63] Cf. note 61 above.

[64] Among the earliest witnesses to this manner of acting is John of Avranches (d. 1079), *De off. eccl.* (PL, 147, 36 B) : *uterque calicem levent et simul ponant.* On the other hand, according to the first appendix to *Ordo Rom.* I (Andrieu, II, 115; PL, 78, 948), the elevation of the chalice is already entirely discontinued in the case where the Pope himself does not celebrate; cf. Ordo of St. Armand (Andrieu, II, 169, 1. 14). Especially stressed was the setting down of the chalice by both together, because it was regarded as a representation of the taking down from the cross by Joseph of Arimathea and Nico-

port the celebrant's arm or concur in touching the foot of the chalice.[65] And on the other hand, this service of the deacon, in accordance with court etiquette, was finished off with a kiss on the celebrant's shoulder.[66]

Later, however, this mark of subservience was allowed to disappear.[67] So even in the eleventh century, when the present full number of crosses first appears, the rule was that the priest lifted the chalice only when he said the words *Per omnia sæcula sæculorum.*[68] This was the prevailing practice during the height of the Middle Ages, was adopted by the old monastic liturgies,[69] and did not cease till the Missal of Pius V. The advantage of this practice was that the rite of elevation was joined to the final words of the canon, the words spoken aloud, and immediately answered by the time-honored *Amen*, so that it retained its importance and made a clear impression on one's consciousness. It was only later that the present method appeared, which joined the elevation with the words *omnis honor et gloria,* and the final words *Per omnia sæcula sæculorum* were not spoken till the chalice and Host had been replaced in their proper position.[70] This practice did not become general in Rome till the fifteenth century.[71] Through it, the elevation of the gifts marked the very climax of the doxology. But there was certainly a double disadvantage in the fact that the final words were not joined to the rite, but were separated from it—by the action of replacing the chalice and Host,[72] as well

demus; Hugo of St. Cher, *Tract. super missam* (ed. Sölch, 45) ; Sölch, *Hugo,* 106.

[65] Ritual of Soissons: Martène, 1, 4, XXII (I, 612 C).

[66] The shoulder kiss appears, as far as I am aware, for the first time in the Pontifical of the Beneventan Cod. Casanat. 614 (11-12th cent.; Ebner, 330), in which different signs point to a Norman origin; here the kiss is still added after the deacon himself has elevated the host. It is further verified among others in the *Ordo eccl. Lateran.* (Fischer, 85) ; in Sicard of Cremona, *Mitrale,* III, 6 (PL, 213, 134 C) ; in Innocent III, *De s. alt. mysterio,* V, 13 (PL, 217, 895) ; in Hugo of S. Cher *(loc. cit.).* In some churches this shoulder kiss was given both before and after the deacon rendered assistance; it was partly customary at the presentation of the paten to the celebrant that followed, where today a kissing of the hand is prescribed. Sölch, 107-109. There is an isolated instance in the *Ordinarium* of Chalon: Martène, 1, 4, XXIX (I, 647 C), where a kissing of the altar was joined with the kissing of the shoulder.

[67] The uncovering and recovering of the chalice by the deacon, as it continues to this day, became his function in the *Ordo eccl. Lateran.* (about 1140; Fischer, 85) ; cf. also *Ordinarium* of Bayeux (13-14th cent.) : Martène, 1, 4, XXIV (I, 629 C), where it is a matter of folding back the corporal.

[68] Bernardus, *Ordo Clun.,* I, 72 (Herrgott, 265) ; Bernold of Constance, *Micrologus,* c. 17, 23 (PL, 151, 988 B, 994 D) ; likewise about 1140 in the Ordo of the Lateran basilica (Fischer, 85).

[69] References in Sölch, 104. So also in the 16th edition of the Roman Missal up to that of Venice, 1563; see Lebrun, I, 467, n. c.

[70] Stephan of Bauge (d. 1136), *De sacr. altaris,* c. 17 (PL, 172, 1301), is the earliest witness. Further proofs in Sölch, 104.

[71] Through John Burchard; see Legg, *Tracts,* 159 f. Cf. P. Salmon, "Les 'Amens' du canon de la messe," (*Eph. liturg.,* 1928), 501 f., 506.

[72] So, e.g., clearly in the Ordo of Card. Stefaneschi (about 1311), n. 53 (PL, 78, 1167 C).

as by the genuflection, added since the fifteenth-sixteenth century.[73] First of all, the elevation was once more overshadowed. And secondly, the detached words *Per omnia sæcula sæculorum*, which by the prominence given them should signalize the conclusion of the canon, now appear to be joined to the *Oremus* that introduces the *Pater noster* as though they were an inaugural piece.[74] In some localities, e.g., in France, it was customary to signalize the *omnis honor et gloria* along with its accompanying rite by ringing the altar bell.[75] The altar missal, prepared by the Abbey of Maria Laach in 1931, has sought to recapture some of its original importance for the whole closing doxology by artistic designing, and particularly by the size of its lettering.

The importance of these words is shared also by the *Amen* in which, according to age-old custom, all the people now join to affirm and corroborate what had been said and done. We have already seen[76] what significance was attached to this *Amen* in ancient times. In the third century we hear a voice enumerating in one breath the several privileges of the people: to listen to the eucharistic prayer, to join in answering *Amen*, to stand at the table and stretch out their hands for the reception of the sacred food.[77] This *Amen* is the people's signature.[78] It was to permit the *Amen* to be shouted aloud that, even in Carolingian times, these final words were not included in the silence which prevailed throughout the rest of the canon.[79]

---

[73] It is still missing, e.g., in the *Ordinarium* of Coutances of 1557 (Legg, *Tracts,* 64.

[74] In point of fact, priests have in all seriousness asked me the question, where does this *Per omna sæcula sæculorum* belong. The difficulty would be solved if the genuflection were placed after the conclusion of the doxology. This suggestion was also made by M. Del Alamo, "La conclusion actual del Canon de la Misa," *Miscellanea Mohlberg,* II, (1949), 107-113.

[75] J. Kreps, "La doxologie du canon," *Cours et Conférences,* VII (Louvain, 1929), 223-230, especially p. 230, with a reference to an affirmative statement of the Congregation of Rites, May 14, 1856.— Lebrun, I, 465, reports the use of incense in French cathedrals, as well as the custom of the deacon and subdeacon kneeling at the right and left in a posture of adoration. According to the Stowe Missal of the 9th century the entire doxology beginning with *Per quem* was sung three times: *ter canitur;* Warner (HBS, 32), 16 f.

[76] Above I, 23; 236.

[77] Dionysius of Alexandria (d. 264-265).

in Eusebius, *Hist. eccl.,* VII, 9 (PG, 20, 656.—Also Chrysostom, *In I. Cor. hom.,* 35, 3 (PG, 61, 300), speaks of this *Amen.* Further witnesses in F. Cabrol, "Amen": DACL, I, 1554-1573, especially 1556 ff.

[78] Augustine, *Serm.* Denis, 6, 3 (PL, 46, 836 Roetzer, 124): *Ad hoc dicitis Amen. Amen dicere subscribere est.*

[79] This is all the more evident, since really only the last words *Per omnia sæcula sæculorum* are said in a loud tone, words that by themselves betray no meaning. Since the time of the canon began to be said in a subdued tone of voice, there has been no attempt to have the loud recital begin with *Per ipsum,* as one would expect from the viewpoint of the text and as Del Alamo (see note 74) actually suggests.—It is quite different in the oriental liturgies, in which silent praying has likewise made great inroads. Here the loud recital in such cases regularly sets in at least at the beginning of the doxology. That holds also for the conclusion of the canon, where, e.g., already in the Byzantine Mass of the 9th century the ἐκφώνησις begins: "and permit us with

one mouth and one heart to praise and ex-
tol thy venerable and glorious Name, of
the Father and of the Son and of the Holy
Ghost, now and forever unto all eternity,"
to which the people answer *Amen* (Brightman, 337). Only in the Armenian Mass is
the proper concluding doxology of the
canon, along with the *Amen* of the people,
included in the silent prayer of the priest,
but nevertheless there follows a blessing
formula prayed aloud, and the *Amen* of the
clergy (Brightman, 444). On the other
hand, in the Egyptian Mass, the *Amen* of
the people is broadened in such a way that
the people join in the doxology of the priest
with Ὥσπερ ἦν (corresponding to our *Sicut
erat* in psalm singing), which even in the
Coptic liturgy is still also used in the
Greek form (Brightman, 134; 180). The
same response of the people also became
customary among the Syrian Jacobites at
an early date (Brightman, 96), for James
of Edessa (d. 708) already testifies to it
(*ibid.*, 493; Hanssens, III, 476). Cf.
Hanssens, III, 481.

Part III

THE COMMUNION CYCLE

1. The Beginnings of a Communion Cycle

IT IS NOT ESSENTIAL TO THE NOTION OF SACRIFICE THAT THE OFFERERS should be invited afterwards to be God's guests at table. But the Sacrifice of Christendom was so instituted, for it is a family celebration, the celebration of the family of God, namely, those who belong to Christ and who, because of Baptism, are bound to Him by ties of most intimate fellowship. Thus they stand before God, a holy people. The *communio sanctorum*, which is holy Church, has to be made manifest in the *sacra communio* of the Sacrament.[1] It has always been regarded as a requirement of every Mass celebration that at least the celebrating priest must receive Communion, and every contrary practice has been condemned, time and again, as an abuse.[2]

In the biblical texts the meal feature of the Eucharist was so much in evidence that Its sacrificial nature has had to be proved. True, even in the nascent Church the oblation was manifestly more than a mere introduction to the meal. It was a first step, to be followed at once by the second step, the meal. Or rather, both formed so complete a unit that participation in one appeared unthinkable without sharing also in the other. There is a clear relationship between this and the fact that those who were unworthy of the Sacrament—not only the unbaptized but often also the penitents—were excluded at the very beginning of the Sacrifice-

---

[1] The word *communio* therefore, even in its application to the Sacrament, denotes in its primary sense not the "union" of the individual with Christ—for then it would have to be *co-unio*—but rather the sublime Good that holds together the society of the faithful. This meaning of the word is still clearly recognized by Bernold of Constance, (d. 1100), *Micrologus*, c. 51 (PL, CLI, 1014 D) : *Nec proprie communio dici potest, nisi plures de eodem sacrificio participent.* Similarly Thomas Aquinas, *Summa theol.*, III, 73, 4 corp.

[2] The XII Synod of Toledo (681), can. 5 (Mansi, XI, 1033), legislates against those priests who, in celebrating more than one Mass on one and the same day, communicate only at the last Mass. In the ensuing centuries the omission of Communion seemed to be rather frequent among priests who for some reason or other celebrated Mass though their consciences were grievously burdened. Numerous ordinances against such a procedure are found even as late as the 10th century, and here and there even in the 14th. Franz, 77 f.; P. Browe, "Messa senza consecrazione e communione," *Eph. liturg.*, 50 (1936), 124-132.

Mass,[3] and that even before the start of the Prayer of Thanksgiving there was another warning by the deacon directed to all those who were not clean of heart.[4] Coming to particulars, in the oriental rites even at present the kiss of peace comes at the very beginning of the Sacrifice-Mass, whereas the western form of the ceremony was relocated in the course of time. In all rites, however, a series of prayers and practices eventually developed around the Communion, as preparation and sequel to it.

According to the oldest accounts, the Communion simply formed the conclusion of the eucharistic service, with no special prayers to accompany it.[5] The preparation consisted in the thankful oblation to God. But already in the fourth century, in the ambit of the Greek Church, we meet with several arrangements of the Mass where the Communion is preceded by at least a prayer of the celebrant begging for a worthy reception, or even by a special prayer as a blessing of the recipients, and after the Communion there follows at least a thanksgiving prayer.[6] Other details of the later oriental order of Communion are also to be noticed in the same documents, in particular the invocation, Τὰ ἅγια τοῖς ἁγίοις, which the priest pronounces after the preparatory prayer, and the psalm chant which accompanies the Communion. Likewise, before the end of the fourth century there appeared in certain Greek sources the prayer which soon became a permanent part of the preparation for Communion in all Mass-liturgies, a prayer which indeed forms the very center of that preparation, namely, the *Pater Noster*.[7]

---

[3] *Supra*, I, 476 f.

[4] Supra, p. 114. However, the tendency to limit the admonition to the Communion, made itself felt in the East also. In the *Canones Basilii*, c. 97 (Riedel, 274) the warnings that are sometimes given before the anaphora, precede the Communion.

[5] *Supra*, I, 22-3, 29. The Gallican church of the 6th century presents an equivalent idea by putting the Communion at the end of Mass: *peractis sollemnibus, expletis missis*. Nickl, *Der Anteil des Volkes*, 55, cf. 65.

[6] The *Euchologion* of Serapion, n. 14-16 (Quasten, *Mon.*, 64-66) contains before Communion a prayer that goes with the breaking of the Host (ἐν τῇ κλάσει εὐχή) and a prayer of blessing (χειροθεσία) over the people, together with a prayer of thanks after Comunion beginning Εὐχαρι-στοῦμέν σοι. The same pattern is presupposed by Theodore of Mopsuestia, *Sermones Catech.*, IV (Rücker, 34-38); similarly it is found in the Egyptian recension of Hippolytus' *Apostolic Tradi-*

tion which goes by the name *Egyptian Church Order* (Ethiopian version: Dix, 11 f.; Brightman, 190-193; cf. Coptic version: Funk, II, 101 f.), but with this difference, that the prayer preceding the blessing is doubled and that after the prayer of thanksgiving there follows once again the prayer accompanying the laying on of hands over the people.—In the *Apostolic Constitutions*, VIII, 13-15 (Quasten, *Mon.*, 227-233) only a prayer by the bishop with a litany as an introduction, precedes Communion, but a thanksgiving and blessing prayer follow. Only a single special form of prayer before and after Communion is presented in the Testamentum Domini (Quasten, *Mon.*, 258 f.). The Our Father does not appear in any of these liturgies.

[7] The oldest testimony would be found in the Mystagogic Catecheses, V, 11-18 (Quasten, *Mon.*, 103-107), if they were really conducted by Cyril of Jerusalem, but the old doubts (above p. 191, n. 25) recur again; for his testimony would be an

2. *Pater noster*

In the Latin area, too, there is evidence since the fourth century of the use of the *Pater noster* at the celebration of the Eucharist.[1] Augustine mentions it time after time.[2] In regard to the Roman Mass there is, indeed, no direct testimony outside the tradition of the canon itself, but it would surely have been remarkable if the Our Father had not by that time come into use at Rome, too.[3] Only in Spain is there any evidence of fluctuation even at a later period, since the IV Council of Toledo (633) had to insist that the Lord's Prayer was to be said every day and not merely on Sunday.[4]

isolated one for a half century, a circumstance that is very suspicious in view of the contradictory evidence found in the very Syrian sphere even in later times (see previous note). The next oldest and clearest testimony from the Eastern Church is in the utterances of Chrysostom: *In Gen. hom.*, 27, 8; *In Eutrop. hom.*, 5; Faustus of Byzantium, *Hist. Armeniæ* (circa, 400), V, 28. Cf. the data in Hanssens, III, 491-493.—For the dfferent readings of the Our Father and its early use in Christian worship, see Frederic H. Chase, *The Lord's Prayer in the Early Church* (Texts & Studies, 1, No. 3; Cambridge, 1891).

[1] Optatus of Mileve, *Contra Parm.* (written 366), II, 20 (CSEL, 26, 56), where he confronts the Donatist bishops with their own practice which contradicts their teaching on Penance, for they grant the remission of sins and then even say the prayer of pardon for themselves, *mox ad altare conversi dominicam orationem prætermittere non potestis et utique dicitis: Pater noster qui es in cœlis, dimitte nobis debita et peccata nostra.* Regarding the allocation of the African Rite of Reconcilition within the Mass cf. Jungmann, *Die Lateinischen Bussriten*, 32; 300 f. If, as can hardly be doubted, a practice in common with Catholics is here presupposed, one is forced to place its beginning already before the outbreak of the Donatist schism (311). Whether Tertullian, *De or.*, c. 11, 18, testifies to the Pater noster in the same location (50 Dekkers, *Tertullianus*, 59 f.) is doubtful; see G. F. Dierks, *Vigiliæ christianæ*, 2 (1948), 253.—Ambrose, *De Sacramentis* (about 390), V, 4, 24 (Quasten, *Mon.*, 168): *Quare ergo in oratione do-*

minica, quæ postea [= after the words of consecration] *sequitur, ait: Panem nostrum?*—Jerome, *Adv. Pelag.* (about 415), III, 15 (PL, 23, 585); cf. *In Ezech.*, 48, 16 (PL, 25, 485) and *In Matth.*, 26, 41 (PL, 26, 198).

[2] Augustine, *Serm.*, 227 (PL, 38, 1101): *ubi peracta est sanctificatio, dicimus orationem dominicam.*—Again in *Ep.*, 149, 16 (CSEL, 44, 362) he says of the principal prayer of the Mass: *Quam totam petitionem fere omnis Ecclesia dominica oratione concludit.* The *fere* shows that Augustine recognizes exceptions. Further passages in Roetzer, 128-130; cf. also *infra*, notes 30, 34 ff.

[3] Jerome, *Adv. Pelag*, III, 15 (PL, 23, 585), sees in the position of the Pelagians, who regard the Our Father before the Communion as superfluous, a departure from the general custom. If it was not already in the Roman Mass during his stay in Rome (382-385), then Jerome had sufficient opportunity from his contacts with the numerous priest pilgrims of the West to keep abreast of Roman practice. Besides, we have every reason to take the testimony of Ambrose, *De sacr.*, V, 4, 24, as a reference to the Roman Mass.—That the Our Father in any event was in the Roman Mass before Gregory the Great, something that Batiffol, *Leçons*, 278, doubts, is already clear from the fact that one Mass of the Leonianum (Muratori, I, 359) contains an embolism between the Preface and the Postcommunion, *Libera nos ab omni malo propitiusque concede, ut quæ nobis poscimus relaxari, ipsi quoque proximis remittamus. Per.*

[4] Can. 10 (Mansi, X, 621).

In the Roman Mass the *Pater noster* stands at the beginning of the preparation for Communion. This is not a categorical position, and as a matter of fact in other liturgies there is a different arrangement. In the non-Byzantine liturgies of the East, as a rule, at least the fraction of the species precedes the Our Father.[5] Even in the non-Roman rites of the West the fraction comes before the *Pater noster*.[6] Thus the gifts are first readied for distribution, the table is set, and only after that does the prayer begin.

The present arrangement of the Roman Mass in this regard goes back to Gregory the Great. As he himself relates, he had been accused of introducing Greek practices; in particular, it was charged that he wanted the Lord's Prayer said right after the canon: *orationem dominicam mox post canonem dici statuistis*. In his letter to Bishop John of Syracuse the pontiff defends himself as follows:

> *Orationem vero dominicam idcirco mox post precem[7] dicimus, quia mos apostolorum fuit, ut ad ipsam solummodo orationem oblationis[8] hostiam consecrarent. Et valde mihi inconveniens visum est, ut precem, quam scholasticus composuerat, super oblationem diceremus et ipsam traditionem, quam Redemptor noster composuit, super eius corpus et sanguinem non diceremus.[9]*

What Gregory means to say is: The Mass of the Apostles consisted simply in this, that they consecrated with the *oratio oblationis;* everything else is a later addition. If some other prayer is to be said over the consecrated gifts, certainly the first prayer to be considered, before any human composition,[10] is the Lord's Prayer. Since Gregory's time this

---

[5] Cf. The survey in Hanssens, III, 504. Originally not only in Byzantium but also in Egypt, the breaking of the Host seems to have taken place after the Our Father; *ibid.*, 517.—On the other hand, the preparations preceding the Our Father are particularly lavish in the East Syrian Mass. They begin with thanksgiving and penitential prayers by the priest, the Psalm *Miserere* among others; then, with more prayers, follows the priest's self-lustration through the washing of the hands, incensing, and then the ceremonious Breaking of the Host and the *Consignatio*. Only then, after a litany and preparatory prayer, is the Our Father said (Brightman, 288-296).

[6] *Missale mixtum* (PL, 85, 558); *Missale Ambrosianum* (1902), 179. For the Gallican Mass see the comparative study in H. Lietzmann, *Ordo missæ Romanus et Gallicanus* (4th ed.; Kleine Texte, 19; Berlin, 1935), 27. The same arrangement probably also for Africa; see Augustine, *Ep.*, 149, 16 (CSEL, 44, 362).

[7,8] *Prex* as well as *oratio oblationis* are designations for the canon; cf. *supra*, p. 102.

[9] Gregory the Great, *Ep.*, IX, 12 (PL, 77, 956 f). The history of the many blunders regarding this text and a final comprehensive clarification of its meaning in Geiselmann, *Die Abendmahlslehre*, 209-217. A detailed discussion of the text from a different angle in Batiffol, *Leçons*, 277 f. There is a different but scarcely happier explanation of the words of Gregory in C. Lambot, *Revue Bénéd.*, 42 (1930), 265-269, who is followed by B. Capelle, *ibid.*, 60 (1950), 238 f.; they interpret as follows: it was the apostles' practice to consecrate the *oblationis hostia* with (ad not in the instrumental but in the concomitant sense; the meaning demanded would be: with added) the Lord's Prayer.

[10] The *prex quam scholasticus composuerat* and for which the *Pater noster* is now

prayer, the Our Father, is said right after the canon, and therefore *super oblationem*, that is, over the sacrificial gifts still lying upon the altar, whereas formerly the prayer was not said till immediately before the Communion, after the consecrated breads had been removed from the altar and broken.[11] It might be that Gregory was impelled to make this change by the practice among the Greeks as he had got to know it in Constantinople.[12] But Gregory went beyond his model. Whereas in Byzantium, as in nearly all the rites of the East, the new prayer-group which starts after the closing doxology of the canon is preceded not only by a renewed invitation to prayer, but also, prior to this, by another greeting of the people,[13] the Roman arrangement omits every such salutation and is satisfied with a simple *Oremus*. This call to prayer, therefore, still comes under the *Dominus vobiscum* and *Sursum corda* of the Great Prayer, the *Eucharistia*. Thus the connection with the canon is quite close. By these means the weighty words which constitute the Our Father are emphasized all the more. The priest pronounces the prayer at the altar in the same fashion as he did the canon. Indeed, the first part of the Lord's Prayer actually forms, to a certain extent, a sort of summary and recapitulation of the preceding eucharistic prayer. The *sanctificetur* is a synopsis of the triple *Sanctus;* the *adveniat regnum tuum* is a kind of epitome of the two epiklesis prayers: *Quam oblationem* and *Supplices*[14]; and the *fiat voluntas tua* sets forth the basic idea regarding obedience from which all sacrifice must proceed. The spirit and disposition in which our Lord Himself had offered up His sacrifice and which we must draw from our co-performance of it, could hardly have been expressed more cogently.

But it would be a mistake to think that the Our Father in this new location right after the canon had acquired an essentially different function and given up its purpose as a preparation for Communion, or even to

substituted was probably of the same sort as the prayers before Communion mentioned above, p. 276, n. 6, or as the *procœmium fractionis* that precedes the fraction and the Our Father in the Coptic Mass (cf. Hanssens, *Institutiones*, III, 486 f.). Baumustark, *Missale Romanum*, 13 f., believes he can even point out a definite text from Roman tradition.

[11] E. Bishop-A. Wilmart, *Le génie du rit romain* (Paris, 1920), 84-87. Thus also F. Cabrol, *The Clergy Review* 1 (1931), 364-366.

[12] Nevertheless a similar pattern appears in a fragment which G. Morin, *Revue Bénéd.*, 41 (1929), 70-73, claims had its origin in N. Africa about 500: *non poteris per orationem dominicam mysterii sacramenta complere, ut dicas ad plenitudinem perfecti holocausti orationem dominicam;* PL, 125, 608 B; cf. *ibid.*, 610 B.

[13] In Byzantium in solemn form: Καὶ ἔσται τὰ ἐλέν τοῦ μεγάλου θεοῦ καὶ σωτῆρος ἡμῶν Ἰησοῦ Χριστοῦ μετὰ πάντων ὑμῶν, whereupon follows the customary answer of the people: Καὶ μετὰ τοῦ πνεύματος σοῦ (Brightman, 337). Similarly in other rites, apparently since earliest times, as can be concluded from *Const. Ap.*, VIII, 13, 1 (Quasten, *Mon.*, 227). Only the Egyptian liturgies are satisfied with the usual salute to the people: Εἰρήνη πᾶσιν. Brightman, 135, 180.

[14] A biblical variation of Luke 11: 2 substitutes a petition for the coming of the Kingdom of the Holy Ghost, for "Thy Kingdom Come:" ἐλθέτω τὸ ἅγιον πνεῦμά σου ἐφ' ἡμᾶς καὶ καθαρισάτω ἡμᾶς.

suppose that Gregory had intended something of the sort when making the new arrangement.[15] The pope's own account of his action gives no hint of such a thing. The canon remains an absolute unit (and therefore it concludes with a doxology), and the Our Father remains a Communion prayer, as it is in all liturgies, only with a closer nexus to the canon than in other rites.[16]

In the life of the ancient Church the Our Father had a close connection with the Communion, even aside from the Mass-liturgy; this is shown by the treatment of the petition for bread in the commentaries on the Our Father, and also in other pertinent remarks of the Fathers. Beginning with Tertullian, the Latin Fathers generally correlate this petition to the Eucharist. The same is done by some of the Greeks.[17] This is certainly very remarkable in regard to a text whose literal meaning obviously signifies the material bread; it seems to presuppose that the faithful were accustomed to recite the Our Father at the reception of Communion, even before it appears in liturgical monuments as part of the liturgy. This

---

[15] Brinktrine, *Die hl. Messe,* 230-233, indeed thinks that Gregory in the given declaration regards the Our Father (which he thinks is meant in the phrase *ad ipsam solummodo orationem consecrarent*) as the prayer of the consecration, not precisely in the sense of transubstantiation, but nevertheless in the sense of a further blessing of the consecrated gifts. In this he follows the commentators of the Middle Ages with whom he is also on common ground regarding the application of this broader conception of the consecration to the fraction and commingling. Brinktrine, therefore, includes the *Agnus Dei* and the Kiss of Peace in the second main division of the Mass, the "eucharistic consecration." But that is no way to gain a better understanding of the original meaning of such customs.—Dix, *The Shape of the Liturgy,* 131, contends that the *Pater noster* was in a certain sense part of the Eucharistic Prayer from the fact that it is said not by the people, but essentially by the priest. But this is only in line with the general exclusion of the people's prayer in the Roman Liturgy.

[16] Certain indications that the Our Father is included in the Eucharistic Prayer appear in Cyril of Jerusalem, *Catech. Myst.,* V, 18; Ambrose, *De sacr.,* VI, 5, 24; Augustine, *Ep.,* 149, 16. But they cannot stand up under closer examination; see I.

Cecchetti, *L'Amen nella Bibbia e nella Liturgia* (special printing of Bollettino Ceciliano, vol. 37; Vatican City, 1942), 21 ff., note 28.

[17] J. P. Bock, *Die Brotbitte des Vaterunsers* (Paderborn, 1911); cf. Chase, *The Lord's Prayer,* 42-53.—Tertullian, *De or.,* c. 6; Cyprian, *De or. Dom.,* c. 18; Juvencus, *Ev. hist.,* I, 595; Chromatius, *In Matth.* tr. 14, 5; are all cited for the eucharistic sense of the bread petition; furthermore a whole series of passages from Hilary, Ambrose, Augustine (Bock, 110 ff.). An explicit denial of the eucharistic sense even among the Greeks is to be found in Gregory of Nyssa (100 f.).—The much-discussed word ($\tau \grave{o} \nu$ $\check{a} \rho \tau o \nu$ $\dot{\eta} \mu \tilde{\omega} \upsilon$ $\tau \grave{o} \nu$) $\dot{\epsilon} \pi \iota o \acute{\upsilon} \sigma \iota o \nu$, that is found in Matth. 6: 11 as well as in Luke 11: 3, as is well known, is often explained by the Fathers since Origen (under the influence probably of the practical application of the Lord's Prayer) to the effect that there is question of a bread that is adapted to the $o \dot{\upsilon} \sigma \acute{\iota} a$, the spiritual nature of man. Ambrose, *De sacr.,* V, 4, 24, renders its *supersubstantialem . . . qui animæ nostræ substantiam fulcit.*—For philological discussions see Quasten, *Mon.,* 169, note 1; W. Foerster, $\dot{\epsilon} \pi \iota o \acute{\upsilon} \sigma \iota o \varsigma$: *Theol. Wörterbuch z. N. Test.,* II (1935), 587-595; Th. Soiron, *Die Bergpredigt Jesu* (Freiburg, 1941), 348-352.

would have been done at the daily house Communion, but also at Communion in church in connection with the Eucharist. The first prayer that the neophytes said in the bosom of the congregation before their first Communion appears to have been the Our Father, even in earliest times, and at least on this occasion it must have been recited by all in common and aloud.[18] In the earliest commentaries on the Mass which mention the Our Father—the *Mystagogic Catecheses* of Jerusalem and the exposition of the Bishop of Milan—the petition for bread is emphatically explained in a sacramental sense;[19] it was therefore also recited in this sense. Ambrose attaches long additions to the passages in question, in which he exhorts to daily reception.[20]

A thing that clearly shows that the Our Father was looked upon as a Communion prayer in the Roman liturgy of the Middle Ages as well as in the extra-Roman liturgies of the West and those of the East, is the fact that it also makes an appearance among the preparatory prayers—in fact, as the most important of them—even where only the Communion is celebrated.[21] That is the case in the *missa præsanctificatorum* (which is nothing else except a Communion service[22] and in most rites of Communion for the sick.[23]

In the Orient, too, the way the Lord's Prayer is fixed in the Mass confirms its role as a Communion prayer. Here as a rule it is inserted in an even older group of prayers. Amongst these there are generally a prayer for a worthy reception and the prayer of inclination said at the blessing

---

[18]Dölger, *Antike u. Christentum,* 2 (1930), 148 ff., with an appeal to Rom. 8: 15; Gal. 4: 6. Cf. The whole discussion, "Das erste Gebet der Tauflinge in der Gemeinschaft der Brüder": *ibid.,* 142-155; A. Greiff, *Das älteste Pascha-ritual der Kirche* (Paderborn, 1929), 126-130.

[19] *Supra,* n. 7 and 1.

[20] Ambrose, *De sacr.,* V, 4, 24-26 (Quasten, *Mon.,* 168-170).

[21] Cf. the chapter "Das Pater noster im Kommunionritus," in Jungmann, *Gewordene Liturgie,* 137-164.

[22] According to the oldest Latin revision of the *Missa Præsanctificatorum* of Good Friday (which originated from the East), in the older Gelasianum, I, 41 (Wilson, 77) the priest after having kissed the cross, should say, *Oremus et sequitur: Præceptis salutaribus moniti. Et oratio dominica. Inde: Libera nos Domine quæsumus. Hæc omnia expleta adorant omnes sanctam crucem et communicant.* Consequently, the entire garniture of prayer, as it were, consisted originally of the *Pater noster.* The

conclusiveness of this fact is not disturbed by the remark of Brinktrine, *Die hl. Messe,* 256, to the effect that it is no surprise that in the Liturgy of the Presanctified the principal prayer is said.

[23] Jungmann, *op. cit.,* 146 ff. In the Roman liturgy the oldest regulations that have come down to us regarding the Communion of the Sick have their origin in the 9th century. But among them, too, there are those that use the *Pater noster* as the very core of the preparation. And this continues into the 16th century. In some cases, as in the 11th century Pontifical of Narbonne, the Communion part of the Mass beginning with the *Oremus* is made to serve for the immediate preparation for the Communion of the Sick. Martène, 1, 7, XIII, (I, 892) . As a trace of the old custom the *Pater noster* is still to be found in a passage of the Roman Ritual (V, 2, 12), namely at the end of the Extreme Unction, where formerly it introduced the Communion.

of the faithful. The Our Father is regularly attached to the first of these;[24] so it belongs to the preparation for Communion. Next the prayer begging for a worthy reception is often so reconstructed that the cleansing of the heart which is sought in view of the reception of the heavenly food, at the same time becomes the preparation for saying the Lord's Prayer worthily.[25] Or else, as in the main Greek liturgies, a transition to the Our Father, having much the same content as the prayer, is spoken aloud: "And make us worthy, Lord, to be able, with trust and without reproach, to venture to call on Thee, the God of heaven, as Father, and to say . . ."[26] Thus we begin to see more pointedly the great esteem displayed for the Lord's Prayer. The independence of the Our Father which we see beginning here was fully achieved in the Greek liturgies of the Syrian milieu, where the Our Father does indeed follow in the same location, after the attention has been directed to the Communion, but where it alone determines the contents of the preceding prayer of preparation. In the East-Syrian anaphora of the Apostles, the prayer reads as follows:

> Let Thy rest, O Lord, dwell amongst us and Thy peace inhabit our hearts, and may our tongues proclaim Thy truth, and Thy Cross be the guard of our souls, since we make our mouth into new harps and speak a new language with fiery lips. Make us worthy, Lord, with the confidence that arises from Thee, to pronounce before Thee this pure and holy prayer which Thy life-giving mouth has taught Thy faithful disciples, the children of Thy mysteries: when you pray, you should pray and confess and say: . . .[27]

The enthusiasm for the grandeur of the prayer which such words as these manifest is also proclaimed, but in a more restrained way, in the introductory words of our Roman Mass.[28] For a man of dust and ashes a certain boldness *(audemus)* is implied in making his own a prayer such as

[24] See the comprehensive proofs in Baumstark, *Die Messe im Morgenland,* 156 f.

[25] Thus in the Liturgy of St. Mark (Brightman, 135 f.) : "Enlighten the eyes of our spirit, that without fault we may partake of the immortal and celestial food, and sanctify us wholly in soul, body, and spirit, that with Thy holy disciples and apostles we may utter this prayer to Thee," whereupon the priest in a low voice joins the Our Father to his prayer (which was also said quietly), and then praying again aloud that he might do so properly, introduces the Our Father recited in common by the people.

[26] Thus in the Byzantine Mass (Brightman, 339). In an expanded version in the Liturgies of St. Mark and St. James (*ibid.,* 135 f.; 59) ; similarly in the Armenian Mass (*ibid.,* 446).—A kindred introduction precedes the Our Father in the Syrian Order of Baptism: see H. Denzinger, *Ritus orientalium,* I (Würzburg), 278, 308, 315.

[27] Brightman, 295. Similar in tone is a version of the Our Father in the East Syrian rite of Baptism, where the introductory words appear in a very expanded form. G. Dietrich, *Die nestorianische Taufliturgie* (Giessen, 1903), 4.

[28] In the Gallic Liturgy also the Our Father is preceded by an introductory formula but one subject to the variation of the formulary and changeable also in content. Still in the Gothic Missal the *audere,* the confident obedience, often constitutes its basic tone. Muratori, II, 522; 526; 535; etc.

this, in which he approaches God as a child does its father.[29] That reference to boldness we have already encountered in the liturgies of the East. In the Fathers it recurs very frequently when they talk about the Our Father.[30] We can better understand the reverence for the Lord's Prayer which is thus manifested, and which is surely appropriate, if we recall that in those days it was not only kept secret from the pagans but was even withheld from the catechumens until shortly before the time when, by Baptism, they became children of the heavenly Father.[31] But even the baptized must always remain conscious of the immense distance separating them from God. Nevertheless, God's Son Himself had put these words on our lips and it was He who ordered us to recite them. It was salutary counsel, it was indeed a divine instruction.[32] The attitude and spirit which this prayer embodies is fitting at this hour when we have in our hands the offering with which the Son Himself met His heavenly Father and meets Him still.

But besides the petition for bread there is another passage in the Our Father which receives special stress in its use at Mass. This is the petition for the forgiveness of sins. Even Optatus of Mileve gives this petition prominence above all.[33] Augustine refers to its presence in the Our Father, and asks impressively: "Why is it spoken before the reception of Christ's Body and Blood? For the following reason: If perchance, in consequence of human frailty, our thought seized on something indecent, if our tongue spoke something unjust, if our eye was turned to something unseemly, if our ear listened complacently to something unnecessary . . . it is blotted

---

[29] A. v. Harnack (in A. Hahn, *Bibliothek der Symbole*, 3rd ed.; Breslau, 1897, 371) calls attention to the fact that in Hermas (Vis. III, 9, 10; Sim., V, 6, 3, 4; IX, 12, 2) only the Church and the Son of God call God Father; see also Ambrose, *De sacr.*, V, 19 (Quasten, 168): *Solius Christi specialis est pater, nobis omnibus in commune est pater . . . Ecclesiæ contuitu et consideratione te ipse commenda: Pater noster.* Cf. *Const. Ap.*, VII, 24, 2 (Funk, I, 410): Thus say the Our Father three times a day and prepare yourselves that you may be worthy of the filiation of the Father, lest calling Him Father unworthily, you may, like Israel, be rejected by Him (Mal. 1, 6, follows).

[30] Jerome, *Adv. Pelag.*, III, 15 (PL, 23, 585). *Sic docuit apostolos suos, ut quotidie in corporis illius sacrificio credentes audeant loqui: Pater.*—Augustine, *Sermo*, 110, (PL, 38, 641): *audemus quotidie dicere: Adveniat regnum tuum.*—Reference

to kindred utterances of the Greek Father in O. Rousseau, "Le 'Pater' dans la liturgie de la messe" (*Cours et Conférences*, VII [Louvain, 1929], 231-241), 233 f.

[31] Rousseau, *op. cit.*, 235, is inclined to look for the origin of this mode of expression with *audere* (τολμᾶν) in the practice of the Catechumenate and more especially in that of the Orient.

[32] The expression in our Roman introductions is already found in Cyprian, *De dom. or.*, c. 2 (CSEL, 3, 267), who says of Christ, *Qui inter cetera salutaria sua monita et præcepta divina, quibus populo suo consulit ad salutem, etiam orandi ipse formam dedit.* Nevertheless it is possible to construe *præceptis salutaribus* as meaning *pr. Salvatoris*, in parallel to *divina institutione = Dei inst.* See Bonifatius Fischer, O.S.B., "Præceptis salutaribus moniti," *Archiv. f. Liturgiewiss.*, 1 (1950), 124-127.

[33] *Supra*, n. 1.

out by the Lord's Prayer in the passage: Forgive us our debts, so that we may approach in peace and so that we may not eat or drink what we receive unto judgment."[34] For Augustine, the Our Father is like washing the face before going to the altar.[35] For that reason it was the practice at Hippo for all, priest and faithful, to strike their breast while pronouncing the words, *dimitte nobis debita nostra*.[36] That the Roman Mass also gave special importance to the final petitions introduced by these words, is shown by the supplement, the so-called *embolism*,[37] which has its counterpart in all the liturgies except the Byzantine.[38]

In the extra-Byzantine liturgies of the East, this supplement regularly accentuates not only the last petition, but the last two, sometimes by just repeating the words,[39] sometimes by a marked expansion. Thus, in the anaphora of St. James, the priest continues: "(Yea, Lord, our God), lead us not into a temptation which we are not able to bear, (but with the temptation grant also the issue, so that we may be able to remain steadfast, and) deliver us from the evil,"[40] thereupon a doxology follows as in all oriental texts. Thus the continuation of the petition for forgiveness is taken up and, with an eye on the future, a plea is made for preservation especially from that evil which would bar us from approaching the sacred repast.

The same is also to be found where (as in the West) only the last petition is taken up. In the Gallic Liturgy the formula in question was again subjected to the variations of the Mass-formulary. Its basic outline, however, for all the various additions made to it, was mostly the same as that which appears in the simplest form in a Sunday Mass of the

---

[34] Augustine, *Serm.*, Denis, 6 (Miscell., Aug., I, 31; Roetzer, 129).

[35] Augustine, *Serm.*, 17, 5, 5 (PL, 38, 127).

[36] Augustine, *Serm.*, 351, 3, 6 (PL, 39, 1541); *Ep.*, 265, 8 (CSEL, 57, 646). Inspired probably by Augustine, the Augustinian Hermit Gottschalk Holden required the same in the 15th century. Franz, 22. A similar stressing of the petition of pardon in St Benedict, *Regula*, c. 13; still Benedict does not speak of the Mass, but of Lauds and Vespers, where one should say the *Pater noster* in a loud tone of voice, because of the words *dimitte nobis sicut et nos dimittimus,* so that one may cleanse oneself of the offenses against charity.

[37] ἐμβολισμός (from ἐμβολή, ἐμβάλλειν) = interpolation.—*Ordo sec. Rom.*, n. 11 (Andrieu, II, 223; PL, 78, 974), speaks of the Lord's Prayer *cum emboli.*

[38] The Byzantine Mass concludes the Our Father simply with a doxology; see below note 49.

[39] So in the East Syrian and the Armenian Mass—Brightman, 296; 446.

[40] Rücke, *Die Syrische Jacobosanaphora,* 49. The brackets indicate those things, like the citation 1 Cor. 10: 13, which are presumably a later addition. In the Greek anaphora of St. James there is the same fundamental text with other amplifications, in which" the evil" is described as a personal principle: ἀπὸ τοῦ πονηροῦ καὶ τῶν ἔργων αὐτοῦ καὶ πάσης ἐπηρείας καὶ μεθοδείας αὐτοῦ; Brightman, 60. The conclusion of the Syrian anaphora of St. James is adopted, with further embellishments, in the Coptic anaphora of St. Cyril: *ibid.*, 182.— Jerome says in two passages, we pray in the Lord's Prayer *ne nos inducas in tentationem, quam ferre non possumus.* Cf. *In Ezech.*, c. 48, 16 (PL, 25, 485 C); *In Matth.*, c. 26, 41 (PL, 26, 198). The addition was also spread elsewhere; see Brightman, 469 f.

Missale Gothicum; it reads: *Libera nos a malo, omnipotens Deus, et custodi in bono. Qui vivis et regnas.*[41] Nor is the Roman form of the embolism to be judged different. That its plea to be freed *ab omnibus malis* is concerned above all with evil in the moral order is clearly seen from the added words: *præteritis, præsentibus et futuris.* Only moral evils, even when they are "past," still lie heavy on the soul. Therefore, in the word *præteritis* there is a renewed stressing of the petition for forgiveness, just as in the *futuris* there is an echo of the petition to be safeguarded from overly hard trial. Then, on the positive side, an all-comprehensive good is included in the petition, the same good already mentioned in the *Hanc igitur* formula: *da propitius pacem in diebus nostris.* Our human wants are all of equal value for the kingdom of God. If a proper peace surround us within and without, then, as we hope, a double result will be more easily forthcoming: we will remain free from sin and will be protected against every disturbance and error. This will then be the correct disposition to have in order to eat the heavenly bread with benefit.

Just as we are accustomed to find it in the orations of Roman saints' feasts, the petition is strengthened by reference to the intercession of heavenly helpers. Here, besides the Mother of God and the protectors of the Roman community, Peter and Paul, the Apostle Andrew is also mentioned. Of course Andrew is mentioned in the *Communicantes* list, being named right after the Princes of the Apostles, just as in the two biblical catalogues (Matthew 10:2; Luke 6:14) his name stands right after Peter's. But it is surely unusual to find his name mentioned right after theirs, all by itself. It is well known that the New Rome on the Bosporus, in rivalry with the old Rome on the Tiber, had early laid claim to the Apostle Andrew, Peter's brother, and "first called" ($\pi\rho\omega\tau\acute{o}\varkappa\lambda\eta\tau\circ\varsigma$)[42] of the Twelve, as its founder. This accounts also for the honor paid to the the apostle at Rome; the prominence given to him—after Peter and Paul, of course—was halfway in opposition to Byzantium, halfway as a gesture of concord. That we are on the right track in our conclusion is shown by a related occurrence among the prefaces of the *Gregorianum,* where special prefaces are provided for only two saints besides the Princes of the Apostles—Anastasia, who was likewise highly revered in Byzantium, and Andrew.[43] Some have thought that the addition of *atque Andrea* was due to Gregory the Great who, before his election as pope, had founded a monastery in honor of St. Andrew and had been abbot there.[44] But the

[41] Muratori, II, 649.

[42] Jno. 1: 35-40.—N. Milles, *Kalendarium manuale utriusque ecclesiæ,* I, (2nd ed.; Innsbruck, 1896), 338. In the year 357 the relics of St. Andrew and at the same time those of St. Luke—therefore those of the brother of St. Peter and the companion of St. Paul—were transferred to Byzantium.

B. Kraft, "Andreas": *LThK,* I, 410 f.

[43] *Supra,* n. 26.

[44] H. Grisar, *ZkTh,* 9 (1885), 582; 10 (1886), 30 f.—That the insertion is not mentioned among the objections that were raised against him speaks rather against Gregory.

addition could have been made earlier than this, since even in the fifth century there was at Rome not only this somewhat uneasy relationship to Byzantium, but even an explicit devotion to the Apostle Andrew.[45] The Middle Anges not seldom added other names here, and this was done even in later times, since the *Micrologus* offered the liberty just for this passage.[46] But in the end they were satisfied with the supplementary phrase, *cum* (later: *et) omnibus sanctis*, which was wanting originally, but which appeared here and there even in early manuscripts.[47]

The conclusion is formed by the ordinary formula *Per Dominum nostrum.*[48] This acts as a close not only for the embolism itself, but also for the *Pater noster* which is merely extended into the embolism. Thus it is an exact parallel to the doxology which, in most oriental liturgies, follows in the same location after the Our Father or its supplement, as the case may be.[49] By this formula we give expression to the fact that even in the

[45] J. Beran. "Hat Gregor d. Gr. dem Embolismus der römischen Liturgie den Namen des hl. Andreas beigtfügt?" *Eph. liturg.*, 55 (1941), 81-87. The shrines of St. Andrew in Rome go back to Popes Simplicius (468-483), Gelasius, I, (492-496), Symmachus (498-514).—For the *atque Andrea* and still more for the selection of just these two prefaces, the only other epoch that comes to mind is the late seventh century when oriental influence of the Vat. Reg. (beginning of the 8th cent.). The words are missing among others in the manuscripts that present the Irish tradition of the canon (Botte, 13; 50). It is not likely that they were stricken out only later on. That there was in the 6th century a version of the embolism without any names of Saints is shown by the example of the Leonianum (above, note, 3).

[46] Bernold of Constance, *Micrologus*, c. 23 (PL, 151, 994 D): *Hic nominat quotquot sanctos voluerit.* The same direction already in the *Roman Ordo,* IV (PL, 78, 984). Already at an early date it appears elsewhere in the form of a supplement; *et beatis confessoribus tuis illis;* Botte, 50 apparatus; Ebner, 425-428, where there are a large number of examples of names from different countries. Michael, John the Baptist, Benedict are especially numerous, in addition at times to the specific patrons of dioceses or convents. Cf. Ferreres, 165; numerous names listed by Leroquais, III, 382.

[47] Botte 50.
[48] With the older position of the word *Deus* in all the old textual sources; *qui tecum vivit et regnat Deus.* Botte, 50. Cf. *supra*, I, 383, n. 38.
[49] This is missing only in the Ethiopian Mass. Otherwise there are two versions. Predominant is the form that made its way into several bibilical texts of Matth. 6: 13 and is found already in the Didache, c. 8, 2 (without the ἡ βασιλεία): ὅτι σοῦ ἐστιν ἡ βασιλεία καὶ ἡ δύναμις καὶ ἡ δόξα εἰς τοὺς αἰῶνας. Cf. Chase, 169 ff. The Armenian Mass gives this wording exactly; Brightman, 446.

The Greek anaphoras of St. James and St. Mark, the East Syrian and the Byzantine Masses present amplifications; the Byzantine doxology (which follows the Our Father without any intermediate text) has in the concluding words the expanded form: . . . δόξα τοῦ Πατρὸς καὶ τοῦ Υἱοῦ καὶ τοῦ ἀγίου Πνεύματος νῦν καὶ ἀεὶ καὶ εἰς τοὺς αἰῶνας τῶν αἰώνων. Brightman 339 f.—The second version that appears among the Copts and West Syrians, inserts a mention of Christ as a connecting link and then continues with the Greek Doxology of the 4th century customary in this area; δι' οὗ καὶ μεθ'οὗ σοὶ πρέπει δοξα . . . Rücker, *Die Jakobosanaphora,* 49; Brightman, 100; 182. This last version therefore is close to the Roman *Per Dominum nostrum.* — Conjectures (that are hardly tenable) regarding an original identity of this doxology with the conclud-

Lord's Prayer we direct our petition to the heavenly Father through Christ, just as with His encouragement, *divina institutione formati,* we pronounced it.

If the Our Father at Mass was designed to serve as a preparation of the assembled people for the reception of Holy Communion, this had to be made clear also in the manner of performance. Actually, the Lord's Prayer was frequently said at Mass by all the people, and in any case it was always said aloud. This might not be entirely expected in ancient Christendom, since the Our Father still remained under the discipline of the secret. Thus a loud rehearsal of the Our Father was excluded from the fore-Mass. True to the command to guard it as a sacred mystery and not even to write it down, it would seem that outside of Mass it was only said quietly, just as the symbol was said only quietly outside of Baptism.[50] Within the Mass, where only those could be present who were full citizens of God's kingdom, there was nothing to hinder its being said aloud. The only question was, by whom was it to be said: whether, like the *Sanctus,* by all the assembly or, like the other prayers of the *Ordo missæ,* by the celebrant in the name of the faithful. Since the prayer was intended as a preparation for everyone to receive the Sacrament, it certainly was appropriate that everyone—the whole people—should take part immediately in the Lord's Prayer, especially since it was certainly quite familiar to everyone.

This solution was the one that became standard in the Orient. Everywhere the rubrics assigned the Our Father to the people,[51] except in the Armenian Mass, where clerics were to sing it with arms outstretched.[52] However, in the Byzantine Mass, too, it became customary for the choir to say it,[53] but always as representative of the people. In the old Gallican

---

ing doxology of the Canon are found in F. Probst, *Liturgie des vierten Jahrhunderts und deren Reform* (Münster, 1893), 198; 264 f.; cf. 221, n. 21. Cf. in opposition Srawley, 163 f.

[50] This explains the still existing custom of saying the Our Father and the Symbol *sotto voce* at the beginning of the Office (before Matins and Prime) and at the end. Cf. Jungmann, *Gewordene Liturgie,* 167 ff. Similarly the further custom belongs here of saying aloud only the beginning and end when it occurs before an oration after the *Kyrie* in the Preces or the corresponding alternating prayers. This later method was first mentioned by St. Benedict, *Regula,* c. 3, who ordered, as an exception, that at both Lauds and Vespers, because of the summons for mutual forgiveness, the whole Our Father be recited in a loud voice, otherwise only the last part, *ut ab omnibus respondeatur: Sed libera nos a malo.*

[51] In the West Syrian Liturgy it is done in this way: the celebrant speaks the first words, "Our Father who art in heaven," and the people then continue. Brightman, 100. The same arrangement among the Maronites. Hanssens, III, 489.

[52] Brightman, 446.—Here also the practice does not seem entirely unanimous. In the Italian translation supplied by G. Avedighian: *Liturgia della messa armena* (4th ed.; Venice, 1873), 53, we read: *Il populo a braccia stese canta il Pater noster.*

[53] Mercenier, Paris, I, 224. Only the director (or chief person) says the Our Father among the Ukrainians; Harnykevitsch, 90. In the Byzantine-Slavic Liturgy

Liturgy also, the Our Father was pronounced by all the people in common,[54] but in the remainder of the West, by the celebrating priest. This was the method already followed in Augustine's African Church,[55] although with provision for both a vital interest and ritual participation by the people.[56] In the old Spanish Mass this participation was manifested by responding *Amen* to every section of the prayer.[57]

Even in the Roman Mass there is not wanting an indication that the Our Father belongs to the people. It is apportioned between priest and people, although in rather unequal parts. Whereas the old sacramentaries and most of the *ordines* contain no reference to this division of the text,[58] and Gregory the Great, in his frequently quoted letter, says tersely that at Rome, in contrast to the practice of the Greeks, the Lord's Prayer is said *a solo sacerdote,*[59] yet we find the responsorial method in the *Ordo* of John the Arch-chanter, therefore at the very latest in the eighth century; the Our Father is concluded *respondentibus omnibus: sed libera nos a malo.*[60] Basically, therefore, the people say the Our Father along with the celebrant.[61] It is the people's Communion prayer.[62]

the Lord's Prayer is frequently sung by all the people together.—Even in the present-day liturgy, as in the older ones, the Greek rubrics mention the people: ὁ λαός. Brightman, 339; 391.

[54] Gregory of Tours, *De mir. s. Martini,* II, 30 (PL, 71, 954 f): A mute woman was miraculously cured on a Sunday at the moment when the *Pater noster* was begun which she then joined the others in praying: *cœpit sanctam orationem cum reliquis decantare.* Cf. Gregory of Tours *Vitæ Patrum,* 16, 2 (PL, 71, 1076), and also Cæsarius, *Serm., 73* (Morin, 294 f.; PL, 39, 2277).

[55] Augustine, *Serm., 58,* 10, 12 (PL, 38, 299; Roetzer, 129): *ad altare Dei quotidie dicitur ista dominica oratio et audiunt illam fideles.*

[56] Above, p. 284.

[57] The *Amen* occurs in five places in the Mozarabic Mass of the *Missale mixtum* (PL, 85, 559) but after the petition for bread the answer is instead, *Quia tu Deus es,* and after the petition against temptation the concluding answer is, *Sed libera nos a malo.*

[58] Among them, strangely enough, is the Codex Pad. of the Gregorianum, which otherwise gives the responses of the people so carefully. It also gives the concluding petition without any remarks whatever. Mohlberg-Baumstark, n. 891; on the other hand cf. n. 874, 893.

[59] Gregory the Great, *Ep., IX,* 12 (PL, 77, 957).

[60] *Capitulare eccl. ord.* (Andrieu, III, 109). This rubric, we are forced to submit, may be of Frankish origin, perhaps a compromise with old Gallican methods. However, the silence of the sacramentaries is explained by the fact that the priest himself had to say the concluding prayer along with the rest and that the sacramentary merely supplied the text for the priest, even though the people also took part in it. Therefore a reference to the people is also missing at the *Sanctus.*

[61] On that account it is a mistake, when Brinktrine, *Die hl. Messe,* 250, considers it "reserved to the priest," and "elevated to a solemn prayer of oblation." Even in Augustine, with whom there is no question at all of the people's joining in, it still remains in the fullest sense a Communion Prayer of the Community. That the Our Father was included in the canon during the Middle Ages is evident; (but that does not necessarily turn it into an oblation prayer) see above, p. 106.—The last phrase which the people pronounce cannot be accounted as equivalent to a simple. *Amen.*

[62] It is therefore a sound solution, if the

In the mouth of the priest the rendition of the Lord's Prayer takes on the distinction of a special musical form, reminiscent of the chant of the preface. Manuscript evidence of our *Pater noster* melodies is not to be found before the peak of the Middle Ages, but on intrinsic grounds, particularly in view of the characteristic cadences, the origin of the melodies is put as early as the fifth to the seventh century. Of the two melodies, the more elaborate one is the earlier.[63] Perhaps even in the days of Gregory the Great this tune served to accent the value of this great prayer.

As is self-evident, the loud rendition of the prayer was continued through the appended embolism.[64] But in the Roman Mass[65] this was done not in the solemn melody of the *Pater noster*, but in a simple recitative tone, like that which we inferred regarding the canon at the *Te igitur*. This manner of performance has been retained till now in the Milanese rite[66] and in the rite of Lyons,[67] as well as in the *missa præsanctificatorum* of our own Good Friday liturgy. But about the year 1000 the Roman Mass changed to a quiet recitation of the embolism, except for Good Friday.[68] It seems that the factor that led to this change was the consideration that the embolism was still within that portion of the Mass which represented the Passion of Christ. The termination of the Passion was the Resurrection, which since the sixth century was increasingly considered as symbolized in the ceremony of commingling,[69] while the fraction that preceded it continued to be referred to the Passion.[70] This whole

Our Father after a long period, a period that has very much lost sight of its function as mentioned, should be prayed almost in its entirety by the people in the community Mass of today. Ellard, *The Mass of the Future*, 203 f., reports also of Masses said by the Pope in St. Peter's (Nov. 5, 1921; May 26, 1922) at which the people were permitted to say the Our Father with him.

[63] Besides today's melodies in the Roman Missal various others appear in medieval manuscripts. The Mass books of the 11th century from Monte Cassino record three of them; Ebner, 101; Fiala, 193, 223. A missal of Minden printed in 1513 contains four *Pater noster* melodies. F. Cabrol, "Le chant du Pater à la messe," III, *Revue Gregorienne*, 14 (1929), 1-7; cf. *JL*, 9 (1929), 304 f.—In contrast to the solemn melodies of the Preface (see above, p. 107) the *Pater noster* melody did not share the development into the double tuba which started in the 12th century. Ursprung, *Die Kath. Kirchenmusik*, 58 f.

[64] Amalar, *De eccl. off.*, III, 29 (PL, 105,

1148-1150) ; *Ordo Rom.*, II, n. 11 (PL, 78, 975 A) ; Commentary of the Clm. 14690 (10th cent.) : Franz, 411.

[65] In the Mozarabic Mass the variable embolism has the melody of the *Pater noster*: *Missale mixtum* (PL, 85, 559).

[66] *Missale Ambrosianum* (1902), 180 f.

[67] Missale of Lyons (1904), 315 f.

[68] The transition was not universal nor simultaneous. The earliest evidence is in the Pœnitentiale Sangallense tripartitum (MS. of 9th cent.) H. J. Schmitz, *Die Bussbücher und das kanonische Bussverfahren* (Düsseldorf, 1898), 189. Also according to the *Ordo Rom.*, IV (PL, 78, 984) the embolism is said *interveniente nullo sono*. Bonizo of Sutri (d. about 1095), *De sacr.* (PL, 150, 862 C)· considers Gregory the Great as the one who introduced the silent praying of the embolism.—By way of exception it is also said silently on Good Friday according to the *Ordo Eccl. Lateran.* (Fischer, 58).

[69] *Infra*, p. 318.

[70] Lupin, *L'idée du sacrifice de la messe*,

section—the canon in the medival sense, also called the *secreta*—would as far as possible continue in silence. The silence was indeed interrupted by the preface and the *Pater noster*, for which chant was prescribed long before, but thus a more mysterious image was created, a triple silence, during the *secreta*, from the *Te igitur* to the *Pater noster*, and during the embolism, which seemed to refer to the three days of rest in the tomb.[71]

An *Amen* appears after the *Sed libera nos a malo*, first in Alcuin's recension of the sacramentary, then by degrees generally.[72] It must have been taken over from the Vulgate edition of the Our Father in the Bible; there is no *Amen* in the original Greek. The question next came up, who was to say this *Amen*. Sometimes it was added to the people's response, and then it was said out loud.[73] But finally, probably because of the growing practice in the Roman liturgy of leaving the *Sed libera nos a malo*, when said aloud, without an *Amen*,[74] it was shifted to the priest, who says it softly before beginning his quiet embolism.[75]

In the later Middle Ages the *Pater noster* was attended by certain external rites, not counting those which today are associated with the embolism.[76] Widespread was the custom of combining with the Lord's Prayer the elevation of chalice and Host, which had been separated from the closing doxology by the signs of the Cross.[77] Various methods were used; sometimes chalice and Host were lifted only during the words *Fiat voluntas tua*,[78] sometimes all through the first three petitions, up to the words *sicut in cœlo et in terra*.[79] Whereas in these two cases the doxo-

---

113-121; 154 f. Jungmann, *Gewordene Liturgie*, 106; 113 f. Cf. *supra*, I, 184, n. 31. —Brinktrine, *Die hl. Messe*, 235, has misunderstood my meaning.

[71] Jungmann, *Gewordene Liturgie*, 106 f.

[72] Lietzmann, n. 1, 31; Brinktrine, *Die hl. Messe*, 252, n. 1.

[73] According to the *Lay Folks Mass Book* (13th cent.), ed. Simmons, 46, the faithful, and not only the choir, were supposed to answer *Sed libera nos a malo, Amen*. The *Amen* is joined to the answer also in John Beleth, *Explicatio*, c. 47 (PL, 202, 54). That the one praying himself joined the *Amen* to his prayer is not unheard of even in the older Christian tradition; cf. precisely for the Our Father already Cyril of Jerusalem, *Catech. Myst.*, V, 18 (Quasten, *Mon.*, 107).

[74] The Liturgy of Baptism excepted; cf. Eisenhofer, I, 175. In this *Amen* of the *Pater noster* we are dealing with a clearly settled arrangement, but not with a convincing and pervasive principle.

[75] Thus already Wilhelm of Hirsau (d. 1091), *Const.*, I, 86 (PL, 150, 1018); *Ordinarium O.P.* of 1256 (Guerrini, 243); *Liber ordinarius* of Liége (Volk, 95).

[76] Regarding the sign of the cross and the kissing of the paten, see below.—The look directed to the host during the Lord's Prayer as prescribed at present is not associated with this prayer as such: cf. *Ordinarium Cart.* (1932), c. 27, 8, where this look is ordered, as far as possible, from consecration to the Communion.

[77] Above, p. 267.

[78] Still so today in the Rite of Lyons; Bünner, 239. So also according to the Rite of Vienne, Martène, 1, 4, 8, 27 (I, 418 A): the priest holds the Sacred Host over the chalice during the first petitions of the Our Father and then raises both at the words *sicut in cœlo et in terra*. Cf. de Moléon, 11; 58.—The showing of the Host *cum incipit Pater noster* appears in 1562 in the first catalog of Abuses of the Mass; *Conc. Tridentinum*, ed. Görres, VIII, 919.

[79] Hugo of St. Cher., *Tract. super mis-*

logical import of the ceremony still remained clearly visible, this was less so when, as happened elsewhere, the elevation was continued during the whole *Pater noster*.[80] Probably quite consciously a new sense was given to the action. Just as in the case of the elevation at *omnis honor et gloria*, where, at the end of the Middle Ages, even the rubric sometimes directed the change, so here, too, the oblatory elevation was turned instead into a "showing" to the people, as at the consecration.[81] This new signification is even more sharply projected when, as happened in some places, the elevation was linked to the words *Panem nostrum:*[82] here (it seemed to indicate) is the bread which we are asking for. In some places, especially in northern France, a practice akin to this arose, namely, that the cleric who held the paten, or the subdeacon to whom he gave it, held it up high, *in signum instantis communionis*, as we read in one place.[83] On the other hand, since the thirteenth century the doxological gesture which accompanied the *per omnia sæcula sæculorum* of the doxology at the end of the canon, was sometimes duplicated at the end of the embolism, the chalice and the little particle of Host being raised when the same words were repeated.[84]

---

sam (ed. Sölch, 44); Cf. Sölch, *Hugo*, 103. As a reason for the prolonged elevation Hugo alleges that the first three petitions referred *ad vitam æternam*, whereas those that follow, when host and chalice are again upon the altar referred *ad vitam præsentem.*—The same custom in the *Ordinarium* von Chalon-sur-Saône: Martène, 1, 4, XXIX (I, 647 C); Durandus, IV, 46, 23; 47, 8.

[80] Missale of the 12th century from Amiens; Leroquais, I, 225. Equally obscure is the meaning of the Elevation, which, according to a Laon Pontifical of the 13th century, lasts from the *Per omnia s. s.* to the *audemus dicere*: Leroquais, *Les Pontificaux*, I, 168.

[81] Monastic Missal of Lyons, 1531; Martène, 1, 4, XXXIII (I, 660 D): *Ostendat populo hostiam.* Similarly in the *Ordinarium* of Coutances of 1557; Legg, *Tracts*, 64. Further examples see Browe, *Die Verehrung*, 64; Dumotet, *Le desire de voir l'Hostie*, 63-65. Cf. also the elevaton of the Body of Christ in the Mozarabic Mass during the Profession of Faith, that is said between the canon and the *Pater noster; Missale mixtum* (PL, 85, 556 a). *et elevet sacerdos corpus Christi, ut videatur a populo.* In this connection we must mention also the custom of our Good Fri-

day liturgy, according to which the sacred Host is elevated after the embolism, *ut videri possit a populo.*

[82] Premonstratension missal of 1578: Legg, *Tracts*, 241. Later on, still so in Langres, France; de Moléon, 58.

[83] Thus according to a Parisian Missal with which a later Premonstratensian custom is in accord. In the latter the elevation occurred at the *Panem nostrum.* See the reference, *JL*, 4 (1924), 252 (according to K. Dom); cf. Waefelghem, 83, n. 2. The custom continues in the Order of the Premonstratensians even to the present day.— According to the *Ordinarium* of Laon: Martène, 1, 4, XX (I, 608 E), the subdeacon raised the paten at the words *sicut in cœlo et in terra.* According to the Missal of Evreux (circa 1400): *ibid.*, XXVIII (I, 644 E), the priest himself elevated it at the *Amen* of the *Pater noster.* The Sarum Missal of the late Middle Ages: *ibid.*, XXXV (I, 669 C), orders the deacon to keep the paten elevated during the entire *Pater noster;* cf. Maskell, 154. A similar custom prevailed at Rouen about 1700; de Moléon, 368. According to the missal of Liége, 1552, the priest elevated the paten during the *Libera;* de Corswarem, 139.

[84] Mainz Pontifikal about 1170: Martène,

In some churches, a considerable emphasis was put on the bodily posture to be taken during the *Pater noster*. On days that did not have a festal character, a *prostratio* was expected of the people.[85] A Mass *ordo* of Bec even demanded the *prostratio* of the celebrant at the embolism.[86] This is bracketed with the fact that at the height of the Middle Ages, prayers for help were often inserted here during times of stress. At first this was done right after the embolism,[87] but later, when the connection of the embolism with the *Pater noster* was no longer so strongly realized, the prayers were inserted between the *Pater noster* and the embolism.[88] Since the Lord's Prayer was less and less conceived as a Communion prayer, this universal prayer of Christendom became the starting point for adding a special prayer in times of need. In 1040 the *consuetudines* of Farfa laid down the rule: After the *Pater noster* a crucifix, Gospel book, and relics are to be set out in front of the altar, the clergy are to throw themselves on the floor and recite Psalm 73: *Ut quid Deus repulisti in finem*, with the corresponding prayer, while the priest at the altar remains silent.[89] In 1194, during the high tide of the Crusades, the Cistercians in-

---

1, 4, XVII (I, 602 B). Statutes of the Carthusians: *ibid.*, XXV (I, 634 C); cf. Legg, *Tracts*, 102.—Also still in Gabriel Riel, *Cananis expositio*, lect., 80, and in the commentary "Indutus planeta" (after 1500): Legg, *Tracts*, 187.

[85] *Capitulare Monasticum* of 817, n. 74 (PL, 97, 392).—John Beleth, *Explicatio*, c. 47 (PL, 202, 54): *animadvertere oportet, cum sacerdos ait: Oremus. Præceptis etc., nos debere prostratos orare usque ad finem orationis dominicæ, si dies fuerint profesti.* On feast days the congregation stood.—Sicard of Cremona repeats the same; *Mitrale*, III, 6 (PL, 213, 134 D).— *Prostratio*, or at least a kneeling position was demanded during the entire canon untill the *Agnus Dei* by the Synod of Trier (1549), c. 9 (Hartzheim, VI, 600). Cf. Synod of Cologne (1536), c. 14 (*ibid.*, VI, 255).

[86] Just as before in the prayer at the foot of the altar and at *In spiritu humilitatis* and as after the Communion at the prayer *Domine Jesu Christi qui ex voluntate*: Martène, 1, 4, XXXVI (I, 674 E; cf. 672 C, 673 B, 675 B).

[87] In a Sacramentary from Tours at the close of the 9th century (Leroquais, I, 53) it is ordered that the deacon *antequam Agnus Dei* should say a long prayer directed to Christ for the afflicted Church, a prayer that begins with *In spiritu humili-*

tatis. The same is found as *proclamatio antequam dicant Pax Domini* among the works of St. Fulbert of Chartres (d. 1029; PL, 141, 353 f.); also in Farfa (*infra*, n. 89)). As an 11th century entry in the Pontifical of Halinardus: Leroquais, *Les pontificaux*, I, 143. A text from Verdun (11-12th cent.) is given by LeClercq, *Revue Bénéd.*, 57 (1947), 224-226. More detailed (with Ps. 119, 120, 122 and oration *contra persecutores* as *clamor in tribulatione* in an Admont manuscript of the 15th century, printed by Franz, 206 f. Cf. The chapter *Quomodo fiat clamor* in Bernhard, *Ordo Clun.*, I, 40 (Herrgott, 231).

[88] This shift also embraced the Nuptial Blessing, which, as prescribed today, is likewise to be inserted before the *Libera nos quæsumus*. In the Gregorianum (Lietzmann, n. 220, 5) this blessing is given *ante quam dicitur Pax Domini*. The mode of expression in the older Gelasianum, III, 52 (Wilson, 226 f.) likely means the same: *dicis orationem dominicam et sic eam benedicis*, and after the formula of the blessing, *Post hæc dicis, Pax vobiscum*. Cf. 10th century, Sacramentary text with the same wording: PL, 78, 268 f. The obscure formulation has probably contributed to the shift.

[89] Albers, I, 172 f. The prayer is the one above (n. 87): *In spiritu humilitatis* (with amplifications).

troduced at this same spot Psalm 78: *Deus venerunt gentes,* as a prayer for the Holy Land.[90] A similar prescription was enjoined by the Dominican General Chapter of 1269.[91] In the same sense John XXII in 1328 extended a decree of Nicholas III,[92] and ordered that at every Mass, after the *Pater noster,* Psalm 121—probably because of the final verse: *Rogate quœ ad pacem sunt Jerusalem,* etc.—be recited by the clerics and other *literati,* along with *Kyrie,* the versicle *Domine salvos fac reges,* and the orations *Ecclesiœ tuœ quaesumus Domine preces* and *Hostium nostrorum.*[93] Likewise the General Chapter of the Franciscans in 1359 enjoined this prayer, and added that the celebrating priest should meanwhile kneel down before the Blessed Sacrament.[94] In the reform of the Mass book in the sixteenth century, these and other similar additions were allowed to drop,[95] but in some places the custom still continued for some time longer.[96]

[90] Schneider (*Cist. Chr.,* 1927), 109. Cf. *ibidem,* 108-114, the whole chapter "Das Suffragium pro pace nach dem Pater noster."

[91] E. Martène, *Thesaurus novus anecdotorum,* IV (Paris, 1717), 1754. Here also Ps. 78, *Deus venerunt,* should be said *cum prostratione,* versicle and oration. Likewise at Sarum in 13-15th century; Legg, *The Sarum Missal,* 209 f.; Frere, *The Use of Sarum,* I, 90 f. The same crusader prayer appears among the Carmelites: Ordinale of 1312 (Zimmermann, 86); among the Calced Carmelites it has survived to the present day; B. Zimmermann, "Carmes": DACL, II, 2171. Cf. also *infra,* with n. 44.

[92] Bona, II, 16, 4 (825): Before the *Agnus Dei* Ps. 121 and Oration, to obtain peace among Christian Princes.

[93] E. Martène, *Thesaurus novus anecdotorum,* II (Paris, 1717), 748 f.; *Corpus Iur. Can.,* Extrav. comm., III, 11 (Friedberg, II, 1284 f.).—The same prayers were especially enjoined upon the Chapter of the Cistercians. Clement VI added a further Oration; Martène, *De Antiquis eccl. ritibus,* I, 4, 9, 5 (I, 420).—In the 14-15th century the Psalm was part of the established rite of the Papal Curia; see Ordo of Peter Amelii, n. 44 (PL, 78, 1295); cf. the exact instructions when the Psalm falls out: *ibid.,* n. 1, 9, 10, etc. (1275, 1278 f., etc.).—These prayers were retained by the Cistercians up to the 17th century, and even later by the Spanish Cistercians as well as by the Calced Carmelites; Schneider (*Cist. Chr.,* 1927), 112-114. In French cathedrals they still pertained to the High Mass rite at the beginning of the 18th century, as a prayer for peace and for the king; so in Auxerre (with Ps. 121, 122); in Sens (with Ps. 121, 66); in Chartres (with Ps. 19); de Moléon, 159; 169; 230. Also the example from Seville, above I, 134, n. 37.

[94] *Analecta Franciscana,* 2 (1887), 194. References in Browe, *JL,* 9 (1929), 47 f. Elsewhere similar prayers were said in connection with the *Agnus Dei;* see *infra,* p. 339 f.

[95] Clearly these are the hymns and prayers (apparently further developed) that were referred to when, as part of the reform resolutions proposed in Germany at the time of the Council of Trent, the suggestion was made that the antiphons and prayers for peace and the thriving of the fruits of the field should be placed, not after the consecration as heretofore, but in some other place. H. Jedin, "Das Konzil von Trient und die Reform des römischen Messbuches" (*Liturg. Leben,* 1939), 42 f.

[96] On June 11, 1605, the Congregation of Rites decided against an ordinance of the Bishop of Osca, who prescribed prayers for rain before the *Libera nos quœsumus* in all conventual Masses. *Decr. auth. SRC,* n. 182.

3. Preparatory Activities in Other Liturgies

In different liturgies, especially those of the East, the reception and distribution of Communion is preceded by a series of preparatory acts and prayers. In the Roman liturgy these acts and prayers either never developed[1] or were reduced to very modest forms and compressed between the embolism and the more immediate Communion prayers. In order to be able to evaluate the meaning of those forms that were retained, it will be worthwhile to make a brief survey of the richer development in the liturgies outside the Roman.

In the rites of the East, the celebrant, after the Lord's Prayer, turns his attention first to the congregation. He pronounces a blessing over the people, then lifts up the species of bread with the words at once invitatory and warning, "The Holy to the holy!" Then follows the fraction (or in some part of the rites it precedes the Lord's Prayer). The fraction is primarily a portioning out of the breads for the Communion of the people, but it also serves as a symbolic expression of certain ideas. With this symbolic fraction there is connected a crossing of the holy species, sometimes very pretentious, and then finally the commingling by putting a particle of the bread into the chalice.[2] After the celebrant's Communion which follows, some of the rites have still another formal invitation to the faithful "to approach in godliness, faith and love."[3]

The blessing of the congregation before the Communion is already developed in some sources of the fourth century.[4] Its original meaning, "that we may be made worthy to take Communion and share in Thy holy mysteries,"[5] is unmistakably expressed in one portion of the oriental liturgies. It is regularly preceded by the usual greeting of the celebrant and the deacon's admonition: Τὰς κεφαλὰς ἡμῶν τῷ κυρίῳ κλίνωμεν, to which the response Σοὶ κύριε is generally given.[6] The benediction then concludes with the usual doxology.

This blessing is found in the Gallic liturgies too. It was given by the bishop, with a solemn formula that varied with each Mass,[7] or by the

---

[1] Duchesne, *Christian Worship*, 186 (with note) supposes that the reason for the absence of such prayers in the older Roman Mass is because the Our Father alone was considered the proper preparation immediately preceding the Communion. Because of its forward shift to its present place a hiatus occurred.

[2] In the rites of the East other than the Byzantine, this group of rites bound up with the breaking of the Sacred Host precedes the Lord's Prayer either partially or entirely. Hanssens, III, 503-518; Baumstark, *Die Messe im Morgenland*, 156-162.

[3] Thus in the Byzantine Mass; Brightman,

395. Similarly with the Armenians and the West Syrians; Baumstark, 164.

[4] Above, p. 276.

[5] Liturgy of St. James; Brightman, 61, 1. 3. Similarly the Liturgy of St. Mark: *ibid.*, 137; Byzantine Liturgy of St. Basil: *ibid.*, 340.

[6] West Syrian liturgy: Brightman, 60; 100; cf. 136, 182.

[7] To the most important remnant of the old episcopal benedictions belongs the collection of *benedictiones episcopales* that originated in Freising (7-9) cent.); see G. Morin, *Revue Bénéd.*, 29 (1912), 168-194. The individual formularies of the Gallican

priest, using a simple unchanging formula.[8] Here, however, the blessing was no longer looked upon as a preparation for Communion,[9] but rather as a substitute for it for those who did not communicate, and who therefore could leave right afterwards.[10] Despite the protest which Pope Zachary had addressed to St. Boniface in 751,[11] the episcopal blessing made its way in northern countries from the Gallic liturgy into the Roman, as a climax of the solemn pontifical service.[12] Therefore the sacramentaries and *ordines* of the Carolingian area which were intended for episcopal use henceforth often contain a reference to this benediction, which usually followed the embolism,[13] but later in many churches was not given till after

and Mozarabic Masses, for the most part, also contain a proper formula of blessing.
[8] According to the *Expositio* of the Gallican Mass (ed. Quasten, 22) the sacerdotal blessing formula is as follows: *Pax fides, caritas et communicatio corporis et sanguinis Domini sit semper vobiscum.* The II Synod of Seville (619), can. 7 (Mansi, X, 539) permits that the priest in the absence of the bishop should also be allowed to impart such a blessing, and the practice is presupposed since then to other Gallic law sources. J. Lechner, "Der Schlussegen des Priesters in der hl. Messe" (*Festschrift E. Eishmann zum 70. Geburtstag* [Paderborn, 1940], 651-684), 652 ff.
[9] The *Expositio* of the Gallican Mass (ed. Quasten, 22) as the formula (preceding note) shows, has preserved a further trace of the original meaning of the blessing; it is given *ut in vas benedictum benedictionis mysterium ingrediatur.*
[10] Already in Cæsarius of Arles (d. 540), *Serm.*, 73, 2 (Morin, 294; PL, 39, 2276 f.) : he who would participate in the Mass with profit must persevere *usquequo oratio dominica dicatur et benedictio populo detur.* Similarly Synods of the 6th century. Cf. Nickl, *Der Anteil des Volkes*, 53-55; Lechner, 651 f.; 673.
[11] Zachary, *Ep.*, 13 (PL, 89, 951 D).
[12] See chapter on Episcopal Benedictions in P. de Puniet, *Le Sacramentaire romain de Gellone* (Special printing from *Eph. Liturg.*, 1934-1938), 80-88; also tables regarding their occurrences in the Gelasian Sacramentary; *ibid.*, 218*-235*. Alcuin also has in his edition of the Gregorianum contributes an extensive collection of benedictions, some of which were partly taken from Mozarabic material; these then reap-

peared in Latin Mass books either as a supplement or distributed among the Mass formularies; Muratori, II, 362-380. Episcopal benedictions from different sources: PL, 78, 601-636. Eisenhofer, I, 97 f., mentions further forms of benediction: See also the collection derived from manuscripts of the 14th century with 287 formulas which, for the most part, are not to be found earlier; edited by W. Lüdtke, "Bischöfliche Benediktionen aus Magdeburg und Braunschweig," *JL*, 5 (1925), 97-122. The *benedictiones episcopales* ultimately made their way into Italy, as testified by Bonizo of Sutri, *De vita christiana*, II, 51 (ed. Perels, 60), and Sicard of Cremona, *Mitrale*, III, 7 (PL, 213, 138 f.). In Rome itself they were unknown.— How highly they were prized in northern countries is seen in the case of Honorius Augustodunensis, *Gemma an.*, c. 60 (PL, 172, 562) who introduces the *benedictio episcopi* as the sixth of the seven *officia* of the Mass.

[13] Gregorianam of Cod. Ratoldi (PL, 78, 244 B) ; *Ordo Rom.*, II, n. 11 footnote, as (PL, 78, 975 A) ; *Ordo Rom.*, VI, n. 11 (PL, 78, 993 f.). The *Pax Domini* appeared as the conclusion of the episcopal blessing, and probably received the form, *Et pax eius sit semper vobiscum;* thus in a Pontifical of Mainz about 1300: Martène, 1, 4, XVIII (I, 603 D) ; thus also in the Pontifical of Durandus (*ibid.*, XXIII [I, 623 C] ; Andrieu, III, 655) ; cf. PL, 78, 30, n. f.—The Abbot of Gregorienmünster also imparted the Pontifical blessing at this place; Martène, 1, 4, XXXII (I, 656 f.). Such, too, was the case at St. James in Liége; Volk, 97. A miniature of the 9th century from Marmoutiers, with

the *Pax Domini*.[14] The Gallic pontifical blessing, like the blessing in the Orient, was usually preceded by the deacon's exhortation: *Humiliate vos ad benedictionem*,[15] which was answered by a *Deo gratias*; then the bishop, with mitre and staff, turned to the people and read the formula of blessing from the *Benedictionale* held before him; at the concluding sentence he made the sign of the Cross three times in three directions.[16] The formula of blessing itself was regularly composed of three members, following the model of the great priestly blessing in the Old Testament (Numbers 6:22-26), which also appeared in the most ancient collections.[17] After each of these three members (usually consisting of well-rounded periods) there was a response, *Amen*, and at the end a special concluding clause. As for content, most of the formulas clung to the pertinent festal thoughts.[18] Thus the original connection with Communion was nowhere visible even in the oldest Latin formulas. Hence this pontifical blessing could be transferred to other positions.[19] But it remained in its original location often [20]

---

the annotation: *Hic benedic populum,* shows Abbot Raganaldus imparting the blessing; H. Leclerq, DACL, I, 3205; III, 75.

[14] Missa Illyrica: Martène, 1, 4, IV (I, 514 f.); Mass order of Séez: PL, 78, 250 A. Both cases deal with the same rubric.—Sicard of Cremona, *loc. cit.*, testifies to the same arrangement.

[15] First in the Sacramentary of Rataldus (PL, 78, 244) and in the *Ordo Rom.*, VI, n. 11 (PL, 78, 993 f.). But cf. already Cæsarius of Arles, *Sermo.*, 76, 2 (Morin, 303; PL, 39, 2284): *Quotiens clamatum fuerit, ut vos benedictioni humiliare debeatis, non vobis sit laboriosum capita inclinare.*

[16] Thus according to the Pontifical of Durandus (Martène, 1, 4, XXIII [I, 622 f.]; Andrieu, III, 653-655), where the conclusion is added: *Et benedictio Dei Patris omnipotentis et Filii et Spiritus Sancti descendat super vos et maneat semper.* Here also directions for an enhancement of the ceremony on solemn feasts.

[17] de Puniet, 82.

[18] Let the first of the episcopal benedictions from Magdeburg and Brunswick, for the First Sunday of Advent, edited by Lüdtke, JL, 5 (1925), 99 f., serve as an example: *Omnipotens Deus, cuius Unigeniti adventum et præteritum creditis et futurum expectatis, eiusdem adventus vos illustratione sanctificet et sua benedictione locupletet.*

Amen.—In præsentis vitæ stadio vos ab omni adversitate defendat et se vobis in iudicio placabilem ostendat. Amen.—Quo a cunctis peccatorum contagiis liberati illius tremendi examinis diem expectetis interriti. Amen.—Quod ipse præstare dignetur, cuius regnum et imperium sine fine permanet in sæcula sæculorum. Amen.

[19] According to the *Ordinarium* of Laon in the late Middle Ages: Martène, 1, 4, XXI (I, 610 B), it was given after the Gospel; cf. above I, 494. As the IV Council of Toledo (633), c. 18 (Mansi, X, 624), remarks with disapproval: *nonnulli sacerdotes* in the 7th century in Spain already tried to push it to the end of the Mass. In the Pontifical of Valencia, written in 1417, it is placed after the *Ite Missa est* as the final blessing. So also in the Parisian manuscript 733 of the Pontifical of Durandus (Andrieu, III, 164 f.). The same seems to have been the case until modern times in Trier, where even today, as I am told, the invitation of the deacon before the Pontifical blessing at this place is retained: *Inclinate vos ad benedictionem.*

[20] There is evidence of this at Salzburg, 1535, in Berthold of Chiemsee (Franz, 727). The abbots of the Cistercians imparted it until 1618; Schneider (*Cist.-Chr.*, 1927), 136-139. De Moléon, *Voyage* (see Register, s. v. Bénédiction) found it still in the 18th century in various French episcopal churches. Further references in Bünner, 278, note 1.

even after the end of the Middle Ages. In the cathedrals of Lyons and Autun this blessing has been retained right down to the present.[21]

After the blessing, all oriental liturgies have an invitation to the faithful: Τὰ ἅγια τοῖς ἁγίοις![22] This exclamation of the celebrant is attested even in sources of the fourth century,[23] and it probably goes back much further.[24] The importance of the occasion is often further accented, as before the reading of the Gospel, by the deacon's call to attention: Πρόσχωμεν, or else by other preparatory prayers.[25] Then, without turning around, the priest raises the Body of the Lord so that all might see.[26] The people respond with a prayer of praise, in the older form of which, still preserved in the Byzantine Mass, the holiness demanded by the reception of Communion is referred back to our Lord Himself: "One is holy, one the Lord, Jesus Christ, to the honor of God the Father."[27] In the remaining liturgies of the East this response of the people has almost everywhere taken a trinitarian turn,[28] which does not let the basic idea stand out so clear.

The chief liturgies of the West, in the more ancient form in which they have come down to us, show no parallels to this elevation or to the words which correspond to it.[29] In later developments the Roman liturgy has

---

[21] Bünner, 277 f.; Schneider, 137.

[22] This form still in use today in the Coptic and Byzantine Mass. Brightman, 184; 393. Elsewhere somewhat altered; see Hanssens, III, 498.

[23] *Const. Ap.,* VIII, 13, 12; Cyril of Jerusalem, *Catech. myst.,* V, 19; Theodore of Mopsuestia, *Sermones catech.,* VI (Quasten, *Mon.,* 107; 229). For further references see Hanssens, III, 499 ff.

[24] Cf. Didache, 10, 6 (*supra,* I, 12).

[25] Both in the Byzantine and in the remaining Greek liturgies; Brightman, 61; 137 f.; 341; cf. Hanssens, III, 494 ff.

[26] The custom is found since the 6-7th century. Previously, as Chrysostom, *In Hebr. hom.,* 17, 4f. (PG, 63, 132 f.) shows, the priest raised only his hand: καθάπερ τις, κῆρυξ τὴν χεῖρα ἄιρων. Hanssens, III, 501.—The performance of the elevation today is varied. In the Byzantine Mass the priest elevates the host upon the diskos. Among the Copts he raises a particle above the chalice. Among the West Syrian Jacobites a double elevation takes place; first the host is elevated upon the diskos and then the chalice; so also among the Maronites. Among the Uniate Armenians the priest, after having elevated the host, takes hold of the chalice and host and turns toward the people; among the disident Armenians the host is dipped instead into the Precious Blood and then elevated once more. Hanssens, III, 494-499.

[27] Brightman, 341; 393; also already *Const. Ap.,* VIII, 13, 13 (Quasten, *Mon.,* 229 f.), where Luke 2: 14 is appended.—Cf. the discussion about *tu solus sanctus,* above I, 354 f.—Baumstark, *Die Messe im Morgenlande,* 158, indicates the possibility that the words of the Apostle, I Cor. 8: 6; Phil. 2: 11, already present an echo of the liturgical formula.

[28] Already in Theodore of Mopsuestia, *Sermones catech.,* VI (Rücker, 36) there is evidence of this: *Unus Pater sanctus, unus Filius sanctus, unus Spiritus sanctus,* where in the catechetical explanation, the same as in a number of later liturgical texts, it was no longer the holiness, but the oneness of the divine nature that was given prominence. Here, as in the later West Syrian liturgy, the formula is extended by adding *Gloria Patri et Filio et Spiritui Sancto;* Rücker, *Die Jakobosanaphora,* 73. See details in Hanssens, *loc. cit.,* especially 498 f., where also further amplifications are presented.

[29] G. Morin, *Revue Bénéd.,* 40 (1928) 136 f., repeatedly refers to traces from the

created counterparts in two different acts: in the elevation of the two species which we join to the consecration, and in the "showing" of the bread before Communion, where the words *Ecce Agnus Dei,* along with the acknowledgment of our personal unworthiness, to some extent correspond to the *Sancta sanctis* and its response.[30]

Among the preparatory acts regarding the Sacrament itself, the oldest and most important one, the one that therefore reappears in all the liturgies, is the fraction or the breaking of the consecrated bread. This is but a continuation of an action which, according to all four New Testament accounts, our Lord Himself performed at the Last Supper: He took the bread, broke it, and gave it to His disciples. The Breaking of the Bread is, in fact, the oldest name used for the celebration of the Eucharist. The more immediate occasion for the breaking or fraction was the necessity of dividing the whole breads for the Communion of the congregation,[31] and, in any case, for the purpose of having a particle to keep for the rite of commingling which followed.[32] The example of the breaking of the bread in the supper room and in the primitive Church must surely have been the factor which determined that the rite would continue not as a *cutting* of the bread, as might easily have been, but as a "breaking"; in other words, this is what determined and determines the choice of a form of bread which could be broken, so that there would be question only of a "breaking" of bread.[33]

In its ritual form, the fraction which was designed to prepare the par-

5th century which lead one to conclude to Latin *Sancta sanctis* and the answer *Unus sanctus* in certain isolated cases. The question has been investigated afresh by L. Brou, "Le 'Sancta sanctis' en Occident," *Journal of Theol. Studies,* 46 (1945), 160-178; 47 (1946), 11-29. As Brou proves, the one certain evidence of the *Sancta sanctis* in the West is found in the British Bishop Fastidius (beginning of the 5th cent.; he calls it a *præfatio*: cf. *infra,* p. 318, n. 33); an uncertain instance is in Nicetas of Remesiana in Dacia (d. after 414). The late Mozarabic commingling formula which somehow appertains here he traces in the *Liber ordinum* (Férotin, 241) and in several of the French Mass-books (since the 11th cent.) described by V. Leroquais. According to Brou the basic text, frequently subjected to variation, must have read: *Sancta cum sanctis et coniunctio corporis et sanguinis D. n. J. C. sit edentibus et bibentibus in vitam æternam. Amen.* (*op. cit.,* 1946, 17). If, therefore, it is conceivable that the *Sancta sanctis* was used

here and there in the Gallic sphere with the complete meaning of the oriental liturgies, a similar assumption (as Brou rightly remarks) would be excluded at Rome where the formula *Si quis non communicat det locum* (see *infra,* p. 341) already fulfilled the same function.—The inscription *Digna dignis* was found in the excavation of the floor of a North African apse; J. Sauer, "Der Kirchenbau Nordafrikas in den Tagen des hl. Augustinus" (*Aurelius Augustinus,* ed. by Grabmann and Mausbach [Cologne, 1930], 243-300), 296.

[30] It has already been emphasized above, note 37, that the elevation of the chalice and host at the *omnis honor et gloria* is not pertinent here.

[31] In this sense the breaking of the host is already intimated by Clement of Alexandria, *Stromata,* I, 1 (PG, 692 B). Cf. Haberstroh, *Der Ritus der Brechung und Mischung nach dem dem Missale Romanum* (St. Gabriel, 1937), 11-33.

[32] Hanssens, III, 513-515.

[33] Nevertheless in the Byzantine Prosko-

ticles for the Communion of the congregation continued along simple lines. In the oriental rites it appears to have been done generally by the celebrant himself. Probably in view of greater Communion days, when more time was required, rather lengthy prayer-texts are in part provided to accompany the rite.[34]

But the fraction which served for symbolism and which culminates in the commingling of the two species is much more elaborate. There are three parts: first, the fraction itself, performed on the Host intended for the celebrant, which is divided into from two to four portions; then the crossing (consignatio), very detailed, especially in the Syrian Liturgy, the particle of Host being crossed either over the chalice or in the chalice;[35] finally, the commingling, in which a particle is dropped into the chalice.

Various ideas are combined in this symbolic rite. Its purpose is, first of all, to manifest and proclaim the unity of the sacrifice performed under the two species. It is, in se, a rather obvious assumption that this is the original meaning of the commingling and therefore the starting-point for the development of the rite. This assumption is confirmed by witnesses from fifth-century Syria, who can hardly be far removed from the source of the rite either as to time or place,[36] and who make the same basic statements regarding the signs of the Cross.[37] Likewise, certain corresponding

---

mide, the bread is cut; the knife used in this instance is called λόγχη, Slavic, kopyo = "lance." Brightman, 356 f.; cf. above, p. 44.

[34] In the Greek Liturgy of St. James they are Psalms 22, 33, 150. (Brightman, 366). Also in the Greek Liturgy of St. Mark (ibid., 138, 1 20), Psalm 150 is intoned.— Extensive prayers accompany the process among the Syrian Jacobites (ibid., 97-99). They revolve about different recollections of Christ's Passion, the piercing with the lance, the Cross, the Resurrection, our guilt and the atonement through the suffering of Christ, the Lamb of God.—In other Mass arrangements, as in the Abyssinian, in general no particular formulas for the fraction are apparent (ibid., 237 f.; cf. nevertheless Hanssens, III, 512 f.); so too in the East Syrian, where, however, the lengthy prayers (among others, Ps. 50; 122; -3; 25; 6, with a washing of hands), that precede the rite of breaking the host, could here be brought in (Brightman, 288 f.).

[35] In the Liutrgy of the Syrian language and also in the Egyptian liturgies the particle referred to is today dipped in the chalice and then the sign of the cross is first made with it. So likewise in the Greek Liturgy of St. James in which the cross is first made with the particle that has been dipped in the chalice over the undipped particle and then the process is reversed (Brightman, 62; MS. of the 14th century; more complicated in the 10th century MS. presented by Hanssens, III, 516 f.). Among the Maronites 18 crosses precede the breaking of the host. In the Ethiopian Mass a special prayer ritual is combined with the breaking of the host and the sign of the cross in which the invocation, Domine miserere nostri Christe is sung by priest and people alternating according to a fixed pattern forty-one times; Hanssens, III, 503-513. Cf. Haberstroh, 13-24; Raes, Introductio, 94-103.

[36] Hanssens, III, 514, hazards the supposition that the rite of the breaking of the host originated in Syria.

[37] Theodore of Mopsuestia (d. 428), Sermones catech., VI (Rücker, 54) cum pane signat super sanguinem figura crucis et cum sanguine super panem et coniungit et applicat eos in unum, qua re unicuique manifestetur ea, quamquam duo sunt, ta-

texts which accompany the commingling in some of the rites emphasize this point of unification in the sacrifice.[38] There is no need, then, to seek a reason for the practice in the merely material order.[39]

A commingling rite of a peculiar sort is the admixture of warm water (ζέον) to the consecrated chalice in the Byzantine liturgy.[40] The practice is ancient.[41] But its meaning is obscure; seemingly its aim is to affirm that the fulness of the Holy Spirit is in the Sacrament or is effected by the Sacrament.[42]

In the Syrian source mentioned, the fraction—taken at first in the sense of an apportionment for the Communion—was given a deeper significance. According to this, it is meant to show how the Lord distributes His presence among many, just as after the Resurrection He made Himself known and "distributed His appearance among many": the women, the disciples

---

men unum esse virtualiter et memoriam esse mortis et passionis . . . Ea de causa fas est deinceps in calicem immittere panem vivificantem, ut demonstretur ea sine separatione et unum esse virtute et unam gratiam conferre accipientibus ea. — Narsai (d. about 502) "He unites them—the Body with the Blood, and the Blood with the Body—that every one may confess that the Body and the Blood are one." Cf. *Hom.*, 21 (*ibid.*, 59).

[38] The Liturgy of St James has the priest say at the same time: Ἕνωσις τοῦ παναγίου σώματος καὶ τοῦ τιμίου αἵματος τοῦ κυρίου .. Ἰησοῦ Χριστοῦ. Then follows a second similar text; Brightman, 62. Cf. the text for the joining of the elements in the East Syrian Mass (*ibid.*, 292). It accompanies the ceremony of the joining of the two now moistened halves of the host; an actual division is missing.

[39] Eisenhofer, II, 201, endeavors to find the origin of the rite of the commingling in the necessity to soften the bread, because (fermented) bread, when kept any length of time (when transported to other churches: *fermentum*, see *infra*.) easily becomes hard; similarly Lebrun, I, 504 f. However, there is clearly question in the oriental rite of a particle from the present Mass. In the Roman liturgy, too, the second mingling was of the same nature. The *fermentum* could be brought only to nearby churches.—Dix, *The Shape of the Liturgy*, 134, supposes that the oriental custom of mingling a particle from one's own Mass was a substitution for the *fer-*

mentum rite which disappeared early. That would be a parallel to the development in the West; see *infra*, p. 309, n. 34. In any event we would then have at the beginning a commingling intended symbolically.

[40] Brightman, 349.

[41] There are evidences of it since the 6th century. Hanssens, II, 235 f.; III, 518 f.

[42] The action is accompanied with the words "Fervor of faith, full of the Holy Ghost"; cf. Rom. 12: 11. Perhaps there is some significance in the fact that the commingling with the particle of the Host, that occurs under a similar formula, immediately precedes, inasmuch as the union of the Body and Blood from which proceeds the warmth of life, is there pushed into relief. K. Burdach, *Der Gral* (Stuttgart, 1938), 148 f., refers to Cyril of Alexandria, *In John* 1, IV, 6, 54 (PG, 73, 580 A), who compares the change of the communicant to the change that takes place when cold water is placed over a hot fire.—Further confirmation is found in something mentioned by L. H. Grondijs, *L'iconographie byzantine du Crucifié mort sur la croix* (Brussels, 1941); see the penetrating review by Countess E. Luchesi-Palli, *ZkTh*, 70 (1948), 369-375. According to Grondijs the custom of the ζέον originated in connection with the teaching of the Aphthartodocetæ promoted by Justinian; according to this teaching the Body of Christ remained incorrupt in death and of course did not become frigid, and therefore warm blood and water issued from it

at Emmaus, the apostles.[43] On the other hand, the symbolism inherent in the primitive Christian and pre-Christian meal ceremony of the breaking of the bread, namely, the fellowship of all at table in the one bread,[44] is nowhere mentioned in the liturgies that have survived.[45] Nor did the symbolism of the Resurrection last long, at least in the ceremony of the fraction itself. By the sixth century, if not earlier, the fraction began to be viewed among the Greeks not as a division and distribution, but rather as a violent separation, a splitting, a sundering, and consequently as a figure of Christ's death on the Cross.[46]

The thought of the Passion is frequently expressed in the prayers and songs with which the oriental liturgies have surrounded the fraction rite in the course of time; this is especially true in regard to the West-Syrian liturgy. "Thus truly has the Word of God suffered in the flesh and was sacrificed and broken upon the Cross . . . and His side was pierced by a lance. . . ."[47] "Father of truth, see Thy Son as a sacrifice that conciliates Thee. . . . See His Blood that was shed on Golgotha."[48] In particular, the connection with the idea of "the Lamb of God that taketh away[49] the sins

---

(76 f.). Inasmuch as later according to the teaching of Niketas Stethatos, the Indwelling of the Holy Ghost, which also bespeaks warmth, and which also continues after death, was substituted in the place of the physical warmth of the body, another symbolic practice could be preserved: In Communion one received the Precious Blood, filled by the Spirit as indicated by the ζέον just as one would not wish to receive the Body of Our Lord under the appearance of ἄζυμα—ἄψυχα (see above, note 19). As a starting point for the custom a profane table practice has been suggested; Hanssens, II, 235.

[43] Theodore of Mopsuestia, loc. cit. (Rücker, 34 f.); cf. Narsai, Hom., 17 (Connolly, 24): "and now He appears in the reception of His Body, to the sons of the church; and they believe in Him and receive from Him the pledge of life."

[44] Above I, 11. Cf. also I Cor. 10: 17; Ignatius of Antioch, Ad Eph., 20, 2.

[45] Nevertheless A. Beil, Einheit der Liebe (Colmar, 1941), 53, reports a Lettish folk custom on Christmas Eve, in which expression is given to the same fundamental idea; the father of the family hands the mother a piece of baked goods which they break in two; the father hands his half to the eldest son, which they break in the same way, while the mother follows the

same procedure with the eldest daughter, etc. This Christmas custom, as I have ascertained through research, is found with insignificant variations (a wafer; the father of the family only starts the breaking; the servants have their own bread, that they also break) in Upper Silesia, Poland, and Lithuania.

[46] Eutychius (d. 582), De Pasch., c. 3 (PG, 86, 2396 A) : ἡ κλάσις . . . τὴν σφαγὴν δηλοῖ. A suggestion along the same lines is Chrysostom, In I Cor. hom., 24, 2 (PG, 61, 200) : In explaining κλῶμεν of I Cor. 10: 16, he says: What He did not suffer on the cross, that for your sake He endured in the sacrifice.—Suggestions of such an interpretation are found moreover in earlier times. Here also belongs the expanded variation of I Cor. 11: 24, (τὸ σῶμα τὸ ὑπὲρ ὑμῶν) κλώμενον, that predominates especially in Egyptian manuscripts and recurs in the Eucharistia of Hippolytus (supra, I, 29) and in the Euchologion of Serapion (supra, I, 34). Cf. Dix, The Shape of the Liturgy, 81; 132 f.

[47] Brightman, 97. The prayer was already extant in the 9th century; Hanssens, III, 518.

[48] Brightman, 98. Also in the Ethiopian Mass, ibid., 239 f.

[49] Ibid., 99. Similarly in the Greek Liturgy

of the world." The thought is even more closely linked with the fraction in the Byzantine Mass, where the priest accompanies the rite with the words: Μελίζεται καὶ διαμερίζεται ὁ ἀμνὸς τοῦ θεοῦ, continuing with the antithetical phrase: "It is divided and yet not separated. It is continually devoured and yet never consumed, but sanctifies the partaker."[50] Still the thought of the Resurrection was not entirely obliterated. The *Ordo communis* of the West-Syrian Mass sees in the fraction a picture of the crucifixion, but then, apparently in reference to the consignation, it also speaks about the Resurrection.[51]

The thought of the Passion was early associated with the fraction rite also in the Gallic liturgies; in fact, it here gained a particular development in connection with the fraction itself. The seventh century *Expositio* of the Gallican Mass even tells of a certain case in which, while the priest was performing the fraction, an angel was seen cutting the limbs of a radiant little child and catching its blood.[52] At the Council of Tours (567) a warning was given to the priests to arrange the particles at the fraction not *in imaginario ordine* but in the shape of a cross.[53] The cruciform arrangement remained as the fundamental one also in the Mozarabic Mass. But it was further elaborated into a representation of all the main points in the work of redemption, in much the same way as the idea of *passio* at the anamnesis (as we have already been able to settle) in many cases gathered around itself all the mysteries of the redemption. Thus arose a second anamnesis, but this one in the language of symbolism. Nine particles were supposed, seven of them composing the cross. Each particle signified a mystery, beginning with the Incarnation and birth down to the glorious reign in heaven.[54] So, here too, the Resurrection has a place beside the Passion. Much more complicated was the arrangement in the Irish-Celtic liturgy.[55] The fraction was accompanied by a special song which is called *confractorium* in the Milanese Mass; it was subject to the

---

of St. James (*ibid.*, 62): ᾽Ιδοῦ ὁ ἀμνὸς τοῦ θεοῦ . . . σφαγιασθεὶς ὑπὲρ τῆς τοῦ κόσμου ζωῆς.

[50] Brightman, 393. Reference was already made *supra*, p. 37, to the persistent designation "Lamb" for the Host.

[51] Renaudot, II (1847), 22.

[52] Quasten, 21. The legend is taken over from the Orient; see Vitæ Patrum, c. 6 (*ibid.*, n. 4).

[53] Can. 3. (Mansi, IX, 793) ; cf. also *supra*, p. 37. It seems that a human figure was formed with the Sacred Body of Our Lord, an abuse against which Pope Pelagius I, about 558, expressed opposition in a letter to the Bishop of Arles; Ph. Jaffé, *Regesta pont. Rom.*, I, (2nd ed.; Leipzig, 1885),

n. 978; cf. Duchesne, *Christian Worship*, 219; P. Browe, *JL*, 15 (1941), 62, note 4.

[54] *Missale mixtum* (PL, 85, 557). The names for the particles are: 1. *corporatio*, 2. *nativitas*, 3. *circumcisio*, 4. *apparitio*, 5. *passio*, 6. *mors*, 7. *resurrectio*, 8. *gloria*, 9. *regnum*. They are arranged as follows:

	1	
6	2	7
	3	8
	4	9
	5	

[55] The number of particles is regulated according to the rank of the feast day; on ordinary days there were only five particles; on the feast of the Saints, 7-11; on Sundays and feasts of Our Lord, 9-13; on

variations of the Church year.[56] In the Mozarabic liturgy the commingling is separated from the fraction by the *Pater noster;* here the former is accompanied by a short variable chant.[57] The thought of the Passion remained conjoined to the fraction even in the explanations of later commentators.[58]

Of the rites here described which developed in the various liturgies between canon and Communion, only the fraction and commingling gained any special importance in the Roman Mass.

4. The Fraction

In the Roman Mass since Gregory the Great, as in the Byzantine Mass, the fraction does not take place till after the *Pater noster* and its embolism have been recited.[1] Years ago on great feast days, when all the people partook of Holy Communion, it must have been a very important activity, which was then carefully regulated, and which led, towards the end of the seventh century, to the introduction of a special chant, the *Agnus Dei.*

The older Roman *ordines* have carefully outlined the proceedings. After the *Pax Domini* was said and the kiss of peace given, the pope took the two Host-breads, now consecrated, which he had himself presented, and after breaking off a small piece, which remained at the altar,[2] laid the two breads on the large paten held out for him by the deacon; then he made his way to his *cathedra,* the deacon following with the paten. Now acolytes stepped up to the altar, taking their stations at both sides of it. They had scarfs over their shoulders, for they were about to bear a

---

the solemn feast of Christmas, Easter, and Pentecost there are 65. Appendix in the Stowe Missal written in Celtic in the 9th century, ed Warner (HBS, 32), 41; cf. the kindred provisions regarding the number and arrangement of the hosts at the Offertory, *supra,* 51 f. From this we understand the warning the bishop gives the newly ordained after their ordination that they should learn *totius missæ atque hostiæ consecrationem ac fractionem et communionem* from well-instructed priests. This admonition came into the Roman Ordination rite through the Pontifical of Durandus (Andrieu, *Le Pontifical Romain,* III, 372f.) and thus clearly originated from the Gallican tradition.

[56] This hymn is verified through the *Expositio* of the Gallican Mass (ed. Quasten, 21): *Sacerdote autem frangente supplex clerus psallit antiphonam, quia ‹Christo› patiente dolorem mortis omnia terræ testata sunt elementa.* In the Mozarabic Mass

the Credo took the place of the fraction chant (PL, 85, 557 f.).

[57] *Missale mixtum* (PL, 85, 119; 560 f.).

[58] Cf. *infra,* p. 309, note 33.

[1] The pre-Gregorian, or rather the Gallic arrangement, is still in the 9th century basically the one found in the Stowe Missal, where the breaking follows immediately upon the concluding doxology; Warner (HBS, 32), 17. The same obtains in the Milanese Sacramentary of Biasca; Botte, 46 Apparatus. To some extent the supposition of Botte, "L'Ange du sacrifice" (*Cours et Conférences,* VII), 218 f., is rather arbitrary; he argues that the breaking formerly followed upon the first half of the *Supplices* and the continuation of the prayer with *ut quotquot* was the conclusion of the prayer for the breaking of the bread.

[2] Until the end of the Mass (Amalar, *De eccl. off.,* III, 35; PL, 105, 1155 A). A

precious burden.[3] They all carried linen bags[4] which, with the subdeacons' help, they held open and ready, and in which the archdeacon placed the breads which lay on the altar. Then they divided to right and left among the bishops and priests who, at a sign from the pope, began the fraction. At the same time, deacons also began the fraction over the pope's paten.[5] This paten was very large; for that reason the first *ordo* stated in one place that two subdeacons brought it over, and obviously it was also held by them during the fraction. In the larger Roman basilicas there was no dearth of such large patens made of gold and silver.[6] One is inclined to wonder why patens were not used in place of the linen bags. As a matter of fact, in the Mass *ordines* of the later Carolingian-Ottonian period,

gloss in the older recension of *Ordo Rom.*, I, n. 19 (Andrieu, II, 101; PL, 78, 946 B) offers a not very enlightening reason for the rite; *ut, dum missarum sollemnia peraguntur, altare sine sacrificio non sit.* Cf. B. Capelle, "Le Rite de la fraction dans la messe romaine" (*Revue Bénéd.*, 1941, 5-40), 15 f., who supposes that this refers to the *fermentum* (see *infra*) that the pope lays aside. However, the circumstance that there is mention here of only one particle argues against this supposition. Cf. also Batiffol, *Leçons*, 92.

[3] Similarly somewhat later other acolytes appear, carrying larger beaker-shaped supplementary vessels for the chalice Communion *(scyphi)*; Ordo of S. Amand (Andrieu, II, 164). In this Ordo the large paten of the pope is carried by the first acolyte (not as in the *Ordo Rom.*, I, by two subdeacons) and held during the breaking of the host. This acolyte wears a silk scarf adorned with a cross; cf. Batiffol, 88.

[4] These appear as the insignia of their office at the consecration of the acolytes, *Ordo Rom.*, VIII, n. 1 (PL, 78, 1000 f.).

[5] Such is the picture the main sources present *Ordo Rom.*, I, n. 19 (Andrieu, II, 98-100; PL, 78, 945 f.); *Capitulare eccl. ord.* (Andrieu, III, 105 f.); Ordo of S. Amand (*ibid.*, II, 164 f.). According to these latter, along with the bishops and presbyters, when necessary, subdeacons also could help along in the breaking. According to a later Frankish appendix in the *Ordo Rom.*, I, (PL, 78, 959 f., n. 50; Andrieu, II, 132, n. 4) the pope also could take part in the fraction; that occurred

on the altar with the use of the paten, and then some of the presbyters and deacons likewise would help along at the altar.

[6] These are among the articles the donation of which has been continuously recorded in the *Liber Pontif.*, beginning with Pope Sylvester I and Emperor Constantine; see the enumeration in Braun, *Das christliche Altargerät*, 216. The Lateran Basilica was most richly furnished by Constantine; it received seven golden and 30 silver patens, each of which weighed 30 (Roman) lbs. = 9. 82 kg. = about 21½ lbs. avoirdupois. Other patens donated weighed between 10 and 35 (Roman) lbs.; thus they corresponded to our large monstrances. In some cases the rim was set with precious stones. A silver vessel from Tomi (6th century) is preserved that measures 60 cm. in diameter, a vessel whose inscription and figurative ornamentation prove it to be liturgical. In other similar cases we are dealing rather with profane objects; Braun, 216-218. The older patens according to the meaning of the word, were more in the form of a deep dish or pan (*patena* = πατάνη). Gregory of Tours, *De gloria martyrum*, c. 85 (PL, 71, 781), tells us of a count, who, having foot trouble had a paten brought to him from the church that he might bathe his feet therein, because he hoped that thus they would be cured. This dish-form of the paten was closely connected with its purpose, a purpose different from that of the paten today and corresponding rather to our present ciborium. In humbler circumstances a smaller paten suffices; thus Gregory the Great *Ep.*, VIII, 4 (PL, 77, 909), required for a church of a nuns' convent in Lucca

patens[7] or (at least optionally) chalices[8] were used in their stead. But then, all of a sudden, the paten loses its function. The introduction of unleavened bread was followed, perhaps not everywhere at once,[9] but certainly not too much later, by the introduction of the small hosts, which changed the whole rite of the fraction as performed up till then, and so likewise rendered the use of the paten superfluous. In the Romano-German Pontifical which originated at Mainz about 950 there is a plan for the bishop's Mass which gives us a glimpse of the new procedure.[10] The subdeacons took their usual place right after the concluding doxology of the canon, and the deacons right after the *Pater noster*, since their function at the fraction dropped out. The archdeacon took the paten as he had always done, but simply handed it to the bishop (*patenam illi accommodans*) after the *propitius pacem*, and nothing special was done with it as far as we can see, but the Gallic episcopal blessing and the kiss of peace followed at once. However, the paten reappeared again at the Communion, along with the chalice held by an acolyte. From the paten the bishop, as the first to receive, took his Communion; the particles had therefore been deposited on it.[11] But a hundred years later, in the Mass *ordo* of John of Avranches (d. 1079), this last use has also disappeared. The paten now is used only as a resting-place for the large

---

a paten of two pounds and a chalice of one-half pound. Individual patens with diameters as high as 31 cm. are still preserved even from the time since the 11th century; Braun, 219 f.—Since the breaking of the particles still plays an important role even today in the Byzantine Liturgy, the diskos used for the purpose (which corresponds to our paten) is considerably larger, with a diameter almost as high as 40 cm. (222).

[7] *Ordo Rom.*, V, n. 10 (PL, 78, 988); after the embolism the bishop takes the paten (that up to this point was carried by the acolytes) from the deacon, kisses it and breaks upon it the Body of Our Lord (*dividat inter eas sacrosanctum corpus consecratum*). After the kiss of peace, the archdeacon hands it to the acolytes *iubeatque unam ante presbyteros et aliam diaconibus coram tenere ut frangat* [read *frangant*] *scilicet oblatas superimpositas.* It appears, therefore, that there is question here of two patens. The one is used thereupon for the Communion of the bishop and the clergy and the other is intended for the Communion of the people. Still provision is made that the particles lying upon them might be distributed upon two or four patens, depending upon the number of

priests distributing Communion; n. 11 (*ibid.*, 990).

[8] *Ordo Rom.*, II, n. 11 (PL, 78, 974): *Subdiaconi autem, postquam . . . audierint: Sed libera nos a malo, vadunt et præparant calices sive sindones mundas, in quibus recipiant corpus Domini . . . donec ex eo populus vitæ sumat confortationem æternæ.* Also in the later section of the *Ordo Rom.*, I, n. 48 (PL, 78, 959) it is appointed, that the acolytes who put themselves at the service of the presbyters for the breaking of the hosts, should hold three chalices, while the deacons proceed with the breaking over the paten (The interpretation which Mabillon, *loc. cit.*, gives this passage is hardly tenable).

[9] Cf. *supra*, p. 36.

[10] *Ordo Rom.*, VI, n. 11 f. (PL, 78, 993 f.).

[11] On the other hand, witnesses are not wanting at this time to testify to the breaking of the bread for the Communion of the people. At all events there is still talk of *fractio oblatarum* in the *Eclogæ* (PL, 105, 1528), as well as in its Amalar model (ed. Hanssens, *Eph. liturg.*, 1927, 162); likewise in the *Expositio "Missa pro Multis,"* c. 19 (ed. Hanssens, *Eph. liturg.*,

Host during its fraction, and then till the Communion.[12] Its use no longer extends beyond the altar. And all this agrees with the fact that precisely in the eleventh century the paten shrinks in size. It now becomes a rule that its diameter should be about the same as the height of the chalice (at first very low),[13] and soon, in fact, that it should not even reach that dimension.

Subsequently the paten gained further use when the custom grew of putting the host on it even at the offertory (as we have seen), and thus making the offering,[14] and this, in turn, especially at private Mass, led to the practice of bringing chalice and paten together to the altar, and further, to fitting the paten to the cup of the chalice, so that it could lie smoothly on the chalice, a rule which was already in effect in the tenth century.[15]

So if the newer form of paten has little in common with the vessel of the same name in the first ten centuries, still reminiscences of the ritual handling of the latter have been transferred to it. At a high Mass it does not remain lying on the altar after the offertory,[16] even though this con-

1930, 42). In the last named, c. 17 is headed: *De subdiacono deferente corpus Christi primum ad frangendum, postea ad communicandum* (40). Cf. further also reports of the 11th and 12th centuries about *integræ oblatæ* that first had to be broken (*supra*, p. 36, n. 32). At Cluny in 1085 Udalricus in discussing the conventual Communion, still speaks of the *patena super quam Corpus Domini fractum fuerit,* that had to be examined carefully for the left-over particles. About the same time Bernold, *Micrologus,* c. 20 (PL, 151, 990 B), also intimates a breaking that follows upon the commingling.

[12] John of Avranches, *De eccl. off.* (PL, 147, 36 f.).—On the other hand, the paten still retains its function at the distribution of Communion about 1140 in the *Ordo eccl. Lateranensis* (Fischer, 86, 1. 13).—Since the small hosts, when on days of Communion they are required in a great amount, could not well remain free and loose upon the altar during the canon, as formerly the communion breads, a vessel came into existence in which they could be held, distributed, and also preserved, the *pyxis* or ciborium in different shapes; cf. Braun, 280-347. True, the *pyxis* or *capsa* as a vessel for the preservation of the Sacrament existed before this (282 ff.), but it is not until the 12th century that frequent mention was made of it and nu-

merous examples preserved. Its use now also for the distribution of Communion most likely led since the 13th century to the practice of supplying the *pyxis* with a permanent base which makes it similar to the chalice (304 ff.). The oldest form (examples from the 12th century) seems to be that which had the cuppa in the shape of a wide shell and thus is in some manner still reminiscent of the older paten. Unfortunately the connection with this transition in the liturgy is not developed by Braun.

[13] As a rule the diameter is now less than 20 cm. In the 10th and 12th centuries as a requisite for traveling paraphernalia besides small chalices there were also small patens of 5 to 8 cm. diameter in use (Braun, 220).

[14] *Supra.* —Related to this is the practice attested in *Ordo Rom., VI,* n. 9 (PL, 78, 992) of using the paten (not yet reduced in size) to receive the gifts of the faithful at the offertory.

[15] Braun, 211.

[16] According to the rite of Vienne it was laid upon the altar at the *Sanctus* and removed again by the subdeacon at the *Pater noster;* Martène, 1, 4, 7, 8 (I, 397 E). So also in several other churches; Lebrun, I, 490. But this remained as an exception.

tracted paten would not be in the way on the altar, which meanwhile had been enlarged; but instead, the subdeacon takes it and holds it, covering it with the ends of the humeral veil, until he returns it to the altar near the end of the *Pater noster*. This is a survival of the function of the acolyte [17] of the seventh-century papal liturgy, who appeared at the beginning of the preface,[18] carrying the paten which he had brought from the *secretarium*,[19] and which he held to his breast under the folds of a cloth thrown over his shoulders, until *medio canone* he turned it over to others; then near the end of the embolism it was carried over to be used at the fraction. It would not be necessary to presume that the undoubtedly remarkable reverence in handling the paten which the earliest *ordines* prescribe was due to some more profound reason, as though a particle of the Eucharist which, as the *sancta*, was displayed at the entrance procession, was still lying on it.[20] Both the fact that the paten is brought in at the start of the Sacrifice-Mass and that it is carried with covered hands correspond wholly with the usual manner of handling holy objects.[21]

The reverent attentions towards the paten were not only retained even after the disappearance of its prime use at the fraction, they were even increased. The kiss which had long been given it by the deacon [22] was

---

[17] An acolyte retained this office also in most Mass arrangements of the Middle Ages. In some cathedrals a *puer* assumes the office, and he then carries a special *cappa;* Sölch, *Hugo,* 111 f. Only since the 11th and 12th centuries does the subdeacon appear more and more in his place. The oldest evidence for this in Ebner, 313; 328; cf. Braun, *Die liturgischen Paramente,* 230.

[18] *Ordo Rom.,* I, n. 17 (PL, 78, 945): *quando inchoat canonem,* does not signify the *Te igitur* as Sölch, 110, assumes and as the rubricians of the Middle Ages explained it (*ibid.,* 109 f.) ; cf. *supra,* I, 97.

[19] Amalar, *De off. eccl.,* III, 27 (PL, 105, 1146 D) : *de exedris.*

[20] Cf. *supra,* I, 70.—Batiffol, *Leçons,* 88; 90 f., has marshalled the points that favor the opinion mentioned. The same supposition is found in Eisenhofer, II, 142; 199 and Sölch, 113. However, this argument is invalidated by what is said in *Ordo Rom.,* I, n. 8, where at the beginning of the Mass the *Sancta* are brought in a *capsa* that can be closed *(capsas apertas)* and that they are clearly laid in this *capsa* for the sole purpose of the Mass celebration since only so many of the particles of the Sacred

Species are to be provided, that only in the case of necessity *(si fuerit abundans)* will some have to be sent back into the *conditorium.* There is, therefore, no apparent reason for taking the *sancta* out of the *capsa* and carrying them open on the paten. Cf. also Capella, "Le rite de la fraction" *(Revue Bénéd.* 1941), 14. Besides it is questionable whether there was any use for it during the Mass; see *ibid.,* 16 ff.

[21] The Book of the Gospels is also thus provided in *Ordo Rom.,* I, long before it is required, namely at the very entry, and is likewise held not with the bare hands, but *super planetas* (n. 5), and besides, it is kissed by the pope (n. 8) just as the paten is kissed by the archdeacon (n. 18), a fact that argues all the more for our opinion, since it is empty. The prepared chalice, too, is taken hold of at the end of the preparation of the offertory gifts only by means of the *offertorium* (n. 15) ; cf. also above. Even today the episcopal mitre is carried only by means of the velum during divine service; this is, moreover, merely a survival of the manner of carrying that one meets at every step in Christian archælology.

[22] *Ordo Rom.,* I, n. 18 (PL, 78, 945).

sometimes offered also by others,[23] above all by the celebrant himself.[24] Since the twelfth century there was added a sign of the Cross made over himself by the celebrant with the paten, sometimes after the kiss,[25] more usually before it,[26] as is customary at present.[27]

In the later Middle Ages the ceremony of blessing which thus originated was elaborated even further and sometimes brought to the very verge of superstition. Instead of one cross there were several.[28] Or the mouth and eyes were touched with the paten;[29] or first the Host was touched with the paten;[30] or else the Host was touched once, the chalice three times.[31] All these excrescences were set aside by the Missal of Pius V.

According to the present Mass book, the paten is kissed right after it is used to make the sign of the Cross, and while the final words of the embolism are still being recited the celebrant genuflects, takes up the Sacred Host and begins the fraction. But this no longer takes place over

[23] *Ordo Rom.*, V, n. 10 (*supra*, n. 7): the patens are kissed by the deacon and sub-deacon, and finally by the bishop celebrant.

[24] Also in the Mass without Levites. Thus for the first time Bernold, *Micrologus*, c. 17 (PL, 151, 988). For pontifical Mass, see *Ordo eccl. Lateran.* (Fischer, 85).

[25] Innocent III, *De s. alt. mysterio*, VI, 1 (PL, 217, 906). This series and others also in the Sarum Missal of the 14th and 15th centuries; Legg, *Tracts*, 264.—Sometimes the sign of the cross took the place of the kiss; *Ordinarium* of Laon (about 1300): Martène, 1, 4, XX (I, 608 E).

[26] Hugo of St. Cher. *Tract. super missam* (ed. Sölch, 46). Durandus, IV, 50, 4, recognizes both methods. — Still numerous missals even of later times make mention only of the kissing of the paten without the sign of the cross; see examples in Sölch, *Hugo*, 114. The quondam Cistercian rite had neither the kissing of the paten nor the sign of the cross; *ibid.*

[27] Still our large sign of the cross, which was hardly known at the time, is not to be presupposed in the 13th century. Where the rubrics give more specific directions it is stated that the priest crosses himself with the paten *in facie sua*, or *ante faciem suam* or *in fronte*—most likely much as we do at present with the host just before Communion. See detailed data in Sölch, 114-117; Lentze (*Anal. Praem.*, 1950), 129.

[28] Mass order of York about 1145 (Simmons, 112): the priest makes the sign of the cross with the paten *in facie*, then *in pectore*, and next the usual large sign of the cross of today.

[29] Thus in a missal of Soissons (14th cent.): Leroquais, II, 335. According to the Sarum Missal of the end of the Middle Ages the priest kisses the paten, places it upon his left eye and then on his right, and thereafter makes with it the sign of the cross; Legg, *Tracts*, 264; Martène, I, 4, XXXV (I, 669 C); cf. Maskell, 156-158. Louis Ciconiolanus in his *Directorium div. Officiorum* which appeared in Rome in 1539 still opposes the custom of touching the right and the left eye at the mention of the names of Peter and Paul: Legg, 211. The same custom was spread in Germany; see Franz, *Die Messe*, 111.

[30] The Mass Ordo of the Carthusians; Legg, *Tracts*, 102. Examples of 14th and 15th centuries from France, Leroquais, II, 233; III, 25, 113, 166. Two Mass orders of the 15th and 16th centuries from Orleans in de Moléon, 198; 200. According to the older statutes of the Carthusians, I, 43: Martène, 1, 4, XXV (I, 634 B), the priest first makes the sign of the cross with the paten, then touches the host with the paten at *da propitius* and kisses it at the word *pacem*. Cf. *Ordinarium Cart.* (1932), c. 27, 10; Missale of Evreux-Jumièges (14-15th cent.): Martène, XXVIII (I, 644 f.).

[31] At the name of the three apostles the priest was supposed to touch the base, the middle, and the rim of the chalice, where-

the paten,[32] but over the chalice, so that no tiny particle might be lost.[33] Thus, according to the present arrangement, the fraction is anticipated, taking place not after, but before the *Pax Domini*. We will come back to this later.[34] The use of the paten during the fraction, which is stressed even at present in the *Pontificale*,[35] is now only suggested by the fact that the Host rests on the paten before the fraction, and the separated portions are deposited on it afterwards.[36]

At present the Sacred Host is broken into three parts.[37] Here, too, we

---

upon the sign of the cross and the kiss followed; *Ordinarium* of Coutances, 1557; Legg, *Tracts,* 65. So also the *Alphabetum Sacerdotum: ibid.,* 47; Missale of S. Pol de Léon: Martène, 1, 4, XXXIV (I, 663 f.); cf. the Lyons monastic missal of 1531: *ibid.,* XXXIII (I, 660 E). A very similar ceremony of touching the chalice already at the offertory in a Pontifical of Noyon (15th cent.); Leroquais, *Les pontificaux,* I, 170.—The earliest evidence of this touching of host and chalice at the embolism I have found in a Hungarian missal of the 13th century: Radó, 62.

[32] This was still the case in Bernold, *Micrologus,* c. 17 (PL, 151, 988 C), and even in the Pressburg Missal D of the 15th century (Jávor, 118).

[33] The transition is evident in Robert Paululus (d. circa 1148), *De Cæremoniis,* II, 39 (PL, 177, 436): *Patenam . . . de manu diaconi suscipit et in altari, ut fractionem super eam faciat, deponit. Nos tamen hanc fractionem ad cautelam facimus super calicem.* The breaking over the chalice already found in the Cod. Casanat. (11-12th cent.): Ebner, 330. The later Middle Ages saw in this breaking over the chalice a symbolical representation of the fact that the Sacred Blood flowed out of the wounds in the Body of Christ; Gabriel Biel, *Canonis expositio,* lect. 80. On the other hand, the Sacramentary of the Papal Court Chapel (about 1290) which rests on the Ordinary of Innocent III (ed. Brinktrine: *Eph. liturg.,* 1937, 206) still has the fraction over the paten. A reminder of it also in Durandus, IV, 51, 3.—Description of the rite, as carried out by Boniface VIII, from a manuscript of Avignon, in Andrieu, *Le pontifical Romain,* III, 43.

[34] Moreover, different accounts indicate that the old liturgy of the city of Rome,

especially outside of the papal stational service, recognized a fraction that preceded the Kiss of Peace and the *Pax Domini.* In the older Gelasianum I, 40 (Wilson, 70-72) it is recorded of the *missa chrismalis* of Maundy Thursday, at which most likely no large crowd of people received Communion: *Ipsa expleta* [i.e., after the embolism] *confrangis,* whereupon follows the second blessing of the oil; then *ponis in ore calicis de ipsa hostia,* whereupon the observation that the *Pax Domini* falls out.—An interpolated passage in Rabanus Maurus, *De inst. cler.,* I, 33 additio (PL, 107, 325) acknowledges that the *Itali* already place a particle *de sancto pane* (therefore a particle separated from their own oblation) in the chalice. It is easily possible that in these cases the rite of commingling a particle separated from the host offered at the celebration represents a later substitute patterned on the rite of commingling the *fermentum* at a non-papal service (see *infra*); cf. Capelle, "Le rite del la fraction" (*Revue Bénéd.,* 1941), 22 ff., 28.

[35] *Pontificale Rom.,* p. 11, De patenæ et calicis consecratione . . . *sanctificet hanc patenam ad confringendum in ea corpus D. n. J. C.*

[36] The latter is not the case, e.g., in the Dominican rite; rather, the priest after kissing the paten lays it to one side, *seorsum a corporali,* because no longer needed. He retains the pieces of the host in his left hand until the *sumptio; Missale O.P.* (1889). 21 f. Thus also already about the middle of the 13th century, Sölch, *Hugo,* 122. The same rite in Sarum: Legg, *Tracts,* 226; 265. Similarly in the *Liber ordinarius* of Liége where, however at the *sumptio* the priest again takes the paten, *tenens sub mento;* Volk, 96, 1. 21.

[37] The breaking into three parts, already

have a survival of ancient memories. According to the Roman *ordines*, the pope, after the kiss of peace, broke off a part of his own host-bread *ex latere dextro*, and this was left on the altar.[38] Then, at his Communion, he again separated a small piece from the Host, and put it in the chalice with the words *Fiat commixtio et consecratio . . .*[39] Although the fraction for practical purposes, namely for apportioning in the Communion of the people, which before was so prominent, had since disappeared, still fractions occasioned by symbolic considerations continued on. This is abundantly clear in regard to the second fraction by the very formula already cited, a formula for the commingling. But it holds even more immediately true of the first fraction. Even several hundred years later the priest was still ordered to break the host *ex dextro latere;*[40] the particle thus removed was then used for the commingling.[41] A second particle was broken off for his own Communion. The third portion remained, as of old, on the altar, but it was now preserved as *viaticum morientium,*[42] or it was also used for the communicants.[43] These three parts were already stipulated by Amalar, and even for him they have their symbolic meaning; the particle mixed with the Sacred Blood refers to the Body of Christ at the Resurrection; the particle for the celebrant's own Communion refers to the Body of Christ on earth, the earthly Church; the particle intended for

mentioned by Amalar *(vide infra)* was and is not universally done in the same manner. For instance, according to Ernulf of Rochester (d. 1124), *Epistola ad Lambertum* (d'Archery, *Spicilegium*, III, 472), the host in many a church was broken into three equal parts: *trium æqualitate partium*. Elsewhere, as it still happens to this day in the Dominican and Carmelite rites, the breaking is first made into two halves. These he then lays diagonally over each other and breaks off a projecting piece from the halves, which piece he then drops into the chalice for the commingling. Sölch, 120-123; *Missale O.P.* (1889), 21; *Missale O. Carm.* (1935), 315.

[38] Above, p. 303.

[39] *Ordo Rom.*, I, n. 19 (PL, 78, 946 C).

[40] Bernold, *Micrologus*, c. 17 (PL, 151, 988 C). Also in the Mass order of Cod. Casanat. of the 11-12th century (Ebner, 330).

[41] Bernold, *loc. cit.*

[42] Bernold, *loc. cit.* St. Thomas, *Summa Th.*, III, 83, 5 ad 8, in explaining the symbolism of the three portions of the broken host quotes the verses: *Hostia dividitur in partes: tincta beatos—Plene, sicca notat vivos, servata sepultos:* "the third part, which is reserved, denotes the

dead." H. Leclercq mentions a missal of Rouen as late as 1516 that still prescribed the reservation of a third of the host for the sick (*CE*, s. v. "host," VII, 492 A).

[43] A practical use of it seems to have been made at least by the 11th century monks of Cluny, among whom Communion was not yet so rare, inasmuch as the third particle was given to the brother who served at the private Mass of the monks. Bernardus, *Ordo Clun.*, I, 72 (Herrgott, 265): *socium tertia [particula] . . . communicat.* Bernold, *loc. cit.*, also has this practice clearly in view: *tertiam autem communicaturis sive infirmis necessario dimittit,* still he alleges as a symbolical signification of this particle: *tertiam [corpus] quod iam requiescit in Christo;* hence the particle is called *viaticum morientium.*—According to John of Avranches (d. 1079), *De off. eccl.* (PL, 147, 36 f.), who also explains this third particle as *viaticum,* the second particle can be used for the Communion of the deacon and subdeacon as well as of the people. Cf. the apportionment of the second particle in the *Ordo eccl. Lateran.* (Fischer, 85 f.). Bishop Ernulf of Rochester (d. 1124), *Ep. ad Lambertum* (d'Achery, *Spicilegium*, III, 472) allots the three particles at High Mass, where

the sick refers to Christ's Body in the grave.[44] This reference to the *corpus Christi triforme* often recurs in the following centuries,[45] although it is not the only explanation given.[46] But then it is readjusted so that the three parts refer to three phases of the Church as militant, suffering, and triumphant;[47] this combination became a constituent element of the Mass commentaries of the later Middle Ages and found its way into popular sermons.[48] The crystallization caused by these symbolic considerations must then have been the reason that this tri-partition of the Host continued even after it had become the practice for the priest to use small Hosts for the distribution of Communion, in particular for the sick, when, therefore, a division into two would have sufficed both to preserve the rite which inhered in the fraction itself and to obtain a particle for the *mixtio.*

5. The Commingling*

In the present-day Roman liturgy the fraction is followed at once by the commingling: the separated particle is dropped into the chalice with an accompanying prayer that had been used in a similar way already in the papal Mass of the eighth century. Thus in the present-day ceremony of the commingling there is a survival of that ceremony in which the celebrating pope, just before his Communion, broke off a particle from his own Host and dropped it into the chalice.[1]

But the Roman liturgy of that time also had a further twofold commingling of the species, which did not, however, form a part of every Mass. The first of these is surrounded by the deepest obscurity. It is mentioned only in the later version of the first Roman *ordo*, which contains the following direction even before the start of the fraction: *cum dixerit:*

hardly anybody receives Communion, simply to the priest, the deacon and the subdeacon in such a manner that the piece in the chalice falls to the priest. The same distribution in Honorius Augustod., *Gemma an.,* I, 63 (PL, 172, 563 D); cf. however, c. 64.—But this last method is expressly rejected by John of Avranches (*loc. cit.*) : *Non autem intincto pane, sed... seorsum corpore, seorsum sanguine sacerdos communicet;* only the people are permitted to communicate *intincto pane.*

[44] Amalar, *De eccl. off.,* III, 35 (PL, 105, 1154 f.). For more detailed explanation see Franz, *Die Messe,* 357, n. 1, and especially de Lubac, *Corpus mysticum,* 295-339, where the dogmatic-historical background as well as the interpretation of Amalar and the gradual change of interpretation are elucidated.

[45] Franz, *Die Messe,* 436; 458; cf. F. Holböck, *Der eucharistische und der mystische Leib Christi in ihren Beziehungen zueinander nach der Lehre der Frühscholastik* (Rome, 1941), 196-199; Haberstroh, 77-82; de Lubac, 333 ff.

[46] Franz, 389 f.; 417; 435 f.; 463, n. 6. Durandus, IV, 51, 20-22.

[47] Among the first to hold this interpretation is a work formerly attributed to Hugh of St. Victor, *Speculum de mysteriis,* c. 7 (PL, 177, 373 B); Franz, 437. Further details in de Lubac, 325 ff., 330 ff., 345 ff.

[48] Franz, 435 f.; 464, n. 1; 669; 692 f.; 697; cf. 654.

[1] *Ordo Rom.,* 1, n. 19 (Andrieu, II, 101; PL, 78, 946) : *de ipsa sancta, quam* [older recension *de qua*] *momorderat, ponit in calicem.*

*See Appendix, p. 532.

Pax Domini sit semper vobiscum, mittat in calicem de sancta.[2] This *sancta* is commonly taken to mean a eucharistic particle from a previous Mass, the same that we noticed in the beginning of Mass at the entrance of the pope.[3] In this way the continuous unity of the eucharistic sacrifice was expressed—the same Mass yesterday and today.[4] But the absence of a rite of this sort in the pertinent parallel documents compels us to suppose rather that the usage was merely a transient or tentative copy of another commingling which took place at the *Pax Domini,* probably with a particle from the oblation itself.[5]

This second commingling was not proper to the papal or episcopal Mass, but to the Mass of the priests in the outlying churches. By an acolyte, the bishop sent the priests of the vicinity a particle of the Eucharist as an expression of ecclesiastical unity, as a token that they belonged to his *communio.* This particle was called the *fermentum.*[6] The priests dropped it into the chalice at this part of the Mass.[7] The practice is ancient indeed.[8] It answered to that awareness, so keen in the ancient Church, that the Eucharist was the *sacramentum unitatis,* that this Sacrament held the Church together, and that all the people of God subject to a bishop should,

[2] *Ordo Rom.,* I, n. 18 (Andrieu, II, 98; PL, 78, 945).

[3] *Ordo Rom.,* I, n. 8 (PL, 78, 941); cf. *supra,* I, 70.—This interpretation, which was already defended by Mabillon in his Commentary, VI, I (PL, 78, 869 f.) is adopted today by most commentators. Duchesne, *Christian Worship,* 163, 185; Batiffol, *Leçons,* 76 f.; 90 f.

[4] This idea is at all events the basis for a Nestorian custom; to the dough that has been prepared for any Mass according to a definite rite a portion is always added from the dough that had been prepared for a previous celebration, so that, in a sense, the same mass of dough is propagated from one Mass to the next. Along with this goes the legend that St. John retained a small piece of the Sacred Bread at the Last Supper and mingled it in the first batch of dough prepared for the Eucharistic celebration of the apostles. Hanssens, II, 169-174; W. de Vries, *Sakramententheologie bei den Nestorianern* (Orientalia christ. anal., 133; Rome, 1947), 194-197.

[5] Capella, "Le rite de la fraction" (*Revue Bénéd.,* 1941), 14-22. Capella assumes that there is question of a mere interpolation (22), to which, consequently, no real rite ever corresponded. Cf., however, *supra,* n. 34.

[6] The name is generally derived from the fact that the communal Eucharist permeates and unites the Church even as leaven permeates the mass of dough (Mt. 13:33). More probable is the notion that the episcopal particle would be mingled with the Sacramental Species of one's own Mass as the yeast is added to the dough; thus also Batiffol, *Leçons,* 34.

[7] A later continuation of the *Ordo Rom.,* I, (Andrieu, II, 115; PL, 78, 948 f.) directs, in case a bishop—or (as finally indicated) a priest—takes the place of the pope: *Quando dici debet: Pax Domini sit semper vobiscum, deportatur a subdiacono oblationario particula fermenti quod ab Apostolico consecratum est . . . ille consignando tribus vicibus et dicendo: Pax Domini sit semper vobiscum, mittit en calicem.*

[8] Irenæus (in Eusebius, *Hist. eccl.,* V, 24) tells about the bishops of the Quartodeciman Easter Practice, to whom the pope nevertheless had sent the Eucharist as a sign of ecclesiastical unity; cf. F. J. Dölger, *Ichythys,* II (Münster, 1922), 535, n. 3. This could have happened during the stay of the bishops in Rome. However, a transporting to a great distance is assumed by Th. Schormann, *Die allgemeine Kirchenordnung,* II (Paderborn, 1915), 419.—To send the Eucharist abroad

if it were possible, be gathered around that bishop's altar and receive the Sacrament from his table of sacrifice.[9]

In the ninth century, both forms of this commingling must have disappeared from the solemn service even in Rome itself. First of all, the commixture of the *sancta* at the *Pax Domini* vanished. The *Ordo* of St. Amand (not purely a Roman document, it is true, but probably reflecting Roman conditions) makes mention only of the use at a papal Mass of a particle from the pope's own Mass, which is dropped into the chalice just before Communion with the words, *Fiat*, etc.[10] On the other hand, the *fermentum* seems to have been still in use, as the same *ordo* indicates.[11] But since it did not come into consideration at a papal Mass, another *ordo* of about the same period adds the note: *Dum vero dominus Papa dicit: Pax Domini sit semper vobiscum, non mittit partem de sancta in calicem sicut ceteris sacerdotibus mos est.*[12] In the Frankish kingdom the only conclusion that could be drawn from this Roman rubric was that the *ceteri sacerdotes* put a particle into the chalice at the *Pax Domini*. And since

was forbidden at the Council of Laodicea (middle of the 4th cent.), can. 14 (Mansi, II, 566) ; transporting, therefore, was in practice here, too.—In Rome also, at least later, a similar law was enacted. To the Bishop of Gubbio Pope Innocent I (d. 417), *Ep.*, 25, 5 (PL, 20, 556 f.), gave this answer to his query *de fermento quod die dominica per titulos mittimus*: Since the priests must remain with their congregations, especially on Sunday, they receive the *fermentum* through the acolyte, *ut se a nostra communione, maxime illa die, non iudicent separatos*. However, this should not be done outside the city; in Rome it was not even customary to send the *fermentum* to churches attached to the cemeteries (*quia*) *presbyteri eorum conficiendorum ius habeant atque licentiam,* which most likely means, even without the *fermentum* they are authorized to hold regular divine service; cf. de Puniet, *The Roman Pontifical* (London-New York, 1932), 225 f.—In the 6th century the *Liber Pontificalis* offers two striking notices of the custom, among them a stipulation, apparently by Siricius (d. 339), that no priest is allowed to celebrate Mass week after week if he has not received the *fermentum* from his bishop. *Liber Pontif.*, ed. Duchesne, I, 216 ; cf. 168, and the remarks of the editor. In later times the sending of the *fermentum* seems to have been restricted to certain solemn feasts; cf. Ma-

billon, *In ord. Rom. comment.*, VI, 2 (PL, 78, 870 f.). An offshoot of the practice under discussion is found in a custom often referred to in the later Middle Ages to the effect that the bishop at ordination (and similarly at the consecration of a bishop) would after Communion hand over to the newly ordained (consecrated) a number of Sacred Particles from which he might communicate further for eight, or according to another rule, for forty days. Cf. among others Fulbert of Chartres (d. 1029), *Ep.*, 3 (PL, 141, 192-195). For further details J. A. Jungmann, "Fermentum," *Colligere Fragmenta* (Festschrift Alban Dold; Beuron, 1952), 185-190.

[9] Cf. *supra*, I, 195 f.

[10] Andrieu, II, 169. This work was compiled by a Frankish cleric in the last decade of the 8th century, using Roman materials, particularly *Ordo Rom.*, I.

[11] Andrieu, II, 151, regarding Holy Saturday; cf. Duchesne, *Christian Worship*, 471.

[12] *Ordo "Qualiter quædam"* (Andrieu, II, 304; PL, 78, 984) : *Dum vero dominus Papa dicit: Pax Domini sit semper vobiscum, non mittit partem de sancta in calicem sicut ceteris sacerdotibus mos est.* This is a Frankish compilation made at either Metz or Besançon between 750 and 900; obviously the editor had in view the version of *Ordo Rom.*, I, represented in

the custom of the *fermentum* was unknown,[13] it was inferred that a fraction had to precede it, all the more because several references in Roman sources seemed to indicate[14] that there was to be a double fraction and commingling, one at the *Pax Domini*, the other(as is clear from the first Roman *ordo*) just before Communion.[15] Naturally, one or the other of these was soon dropped, although for a time there was some confusion and hesitancy as to which one should be retained.[16] It was not long before the first of the two gained the upper hand.[17] Symbolism was probably a determining factor in this decision, because thus the commingling which represented the Body of Christ returned to life preceded the peace greeting of the *Pax Domini;* for indeed our Lord first rose from the dead, and only then did He bring peace to heaven and earth.[18]

Probably in connection with such ideas (which we have likewise encountered in the Orient), the reference to our Lord's death on the Cross was emphasized by a single cross[19] or later more often by a triple cross,[20]

the St. Gall MS. 614 (Andrieu, II, 98; cf. 286 f.). The rubric fitted to suit Carolingian circumstances, and in part badly mutilated, recurs in a number of 11th century arrangements for pontifical Mass. It appears best preserved in the Missa Illyrica: Martène, 1, 4 (I, 515 A) : At first a double formula is specified for the commingling after the *Pax Domini; Hæc sacrosancta commixtio* and *Fiat commixtio et consecratio.* Then it reads : *Non mittat episcopus in calicem partem oblatæ, ut presbyteri solent, sed expectet donec finita benedictione episcopus communicare debeat et tunc accipiens partem, quam antea fregerat, teneusque super calicem immittat dicens: Sacri sanguinis commixtio . . .* Similarly in the Mass arrangement of Liége and Gregorienmünster; Martène, 1, 4, XV f. (I, 592 f., 600) ; also in a Missale of the 13th century from St. Lambrecht (Köck, 23). Only the second half (*finita benedictione . . .*) is found in the Mass of Séez (PL, 78, 250), in a modified form and in a sense difficult to understand.— Cf. the study of this rubric by Capelle (*Revue Bénéd.,* 1941), 32-34.

[13] This holds at least for the period under consideration. For an earlier period study canon 17 of the Synod of Orange (441) ; regarding the puzzling text, cf. Haberstroh, 28.

[14] *Supra*, n. 34.

[15] Actually the double commingling—and along with that evidently the double fractions—is retained in the *Ordo Rom.*, II,

n. 12 f. (PL, 78, 975), therefore in an ordo in which the rite of the Pope's Mass was adapted to the conditions of the late Carlovingian episcopal churches.—However, the double commingling and fraction is already provided for in the *Capitulare eccl. ord.* (Andrieu, III, 105 f.).

[16] Amalar, *De eccl. off.*, III, 31 (PL, 105, 1151 f.), bears witness to the fluctuation inasmuch as he is unable to explain the twofold commingling, of which he reads in the *libellus Romanus;* he is inclined to retain the first commingling. Also Rabanus Maurus, *De inst. cler.*, I, 33 additio (PL, 107, 325), speaks of the variation in practice. The uncertainty seems to have resulted at times in the entire omission of any commingling; *Ordo Rom., IV*, n. 12 (PL, 78, 994).

[17] This one alone is found in Remigius of Auxerre (d. 908), *Expositio* (PL, 105 1270B) ; cf. *idem., In I Tim.,* c. 2 (PL, 117, 788 C). Likewise *Ordo Rom.,* III, n. 16 (PL, 78, 981 f.).

[18] Amalar, *loc. cit.*—Likewise later Bernold, *Micrologus,* c. 20 (PL, 151, 990 B).

[19] Sacramentary of Cod. Pad. (Mohlberg-Baumstart, n. 893) ; Ordo of S. Amand (Duchesne, *Christian Worship,* 462). In Amalar, *loc. cit.,* this sign of the cross becomes a fourfold touching of the chalice rim, because in the cross the *hominum genus quattuor climatum* attained unity and peace. Likewise *Ecloga* (PL, 105, 1329).

[20] The triple cross appears in isolated

formed with the particle over the chalice. Thus the "consignation" which we found in the oriental liturgies appears in its simplest form also in the Roman Mass before the commingling.

The commingling itself is regularly accompanied by the formula already quoted. It is surprising that this formula is not marked in the older sacramentaries; obviously this was because it was not designed to be said aloud but, like certain salutations and directives at the beginning of Mass, was said in a quiet speaking tone and came into use only secondarily. Like these greetings and directions therefore, it is to be found only in the *ordines,* where the old wording is as follows: *Fiat commīxtio et consecratio corporis et sanguinis D. n. J. C., accipientibus nobis in vitam æternam. Amen.*[21] This version continued in use, unchanged, especially in Italian Mass books.[22] In the preparation of the reform of the missal at the Council of Trent, theological doubts were loudly raised against this formula, for on the face of it, its meaning—leaving aside the word *consecratio* for a moment—clearly was: let there be a commixture of our Lord's Body and Blood, (let it bring) us recipients to life everlasting. Thus, the formula could be construed as though, in consequence of it, the Body and Blood of Christ would be united to each other only after the commingling, and not already at the consecration of the two species,[23] so that the Utraquists had grounds for arguing that Communion under one kind was insufficient.[24] So the change to the present reading was proposed:

manuscripts of the *Ordo Rom.,* I, n. 18 f., and indeed, now at the first commingling, now at the second, in which it is accompanied with the *Fiat* formula (Hittorp, 14 a); so also the *Ordo Rom.,* II, n. 13 (PL, 78, 975). This sign of the cross must have come into use already in the 8th century, to judge from the evidence of three texts of the works of Johannes Archicantor (Silva-Tarouca, 199 a. 200 b with Apparatus; Datierung der Hss S. 179 f.). The manuscripts H (8th and 9th cent.) and V of the *Capitulare* have the sign of the cross preceding both of the two comminglings. Perhaps it is Roman, since it also appears in the Cod. Pad. (previous note)—Cf. also *Ordo Rom.,* IV (PL, 78, 984): *faciens crucem de ea tribus vici bus super calicem nihil dicens,* where the omission of the accompanying formula is one of the few exceptions. In the Ordo S. Amand (previous note) and in the *Ordo Rom.,* II, n. 13, the cross is made at the commingling in the second place before Communion.

[21] *Ordo Rom.,* I, n. 19 (PL, 78, 946; Stap-per, 28). Here, as well as in the *Ordo Rom.,* II, n. 13 (PL, 78, 975), follows a *Pax tecum* addressed to the archdeacon who holds the chalice, to which he answers in the usual way. The commingling formula is already missing in the St. Gall MS. 614 of *Ordo Rom.,* I Andrieu, II, 101 f.); see Capelle, "Le rite de la fraction" (*Revue Bénéd.,* 1941), 25.

[22] See the texts printed by Ebner, 299 ff.; with a *In nomine P. et F. et Sp. S.* mentioned first; *ibid.,* 295. Also almost universally in Styrian Mass-books; Köck, 127 ff.

[23] The explanation in Amalar, *De eccl. off.,* III, 31 (PL, 105, 1152 B) while not going quite so far, does actually follow this line: *Quæ verba precantur, ut fiat corpus Domini præsens oblatio per resurrectionem, per quam veneranda et æterna pax data est, non solum in terra sed etiam in cælo.*

[24] *Concilium Tridentinum,* ed. Görres, VIII, 917; Jedin. "Das Konzil von Trient und die Reform des Römischen Messbuches" (*Liturg. Leben,* 1939), 46; 58.

Hæc commixtio . . . fiat accipientibus nobis in vitam æternam; here there is no longer any possible question of a commingling taking place beyond the visible performance; it is now merely the expression of a wish that this external ceremonial commingling may avail us for salvation. It has been established that this is the only change in the Tridentine Missal that was aimed at the Reformers.[25] The word *consecratio,* which stayed in the text in spite of the objections brought against it, and in spite of the fact that it was missing in some medieval texts here and there,[26] must be rendered by "hallowing" in the sense that through the commingling a sacred token* or symbol is effected in the sacramental species and mediately in the Body and Blood of Christ.[27]

The idea of the formula we have been considering, along with the rite itself, might possibly have come from the Syrian country where the symbolic fraction and commingling originated. For the Greek liturgy of St. James has the accompanying phrase: Ἥνωται καὶ ἡγίασται καὶ τετελείωται εἰς τὸ ὄνομα τοῦ πατρός . . .[28] The act of commingling is here

---

[25] Jedin, 58. That the formula was already understood in this sense even in earlier times is shown by many variants, e.g., *Fiat hæc commixtio* (Ebner, 310, 341, 346; Köck, 6 f.); cf. the contaminations with the formula *Hæc sacrosancta (infra)*; e.g., Ebner, 348.

[26] Amalar, *De eccl. off.,* III, 31 (PL, 105, 1152 B); Rabanus Maurus, *De inst. cler.,* I, 33 additio (PL, 107, 325); John of Avranches, *De eccl. off.* (PL, 147, 36 D); Innocent III, *De s. alt. mysterio,* VI, 2 (PL, 216, 907); Styrian Mass-books, Köck, 127; 129.

[27] Cf. Gihr, 745-746; Brinktrine, *Die hl. Messe,* 243 f. The latter refers to a general tendency in liturgies, to end a consecration or blessing with a commingling of some sort (salt, oil) where a liquid element is involved, or with an anointing if there is question of a solid substance. In the Holy Eucharist there is the further impetus given by the fact that the sacrament has a dual form. As a matter of fact, we can follow Brinktrine in speaking of a consecration rite, in which the word "consecration" is understood in a wider sense. Later, indeed, our formula *Fiat commixtio et consecratio* is joined in passing to the idea that even by commingling a consecrated particle with the mere wine, e.g., before Communion of the sick, the wine could be transubstantiated into the

Blood of Christ. M. Andrieu, *Immixtio et consecratio (Paris,* 1924). Cf. *ibid.,* 10 f. and 218, n. 2, the significance of *consecratio* in the legend of St. Lawrence in Ambrose, *De off.,* I, 41 (PL, 16, 90): *cui commisisti Dominici sanguinis consecrationem,* where the word possibly means only the mingling of consecrated with unconsecrated wine. Haberstroh, 66-68, is inclined to assume a similar meaning for the *Fiat . . . consecratio* spoken by the pope in the *Ordo Rom.,* I, n. 19. Since, according to the Ordo of S. Amand (Duchesne, 462) the particle placed by the pope in the chalice was transferred before Communion of the people to a vessel especially prepared for the purpose, already containing wine and some drops of the Precious Blood, clearly for the further sanctification of the wine, it may be said that the pope intended by this commingling to begin the sanctification of the wine for the Communion of the people. Similar explanation in de Puniet., *The Roman Pontifical,* 190.

[28] Brightman, 62; cf. a first formula *supra* p. 300, n. 38, and the Syrian references at the *Agnus Dei* that we shall take up later.— In Spain the *coniunctio panis et calicis* is already presupposed as a firmly established rite by the IV Council of Toledo (633), can. 4 (Mansi, X, 624).

clearly and simply designated as a union and hallowing and consummation—just as in the original Latin formula and somewhat more reservedly
in the new (where the stress is no longer on the characterization, but on
the blessing). We are therefore justified in regarding the thought that
both species represent one Sacrament and contain the one Christ as the
original meaning of the Roman rite of commingling.[29]

But in Carolingian territory, at least since the ninth century, a second
formula was rife. This one presented, in somewhat more verbose a vein,
the thoughts that were stressed in the Missal of Pius V. It was in general
use in northern France and in England till the reform of the missal, and in
the Dominican rite is used even at present. It is worded as follows:[30] *Hæc
sacrosancta commixtio corporis et sanguinis D. n. J. C. fiat (mihi) omni-
bus(que) sumentibus salus mentis et corporis et ad vitam (æternam
promerendam et) capescendam præparatio salutaris. (Per eundem.)*[31]
The word *consecratio* is wanting here, and we can probably affirm that
the *commixtio* is here understood only in the concrete sense as "this mixture,"[32] leaving out, therefore, any sort of interpretation of the commingling rite and any reference to it, and turning the formula merely into an
act of desire for Communion.[33] The original Roman formula, too, has

---

[29] Cf. too Haberstroh, 62-70.

[30] In brackets are set the amplifications
that appear above all in later English texts,
but also in the Dominican and Carmelite
missals and as early as 1100 in a missal
of Arles; (Lebrun, *Explication,* I, 508,
note); vide the Mass arrangement of
Sarum: Legg, *Tracts,* 14; 226.

[31] Mass-ordo of Amiens (9th cent.), ed.
Leroquais (*Eph. liturg.,* 1927), 443. Further examples from France of the 10-15th
centuries, Martène, 1, 4, V-VIIII; IX;
XV; XXVI-XXVIII (I, 527, 534, 537,
540, 567, 592, 638, 641, 645); Lebrun, I,
508, note. Also (and in part with the opening *Fiat hæc*) in Italian Mass-books;
Ebner, 323, 330, 348; Fiala, 213. A freer
version *(Fiat nobis et omnibus)* in the
Sacramentary of Fulda (Richter-Schönfelder, n. 22); also in a Sacramentary of
the Fulda type from the 11th century in
Ebner, 258. This Fulda type and the ordinary one, one after the other in the Missal of Remiremont (12th cent.); Martène,
1, 4, 9, 9 (I, 425 A). A shortened form
(Fiat hæc) in the missals of Regensburg
and Freising of the late Middle Ages
(Beck, 268; 308). Similar short forms in
the Mass-books of Styria (Köck, 10, 13,

et al.). An isolated formula *(Commixtio
sancti corporis)* in the Sacramentary of Le
Mans (9th cent.); Leroquais, I, 30. In
Spain at times with a Gallican concluding
formula, *te præstante rex regum . . .* Ferreres, p. XXIX, CVIII, 179; so still in
the present-day Missal of Braga (1924),
325.

[32] This meaning is obviously to be supposed when in the Missa Illyrica the administration of the chalice *(calicem vero
cum sacrosancta commixtione dando)* to
the priests at High Mass is accompanied
with the formula: *Hæc sacrosancta commixtio corporis et sanguinis D. n. J. C.
prosit tibi ad vitam æternam;* Martène, 1,
4, IV (I, 516 C). At the commingling itself this Mass-*ordo* contains three formulas, namely the two cited above and a
third formula for the commingling rite of
the bishop: *Sacri Sanguinis commixtio
cum sancto corpore D. n. J. C. prosit omnibus sumentibus ad vitam æternam* (515 B).
But aside from the kindred Mass arrangements cited above in note 11, it appears
very rarely. Isolated examples from Italy
(11 and 12th cent.), see Ebner, 164, 297.

[33] In a Dominican Missal of the 14th century the formula begins *Hæc sacrosancta*

nothing to say regarding any further meaning of the commingling rite. But the thought of the Resurrection, which, among the Syrians, had been linked first with the fraction and then with the commingling,[34] was associated with the latter by the Carolingian commentators on the liturgy,[35] and in this relationship remained as an element in the explanation of the Mass all through the Middle Ages[36] and even down to the present.[37] On the other hand, the fraction was not until somewhat more recent times linked to the Passion of Christ, as signifying Christ's death,[38] a signification on which later theologians, even post-Tridentine ones, placed a great deal of importance.

According to Amalar, whose attitude it probably was that ultimately decided the anticipation of the commingling ceremony, this ceremony, along with the accompanying phrase, ought to be placed before the *Pax Domini,* in the short pause after the conclusion of the embolism and the *Amen,* during which the fraction of the Host and the crossing of the chalice would already have occurred; for it was not till after His Resurrection that our Lord appeared to His disciples and saluted them with His greeting of peace. Allegorical considerations appear to have had so

---

commixtio; Ebner, 114. A later weakened *commixtio et consecratio* is evidently the basis of the commingling formula of Milan, *Commixtio consecrati corporis et sanguinis D. n. J. C. nobis edentibus et sumentibus proficiat ad vitam et gaudium sempiternum; Missale Ambrosianum* (1902), 179. A strong leaning towards a blessing formula is evident in the Mozarabic commingling formula (which is not too clear) : *Sancta sanctis et coniunctio corporis D. n. J. C. sit sumentibus et potantibus nobis ad veniam et defunctis fidelibus præstetur ad requiem; Missale mixtum* (PL, 85, 561 f.). Here the *sancta sanctis* is probably only a literary reminiscence of the oriental Τὰ ἄγια τοῖς ἀγίοις and signifies only: the species of the bread to that of the wine. This meaning is clearly evident in the parallels from Angers adduced by Lesley (*ibid.,* 561) ; *Sanctum [Sancta] cum sanctis.* Cf. Martène, 1, 4, 9, 2 (I, 419).

[34] *Supra,* p. 300. The idea of the Resurrection at the commingling was all the more natural to ancient thinking because it was customary to consider the soul as joined to the blood. Therefore with the blood the soul also returned to the body. Even Durandus, IV, 51, 17, mentions the idea, with an appeal to Aristotle.

[35] Amalar, *De eccl. off.,* III, 31 (PL, 105, 1152 A) ; *Expositio* "Missa pro multis." ed. Hanssens (*Eph. liturg.,* 1930), 42; *Expositio* "*Introitus missæ,*" ed. Hanssens (*Eph. liturg.,* 1930), 45.

[36] Bernold, *Micrologus,* c. 20 (PL, 151, 990) ; Durandus, IV, 51, 17, Cf. *supra,* the interpretation of the three portions of the broken host.

[37] Gihr, 744 f.—In view of the allegorizing about the Passion of Christ which was connected with the concluding part of the canon and which actually became ritually effective there, one must acknowledge a certain justification for the application to the Resurrection. Of course the idea can hardly be carried out in the liturgical process, not only because there is little support for it, but also because the overlapping of words and ceremonies scarcely leaves room for it.

[38] The idea is clearly expressed by Humbert of Silva Candida (d. 1061), *Adv. Græcorum calumnias,* n. 31 (PL, 143, 950 D), and by Lanfranc (d. 1089), *Liber de corp. et sang. Domini,* c. 14 (PL, 150, 424 A). Cf. Haberstroh, 74-76; Lepin, 113 ff. A slight but isolated indication also in Remigius of Auxerre, *In I Cor.,* c. 11 (PL, 117, 572).

powerful an influence that in at least one area[39] they were able to over-rule the explicit direction of the Roman *ordo* which says: *Cum dixerit: Pax Domini.*[40] Thereafter only the partition of the Host was anticipated, being linked with the concluding formula, *Per Dominum*, in lieu of a pause.[41] The crossing then was joined to the *Pax Domini*,[42] for this latter was by degrees interpreted as a formula of blessing. Therefore it was put in the same place where formerly the pontifical blessing had been inserted, being treated as the final phrase which the bishop added upon his return to the altar.[43]

However, only in one portion of the post-Carolingian Mass plans did this commingling follow immediately;[44] but it was this arrangement that was adopted in Italy[45] and therefore also the one definitely fixed in the Missal of Pius V.

By far the greater portion of the Carolingian Mass plans contained a different arrangement. True, they did not hold to the original Roman pattern, where the commingling was linked to the Communion[46] or, at any

---

[39] Remigius of Auxerre, *Expositio* (PL, 105, 1270 B) : first by reason of the commingling does the priest wish peace to the Church.

[40] *Ordo Rom.*, I, n. 18 (PL, 78, 945). Likewise *Ordo Rom.*, III, n. 16 (*ibid.*, 981). On the other hand, *Ordo Rom.*, V, n. 10 (*ibid.*, 988) says: *dicendo: Pax Domini.* Moreover, both *Capitulare eccl. ord.* and *Breviarium eccl. ord.* already have: *Mittit in calicem (. . .) et dicit: Pax Domini* (Andrieu, III, 105; 182).

[41] Bernold, *Micrologus*, c. 23 (PL, 151, 988 C). So also in the Georgian Liturgy of St. Peter (Codrington, 162; cf. 20) which duplicates the Latin Mass as performed towards the end of the 10th century in the domain of Beneventum (*ibid.*, 107; cf. 25 f.). On the other hand, the pause after *Amen* is still presupposed in the Cod. Casanat., 614 (Ebner, 330) at the turn of the 11th century, and even somewhat later perhaps in the *Ordo eccl. Lateranensis* (Fischer, 85).

[42] Expositio "Introitus Missæ" (written since the 10th century; follows Amalar), ed. Hanssens (*Eph. liturg.*, 1930), 45. *Quare panis cum cruce in vinum mittitur dicente sacerdote: Pax Domini . . .?* In the Sacramentaries, Brinktrine, *Die Messe*, 302, established a first sign of the cross at the *Pax Domini* in a manuscript of the 11-12th centuries, (the Cod. Casanat., 614, just mentioned); but it was not till the

13-14th centuries that this sign of the cross became general.

[43] *Supra*, p. 295, n. 13.

[44] *Ordo Rom.*, III, n. 16 (PL, 78, 981). More frequently the commingling coincides with the *Pax Domini*; *Ordo Rom.*, V, n. 10 (PL, 78, 988) ; John of Avranches, *De off. eccl.* (PL, 147, 36 D) ; Bernold, *Micrologus*, c. 17, 23 (PL, 151, 988, 995). Above all, for the non-episcopal Mass, the Missa Illyrica and the related texts must be cited here; *supra*, n. 11.

[45] *Vide* examples since the 11th century in Ebner, 299; 301; 307; 310; 316; 330; 335; 348. Contrary to the statements of Sölch, *Hugo*, 127, I was able to find only two examples in which clearly something else, namely the *Agnus Dei*, precedes; Ebner, 297; 335 (Cod. F. 18) ; cf. 4.—In the northern countries this arrangement is rare after the 11th century; Missal of Remiremont (11-12th cent.) : Martène, 1, 4, 9, 9 (I, 423) ; Statutes of the Carthusians : *ibid.*, 1, 4, XXV (I, 634 C) ; Augsburg Missale of 1386 (Hoeynck, 374) ; the Mass-*ordo* of Ratisbon about 1500 (Beck, 269) ; even Durandus, IV, 51, 18, for allegorical reasons, champions this plan.

[46] This arrangement was retained in the pope's Mass even in the 14th century; v. *Ordo Rom.*, XIV, n. 17 (PL, 78, 1191) : The pope with two fingers of either hand takes hold of the still unbroken halves of

rate, followed the kiss of peace and the fraction (insofar as there was still question of one).[47] But the commingling often occurred after the *Agnus Dei* in those churches where it had already become customary for the priest to recite it.[48] And so the priests kept the sacred particle in their hands during the *Agnus Dei* with the purpose (as Durandus says) *ut eorum oratio efficacior sit pro eo quod tenentes eam in manibus . . . oculo corporali et mentali reverenter intuentur.*[49] In this case, then, we have a secondary reshifting which likewise rests on Amalar's solution and which in the main has disappeared since 1570.

Since Amalar had indicated for the rite of commingling a place at the *Pax Domini,* the very spot where, according to the practice of the ancient Church, the space-encircling unifying force of the Eucharist had been represented by the admixture of the *fermentum,* our modest rite had gained an additional significance beyond its original meaning of representing the intrinsic unity of the Sacrament under two kinds, borrowing from the farther-reaching significance of its sister rite the symbolism of Communion of church with church. The accompanying *Pax Domini* could easily add support to these latter ideas. On the other hand, the rite of fraction and commingling, as now in use in the Roman Mass, has lost

---

the host and says the *Domine non sum dignus.* After the sign of the cross with the Sacred Species of Bread *reverenter sumat totum illud quod est extra digitos prædictos, et quod infra digitis remanet ponat in calice cum sanguine dicens: Fiat commixtio . . .* Cf. *supra,* n. 1.

[47] This arrangement appears as an alternate plan in Amalar, *De off eccl.,* III, 31 (PL, 105, 1151 D) (*ut*) *aliqui reservent immissionem, usquedum pax celebrata sit et fractio panis.* It is still to be recognized in the Sacramentary of Ratoldus (d. 986) (PL, 78, 244), where the formula of commingling is raised to the dignity of an oration. After the *Pax Domini* the bishop gives the *cantor* the signal for the *Agnus Dei: Interim osculetur archdiaconum et ceteros. Inde vertens se ad altare dicat hanc orationem: Dominus vobiscum. Resp. Et cum spiritu tuo. Hæc sacrosancta commixtio . . . salutaris. P. D.*—Also, where the rubric mentioned above, n. 11, still survived, the commingling took place, at least at the bishop's Mass, only after the kiss of peace; cf. also the older version of the Greek Liturgy of St. Peter as witness to the liturgy of the early 10th century in central Italy (Codrington, 136).

[48] Mass-*ordo* of Amiens (ed. Leroquais:

Eph. liturg., 1927, 443); Sacramentary of Fulda (Richter-Schönfelder, n. 22); further, from the 10-11th century the *ordines* in Martène, 1, 4, V-VIII (I, 527, 533 f., 537, 540), likewise the Mass plans, generally later, from France in Martène and Leroquais; v. also *Liber ordinarius* of Liége with its Dominican model (Volk, 96). The same arrangement holds also in Spain (Ferreres, 179) and especially in the English Mass-books of the later Middle Ages; *v.* Martène, 1, 4, XXXV (I, 669); Legg, *Tracts,* 14, 226, 265; *ibid.,* 47 f.; 65, further examples from the 16th century. — The rite survives still today among the Dominicans; *Missale O.P.* (1889), 21. Among the Cistercians the priest let one of the three broken pieces which he held in his hands fall into the chalice after the *Agnus Dei;* the second, set aside for the Communion of the Levites he laid upon the paten, after imparting the kiss of peace; and the third he retained for his own Communion. Schneider (*Cist.-Chr.,* 1927) 139 f.—In certain isolated cases the commingling took place already after the first *Agnus Dei*: Mass-*ordo* of Bec: Martène, 1, 4, XXXVI (I, 674 C); Sacramentary from Arezzo (11th cent.): Ebner, 4.

[49] Durandus, IV, 51, 18.

some of its importance, since it does not occupy a place in the pause mentioned above and, as a consequence, appears simply as an accompaniment
to the close of the embolism and the *Pax Domini*, texts which have no
immediate relevance to the rite. Thus few celebrants will find it possible
to keep in mind the significance of the venerable rite. And for the other
participants, the rite has hardly any purpose at all, since it is perceptible
only to those close to the altar. Besides, the ancient song that formerly
accompanied the fraction, the *Agnus Dei*, did not follow the change of
position of the rite as we have it now, but continued to occupy the position of the older fraction, as we shall see. Scarcely anywhere else has the
transparency of the liturgical procedure suffered so much by later contraction and compression as here in the purlieu of the fraction and commingling, although the elements of the ancient tradition have been faithfully preserved.[50]

6. *Pax Domini* and the Kiss of Peace

Whether we study the development of the Roman Communion rite or
confine our attention to the external picture of the Mass as it is today
(where the *Pax Domini* is taken up right after the close of the embolism),
we must deal with the kiss of peace. For the *Pax Domini* was regarded as
a signal and an invitation to the faithful to exchange the kiss of peace
with each other. Nowhere is this indicated in any explicit rubric, but it
follows from parallels in the African liturgy[1] and from the actual procedure outlined in the oldest *ordines*.[2] Even in documentary sources of the
tenth century the fact that the *Pax Domini* is omitted on Good Friday

[50] Abbot Capelle arrives at the same conclusions, "Le rite de la fraction" (*Revue
Bénéd.*, 1941). 5 f., 39 f. Here he also
points out a method that could be a remedy.
The priest would say the oration for peace,
Domine J. C. qui dixisti before the *Pax
Domini*. The breaking and commingling
would follow after the *PaxDomini*, accompanied by the singing of the *Agnus Dei*,
which the priest himself would also recite
after these actions.

[1] Augustine, *Sermo*, 227 (PL, 38, 1101):
Post ipsam [*sc. orationem dominicam*]
*dicitur: Pax vobiscum, et osculantur se
Christiani in osculo sancto.* Cf. *Enarr. in
ps. 124*, 10 (PL, 37, 1656), where also the
answer of the people, *Et cum spiritu tuo,* is
attested. Other passages in Roetzer, 130 f.
Moreover, in the *Apostolic Constitutions*,
VIII, 11, 8 f. (Quasten, *Mon.*, 210), the in-

vitation to the Kiss of Peace is mentioned
as occurring in a similar manner, even before the beginning of the Eucharistic prayer; the bishop gives the salutation: 'Η
εἰρήνη τοῦ θεοῦ μετὰ πάντων ὑμῶν; and the
people answer: Καὶ μετὰ τοῦ πνεύματος σοῦ,
whereupon the deacon recites the express
summons to the Holy Kiss, using the words
of I Cor. 16: 20.
[2] *Ordo Rom.*, I, n. 18 (Andrieu, II, 98; cf.
II, 57 f.): *Et cum spiritu tuo. Sed archidiaconus pacem dat episcopo priori, deinde
et ceteri per ordinem et populus. Capitulare
eccl. ord.* (Andrieu, III, 124; cf. 105):
*respondentibus omnibus: Et cum spiritu
tuo, statim, sicut supra dictum est, debet
clerus et populus inter se pacem facere, ubi
stare videntur*—Ordo of St. Amand (*ibid.*,
II, 169).—The connection is clearly recognized in the Carlovingian *Expositio
"Dominus vobiscum"* (PL, 138, 1172 f.).

was explained *quia non sequuntur oscula circumadstantium.*[3] The arrangement of the present-day high Mass, where the kiss of peace is not given till after the *Agnus Dei* and another prayer for peace are said, is (as we shall see) the result of more recent developments.

By placing the kiss of peace just before the Communion, the Roman Mass (along with the African already mentioned) assumes a position apart, for all the other liturgies have it at the beginning of the Sacrifice-Mass. The original place of the kiss of peace was, in reality, at the end of the service of reading and prayers rather than at the start of the Sacrifice-Mass. According to the ancient Christian conception, it formed the seal and pledge of the prayers that preceded it.[4] But after the service of readings and prayers had been joined to the celebration of the Eucharist, regard for our Lord's admonition (Matthew 5:23 f.) about the proper dispositions in one who wishes to make an offering would probably have led to placing the kiss of peace (as guarantee of fraternal sentiment) closer to the moment when one is "bringing his gift before the altar." [5]

At a very early date the Roman liturgy went a step further.[6] In opposition to the practice which the Bishop of Gubbio had in view, of announcing the kiss of peace *ante confecta mysteria,* Pope Innocent I, in his reply in 416, insisted that it was not to be proclaimed till after the completion of the entire sacrifice; for, he asserted, the people ought by means of it to make known their assent to all that had gone before.[7] Here again attention is immediately drawn to its function as a seal and guarantee. But ultimately (when, as a result of Gregory the Great's rearrangement, the *Pater noster* was placed directly after the close of the canon and there was no proclamation of the kiss of peace until after the embolism), it was

[3] *Ordo Rom. antiquus* (Hittorp, 67, recte, 69). Likewise Sicard of Cremona, *Mitrale,* VI, 13 (PL, 213, 321.— Cf. Maundy Thursday in the older Gelasianum, I, 40 (Wilson, 72): *non dicis: Pax Domini, nec faciunt pacem.* Similarly in today's *Missale Romanum* the rubrics on Holy Saturday: *Dicitur Pax Domini sit semper vobiscum, sed pacis osculum non datur.*

[4] Justin, *Apol.,* I, 65 (*supra* I, 22). Tertullian, *De or.,* 18 (CSEL, 20, 191), calls the Kiss of Peace the *signaculum orationis;* with it we should conclude the prayer in common, even if we are celebrating a feast day; only on public feast days is the Kiss omitted, since it is also the expression of the joy of life (cf. the previous note). Origen, *In Rom. hom.,* 10, 33 (PG, 14, 1282 f.) also speaks of the custom called forth by Rom. 16: 16 (among others), *ut post orationes osculo invicem suscipiant*

fratres, Hipolytus, *Trad. Ap.* (Dix, 29): "When the prayer (after the instruction) is ended, the catechumens should not give the Kiss of Peace, because their kiss is not yet pure; but the baptized should greet each other (ἀσπάζεσθαι), men the men, and women the women. But the men, should not greet the women." After baptism the newly baptized take part in the prayers of the faithful and then exchange the Kiss with them (Dix, 39). For further ancient Christian evidences see Quasten, *Mon.,* 16, note 2, and in the Register, p. 374, under *osculum.*

[5] Cf. Baumstark, *Liturgie comparée,* 145.

[6] The north African liturgy even earlier; Dekkers, *Tertullianus,* 59 f.; Roetzer, 130 f.

[7] Innocent I, *Ep.,* 25, 1 (PL, 20, 553): . . . *per quam constet populum ad omnia . . . præbuisse consensum ac finita*

quite natural that the kiss appear as an illustration of the *sicut et nos dimittimus*. Perhaps it was this phrase which first drew it towards the conclusion of the *Pater noster*.

As a matter of fact, even in Gregory the Great's time the kiss of peace was regarded as a natural preparation for Communion. A group of monks, threatened by shipwreck, gave each other the kiss of peace and then received the Sacrament which they carried with them.[8] The same opinion predominated at this period also outside the area of the Roman liturgy. Sophronius (d. 638) pictures St. Mary of Egypt giving the kiss of peace to the aged monk who brings her the Mysteries, whereupon she receives the Body of the Lord.[9] In the arrangement for Communion of the sick in the Celtic Church, the Book of Dimma, about 800, stipulates: *Hic* [after the Our Father and the embolism belonging to it have been recited] *pax datur ei et dicis: Pax et communicatio sanctorum tuorum, Christe Jesu, sit semper nobiscum. R. Amen*, whereupon the Eucharist is given.[10]

In the Carolingian area also the same succession (of kiss of peace and distribution of Communion) is found both at Communion of the sick[11] and at public service.[12] Indeed the kiss is often restricted to the communicants. The *canones* of Theodore of Canterbury, in one version (eighth century), contain the rule: *qui non communicant, nec accedant ad pacem neque ad osculum in ecclesia*.[13] The rule was also known in the Carolingian Church, but there, alongside the severe regulation, a milder interpretation also appeared, which did not make restriction so narrow.[14] Nevertheless,

---

esse pacis concludentis signaculo demonstrentur.

[8] Gregory the Great, *Dial.*, III, 36 (PL, 77, 307 C); cf. the same, *In ev.*, II, 37, 9 (PL, 76, 1281 A).

[9] Sophronius, *Vita s. Mariæ Aeg.*, c. 22 (PL, 73, 87 B). In the two witnesses cited by Mabillon in his commentary the Kiss of Peace is joined with the Communion: Jerome, *Ep.* 62 al. 82 (PL, 22, 737); Paulus of Merida (7th cent.), *Vitæ patrum*, c. 7 (PL, 80, 135 B).

[10] F. E. Warren, *The Liturgy and Ritual of the Celtic Church* (Oxford, 1881), 170. The formula quoted corresponds to our *Pax Domini;* cf. formula connected with the Kiss of Peace in the Mass in the Stowe Missal (*ibidem.*, 242): *Pax et caritas D. n. J. C. et communicatio sanctorum ominum sit semper vobiscum.* The liturgy of Milan uses *Pax et communicatio D. n. J. C. sit semper vobiscum*, whereon still follows: *Offerte vobis pacem. Missale Ambrosianum* (1902), 181 f.

[11] The 9th century Ordo for the Sick from Lorsch, edited by C. de Clerq: *Eph. liturg.*, 44 (1930), 103, contains the rubric: *Hic pax datur et communicatio* and then the formula: *Pax et communicatio corporis et sanguinis D. n. J. C. conservet animam tuam in vitam æternam.* Likewise Theodulph of Orleans (d. 821), *Capitulare*: Martène, 1, 7, II (I, 847 C); cf. the somewhat later ordo for the sick from Narbonne: *ibid.*, 1, 7, XIII (I, 892 B).

[12] Sacramentary of Ratoldus (10th cent.; PL, 78, 245): *Et episcopus communicet presbyteros et diaconos cum osculo pacis.*

[13] n. 50; P. W. Finsterwalder, *Die Canones Theodori* (Weimar, 1929), 274.

[14] Walafried Strabo, *De exord, et increm.*, c. 22 (PL, 114, 950 C): The *pax* remains licit for those who are not excluded *iudicio sacerdotali* from Communion and therefore are not *extra communionem*. In point of fact, several of the ordinances at the

at least in monasteries, it was still the rule even in the year 1000 that on Communion days, and only on these, the brethren received the *pax*. This was true in England [15] as well as on the continent.[16] The kiss of peace was a pre-condition for Communion,[17] or at least a fitting preparation for it,[18] and in reverse, the deacon and subdeacon at high Mass, who were to re-

time of Charlemagne required that all participate in the Kiss of Peace; thus the Frankfort Synod of 794 (c. 48; Mansi, XIII, App., 194) : *omnes generaliter pacem ad invicem præbeant.* Cf. Nickl, *Der Anteil des Volkes,* 48 f.

[15] *Concordia Regularis* of St. Dunstan (PL, 137, 483 A, 495 A). A report about Winchester in G. H. Ritchin, *Compotus rolls* (1892), 176, quoted by Browe, *Die häufige Kommunion,* 65, n. 22.

[16] Capitula monachorum ad Augiam directa (Albers, III, 106) ; Consuetudines Cluniacenses (before 1048; Albers, II, 48; cf. however p. 38) ; Consuetudines monasteriorum Germaniæ (Albers, V, 28). Liber usuum O. Cist. (12th cent.), c. 66 (PL, 166, 1437) : *In die Nativitatis Domini, Cænæ, Paschæ, Pentecostes debent fratres pacem sumere et communicare.* In the later Consuetudines Cluniacenses of the Abbot Udalrich (circa 1080), I, 8 (PL, 149, 653) the bond between Communion and the Kiss of Peace is already somewhat less rigid.

[17] A remnant of it is a custom still much in use today, that the communicant kiss the ring of the bishop administering Communion, or as the *Cæremoniale Episcoporum,* II, 29, 5 declares, the hand. Although a kissing of the hand just before receiving Communion was customary in the ancient church (v. *infra*) still the present-day use seems to be derived from the mutual Kiss of Peace that was exchanged at the altar, or at least was inspired by it. The transition to the kissing of the hand on the part of the one receiving Communion is evident in John of Avranches (d. 1079) *De off. eccl.* (PL, 147, 37 B) : *Dum ergo sacerdos ministris communionem porrigit, unumquemque primitus osculetur et post qui communicandus est, manu sacerdotis osculata, communionem ab eo accipiat.* The suppression of the Kiss on the part of the celebrating bishop, who is already occupied with the administration of the Sacrament

(even though he does not himself carry the paten with the particles, but an acolyte) is already shown in *Ordo Rom.,* VI (10th cent.), n. 12 (PL, 78, 994), according to which henceforth only priest and deacon kiss the bishop, whereas the subdeacon kisses the bishop's hand. On the contrary, the Sacramentary of Ratoldus (d. 986) mentions only the kiss of the bishop (for priest and deacon) (PL, 78, 245 A).—On the other hand, in the tradition of the city of Rome the mutual kiss among the immediate assistants lasted a much longer time. *Ordo eccl. Lateran.* (Fischer, 85, 1. 40; cf. 86, 1. 23) : *(episcopus) communicat diaconum dando ei pacem, illo osculante manum eius.* According to Innocent III, *De s. alt. mysterio,* VI, 9 (PL, 217, 911 f.) the pope, after his own Communion, gives the deacon *particulam unam cum osculo,* the subdeacon receives the kiss when he receives the Precious Blood from the deacon. Also according to the somewhat later *Pontificale Romanæ Curiæ* (Andrieu, *Le Pontifical Romain,* II, 350) the newly ordained priests and deacons kiss the hand of the bishop before Communion and then receive from him both Communion and the Kiss of Peace; similarly in the Pontifical of Durandus (Andrieu, III, 348).— Our *Cæremoniale episc.,* I, 9, 6; 24, 3 f., decides in the same sense, that at a High Mass the deacon and subdeacon should not receive the *pax* with the others (insofar as they do not wish to celebrate as priests themselves) but only when the bishop offers them Communion, when they, as well as the canons receiving Communion, *primo manum, deinde faciem episcopi,* while the other clerics and the lay people kiss only the hand of the bishop (II, 29, 3, 5); cf. the Ordo of Stefaneschi, n. 53; 56; 71 (PL, 78, 1168 B, 1172 C, 1191 D), where the pope first administers Communion and then imparts the *pax.*

[18] Later evidence for this idea in Brinktrine, *Die hl. Messe,* 250.

ceive the *pax* were for a long time obliged also to receive Holy Communion.[19] In fact, amongst the Cistercians there was a regulation even for private Mass that the server receive *pax* and Communion each time,[20] until in 1437 Eugene IV rescinded this obligation of the *ministri altaris* as dangerous.[21] But even so, the connection between kiss of peace and Communion survived for a long time.[22]

Elsewhere the kiss of peace gradually became a sort of substitute for Communion.[23] Not only was the kiss exchanged at the altar, but all the people participated. The ancient way of exchanging the kiss of peace

---

[19] See below, p. 387.

[20] Liber usuum, c. 54 (PL, 166, 1429): *(minister) pacem et communionem semper accipiat, excepta missa defunctorum, in qua nec pacem sumere nec communicare licet.* Aside from the communicants only guests received the Kiss of Peace among the Cistercians (Schneider, *Cist.-Chr.*, 1928), 8.

[21] Browe, "Die Kommunionvorbereitung im Mittelalter" (*ZkTh*, 1932), 413.

[22] According to the statutes of a convent of Cistercian nuns in Lower Germany, 1584, edited by J. Haus (*Cist.-Chr.*, 1935), 132 f., the Kiss of Peace was given before Communion on Communion days starting with the abbess. See *Rituale Cist.* (Paris, 1689), 93, according to which the server if he or someone else wishes to receive Communion, hands the priest the *instrumentum pacis*, then kisses it himself and passes it on. Cf. on the contrary the statement of Balthasar of Pforta (1494) in Franz, *Die Messe*, 587, according to which the Cistercians in Germany at the time (except in the case the server received Communion?) gave the *pax* only at High Mass, whereas the secular clergy imparted it to the server by means of the crucifix also at private Mass. The *pax* for the *frater servitor* also without Communion was firmly retained in private Mass by the Dominicans in the *Ordinarium* of 1256 (Guerrini, 244); likewise in the *Ordinarium* of Liége (Volk, 101, 1. 33).

[23] Cf. *supra*, note 14. The Consuetudines of Udalricus of Cluny (circa 1080) orders one half of the choir to give and receive the Kiss of Peace daily; Communion remains free (I, 6; PL, 149, 652). John Beleth (d. 115), *Explicatio*, c. 48 (PL, 202, 55 D), mentions a triple substitute, introduced after Communion at every Mass was no longer demanded: *singulis diebus,* the Kiss of Peace; on Sundays, the blessed bread; and in Lent, instead of that, the *oratio super populum.* Durandus repeats the same, IV, 53, 3.—Sicard of Cremona, *Mitrale*, III, 8 (PL, 213, 144), and Hugo of S. Cher, *Tract. super missam* (ed. Sölch, 51) express themselves in the same manner. Beleth's evaluation of the Kiss of Peace is taken over literally by Pope Innocent III, *De s. alt. mysterio*, VI, 5 (PL, 217, 909). Further witnesses with like sentiments, from the 12th and 13th centuries, in Browe, *Die Pflichtkommunion*, 186. Ludolf of Saxony (d. 377), *Vita D. n. Jesu Christi*, II, 56 (Augsburg, 1729: p. 557), regards the Kiss of Peace as a substitute for the Communion; so also the Hollander William of Gouda (15th cent.): see P. Schlager, "Uber die Messerklärung des Franziskaners Wilhelm von Gouda," *Franziskan. Studien*, 6 (1919), 335. — In the transition period about the 11th century, a time when Communion was already very rare, the Kiss of Peace even at High Mass must have been out of use in many a place, because it is no longer mentioned in the otherwise very detailed rubrics of the Mass-plans; thus in that of Séez (PL, 78, 250 B). Durandus, IV, 53, 8, mentions another basic reason why the monks no longer made use of the Kiss of Peace, but even at this time (for the earlier period, cf. *supra*, n. 7 f., 14 f.) this reason applies only to a particular practice, which took a more stringent view of the worldly and passionate element of the kiss; more information in Lebrun, I, 522-524.

would not entail the disturbance and confusion in the service that we would be led to expect today, for then the kiss was not continued from person to person, but merely exchanged between neighbors.

The first Roman *ordo* says explicitly: When the *Pax Domini* has been spoken, the archdeacon gives the kiss of peace to the first bishop, *deinde et ceteri per ordinem et populus.*[24] At the given signal, therefore, those in the nave of the church greeted each other with the kiss. But many of the later manuscripts of this *ordo* have introduced an inconspicuous but very important change: *deinde ceteris per ordinem et populis.*[25] Thus the kiss of peace is made to proceed from the altar and, like a message or even like a gift which comes from the Sacrament, is handed on "to the others and to the people." The new rule is clearly expressed in a plan for Mass, which is placed at the beginning of the tenth-century Romano-German Pontifical and its derivatives: *presbyter accipiat pacem ab episcopo eandem ceteris oblaturus.*[26]

With this in view it was only natural that the kiss of peace was no longer received from the deacon but from the celebrant himself, and even he "received" it. Therefore he first kissed the altar: *osculato altari dat pacem astanti.*[27] Even this was not fully satisfactory, and efforts were made to indicate even more plainly the source from which the peace was to be derived. According to a pontifical from lower Italy, about 1100, the celebrant kissed first the altar, then the book, and finally the Sacred Host, before he offered the deacon the kiss of peace.[28] Elsewhere, as in France, as a rule only the Host was kissed.[29] In England, however, during the

---

[24] *Ordo Rom.*, I, n. 18 (Andrieu, II, 98). Every change of place is expressly excluded in the *Capitulare eccl. ord.* (*supra*, note 2). Cf. Nickl, *Der Anteil des Volkes an der Messliturgie*, 49 f.

[25] Thus Mabillon (PL, 78, 945 B), and a number of later MSS.

[26] *Ordo Rom.*, VI, n. 12 (Hittorp, 8; PL, 78, 994). That this new order is already to be supposed in Remigius of Auxerre, as Sölch, *Hugo*, 129 f., assumes, need not be taken as conclusively proved.—The older custom is still clearly testified by Amalar, *De eccl. off.*, III, 32 (PL, 105, 1153), but also in the *Ordo Rom.*, III (11th cent.), n. 16 (PL, 78, 982 A): . . . *per ordinem ceteri; atque populus osculantur se in osculo Christi*. The two methods of the Kiss of Peace overlap each other therefore in point of time; cf. Synod of Santiago de Compostela (1056), can. 1 (Mansi, XIX, 856): *omnibus intra ecclesiam stantibus pacis osculum sibi invicem tribuatur.*

[27] Bernold, *Micrologus*, c. 23 (PL, 151, 995); Sakramentar von Modena (vor 1174): Muratori, I, 93. A Sacramentary of the 11th century from Arezzo (Ebner, 4) has the priest first kiss the altar, *tunc osculetur omnes.*—The provision that the priest receive the *pax* from the bishop also in the *Ordo Rom.*, VI (previous note).

[28] Ebner 330 (Cod. Casanat. 614); it occurs at specified places in the prayer for peace, *Domine Jesu Christe.*

[29] John Beleth, *Explic.*, c. 48 (PL, 202, 54); Herbert von Sassari, *De Miraculis* (written, 1171), I, 21 (PL, 185, 1298 A). Important authorities espoused the kissing of the Host; Hugo von S. Cher, *Tract, super missam* (ed. Sölch, 49); Albert the Great, *De sacrificio missæ*, III, 21, 5 (Opp., ed. Borgnet, 38, 159 f.).—The custom lasted beyond the Middle Ages in French churches; Ordinarium of Coutances, 1557: Legg, *Tracts*, 66; Lebrun, I, 518, note c.

thirteenth century this custom was stopped as being less seemly.[30] Here, and in part also in France, it was customary to kiss instead the brim of the chalice and in addition generally the corporal or the paten,[31] while in Germany the prevailing practice was to kiss the altar and the book.[32] Altar and crucifix are also mentioned for this.[33]

The participation of the people continued for several centuries, especially after the kiss of peace was everywhere extended beyond the circle of communicants, and in particular when it was brought from the altar.[34] Therefore the old rule which is found in earlier Christian sources[35] was repeated, namely, that men may give the kiss of peace only to men, and women to women.[36] This rule was very easy to keep when—as was usually

---

[30] First of all, in 1217 by a decree of Bishop Richard of Salisbury, Sölch, *Hugo,* 131. —The East Syrian Liturgy offers a parallel to such considerations, for the kissing of the Sacred Host was at one time prescribed, but the caution is added, that it is to be be done figuratively, without touching the lips; Brightman, 290.

[31] Mass-*ordo* of Sarum (Legg, *Tracts,* 265; Legg, *The Sarum Missal,* 226, note 5); Missale of York (Simmons, 112 f.). *Missale O. Carm.* (1935), 317, where pall and chalice are kissed.— Only the kissing of the chalice is customary in the later Dominican rite (Guerrini, 243); in the *Liber ordinarius* of Liége (Volk, 96)), in the Missale of S. Pol de Léon: Martène, 1, 4, XXXIV (I, 664). Cf. Sölch, *Hugo,* 131 f.

[32] This kiss is prescribed (among others) in the Pontifical of Mainz about 1170: Martène, 1, 4, XVII (I, 602 C); the Regensburg Missal about 1500: Beck, 269. Cf. Franz, *Die Messe,* 587 f.; Sölch, *Hugo,* 130 ff., note 199 and 207.—In the north, about 1500, it was the more common practice to kiss both the book and paten; *v.* Bruiningk, 87, n. 2; Yelverton, 20. The Breslau Missal of 1476 mentions paten and book: Radó, 163.—Above all the kiss was implanted on the picture of the Lord (mostly the Lamb of God) that was inserted at the end of the canon; traces of the kissing can still be recognized; Ebner, 448 f. In a book printer's contract of the Bishop of Upsala of Feb. 23, 1508, a special stipulation was made, *etiam una crux in margine pro osculo circa Agnus Dei;* J. Freisen, *Manuale Lincopense* (Paderborn, 1904), page XLVI.

[33] Hungarian Missals of the 13th (Radó, 62) and the 15th centuries (Jávor, 118); Mass-commentary of William of Gouda: Schlager, Franziskan. Studien, 6 (1919), 335.

[34] Cf. Franz, 587-594. In the Credo of Poor Hartmann (circa 1120), Verse 857-859, is mentioned "the kissing which the people do at Mass"; see R. Stroppel, *Liturgie und geistliche Dichtung zwischen 1050 und 1300* (Frankfort, 1927), 77 f. — Also the Benedictine *Liber ordinarius* of Liége (Volk, 96) declares again: *subdiaconus uni acolythorum* [*det pacem*], *ille vero deferat extraneis;* the subdeacon himself could impart the *pax* to an *excellens persona.*

[35] *Supra,* note 4. It is clear that the old rule was first introduced as the result of experience. The remark of Tertullian, *Ad uxor.,* II, 4 (CSEL, 70, 117), that a pagan husband would not tolerate that his wife should dare to approach a brother for the Kiss of Peace, obviously stems from a previous period before the rule was in effect. Cf. also *supra,* p. 322, the example in Sophronius, and on the other hand the warning remarks in Clement of Alexandria, *Pædag.,* III, 81 (GCS Clem., I, 281).

[36] Thus Amalar, *De eccl. off.,* III, 32 (PL, 105, 1153); and again John Beleth, *Explicatio,* c. 48 (PL, 202, 54 f.); Durandus, IV, 53, 9. The rule shows that in general it must have been as a matter of fact an actual *osculum oris.*—An uninterrupted passage of the Kiss of Peace from the altar was thereby naturally excluded for the women. According to an old French custom, however, the priest gave the Kiss of Peace to the groom in a bridal Mass,

the case—the old ordinance regarding the separation of the sexes was still observed.[37]

Nevertheless we feel it would always have been somewhat risky to employ a token of the deepest confidence, such as the kiss is, only in the tiny circle of a young community borne up by high idealism, but even as a permanent institution in public assembly. Of course conditions of ancient culture must be taken into account.[38] Still, in all Christian liturgies in the course of time a certain stylizing was effected, in which only a discreet indication of the former kiss remained. Aside from the Byzantine liturgy (where the kiss is executed in this restrained form only by the celebrant and deacon, and by no one else,[39] this symbolic gesture has been retained also for the people in all the rites of the East. Among the East Syrians it is customary for each one to clasp the hands of his neighbor and kiss them. Among the Maronites the faithful clasp the neighbor's fingers with their own, then kiss the latter. Even more reserved are the Copts, who merely bow to their neighbor and then touch his hand, and the Armenians who are—partly—satisfied with a mere bow.[40]

Such a stylizing is also found in the present Roman liturgy in the kiss of peace given within the ranks of the clergy at high Mass, the only time it is still practiced. Here it is a light embrace, *sinistris genis sibi invicem appropinquantibus.*[41] A different stylization for the kiss of peace in the whole congregation had its origin in England, where the finer touch had also been shown in regard to the kissing of the Host. This is the kiss of peace given by means of the *osculatorium,* a plaque (often richly orna-

---

who in turn imparted it to the bride; P. Doncœur, *Retours en chrétienté* (Paris, 1933), 119 f.

[37] As Sölch, 133, remarks, the prescription was at that time violated most frequently in monastic churches.

[38] Cf. J. Horst, *Proskynein* (Gütersloh, 1932), 50 f.: In general the kiss had a different meaning in ancient times from what it has today. Among non-related people it was a mark of respect rather than affection.

[39] The priest kisses the gift offering, the deacon his own stole; Brightman, 382, 1. 26. In the Pontifical rite, however, a real Kiss of Peace takes place among the clergy. The bishop's shoulders and right hand are kissed, and both shoulders of the Archimandrites and priests, with the words "Christ is among us," to which the response is given, "He is and will be." A. v. Maltzew, *Liturgikon* (Berlin, 1902), 232

[40] Brightman, 584 f.; Hanssens, *Institutiones,* III, 317-321. Here still further

statements concerning the generally more elaborate form in which the celebrant and his assistants give each other the Kiss of Peace, and the accompanying prayers. According to Cl. Kopp, *Glaube u. Sakramente der koptischen Kirche* (Rome, 1932), 128, the form in vogue among the Copts today consists in this that each one extends his hand right and left to his neighbor. According to J. M. of Bute, *The Coptic Morning Service* (London, 1908), 92, each one then kisses his own hand. In fact, the manner of the Kiss of Peace in the Orient seems to have varied not only between the Uniates and non-Uniates, but also within the individual communities, as a comparison of the statements made above with those by Raes, *Introductio* (1947), 86, forces us to assume.

[41] *Missale Rom., Ritus serv.,* X, 8; cf. *Cæremoniale episc.* I, 24, 2.—Gavanti-Merati, *Thesaurus,* II, 10, 8, n. XLIII (I, 330) mentions different methods in which the indicated embrace is carried out.

mented) called a pax-board or pax-brede.[42] It put in a first appearance after 1248 in English diocesan statutes, then gradually spread to the continent where, however, the earlier manner of communicating the kiss long remained in vogue.[43] Charles V, in his efforts for reform, had also determined on the renewal of the kiss of peace, *ubi mos eius dandi exolevit*, with the employment of the pax-board.[44] The kiss of peace with the *instrumentum pacis* is also provided in the Missal of Pius V of 1570 and in the *Cæremoniale episcoporum* of 1600. In this way it can, at high Mass, be communicated also to the laity. Outside of high Mass, both at the *missa cantata* and the low Mass, this is the only manner of giving the kiss of peace that is considered, both for the clergy of all ranks and for the laity.[45] Thus, the kiss of peace, like the incensation at solemn services, could in the last few centuries be regarded most often as a privilege of persons of rank. But precisely this restriction was the occasion for unedifying disputes about precedence (for the principle of handing it on from person to person involved a certain order or gradation), which was in direct contradiction to the very meaning of the ceremony. For these and similar reasons, the kiss of peace even with the pax-board was im-

[42] Braun, *Das christliche Altargerät*, 557-572; illustrations on plates 116-120.—The pax-tablet, called of old in England the Pax-board (Pax-brede), consisted of a small tablet of wood or ivory or metal (even gold or silver) upon which was graven or painted the figure of Our Lord or of a saint or sometimes symbolic figures, and usually encased in a frame with a handle at the back so that it could stand on the altar during Mass.

[43] The *osculum oris* is expressly stipulated in the old Cistercian and Premonstratensian rites: *divertat os suum ad diaconum osculans illum . . . Liber usuum*, c. 53 (PL, 166, 1426 C); Waefelghem, 87.—The German Augustinian, John Bechofen still had occasion at the turn of the 15th century to recommend the pax-tablet: *honestior est cautela ut per pacificale sive tabulam imaginem Christi aut sanctorum reliquias continentem fiat, ne sub specie boni aliquid carnalitatis diabolico inflatu surripiat.* Franz, *Die Messe*, 594. Inventories of churches in the diocese of Ermland, in East Prussia, testify to the later popularity of the pax-tablets in Germany; some churches show as many as six and eight; Braun, 559.—In Rome also the pax-tablet came into use at the turn of the 15th century, apparently through John Burchard; v. Lebrun, 519 f.

[44] *Formula Reformationis* (1548), tit. 12 (Hartzheim, VI, 756; Braun, 560). The Kiss of Peace by means of a cross (as a substitute for the pax-tablet) of a "Heilthumbs" (reliquary) is discussed in detail in the "Keligpuchel" (Chalice Book) of Bishop Berthold of Chiemsee that appeared 1535: Franz, 727.

[45] *Missale Rom., Ritus serv.*, X, 3; *Cæremoniale episc.*, I, 24, 6, 7. The latter passage, it is true, discusses only the choir of clerics and the *laici, ut magistratus et barones ac nobiles* as receivers of the *pax*, but the directions of the *Missale* contain no such restrictions. According to Gavanti-Merati, *Thesaurus, II*, 10, 8 (I, 329) the *instrumentum pacis* is handed by the subdeacon to those lay people, *quos diaconus incensavit*, and then by the acolyte to *laicis aliis*. Cf. *supra*, n. 33.—Ph. Hartmann-J. Kley, *Repertorium rituum* (Paderborn, 1940), 477 f., remarks, "where it is the custom, also the bridal couple, but otherwise never the woman at a High Mass" should receive the *pax* by means of the *pacificale*. According to the *Ordo* of John Burchard (1502), the server hands the tablet to be kissed without restriction to *interessentibus missæ*, first to those of higher rank and lastly to the women. Legg, *Tracts*, 162.

practicable and, except on certain extraordinary occasions and in a few areas here and there,[46] could continue only in various religious groups.[47]

Today the kiss of peace is preceded not only by the *Pax Domini*, but by a special prayer for peace which, however is separated from the announcement (the *Pax Domini*) by the commingling formula and by the *Agnus Dei*, which is now also said by the priest. Even as late as the ninth century the Carolingian source documents present the kiss of peace as given right after the *Pax Domini*.[48] Frequently the *Agnus Dei* was still only sung by the choir without being said by the priest, and therefore did not form any interruption before the kiss.[49]

A prayer for peace before the *pax*[50] is still missing even in some late medieval Mass plans.[51] Only the commingling formula had to be inserted after the *Pax Domini*, since the latter, of course, was coupled with the preceding triple crossing.[52]

Our prayer for peace, *Domine Jesu Christe qui dixisti*, made its appearance since the eleventh century, first of all in German territory.[53] It replaced an older prayer for peace.[54] From then on it recurred regularly,

---

[46] It is reported from the diocese of Valencia in Spain that the men still give each other the Kiss of Peace, imparted to them by two acolytes who receive it from the priest. Kramp, "Messgebräuche der Gläubigen in den ausserdeutschen Ländern" (*StZ*, 1927, II), 361.

[47] Sölch, *Hugo*, 132, names the Dominicans, Carthusians, and Carmelites. Also, so I am informed, the pax-tablet is in use among the Capuchins within their own community at Mass on Sundays and feast days.—In modern times a revival of the Kiss of Peace has been attempted in parts of Europe; *v.* Parsch, *Volksliturgie*, 18; 224.—R. B. Witte, *Das katholische Gotteshaus* (Mainz, 1939), 260 f., declares a *pacificale* as among the requirements for the furnishing of a church.

[48] Cf. aside from Amalar, Walafried Strabo, *De exord. et increm.*, c. 22 (PL, 114, 950); *Expositio "Introitus missæ quare,"* ed. Hanssens (*Eph. liturg.*, 1930), 45. Also in John of Avranches, *De off. eccl.*, (PL, 147, 36 f.), only the words for the commingling apparently still precede the Kiss of Peace.

[49] *Vide infra.*

[50] According to the original arrangement, moreover, the priest for the most part first kisses the altar and then says the prayer for peace; *v.*, e. g., passages cited below, n. 55.

[51] *Vide* Styrian Missalia in Köck, 128-132; Ordinarium of Coutances (1557): Legg, *Tracts*, 66.—Among the Dominicans it is still missing today, *Missale O.P.* (1889), 21 f., as it was in the Ordinarium of 1256 (Guerrini, 243). The same holds for the Carthusians; cf. their statutes: Martène, 1, 4, XXV (I, 634 C).—On the other hand, in several Mass arrangements not only the prayer for peace, but also one of the Communion prayers precedes the Kiss of Peace; *v.* Ebner, 299; 338; Martène, 1, 4, IV, XXXV f. (I, 515, 593, 669, 674).

[52] *Supra*, pp. 318 f.

[53] South German Sacramentary of the Cod. 1084 of Bologna, apparently from Regensburg: Ebner, 7. Mass of Flacius Illyricus: Martène, 1, 4, IV (I, 515 B).

[54] This appears for the first time in the Sacramentary of S. Amand (end of the 9th century; dating see Leroquais, I, 56, 58; text *v.* Netzer, 244) and with a better text in the Sacramentary of Fulda (10th cent.), where it reads: *Qui es omnium Deus et dominator, fac nos pacificando digne operari in hora ista, amator humanitatis, ut emundatos ab omni dolo et simulatione suscipias nos invicem in osculo et dilectione sancta, in quo manet vera pacificatio et caritas et unitatis coniunctio;* Richter-Schönfelder, n. 23. The prayer recurs, partly with altered address (among others

even in Italian Mass plans,[55] and thus was introduced into the Missal of Pius V. It is the first formal prayer in the *Ordo missæ* addressed to Christ. This address to Christ which is already found, in a different way, in the *Agnus Dei,* and which has here been continued obviously in view of the Communion about to be received, is retained also in the following Communion prayers.

This prayer for peace is a prayer for the priest in preparation for giving the *pax.* It presupposes the kiss of peace, which starts here at the altar and thence is continued through the church. Therefore, the priest begs the Lord—in view of the promise He made (John 14:27)—not to look upon his sins, but rather upon the confident attitude of the people gathered in church;[56] to disregard the unworthiness of His representative and grant peace and concord through this sacred symbol of a kiss. The prayer, therefore, gains its full meaning only when supported by the performance of the rite.

When the kiss of peace was omitted, the *Pax Domini* no longer had to be omitted with it,[57] but perhaps this prayer would be left out.[58] However, since the *pax* is almost generally omitted, except at high Mass, the prayer, in which the priest pleads for peace and concord for the Church, offers a substitute for it. Other formularies of such a prayer never made much headway.[59]

Even in Carolingian times the kiss of peace was still given without any accompanying greeting aside from the *Pax Domini.*[60] But after the practice began of letting the kiss proceed from the altar, it became customary for the priest to combine it with a special blessing. The oldest version of such a blessing—which, however, became rarer later in the Middle Ages—still regarded the kiss of peace as a preparation for Communion: *Habete vincu-*

Quies omnium) and with the conclusion *Per Christum,* in Mass arrangements of the 10th and 11th centuries from France and Italy: Martène, 1, 4, VI, VIII, X (I, 534, 540, 551); *ibid.,* 1, 4, 9, 9 (I, 423 D, 425 D); Ebner, 4; 301; 338 f.; Leroquais, I, 162; 171; II, 18; 100; 226. It is a poor translation of a formula of the Greek liturgy of St. James; Brightman, 43; cf. *ibid.,* LIV, 1. 18.

[55] Ebner, 297, 299, 301, 307, etc.; Fiala, 213.

[56] Cf. in an earlier passage: *Quorum tibi fides cognita est,* etc.

[57] *Supra* with n. 3.

[58] This rule as at present is already found in Durandus, IV, 53, 8, but applied only in the Mass of the Dead, and not on Maundy Thursday; *v. ibid.,* VI, 75. Cf. *supra,* n. 3.

[59] In several texts of the late Middle Ages

the priest says instead a prayer for external peace: *Da pacem Domine in diebus nostris quia non est alius qui pugnet pro nobis nisi tu Deus noster.* Missale of Fécamp (about 1498): Ferreres, p. XXIV. Likewise in the Missale of Evreux-Jumièges (about 1400), where a short prayer precedes: *Domine Jesu Christe, qui es vera pax et vera concordia, fac nos tecum participari in hac hora sancta. Amen.* Martène, 1, 4, XXVIII (I, 645). Cf. further *Alphabetum sacerdotum:* Legg, *Tracts,* 48.

[60] Only in the Communion of the sick, where the Kiss of Peace immdiately precedes the administration of the sacrament, is there at times an accompanying prayer, derived from an invitation corresponding to our *Pax Domini* and used at the same time as a formula for the administration of the sacrament; *vide supra,* p. 323, from

lum pacis et caritatis, ut apti sitis sacrosanctis mysteriis.[61] Those who handed on the kiss and those who received it were to say together: *Pax Christi et ecclesiæ abundet in cordibus nostris.*[62] In other cases this phrase is featured at least as the response of the *ministri,*[63] or it is put into the mouth of the celebrant, usually in combination with the aforementioned prayer, and with the variation: *in cordibus vestris.*[64] But then the simpler *Pax tecum,* the greeting which we heard from the lips of our Saviour Himself, with the answer of the recipient, *Et cum spiritu tuo,* comes more and more into use.[65]

7. Agnus Dei

After the answer to the *Pax Domini* has been given, the choir (according to present custom) at once begins the singing of the *Agnus Dei.* The chant is continued while the priest quietly recites the *Agnus Dei* and the following prayers, and while he receives Communion, so that we get the impression that here we have a Communion song. On the other hand, the final petition, *dona nobis pacem,* seems to suggest some relation between

the Book of Dimma.—In the Rituale of St. Florian (ed. Franz; Freiburg, 1904, 82) the formula is given a more definite form: *Pax et communicatio corporis et sanguinis* . . . Sometimes such a formula follows the formula of administration; *v. infra,* p. 389, n. 117.—Behind all this seems to be a blessing formula with which (according to the *Expositio* of the Gallican Mass) the priest also could bless the people after the *Pater noster* (*supra,* p. 295, n. 8).

[61] Missa Illyrica: Martène, 1, 4, LV (I, 515 C). It seems that here the formula was generally dispensed with. The formula is more common in Italy in the 10th and 13th centuries Ebner, 297; 299; 302; 307; 330, etc. In the Missal of the Hungarian Hermits of St. Paul the priest still says the *Pax Christi et caritas Dei maneat semper in cordibus nostris. Amen,* after the prayer for peace and before the *Habete;* Sawicki, *De missa conventuali,* 148.

[62] Missa Illyrica: *loc. cit.* A Salzburg Missale of the 12-13th century: Köck, 131; for Italy since 11th century; *v.* Ebner, 307; 330, 356; Muratori, I, 94.

[63] Italian Mass orders since the 11th century: Ebner, 299, 302.

[64] Martène, 1, 4, 9, 9 (I, 423 D); *ibid.* (I, 652 A); late medieval Missals from Regensburg and Freising: Beck, 269, 309. Since 1510 also in the Augsburg Missale:

Hoeynck, 375. Similarly in the commentary of William of Gouda: Schläger, *Franziskan. Studien,* 6 (1919), 335.

[65] At first and as the only formula in Bernold, *Micrologus,* c. 18, 23 (PL, 151, 989; 995). Likewise somewhat later in Italy; Ebner, 317, about 1290 also in the papal court chapel; Brinktrine (*Eph. liturg.,* 1937), 207; otherwise connected with other formulas (Ebner, 336; Köck, 131), or in various elaborations as the words of the celebrant; thus in the Dominican Mass-arrangement of 1256 (Guerrini, 243): *Pax tibi et Ecclesiæ sanctæ Dei;* Missale of Evreux-Jumièges: Martène, 1, 4, XXVIII (I, 645 B): *Pax tibi, frater, et universæ Ecclesiæ Dei.* Likewise in Sarum; *ibid.,* XXXV (I, 670 A); cf. Maskell, 170. Also in the Mass-arrangements of northern France in the 16th century; Legg, *Tracts,* 48; 66. In Rouen: *Pax mihi, Domine Jesu Christe, et Ecclesiæ sanctæ tuæ. Et tibi frater.* Martène, 1, 4, XXXVII (I, 678 B). For a renewal of the *Pax.* A Beil, *Einheit in der Liebe* (Colmar, 1914), 106, n. 46, makes the proposal that the *Pax tecum* be simply taken up and repeated by the congregation. But according to what has been said above this repetition would in any event be superfluous. Besides, the answer to the priest's *Pax Domini* already voices agreement with the idea of the Kiss of Peace

the chant and the wish expressed in the *Pax Domini*. What is really the original meaning of the *Agnus Dei?*

Regarding the introduction of the *Agnus Dei* into the Roman Mass, the *Liber pontificalis* has this to tell: Pope Sergius I (687-701) had decreed *ut tempore confractionis dominici corporis "Agnus Dei qui tollis peccata mundi miserere nobis" a clero et populo decantetur.*[1] The older Roman *ordines* direct that after the archdeacon has distributed the consecrated breads to the acolytes so that the fraction can begin, he should give a signal to the singers for the start of the *Agnus Dei,*[2] which is coupled with the fraction.[3]

So the *Agnus Dei* was a chant to accompany the fraction, a *confractorium,*[4] designed to fill out the interval after the *Pax Domini*, which was given over to the activity of breaking the breads.[5] The one occasion when it is not used for this is on Holy Saturday, a custom which goes back to times immemorial.[6] Otherwise, it continued to have the character of a fraction chant until the fraction itself was rendered superfluous by the introduction of unleavened bread and small particles. It is surprising to read that Sergius I was the one who introduced the song; indeed, that statement has been contested in various ways.[7] However, the *Agnus Dei*

and forms a counter salute at least to the priest.

[1] *Liber pont.,* ed. Duchesne, I, 376.

[2] *Ordo Rom.,* I, n. 19 (PL, 78, 946) ; *Ordo Rom.,* II, 13 (PL, 78, 975). The connection is still clearer in the Ordo of S. Amand (Duchesne, *Christian Worship,* 461) : *Annuit archidiaconus schola ut dicatur Agnus Dei. Et interim, dum confranguntur, iterum respondunt acolythi qui sciffos et amulas tenent, Agnus Dei.*

[3] *Capitulare eccl. ord.* (Silva-Tarouca, 200) : *confrangunt separatim unusquisque in ordine suo cantantibus omnibus semper: Agnus Dei;* cf. *ibid.* (206) : *confrangunt ipsum corpus Domini cantantibus interim clericis semper: Agnus Dei. Ordo Rom.,* I, n. 48 (PL, 78, 959) : *quod tamdiu cantatur usque dum complent fractionem.*

[4] Cf. *supra,* pp. 302 ff.

[5] According to the Ordo of S. Amand (Duchesne, *Christian Worship,* 461), in which the *Agnus Dei* is provided as usual as a chant for the schola, the priests and deacons should quietly pray Ps. 118 while they are busy with the fraction. In the Sacramentary of Ratoldus (PL, 78, 244 C) and in that of Echternach (11th cent.; Leroquais, I, 122) there still appears a Gallican prayer for the fraction: *Emittere digneris Domine sanctum angelum . . .* Cf.

also Cagin, *Te Deum ou illatio,* 226 ff.

[6] The reason generally alleged for the omission, namely the great antiquity of the Easter Vigil Mass, is not entirely pertinent. Rather the same reason holds as was alleged for the omission of the *Kyrie* in the same Mass; the *Agnus Dei* was already sung in the litany; cf. *Ordo Rom.,* I, n. 45 ; Appendix, n. 9 f. (PL, 78, 957 ; 964). The rule, moreover, was not observed everywhere ; in individual cases the opposite was specifically provided for ; *vide Breviarium eccl. ord.* (Silva-Tarouca, 211) ; Holy Week *ordo* of Einsiedeln (Duchesne, *Christian Worship,* 484.

[7] E.g., by Silva-Tarouca, in the edition of the *Ordo* of John Archicantor (p. 183 f.). The author of this Ordo had already left Rome in 680, but in the Ordo he wrote soon after in England he already included the *Agnus Dei* (*supra,* n. 3). Silva-Tarouca considers the possibility that the information of the *Liber Pontificalis* was merely taken from a Sacramentary that bore the name of Sergius. Besides, we must take into consideration the rather marked revision of this Ordo (*supra,* I, 66) ; but this incorporates essentially Gallican characteristics and not Roman. — That the author of the reports regarding Sergius I is inclined to ascribe more to him than is

could not have had a place in the Roman Mass very much earlier.[8] Even if it was not brought into Rome by Sergius himself, a Syrian by descent, still it was during the later seventh century, in the train of that great inrush of Greek clerics from the eastern lands overrun by Islam, above all Syria;[9] for it is manifestly an element from the Eastern liturgy. In the East it had become the practice since the sixth century to regard the breaking of the species of bread as a reference to our Lord's Passion and death.[10] In the East, too, since an even earlier date, the sacrificial gifts had been designated as the "Lamb,"[11] an expression occasioned, no doubt, by St. John's Apocalypse.[12] And here, finally, especially in the liturgy of the West Syrians, liturgical texts—some of them coming from this earlier period—are found which have a reference to the Sacrament and are especially used during the fraction, and these texts speak of the Lamb of God who taketh away the sins of the world.[13]

his due, is shown at all events by his statement that Sergius introduced the processions on the four feasts of the Blessed Virgin Mary, whereas according to A. Baumstark it is established that three of them already existed at an earlier time; Mohlberg-Baumstark, *Die älteste erreichbare Gestalt*, 155 f.—In favor of Sergius it is pointed out that he could have introduced the *Agnus Dei* as an answer to the prohibition issued at the Synod of Trullo (692) forbidding any representation of the Lamb of God, can. 82 (Mansi, XI, 977); cf. Duchesne, *Le liber pont.*, I, 381; K. Künstle, *Ikonographie der christlichen Kunst*, I (Freiburg, 1928), 122; 558.

[8] That in Rome a different fraction hymn preceded it as Cagin, *Te Deum*, 231 f.; 236, 495, assumes, is possible, but cannot be proven. In any case the use of Psalm 118 mentioned above, note 5, is striking.

[9] Cf. Bishop, *Liturgica historica*, 145 f.— Pope Theodore I (642-649) was a native Palestinian.

[10] *Supra*, p. 301. The same idea is carried even further in the Byzantine rite. During the πρόθεσις at the beginning of Mass the bread is arranged and divided in realistic fashion into a true θύειν; the ἁγία λόγχη is used and as accompaniment passages are selected not only from John 1 : 29 but from the Prophet of the Passion (Is. 53 : 7, 8) and from the account of the Passion (John 19 : 34, 35). Brightman, 356 f.

[11] *Supra*, p. 37. There is probably a connection between this mode of expression and the fact that, where the Latin Fathers use

the generic term *hostia*, the ancient Greek church substituted the more concrete ἀμνός, ἀρνίον, for the lamb was the most common sacrificial animal of ancient times. Origen, *In Joh. hom.*, X, 12, al. 17 (PG, 14, 336 B): Is this [Eucharist] not the flesh of the Lamb that takes away the sins of the world?—Gregory of Nyssa, *In Christi resurr. hom.*, 1 (PG, 46, 601 C): Isaac, like Christ, was only-begotten and lamb at the same time.—Chrysostom, *In I Cor. hom.*, 41, 4 (PG, 61, 361): In the prayer of petition we approach the Lamb that lies before us.—Other passages in A. Nägle, *Die Eucharistielehre des hl. Johannes Chrysostomus* (Freiburg, 1900), 153 f. —Passio Andreæ (Lipsius-Bonnet, *Acta apost. apocrypha*, II, 1, p. 13 f.): To the almighty, one, and true God, I offer daily a spotless lamb that continues unimpaired and alive even after all the faithful have eaten its flesh and drunk its blood.

[12] Apoc. 5: 6 ff.: ἀρνίον ἑστηκὸς ὡς ἐσφαγμένον; cf. thereto Th. Schermann, *Die allgemeine Kirchenordnung*, II (Paderborn, 1915), 403-405, from which light is thrown upon the sacrificial character of the Eucharist according to the mind of the most ancient church.

[13] *Supra*, p. 301.—Jungmann, Die Stellung Christi, 229 f. The Egyptian anaphora of St. Gregory, which must have had its beginning on Syrian soil about the 16th century, has a prayer between the Eucharistic prayer and the Communion that begins with an address to the Lamb of God: Ὁ ἀμνὸς τοῦ θεοῦ ὁ αἴρων τὴν ἁμαρτίαν τοῦ

From all that has been said we can see at once that the address to the
Lamb of God patently does not refer to Christ simply, but rather to Christ
present in the Eucharist as a sacrificial offering; in the same way, just
before the distribution of Communion, when the priest holds the Sacrament upraised before the faithful with the words, *Ecce Agnus Dei,* it is
the sacramental Christ who is meant. In the liturgy of the city of Rome
during the first thousand years this would perhaps be rather strange and
unexpected if the prayer under scrutiny were a formal oration said by the
priest and not rather a hymnic element intended first of all for the congregation, for in its whole rather imposing store of prayers there is scarcely
even one exception to the rule that the prayers be addressed to God. Among
the prayers apportioned to the congregation, however, the Roman Mass
had long appropriated the *Kyrie eleison;* now, for the same purpose, it
took over the *Agnus Dei.* In the interval between consecration and Communion this hymn represents a reverential and, at the same time, humble
greeting of Him who has been made present under the form of bread. We
might compare it to what occurred some five hundred years later when,
under the impulse of a new wave of eucharistic devotion, the silence of the
consecration and the elevation of the bread was broken by the introduction of hymns which were engendered not only by the Latin genius but
by a new attitude towards the Sacrament—hymns like *Ave verum corpus*
and *O Salutaris hostia.*[14] An indication of the close kinship between these
two scenes is to be found in the fact that the beginnings of the more recent
rites of adoration before the Blessed Sacrament were introduced in the
twelfth century at the *Agnus Dei,* and then gradually transferred to the
elevation.[15] On the other hand, the note of reverence and adoration at the
Agnus Dei was later on frequently fortified by the priest not putting the
two halves of the Host back on the altar after the fraction, but continuing
to hold them raised over the chalice till the Communion[16] or else—according to a widespread custom—holding the particle intended for the commingling over the chalice during the *Agnus Dei.*[17]

According to the *Liber pontificalis,* the *Agnus Dei* was sung by clergy

κόσμου; Renaudot, I (1847), 110. The
same address, combined with the *Miserere
nobis,* is indeed present much earlier already in the *Gloria,* but without any relation to the Eucharist; in fact there is a
repetition of the same invocation, so that
one might speak of a sort of litany that is
present here as with the *Agnus Dei;* cf.
supra, I, 353 f.
[14] *Supra,* p. 215 ff. O Casel, *JL,* 7 (1927),
183, underlines the differences.
[15] *Supra,* p. 206, n. 22.
[16] *Infra,* p. 351. That the ceremony was thus
understood is shown by a passage from a
Dominican source, a passage given by Mar-

tène, 1, 4, 9, 4 (I, 420 B) : *Datum est
Ordini nostro, ut in missa post Agnus Dei
ante communionem tenerent fratres hostiam elevatam super calicem, ut sic adorare-
tur ab universo populo tamquam verum
corpus et sanguis Christi.*—Separated from
the *Agnus Dei* only by the commingling
formula, the Westminister Missal, ed. Legg
(HBS, 5), 517, has a relevant *oratio
singulis dicenda* beginning with: *Adoramus sanctum corpus tuum atque sanctum
sanguinem tuum, Domine Jesu Christe,
cuius effusione omnes redempti sumus,
tibi gloria . . .*
[17] *Supra,* p. 320.

and people. That the priest also said it—at least in some localities—is extremely unlikely. References here and there which seem to point to such a practice do not stand up under closer investigation.[18] Most of the older sacramentaries, which as a rule present only the prayer texts of the celebrant, do not contain the *Agnus Dei*. And that is true down to the eleventh century.[19] Only then does it begin to appear regularly in the sacramentaries, with all indications that the priest is also to say it.[20] On the contrary, the older sources often expressly mention the singing by the people or by the clergy around the altar.[21] The members of the *chorus* or the *clerus* (which is the same thing) would naturally have been the chief performers in most cases, and therefore even at an early period they alone are mentioned.[22]

A refinement, in keeping with the grand pontifical liturgy, is the direc-

---

[18] Some manuscripts of the Gregorianum instance the *Agnus Dei* at the end of the canon after the *Pax Domini;* Botte, 50. Still this citation can also have the same meaning as the enumeration before the canon of the Gregorianum of the various parts that belong to the Order of the Mass, Introit, *Kyrie*, etc.; Lietzmann, n. 1. The *Ordo "Qualiter quædam orationes"* (PL, 78, 984; cf. 284) seems to say: (. . . *mos est.) Dum confringit, Agnus Dei dicit* (sc. *pontifex*). But the text, suspect already from the mere fact that the *Agnus Dei* is strangely ascribed to the pope, stands on precarious ground. According to Hittorp it runs thus: . . . *mos est, dum confringunt. Interim vero dicitur Agnus Dei.* According to St. Baluze, *Capitularia regum Francorum*, II (Paris, 1677), 1368, it reads: *mos est dum confringunt et Agnus Dei dicunt.* D. Georgius, *De liturgia Romani pontificis*, III (Rome, 1744), 369 gives the same reading; thus also Gerbert, *Monumenta*, II, 166. That then must be the original form of the text. Cf. also in the same sense Capelle, "Le rite de la fraction" (*Revue Bénéd.*, 1941), 21.—More striking is the fact that, according to the *Ordo Rom.*, I, n. 19 (PL, 78, 946) the officials of the court say the *Agnus Dei* before the fraction; apparently this is because during the fraction they are busied with the invitations.

[19] The otherwise wordy Missa Illyrica does not mention it; Martène, 1, 4, IV (I, 515); no more so the Mass arrangement of Séez, PL, 78, 250. Also Bernold, *Micrologus*, c. 23 (PL, 151, 995), does not

mention it among the texts to be uttered by the priest, yet, like earlier commentators, he repeats the statement regarding Sergius in c. 18 (989).

[20] Cf. *infra*, note 28. There seems to have been some uncertainty about where the priest was to insert the *Agnus Dei* which meanwhile had been turned into a Communion hymn. This is seen in the fact that in one Central Italian sacramentary of the 11th century (Ebner, 299) the *Agnus Dei* follows the communion of the chalice.— Durandus, IV, 52, 3, discusses only the variation in bodily attitude assumed at the *Agnus Dei;* some say *manibus super altare positis*, therefore with hands resting upon the altar; others *manibus iunctis, parum super altare inclinati.* The expression of humble petition in the latter attitude has gone over into the *Missale Romanum* for the beginning of the prayer. The striking of the breast, however, is not mentioned by Durandus. It appears in the *Ordo Rom.*, XIV (about 1311), n. 71 (PL, 78, 1190 C).

[21] Remigius of Auxerre, *Expositio* (PL, 101, 1270 D): *Inter hæc* [Kiss of Peace] *cantatur ab omnibus et cantando oratur dicentibus: Agnus Dei.* A Central Italian sacramentary of the close of the 11th century (Ebner, 301): *Interea . . . chorus sive alii circumstantes dicant Agnus Dei tribus vicibus.* Sicard of Cremona, *Mitrale*, III, 8 (PL, 213, 139).

[22] *Expositio "Primum in ordine"* (9th cent.; PL, 138, 1185 f.); Hildebert of Le Mans, *Versus* (PL, 171, 1192 B). Cf. Sacramentary of Ratoldus (d. 986) (PL, 78,

tion in the first Roman *Ordo,* which delegates the *Agnus Dei* to the *schola.* That does not mean, of course, that the *schola* alone was to undertake the singing, as was the case later.[23] It could well mean that the *schola* was to intone it and to alternate with the rest of the clergy and the people, as in the *litania,*[24] the stylistic structure of which either the repetition of the entire invocation or else the final petition in each phrase, *miserere nobis.*[25] In any case, outside the papal stational services the *Agnus Dei* was largely a popular chant. Therefore the oldest melody to which it was sung, the one still used at ferial and Requiem Masses, is very simple. Not till the eleventh and twelfth centuries were newer and richer melodies added,[26] an indication that the simple hymn had been transferred to the choir.[27] Soon after this we begin to read reports that the priest at the altar also says the *Agnus Dei.*[28]

The *Agnus Dei* early lost its original purpose, since the fraction was gradually abandoned after the ninth-tenth century. Up to this time the *Agnus Dei* actually appears as an accompaniment of this function.[29] But about this time it also appears in other positions, as the song accompanying the *pax*[30] or simply as a Communion song.[31] When, in some instances

244 B): *annuente episcopo dicat cantor Agnus Dei.* See John of Avranches, *De off. eccl.* (PL, 147, 37 C); Innocent III, *De s. alt. mysterio,* VI, 4 (PL, 217, 908); cf. Durandus, IV, 52, 3 f.

[23] *Ordo Rom.,* XI (12th cent.), n. 40 (PL, 78, 1040); cf. *Ordo Rom.,* V, n. 11 (PL, 78, 990).

[24] *Supra,* I, 335 ff. Cf. the statements of the *Capitulare* and the Ordo of S. Amand (*supra,* n. 2).

[25] A response to the beginning of the Schola (by the acolytes) is expressly certified by the Ordo of S. Amand (*supra,* n. 2) and likewise by the Einsiedeln *Ordo* for Holy Week (Duchesne, *Christian Worship,* 484).

[26] Wagner, *Einführung,* I, 116; Ursprung, *Die kath. Kirchenmusik,* 57.

[27] This must have been partly the case in the 10th century, since the first *Agnus Dei* tropes appear in this period. Blume-Bannister, *Tropen des Missale,* I (Analecta hymnica, 47), p. 373 ff.

[28] *Liber usuum O.Cist.* (shortly after 1119), c. 53 (PL, 166, 1426 C). A Missale of Cologne of the year 1133 and other Mass-books of the same time in Lebrun, *Explication,* I, 509 f. *Ordinarium O.P.* of 1256 (Guerrini, 243) and the Liége *Liber ordinarius* (Volk, 96: besides the deacon and the subdeacon, the two acolytes say it

along (with the priest). Noteworthy in the same *Ordinarium O.P.* (243 f.) is the statement that during the singing of the *Agnus Dei,* the *Pax* should not be imparted any further.

[29] Amalar, *De eccl. off.,* c. 33 (PL, 1153); Walafried Strabo, *De exord. et increm.,* c. 22 (PL, 114, 950); *Ordo Rom.,* II, n. 13 (PL, 78, 975); *Ordo Rom.,* III, n. 16 (PL, 78, 982). Also in the older version of the Greek Liturgy of St. Peter (Codrington, 136), i.e., toward the middle of the 10th century in a Central Italian model (*ibid.,* 106).

[30] Rabanus Maurus, *De inst. cler.,* I, 33 (PL, 107, 324); Florus, *De actione miss.,* c. 89 f. (PL, 119, 71 C); Remigius of Auxerre, *Expositio* (PL, 101, 1270).

[31] Expositio "Quotiens contra se" (beginning of the 9th cent.; PL, 96, 1500 C): *Inter communicandum;* Expositio "Primum in ordine" (beginning of the 9th cent.; PL, 138, 1185 C); Expositio "Dominus vobiscum" (PL, 138, 1173 C); *Ordo Rom.* V, n. 11 (PL, 78, 990); *Ordo Rom.* VI, n. 13 (PL, 78, 994); revised version of the liturgy of St. Peter (Codrington, 144, l. 3; 153, l. 15; 162, l. 20); Ivo of Chartres (d. 1117), *De conven. vet. et novi sacrif.* (PL, 162, 560 B); Innocent III, *De s. alt. mysterio,* VI, 4 (PL, 217, 909); Durandus IV, 52, 1.

even later, the fraction was still customary, the *Agnus Dei* was no longer intrinsically connected with it.[32]

As regards the wording—based on the testimonial of the Baptist (John 1:29)—the first thing that occasions surprise is the vocative form *agnus*. This is in keeping with a grammatical rule which is in effect in many languages: from a feeling of reverence, religious terms are apt to be handled as indeclinable.[33] For the biblical *peccatum* is substituted a plural, *peccata*, which is substantially contained in it.[34] And as in other similar cases, only one all-inclusive petition—according to strict Roman usage—is joined to the invocation, namely, *miserere nobis*.

Originally the one simple verse was repeated as often as necessary, just as the *Kyrie eleison* or the *Christe eleison*, as the case might be, could be repeated as often as one pleased.[35] But when the time period necessitated by the fraction fell out, the song itself (which no one wanted to drop) gradually assumed the hallowed number three. The earliest testimonies to this change begin even in the ninth century.[36] Thus a hymn developed, short in its wording but impressive in its import, capable (especially within the limits in which it appears) of being compared to the hymns of the Apocalypse. The Lamb that is our sacrifice and will become our food, in which the paschal lamb of the Old Testament has found its fulfillment, is the triumphant Lamb of the end of the world, that opens the books of mankind's fate. And as from the heavenly Church the canticles of thanksgiving sung by the elect resound to His praise, so also a plea rises aloft from the assembly of the redeemed who still wander through the pilgrimage of life. All this is made even plainer if we take into account the symbolic reference to our Lord's Passion and Resurrection which followed at the fraction and commingling.

Originally the same plea, *miserere nobis*, was sung unchanged at every repetition, as is still done in the Lateran Basilica. But here and there even in the tenth century,[37] and with increasing frequency in the eleventh, a

---

[32] That is the case, e.g., in the *Ordo eccl. Lateran.* (Fischer, 48) : On Communion days the priests should divide the *oblatæ* after the (first) *Agnus Dei.*

[33] Suggestion made by Prof. W. Havers. Cf. the vocative *Deus,* the word *sancta* (above, I, 70).—By way of exception there is the vocative *agne Dei* which we encountered above, I, 339.

[34] Is. 53 : 5, 7.

[35] *Supra,* I, 339.

[36] Mass-*ordo* of Amiens (2nd half of 9th cent.), ed. Leroquais (*Eph. Liturg.,* 1927), 443. Perhaps the Holy Week Ordo of Einsiedeln belongs here (Duchesne, *Christian Worship,* 484) with the somewhat puzzling statement *Et Agnus Dei cantat schola cantorum et respondent III* [= *tertio* = up to 3 times?] *acolythi stantes ad rugas tenentes scyphos* . . . Further proofs from the 10-11th centuries have been collected by Codrington, *The Liturgy of St. Peter,* 54. In John of Avranches, *De off. eccl.* (PL, 147, 37), only a double *repetition* can be intended, therefore not a double, but a triple singing of the invocation.

[37] *Agnus Dei* tropes with the concluding petition, *dona nobis pacem* in the 10th century Tropers of St. Martial, Winchester, and Reichenau. Blume-Bannister, *Tropen des Missale,* I, p. 373, 385 (n. 385, cod. A. B. C. Y; n. 419 cod. A), etc.

substitution was made in the third place (except often on Holy Thursday,[38] by singing *dona nobis pacem*.[39] The first occasion for this change was probably the transfer of the song to accompany the Kiss of Peace.[40] Periods of external distress, which recur so often, would then probably have led to the retention of this petition for peace.[41] Indeed, the whole *Agnus Dei* was regarded as a prayer for peace, and the plea for external peace was thus appended to the affirmation of inward peace which was inherent in the ceremony of the kiss of peace,[42] or else a special prayer to obtain peace was added to the *dona nobis pacem,* as the Salzburg synod of 1281 decreed for a certain period,[43] or—as an echo from the period of the Crusades—a prayer for the deliverance of the Holy Land was added, as is attested in England.[44] One change of the *miserere* soon led to another. In the Requiem Mass, as early as the eleventh century, the words *dona eis requiem* are substituted, and in the third place *requiem sempiternam*.[45]

Another indication of the effort to give the *Agnus Dei* special importance is seen in the prescription that it is to be sung or said *non continuo, sed interpolate ac seiunctim cum oratione interposita*.[46] Thus it often [47] hap-

[38] Durandus, IV, 52, 4. Later examples in Ferreres, p. XXX, 178. The reason for the omission of the petition for peace lay, as the rubrics of Ferreres and others show, in the fact that the *Pax* was also omitted here; cf. also Gerbert, *Vetus liturgia Alemannica,* I, 381 f. In the *Missale Romanum* the rubric *Agnus Dei dicitur de more is* evidently directed against this exception.

[39] Leroquais, I, 162; 197; 232. Ivo of Chartres (d. 1117), *De conven. vet. et novi sacrif.* (PL, 162, 560 C). A Mass-*ordo* of the 11th century from Bologna and the Georgian version of the Greek Liturgy of St. Peter (which traces back to the custom of Beneventum towards the end of the 10th century) have the *dona nobis pacem* at the second *Agnus Dei* (Codrington, 54, 162).

[40] *Supra,* p. 337.

[41] See the argument in Innocent III, *De s. alt. mysterio,* VI, 4 (PL, 217, 908 D).

[42] Cf. Missale of Remiremont (12th cent.) : Martène, 1, 4, 9, 9 (423 C), where the prayer of the priest for the Kiss of Peace is understood as an introduction to the *Agnus Dei*; of the two formulas provided for the purpose, the first concludes: *et præsta ut cum fiducia audeamus dicere: Agnus Dei.*

[43] Can. 16 (Mansi, XXIV, 402): the clergy everywhere, throughout the year specified, were to say three Our Fathers, Versicle, and the Oration *Deus a quo sancta desideria* after the third *Agnus Dei*. Cf. the kindred insertions before the embolism *supra,* pp. 292 ff.

[44] A Missale of Sarum in Martène, 1, 4, 9, 5 (I, 421) : Pss. 76, 66 and 20 with *preces* and three orations should be said *a prostratis.* Similarly, but already inserted after the *Pater noster,* in the Missal of St. Lambrecht of the 14-15th century; Köck, 50. Cf. *supra,* p. 292 f. Martène, *loc cit.,* knows of similar prayers in French churches of the late Middle Ages.

[45] John Beleth, *Explicatio,* c. 48 (PL, 202, 55). The *dona eis requiem sempiternam* is noticed by Leroquais, I, 162, in the Sacramentary of Soissons (11th cent.).

[46] John Beleth, *Explicatio,* c. 48 (PL, 202 202, 55 A). Likewise an apparently older source in Martène, 1, 4, 9, 4 (I, 419 E) : *mixtim cum privata oratione.* The *Liber Ordinarius* of Liége (Volk, 103) speaks of a *Pater noster quod a singulis dicitur inter primum et secundum Agnus.*

[47] *Ordo eccl. Lateran.* (Fischer, 85 f.) ; cf. the division already in the Missal of Remiremont (12th cent.) : Martène, 1, 4, 9, 9 (I, 423 D). In the cathedral of Tours *clericuli* had to entone the second *Agnus Dei* after the Communion; Martène, 1, 4, XIX (I, 606 E) ; cf. XXII (612 E). According to the Mass-arrangement of the

pened, and still does among the Carthusians,[48] that only one *Agnus Dei* was sung after the *Pax Domini*, the second and third not being taken up till after the Communion. Thus, insofar as a Communion of the assistants or of the people followed, the *Agnus Dei* became even more of a Communion song, with the *communio* of the Proper of the Mass added as sequel.[49]

Like so many other chants of the Mass, the *Agnus Dei* also was overspread with tropes, especially in the later *Middle Ages*. These tropes are a good index of the notions that were at that time associated with the *Agnus Dei*.[50]

8. Concluding Rites before the Communion

In many sacramentaries of the earlier Middle Ages the Mass *ordo* closes with the *Agnus Dei*, if it has not already ended with the *Pax Domini*. This should not be surprising, for according to the older system the only thing that followed in the way of priestly prayers was the post-communion (after the communion), which, being a variable text, did not really belong to the *ordo* of the Mass.

At the same time—to follow the conceptions of this and the following period further—the *Agnus Dei* formed the conclusion of the canon, the point at which the priest once more emerged from the sanctuary of the sacrificial and commemorative celebration. Since for a long time the *Te igitur* was not to be started till after the *Sanctus* and *Benedictus* had been sung, the *Agnus Dei* was the first song after the beginning of the canon—

---

monastery of Bec the priest says the commingling prayer between the first and second *Agnus Dei;* Martène, 1, 4, XXXVI (I, 674 C).

[48] Cf. Martène, 1, 4, 9, 4 (I, 419 f.) ; *ibid.*, 1, 4, XXV (I, 634 D). *Ordinarium Cart.* (1932), c. 27, 14. The celebrant also pronounces the 2nd and 3rd *Agnus* only after the Communion; *ibid.*, c. 2, 17.—A trace of this is also found in the rite of Lyons (Buenner, 256; 281 ff.) : insertion of the *Venite populi* after the first *Agnus*. Moreover until 1780 at a non-pontifical Mass in the liturgy of Lyons only one *Agnus Dei* was generally sung; Buenner, 280 f.

[49] Cf. *supra*, p. 337. *Ordo eccl. Lateran.* (Fischer, 86; cf. 12). So also in *Ordo Rom.* V, n. 11 (PL, 78, 990 A).

[50] Blume-Bannister, *Tropen des Missale,* I, pages 373-405. Eighty-six numbers are here reproduced consisting mostly of three verses, hexameters in great part, of which one verse was to be inserted each time be-

tween the invocation and the petition *miserere nobis*, resp. *dona nobis pacem*. Accordingly the content is mainly an elaboration of the invocation in such manner that attributes and claims to honor of the divinity as well as the humanity of Christ are extolled. A widely spread Tropus that appeared in the 10th century runs as follows:

Agnus Dei . . . mundi. Qui patris in solio residens per sœcula regnas—miserere nobis.

Agnus Dei . . . mundi. Tu pax, tu pietas, bonitas, miseratio, Christe—miserere nobis.

Agnus Dei . . . mundi. Singula discutiens cum sederis arbiter orbis—miserere nobis.

Blume, 374 (n. 386). The earliest example is already cited in the commentary based on Amalar, "Missa pro multis," ed. Hanssens (*Eph. liturg.*, 1930), 42: *Qui resurrexisti, Agnus Dei consecratus et vivificatus.*

prescinding from the closing formulas and the *Pater noster* of the priest—to break through the stillness. Even as late as 1549 a synod of Trier objected to the practice of singing any antiphons at all after the consecration till this moment of the Mass;[1] the organ, too, was supposed to be silent till the *Agnus Dei*, and all were to be on their knees or stretched out on the floor, meditating *silenter* on the Passion of Christ.[2]

But even in an earlier period the portion of the Mass where the *Agnus Dei* was inserted marked the end of the Mass in a different and more profound sense. When general participation in Communion was no longer taken for granted, it would seem that no one at first expected the non-communicants to remain during the Communion. In the Gallic liturgy the solemn blessing after the *Pater noster* formed an ostensible termination, you might say, a sort of formal dismissal of the faithful who were not communicating, and it was actually so understood.[3] In Rome the forms were much plainer, but the views were the same. In the sixth century it had already become a time-honored practice for the deacon to call out before Communion: *Si quis non communicat, det locum*, that is, the non-communicants should make room, which in practice meant that they had to leave.[4] For, in view of the Roman manner of distributing Communion, which was done not before the altar to those who came up, but in the nave of the church to all present, any other solution was difficult.

A further step in this arrangement is found in other Roman sources of the seventh and eighth centuries. After the *Pax Domini* the announcements were made regarding the next stational service, pertinent feasts of martyrs, fast days and other ecclesiastical affairs, the time set aside [5] for these an-

---

[1] Cf. *supra* I, 124, note 121; 134, note 37.

[2] Can. 9 (Hartzheim, VI, 600).

[3] Cf. *supra*, I, 235; II, p. 295.

[4] Gregory the Great, *Dial.*, II, 23 (PL, 66, 178 f.), in the life of St. Benedict tells of two nuns, who despite the saint's threat to exclude them from Communion failed to curb their tongues and so died and were buried in the church; they were seen by someone to arise from the grave and leave the church with the others every time the summons mentioned was issued. The passage is to a great extent falsely explained, as if there were question here of the dismissal of the penitents before the Mass of the Faithful, thus, e.g., F. Probst, *Die abendländische Messe von 5-8 Jahrhundert* (Münster, 1896), 115. Also the reference to the similar summons: οἱ ἀκοινώνητοι περιπατήσατε, in Timothy of Alexandria (d. 385), *Responsa canonica* (PG, 33, 1301 C), where the summons before the Eucharistia

is discussed, involves only an external parallel. But there is question rather in our case of a summons addressed before Communion to non-communicants; this is shown especially by the continuation of the story: As Benedict sent an offering for the two nuns and this was offered up, and when the summons again was given, *et a diacono iuxta morem clamatum est ut non communicantes ab ecclesia exirent*, the mysterious incident failed to recur; Cf. Jungmann, *Die lateinischen Bussriten*, 23 f. —As everyone knows, this call is introduced in the *Pontificale Romanum* as among the duties of the exorcists. How this came about, see de Puniet, *The Roman Pontifical*, 134.

[5] In the later Gelasianum (Mohlberg, n. 1566): *Post hæc commonenda est plebs pro ieiuniis primi, quarti, septimi et decimi mensis temporibus suis, sive pro scrutiniis vel aurium apertione sive orandum pro in-*

nouncements being either before the Communion in general or (after the celebrant had communicated) before the Communion of the congregation,[6] that is, before the *Agnus Dei,* insofar as this had become a Communion song.[7]

In Rome, just as in the area of the Gallic liturgy, only those remained at the Communion who were really going to receive. Efforts to get a stricter idea under way and to insist on the presence of all the people also at Communion first cropped up in Spain.[8] This idea then took hold all through the land of the Franks in conjunction with the adoption of the Roman liturgy. In the Gelasian Sacramentaries, which were substituted for the Gallican since the turn of the seventh century, both a text and a suitable location were wanting for the accustomed Gallic blessing after the *Pater noster.* But on many days a prayer *super populum* was provided after the post-communion, and besides, as an appendix to the canon of the Mass, a special selection of other formulas of such a blessing were offered under the title: *Item benedictiones super populum.*[9] The Gallic benedictions after the *Pater noster* were kept in part, but only at pontifical Mass.[10]

firmis vel ad nuntiandum natalicia sanctorum. Post hæc communicat sacerdos cum ordinibus sacris et cum omni populo. The older Gelasianum, III, 16 (Wilson, 236), is in agreement. Cf. similar references in Martène, 1, 4, 9, 7 (I, 422 C) and in Mohlberg-Manz, n. 1566. The formula, that elsewhere quickly disappeared in the Frankish tradition, is still found in the Sacramentary of Reims in the 10th century; U. Chevalier, *Sacramentaire et martyrologe de l'abbaye de S. Remy* (Bibliothèque liturg., 7; Paris, 1900), 344 f.
[6] *Capitulare eccl. ord.* (Silva-Tarouca, 200); *Ordo Rom.* I, n. 20 (PL, 78, 946 f.); *Ordo Rom.* II, n. 14 (PL, 78, 975). According to these sources the announcements take place after the fraction has been completed and the *Agnus Dei* accompanying it has been sung and after the pope himself has communicated, but before the Communion of the clergy and the people. The Breviarium (Silva-Tarouca, 200) also has the Communion of the *clerici* precede, the Ordo of S. Amand (Duchesne, *Christian Worship,* 462) has it at least begin. The *Ordo Rom.* XI (12th cent.), n. 34 (PL, 78, 1038) still has the regional subdeacon announce the Station *ante communionem;* not until all this is done is the Communion chant intoned. *Deo Gratias* is the response to the announcement, as the last three sources and also the *Ordo Rom.*

I, n. 20 (Stapper, 29; missing however in Mabillon) note.
[7] According to the order of the scrutinies of Clm. 6425 (11th cent.) which corresponds to the *Ordo Rom.* VII, the announcement of the scrutinies at the Sunday service should take place before the *Agnus Dei;* see the evidences in H. Mayer, *ZkTh,* 38 (1914), 372. Naturally in that case as well as in that of the *Ordo Rom.* XI, there is question only of a custom long since crystallized; that becomes evident from the contemporary *Ordo eccl. Lateran.* (Fischer, 87, 1. 9), according to which the announcement of the feast days takes place before the *Postcommunio.*
[8] Here the IV Synod of Toledo (633), can. 18 (Mansi, X, 624), points out an opposite custom that was developing; *Nonnulli sacerdotes post dictam orationem dominicam statim communicant et postea benedictionem in populo dant;* this is now forbidden.
[9] Mohlberg, n. 1569-1581. Cf. for the related manuscripts the Concordance-tables of Manz, *ibid.,* p. 339, and the further data in de Puniet, *Le pontifical de Gellone* (special printing from the *Eph. liturg.,* 1934-1938) 216 f.
[10] One group of the manuscripts of the later Gelasianum contains as an addition to the Gelasian formulas a further appendix of *Benedictiones episcopales super populum,*

All the more eagerly, then, must these benedictions have been adopted. As a natural result the old direction, in these new circumstances, was taken to mean that the people were to remain, according to the Roman pattern, till this last prayer of blessing, therefore also during the Communion. This interpretation of the law became so firmly established in the course of the century that it could not be dislodged even with the ultimate adoption of the Gregorian Sacramentary which began about 785, even though here the *oratio super populum* was no longer to be found during the Lenten season.[11]

9. Communion of the Priest: Preparatory Prayers

In the early Church, because the concept of the Mass as a sacred repast, a meal, the δεῖπνον κυριακόν, was so much to the fore, it was taken for granted that the Mass would culminate in the reception of the Sacrament by all the participants. In Justin's time this was so much a matter of course that the deacons, as he remarked in both of his accounts, even brought some of the hallowed gift to the absent.[1] A fixed order was followed in arranging the reception, as we discover somewhat later: the leader (bishop or priest) of the assembly was the first to receive "so that it may be made clear that he has offered the sacrifice for all, according to the established

partly of Gallican coinage; de Puniet, 218-236. Cf. *supra*, pp. 296 f.

[11] The name *benedictio super populum* was now transferred to the Postcommunion. Thus already in the *Expositio "Primum in ordine"* (PL, 138, 1186) which originated in 800, unless this designation actually conceals the survival of an *oratio super populum*. In any case *v.* the proximately contemporaneous *Ordo Angliberti* (Bishop, *Liturgica historica*, 323): the communicants should be able to hear the *benedictionem sive completionem missæ* (in the Gregorianum the Postcommunio was commonly called *Ad complendum*. Perhaps the Gregorian background and the same mode of expression is to be presupposed in the demand of the *Admonitio generalis* of Charlemagne of 789, c. 71 (MGH Cap., I, 59): *ut non exeant ante completionem benedictionis sacerdotalis;* also in the collection of capitulars of Ansegisus (completed 827), I, 67 (MGH Cap., I, 403). Amalar, *De eccl. off.,* III, 36 f. (PL 105 1155 f.) calls the Postcommunion *ultima benedictio,* the *oratio super populum* of Lent he terms *ulterior ultima benedictio.*

The same designation of the Postcommunio in Rabanus Maurus, *De inst. cler.,* c. 33 (PL, 107, 324); *idem., Additio de missa* (326); Walafried Strabo, *De exord. et increm.,* c. 22 (PL, 114, 951). After all that has been said, it will not be necessary to follow the line of thought presented by J. Lechner, "Der Schluszsegen des Priesters in der hl. Messe" (*Festschrift E. Eichmann* [Paderborn, 1940]), 676 ff. In discussing this new designation of the Postcommunion by the Carolingian liturgists, he speaks of "an interpretation arranged *ad hoc*" (677), of "an erudite exegesis that is artificially contrived" (679) in an endeavor to find in the synodal stipulations of the 6th century (which demanded that the faithful remain for the blessing) a support for the requirement that they remain till the end of Mass. This new designation of the Postcommunion as *benedictio* was made all the easier, after the intermediate Gelasian stage, by the fact that at all sacerdotal orations the faithful assumed the same bodily posture as at the imparting of a blessing; cf. *supra,* I, 370 f.; II, pp. 141 f.

[1] *Supra* I, 22 f.

order of priestly service":[2] next came the other members of the clergy, in order of their ecclesiastical rank; and finally the people.[3]

Even in the most ancient Roman *ordines*, the Communion of the assembled congregation, at least at the stational services, formed a natural termination, which appeared like the exact counterpart of the offering of the gifts by the congregation at the start of the Sacrifice-Mass. Here, too, the pope himself received the Sacrament first; he took the bread and partook from the chalice held by the archdeacon. Then he distributed the Body of the Lord to the bishops and priests, and started off the distribution to the people by stepping down (followed by the archdeacon with the chalice), first to the noble men and then over to the noble ladies, to give them the Sacrament.[4]

In the fuller development of the Mass-liturgy, as it proceeded eventually on Frankish soil, the Communion of the celebrant assumed a more prominent position, to such an extent, in fact, that as time went on it alone began to be considered an integral part of the liturgy. Its rite was regulated more and more, and encompassed by special prayers which the priest was to say softly to himself. Even here the comparison to the offertory is marked, for in the offertory, too, a similar evolution took place, although in a somewhat different rhythm. But neither in the offertory nor in the Communion was the original design destroyed by this development; it is still clearly manifest at present. So just as the offertory activity of the congregation is still recalled in the offertory chant which grew around it, and still finds its conclusion in the *oratio super oblata* that marks the close, so the Communion chant which was designed to accompany the Communion of the people has been retained throughout all the changes in the ceremony, and so too until now—and especially in our own day—the Communion cycle closes with a community prayer (corresponding to the oration mentioned above), called the post-communion.

The Communion of the priest is at present introduced by two lengthy prayers in oration style, subjoined to the prayer for peace, and it is accompanied by a series of shorter prayer-phrases which continue even after the consumption of the Precious Blood. This cycle of silent prayers—like the parallel structure around the offertory—was added to the Roman Mass in the area of the Gallo-Frankish Church. Like the former, they are mainly shoots that grew from the still living roots of the abandoned Gallican liturgy. But to a higher degree even than the prayers at the offertory, they are private prayers, as the "I"-form which is their very basis clearly betrays. We will also have occasion to establish that they were all originally designed to serve for the devotion of the other communicants as well.[5] This

---

[2] Theodore of Mopsuestia, *Sermones catech.*, VI (Rücker, 36).

[3] See enumeration *Const. Ap.*, VIII, 13, 14 (Quasten, *Mon.*, 230): Priests, deacons, subdeacons, lectors, singers, monks (ἀσκηταί deaconesses, virgins, widows, children, people.

[4] *Ordo Rom.* I, n. 19 f. (PL, 78, 946 f.). As a mark of distinction the Communion of the regionary clergy and certain officials of the court takes place at the Cathedra of the pope. [5] *Infra*, pp. 367 f.; pp. 400 ff.

is not strange. The oriental liturgies, too, have the priest prepare himself for Communion by private prayer, and at least the Byzantine has him make a private thanksgiving at once after Communion.[6] The prevailing address to Christ and the partly unusual concluding formulas[7] are also in keeping with the non-Roman origin of these prayers.

The oldest texts are again found in the Sacramentary of Amiens, which belongs to the ninth century. It presents two preparatory prayers, the first of which is the one that is still used at present as the first prayer: *Domine Jesu Christe, Fili Dei vivi.*[8] But it is clear that we do not here have the beginnings of all later Communion prayers, but only one sample of such creations, for the first prayer here shows one isolated variant,[9] while the other prayer[10] apparently does not generally recur in the later transmission of such texts.

Our second preparatory prayer, *Perceptio*, also is met already in the tenth century, in two books stemming from the northeast portion of the Carolingian domain,[11] and in both cases it precedes its companion formula. In contrast to our first prayer, this formula as a rule makes mention only of the Body of our Lord,[12] as it does at present. For this reason it was in later times preferred for the Good Friday Communion, where only the species of bread was received.

Often (as was the case already in the Sacramentary of Fulda) these two formulas are accompanied by a third which is addressed to God the Father. This prayer frequently took the place of the others. But even at its first

[6] Baumstark, *Die Messe im Morgenland,* 163.

[7] Thus in the Sarum Missal of the 13th century (Legg, *The Sarum Missal,* 226 f.) our first communion oration *Domine Jesu Christe* has a Gallican conclusion, *Salvator mundi qui vivis* . . . In the Missale of Lucca (11th cent.; Ebner, 305) the *Salator mundi* is taken into the invocation. Other examples, see also *infra* n. 11, 14.— The only thing noteworthy regarding details in the form of today's concluding formula of the communion prayers, as well as that of the preceding prayer for peace, is that it reflects the variation of expression from the early Middle Ages, whereas according to a later rule it ought to be *qui vivis et regnas in sæcula sæculorum,* at all events with the Trinitarian extension as in the second communion prayer).

[8] Leroquais (*Eph. liturg.,* 1927) 444; Sacramentary of Le Mans (also from the 9th cent.) : Leroquais, *Les sacramentaires,* I, 30.

[9] Namely after the *fac me* the inserted invocation *Domine Deus meus.* The prayer

coincides for the rest in the first half with today's text; the continuation runs mostly as follows in the oldest texts as well as in the Sacramentary of Ratoldus (PL, 78, 244) : . . . *per hoc sacrum corpus et sanguinem tuum a cunctis iniquitatibus et universis malis meis, et fac me tuis obœdire prœceptis et a te nunquam in perpetuum separari. Qui cum Patre.*

[10] *Da mihi Domine peccatori* . . . related, as far as content is concerned, to the present-day oration *Perceptio.*

[11] Sacramentary of Fulda (Richter-Schönfelder, n. 24), with the variation *Perceptio corporis et sanguinis tui* and with the Gallican conclusion *Te donante qui;* Sacramentary of Ratoldus of Corbie (PL, 78, 244).

[12] The addition *et sanguinis* as in the Sacramentary of Fulda (and in that of Corbie;) occasionally also later; thus as a supplement in the Sacramentary of the Papal Court Chapel of the 13-14th centuries; Brinktrine (*Eph. liturg.,* 1937), 207; in Missale of Riga (supplement of the 15th century) : *v.* Bruiningk, 87.

appearance it presented itself not as a component of liturgical prayer, but as a private prayer:[13]

> Domine, sancte Pater, omnipotens æterne Deus, da mihi corpus et sangui-nem Christi filii tui Domini nostri ita sumere, ut merear per hoc remis-sionem peccatorum accipere et tuo Sancto Spiritu repleri. Quia tu es Deus et in te est Deus et præter te non est alius, cuius regnum permanet in sæcula sæcuorum.[14]

A series of still other formulations of a prayer of preparation appear here and there, but never gained widespread use. Some of them,[15] like the prayers

[13] Noticed for the first time in the prayer-book of Charles the Bald (d. 877), ed. Fel. Ninguarda (1583), 115 f.

[14] In the 9th century still in a Sacramen-tary of Tours (Leroquais, I, 49). In the 10th century in the Sacramentaries of Fulda (Richter-Schönfelder, n. 26), Char-tres (Leroquais, I, 76), of Ratoldus (PL, 78, 245). The formula, in which the Gal-lican concluding formula (Quia tu . . .) often varies, was still widespread in the later Middle Ages; it formed part of the permanent Mass order in Normandy and in England; Martène 1, 4, XXVI-XXVIII (I, 638, 641, 645, 669) ; Legg, Tracts, 14 f., 66, 226. In a more expanded version in two Communion devotions at the turn of the 11th century, ed. A. Wilmart, "Prières pour la communion en deux psautiers du Mont-Cassin (Eph. liturg., 43 ([1929]), 320-328), 323 ; 326. Cf. Fiala, 213.

[15] Aside from shorter texts in an optative form the following are to be noted : in the Sacramentary from Thierry of the end of 10th century a formula Da mihi Domine corpus, with the petition for a worthy re-ception now and at the hour of death ; Mar-tène, 1, 4, X (I, 551 D). A formula Fiat mihi obsecro Domine (corresponding to our Perceptio in content), among others in the Missa Illyrica; Martène, 1, 4, IV (I, 515 D) ; cf. ibid., XV (I, 593 E). A for-mula Præsta mihi peccatori misericors Christe, with a petition for a very fruitful reception, in the Sacramentary of Subiaco from the year 1075; Ebner, 339. In the Mass-arrangements of the Middle Ages about the 11-12th centuries, formulas were circulated that began with Domine Jesu Christe propitius esto mihi peccatori et ne respicias, and the petition that the recep-tion might not redound to one's judgment; Ebner, 331; cf. 101, 102, 183, 341, 346,

348. The same as a private prayer in a Communion-arrangement of Montecas-sino; Wilmart (previous note), 326. Like-wise with another extension (. . . esto pec-catis meis per assumptionem corporis . . .) in the Missal of Remiremont (12th cent.) : Martène, 1, 4, 9, 9 (I, 424) ; also in the Vorau Missal of the 15th century, Köck, 134; it is a Postcommunio of the Fulda Sacramentary (Richter-Schönfelder, n. 2185). Ebner notices another formula from Italian Mass books that begins with Do-mine J. C. Fili Dei vivi ne indignum me iudices (189), and another with Domine J. C. qui in cœna (256).—Oftentimes lengthy formulas are found with the be-ginning Domine, non sum dignus; con-cerning these vide infra, p. 355.—Two Mis-sals of Tortosa (15th and 16th cent.) con-tain a prayer, Domine Jesu Christe Fili Dei vivi, pone passionem tuam, crucem et mor-tem tuam inter iudicium tuum et animam meam, whereupon petitions and interces-sions follow; Ferreres, 186; the prayer is reminiscent of the Admonitio morienti of St. Anselm. (PL, 158, 687).—English Mass-books propose a prayer during which the priest holds the Host in his hands, Deus pater, fons et origo totius bonitatis, qui . . . Unigenitum tuum . . . carnem sumere volu-isti, quam ego hic in manibus meis teneo . . .; Martène, 1, 4, XXXV (I, 670 B) ; Legg, Tracts, 15; 227; Ferreres, 187; 188; Maskell, 174. In England, and also in France, an offering up of the Body and Blood of Christ for the souls in Purga-tory and for one's sins, Agimus tibi Patri gratias; Martène, 1, 4, 9, 9 (I, 426 B) ; Legg, The Sarum Missal, 227; the same, Missale Westmonasteriense (HBS, 5), 519. As a 12-13th century supplement in the Missal of St. Vincent: Fiala, 217 ; 224. —A further supply of Communion prayers,

already mentioned, are marked entirely by a tone of humble petition. Others have a hymnic character.[16]

However, some Mass books even in the tenth [17] and the eleventh centuries did not take up any of these new Communion prayers.[18] On the other hand, Bernold of Constance tells of many prayers which some associate with the kiss of peace and the Communion. And he agrees with other custodians of a good tradition in maintaining that one ought to lose no time over such *privatæ orationes* which are in use *non ex ordine, sed ex religiosorum traditione,* and that one ought to be satisfied with the one oration *Domine Jesu Christe, qui ex voluntate Patris,*[19] which is to be said

among them two Apologies, in a Premonstratensian Missal of the 14th century from Chotieschau; see Lentze, *Anal. Præm.,* 27 (1951), 17; cf. *ibid.,* 26 (1950), 140. Even the Sacramentary of Boldau in Hungary (circa 1195) already contains three apparently independent, but extensive preparatory prayers in the appendix of the Mass-*ordo,* ed. Kniewald: *Theologia,* 6 (Budapest, 1939), 25 f.

[16] If we prescind from the short greetings with which we shall deal later on, we find such hymnic inserts especially, though not exclusively, in the Mass-books of Styria. According to the Mass-arrangement of Seckau (12th and 14th cent.) the priest said *Gloria æterno Patri et Agno mitissimo qui frequenter immolatur permanetque integer* . . . Köck, 127; 129; cf. 53, 128, 133 (in connection with the ablution).—A Mass-book of St. Lambrecht, 14-15th century, proposes in the same place a prayer in five hexameters beginning with *Te veneranda caro,* followed by several other peculiar comositions (Köck, 130). A Mass-book from Vorau (14-15th cent.; Köck, 133; cf. 79) has the hymns *O vere digna hostia* and *O salutaris hostia* immediately after the Communion. Another proposes the *Anima Christi* to be prayed before Communion (15th cent.; Köck, 76; 132). A broadened version of the same from the 15th century in a Missal of Cambrai (Wilmart, *Auteurs spirituels,* 21 f.). A Missal of the 13th century from Stift-Schlägl, Cpl. 47-1, uses the hymn *Jesu nostra redemptio* before Communion (M. J. Waefelghem, in *Analectes de l'Ordre de Prémontré* [1912], p. 140). This, along with further stanzas of the hymn and various Scripture phrases, was still in use later

in the liturgy proper to the Premonstratensians (Lentze, *Anal. Præm.* [1950] 144).—The Mass-arrangement of the monastery of Bec: Martène, 1, 4, XXXVI (I, 674), places at the priest's disposal *pro animi desiderio* before Communion the hymn *Ave verum corpus* and a lengthy prayer *O panis angelorum.*—The Regensburg Missale about 1500, places here the distych *Ave salus mundi* (Beck, 270); cf. *supra,* p. 215. The same with the beginning *Salve salus mundi* in the Ordinal of the Carmelites of 1312 (Zimmermann, 83); cf. also Missale of Carmelites of 1663 (Ferreres, 187) and the present-day *Missale O. Carm.* (1935), 318.—In a Missal of Passau of the 14th century a prayer begins *Salve rex fabricator mundi* whereupon the *O vera digna hostia* mentioned above follows; Radó, 102.—A Missal of the 14th century from Gerona has the priest pray *Adoro te, Domine J. C. . . . quem credo sub hac specie quam teneo sive video;* Ferreres, p. XLVI.

[17] Leroquais, I, 66, 72, 84, 90.

[18] From the 11th century, cf. Leroquais, I, 106, 108, 120, 127; Ebner, 7, 53, 65, 105, etc. Even some isolated manuscripts of the 12th century still conclude the Mass-*ordo* with *Fiat commixtio* or with the *Agnus Dei;* Ebner, 36, 89, etc.; an Admont Missal of the 13th century that concludes with *Agnus Dei* in Köck, 3.

[19] Bernold, *Micrologus,* c. 19 (PL, 151, 989); cf. c. 23. Sicard of Cremona (d. 1226); *Mitrale,* III, 8 (PL, 213, 141 f.) is equally reserved. So also Durandus (d. 1296), IV, 54, 10, who otherwise explains every word in detail, handles the preparatory prayers but briefly, evidently because

bowed. As a matter of fact, this prayer does not seldom appear all alone.[20] How much a favorite it was is attested also by the different variants.[21]

But the eagerness for an increase of such prayers was even stronger. Some wanted first a prayer addressed to God the Father, and only then one addressed to the Son.[22] Finally, the wish was expressed that a prayer should be added addressed to the Holy Ghost,[23] or at any rate one for the grace of the Holy Ghost.[24] Or else free rein should be given to the private devotion of the celebrant. Even in the sixteenth century there were those who upheld this opinion and put it into practice.[25] In the Mass plans of Middle Italy, where the monasteries had obviously borrowed their prayer material from the sister establishments of the North, the two prayers come to the fore side by side with increasing frequency since the eleventh century. But the first of them, *Domine Jesu Christe*, in these and other

he regards them as matter for private devotion. Cf. Sölch, *Hugo*, 138 f.

[20] Missale of Monte Cassino (11-12th cent.) Ebner, 310; Sacramentary of Modena (before 1173): Muratori, I, 94; *Ordinarium O.P.* of 1256 (Guerrini, 244) and *Liber ordinarius* from Liége (Volk, 96); Ordinarium of the Carthusians; Legg, *Tracts*, 102; cf. Martène, 1, 4, XXV (I, 634 C) and even later, e.g., *Missale Cart.* (1713), 222; also in a *Missale itinerantium* from Cologne, 1505: Beck, 337.

[21] Three modifications, among them one with an intercession for the departed and one with prayer for the living in the Missale of Fécamp, circa 1400. Martène, 1, 4, XXVII (I, 641 f.).

[22] This arrangement frequent in the northern French and the English Mass-books; thus already in the Missale of Robert of Jumièges from the 11th century, ed. Wilson (HBS, 11), 47 f. So also in the following period; *v.* Legg, *Tracts*, 15; 48; 66: 227; Martène, 1, 4, XXVI-XXVIII (I, 638, 641, 645); cf. *ibid.*, 1, 4, 9, 9 (I, 425 C).

[23] Such a prayer *(Domine Sancte Spiritus)* is handed down in several Mass-arrangements from monasteries in Southern Italy; Ebner, 348, 157; Fiala, 204. In the two last cases (Missale of the 15th century from Monte Vergine and a missal of the 12th century from St. Vincent) as well as in the Communion devotions at the end of the 11th century from Monte Cassino, ed. Wilmart (*Eph. liturg.*, 1929), 326, it has its place in fact after a prayer each to God the Father and God the Son. Wilmart

(228) traces the core of the formula back to Peter Damian (PL, 145, 922 C). In the Missale from Monte Vergine and in the second version of the Communion devotion mentioned (*ibid.*, 326 f.) a prayer to each of the Divine Persons also follows after the Communion.

[24] Hugo of S. Cher, *Tract. super missam* (ed. Sölch, 49 f.) testifies that some say the prayer *Assit nobis, quæsumus Domine, virtus Spiritus Sancti* or *Veni Sancte Spiritus* for the purpose of rounding out the series to the whole Trinity. He himself does not recommend this.—Cf. Sölch, *Hugo*, 139-142.

[25] Jod. Clichtoveus (d. 1543), *Elucidatorium* (Basle, 1517), 150 v., discusses the Communion prayer *Domine Jesu Christe* and *Perceptio* and then adds: *Alii vero (quisque pro more suæ ecclesiæ) alias orationes secundum devotionis suæ affectum et recte quidem dicunt.*—St. Francis Xavier inserted in this place a prayer for the conversion of the heathens; G. Schurhammer, *Der hl. Franz Xaver* (Freiburg, 1925), 241.—John Bechofen (circa 1500) is somewhat stricter, inasmuch as he would permit the addition of such prayers only mentally, but not vocally; Franz, *Die Messe*, 594 f. Louis Ciconiolanus, *Directorium div. off.* (Rome, 1539; Legg, *Tracts*, 211), also inserts, after the *Domine non sum dignus*, a prayer that apparently does not occur elsewhere *(Domine Jesu Christe, da mihi . . .)* which the priest should say *submissa voce vel potius mente.*

uses very frequently follows the reception of Communion;[26] this is true less often of the second formula, *Perceptio*.[27]

In these arrangements of the prayers is revealed the attitude towards the Sacrament which prevailed even at the height of the Middle Ages, an attitude which was concerned less with a special preparation of the soul as such, but rather with the production of the *opus operatum* which is to be sought from God.[28] Since the last years of the eleventh century the two formulas appear at one or another time in Italy in the present-day arrangement,[29] and even outside Italy the same arrangement had made its way before Pius V.[30]

In the arrangement as we have it now, the two prayers serve as a final preparation for the reception of the Sacrament. Prescinding from the Great Prayer itself, there was already a first preparation in the Lord's Prayer, in which we asked the heavenly Father for the sacred bread. In this second step we turn our prayer to Christ, a course which is undoubtedly to be expected even in liturgical prayer. But all the same, even in this we do not lose sight of the gift character of the Sacrament. In other words, our prayer is directed not to Christ as present under the form of bread, but always to Christ who "liveth and reigneth" in heavenly majesty and who, "by this, His most holy Body and Blood," will deliver us from sin and sorrow. The idea of the heavenly Christ and his heavenly existence is so strong that it is not eclipsed even by the sacramental nearness. In the *Agnus Dei* the latter could flash momentarily. But the mood which prevails in the popular devotion since the late Middle Ages, and which has found an outlet in the Fourth Book of the *Imitatio Christi*, and in subsequent prayerbook literature—that mood here was stopped short and not permitted to turn the reception of Communion into a meditative visit to the Blessed Sacrament.[31] Instead, a complete view of the Christian world of faith is maintained and not even in the moment of reception is it forsaken in favor of a partial view.[32]

---

[26] Ebner, 5; 20; 101; 102; 305; 311; 334; 339; 349; cf. 157 f. Similarly in old Italian Mass-orders; see, e.g., Martène, 1, 4, IV; V; VIII; XIII; XV (I, 516, 528, 541, 579, 594). Enumeration from Leroquais in Eisenhofer, II, 211.

[27] Cf., however, earlier and later Mass-orders in France and on the Rhine. Martène, 1, 4, VIII; XVII; XXVI; XXVIII; XXXII f. (I, 541, 602, 638, 645, 657, 661); Leroquais, I 140; 186; 197, etc.—That the Communion prayers, on the other hand, often occur even before the Kiss of Peace and the pertinent prayers was already noted above, p. 340, n. 50.

[28] For the rest Gihr, 762, rightly calls attention to the fact that the prayer *Domine*

Jesu Christe was formulated in such a general way (*per hoc sacrosanctum corpus* . . .) that it did not have to refer exclusively to the Communion, but could also be understood as a petition for the fruit of the Sacrifice.

[29] Ebner, 299; 317; 335; Mass-*ordo* of John Burchard: Legg, *Tracts*, 162 f.

[30] Mass-*ordo* "Indutus planeta": Legg, 187; Freising Missale of 1520: Beck, 309.

[31] Amalar, *Ep. ad Guntrad.* (PL, 105, 1339), offers an early example of this manner of meditating.

[32] The inclination to complete this transition is certainly evident in many a Massbook of the Middle Ages. Thus already in a text dated about 1100 our oration *Domi-*

This complete view is unfolded in a wonderful way, briefly, concisely, in the very first Communion prayer, *Domine Jesu Christe*. As someone has rightly said, a whole theology is contained in this one prayer. We can also say that in it the grand concepts of the anamnesis once more come to life. Grand, indeed. Before our mind's eye appears again the picture of Him whose Body and Blood will soon be our nourishment. At the very start of the prayer our gaze is fixed on the Christ whom we in this solemn moment call—as Peter did (Matth. 16:16)—the Son of the living God. Then our look takes in His momentous work of renewing and reviving the world *(vivificasti)*, that work which will be continued in one tiny point in the Sacrament about to be received; our look takes in the well-spring of this work in the grace-laden decree of the heavenly Father[33] and in the obedience unto death of the Son; it takes in the completion of that work in the operation of the Holy Spirit. Grand, too, is the plea which we now direct to the Lord, confiding in His most holy Body and Blood which He has vouchsafed to us as a sacrifice and which He wills to grant us as a repast; the things we ask are things of magnitude: deliverance from all sin, the strength to be true to His commandments, and—the same petition which we made in the instant before the consecration—the grace of final perseverance, so that we may never be separated from Him. Here, in bold strokes, the whole pattern of Christianity is presented to view.

The second prayer, *Perceptio*, recalling the Apostle's earnest words about an unworthy reception (1 Cor. 11:29), seizes upon one negative point in the first prayer, the curbing of sin. Whoever dares to receive *(præsumo)* may not be conscious of any grave fault; he that eats unworthily, eats the judgment unto himself. But who is really worthy? All that each and everyone can do is raise a humble prayer for the Lord's leniency *(pro tua pietate)*. The positive side of the petition blends the objects that are stipulated as the effect of the Sacrament in numerous formulas of the post-communion: protection of soul and body and the cure of our manifold weakness. Even if the body is not the direct subject of grace, yet it is the recipient of the sacramental tokens and is destined to secure those rays of grace which issue from the spiritual center of man's essence.

ne *Jesu Christe* is characterized as a prayer of St. Augustine *ad Filium quem ante se tenet;* Martène, 1, 4, 9, 9 (I, 425 C). The custom of holding the Blessed Sacrament in one's hands during these prayers was already mentioned above. But there is no necessary connection between these prayers and this deportment, as the Communion-prayer above (n. 15), *Deus Pater fons,* shows. The attention is thereby merely directed all the more intensively to the Sacrament, as happens similarly when, according to the prescription of the *Missale Romanum, Ritus serv.* X, 3, the prayers after the *Agnus Dei* are said *oculis ad sacramentum intentis.*

[33]Cf. Eph. 1: 5, 9, 11, et al.

10. Communion of the Priest: Ritual Procedure

As before the priest's Communion, so also during it, the old liturgy had no accompanying prayers. In some individual places this situation lasted a long time, even when some preparatory prayers had been admitted. The conduct of the Communion itself was one of utmost simplicity, even if not the same everywhere. Any previous genuflection here or elsewhere was unknown till very late in the Middle Ages.[1] The priest simply retained the posture he had, until now. He uncovered the chalice,[2] then conveyed first the Host and next the chalice to his mouth. A previous sign of the Cross with the Host appears here and there since the thirteenth century.[3] According to the system still observed by the Dominicans, the priest held the two halves of the Host just as they were at the fraction, in the left hand, while the right rested on the node of the chalice.[4] In this case the *sumptio corporis* was—and is—done with the left hand,[5] and then the chalice was taken up at once.[6] But elsewhere the practice of making a sign of the Cross over himself with the Body of the Lord before the reception entailed an increasing employment of the right hand,[7] even when it was not already in use. When—as at the grand pontifical service—the Communion of the celebrant did not take place at the altar, care was exercised in olden times that he should be facing East, as at solemn prayer.[8]

[1] Cf. *supra* I, 123.—The two genuflections customary today are proposed in the Mass arrangement of John Burchard (Legg, *Tracts,* 163 f.), still the second does not occur after the uncovering of the chalice, but only after the *Quid retribuam* that follows. The second genuflection is still missing in the monastic Missal of 1531 from Lyons; Martène 1, 4, XXXIII (I, 661 B).
[2] Another Minorite Missal about 1300 provides for the removal of the pall already before the words *Panem cœlestem.* Ebner, 351; cf. 317.
[3] Ebner, 317; 351; Martène, 1, 4, XXXVIII; XXXV (I, 661 B, 670 C). A sign of the cross with the chalice is not especially mentioned. Such a sign, on the contrary, is specified in the Mass-book of Salzburg of the 12-13th century: Köck, 131; both signs of the cross are indicated in Durandus, IV, 54, 11.
[4] A related custom is that in the Pressburg Missal D (15th cent.) according to which the priest takes the Body of the Lord together with the paten in his hands before the oration *Perceptio Corporis:* Jávor, 119.
[5] Sölch, *Hugo,* 145 f. In the 13th and 14th centuries the papal liturgy gives evidence of the Communion with the left hand: Ordo of Stefaneschi, n. 53 (PL, 78, 1168); cf. Sölch, *loc. cit.*—A form of respect that is strange to our way of thinking is the one adopted in the Mass arrangement "Indutus planeta" (origin period to 1244): Legg, *Tracts,* 187: The priest should lift the host upon the paten and take it thence, not with his hands, but with his tongue. Cf. also Ebner, 151, 166. This method also is mentioned at the turn of the 15th century by Balthasar of Pforta (Franz, 540, n. 2), but he does not recommend it. It appears in 1562 among the lists of *abusus missæ; Concilium Tridentinum,* ed. Görres, VIII, 923. Regarding the origin of the custom, a Franciscan Missal of the 13th century (Leroquais II, 129), reports that the practice was introduced at the Roman Curia under Gregory IX (1227-1241).
[6] Durandus, IV, 54, 12, wanted to see the Communion of the chalice emphasized over the drinking of the ablution by having the priest take hold of the chalice with both hands and drink it in three draughts.
[7] Cf. Sölch, *Hugo,* 146 f.
[8] *Ordo Rom.* V, n. 10 (PL, 78, 989): *qui*

Even in later texts, when at times mention is made of a meditative pause either before or after the *sumptio*,[9] still a further direction is given that the priest must take the sacred meal *festinanter*, as did the Israelites at the exodus,[10] and he may not, by his own private devotion, keep the participants waiting.

Regarding the accompanying prayers at the priest's Communion, the texts of the earlier Middle Ages give indications of three motifs in their introduction. The first was the desire to give proper expression to the veneration of the Sacrament. It is the same desire from which proceeded the *Agnus Dei*, and later the elevation and salutation of the Sacrament right after the consecration. The texts composed for this we find in the earliest and purest form in the Missal of Troyes written about 1050,[11] where no other type of text is given.

First, a passage from the Acts of the Martyrdom of St. Agnes is cited: *Ecce, Jesu benignissime, quod concupivi iam video; ecce, rex clementissime, quod speravi iam teneo; hinc tibi quæso iungar in cælis, quod tuum corpus et sanguinem, quamvis indignus, cum gaudio suscipio in terris.* Then follows a double salute of the Sacrament, to which each time is added a short prayer: *Ave in ævum, sanctissima caro, mea in perpetuum summa dulcedo;* and then the prayer referring to the species of bread, *Perceptio.*[12] Then a greeting of the chalice: *Ave in æternum, cælestis potus, mihi ante omnia et super omnia dulcis;* and to this as a prayer, the words, *Cruor ex latere D. n. J. C. mihi indigno maneat ad salutem et proficiat ad remedium animæ meæ in vitam æternam. Amen.*

Of these, only the two salutations, *Ave in ævum* and *Ave in æternum*, gained a wider acceptance,[13] which they kept all through the Middle Ages,[14]

---

surgens vertat ese ad orientem et communicet. We may follow Mabillon (PL, 78, 946, note k) in surmising that the same directional turn is to be presupposed at the Communion of the Pope *ad sedem* in *Ordo Rom.* I, n. 19.

[9] Hugo of S. Cher requires such a *meditari* before the reception; so also the Dominican Missal of today and the statutes of the Carthusians (though here it is a modern regulation) ; Sölch, 142. The Missal of Bangor about 1400 (Maskell, 182) gives an express instruction: *Hic debet sacerdos intime meditari de incarnatione, caritate, passione et de dira morte Jesu Christi, quas pro nobis passus est . . .* The *Missale Rom., Ritus serv.* X, 4, requires such a moment of meditation after the *sumptio corporis.*

[10] Franz, 518; 610.

[11] Martène, 1 4, VI (I, 534). Similarly complete, but with an inversion and the addition of other accompanying words, in the Missal of Remiremont; *ibid.*, 1, 4, 9, 9 (I, 424).

[12] Shortened at the end: . . . *tutamentum animæ et corporis. Amen.*

[13] Ebner, 63; 336; 338; Leroquais, I, 199; 225; 232; 259; Legg, *The Sarum Missal*, 227 f. A number of French manuscripts of the 12-16th centuries in Wilmart, *Auteurs spirituels* 20, n. 1.

[14] From the later Middle Ages should be mentioned, for England: Martène, 1, 4, XXXV (I, 679 C) ; Maskell, 180 f.; cf. Ferreres, 189-191 (nn. 691, 693 f., 696) ; Frere, *The Use of Sarum*, I, 86 f. For France: Lebrun, I, 537, note a. For Germany: Hoeynck, 375 (cf. Franz, 753) ; Beck, 270, 309. For Hungary: Radó, 43, 62, 71, 76, 84, 123. And in Sweden since the end of the 14th century: Segelberg, 258; Freisen, *Manuale Lincopense*, p. XXX, LI. — Differently worded is

mostly in connection with the pertinent phrase used at the distribution, *Corpus D. n. J. C.,* etc., which was added immediately. The phrase from St. Agnes seldom recurs.[15] On the other hand, the salutation was more frequently expanded. And just as the salutation—sometimes even to the wording—was used since the thirteenth century for the veneration of the Sacrament at the consecration; so, in reverse, the forms which were created for the consecration were later used also before Communion.[16]

The second motif consists of short scriptural passages which were suited to accompany the Communion. There was above all Psalm 115:3 f. (12 f.) which presented the phrase *Calicem salutaris accipiam* as a happy accompaniment for the reception of the chalice, but also the words *Quid retribuam Domino* as an expression of awed thankfulness for the Communion. As a matter of fact, we find it used already since the beginning of the eleventh century in its present-day length and in the place it occupies today, and even, as now, continued with the phrase from Psalm 17:4, *Laudans invocabo Dominum et ab inimicis meis salvus ero.* Here, too, it is preceded by a phrase composed as a parallel for the reception of the bread: *Panem cœlestem accipiam et nomen Domini invocabo.*[17] Here, of course, the scriptural passage is farther removed from its literal meaning than it was in its first and more ancient use at the offering of the chalice.[18] In the psalm the singer speaks out his resolve to make a thank-offering for his delivery from a great peril and in so doing (as was probably part of the ritual of a thank-offering) to raise the cup to praise God. But here the cup which we intend to pick up itself contains the welfare and therefore the reason for thanksgiving, and next to the cup lies the bread from heaven. At this moment both of them are not so much gifts we offer up to God as rather that sacred repast to which we are now invited. But since we eat of this meal, it behooves us, as it behooved the psalmist, to praise the Lord because, as His guests at table, we are delivered from every earthly peril and safeguarded even if—as it added from Psalm 17:4—our enemies beset us on all sides.[19]

---

the greeting in the Pontifical of Mainz about 1170: Martène, 1, 4, XVII (I, 602 C): *Ave sanguis et sanctissima caro, in quibus salus mundi est et vita.*

[15] Ebner, 336; Leroquais, I, 199; II, 54; Radó, 71; 84.—With a double greeting in several Mass-books of the 13-15th centuries from Gerona; Ferreres, 190; Leroquais, III, 98 f. Perhaps, however, the saint's words, as we shall yet see, acted as the occasion for inserting other words from her *Passio.*—I find the formula *Crux ex latere* in the Sacramentary of Caen (11th cent.): Leroquais, I, 183.

[16] Cf. the material *supra,* n. 16.

[17] Mass-*ordo* of Séez: PL, 78, 250; Missa Illyrica: Martène, 1, 4, IV (I, 515).—For

calicem salutaris we find substituted, in accordance with John 6: 32 f., the word *panem cœlestem,* the name frequently used in the Old Testament (Ps. 77: 24; 104: 40 Wisd. 16: 20) for the Manna. The Augsburg missal of 1386 has the supplement: *(accipiam) de mensa Domini.*

[18] *Supra,* p. 55.

[19] Cf. the same idea Ps. 22: 5.—A similar notion of strengthened confidence in the midst of hostile threats finds expression in an antiphon for the Communion in the Antiphonary of Bangor; ed. Warren (HBS, 10), 30: *Corpus Domini accepimus et sanguine eius potati sumus. Ab omni malo non timebimus, quia Dominus nobiscum est.*

In later years this combination of psalm passages appears in more or less complete form in most of the German Mass plans [20] and also in the majority of the Italian—here since the eleventh century [21]—while in France it is less frequent. In Normandy and England it is absolutely unknown.[22] Sometimes, to be sure, only portions are used, or a different order is chosen, or a different method of interweaving them with the other texts.[23] In Spain the *Panem cœlestem* is occasionally continued with the phrase from Psalm 77:25 about the bread of angels.[24] Again the last words before the reception of Communion are formed from Psalm 50:11 f.[25] or Psalm 50:11-14, the celebrant striking his breast as he recites the verses.[26] Here we have the same penitential concept that is behind the prescriptions of our ritual, which lays down that at Communion for the sick the Psalm *Miserere* is to be recited on the way.[27] It presupposes some what the same spiritual experience that agitated the soul of the Apostle Peter at the miraculous draught of fishes; the nearness of the Son of God draws from our lips the anguished cry: "Depart from me, O Lord, I am a sinful man" (Luke 5:8).

Especially in later times, similar exclamations, in which an acknowledgment of sinfulness is combined with confidence in God's mercy, are frequently extracted from the New Testament, to be used at the moment of Communion. Thus, there is the prayer of the tax collector: *Deus, propitius esto mihi peccatori* (Luke 18:13),[28] or the exclamation of the prodigal son: *Pater peccavi . . .* (Luke 15:18 f.)[29] or the servant's plea for indulgence: *Patientiam habe in me, Domine, peccavi, et omnia reddam tibi* (cf. Matthew 18:26),[30] But other phrases that express only unreserved

---

[20] Köck, 128-132; Beck, 270; 309 f.; Hoeynck, 35; Franz, 753.

[21] Ebner, 302; 310 f.; 317; 331; 334; 336, etc.

[22] Cf. e. g., the Mass arrangements offered by Martène, 1, 4, XXVI f., XXXV-XXXVII (I, 638, 642, 670, 674, 678); Legg, *Tracts*, 15; 66; 227.——Also the Dominican Mass arrangement (Guerrini, 244) and that of the Carthusians (Legg, 102) do not have the Psalm phrase.

[23] Thus Ps. 17: 4 at times already precedes the *Quid retribuam*, (Köck, 128; 132; v. Bruiningk, 88) or else it comes only after the *sumptio* formula (Ferreres, 189). Sometimes the *Panem cœlestem* is missing entirely (e.g., Ebner, 297) or else it is not found till after the *Domine non sum dignus* (Ebner, 302; 334).

[24] Mass-book of the 15th century from Valencia; Ferreres, 189.

[25] Cologne *Ordo celebrandi* (14th cent.): Binterim, IV, 3, p. 225.

[26] Monastic missal of 1531 from Lyons: Martène, 1, 4, XXXIII (I, 661).

[27] *Rituale Rom.* IV, 4, 13. The beginning of the Psalm also in connection with the sprinkling with holy water; *ibid.*, IV, 4, 15.

[28] The 15th century Missal of Styria, Köck, 132, 134; Regensburg Missal of 1500: Beck, 270; Rituale of the Bursfeld congregation (15th cent.): Martène, *De antiquis monach. ritibus*, II, 4, 3, 17 (*De ant Eccl. ritibus*, IV, 186). In all cases named the plea is combined with the *Domine non sum dignus*. Cf. the formula elaborated into a longer prayer *supra*, p. 346, n. 15.

[29] Missal of the Evreux-Jumièges (about 1400): Martène, 1, 4, XXVIII (I, 645 B).

[30] Missal of Vorau (15th cent.): Köck, 134.

trust also find a place, phrases like the last prayer of the dying Saviour (Luke 23:46): *Pater, in manus tuas commendo spiritum meum,*[31] or a daring adaptation of St. Paul's words (1 Cor. 13:12): *Cognoscam te, cognitor meus, sicut a te cognitus sum . . .*[32] or the trinitarian blessing (Matthew 28:19): *In nomine Patris et Filii et Spiritus Sancti.*[33]

However, the oldest of such phrases, combining both humility and confidence, is the *Domine non sum dignus* of the centurion of Capharnaum (Matthew 8:8). It had already been used since the tenth century as a reinforcement of longer prayers preceding the reception.[34] Then it was thought sufficient to use only a shortened version, substituting for the clause beginning with *sed tantum*—which could not be used directly— some other scriptural saying: *(sed) salvum me fac et salvus ero, quoniam laus mea tu es* (Jer. 17:14),[35] or the words from Matthew 8:2 already cited: *sed si vis, potes me mundare,*[36] or an allusion to the words of the promise (John 6:55 ff.): *sed tu Domine qui dixisti: Qui manducat carnem meam.*[37] There is no mention here of any repetition of the phrase. But at the same time in Italy the practice began of using the words of the centurion as they are, repeating them three times, either with no change at all,[38]

---

[31] Seckauer Missal of the 14th century: Köck, 129.

[32] Sacramentary of Vich (11-12th cent.): Ferreres, 186.

[33] *Alphabetum sacerdotum* (about 1500): Legg, *Tracts,* 48; Styrian Missals of the 15th century: Köck, 77; 132, in the latter place before both the first and the second *sumptio.* Likewise already in the Missals of the 13th century from Schägl mentioned above, p. 347, n. 16: In the Sarum rite since the 14th century added to both *sumptio* formulas; Frere, *The Use of Sarum,* I, 86 f.; Martène, 1, 4, XXXV (I, 670 C).

[34] Sacramentary of S. Thierry (end of 10th cent.): Martène, 1, 4, X (I, 551 C): *Domine . . . tectum meum, sed invoco te cum beatæ Mariæ et omnium sanctorum meritis quatenus in me venias et mansionem facias, et obsecro, ut non intres ad condemnationem et iudicium, sed ad salutem animæ meæ et corporis mei . . . et libera me per . . .* (phrases from our first Communion oration follow). Likewise in the Sacramentary of Moissac (11th cent.): Martène, 1, 4, VIII (I, 540 f.): *Domine Jesu Christe, non sum dignus te suscipere. sed tantum obsecro, propitius esto mihi peccatori et præsta* (the petition as in the *Perceptio* follows). Later frequently in French Mass-books in part with elabora-

tions; see *ibid.,* 1, 4, 9, 9 (I, 425 B); Leroquais, I, 204; II, 25; 32; 315, etc. Also with the continuation: *propitius esto mihi peccatori per assumptionem . . .* (cf. *supra* p. 346, n. 15); Leroquais, II, 375; III, 73. Other free extensions in the Styrian Mass books: . . . *tectum meum, sed propter misericordiam tuam libera me a peccatis et angustiis et necessitatibus meis;* Seckau Missale of the 14th century (Köck, 129) *. . . tectum meum, sed propter magnam clementiam tuam veni in cor meum et munda illud . . . intra in animam meam, sana et sanctifica eam . . . Salvator mundi;* Vorau Missale of the 14-15th century (Köck, 133).

[35] Salzburg Missale of 12-13th cent.: Köck, 131; Styrian Missals of the 15th century: *ibid.,* 77, 132; Missale of 1519 from Aquileja: Weth(*ZkTh* 1912), 419; Passau Missale of 14th century: Radó, 102; Augsburg Missale of 1386; Hoeynck, 375; two missal manuscripts of the 15th century from Amiens in Wilmart, *Auteurs spirituels,* 20 f. Cf. Leroquais, II, 81 (Sens, 13th century).

[36] Vorau Missale of the 15th century: Köck, 134.

[37] French Mass-books since the 12th century: Leroquais, I, 261, 328; II, 17, 60.

[38] Ending with *puer meus:* Sacramentary

or by using only the first half,[39] or finally inserting *anima mea* in place of *puer meus* in the second half of the phrase, just as is done nowadays.[40] Outside Italy this shorter *Domine non sum dignus* is seldom found before Pius V; [41] it is most frequent in German Mass plans.[42] Even in Italy its ascendancy was only gradual.[43] And striking the breast while saying the words seems to have come into vogue quite late.[44]

How closely associated the centurion's words are with the reception of Communion is seen in the fact that they were used also in oriental liturgies. In the Ethiopian Mass *ordo* the words form the beginning of a lengthy Communion prayer,[45] and the Byzantine liturgy contains amongst its semi-liturgical Communion prayers also some with the same beginning.[46] Even

of Modena (before 1174) : Muratori, I, 94; Sacramentary of St. Peter in Rome (about 1200) : Ebner, 336; Sacramentary from the chapel of the papal court (about 1290) : Brinktrine (*Eph. liturg.*, 1937), 208; Missale of St. Lambrecht (in the beginning of the 13th cent.) : Köck, 23.

[39] . . . *sub tectum meum*. Earliest evidence (with a threefold repetition) in a Central Italian monastic Sacramentary of the 11th century; Ebner, 302; cf. *ibid.*, 331, 334, 339, 348. Cf. too the Missale of Bayeux (12th cent.) : Leroquais, I, 237. Without any indication that it is to be continued, mentioned as a prayer for the communicants in the *Enarrationes in Matth.*, c. 8 (PL, 162, 1321), now generally ascribed to Gottfried of Babion (about 1100; but cf. W. Lampen, *Antonianum*, 19 [1944], 144-149).

[40] In a Sacramentary of the 12-13th cent. from lower Italy; Ebner, 325, also with a threefold repetition. Here again the trail leads back to Normandy, where a Missal of the 12th century proposes the *anima mea*: Leroquais, I, 241; cf. II, 135. The 13th century missal from Schlägl mentioned above (p. 427, n. 16) concludes the formula with *sanabitur et mundabitur corpus et anima mea* (Waefelghem, *loc. cit*, 140).

[41] Still Durandus, IV, 54, 10, is familiar with it. Cf. Browe, *JL*, 13 (1935), 48; but the Franciscan Missal of the 13th century mentioned here is hardly of French origin. In Spain the triple *Domine non sum dignus* appears in the Missal of Tarragona, 1499; Ferreres, 188.

[42] Gregorienmünster (14-15th century) : Martène, 1, 4, XXXII (I, 657 A) ; Re-

gensburg (about 1500) and Freising (1520) : Beck, 270; 309.

[43] A Mass arrangement of the 11-12th cent. from Monte Cassino presents it, but as a supplement of the 12-13th century: Ebner, 310, n. 2.

[44] It is noted in the Missals of Tarragona of 1499 (Ferreres, 188) and Vich, 1547 (*ibid.*, CVIII). John Trithemius (d. 1516) reports as an old monastic tradition, that this was done at the triple *Deus propitius esto mihi peccatori;* Martène, 1, 4, 10, 14 (I, 440) ; cf. also Gabriel Biel, *Canonis expositio,* lect. 82; Missal of Schlägl (15th cent.) : Lentze (*Anal. Præm.,* 1950), 139.

[45] Brightman, 239: "O Lord, Lord, it in no wise beseemeth thee to come under the roof of my polluted house, for I have provoked Thee and stirred Thee to anger . . ." (there follows an acknowledgment of faults and, after reference to the redemptive will of Christ, a petition that the mystery might not redound to one's judgment).

[46] O Lord, I am not worthy that Thou shouldst enter beneath the unclean roof of my soul, but as Thou wert pleased in the cave to lie in the manger for senseless beasts, and as Thou didst receive the sinner who, stained even as I, approached Thee in the house of Simon the Leper, so too come into the manger of my senseless soul and enter my soiled body, this body of death and full of leprosy. And as Thou didst not despise the unclean mouth of the sinner who kissed Thy stainless feet, so do not despise me, my Lord and my God, me a poor sinner, but in Thy goodness and love for mankind make me worthy to partake of Thy Body and Blood." M. Daras, "Les prières préparatoires à la S. Com-

the Fathers had already shifted the centurion's phrase to the reception of Holy Communion.[47]

Although in the broad perspectives of liturgical prayer the notion of a visit is not one of the fundamental ideas in the contemplation of the Eucharist, still, in this biblical phrase, it is taken up for an instant as a relevant simile. And there is nothing to hinder our considering the *Agnus Dei* as a background, or to find in the *Domine* an echo of the title by which the Lamb is addressed in St. John's revelations according to the Vulgate (Apoc. 5:19), that Lamb who, together with Him who sits on the throne, receives the adoration of the four living creatures and the four-and-twenty elders.[48] Not only His coming, but even the word which we beg of Him *(dic verbo)* brings health to the sick—and every recipient acknowledges himself sick in soul. However, by not declining the visit (as did the humble centurion), but instead longingly awaiting it, we alter the sense of the plea. We think now not of the word that substitutes for His visit, but of the word that prepares us for it.[49]

A third motif of words to accompany the reception of the Sacrament—in this case to accompany it immediately—are the formulas for the distribution which came into use in the early Middle Ages, at first for Communion of the sick.[50] These formulas were simply turned into formulas for reception, usually with only a change of *te* and *animam tuam* to *me* and *animam meam*. An early and as yet isolated example is once again offered by the Sacramentary of Amiens, which presents after the two preparatory prayers,[51] a single formula under the heading *Alia*. This formula, meant for the double reception, reads as follows: *Corpus et Sanguis D.n.J.C. prosit mihi in remissionem omnium peccatorum et ad vitam æternam in sæcula sæculorum.*[52] Both the reserve discernible here and the effort here seen to enrich the expression is found in the Sacramentary of St. Thierry (end of the tenth century) which offers only a formula for the chalice Communion, probably out of consideration for the fact that the longer prefatory prayers immediately precede the *sumptio corporis;* it runs as follows: *Sanguis D. n. J. C., qui ex latere suo processit, salvet*

---

munion" (*Cours et Conférences*, VII; Louvain, 1929), 255, with reference to Pl. de Meester, La divine liturgie de s. J. Chrysostome (Rome, 1920 = 1st ed., not available to me).—Cf. also the third and fourth prayer in the Byzantine Communion office: Ὡρολόγιον τὸ μέγα (Venice, 1875), 417-419.

[47] Examples in Bona II, 17, I (838).

[48] The same invocation at the end of our litanies: *Agnus Dei . . . parce nobis, Domine.*

[49] The English translations commonly found do not render this turn of thought adequately: "Lord, I am not worthy that

Thou shouldst come under my roof; but only speak a word . . ." This "but" is ambiguous, either rejecting the former sentence ("Don't come") or only suggesting a partial opposition ("Come despite the unworthiness, for Thou canst remove it by a word").

[50] See below, pp. 390 ff.—Also in the oriental liturgies, the Armenian excepted, the *sumptio* formulas used by the celebrant are as a rule derived from the formulas for administering the Sacrament. Baumstark, *Die Messe im Morgenland*, 163.

[51] *Supra*, p. 345.

[52] Leroquais (*Eph. liturg.*, 1927), 444.

animam meam et perducat in vitam æternam. Amen.[53] Some Mass books even after the year 1000 still contain no sumption formula.[54] English Mass arrangements avoided them even in the later Middle Ages,[55] and the Carthusians even at the present have none.[56]

But in general they crop up everywhere, usually for Host and chalice separately,[57] and sometimes accompanied by a third formula which originally was an independent chalice formula.[58] Very frequently the second formula has the wording *Corpus et sanguis*, in view of the particle included at the commingling; this was partially the practice in Normandy and England.[59] As a rule, the formulas are spoken before the sumption, as is the present-day practice. Still, even in the late Middle Ages examples are to be found where they follow the sumption.[60]

The formulas present almost the same picture which we will encounter in the formulas for the distribution. Within the basic framework there is

[53] Martène, 1, 4, X (I, 551 E). On the other hand, the Sacramentary of S. Gatien-Tours, from the same period, has only one formula: *Corpus D. n. J. C. conservet animam meam in vitam æternam. Amen,* to be said only after the Communion of the Chalice; Martène, 1, 4, VII (I, 537 C). The same thing in a 15th century missal of Vorau: Köck, 134.

[54] The Missal of Troyes (about 1050), which already proposes three different administering formulas, has no sumption formula aside from the greetings mentioned above, a sumption formula is likewise missing in many an Italian Mass-arrangement of the 11-13th centuries; Ebner, 305, 326, 335, 348.

[55] See the Sarum Ordinary, Legg, *Tracts,* 15; 227 f. In the later Sarum rite, on the other hand, sumption formulas have been incorporated which are introduced by *In nomine Patris . . .*; see *supra,* n. 33.

[56] Cf. Legg, 102.—Regarding other monastic liturgies, cf. Sölch, 144. The liturgy of Lyons has no formula for the Communion of the Chalice; Bünner, 242.

[57] Examples of separate *sumptio* formulas already in the 11th century, among others in the Missa Illyrica: Martène, 1, 4, IV (I, 515 f.—A single formula for both is rare in later times, but is certified for the rite of Lyons by de Moléon, 59, 65. Likewise among the Dominicans; *Missale O.P.* (1889), 22: *Corpus et sanguis D. n. J. C.*

custodiant me in vitam æternam. Amen. Cf. Sölch, *Hugo,* 143 f.

[58] In a central Italian Sacramentary of the 11th century in Ebner, 299 (with the rubric: *Ad calicem cum ceperit se confirmare*): *Communicatio et confirmatio s. sanguinis tui, Domine J. C., prosit mihi in remissionem omnium peccatorum meorum et perducat me in vitam æternam. Amen.* (Then follows the formula *Sanguis D. n. J. C. conservet animam meam in vitam æternam. Amen.*) The formula mentioned appears in this version also in the north, where it is evidently indigenous; Massordo of Séez (PL, 78, 250 C); Missal of Liége: Martène, 1, 4, XV (I, 594 A).—For Italy see Ebner, 14; 1; 200; 331; 341; for Styria: Köck, 129, 131; also in the Augsburg Missale of 1386: Hoeynck, 376. In the Missa Illyrica (Martène, 1, 4, IV [I, 515 E], it is changed to include both species: *Communicatio et confirmatio corporis et sanguinis D. n. J. C. prosit mihi . . .*; in this form it is found elsewhere: Köck, 130; Beck, 271.

[59] Martène, 1, 4, V, XXVI, XXVIII, XXXI f., XXXVI (I, 528, 638, 645, 652, 657, 674); Ebner, 334; Legg, *Tracts,* 49, 66; Maskell, 182. The Mass-*ordo* of York about 1425 (Simmons, 114) presents such a double formula to follow upon the single formulas.

[60] Hugo of S. Cher, *Tract. super missam* (ed. Sölch, 50); cf. Sölch, *Hugo,* 142 f. with n. 256. This shifting is to be judged in the same way as in the case of the Communion prayers; above, p. 348 f.

the greatest variation, so that even in the Mass *ordo* the identical version of the formula for both Host and chalice is studiously avoided. Thus, frequently there is a recurrence of the combination: *Corpus D. n. J. C. sit mihi ad remedium sempiternum in vitam æternam. Amen* and *Sanguis D. n. J. C. custodiat me in vitam æternam. Amen.*[61] In some instances, here and there the designation of our Lord is changed: *Corpus Domini mei;*[62] *sit remedium* is often replaced by *prosit, proficiat,*[63] and *custodiat* by *conservet*[64] or also *mecum permaneat.*[65] To the words *me* and *mihi* an addition is made of the qualification *peccator* as a humble self-designation.[66] Even more frequently, as the examples have shown, *animam meam* is substituted for *me* and *mihi* even in earlier times, sometimes also *corpus et anima mea.*[67] In more recent times an expansion of the formula appears: . . . *et omnibus fidelibus defunctis (proficiat) ad veniam et vivis ad salutem et conservet me ad vitam æternam.*[68]

11. Communion of the Faithful: Frequency

As we have already seen, the Communion of the celebrating priest is generally followed by the Communion of the rest of the congregation. This is in accord both with the original practice and also with the established plan of the Roman Mass. This pattern, which in our own day has again come to be taken for granted more and more, was subjected, during the course of centuries, to several fluctuations and violent upheavals. These fluctuations and upheavals have had their effect upon the liturgical design of the people's Communion. They also led to the result that in the expla-

[61] In Italian Mass arrangements of the 11-12th century; Ebner, 323; 338; 339. Likewise in the Missal of Remiremont (12th cent.) where in addition a second pair of formulas appears: *Corpus D. n. J. C. mihi proficiat ad remedium animæ meæ: Sanguis D. n. J. C. conservet animam meam in vitam æternam.* Martène, 1, 4, 9, 9 (I, 424).—On the other hand, there are also Italian Mass-books that present exactly parallel expressions; see from the 11-13th centuries, Ebner, 302; 307; 311; 317. Later the parallelism becomes more frequent also elsewhere; it is found, e.g., in the Pontifical of Mainz about 1170; Martène, 1, 4, XVII (I, 602 C D). Further examples: Köck, 132; Beck, 270 f.; Legg, *Tracts*, 48 f.; 66.

[62] Examples of the 11th and 12th century: Martène, 1, 4, V (I, 528 A); *ibid.*, 1, 4, 9, 9 (I, 424 A). At the chalice prayer two Hungarian Missals of the 14th century insert: *(Sanguis D. n. J. C.) quem vere con-fiteor de latere eius profluxisse;* Radó, 84, 96.

[63] Both by preference, e.g., in the Styrian texts; Köck, 127-134.

[64] Ebner, 299; 307; 311, etc.

[65] Ebner, 150.

[66] Sarum missal: Martène, 1, 4, XXXV (I, 670 C); missal of the 15th century of Valencia: Ferreres, 189 (n. 692 f.). English Mass-*ordo* of Bec: Martène, 1, 4, XXXVI (I, 674 E): *mihi, Domine, famulo tuo peccatori;* cf. *ibid.*, XXVIII (I, 645 D).

[67] For the latter see Missale of Fécamp: Martène, 1, 4, XXVI (I, 638 C); Missale of Riga (14-15th cent.): *v.* Bruningk, 88. Also in many Premonstratensian Missals of the 12th and 13th centuries; Sölch, *Hugo*, 144, n. 261.

[68] Præmonstratensian Missal of the 15th century from Stift Schägl: Lentze (Annal. Præm., 1950), 139 f.

nation of the Mass, even down to the present, the Communion of the people was sometimes treated as a sort of foreign element that did not belong to the structure of the Mass-liturgy and could therefore be disregarded.

Up to the fourth century it was not only a rule that the faithful communicated at every Mass; but Communion was even more frequent than the celebration of Mass, which was usually restricted to the Sunday. On Sunday, the consecrated bread could be received not only to be eaten there and then, but also to be taken home.[1] There it was to be carefully preserved so that it could be eaten day after day before every other food.[2] This practice actually continued in Egypt even much longer,[3] and we find in particular the monks and hermits of the desert, who generally attended the celebration of the Eucharist on Saturdays and Sundays, making good use of the custom. Often they did not partake of the Eucharist till the ninth hour, when they began their spare meal.[4] In those days, and even later, it was customary to take the Eucharist along on journeys of greater length.[5] But in general, after the Church had finally gained free-

---

[1] Ps.-Cyprian (probably Novatian), *De spectaculis*, c. 5 (CSEL, 3, 3, p. 8, l. 11): *dimissus e dominico et adhuc gerens secum, ut assolet, eucharistiam.*

[2] Tertullian, *Ad uxorem*, II, 5 (CSEL, 70, 118): *Non sciet maritus, quid secreto ante omnem cibum gustes?* Cf. *De or.*, c. 19 (CSEL, 20, 192): on feast days one could take the Eucharist home, so as to partake of it in the evening. Hippolytus, *Trad. Ap.* (Dix, 58 f.): *Omnis autem fidelis festinet, antequam aliquid aliud gustet, eucharistiam percipere.* Regarding the later twisting of the prescription see Dix, p. LVIII. Cyprian, *De lapsis*, c. 26 (CSEL, 3, 256) reports of a woman who preserved the Eucharist *(Domini sanctum)* in an *arca* in order to be able to partake of it. Cf. F. J. Dölger, *Icthys*, II (Münster, 1922), 570, n. 4; Eisenhofer, II, 306 f.

[3] Basil, *Ep.*, 93 (from the year 372; PG, 32, 485): "In Alexandria and Egypt every lay person has it (the Eucharist) regularly with him in his home and takes it as often as he wishes." Moreover, the custom is supposed for Rome by Jerome, *Ep.*, 49, 15 (CSEL, 54, 377). Dölger explains an obscure text in Zeno of Verona, lib. I, 5, 8 in the same sense; *Antike u. Christentum*, 5 (1936), 243 f.—Further evidence is also seemingly found in Augustine, *Opus Imperf. c. Julian.*, III, 162 (PL, 45, 1315); see Roetzer, 179.—In regard to the

West Syrians even as late as the 6th century we read that they are accustomed to take home with them on Maundy Thursday enough of the Eucharist to last the year, and to preserve it in a locked cabinet; John Moschus, *Pratum spirituale*, c. 79 (PG, 87, 2936 f.).

[4] Basil, *loc. cit.*, Rufinus (d. 410), *Historia monach.*, c. 2 (PL, 21, 406 B).— Palladius, *Historia Lausiaca* (about 420; there is question here, however, of a revision into which material from a later period was woven), c. 10; 52 (PG, 34, 1027 D, 1147 B C). — According to Chrysostom, *In Hebr. hom.*, 17, 4 (PG, 63, 131) there were Fathers of the Desert who received Communion once a year or even once in two years. Further data in Hanssens, II, 301 f.

[5] Ambrose, *De excessu fratris sui Satyri*, I, 43 (PL, 16, 1304); cf. Dölger, *Antike u. Christentum*, 5 (1936), 232-247: "Die Eucharistie als Reiseschutz." Dölger also offers samples of abuses and faults that crept in with the custom of using the Blessed Sacrament as travel tutelage.— Gregory the Great, *Dial.* III, 36 (PL, 77, 304 C; see above, p. 323).—Later examples in P. Browe, "Zum Kommunionempfang des Mittelalters" *JL*, 12 [1934]), 177; Bona, II, 17, 5 (850 f.); Corblet, I, 527-535. After the 13th century the custom continues into the 18th century as a

dom and peace, the reception of the Sacrament was restricted to the divine services which had meanwhile increased in frequency.[6] About the fourth century, therefore, Communion of all the faithful present was generally an integral part of the regular course of the eucharistic celebration.

But then, with unexpected rapidity, the frequency of reception, at least in some countries, took a sharp drop.[7] Already Chrysostom, among the Greeks, complained: "In vain do we stand before the altar; there is no one to partake."[8] In Gaul, too, the Synod of Agde (506) found it necessary to insist on Communion three times a year, on Christmas, Easter, and Pentecost, as a minimum.[9] And this demand was repeated time and time again till the very height of the Middle Ages, sometimes with the addition of Maundy Thursday.[10] In the Carolingian reform the attempt was made to re-introduce Communion every Sunday, especially on the Sundays of Lent,[11] but the result was at best temporary.[12] From the eighth century onward, the actuality seems generally not to have gone beyond

privilege of the popes, for which there was a special ceremonial on their journeys. The Sacrament was carried in a sort of tabernacle upon a richly adorned litter, and had its own retinue of mounted clerics; Corblet, I, 529 ff. (with illustrations), Righetti, *Manuale*, III, 505 f.—According to Gabriel Sionita (d. 1658) it was at that time still customary among the Maronites to give people who undertook a dangerous journey and soldiers in war the Eucharist to carry with them. Hanssens, II, 500.

[6] A certain combination of the domestic Communion with the times of persecution is surely apparent in the following incident: When, in 510, a persecution seemed about to break out in the battle with the Monophysites, Bishop Dorotheus of Thessalonica permitted the Eucharist to be distributed in baskets, *canistra plena . . . ne imminente, sicut dicebant, persecutione communicare non possent;* Hormisdas, *Ep.* 102 (Thiel, 902); cf. Duchesne, *Christian Worship*, 249, n. 3.

[7] J. Hoffmann, *Geschichte der Laienkommunion bis zum Tridentinum* (Speyer, 1891); H. Leclercq, "Communion quotidienne": DACL, III, 2457-2462. P. Browe, Die Häufige Kommunion im Mittelalter (Münster, 1938); the same, *Die Pflichtkommunion im Mittelalter* (Münster, 1940); the same, *De frequenti communione in Ecclesia occidentali usque ad annum c. 1000 documenta varia* (Textus

et documenta, ser. Theol., 5; Rome, 1932). —The I Synod of Toledo (400), can. 14 (Mansi, III, 1000 D), forbade anyone to take the Eucharist with him out of the church. Also, according to Abbot Schenute (Schenoudi; d. about 451), the priest or deacon should not surrender to anyone even so much as a grain of it; J. Leipoldt, *Schenute von Atripe* (TU, 25, 1; Leipzig, 1904), 184.

[8] Chrysostom, *In Eph. hom.*, 3, 4 (PG, 62, 29); cf. *In I Tim. hom.*, 5, 3 (PG, 62, 529 f.); *In Hebr. hom.*, 17, 4 (PG, 63, 131 f.). Also Ambrose, *De sacr.* V, 4, 25 (Quasten, *Mon.*, 169), in attacking those who communicate only once a year, makes a side-remark: *quemadmodum Græci in Oriente facere consuerunt.*

[9] Can. 18 (Mansi, VIII, 327): *Sæculares qui Natale Domini, Pascha et Pentecosten non communicaverint, catholici non credantur nec inter catholicos habeantur.*

[10] Browe, *Die Pflichtkommunion*, 33-39.

[11] Browe, 29-33.

[12] The fact that Walafried Strabo, *De exord. et increm.*, c. 22 (PL, 114, 950), discusses the question whether it is permitted the faithful to communicate at every Mass even several times a day, is definite evidence of the frequency of Communion; he answers the question in the affirmative. Cf. also what is said below about the Communion chant; *infra*, p. 396.

what the Lateran Council of 1215 established as a new minimum: Communion at Easter.[13]

It was only in monasteries that the Sunday Communion continued to be the rule in the early Middle Ages,[14] and among the Cluniacs,[15] and Cistercians even later. But the lay brothers had to be content with a much more restricted quantity; for example, in a monastery as zealous for reform as Camaldoli, the lay brothers received only four times a year.[16] A similar rule was in force in the military orders[17] and quite generally also in convents of women.[18]

How could the eagerness to receive the Sacrament reach such a low state? And how could it continue even through a period we are accustomed to regard as the flowering period of ecclesiastical life, the central Middle Ages? Obviously the reason could not have been the lukewarmness and even coldness of Christians so often remarked upon, and admittedly on the increase since the earlier years of the Church. Otherwise, this regression would have been halted at least at the gates of the many monasteries which were borne on the crest of religious enthusiasm. Certainly the mass of those in the Roman Empire who, after Constantine, were converts for external reasons only, and who, therefore, were believers only externally, must have had a debilitating effect on religious life, just as among the Germanic tribes that were but superficially missionized a profound understanding of the sacramental life unfolded very slowly. But it is certainly surprising that this regression should be most noticeable in those countries where the struggle against Arianism had led to a one-sided stressing of the divinity in Christ and in the process had brought about a religious attitude which in turn produced in those very same countries—namely, in the Greek Orient and in the milieu of the Gallic liturgy—corresponding modifications of liturgical prayer and a novel form of language in respect to the Eucharist. The humanity in Christ, Christ's mediatorship which draws us to Him, receded into the shadows. The tremendous distance that separates us from God and the saints gains greater and greater power over the Christian mind in spite of the strong hold which traditional teaching had. It became customary to speak of the awesome table of the Lord, of the *mysterium tremendum*.[19] No wonder, then, that people hardly dared

---

[13] Browe, 43 ff.

[14] Browe, *Die häufige Kommunion*, 60-68; 74-77.

[15] At Cluny the monks could receive at least three times a week, and in some monasteries of the reform in the 10th century they could go to Communion daily. E. Tomek, *Studien zur Reform der deutschen Klöster im II Jh.* (Vienna, 1910), 204, 306 f., 315.

[16] *Ibid.*, 77; cf. 71 ff., 86 f.

[17] *Ibid.*, 84 f.

[18] Among the Benedictine nuns there were convents where Communion was received only three times a year, but then also, especially since the Reform Bull of Gregory IX (1235), some where it was received every month. Among the Poor Clares the rule required confession 12 times a year and Communion seven times. Browe, *Die häufige Kommunion*, 88-97.

[19] Cf. Jungmann, *Die Stellung Christi im liturgischen Gebet*, 217 ff.; Browe, *Die häufige Kommunion*, 152.

approach. Where the upheavals in the structure of liturgical prayer were least violent, namely in Rome, the ancient traditions of a frequent Communion, naturally connected with the celebration of the sacrifice, continued the longest.[20]

Since the early Middle Ages an additional hindrance to frequent Communion developed—the change of the penitential discipline. In contrast to the unrestricted—perhaps often too unrestricted—manner of an older Christendom, the *probet se ipsum homo* of the Apostle (1 Cor. 11:28) was soon explained not merely as demanding a preliminary sacramental confession for *criminalia peccata* but, with increasing positiveness since the tenth century, as requiring sacramental confession before each and every reception of Communion.[21] But in the Middle Ages, with the prevailing parish restrictions and the often insufficient organization of the cure of souls, not only was there no willingness, but to a great extent even no possibility to confess and thus to communicate frequently.[22] In addition, various cases of exclusion from the Sacrament were established in the spirit of the Old Testament purification laws, especially for married people and women.[23] And on the other hand, greater and greater requirements

[20] For the 7-8th century there is the evidence of the Roman *ordines*, which are concerned primarily with the stational services; but these were held practically every day in Lent. And there are other evidences along the same line. In the Gregorianum we find some of the formulas of the *oratio super populum* inserted in the 7-8th century, which presuppose the Communion of the people, even though, as blessing formulas, they would not necessarily contain any ideas connected with Communion; thus the formulas for Ash-Wednesday and for the Thursday of the first week in Lent; Lietzmann, n. 35, 5; 42, 4. Granted that these formulas were borrowed from older sacramentaries, yet their particular choice is remarkable, for only a small portion of the pertinent formulas in these sacramentaries makes any mention of Communion. Also according to Bede (d. 735), *Ep. 2 ad Egbertum* (PL, 94, 666 A), Christians of every age went to Communion every Sunday in Rome at that time. In 866 Pope Nicholas I, *Ep.* 97, n. 9 (PL, 119, 983), being asked by the Bulgarians whether they should go to Communion every day during Lent answers in the affirmative, provided they have the right disposition.

[21] Browe, "Die Kommunionvorbereitung im Mittelalter" (*ZkTh*, 56 [1932], 375-

415), 382 ff. Communion without previous confession appears as a matter of accusation in the *Confiteor* formulas. However, the first example thus cited by Browe: Alcuin, *De psalmorum usu*, II, 9 (PL, 101, 499 C), does not really seem to belong to Alcuin; see below, p. 368, n. 5.

[22] Browe, *Die häufige Kommunion*, 139-143.

[23] The reception of Communion on the part of a woman in her menstrual period was disapproved already by Dionysius of Alexandria, *Ep. can.*, c. 2 (PG, 10, 1281 A), and by the Testamentum Domini, I, 23 (Quasten, *Mon.*, 257). Jerome, *Ep.* 49, 15 (CSEL, 54, 376 f.), requires married people to abstain from their marriage rights for several days before Communion. According to Cæsarius of Arles, *Serm.* 44 (Morin, 189; PL, 39, 2299) married people, after intercourse, should in fact stay away from church for 30 days. Further references, see PL, 39, 2299, note a. A milder practice is advocated in the *Ep.* IX, 64, n. 10 (PL, 77, 1195-1198) to St. Augustine of England which is ascribed to St. Gregory the Great (see *supra* I, 98, note 35).—The penitential books required 3 to 8 days' abstention; see W. Thomas, *Der Sonntag im frühen Mittelalter* (Göttingen, 1929), 110.—The Pontifical of Narbonne (11th c.), in Martène, 1, 7, XIII

were set down for the preparation. A synod of Coventry in 1237 desired a previous fast of half a week for lay people. Elsewhere, six days' abstinence from flesh meat was required.[24] Whoever had not already acquired a high degree of perfection and was not supported by devotion of the most definite sort should, like the centurion, consider himself unworthy, rather than, like Zacchæus, have the Lord often lodge with him.[25] For people said to themselves—and herein a genuinely religious judgment of the problem is once more revealed—"from the frequent celebration a low esteem is sure to develop, but from the infrequent celebration grows reverence for the Sacrament."[26]

The eucharistic wave that passed over Christendom from the end of the twelfth century on, did indeed magnify the cult of the Sacrament, but not the frequency of its reception. On the contrary, the notion grew that frequent gazing upon the Eucharist could in some way replace the sacramental reception. The idea of spiritual communion developed. With an appeal to the Augustinian *Crede et manducasti*, this form of piety, when one turned with loving faith to Christ, contemplated His Passion with profoundest love, devoutly assisted at Holy Mass or looked up at the Sacred Host, was explained as a work scarcely less valuable than sacramental Communion itself.[27] In the later Middle Ages, the desire for sacramental Communion was regarded as a requisite for such a *spiritualis communio*,[28] in fact as its essential mark. At a time when frequent Communion was made almost impossible by exaggerated requirements, this desire must really have been a genuine one for many people.

A certain justification for the existing practice of infrequent Communion was found in the Middle Ages in the thought that the priest surely communicates and does so as representative of the entire community. This idea of a representative activity is brought out time and again,[29] and

---

(I, 893 D), prescribes, *ut illi qui defuncti corpus laverint, per septem dies non accedant ad altare nec corpus Domini offerre nec participare præsumant, quia lex Veteris Testamenti hoc prohibet.* Later on, such prescriptions were gradually watered down, but even as mere counsel they still exercised a great deal of authority; Browe, *Die häufige Kommunion*, 8, 19, 120, 153 f.
[24] Browe, *Die häufige Kommunion*, 146.
[25] *Ibid.*, 152-158.
[26] Peter of Blois (d. about 1204), *Ep.* 86 (PL, 207, 267 A).
[27] Browe, "Die Kommunionandacht im Altertum und Mittelalter" (*JL*, 13, 1935) 56-61.—A pertinent sample in the *Imitatio Christi*, IV, 10, 25. For a positive theological evaluation of the exercise under discussion see J. Auer, "Geistige Kom-

munion," *Geist u. Leben*, 24 (1951), 113-132.
[28] Browe, *loc. cit.*
[29] As Herbord, *Dialogus de Ottone*, II, 18 (Jaffe, Bibliotheca rerum Germanicarum, V, 761), reports, Otto of Bamberg (d. 1139) advised the newly converted Pomeranians to come to Mass frequently; in case they could not then themselves communicate, they should do it through the priest, *saltem per mediatorem vestrum sc. sacerdotem qui pro vobis communicat . . . communicate.* Berthold of Regensburg (d. 1272), *Predigten,* (ed Pfeiffer, I, 502), says of the communicating priest, "he nourishes his own soul and us all"; for all participants formed with the priest one body of which he is the mouth (*ibid.*, II, 686). Cf. Browe (*JL*, 13, 1935), 61, n. 61.—

there was even a tendency to put the idea into effect in other instances. A Trier synod of 1227 had to prohibit the practice of priests receiving the Body of the Lord in place of the sick.[30] Even the faithful—especially in convents of women—began somehow to practice such a representative Communion—Communion in place of someone else. Thus in the thirteenth century there are evidences of the practice of receiving or, to use a better term, "offering up" [31] Communion for others, especially for the dead.[32] So even this practice is one of the fruits of the infrequent Communion during these centuries.

Towards the end of the Middle Ages, other forces came into play, forces aimed at favoring and promoting a more frequent reception of the Eucharist. These new aims were decidedly encouraged at the Council of Trent and finally gained a complete triumph through the action of Pius X.[33]

So, in the two thousand years of the Church's history, we see two viewpoints the most opposite imaginable enjoying the field: on the one hand, the undiscerning confidence that he who by Baptism was implanted in Christ and accepted into the Kingdom of God, should also be allowed to regard the bread of heaven as his daily food; on the other hand, that feeling of reserve and timidity that looked more to human weakness than

---

Durandus, IV, 56, 1: it was decided because of human sinfulness that we receive the Sacrament of Communion three times a year *et sacerdos quotidie pro omnibus.* According to Ludolf of Saxony (d. 1377), *Vita D. n. Jesu Christi,* I, 37, 7 (Augsburg, 1729: S. 164) the Eucharist is called our daily bread *quia quotidie ipsum sumimus per ministros Ecclesiæ, qui hoc sacramentum percipiunt pro se et pro tota communitate.* — Cf. the reasons that Honorius Augustod., *Gemma an.* I, 36 (PL, 172, 555; *supra* I, 117, n. 81) alleges for the daily celebration of Mass.

[30] Can. 3 (Hartzheim, III, 527)).

[31] See the excursus on the offering of Communion in Browe, *Die häufige Kommunion,* 167-174, where, however, other reasons for its origin are sought.—From the ranks of the Beguines of Strassburg in 1317 we hear of one who gave the assurance that the Communion of a lay person would profit as much for the redemption of a departed soul as the Mass of the priest; *ibid.,* 166.— Post-Tridentine theologians make it clear that there can be question in the aforesaid practice only of the *opus operantis* of one's own personal devotion at the reception of Communion and the accompanying prayer of petition; *ibid.,* 172 ff. Moreover, from olden times a very similar

form of expression is found in the formulas of *Postcommunio,* where the prayer is said that this Communion (*sacramenta quæ sumpsimus, cœlestis participatio sacramenti*) may redound to the salvation of someone (e.g., one's departed parents); cf. J. Tschuor, *Das Opfermahl* (Immensee, 1942), 221-229, where it is correctly emphasized that one need not separate the Communion from the Sacrifice.

[32] The custom has had its effect on the liturgical books also; the Missal of Valencia, 1492 (Ferreres, p. XC) expands the Communion chant of the Requiem Mass with the words: *pro quarum commemoratione corpus Christi sumitur.*—Moreover, according to the principle mentioned above, the Communion of the Faithful was not customary at a Requiem Mass. It was still declared as inappropriate in 1630 by B. Gavanti; see the arguments in Thesaurus, II, 10, 6 (I, 319-323). L. Paladini, "La controversia della Communione nella Messe," *Miscellanea Mohlberg,* I (1948), 347-371, especially 354-356. The Congregation of Rites allows the administration of Communion at a Requiem Mass, even with previously consecrated particles, in the decision of June 27, 1868; *Decreta Authentica SRC.,* n. 3177.

[33] E. Dublanchy, "Communion fréquente":

to the grace-made dignity of the Christian, and which hindered even the pious from often approaching the holy mystery.

Aside from the state of grace, another condition was stipulated even in early days both for the priest and for the faithful: to remain *fasting* before the reception of the Sacrament. This requirement was already silently fulfilled in the ancient practice of taking the Sacrament "before every other food."[34] But by the end of the fourth century this condition was more or less explicitly imposed,[35] although some few exceptions were still granted, especially on Maundy Thursday, when the pattern suggested by the Last Supper was to be copied.[36] All through the Middle Ages the precept of fasting was not only strictly adhered to with regard to Holy Communion, but was even repeatedly prescribed for attendance at Mass (as in a synod of Brixen as late as 1453),[37] or at least it was counseled for Mass.[38]

DThC, III, 515-552; Eisenhofer, II, 309 f.

[34] This oft-recurring formula (see the references in n. 2) is understood by J. Schümmer, *Die Altchristliche Fastenpraxis* (LQF, 27; Münster, 1933), 108, only to the effect that the Eucharist should be taken as a protection against poison in the sense of a *prægustatio*, as the text of Hippolytus, *Trad. Ap.* (Dix, 58) certainly seems to indicate. So, too, J. M. Frochisse, "A propos des origines du jeûne eucharistique," *Revue d'hist. eccl.*, 28 (1932), 594-609, especially 595 ff. Even at present we are aware that the reception of the Sacrament should redound *ad tutamentum mentis et corporis*. This sort of consideration need not exclude the other, based on reverence. But with even greater necessity because of the undoubting faith in the real presence of the Body of Christ, which after all was the foundation of the practice, it had to include the further idea that priority be given to the Sacred Nourishment as such. Schümmer himself feels obliged to establish this in another connection (221) and to confirm it with a reference to the Jewish practice of not eating the paschal meal on a full stomach. And thus he concludes here that even at the time of Tertullian fasting was not only actual but considered obligatory. So also Dekkers, *Tertullianus*, 63. To bolster this opinion we might allege the further fact that even in pagan antiquity such prescriptions of fasting had to be observed when anyone intended to appear before the deity. Cf. R. Arbesmann, *Das*

Fasten bei den Griechen und Römern (Geissen, 1929), 72-97, especially 96 f.

[35] Indications in Basil, *De ieiun. hom.*, I, 6 (PG, 31, 172 B; in the Roman breviary on *Lætare* Sunday); Chrysostom, *In I Cor. hom.* 27, 5 (PG, 61, 231).—Gregory of Nazianzen, *Orat.*, 40, 30 (PG, 36, 401), emphasizes the point that the Eucharist is held not after but before the meal. Similarly Ambrose, *In ps. 118 expos.* VIII, 48 (CSEL, 62, 180).—Timotheus of Alexandria (d. 385), *Responsa canonica* (PG, 33, 1307 A); still the decision rendered by him has more than one possible interpretation; cf. Frochisse, 608.—Cf. also J. Burel, "Le jeune eucharistique," *La Vie et les Arts liturg.*, 9 (1922-23), 301-310; review thereof *JL*, 3 (1923), 138 f.—But by 400 the prescription appears in all clearness in Augustine, *Ep.* 54, 6 (CSEL, 34, 166 f.), who regards the Eucharistic fast as apostolic tradition observed by the universal Church.—Regarding history and canonical prescriptions cf. Anglin, *The Eucharistic Fast* (Washington, D. C., 1941).

[36] A. Bludan, *Die Pilgerreise der Aetheria* (Paderborn, 1927), 313 f. The Trullanum (692) rejects this exception, a proof for its long survival.

[37] *Sicut enim celebrans debet esse jejunus, ita et audientes, quia, ut canon dicit, simul cum ipso sacerdote hostiam offerunt.* (Quoted by Franz, *Die Messe*, p. 63). Cf. *supra*, I, 190, note 46.

[38] P. Browe, "Die Nüchternheit vor der Messe und Kommunion im Mittelalter,"

It has been left to our own day to make bigger and bigger inroads into the law of strict eucharistic fast.[39] After various concessions had been made in favor of the sick, the military, and those working night hours, the culmination of all such indulgence was reached on the feast of Epiphany, 1953, when, in a special Apostolic Constitution, Pope Pius XII, while restating the basic principles governing the law, promulgated for the whole world certain mitigations dictated by the changed conditions of modern society.[40]

12. Communion of the Faithful: Preparatory Prayers

As long as the Mass, throughout its course, remained a common celebration of both priest and people, there was no reason to think of other prayers for the Communion of the faithful than those they said with the priest, and the priest with them. The Mass itself moved on towards the sacred repast. This was true also of the ancient Roman Mass, in spite of the special poverty which its prayer-plan shows in the area of the Communion.[1]

But when, during the Carolingian epoch, the Roman Mass was transplanted to the land of the Franks, it was apparent that the Frankish clergymen did not feel at home in its rhythm. The result: attempts to readjust and build up the prayers, particularly in the Communion cycle. Even the faithful—in that thin layer of people who had mastered Latin—took an attitude towards the antique severity of the Roman Mass that could hardly have been more favorable than that of the clerics. So it is no surprise to learn that a large portion of the priest's new Communion prayers—those that he begins to recite in a low tone as he inserts them in his Mass *ordo*—are prayers of the faithful, or at least of the assisting and participating clerics and monks. The prayers which are still in use at the present, all of them, appear in this double role. The convergence is here more complete than in the parallel occurrence in the oblation cycle.[2]

Eph. liturg., 45 (1931), 279-287; Franz, Die Messe, 62 f.; Bilfinger, Die mittelalterlichen Horen (Stuttgart, 1892), 86-89.

[39] For the sick a concession by Pius X in 1906: Acta S. Sedis, 49 (1906), 499-510. A special grant for Russia: see Bouscaren, Canon Law Digest, I (Milwaukee, 1943), 202. Many favors during the war period (World War II), especially for the military and for those working on night shifts, the concessions differing in each locality.

[40] The Apostolic Constitution Christus Dominus of Jan. 6, 1953:AAS, 45 (1953), 15-24, with official instructions and commentary by the Holy Office, ibid., 47-51.— The most notable innovation was the declaration that drinking plain water no longer breaks the fast. See John C. Ford, S.J., The New Eucharistic Legislation (New York, 1953).

[1] Cf. supra, pp. 234 ff., pp. 279 ff.

[2] Supra, p. 46, n. 22; p. 54, note 60; etc.— Something similar occurs in the Byzantine rite where even now the faithful are directed to say before the Communion the same prayer Πιστεύω κύριε which the priest says quietly. Brightman, 396 b.

The prayer to God the Father that usually occupies the first place, *Domine sancte Pater*,[3] we encounter first in the prayer book of Charles the Bald.[4] Also the prayer *Domine Jesu Christe, fili Dei vivi* appears about the same time in private collections of prayers, amongst others in one version of the Communion Devotions of Monte Cassino (written during the closing years of the eleventh century), where it is used as a prayer after Communion.[5] It is also inserted in the Mass plan of the Alsatian monastery of Gregorienmünster (eleventh century), with the rubric: *Quando ad sumendum corpus et sanguinem dominicum accedimus, dicimus;*[6] it was therefore a prayer for communicants. The same is true of the prayer *Perceptio corporis*. In one instance it appears as a second formula, introduced by the word *Item*, under the heading: *Communicantes singuli dicant.*[7] For the prayers that follow in our order of Communion, parallels are to be found in the Missal of St. Lawrence in Liége (first half of the eleventh century), which contains the direction: *Cum aliquis corpus Christi accipit, dicat: Panem cœlestem accipiam et nomen domini invocabo. Item: Corpus D. n. J. C. sit mihi remedium sempiternum in vitam æternam.*[8] This latter is not the only sumption formula which has been appropriated for the faithful.[9] The *Domine non sum dignus* was already recommended to laypeople since the eleventh century.[10] As a matter of fact, it is found in the Communion Devotions of Monte Cassino cited above, as the last of the prayers spoken before Communion,[11] and since the thirteenth century the custom began in monasteries of reciting it in common before Communion.[12]

---

[3] *Supra*, p. 346.

[4] *Ibid.*, note 13. The book also contains (*op. cit.*, 116) the slightly changed oration *Quod ore sumpsi Domine*, worded in the singular, as a prayer after Communion.

[5] A. Wilmart, "Prières pour la Communion en deux psautiers du Mont-Cassin" (*Eph. liturg.*, 1929), 324. The prayer is also contained in several earlier collections: as the second of three prayers *ante communionem* in the collection *De psalmorum usu* (PL, 101, 508 C), made about 850 in an Italian monastery and later attributed to Alcuin (for the dating see A. Wilmart, "Le manuel de prières de s. Jean Gualbert" [*Revue Bénéd.*, 1936, 259-299], 265) ; in the *Libellus of Fleury*: PL, 101, 1408 A.

[6] Martène, 1, 4, XVI (I, 600 D).

[7] Salzburg Missal of the 12-13th cent.: Köck, 131. The formula appears here, as so often also in the priest's Mass-*ordo*, after the reception. The first formula, which all are supposed to say, is a sumption formula: *Corpus D. n. J. C. proficiat mihi ad salutem corporis et animœ in vitam æternam. Per.*

[8] Martène, 1, 4, XV (I, 593 D).

[9] Cf. *supra*, n. 7. A Missal of lower Italy from the 12-13th cent (Ebner, 346 f.) allots the sumption formula *Perceptio* to the communicants.

[10] Browe, "Mittelalterliche Kommunionriten" (*JL*, 15, 1941), 32, mentions these authors: Anselm of Laon (d. 1117), *Enarr. in Matth.* c. 8 (PL, 162, 1321) ; Bruno of Segni (d. 1123), *Comment. in Matth.*, II, 8, 25 (PL, 165, 141) ; Baldwin of Flanders (d. 1190), *De sacr. altaris* (PL, 204, 773B) ; Ludolf of Saxony (d. 1377), *Vita D. n. Jesu Christi*, I, 42, 8 (Augsburg, 1729: p. 190). Cf. *supra*, note 45, p. 356.

[11] Wilmart, 324.

[12] Browe, "Mittelalterliche Kommunionriten" (*JL*, 15, 1941), 32. That is why is said in convents of nuns *Domine, non sum digna*, which in turn on occasion was transferred to the words spoken by the

The Communion Devotions of Monte Cassino [13] gives us a good picture of the manner in which zealous monks prepared themselves for Communion. The *Ordo ad accipiendum corpus Domini* begins with Psalms 50, 15 and 38. *Kyrie, Pater noster,* and *Credo* follow, and then, in a free version, formulas of the *Confiteor* and *Misereatur*. After several versicles come the Communion prayers proper, addressed in turn first to God the Father, then to the Son, and then to the Holy Ghost.[14] Next follows the centurion's protestation, said three times.[15] After the reception of the Sacrament the Communicant says three times: *Verbum caro factum est et habitavit in nobis,*[16] and then the doxology: *Tibi laus, tibi gloria, tibi gratiarum actio in sæcula sæculorum, o beata Trinitas.* Among the prayers that follow we find, besides the *Domine Jesu Christe Fili* already mentioned, the prayer *Corpus tuum Domine quod sumpsi.*[17] A few other formulas present variations on the prayer for the purifying and strengthening effect of the Sacrament.[18]

It is astonishing that this group of prayers, which since the end of the Carolingian era had been transferred from the private sphere into the liturgical prayers even of the priest, after a few centuries played no special role in private Communion devotions. While the prayers in the priest's Mass *ordo* became more and more fixed, private piety in the pre-Gothic period took a new direction. By the eleventh century we encounter the salutations of the Blessed Sacrament [19] which even found a place in the Mass books [20] and which reached their climax in the elevation of the Sacred Host at the consecration. In connection with these a new mode of speech gradually broke through. No more is the Body and Blood of Christ kept in view, but simply Christ, who is desired and greeted as the guest of our souls. The fundamental tone is produced not by the phrase "Who eats My flesh and drinks My blood" (John 6:53 ff.) but by that other phrase "who eats Me" (John 6:58). As a result, the contemplation of Christ's

---

priest (*ibid.,* 31), thus, e.g., also in the Roman Missal printed at Venice in 1563: Lebrun, I, 556.

[13] First version: Wilmart (*Eph. liturg.,* 1929), 322-325.

[14] In the second version one prayer apiece to each of the Three Divine Persons (326) ; in the first are two formulas to the Father.—One part of the formulas is already dealt with *supra*. The texts in general show a tendency to sentimental elaboration.

[15] Only to the *sub tectum meum*. In the second version there is a long preceding prayer beginning with th same phrase, similar to the prayer mentioned above, p. 355, n. 34.

[16] Likewise in the Lower Italian Missal of the 12-13th cent. in Ebner, 347.

[17] The missal just mentioned in the previous note (Ebner, 347) has the communicating clerics say *Quod ore sumpsimus* and then *Corpus D. n. J. C. quod accepi.*

[18] Wilmart, 327, rightly emphasizes "une préoccupation morale" as a recognizable trait of these Communion prayers.

[19] Wilmart, *Auteurs spirituels,* 20 ff., 373 f. ; Browe, *Die Kommunionandacht (v.* below, n. 21), 49. The Sacramentary of Fonte Avellana (before 1325), without mentioning any other prayers, has the communicants pray together (*Ad sonitum patenæ hanc fratres orationem dicant*): *Huius sacramenti susceptio fiat nobis, Domine, omnium peccatorum nostrorum remissio. Per Christum.* PL, 151, 887 f.

[20] *Supra,* p. 352.

Passion, which had been brought to the fore in the allegorical explanations of the Mass, and (in general) the reminiscent preoccupation with our Lord's life and suffering, had their effect on the preparation for Communion.[21]

It is against this background that we must evaluate the appearance, towards the end of the Middle Ages, of a special series of prayers within the Mass for the case when Communion was to be distributed to the faithful. And as time went on, the rite thus inserted into the Mass became more and more identical with that used when Communion was distributed outside of Mass, as was necessary at least for the Communion of the sick and dying. This development had been preceded by substantially the reverse procedure. For the oldest rites for the Communion of the sick which we know of transported, as far as possible, the Communion part of the Mass into the sick-room. The *Pater noster* was said, with its introduction and its embolism, the kiss of peace was given with a formula corresponding to the *Pax Domini*, and then the Sacrament was presented to the sick.[22]

After the eleventh century, however, this rite for the Communion of the sick grew less common. It was broken up and various other elements assumed a more prominent role in it, especially a confession of sin and a profession of faith. Of course a confession of sin was long a part of the correct preparation for Communion, in fact fundamentally it was a part of it from the very beginning. But it did not always come right before the reception of the Sacrament.[23] In the prayer book of Charles the Bald the imperial petitioner is admonished: *Confitenda sunt peccata secreto coram Deo, antequam vestram offeratis oblationem vel communicetis.*[24] To be sure, at the Communion of the sick these requirements were of necessity drawn closer together. As one twelfth-century source puts it, the sick person should recite *suum Confiteor,*[25] after which the *Misereatur*

---

[21] Browe, "Die Kommunionandacht im Altertum und Mittelalter," *JL,* 13 (1935), 45-64, especially 53 ff.—The sublime meditations offered in the *Imitatio Christi,* IV, 6 ff., as *exercitium ante communionem,* are something very different.

[22] To be exact, certain formulas of the Gallican Mass survive therein; thus clearly in the Ritual of St. Florian (12th cent.), ed. Franz (Freiburg, 1904), 82. Still the pertinent section of the Roman Missal, beginning with the *Præceptis salutaribus,* was used, and even with a Fore-Mass preceding. Thus in the Pontifical of Narbonne (11th cent.): Martène, 1, 7, XIII (I, 892) ; cf. Jungmann, *Gewordene Liturgie,* 149-156. In the *missa præsanctificatorum* we have a form taken from the Com-

munion of the Mass and developed to a greater solemnity; see *ibid.,* 144-146. In the Orient the rite of the Mass of the Presanctified in its essentials was frequently used for Communion outside of Mass: Hanssens, *Institutions,* II, 99 f.

[23] Cf. above I, 18, 494.

[24] ed. Ninguarda (*v. supra n.* 22) 113; cf. also the Communion order of Monte Cassino, *supra,* p. 369.

[25] Ritual of St. Florian, ed. Franz, 82. Browe, "Mittelalterliche Kommunionriten" (*JL,* 15, 1941), 28 f., refers to other examples, among them one from the 11th century. Still the *Confiteor* is missing even in later documents; so in the older revisions of the *Pontificale Romanum* of the 13th century (ed. Andrieu, II, 493).

follows, along with the *Indulgentiam* (embodying the absolution)[26] and the rest of the Communion rite.

Already in the sources of the eighth and ninth centuries there is evidence here and there of a profession of faith made by the sick, usually in the form of the Apostles' Creed.[27] However, it never became a general practice. But when, in the eleventh and twelfth centuries, it was drawn into closer relation with the Communion, it again appears.[28]

Both elements were then transferred to the order of Communion at Mass. The liturgies of the religious orders in the twelfth and thirteenth centuries usually indicate the *Confiteor* before the Communion of the brethren.[29] Soon, in the form of the *culpa* or "open confession," it gained entrance into the parish churches, where it was generally recited by the entire congregation.[30] Since the thirteenth century we sometimes find, in some form or other, a profession of faith in the truth of the Sacrament, made before the Communion of the Mass.[31] It appears in the form of a

---

[26] Cf. *supra* I, 305 ff., 492 ff.

[27] P. Browe, "Die Sterbekommunion im Altertum und Mittelalter; 5. Die Ablegung des Glaubensbekenntnisses," *ZkTh*, 60 (1936), 211-215; cf. the Dimma Book (F. E. Warren, *The Liturgy and Ritual of the Celtic Church* [Oxford, 1881] 169); Theodulf, *Capitulare*, II (PL, 105, 222 C). —An example from the 13-14th cent. in Martène, 1, 7, XXVI (I, 948).—Also the ritual of the diocese of Schwerin of 1521 (ed. A. Schönfelder [Paderborn, 1906], 24 f.) demands the Apostles' Creed.

[28] Ritual of St. Florian (Franz, 82): *Ecce, frater, corpus D. n. J. C., quod tibi deferimus. Credis hoc esse illud, in quo est salus, vita et resurrectio nostra?* Rituale of Bishop Henry I of Breslau (d. 1319) (ed. Franz [Freiburg, 1912] 33): *Credis, quod hoc sit Christus, salvator mundi?* In an *Ordo* for the Sick from Gerona (about 1400) there is required from the sick person first a Christological profession of faith consisting of seven articles and then, after the prayer that accompanies the Kissing of the Cross, the profession of faith in the Sacrament; T. Noguer i Mosqueras, "Un text liturgic en Català," *Analecta sacra Tarraconensia*, 12 (1936), 451-462. Further examples in Browe, "Die Sterbekommunion" (*ZkTh*, 1936), 213 ff.

[29] Browe, "Mittelalterliche Kommunionriten" (*JL*, 15, 1941), 29. Only the Carthusians to this day have not accepted the *Confiteor* in this place, and likewise Do-

mine, non sum dignus. The Cistercians omit it when only the assistants communicate (*ibid.*).

[30] Browe, 30. There is evidence that at the same time a penance was imposed as in other analogous cases (above I, 493, note 18). See *Ritus communionis catholicus* (before 1557) of Duke Albrecht IV of Bavaria, as well as other accounts in H. Mayer, *ZkTh*, 38 (1914), 276 f. Confession of sins and the imposing of penance also in the Hungarian Rite of Communion of the 16th century; G. Péterffy, *Sacra concilia Ecclesiæ Rom. cath. in regno Hungariæ* (Pressburg, 1742), 240.

[31] In the *Queste del St. Graal* (about 1220) ed. Pauphilet 167 (in Browe, 24) one of the heroes confesses to the priest's question what he is holding in his hands, "You hold my Savior and my Redemption under the species of bread."—Browe, 24 ff., calls attention to the fact that often, specially since the middle of the 13th century, instead of a question pertaining to faith, a sermonette was delivered urging the people to religious and worthy reception. Still this address often takes the place of the customary sermon, or in convents is given on the day before (25 f.). In later times and into the 20th century the Communion addresses preceding the Communion, especially a General Communion, became indeed more frequent. They were declared permissible (as "fervorini") by decree of the Cong. of Rites, April 16, 1853: *De-*

question by the priest and an answer by the people, especially after the Reformers began to attack the Sacrament.[32]

A very happy method of making such a profession of faith was found when, in place of the questions about faith and the knowledge of faith, the more quiet and harmonious form we have in our *Ecce Agnus Dei* appeared. By its pertinent and pregnant designation of the Blessed Sacrament as the Lamb of God it takes up the message of the *Agnus Dei* chant which preceded. It can surely be put on a par with the *Sancta sanctis* of old.[33] The earliest witness to the use of these words before Communion seems to be the Synod of Aix (1585), where they were prescribed along with the accompanying *ritus*.[34] In order to attain their purpose as an acknowledgment of belief in the Eucharist they were often—even to very recent times—spoken in the vernacular, just as was done earlier with regard to the questions about faith, and even as was done with the *Domine non sum dignus* following. Quite a number of synods and diocesan rituals, even in the eighteenth century and later, both in Germany and France, expressly ordered this use of the vernacular.[35] Then this group of formulas, *Confiteor* with the accompanying words of absolution, *Ecce Agnus Dei,* and *Domine non sum dignus,* were introduced into the order of Communion in the Roman Ritual of 1614. There it was naturally given in Latin, and insofar as the Roman Ritual took the place of the diocesan rituals, this resulted in the exclusion of the vernacular. Now the *Confiteor*

---

creto auth. SRC, n. 3009, 4.—In rituals, printed texts for the purpose are provided; see, e.g., for the ecclesiastical province of Salzburg, in the 16th century, Mayer, *loc. cit.,* 277 ; for Constance, A. Dold, *Die Konstanzer Ritualientexte* (LQ, 5-6; Münster, 1923), 42 f.

[32] Thus, the Dominican General Chapters of 1569 and 1583 prescribed the following form for the Communion of the laity ; after the confession of sins the priest holds the Sacrament before the communicant, saying : *Credis hunc esse verum Christum Deum et hominem?* The communicant answers *Credo.* Then follows the *Domine, non sum dignus. Monumenta Ord. Fr. Præd. hist.,* 10 (1901), 239 ; Browe, 27. In the *Rituale Sacramentorum Romanum* (Rome, 1584), 297, composed by Cardinal Santori, occurs the question *Creditis hoc esse verum Christi corpus, quod pro vobis traditum fuit in mortem?* After an affirmative *Credo* there follows a second more general question. Similar questions in the Hungarian Communion Rite of the 16th century ; Péterffy (*supra,* n. 30), 241.

[33] Another case to the point is the expression with *Ecce* above in n. 28.

[34] Hardouin, X, 1525.—Lebrun, I, 556.

[35] Browe, "Mittelalterliche Kommunionriten" (*JL,* 15, 1941), 30 f. ; Corblet, II, 20. Thus also, e.g., for ages the *Manuale Sacrum* of the Diocese of Brixen ; the edition of 1906 precribes (p. 102) that the *Agnus Dei* be said first in Latin then in German, the *Domine non sum dignus* only in German, provided of course that Communion was administered outside the Mass. But the answer from the Cong. of Rites, July 4, 1835, to the Swiss Capuchins was different : *Decreta auth. SRC,* n. 2725, 5. According to the Synod of Aix cited above, the *Domine non sum dignus* could be said by the server instead of by the priest. There is a certain solemnity given to the *Domine non sum dignus,* as is reported customary among the Latin Catholics of Rumania, where on special Communion days it is sung by the choir and the congregation ; Kramp, "Messgebräuche der Gläubigen in den ausserdeutschen Ländern" (*StZ,* 1927, II), 360.

is to be recited by the Mass-server *nomine populi*, and the *Domine non sum dignus* is to be said by the priest.[36]

The acceptance of these prayers into the Roman Missal was a matter of course.[37] From what we have said we see that it was entirely in keeping with long usage. However, in our day, when we have learned to follow the procedure of the Mass from start to finish, we find the *Confiteor* especially a rather unnecessary repetition, since, even without considering the community type of Mass, every attempt to participate at the sacrifice demands from the very beginning the humble acknowledgment of sin.[38] At the Communion of the ordination Mass, the *Ecce Agnus Dei* and the *Domine non sum dignus* are wanting, and at the Communion of newly-ordained priests the *Confiteor* also is omitted.[39]

That these interpolations before the dispensing of Holy Communion could so easily succeed in gaining general acceptance during the last years of the Middle Ages is linked in some way with the fact that even from ancient times it was customary on occasion to stop momentarily at this place and use the sacred moment for important explanations. It is already recounted of Novatian that he exacted from his followers an oath of fealty before he let them approach for Communion.[40] In the early Middle Ages similar demands and explanations were customary when Communion was dispensed at a Mass which had been preceded by an ordeal.[41] From this, it was but a short step to consider the religious profession as a kind of sacred oath which was sealed with the reception of the Sacrament. An example of this sort is seen in French Franciscan circles in the year 1331.[42] In the Society of Jesus [43] it became an established institution to take the

---

[38] *Rituale Rom.* (1925), IV, 2, 1. 3.

[37] *Missale Rom., Ritus serv.* X, 6.

[38] Already in 1680, N. Letourneux, French preacher and ascetical writer, made reference to the unsuitableness of repeating the *Confiteor* and the *Domine non sum dignus;* see Trapp, 10.

[39] *Pont. Rom.*, De ord. presbyteri; in the case of the priests the reason given is: *quia concelebrant Pontifici.*

[40] Eusebius, *Hist. eccl.*, VI, 43, 18.

[41] P. Browe, "Zum Kommunionempfang des Mittelalters; 5. Die Kommunion vor dem Ordal und dem Duell," *JL,* 12 (1934), 171-173. A Missal of the 12-13th century from the neighborhood of Siena, in the *Missa quando lex agitur*, has this rubric; *sacerdos cum ad communicandum accerserit, ita adiuret eum: Adiuro te, homo, per Patrem et Filium et Spiritum Sanctum et per tuam christianitatem et per istas reliquias quæ sunt in ista ecclesia, ut præsumas es.* non ullo modo communicare, si cul-

pabilis es. Ebner, 254 f. In the plural form and with some elaborations in the Ritual of St. Florian (12th cent.), ed. Franz, 119; also in Franz, *Die Messe*, 214. Similarly already in two manuscripts of 9 and 10th centuries copied among others in P. Browe, *De ordaliis*, II (Textus et Documenta, ser. theol. II; Rome, 1933), 7.— As is apparent, the Communion of the accused also served as a means of ascertaining the truth. As a "Lord's Supper Test" it was of course encompassed with superstition. Essentially, though, it was a particularly solemn form of the oath of purgation; G. Schnürer, *Kirche und Kultur im Mitteelalter,* II (Paderborn, 1926), 54.

[42] General chapter of Perpignan, *Constitutiones*, III, 8: *Archivum Franciscanum hist.,* 2 (1909), 281.

[43] *Constitutiones S. J.,* V, 3, 2-4. (Institutum S. J., II; Florence, 1893, 89); I. Zeiger, "Professio super hostiam. Ursprung und Sinngehalt der Professform

vows a moment before receiving the Sacrament, an example which has been imitated in many later congregations.

13. Communion of the Faithful: Ritual Shape

Regarding the problem of the place to be occupied by the faithful when receiving Holy Communion, there have been various solutions in the course of time.[1] When all or a great part of those present communicated, the manner described in the Roman *ordines* had certain advantages: the faithful remain in their place, and the clergy bring them the Sacrament.[2] In other localities, as early as the fourth century, the faithful went up to the altar.[3] In Gaul that was the old traditional practice. The gates which separated the sanctuary (and consequently the place of the clergy) from the people were left open at this time; the faithful ascended the steps to the altar, a right which the Synod of Tours (567) expressly ratified,[4] and which was not curtailed till the Carolingian period.[5] After that it still remained at least the privilege of monks, and frequently also of nuns. It was seldom granted to the laity to receive at the main altar, as was the case with the Augustinian Canons according to a rule confirmed in 1116 for the foundation of Ravenna.[6] Usually lay people received Communion at a side altar where the Sacrament had been placed beforehand, or where a special Mass was said.[7] This was especially the case where (as frequently happened since the Romanesque period in churches with many priests) the choir was separated from the nave of the church by a high

in der Gesellschaft Jesu" *Archivum historicum S. J.,* 9 (1940), 172-188.—One often reads in the lives of the saints since the late Middle Ages how they made their final declaration in the presence of the Eucharist before receiving it as Viaticum; thus, e.g., St. Thomas Aquinas. In the same manner L. Ricci before his death on Nov. 19, 1775, the last General of the Society of Jesus before its dissolution, solemnly asserted in the presence of the Host his innocence and that of the Society; B. Duhr, "Lorenzo Ricci," *StZ,* 114 (1928, I), 81-92, especially 88.

[1] Browe, "Mittelalterliche Kommunionriten 4. Der Ort des Empfanges," *JL,* 15 (1941), 32-42.

[2] Above I, 73. In certain circumstances this method was to be found in use even later. At the place of pilgrimage Maria Luschari in Carinthia it was still customary in the 19th century for the priest to go up and down from the High Altar to the main entrance administering Communion: A.

Egger, *Kirchliche Kunst-und Denkmalpflege* (2nd ed., Brixen, 1933), 204, n. 3.

[3] The Council of Laodicea, can. 44 (Mansi, II, 571), certainly recognizes the custom, but rejects the approach of the women to the altar.

[4] Can. 4 (Mansi, IX, 793). Further data in Browe, 36 f.

[5] Cf. the restrictions regarding the Offertory Procession; *supra,* p. 9, n. 43. In Rome also, in the 9th century laws were made forbidding the laity to enter the presbyterium; Browe, 36. Through the IV Council of Toledo (633), can. 18 (Mansi, X, 624), it had already been decreed in Spain, *ut sacerdos et levita ante altare communicent, in choro clerus, extra chorum populus.*

[6] E. Amort, *Vetus disciplina canonicorum,* (Venice, 1747), 376. A rule of the Humiliati that originated about 1310 still permits men to enter the choir; Browe, 40.

[7] Cf. Browe, 40.

wall, the so-called screen. Here Communion was usually given at a transept-altar erected outside the screen.

In the North African Church of ancient times, and elsewhere, too, the method adopted was for the faithful to approach the rail which surrounded the altar. Augustine warned the guilty who had lost their right to Communion not to approach "lest they be sent away from the rail *(de cancellis).*"[8] A similar custom must have existed in the Orient.[9] During the Carolingian era, too, we find mention made of these rails. These rails, however, were not so low as those of today; they reached as high as the chest.[10] Consequently, the faithful were able to receive standing.

Since the thirteenth century it was customary here and there to spread a cloth (held by two acolytes) for those communicants kneeling at the altar.[11] Later on, in the sixteenth century, this cloth began to be laid over a table or a bench which had been placed before the communicants between the nave and the *presbyterium.* This was found very convenient for an orderly coming and going. Various synods now laid down prescriptions along these lines.[12] However, in place of table or bench, solid rails of wood or stone gradually came into use, but they were calculated for kneeling and hence were made lower—our Communion rail, which since the seventeenth century has almost everywhere taken the place of the former screen.

When the faithful go to Communion we say nowadays: They approach the Lord's table. This had never meant the Communion rail or any of its forerunners, but from the very beginning it always meant only the altar-table, the *mensa Domini* at which the Sacrament was confected, and from which it was distributed. Nevertheless, it still remains a splendid task for the church-architect so to arrange and align the structure mentioned as to trace the connection with the holy table which we actually approach when we kneel at the Communion rail.

---

[8] Augustine, *Serm.,* 392, 5 (PL, 39, 1712). —Cf. Zeno of Verona, *Tract.,* II, 30 (PL, 11, 476 B).

[9] Cf. *supra,* note 3.—Theodore of Mopsuestia, *Sermones catech.* VI (Ruecker, 36): to communicate at the altar was the privilege of the clergy. But cf. the example from Eusebius, *Hist. eccl.* VII, 9, cited above, p. 273, and the practice contested at Laodicea (above, note 3).—See also the provisions regarding the oblation of gifts, above, p. 9, note 43.

[10] Walafried Strabo, *De exord. et increm.,* c. 6 (PL, 114, 926 B), says that as a rule they are only so high that while standing one might support one's elbows upon them. J. Braun, *Der christliche Altar,* II, 660, gives the general height of these balustrades as 0.80-1.20 m. (2 ft. 6 in.—3 ft. 5

in.). The *cancelli* were then similar to those in any present-day court or chancery.

[11] *Ordinarium O.P.* (Guerrini, 247) ; *Liber ordinarius* of Liége (Volk, 99, 1. 18). In both sources the priest, who evidently does not carry the Pyx with the Sacred Particles himself, is directed each time to take the host in his right hand and to hold the paten in his left *supponendo eam hostiæ, et sic transferat usque ad fratrem communicandum.* The cloth mentioned before could according to the Ordo of Stefaneschi, n. 56 (PL, 78, 1172 B), also be the velum for the chalice.—Cf. also the teaching of the Mainz pastor Florentius Diel about 1500 to the faithful anent the Communion Cloth; *supra,* p. 16, n. 81.

[12] The oldest is from Genoa, 1574; Browe, 41 f.

That the Body of the Lord should be received kneeling is a custom which slowly and gradually gained the ascendancy in the West [13] between the eleventh and the sixteenth centuries.[14] Prior to that, it was the practice, as we have said, to stand while communicating.

The changes of bodily bearing are mirrored, amongst others, in the picturizations of the Last Supper. While the exegete must surely conclude from the accounts at hand that the disciples received the divine bread in the same posture which they had assumed during the meal,[15] art, delving into the very core of the matter, has preferred to sketch the event in accordance with contemporary Communion rites.[16] A Gospel codex of Rossano, which originated in Egypt about the year 500, pictures our Lord standing while giving His disciples, also standing, Communion under the form of bread.[17] In reverse, the Evangeliary of Bernward of Hildesheim (d. 1024) shows the apostle Judas receiving the Eucharist kneeling.[18] That this practice, however, had not yet become common everywhere can be seen from the statutes of the various religious orders in the eleventh, twelfth, and thirteenth centuries, which expressly prescribe it. For parochial churches in several dioceses it was not till much later that its introduction was recommended. Thus we read in a Paderborn memorandumbook printed in 1602 that the custom was to be introduced there *ubi commode fieri poterit*.[19] In the rite of the Roman Curia, on the other hand, it had become so firmly rooted as early as the fourteenth century that, as today, outside of the celebrant, only the bishop stood when receiving Communion at his consecration Mass.[20]

---

[13] In the Byzantine Liturgy to this day the faithful receive Communion while standing. The Gallician Ukrainians, who receive kneeling, are an exception.

[14] P. Browe, "Mittelalterliche Kommunionriten; 4. Aeussere Verehrung des Sakramentes beim Empfang," *JL*, 15 (1941), 42-48; B. Kleinschmidt, "Zur Geschichte des Kommunionritus," *Theol.-prakt, Quartalschrift*, 59 (1906), 95-109, especially 96 f.

[15] Mark 14: 18: ἀνακειμένων αὐτῶν. Cf. Matt. 26: 20; Luke 22: 14.

[16] Cf. E. Dobbert, "Das Abendmahl Christi in der bildenden Kunst bis gegen Schluss des 14th cent.," *Repertorium für Kunstwissenscraft*, 13 (1890), 281-292, with seven other articles to 18 (1895), 336-379.

[17] Illustration in O. Gebhardt-A. Harnack, *Evangeliorum codex græcus purpureus Rossanensis* (Leipzig, 1880), table 9 and 10; on the basis of photographs, with detailed description, A. Haseloff, *Codex purpureus Rossanensis* (Berlin, 1898), table 6 and 7, respectively pages 102-106. — Similarly the somewhat later Syrian Gospel Codex of Rabulas; O. Wulff, *Altchristliche und byzantinische Kunst*, I (Berlin, 1918), 294.—Pertinent pictures from later times in the work of Dobber, "Das Abendmahl," *Repertorium*, 15 (1892), 507; 509; 511 ff.; 517; 519; Braun, *Das christliche Altargerät*, table 10 and 41.—Literary evidence for the standing position in the West is supplied by the *Regula Magistri* that belongs perhaps to the 6th century; c. 21 (PL, 88, 988): *erecti communicent et confirment*.

[18] Dobbert, *op. cit.*, 18 (1895), 365.

[19] Brinktrine, *Die hl. Messe*, 267. Further data in Browe, 46-48.

[20] Ordo of Stefaneschi, n. 56 f. (PL, 78, 1172 B.D.). At the solemn Pontifical Mass the ministering Cardinal Deacon also receives standing; Brinktrine, *Die feierliche Papstmesse*, 36. The Pope communicates while seated, a custom for which there is

For evident reasons the standing position was the rule for the chalice Communion, and this position was retained also for the ablution wine.[21]

Apropos of the Communion which was received standing, the question arises, whether in this case there was not perhaps some sign of adoration or reverence connected with the reception. For the period which witnessed anew the increase in that eucharistic devotion which brought with it the change to reception while kneeling, signs of veneration could naturally be taken for granted. St. Hildegard had her nuns approach Communion dressed in white, adorned like brides, with a crown which displayed on the forehead the picture of the *Agnus Dei*.[22] About the same time, when the Canons of the Lateran went to Communion they all wore the cope.[23] In Cluny, they were still speaking of the custom practiced by the Fathers of approaching *discalceatis pedibus*.[24] Reverence was also shown by bodily movement. The *Consuetudines* of Cluny, written down by Udalricus about 1080, demand a genuflection before receiving.[25] Elsewhere it was cus-

---

apparently no evidence before the 12th century. Browe, 46.

[21] Browe, 44 f.

[22] Hildegard of Bingen, *Ep.* 116 (PL, 197, 336 C; 337 f.). The precise relationship of the dress described to the approach to Communion may be in some doubt, but it can be safely assumed to correspond. A MS. in the municipal library of Trier, about 1403, mentions among the relics of St. Matthias in Trier the "communion coronet" of St. Hildegard.

[23] *Ordo eccl. Lateran.* (Fischer, 12, 1. 15; 86, 1. 16). But when approaching there is a genuflection for the bishop (*ibid.*, 86, 1 22).

[24] Odo of Cluny, *Collationes* II, 28 (PL, 133, 572 C). Once again the custom was revived, in the 15th century, where a Low German "rule for lay people" originating in the Windesheim Congregation, demanded that the communicant lay aside his weapons and shoes; R. Langenberg, *Quellen und Forschungen zur Geschichte der deutschen Mystik* (Bonn, 1902), 96; cf. p. 145. Older data and explanation of the custom in Ph. Oppenheim, *Symbolik und religiöse Wertung des Mönchskleides im christlichen Altertum* (Münster, 1932), 96 f. The practice is grounded not only on a text of Ex. 3: 5, but also on the idea that one should strip oneself of everything that might remind one of death (leather from killed animals), when appearing in the presence of God. For that reason the monks of Pachomius before receiving Communion laid aside their leathern mantles and girdles. In this connection should be mentioned the baptismal robe of white linen; see F. van der Meer, *Augustinus als Seelsorger* (Cologne, 1951), 433. Concerning linen as cultural clothing see E. Stommel, *Münchener theol. Zeitschrift*, 3 (1952), 19 f.

[25] II, 30 (PL, 149, 721 B). This genuflection is also emphasized by Peter of Cluny (d. 1156), *Statuta* n. 4 (PL, 189, 1027 B). A preceding genuflection is verified earlier in the Orient, among the East Syrians already in the 6th century and also among the Greeks (triple genuflection) in the 10th century; Browe, 43.—Among the Cistercians, after the introduction of receiving in a kneeling posture, a *prostratio* was further required before ascending the altar; *Liber usuum O. Cist.*, c. 58 (PL, 166, 1432). As is known, the practice regarding these genuflections varies to this day. Even the prior genuflection in any event requires a strictly ordered approach. A genuflection after receiving Communion is not perhaps at variance with the rubric of today; but in the Middle Ages such a genuflection was not customary at all. Some Orders, like the Cistercians, required a bow after receiving. Browe, 44.—On the analogy of the present-day Roman rubrics, there is no other reverence *required* either before or after Communion outside the kneeling at the reception; see Th. Schnitz-

tomary to kiss the floor or the priest's foot.[26] A threefold inclination was already prescribed in the rule of St. Columban (d. 615).[27]

St. Augustine seems to have had something similar in mind when he remarked that no one partook of this Flesh *nisi prius adoraverit*,[28] but we find nothing further about a bodily gesture except that the faithful were to approach *conjunctis manibus*.[29] According to Theodore of Mopsuestia the communicant should draw near with lowered eyes, both hands extended, and at the same time he should speak a word of adoration, since he is to receive the Body of the King.[30]

A clear picture of the procedure at Communion in the fourth century is given us in the *Mystagogic Catecheses* of Jerusalem:

> When you approach, do not go stretching out your open hands or having your fingers spread out, but make the left hand into a throne for the right which shall receive the King, and then cup your open hand and take the Body of Christ, reciting the *Amen*. Then sanctify with all care your eyes by touching the Sacred Body, and receive It. But be careful that no particles fall, for what you lose would be to you as if you had lost some of your members. Tell me, if anybody had given you gold dust, would you not hold fast to it with all care, and watch lest some of it fall and be lost to you? Must you not then be even more careful with that which is more precious than gold and diamonds, so that no particles are lost? Then, after you have partaken of the Body of Christ, approach the chalice with the Blood without stretching out your hands, but bowed, in a position of worship and reverence, and repeat the *Amen* and sanctify yourself by receiving the Blood of Christ. Should your lips still be moist, then touch them with your hands and sanctify your eyes and your forehead and the other senses. Then tarry in prayer and thank God who has made you worthy of such mysteries.[31]

Most of the details found in the picture presented above are corroborated

---

ler, "Kniebeuge nach der Kommunion?" *Katechetische Blätter*, 75 (1950), 459-461.

[26] The Ordinarium of the Dominicans about 1256 (Guerrini, 247) rejects these customs and requires only the genuflection; likewise the *Liber ordinarius* of Liége (Volk, 99). Cf. Browe, 43 f.

[27] *Regula*, ed. Seebass (*Zeitschr. f. Kirchengesch.*, 1897), 227. Browe, who refers to this testimony (42 f.), also mentions two rules for nuns that are derived from it.

[28] Augustine, *Enarr. in ps.* 98, 9 (PL, 37, 1264).

[29] Augustine, *Contra ep. Parmen.* II, 7, 13 (CSEL, 51, 58, 1. 16). Similarly already the Passio Perpetuæ, c. 4, 9; see Dekkers, *Tertullianus*, 87 f. Cf. below, note 34.

[30] Theodore of Mopsuestia, *Sermones catech.*, VI (Rueker, 36). Extending or stretching both the hands clearly accom-

panies the more remote act of approaching while they are folded immediately before receiving, as Augustine also emphasizes. Cf. the row of approaching Apostles in the illustration of the Last Supper in the Codex Rossanensis (above n. 17), the one next to Our Lord bows, kissing the Lord's right hand, from which with both hands he has just received the Sacred Bread; the one following has his folded hands still covered, while the rest have them open and outstretched. One who has evidently already received the Sacrament, holds both hands uplifted in prayer. The illustration of the Chalice Communion parallels this every respect. Cf. the discussion of the picture in Haseloff, 102-106, who also claims to be able to see the folded hands of the one receiving.

[31] Cyril of Jerusalem, *Catech. myst.*, V, 21 f. (Quasten, *Mon.*, 108-110).

for the period of Christian antiquity not only by the texts cited before and by pictures and drawings, but also in many other sources:[32] the giving of the Eucharist into the hand of the communicant,[33] the placing of both hands together open and in cruciform,[34] the blessing of the senses with the sacramental species,[35] the admonition to take great care in handling them,[36] and the immediate reception of the eucharistic bread before proceeding to partake of the chalice. However, there are a few sources which advise the communicant to remain in prayer momentarily before the reception; one should keep in mind the power of Him whose Body is held in one's

[32] F. X. Funk, *Kirchengeschichtliche Abhandlungen*, I (Paderborn, 1897), 293-308: "Der Kommunionritus."

[33] F. J. Dölger offers the most important proofs for the first centuries; *Ichthys*, II (Münster, 1922), 513 f.; the same, *Antike u. Christentum*, 3 (1932), 239, n. 34; 5 (1936), 236 f.; see also Bona, II, 17, 3 (841-847). An early testimony in Tertullian, *De idolol.*, c. 7 (CSEL, 20, 36): the Christian who sacrificed to the gods, dares *eas manus admovere corpori Domini, quæ dæmoniis corpora conferunt . . . O manus præcidendæ!*—Dionysius of Alexandria, in Eusebius, *Hist. eccl.*, VII, 9, 4; Pope Cornelius to Fabius, in Eusebius, VI, 43, 18. According to the inscription of Pectorius the Christian should eat and drink ἰχθὺν ἔχων παλαμαῖς (Quasten, *Mon.*, 26).—The last clear testimonies are from the 8th century: *Capitulare eccl. ord.* (Silva-Tarouca 201): *pontifex . . . communicat populum qui manus suas extendere ad ipsum potuerit*: cf. Nickl, *Der Anteil des Volkes*, 65 f.—Beda (d. 735), *Hist. eccl.*, IV, 24 (PL, 95, 214 D). Later traces, but no longer unequivocal in meaning, in Funk, 298—In the Orient the witnesses for the extending of the hands continued until about the same time; it is still certified by John Damascene, *De fide*, IV, 13 (PG, 94, 1149).

[34] Theodore of Mopsuestia, *Sermones catch.* VI (Ruecker, 36 f); Trullan Synod (692), can. 101 (Mansi, XI, 985 f.), here also the prohibition to use a golden platter instead of the bare hands; John Damascene, *loc. cit.* Iconographic testimony in J. Stefănescu, *L'illustration des liturgies dans l'art de Byzance et de l'Orient* (Brussels, 1936), ill. 73, 75.—The extending of the hands discussed here is still customary in

the Byzantine Liturgy at the Communion of the deacon and at the reception of the *Antidoron* by the faithful. Pl. de Meester, *La divine liturgie de s. Jean Chrysostome* (3rd ed., Rome, 1925), 135.

[35] The custom is first mentioned by Aphraates, *Hom.*, 7, 8 (BKV, Select writings of Syrian Church Fathers [1874], 99). It seems to have originated with the Syrians, perhaps on the basis of Ex. 12: 7 ff. Cf. Dölger, *Antike u. Christentum*, 3 (1932), 231-244. A kissing of the Eucharistic Bread that one held in the hands is also connected with this; cf. *ibid.*, 245 ff. The "blessing of the senses" is found still today in the East Syrian Mass. After the priest has performed the fraction and consignation, he makes a sign of the cross with his thumb upon his own forehead and that of the deacons; Brightman, 292, l. 34.—Related customs took on new forms later on in the West in combination with the priest's ablution after Communion; see below, p. 418.—The application of the Eucharist as a means of protection and good health was not uncommon. Augustine, *Opus imperf. c. Julianum*, III, 162 (PL, 45, 1315) without disapproval, reports of a woman who made a compress with the Eucharist for her blind boy. Cf. the use of the Eucharist as a protection for a journey, *supra*, p. 360. In the Middle Ages these views and methods became more coarse and appear even for the purpose of business and profit. Since the 12th century the Church was obliged to take a firm stand against the abuse of the Sacrament for such purposes and even as a talisman.

[36] Tertullian, *De corona mil.*, c. 3 (CSEL, 70, 158): *Calicis aut panis etiam nostri aliquid decuti in terram anxie patimur.* Other passages in Quasten, *Mon.*, 109, n. 2.

hands, acknowledge one's own sinfulness and unworthiness, and praise the Lord *qui tale dedit tali*.[37] A prayer for this moment, first attested in the fifth century,[38] is still in use in Egypt today.[39] Only after this prayer had been said was the Body of the Lord received. In the West, too, the customary manner of receiving Communion in early medieval times was similar to this.[40] We see this more plainly in the Communion of clerics by whom the practice of taking the Communion in the hands was retained longest. At the papal Mass in the eighth and ninth centuries, after the bishops and priests had received the Body of the Lord, they went to the left side of the altar, placed their hands with the Sacrament on the altar and communicated; the deacons did the same on the right side of the altar.[41] The practice was not much different even in the pontifical Mass of the tenth century.[42]

The laity intending to receive Communion were expected to wash their hands beforehand.[43] It is not clear, however, if this washing of the hands was demanded only as needed or if it represented a settled ritual prescription: the latter seems probable, for it was customary since ancient times to wash the hands before prayer.[44] Be that as it may, in the plans for the great basilicas, a fountain was placed in the fore-court.[45] That it was not intended merely as an ornament is seen clearly from the fact that in front of St. Peter's Basilica in Rome, behind the splendid Constantinian fountain, a second, more modest one was erected by Pope Symmachus in order to satisfy the need.[46] In Gaul, the women were not permitted to receive the Body of the Lord in their bare hands, but were obliged to cover them with a white cloth.[47]

[37] Theodore of Mopsuestia, Sermones catech., VI (Ruecker, 37 f.).

[38] Testamentum Domini I, 23 (Quasten, Mon., 258) : *Sancta, sancta, sancta Trinitas ineffabilis, da mihi, ut sumam hoc corpus in vitam, non in condemnationem. Da mihi, ut faciem fructus, qui tibi placent, ut cum appaream placens tibi vivam in te, adimplens præcepta tua, et cum fiducia invocem te, Pater, cum implorem super me tuum regnum et tuam voluntatem, nomen tuum sanctificetur, Domine, in me, quoniam tu es fortis et gloriosus et tibi gloria in sæcula sæculorum. Amen.*

[39] In the Coptic Liturgy as a prayer that the priest says, and in the Ethiopian as a prayer that each one of the faithful should say as of yore after the reception and before the actual eating of the Body of Christ. Cf. the text of the prayer in the Arabic version of the Testamentum Domini (Quasten, Mon., 258, n. 3).

[40] Cf. the *coniunctis manibus* in Augustine, supra, p. 378.

[41] *Ordo* of S. Amand (Andrieu, II, 165; cf. 170).

[42] *Ordines* for episcopal Mass "In primis" and "Post quam" (Andrieu, II, 335, 361; PL, 78, 989; 994).

[43] Athanasius, *Ep. heort.*, 5 (from the year 333), n. 5 (PG, 26, 1383 A) ; Chrysostom, *In Eph. hom.*, 3, 4 (PG, 62, 28 f.) ; Cæsarius of Arles, *Serm.*, 227, 5 (Morin, 854; PL, 39, 2168) : *Omnes viri quando communicare desiderant, lavant manus suas, et omnes mulieres nitida exhibent linteamina, ubi corpus Christi accipiant.*—Cf. Benedict XIV, *De s. sacrificio missæ*, I, 12, 3 (Schneider, 73).

[44] Hippolytus of Rome, *Trad. Ap.* (Dix, 61; 65 f.).

[45] Cf. Eusebius, *Hist. eccl.*, X, 4; Paulinus of Nola, *Ep.* 32 (PL, 61, 337).

[46] Beissel, *Bilder*, 254-256.

[47] Cæsarius, *loc. cit.*—The same decision at the Synod of Auxerre (578 or 585), can. 36 (Mansi, IX, 915). This same small

Before receiving the eucharistic bread the faithful often kissed the hand of the one giving them Communion.[48] Even today the Byzantine deacon does the same before taking the sacred bread.[49]

In giving the Eucharist into the hands the danger arose that the Eucharist was sometimes misused. Spanish synods found it necessary to decree that whoever receives the Eucharist and does not eat It should be considered as *sacrilegus*.[50]

Even stronger than this worry about possible misuse was the influence of the growing respect for the Eucharist. Both together led to the practice of placing the Sacred Host in the mouth. Even though there may be some isolated instances of this practice in earlier times,[51] the method dates substantially from the ninth century.[52]

A general prescription of the Council of Rouen (*c.* 878) reads as follows: *nulli autem laico aut feminæ eucharistiam in manibus ponat, sed*

---

cloth is not to be confused with the *dominicale* that was prescribed for them over and above. This latter was a veil of some sort; cf. Funk, *Der Kommunionritus,* 296 f. The former, according to H. Melcher, *Bibel u. Liturgie,* 8 (1933-34), 247 f. would still be retained, transformed, in the white cloth with which First Communicants in some places hold their candles or carry suspended from their belts.

[48] Codex of Rossano, *supra,* note 17.

[49] Brightman, 395, 1. 2.—Modern commentators (Fortescue, 374; Batiffol, 289) in referring for this kiss to the story of the Viaticum of St. Melania, Dec. 31, 439, are laboring under a misunderstanding for which the editor of the Life is the first to be blamed; see M. Cardinal Rampolla, *Santa Melania Giuniore* (Rome, 1905), 39, and the commentary 257-259. The narrative reads as follows (c. 68): *accepitque eadem hora communionem de manu episcopi et completa oratione respondit Amen. Exosculatur vero dexteram sancti episcopi* . . . After the reception therefore there followed an oration like our *Postcommunio,* prayed by the bishop, to which Melania answered *Amen* (cf. Rampolla, 39, l. 21), and only then is mention made of the kissing of the hand, which was thus rather a kind of farewell; cf. *infra,* n. 5.— The kissing of the hand as Communion is placed in the mouth is verified for Cluny; Udalricus, *Consuet. Clun.,* II, 30 (PL, 149, 721 B). The Premonstratensians also prac-

ticed it. Regarding kissing the hand when the bishop administers Communion as at present, see above, p. 324, n. 17.

[50] Council of Saragossa (380), can. 3 (Mansi, III, 634); Council of Toledo in 400, can. 14 (Mansi, III, 1000). Cf. the later medieval practices discussed above.

[51] The well-known anecdote reported by John Diaconus (d. before 882), *Vita s. Gregorii* II, 41 (of a matron who laughed at the reception of the Sacrament from the hands of the pope, because she recognized in the sacred particle the bread she herself had offered, whereupon the pope immediately withdrew his hand *ab ore ejus*) will have to be eliminated from consideration; cf. above, p. 32, n. 2.—As the earliest examples from Gaul, P. Browe, "Die Kommunion in der gallikanischen Kirche der Merowinger-un Karolingerzeit" (*Theol. Quartalschrift,* 1921), 49, mentions some individual cases for the 7th century, which however could still be conditioned by circumstances (sickness). That Communion should be placed into the mouth of the sick is especially emphasized by the so-called *Statuta ·Bonifatii* (9th cent.), can. 32 (Mansi, XII, 386): *infundatur ori eius eucharistia.*

[52] A Synod of Cordova (839) inveighs against the sect of the Casians who resisted the practice of placing the Eucharist in the mouth of the communicant. C. J. Hefele, *Conciliengeschichte,* IV (2nd ed.; Freiburg, 1879), 99.

tantum in os eius.[53] The change of custom is contemporaneous with the transition from leavened to unleavened bread, and is probably related to it.[54] The delicate pieces of thin wafer almost invited this method of distribution, since, unlike the pieces of unleavened bread formerly used, they easily adhered to the moist tongue. At the synod of Rouen a further rule was established that at high Mass the priest was to give the Eucharist into the hands of the deacon and subdeacon as *ministri altaris.*[55] During the tenth and eleventh centuries this right was narrowed down to priests and deacons.[56] Then it disappeared entirely, although there are isolated accounts still of the laity taking the Sacrament into their own hand.

This manner of distributing the Sacrament removed the worry about the recipient's clean hands, and also the greater worry that small particles of the sacred bread would be lost or that something had to be done about purifying the fingers, as had become the custom for the priest. The Communion cloth later introduced and, since 1929, the Communion paten or plate[57] are expressions of further increased care in the direction mentioned.

Giving the chalice to the Christian people lasted longer than giving the eucharistic bread into the hand. Naturally, with regard to the chalice, there was even greater insistence in the warning not to spill anything,[58] but even with the best will in the world it was often of no avail. However, for centuries the Communion of the chalice continued unchanged for the laity, and even today such a Communion takes place in the Liturgy of the East Syrians and the Abyssinians.[59] All drank from the same chalice,[60] which was either the consecration chalice[61] or a special distribution chalice, originally called *calix ministerialis* in Rome. When necessary, several such chalices were used.[62]

---

[53] Can. 2 (Mansi, X, 1199 f.). Pertinent illustrations since the 9th and 10th centuries; Dobbert, "Das Abendmahl," *Repertorium,* 18 (1895), 365; 367.

[54] Cf. above, p. 12.

[55] Can. 2 (Mansi, X, 1199 f.).

[56] *Ordo "Postquam"* (Andrieu, II, 361; PL, 78, 994). Of the subdeacon it says: *ore accipiant corpus Christi.*—The later regulation in the Missa Illyrica: Martène, 1, 4, IV (I, 516 B).

[57] J. Braun, "Kommunionteller," *LThK,* VI, 108. In certain places the communion paten was already in use earlier. Two decrees of the Congr. of Rites of 1853 and 1854 treated of the matter: Martinucci, *Manuale decretorum,* n. 499 f. Moreover, a sort of communion paten was already used in Cluny; it was a flat, golden plate which the acolyte held as he accompanied the movement of the priest's hand when he dipped the particle into the chalice held by the subdeacon and then placed it upon the tongue of the communicant. Udalricus, *Consuet. Clun.,* II, 30 (PL, 149, 721). Cf. too, *supra,* n. 11.

[58] Hippolytus, *Trad. Ap.* (Dix, 59).

[59] Brightman, 241; 298.

[60] Gregory of Tours, *Hist. Franc.,* III, 31 (PL, 71, 264), reports that among the Arians one chalice was used for the *reges* and another for the common people; clearly such was not the case among Catholics.

[61] That is clearly the presupposition, e.g., in the minature of an Athos Manuscript of the 9-10th century; one of the communicants who has come forward is drinking from the large chalice that stands at the edge of the altar. Braun, *Das christliche Altargerät,* table X; cf. *ibid.,* 79.

[62] Braun, 247.

But with the use of a special Communion chalice they soon found another solution, a solution which in a certain measure lessened the danger of irreverence towards the sacred contents. A small amount of the Precious Blood was poured into a chalice which contained other non-consecrated wine. Evidently a custom of this kind must have been known in early times in the Orient.[63] Perhaps the Council of Laodicea had something like this in view when it forbade the deacon to "bless the chalice," ποτήριον εὐλογεῖν.[64] At any rate, this custom is to be found in the Roman *ordines* since the seventh century:[65] the acolytes held vessels of wine in readiness, into which, after the Communion of the celebrant, a part of the Precious Blood from the *calix sanctus* (which alone was allowed to be consecrated) was poured. This mixture could still be called *sanguis Dominicus*, as the third Roman *ordo* remarks, *quia vinum etiam non consecratum sed sanguine Domini commixtum sanctificatur per omnem modum.*[66] In the same manner the Communion chalice was provided for in monastic *Consuetudines* up to the twelfth century:[67] before the contents of the consecrated chalice given to the brethren were used up, it was permitted to add wine for the remaining communicants. The "sanctification" of the wine by touching the particle of the Holy Host to it was another practice, especially in the case of Communion for the sick.[68]

The Roman *ordines* bring to our attention a second prescription: the faithful are not permitted to drink directly from the chalice, but by means of a tube *(pugillaris)*[69] or reed, also called *calamus* or *fistula.*[70] For the

[63] According to the decision of James of Edessa (d. 708) a cleric, who, after the administration of the chalice, consumed from it the Precious Blood mixed with water was not considered to have broken his fast; see text and explanation in Hanssens, *Institutiones*, II, 303.

[64] Can. 25 (Mansi, II, 567). One could also conjecture the blessing with a consecrated particle. Andrieu, *Immixtio et consecratio*, 218; cf. *ibid.*, 10, also the reference to the St. Lawrence legend in Ambrose, *De off.* I, 41 (*supra*, n. 26).

[65] *Ordo Rom.* I, n. 20 (Andrieu, II, 103, 1. 7; PL, 8, 947 A). Even plainer is the description of the *Capitulare eccl. ord.* (Andrieu, III, 107): *per omnia vasa quod acolythi tenere videntur, de calice sacro ponit [archidiaconus] ad confirmandum populum.*

[66] Frankish extract from *Ordo Rom.* I (Andrieu, II, 249; PL, 78, 982 C); cf. Amalar, Liber off., I, 15 (Hanssens, II, 546): *Sanctificatur enim vinum non consecratum per sanctificatum panem.*—It is not neces-

sarily said that this *sanctificatio* is to be understood as a transformation into the Precious Blood; cf. *supra*, p. 316, note 27. —However, in England the wine taken after Communion by the faithful was called "housel-sipping," and the term "housel" (Old English *husel* = sacrifice) was the popular name for sacramental Communion; see E. Peacock (ed.), *Myrc's Duties of a Parish Priest* (EETS, OS, 31 [1868]), 70.

[67] Mabillon, *In ord. Rom. commentarius*, 8, 14 (PL, 78, 882).

[68] Also at Mass.

[69] *Ordo Rom.* I, n. 3; 20 (Andrieu, II, 3, 103; PL, 78, 939; 947); *Ordo sec. Rom.*, n. 14 (Andrieu, II, 225 1. 15; PL, 78, 976).

[70] Braun, *Das christliche Altargerät*, 240-265. The references in Braun, 254 f., show how reluctantly this tube or siphon was accepted in the land of the Franks. In fact the older Romano-Frankish *ordines* — Mabillon's *Ordo Rom.* III (Andrieu, II, 250) is merely an excerpt from *Ordo Rom.* I—make no mention of it whatever.

Communion of the faithful at the stational services a number of these tubes was kept on hand. They also seem to have served for the clergy, for besides the silver there are also golden ones.[71] The use of the tube spread everywhere from Rome; it even frequently remained in use in taking the ablution wine after the Communion chalice had been abrogated.[72]

In some places outside of Rome a third way was practiced: the Sacrament was given to the faithful in the form of consecrated bread which had been dipped into the Precious Blood and so was soaked with it *(intinctio)*. This method was first attested by the Third Synod of Braga (675) which discountenanced it,[73] just as happened later at the synod of Clermont (1096).[74] However, it must have been widely spread in northern countries,[75] especially as a method of making it possible to give Communion under both species to the sick.[76] In most of the rites of the East and especially in the Byzantine rite this is at present the ordinary way Communion is dispensed to the faithful.[77]

---

[71] Even today, as everyone knows, the pope uses such a siphon in the solemn papal Mass for his own Communion. Innocent III, *De s. alt. mysterio*, VI, 9 (PL, 217, 911 B) mentions its use in this respect. For the Communion of the bishop in the pontifical services, there is mention of it already in the *Ordo Postquam* of the bishop's Mass (Andrieu, II, 361; PL, 78, 994).

[72] Braun, 257 f.

[73] Can. 2 (Mansi, (XI, 155).

[74] Can. 28 (Mansi, XX, 818).

[75] Udalricus,*Consuet. Clun.* II, 30 (PL, 149, 721); cf. *supra*, n. 57. John of Avranches (d. 1079), *De off eccl.* (PL, 147, 37); he emphasizes that this method is applied *non auctoritate sed summa necessitate timoris sanguinis Christi effusionis.*—Ernulf of Rochester (d. 1124), *Ep. ad Lambertum* (d'Achery, *Spicilegium*, III, 471 f.), presupposes this method as generally in use, even if only *nova consuetudine*, and defends it. The *Liber officiorum* of Trier (middle of 11th cent.) and likewise Bernold of Constance, *Micrologus*, c. 19 (PL, 151, 989 f.), which both argue against the practice, the former putting it parallel with the morsel of Judas, give testimony to its wider spread. Franz, *Die Messe*, 374; 415; cf. also Bona, II, 18, 3 (872 ff.); Hoffman, *Geschichte der Laienkommunion*, 111 f.

[76] For that reason it was prescribed by

Regino, *De Synod. causis*, I, 70 (PL, 132, 206); Burchard of Worms (d. 1025), *Decretum*, V, 9 PL, 140, 754); Ivo of Chartres (d. 1116), *Decretum*, II, 19 (PL, 161, 165). The wide diffusion of this procedure is further certified through the frequency with which the following formula of administration occurs in the 11th and 12th centuries, *Corpus D. n. J. C. sanguine suo tinctum conservet...*; Browe, "Die Sterbekommunion" (*ZkTh*, 1036), 218 f.; Andrieu, *Immixtio et consecratio*, 136 f.

[77] The particles that have been dipped into the chalice and thus moistened with the Precious Blood are taken out by means of a small spoon and placed in the mouth. Among the Armenians this is done without the small spoon; Brightman, 573; cf. Baumstark, *Die Messe im Morgenland*, 164. This was the prevailing method of administering Communion in the Orient already in the 11th century; Funk, 304 f. At the same time in the Byzantine Liturgy, outside the sphere of the Union, according to the prevalent procedure the particles that are to be used for the Communion of the Faithful are not as a rule consecrated, so that only the Precious Blood is received, along with a symbol of the other species, the exact reverse of what happens in the Roman Mass of the Presanctified; Hanssens, *Institutiones*, II, 200-203. For further details regarding the Oriental Communion rite see Raes, *Intro-*

Since the twelfth century the chalice Communion was discontinued more and more in the West.[78] Developments in dogma which led to a clearer understanding that *per concomitantiam* the entire Christ is present under both species seemed to have been decisive in bringing this about.[79] The command of Christ, "Eat and drink," could be regarded as fulfilled by the priest who stands at the altar as head of the congregation.[80] In fact Communion under one species was not unknown even in earlier times. Communion was given to infants and young children after Baptism under the form of wine.[81] Occasionally, too, this was done in the case of those mortally sick.[82] In Communion at home, of course, only the form of bread was generally under consideration.[83]

At the time the *Summa theologica* of St. Thomas (d. 1274) was being completed, the chalice Communion had not as yet disappeared everywhere, for the author mentions the practice of not giving the Precious Blood to the people and of having the priest alone consume it, and he qualifies the practice merely as the well-founded custom of some churches.[84] On special occasions the lay chalice was still retained in the fourteenth century and even later, as at the coronation of emperors and kings,[85] and at the Easter-Sunday Mass at the *Capella papalis*,[86] where *quicumque voluerit vere confessus et pœnitens* was permitted to communicate in this

---

ductio, 103-107; L. Corciani, *Eph. liturg.*, 58 (1944), 197 f.

[78] Funk, 306-308; Corblet, I, 613-619.

[79] Cf. *supra*, I, 118.

[80] Cf. *supra*, p. 364, with n. 29.

[81] Cyprian, *De lapsis*, c. 25 (CSEL, 3, 255). Further evidence from early times, see Eisenhofer, II, 265 f.—J. Baumgärtler, *Die Erstkommunion* (Munich, 1929), 30 ff., thinks the Baptismal Communion of children did not originate till about the time of Augustine; cf. to the contrary *ZkTh*, 54 (1930), 627 f. For the Middle Ages see the chapter "Die Taufkommunion" in Browe, *Die Pflichtkommunion im Mittelalter*, 129-142.—The Baptismal Communion went out of use by the 12th century. But the memory of it lingered for a long time in the administration of the wine of ablution; see below.—In the Oriental Rites, outside the sphere of the Union, the Baptismal Communion is still administered to this day; see Baumgärtler, 87-89; 100; 124 f. Among oriental Catholics it is still practiced by the Copts; L. Andrieux, *La Première Communion* (Paris, 1911), 73-77.

[82] Statuta eccl. antiqua (6th cent.), can. 76 (Mansi, III, 957): *Infundatur ori eius eucharistia*. Later on, the effort was gen-

erally made to preserve the double form by means of the *intinctio*; cf. Browe, "Die Sterbekommunion" (*ZkTh*, 1936), 218 ff.

[83] Cf. *supra*, p. 384; *Hoffmann, Geschichte der Laienkommunion*, 76 f.

[84] St. Thomas, *Summa theol.*, III, 80, 12: *In quibusdam ecclesiis.*—Cf., e.g., a Mass-ordo of lower Italy of the 12-13th century in Ebner, 346 f.; this presents a special formula *ad confirmandum* for the administration of Communion to the people: *Sanguis D. n. J. C.*—The Synod of Exeter (1287), can. 4 (Mansi, XXIV, 789) desires the faithful, moreover, to be taught: *hoc suscipiunt in calice quod effusum de corpore Christi*.

[85] Browe, "Zum Kommunionempfang des Mittelalters, 3. Die Kommunion bei der Krönung der Kaiser und Könige," JL, 12 (1934), 166-169). In France the tradition continued unbroken until Louis XIV (168 f.), in Germany, with an interruption in the 15-16th century, until Francis II (168).

[86] Ordo of Petrus Amelii, n. 85 (PL, 78, 1331 f.). Martin V did away with the practice; see the report in Gerbert, *Vetus liturgia alemannica*, 393.

way. Also in some monasteries of the old orders the chalice Communion was still retained for a long time, in part even beyond the Middle Ages.[87] A certain reminder of this is seen in the ablution chalice which remained customary in part until the last centuries.[88]

When the chalice Communion was already practically forgotten, it was seized upon by hostile groups and made a symbol of their movement. Thereupon, after first being forbidden,[89] the lay chalice was granted in 1433 for Bohemia. After the Council of Trent, the use of the chalice was granted for Germany, under certain specified conditions, but after some unhappy experiences the concession was withdrawn, for Bavaria in 1571, for Austria in 1584, and for Bohemia and in general, in 1621.[90]

According to ancient tradition it was the deacon who passed the chalice at solemn services.[91] Evidences for this are found as early as the third century.[92] In the Roman liturgy this arrangement is clearly witnessed by the Roman *Ordines* and their offshoots.[93] In the oldest descriptions, those in Justin, it was the principal task of the deacons to distribute the Eucharist,[94] and likewise to bring it to the absent.[95] Of this office of theirs a

---

[87] Browe, *Die häufige Kommunion*, 51 f.
[88] *Infra*, p. 413 f.
[89] Council of Constance (1415), sess. 13 (Mansi, XXVII, 727 f.) ; Council of Basle (1437), sess. 30 (Mansi, XXIX, 158).
[90] A. Herte, "Kelchbewegung" : *LThK*, V, 920 f. ; Hoffmann, *Geschichte der Laienkommunion*, 189-209. See also P. J. Toner, "Communion under Both Kinds," *CE*, 4, 175 ff., especially 178-179.
[91] In later times he stood by on the gospel side of the altar, while the priest administered the species of bread on the epistle side. Thus, among others, in the old rite of the Cistercians; Schneider (*Cist.-Chr.*, 1927), 196 f.
[92] Cyprian, *De lapsis*, c. 25 (CSEL, 3, 255 Z. 15) ; Augustine, *Serm.*, 304, 1 (PL, 38, 1395) ; *Const. Ap.*, VIII, 13, 15 (Quasten, *Mon.*, 230) ; Testamentum Domini, II, 10 (Quasten, *Mon.*, 273) ; Johannes Moschus, *Pratum spirituale*, c. 219 (PG, 87, 2109 C).
[93] *Ordo Rom.* I, n. 20 (Andrieu, II, 103 f. ; PL, 78, 947), etc.—The deacon still appears as administering the chalice Communion (in monasteries) in a 15th century Missal from Monte Vergine: Ebner, 157. Cf. the parallel function of the deacon at the Offertory, above, I, 71; 11.
[94] See above, I, 22 f. Also according to Isidore of Seville, *De eccl. off.*, II, 8, 4 (PL, 83, 789), the *dispensatio sacramenti* is sim-

ply the deacons' duty. According to Hippolytus, *Trad. Ap.* (Dix, 41), on the contrary, their work is to handle the chalice and that only if there are not enough presbyters present.
[95] In a way it is not surprising that lay people, under circumstances, took Communion to the sick, as did the lad during the time of Dionysius of Alexandria, who brought it to the aged Serapion (Eusebius, *Hist. eccl.*, VI, 44). In the Roman pontifical services acolytes appear as carriers of the Eucharist, though by no means as administrators; (see above). But in the Lateran Basilica in the 11th century we see even subdeacons administering Communion (*Ordo eccl. Lateran.*, ed. Fischer, 86, 1. 29). At the Synod of Nîmes (394) can. 2 (C. J. Hefele, *Conciliengeschichte*, II [2nd ed.; Freiburg, 1875], 62) and in episcopal and papal decrees in the time thereafter, among others even at the Synod of Paris (829), can. 5 (Mansi, XIV, 565), reference is made to the not infrequent abuse of women administering Communion. There seems too have been question chiefly of Viaticum, which ought to be administered at the last moment and which the pastor then, in given circumstances, entrusted for the specific purpose to someone in the house; see the warning in the Admonitio Synodalis of the 9th century (PL, 96, 1376 C). Browe, "Die Sterbe-

remnant is found even today. At the ordination to diaconate the bishop calls the deacons *comministri et cooperatores corporis et sanguinis Domini*,[96] and the *Codex Iuris Canonici* still describes the deacon as *minister extraordinarius sacræ communonis*.[97]

The connection between the office of deacon and the Sacrament was, for that matter, even closer during the Middle Ages, since it was taken for granted that at solemn high Mass he should communicate himself, a right that is still his among the Greeks and Armenians,[98] and which the subdeacon also enjoyed. In this connection the Communion chalice also survived,[99] especially in many French monasteries. At St. Denis, even as late as 1760, the deacon and subdeacon received under both species on all Sundays and feast days during the high Mass at which they served.[100] In other places, in old foundations and cathedrals, the same custom was still observed at least as late as the twelfth century.[101]

---

kommunion" (*ZkTh*, 1936), 7 ff. Still there are available statements and accounts from England until the 13th century which are milder in their judgment of this case; Browe, 11 f. Not a few theologians still later favor a mild decision; see Corblet, I, 286, n. 2. In the Orient, too, the practice was less strict. According to the Synod *in Trullo* (692), can. 58 (Mansi, XI, 969) it was permissible for a lay person to administer Communion, if no priest, bishop, or deacon were present. Among the West Syrian Jacobites, deaconesses in convents of nuns in similar circumstances were permitted to administer Communion to their fellow Sisters and to little children, not indeed directly from the altar, but from a special container; C. Kayser, *Die Kanones Jakobs von Edessa* (1886), 19; Browe, 11, n. 65.—For the sake of convenience also in later times lay people were permitted on occasion to bring Communion to the sick. Various prohibitions are directed against this practice. Such a one appears, e.g., in the collection of Canons of Bishop Ruotger of Trier (927), can. 6 (*Pastor bon.*, 52 [1941], 67): pastors should not permit Communion to be brought to the sick *per rusticos et immundos, sicut fieri solet*, but should either bring it themselves or *per clericos suos;* see also Decretum Gratiani, III, 2, 29 (Freidberg, I, 1323 f.); cf. Browe, 9-11.

[96] *Pontificale Rom.*, De ord. diaconi.

[97] Can. 845, § 2. In the note the connection is made with the old law. Evidences since

the 4th century for the restriction of this right of the deacons to cases when no priest is present, in Martène, 1, 4, 10, 5 (I, 431 C). Cf., too, Corblet I, 283.

[98] Baumstark, *Die Messe im Morgenland*, 162.

[99] At times only the deacon was permitted the chalice Communion; thus in the 13th century among the Carthusians, where, however, since 1259 it was entirely abrogated. Browe, *Die häufige Kommunion*, 51.—Earlier also in the Communion rite a distinction was often made between deacon and subdeacon. Thus the Sacramentary of Ratoldus (d. 986) (PL, 78, 245 A), decrees that the bishop administer Communion to priest and deacons *sicco sacrificio*, to subdeacons *misto sacrificio*, that is, the former receive the Precious Blood separately from the chalice, while the latter, like the faithful, together with the host by means of the *intinctio*. Deacons also retained for a longer time the right to receive the Host in their hand; see above n. 56.—Among the oldest *Ordines* only that of S. Amand (Andrieu, II, 166) makes any pertinent statement: while the deacons communicate at the altar just as the bishops and priests (above, p. 380), the subdeacons do so only after the Communion of the people, and no special rite is mentioned in their regard.

[100] Browe, *Die häfige Kommunion*, 52. Cf. the information from the 18th century in de Moléon 149; 263; 290 f.

[101] Browe, 53.

The distribution of the Sacrament was accompanied with corresponding words even in the early Christian era. The ordinary form of distribution was Σῶμα Χριστοῦς,[102] *Corpus Christi.*[103] This had the significance of a profession, as the Arabic *Testamentum Domini* explicitly indicates when it describes the formula: *unicuique, cum panem gratiarum actionis participat, sacerdos testimonium perhibeat id esse corpus Christi.*[104] Hence special stress was laid upon the recipient's answer of *Amen.*[105] The same was repeated with the chalice,[106] where, however, the formula was often expanded: Αἷμα Χριστοῦ ποτήριον ζωῆς. [107] Also when giving the species of bread, expanded formulas were in use at an early period.[108] Such expanded versions are also seen in the later oriental liturgies. Reverential epithets were added, as in the Greek liturgy of St. Mark: Σῶμα ἅγιον (resp. Αἷμα τίμιον) τοῦ κυρίου καὶ θεοῦ καὶ σωτῆρος ἡμῶν Ἰησοῦ Χριστοῦ.[109] Besides this, where possible, the recipient was even mentioned by name,[110] and when the occasion demanded, with his ecclesiastical title, as in the

---

[102] *Const. Ap.*, VIII, 13, 15 (Quasten, *Mon.*, 320); Theodore of Mopsuestia, *Sermones catech.*, VI (Ruecker, 37).

[103] Ambrose, *De sacr.*, IV, 5, 25 (Quasten, *Mon.*, 161); Augustine, *Serm.* 272 (PL, 38, 1247); cf. Roetzer, 133.

[104] A. Baumstark, "Ein ägyptische Mess- und Taufliturgie vermutlich des 6 Jh." (*Oriens christ.*, 1901), 29; Quasten, *Mon.*, 258, n. 1.

[105] In all the passages named. The Mystagogical Catecheses of Cyril of Jerusalem, V, 21 (Quasten, *Mon.*, 108 f.) and the Syrian *Testamentum Domini*, I, 23 (*ibid.*, 258) verify only this *Amen;* likewise already Pope Cornelius according to Eusebius, *Hist. eccl.*, VI, 43, 19. Augustine also mentions repeatedly only the *Amen* of the recipient. Further data in Bona, II, 17, 3 (842 f.). As Odilo Heiming, *Liturgie und Mönchtum*, 3 (1949), 84, notes, Milan has lately been permitted to resume the old formula for distribution, *Corpus Christi*, to which each one replies, *Amen.*

[106] Theodore of Mopsuestia, *loc. cit.;* the Arabian Testamentum Domini (Baumstark, *loc. cit.*, 29).

[107] *Const. Ap.*, VII, 13, 15 (Quasten, *Mon.*, 230 f.); similarly the Sahidic Ecclesiastical Canons: Brightman, 462.

[108] Hippolytus, *Trad. Ap.* (Dix, 41): *Panis cœlestis in Christo Jesu;* the chailce formula is modified because of the three chalices (above I, 15). The formula mentioned is expanded in the baptismal Mass

of the Sahidic Ecclesiastical Canons (Brightman, 464): "This is the bread of heaven, the body of Christ Jesus." Likewise in the Ethiopian anaphora of the Apostles of the Abyssinian Jacobites (Brightman, 240 f.): "The bread of life, which came down from heaven, the body of Christ." In the Canons of Basil, c. 97 (Riedel, 275): "This is the body of Christ that He offered for our sins." Marcus Eremita, *Contra Nestorianos*, c. 24 (Brightman, p. CIV to p. 523) testifies in 430 to the formula Σῶμα ἅγιον Ἰησοῦ χριστοῦ εἰς ζωὴν αἰώνιον.

[109] Brightman, 140. A laudatory character of a different sort is found in the Ethiopian formulas, several of which are generally used together. Brightman, 240 f. with the notes; in the anaphora of Our Lord: "The body of Jesus Christ, which is of the Holy Ghost, to hallow soul and spirit"; in the anaphora of the Elders: "The holy body of Emmanuel our very God which He took of the Lady of us all."

[110] This naming of the recipient is also in that East Syrian Mass, where the formula in Brightman, 298, is given again, "The Body of Our Lord to the discreet priest (or: to the deacon of God, or: to the circumspect believer) for the pardon of offenses." It seems to be a question of a general Syrian tradition both in the matter of naming the recipient and in the solicitous petition made in his regard; cf. the formula among the West Syrian Jacobites, *ibid.*,

Byzantine Mass, where, as also with the Syrians,[111] the wish was added: "For the forgiveness of his sins and unto eternal life." [112] Or the profession character of the formula was underlined, as with the Coptic: "This is in truth the Body and Blood of Emmanuel, our Lord," whereupon the communicant answered: "Amen. I believe." [113]

In the liturgy of the city of Rome in the early Middle Ages the old tradition of handing out the sacramental species with a corresponding phrase seems to have been broken. Not only are the sacramentaries silent about this, but also the *ordines* which faithfully give us the words for the commingling, *Fiat commixtio*, which are about on a par. What later appears among the Franks is not the ancient profession, "The Body of Christ," which demands the actualizing *Amen* of the communicant, but instead is a blessing which is said, in general, only by the priest.[114] Perhaps we have a link which represents the connection with the old form of distribution; according to some sources the newly-baptized child was given the Sacrament with the words: *Corpus D. n. J. C. in vitam œternam.*[115]

The basic form of this blessing, from which the later formularies branch off and which reaches back to the eighth century,[116] seems to have been as follows: *Corpus et sanguis D. n. J. C. custodiat te in vitam œternam.*[117]

---

103 f.—In the Armenian formulary (*ibid.*, 452) the Syrian and Roman methods seem to be joined.

[111] Preceding note.

[112] Brightman, 395 f.: Μεταλαμβάνει ὁ δοῦλος τοῦ θεοῦ N. τὸ τίμιον καὶ ἅγιον σῶμα καὶ αἷμα . . . .

[113] Brightman, 186.—The *Amen* of the recipient is also mentioned in the Ethiopian liturgy and in the West Syrian liturgy of the Jacobites by an explicit rubric (*ibid.*, 421).

[114] The *Amen* would indeed be apposite, in view of the prayer for blessing, and in fact is generally, though not always, joined to the expression in the manuscripts. But that, as a rule it was said by the priest and not (as is still done today after ordination to subdiaconate and diaconate) by the recipient, was quite to be expected, once Communion began to be administered to the mouth. If the recipient is still to say the *Amen*, then, as is self- evident, it must be said before receiving the Sacrament. In some French churches in the 18th century the faithful were required to say this *Amen;* de Moléon, 216; 246.

[115] Sacramentary of Gellone (about 770-780): Martène, 1, 1, 18, VII (I, 188 B); Baptism-*ordo* from M.-Gladbach: *ibid.*, XIV (I, 204 D). But other parallel

sources have: . . . *sit tibi in vitam œternam*: *ibid.*, V (I, 183 C).

[116] A unique formula of similar antiquity appears in the Communion of the Sick in the Celtic Dimma Book (8-9th cent.) *Corpus et Sanguis D. n. J. C. Filii Dei vivi conservat animam tuam in vitam perpetuam;* F. E. Warren, *The Liturgy and Ritual of the Celtic Church* (Oxford, 1881), 170. Later administering formularies for Viaticum in Browe, "Die Sterbekommunion" (*ZkTh*, 1936), 220 f.

[117] Cf. Theodulf of Orleans, *Capitulare,* II (PL, 105, 222 C), where the formula reads: *Corpus et sanguis Domini sit tibi remissio omnium peccatorum tuorum et custodiat te in vitam œternam.* It is therefore already amalgamated with a second formula. Stowe Missale (in the beginning of the 9th cent.), ed. Warner (HBS, 32), 32: *Corpus et sanguis D. n. J. C. sit tibi in vitam œternam.* In the Sacramentary of S. Thierry (end of the 10th cent.): Martène, 1, 4, X (I, 551 E), the basic form above is presented with the variation *animam tuam* for *te.* The same wording appears as the formula at the combined administering of both species in the Sacramentary of S. Remy-Reims (according to Andrieu, 10th cent., note 800; PL, 78, 539 B). But in the separate administering

We meet similar forms after the ninth century also at the distribution at Mass.[118] And these formulas of distribution are found in many different shapes. This is all the more worthy of remark because the sumption formulas were not so frequent even as late as the eleventh century, and because, on the other hand, the Communion of the faithful since that time has been given less consideration in the Mass plans. Although these distribution formulas all are built upon the schema mentioned above, no value was laid upon keeping to any special text. In fact, the fashion seems to have been to try for variety.

The Missal of Troyes, which was written about 1050, gives us three versions. The first is *Corpus D.n.J.C. maneat ad salutem et conservet animam tuam in vitam æternam. Amen.* Then, while giving the precious Blood, a different turn is given to the phrase: *Sanguis D. n. J. C. sanctificet corpus et animam tuam in vitam æternam.* Finally, with the superscription *ad utrumque* (evidently for a combined distribution) follows the formula: *Perceptio corporis et Sanguinis D. n. J. C. prosit animæ tuæ in vitam æternam. Amen.*[119] The somewhat older Mass of Flaccius Illyricus gives three different versions, one for the Communion of the priest and the deacon,[120] one for the rest of the clergy, and one for the people.[121] A special prayer with which the priest introduced the giving of the Sacrament to the faithful is encountered in sources of the eleventh and twelfth centuries.[122]

the first formula here is the same as above, *Corpus D. n. J. C. custodiat te in vitam æternam* (likewise in Ps.-Alcuin, *De div. off.*, c. 19 PL, 101, 1219), in the second, *Sanguis D. n. J. C. redimat te in vitam æternam,* after which there follows a formula that incorporates the Kiss of Peace: *Pax D. n. J. C. et sanctorum communio sit tecum et nobiscum in vitam æternam* (PL, 78, 537 A; cf. above n. 59).—Cf. the Order for the Sick of the Salzburg Romano-German Pontifical (11th cent.; see Andrieu, *Les ordines,* I, 207; 352 f.), where likewise there is first the above *Corpus et Sanguis* formula (with *animam tuam*), followed by *Pax et communicatio* (similar in wording to the above, p. 323, n. 11); Martène, 1, 7, XV (I, 905 B).

[118] Synod of Rouen (about 878), can. 2 (Mansi, X, 1199 f.) prescribes the formula: *Corpus Domini et sanguis prosit tibi ad remissionem peccatorum et ad vitam æternam.* Probably about the same time the Interpolater of Paulus Diaconus, *Vita s. Gregorii* (PL, 75, 52) has Pope Gregory the Great uttering these words while administering Communion during Mass: *Corpus D. n. J. C. prosit tibi in remissio-*

nem omnium peccorum et vitam æternam. —Johannes Diaconus (d. before 882), *Vita s. Gregorii,* II, 41 (PL, 75, 103), ascibes this formula to the Pope: *Corpus D. n. J. C. conservet animam tuam.*—Regino of Prüm, *De synod. causis,* I, 70 (PL, 132, 206) presents this for the Communion of the Sick: *Corpus et sanguis Domini proficiat tibi,* etc.

[119] Martène, 1, 4, VI (I, 534 D).

[120] In this case a real reason is apparent; the Body of the Lord is put in their hand with either *Pax tecum* or *Verbum caro factum est et habitavit in nobis.* Then the chalice with the commingling formula cited above, n. 31.

[121] These two read: *Perceptio corporis et sanguinis D. n. J. C. sanctificet corpus et animam tuam in vitam æternam. Amen,* and *Corpus et sanguis D. n. J. C. prosit tibi in remissionem omnium peccatorum et ad vitam æternam. Amen.* Martène, 1, 4, IV (I, 516).

[122] A prayer in the missal of Troyes, found immediately before the formula for administration, clearly has this function; it reads: *Concede, Domine Jesu, ut sicut hæc*

A more detailed enumeration of the different versions in which the formula appears would be without value, for there seems to be hardly any difference in the meaning, and no expansions worth mentioning appear.[123] Every member of the traditional schema has its variants. For *Corpus (et sanguis)*[124] *D. n. J. C.* we sometimes find *Perceptio corporis . . .;*[125] for *custodiat*, as we saw before, we often find *sanctificet* or *conservet* or (with a dative construction) *prosit* or *proficiat*[126] or *propitiatus sit*[127] or *sit remedium sempiternum.*[128] For *te* and *tibi* the words *anima tua* are inserted, or sometimes also *anima tua et corpus*[129] or (as above) *corpus et anima tua.* For *in vitam æternam*, which as a rule recurs as the only unchanging element, we often find *ad* (or *in*) *remissionem (omnium) peccatorum (tuorum).*[130] It is almost astounding that from the midst of this confusion the seemingly oldest wording was finally chosen: in ordinary use with *custodiat animam tuam*, and at the ordination of subdeacon and deacon with the simple *custodiat te.*[131]

14. The Communion Chant

It is so natural that the distribution of Communion should be accompanied by song, particularly when a large crowd is to receive and the divine service is somewhat solemn, that even in our own day, when the

sacramenta corporis et sanguinis tui fidelibus tuis ad remedium contulisti, ita mihi indigno famulo tuo et omnibus per me sumentibus hæc ipsa mysteria non sint ad reatum, sed prosint ad veniam omnium peccatorum. Amen. Martène, 1, 4, VI (I, 534 C). With non-essential variations in related sources, *ibid.,* IV, XV, XVI (I, 515 B, 593 B, 600 B) ; 1, 4, 9, 9 (I, 423 D). Here, however, the prayer either precedes or immediately follows the Kiss of Peace.
[123] The case in the 15th century Missal of Vorau, which attaches *Pax tecum* to the administering formula, is an isolated one ; Köck, 134.
[124] The addition of *et sanguis* pertains to the combined administering of both species. This was especially widespread in the administration of Viaticum; see Ivo of Chartres, *Decretum*, II, 19 (PL, 161, 165). Further examples of corresponding formulas in Andrieu, *Immixtio et consecratio*, 124 ff. However, special formulas with *Sanguis D. n. J. C.* are frequently cited both in the administration of Viaticum and within the Mass; thus in the Missal of Troyes; Martène, 1, 4, VI (I,

534 D) ; in a Central Italian missal of the end of the 11th century: Ebner, 299; also in a Salzburg Missal of the 12-13th century: Köck, 134. Older examples see above n. 116 ff.
[125] Besides the other examples just mentioned see Ebner, 399, 346; Martène, 1, 4, XIII ; XV (I, 579 D, 594 B) ; Köck, 134 (n. 761).
[126] Köck, 134 (n. 17 b). So also Bernold of Constance, *Micrologus*, c. 23 (PL, 151, 995 B) ; *Corpus et sanguis D. n. J. C. proficiat tibi in vitam æternam.*
[127] Ebner, 299.
[128] Ebner, 297; Köck, 134 (n. 1 a).
[129] For the latter see Ebner, 339; 346; Köck, 134 (n. 761) ; Binterim, IV, 3, page 226.
[130] Martène, 1, 4, IV (I, 516 C) ; Köck, 134 (n. 272). The Mass-arrangement of Séez (PL, 78, 250 D) presents a unique version: *Perceptio corporis Domini nostri sit tibi vita et salus et redemptio omnium tuorum peccatorum.*
[131] *Pontificale Rom.*, De ord. presbyteri. The Carthusians also used the latter version: *Ordinarium Cart.* (1932), c. 27, 14.

original Communion chant no longer seems sufficient, other substitutes are pressed into use. Among the three ancient *schola* songs of the Roman Mass, introit, offertory and communion, the oldest without doubt is the communion.

We first come upon a Communion song in the liturgies of the fourth century. Here it appears at first as a responsorial song, hence one in which the people responded in the ancient Christian manner of congregational singing, answering verse for verse, with an unchanging refrain, as the precentor chanted a psalm. At least Chrysostom mentions that the "confirmed"—he is therefore treating about the very core of the eucharistic celebration—responded (ὑποψάλλουσιν) constantly with the verse "The eyes of all look hopefully to Thee and Thou givest them their food in due time."[1] Evidently Psalm 144 was being sung. A similar participation of the people was presupposed for Psalm 33, since Jerome remarks: *Quotidie cœlesti pane saturati dicimus: Gustate et videte, quam suavis est Dominus.*[2]

We meet with this Psalm 33 as a Communion song almost everywhere in ancient Christendom.[3] There is evidence of the use either of the whole psalm,[4] or of the ninth verse already cited,[5] as in the Liturgy of Jerusalem[6] and other places,[7] or else of the sixth verse, with which Augustine repeatedly directs the faithful to the table of the Lord: *Accedite ad eum et illuminamini.*[8] In various forms, or in combination with the other psalms or with hymns, we encounter these two psalm verses in future times among ‛the Communion songs of the West,[9] just as Psalm 33 is also found at different parts of the Mass in the Orient.[10]

---

[1] Chrysostom, *In Ps. 144 expos.*, 1 (PG, 55, 464) ; cf. Brightman, 475.

[2] Jerome, *In Isaiam comment.*, II, 5, 20 (PG, 24, 86 D).

[3] Cf. the survey in H. Leclercq, "Communion": DACL, III, 2428-2433.

[4] *Const. Ap.*, VIII, 13, 16 (Quasten, *Mon.*, 231). The psalm is intoned by one singer ; *ibid.*, 14, 1 (231): παυσαμένου τοῦ φάλλοντος. Thus responsorial chanting is also presupposed here.

[5] Besides the obvious sense of the verse, the Greek text contains a suggestion of Christ's name: ὅτι χρηστὸς ("η" pronounced like "ι" ὁ κύριος Cf. F. J. Dölger, *Ichthys*, II (Münster, 1922), 493.

[6] Cyril of Jerusalem, *Catech. myst.*, V, 20 (Quasten, *Mon.*, 198) : "You hear then the voice of the one singing the Psalms, who invites you with divine melody to partake of the Holy Mysteries and says, Taste . . . ." Here, again, it could be the responsory verse that is first intoned by the

leader. In the Greek liturgy of St. James (Brightman, 63), however, only this verse appears, followed by other chants.

[7] Armenian Liturgy (Brightman, 449 f.) ; Ambrose, *De myst.*, 9, 58 (Quasten, *Mon.*, 136).

[8] Augustine, *Serm.*, 225, 4 (PL, 38, 1098) ; *Serm. Denis*, 3, 3 (PL, 46, 828). See the further reference to Communion Psalms in Roetzer, 134 f.

[9] Cassiodorus, *In Ps. 33* (PL, 70, 234 f.; 235 f.; 240 D) ; in the Liturgy of Milan in the Transitorium (= Communion chant) at Easter : *Missale Ambrosianum* (1902), 192. Also in the Roman Mass, Ps. 33 : 9 still appears today on the 8th Sunday after Pentecost. In older antiphonaries it forms the antiphon to Psalm 33; see Hesbert, n. 180.

[10] Now in the Byzantine liturgy the Psalm is commonly prayed at the end of the Mass, during the distribution of the blessed bread, or during the ablution of the ves-

In a special version this psalm survives in the Mozarabic liturgy, where the so-called *antiphona ad accedentes,* used during the greater part of the year, reads as follows:

> *Gustate et videte quam suavis est Dominus, alleluja, alleluja, alleluja. Benedicam Dominum in omni tempore, semper laus eius in ore meo, alleluja, alleluja, alleluja. Redimet Dominus animas servorum suorum et non relinquet omnes qui sperant in eum, alleluja, alleluja, alleluja. Gloria et honor Patri et Filio et Spiritui Sancto in sæcula sæculorum. Amen. Alleluja . . .*[11]

The pendent *Alleluia* at the end of every verse is evidently the response with which the faithful were accustomed to answer.[12] The oriental liturgies also show traces of this responsorial use of the *alleluia* in their *Communion* songs;[13] this is especially plain in the Armenian rite which also uses the alleluiatic Psalm 148,[14] and in the Coptic which employs the alleluiatic Psalm 150.[15]

So, whereas in the ancient period the communicants themselves as a rule took part in this song,[16] we find in the later sources immediately available of both Eastern and Western liturgies, that this Communion song or one of the Communion songs[17] was turned over to the choir. Hand in hand with this, we find, besides the enriching of the melodies, an increased use of other texts; among others they used hymns of their own composition. The Irish-Celtic liturgy of the seventh century had such a hymn, built up in eleven double verses, which began as follows:

> *Sancti venite, Christi corpus sumite,*
> *Sanctum bibentes quo redempti sanguine,*

---

sels; Hanssens, III, 533 f.; but it appears especially at the Communion in the Missa præsanctificatorum.

[11] *Missale mixtum* (PL, 85, 564 f.).—Also in the Cathedral of Belley (Rite of Lyons) at the Easter High Mass an antiphon *Gustate et videte* was inserted after the first *Agnus Dei.* Buenner, 256, n. 1.

[12] Cf. above I, 422 ff. Cf. also Leitner, *Der gottesdienstliche Volksgesang,* 167 f.—The two first verses, likewise with added *Alleluia,* also in the Stowe Missal; ed. Warner (HBS, 32), 18; cf. the Antiphoner of Bangor, ed. Warren (HBS, 10), 30 f.

[13] East Syrians: Brightman, 299; West Syrian Jacobites: *ibid.,* 102 f.

[14] Brightman, 449 f.

[15] Brightman, 185. The same Psalm, too, still in the Ethiopian Liturgy: *ibid.,* 240 (see corrigenda, page CIV).

[16] Cf. also Aurelian (d. 551), *Regula ad monachos* (PL, 68, 596 B): *psallendo omnes communicent;* also in the rule for nuns (PL, 68, 406 B).—A. Dohmes, "Der Psalmengesang des Volkes in der Eucharistischen Opferfeier der christlichen Frühzeit (*Liturg. Leben,* 1938), 147 f., believes that from what ancient witnesses have to say we can argue only to a rather narrow extension of congregational singing at the Communion. The conclusion depends, to some extent, on how we rate this *Alleluia* which here appears.

[17] Already in the *Apostolic Constitutions,* VIII, 13, 13 (Quasten, *Mon.,* 229 f.), besides Psalm 33 mentioned as a first Communion song (here still sung by the people), we find mention of a combination of Luke 2: 14; Matt. 21: 9; Ps. 117: 26 f.; of which Psalm 117: 27 b and Mt. 21: 9 still survive in the same place in the Armenian liturgy; Brightman, 24; 453.— Sometimes a distinction is made between a chant at the Communion of the clergy and

Salvati Christi corpore et sanguine
A quo refecti laudes dicamus Deo.[18]

The Roman liturgy at first clung to the chanting of psalms, but in such a way that the Communion psalm changed according to the ecclesiastical year.[19] As the first Roman *ordo* prescribed, the *schola* was to intone the *antiphona ad communionem* as soon as the pope began to distribute Communion in the *senatorium*. Then came the psalmody *(psallunt)* until all the people had communicated. When the archdeacon saw *quod pauci sunt ad communicandum,*[20] he gave the *schola* a sign for the *Gloria Patri,* after which the verse was again repeated: *et tunc repetito versu quiescunt.*[21] The communion was therefore an antiphonal song of the *schola cantorum* similar to the introit, consisting of a psalm sung alternately by two semi-choruses, and with a pre-verse which was repeated at the end.

The introduction of this antiphonal manner of singing at the Communion, as at the offertory, took place in North Africa in St. Augustine's time,[22] and could not have been much later in Rome.[23] The absence of the Communion song on Holy Saturday recalls the time before the introduction of the chant.

Whereas at the offertory the responsorial form replaced the antiphonal, at the Communion the antiphonal manner of singing continued unchanged for centuries. It was thought important that the song should actually accompany the distribution of Communion. A Carolingian explanation of the Mass remarks that during the Communion "soft melody should touch the ear [of the faithful] so that hearing this sound they would busy themselves less with distracting thoughts and . . . their hearts would be moved to humble love for that which they receive."[24] The oldest manuscripts of the Mass song-book, which belong to the eighth-ninth century, give us the same picture for the communion as for the introit: the antiphon (the same which today forms the entire communion in the Roman Missal) is intoned; thereupon follow the initial words of the psalm, or

such a one at the Communion of the people; cf. following note.

[18] Antiphoner of Bangor (ed. Warren [HBS, 4]), fol. 10 v.; PL, 72, 587), with the heading: *Ymnum quando communicarent sacerdotes.* The manuscripts read *sanguine* in the second line, though most editors correct it to *sanguinem.*

[19] The Communion song in the Byzantine (χοινωνιχόν) and East Syrian liturgy is subject to the seasonal changes in the Ecclesiastical year; Baumstark, *Die Messe im Morgenland,* 162 f.

[20] Cf. Ordo of S. Amand (Andrieu, II, 167 l. 11).

[21] *Ordo Rom.* I, n. 20 (PL, 78, 947); *Ordo Rom.* II, n. 14 f. (PL, 78, 976 B).

[22] Augustine, *Retract.* II, 11 (see above), p. 27.

For the interpretation of the text, cf. Dohmes, 148, who supposes that the people first of all sang only antiphonally. Insofar as only Psalm 33 was dealt with, this is quite possible.

[23] P. Pietschman, "Die nicht dem Psalter entnommenen Messgesangstücke auf ihre Textgestalt untersucht" (*JL,* 12 (1934], 87-144), 91, on the basis of his study of the texts, reckons with the possibility that the *Communio* of the Roman Missal was introduced on the authority of Augustine.

[24] Expositio "Primum in ordine" (before 819; PL, 138, 1186).

else, in those many cases in which the introit psalm is simply to be repeated, the remark: *Psalm. ut supra.*[25]

In a few scattered Frankish manuscripts we find something similar to what we discovered in regard to the introit,[26] namely, a second psalm verse, under the heading *Ad repet.*,[27] the function of which has hitherto been a riddle. But the riddle is solved if we hark back to the *trecanum*, the Communion song of the Gallican liturgy.[28] Here we have what proves to be a remnant from the Gallican liturgy, so strongly Trinitarian in character, where, in the interweaving of antiphon, psalm verse and *Gloria Patri*, this extra verse served to round out the picture of the circumincession of the three divine Persons.

Other expansions of the *communio* also put in an appearance, especially by the repetition of the antiphon.[29] Apropos of this, it seems that during

[25] Hesbert, *Antiphonale missarum sextuplex*. Of the five manuscripts printed here that offer the antiphonal chants, the Psalm for Communion is regularly missing only in that of Rheinau (about 800).—In some manuscripts the starting point is not the opening of the psalm, but, according to the occasion, some other remarkable verse, e.g., in Ps. 33 the verse *Gustate* (Hesbert, n. 44) or on Pentecost Tuesday in Ps. 50 *Cor mundum crea* (ibid., 108).

[26] *Supra*, I, 325 f.

[27] Chiefly two of the oldest antiphonary manuscripts in Hesbert, those of Campiègne and of Senlis, again offer the verse mentioned but as a rule not in the same formulary. In the Senlis manuscript, on Sexagesima Sunday we find the antiphon *Introibo* in use today, followed by the psalm *Judica*, to which furthermore is added, *Ad repet.: Spera in Deo* (Hesbert, n. 35). The key to the manner and method of performance is perhaps furnished in the *Capitulare eccl. ord.* (Silva-Tarouca, 260, line 36) according to which the priest gives a sign to conclude the singing with *Gloria Patri*, and then: *post Gloria repetant verso de ipso psalmo et novissime canent ipsa antiphona et sic laudem sanctæ Trinitatis debit peragere.*

[28] In the *Expositio* of the Gallican liturgy (ed. Quasten, 23) the Communion song is described as follows: *Trecanum vero, quod psallitur, signum est catholicæ fidei de Trinitatis credulitate procedens. Sicut enim prima (pars) in secunda, secunda in tertia et rursum tertia in secunda et secunda rotatur in prima, ita Pater in Filio*

mysterium Trinitatis complectitur, Pater in Filio, Filius in Spiritu Sancto, Spiritus Sanctus in Filio et Filius rursum in Patre. If in this description of the Gallican "Triad" we set down the antiphon for the first member, the psalm for the second, and the *Gloria Patri* for the third, we have the following pattern: Antiphon (1)—Psalm (2)—Gloria Patri (3)—Psalm (2)—Antiphon (1), i.e., the succession as in the *Capitulare* that, to be sure, expressly emphasizes the *laus sanctæ Trinitatis*. In point of fact, one can say that we have here a remote symbol of the Most Holy Trinity, where 1 continues in 2 and 2 in 3 and 3 in 2 and 2 in 1, and thus leads to the completion of the circle (*rotatur*). The design of the song becomes a picture of the Divine Perichoresis, that occupied the attention of the Fathers so much. Cf. especially the arguments in Gregory of Nyssa, *Adv. Maced.*, c. 22 (PG, 45, 1329) regarding the ἐνκύκλιος τῆς δόξης περιφορά in the Divine Persons. The same plan is the basis of the presentation that the same *Capitulare* gives of the *Introit* (Silva-Tarouca, 205; *supra* I, 323, n. 13), only that there, for the heightening of the solemnity no doubt, the antiphon is repeated after each verse, and thus the interplay of verses is strengthened.—Regarding the various attempts to explain the meaning of *trecanum*, see L. Brou, *Journal of Theol. Studies*, 47 (1946), 19.

[29] According to the *Ordo* of S. Amand (Andrieu, II, 166 f.) the subdeacons should repeat the antiphon at the beginning; what is repeated at the end is not entirely clear.

the ninth century the subdeacons formed a sort of counter-choir to the *schola* of chanters.[30] And then, according to Carolingian prescription, all the people were to join in at the *Gloria Patri.*[31]

Although the development of the Communion song thus ran parallel in part to the introit, yet in contrast to the latter, the psalm began to be dropped very soon. The psalm begins to be missed in the manuscripts during the tenth century,[32] and by the twelfth century it is found only very seldom.[33] The remarks of the exponents of the liturgy correspond; Bernold of Constance still mentions the addition of the psalm with the *Gloria Patri* but with the quiet limitation, *si necesse fuerit.*[34] The embellishment by tropes which started in the tenth century, fell into decay even before it could be properly developed.[35] When we take into consideration the ability of liturgical creations to survive, then this phenomenon more or less matches the fact that in the Carolingian reform, which faithfully copied the practices of the city of Rome, Sunday Communion was once again on the increase,[36] but when this slowed down, the grounds for a Communion song also crumbled.[37] All that remained was the antiphon, which in the thirteenth century gets the name *communio.*[38]

Cf. the theory in this matter of J. N. Tommasi rejected by Wagner, *Einführung,* I, 65, n. 2. The Stowe Missal, ed. Warner (HBS, 32), 18, presents as Communion song a whole line of verses, each ending with *Alleluia,* formulated from well-selected phrases of Scripture; towards the end of the verse *Venite benedicti* (Matt. 25: 34) is repeated three times in connection with the *Gloria Patri.*

[30] Also in the tradition of the *Ordo Rom.* I, n. 20, as proffered by Mabillon (PL, 78, 947 B; Andrieu, II, 105; this is the original reading: see *ibid.,* II, 7, note 4) the Schola begins the antiphon for Communion *per vices cum subdiaconibus.*

[31] Cf. *supra,* I, 237, n. 20.

[32] Ursprung, *Die Kath. Kirchenmusik,* 57.

[33] Wagner, *Einführung,* I, 119. Another manuscript of the Leipzig of the 13th century is mentioned *ibid.,* that presents the Psalm. In Lyons in the 18th century the Communion at solemn feasts was sung with a verse from the Psalm and the *Gloria Patri,* just like the *Introit;* de Moléon, 59. —On the other hand, cf. the Rheinau manuscript (above, n. 25).

[34] Bernold of Constance, *Micrologus,* c. 18 (PL, 151, 989 B).—Innocent III, *De s. alt. mysterio,* VI, 10 (PL, 217, 912) speaks of the alternate singing *(reciprocando cantatur),* which he interprets, with

Amalar, *De eccl. off.,* III, 33, 2 (Hanssens, II, 365) as referring to the reciprocal account of the disciples after the appearance of the Risen Savior. Durandus, IV, 56, 2, has already probably only a literary knowledge of the practice.

[35] The tropes for Communion which, like those for the *Introit,* either introduce the antiphon, or carry it through, belong almost entirely to the 10th and 11th centuries; see text in Blume, *Tropen des Missale,* II (*Analecta hymnica,* 49 (pages 343-353.

[36] *Supra.*

[37] It is worth remarking that a verse *(Requiem æternam)* and even a repetition of a part of the antiphon *(cum sanctis tuis)* has been retained to this day in the Mass of the Dead at which Communion of the Faithful was not at all customary in the Middle Ages. This instance, however, was unique even within the Mass of the Dead. Cf. B. Opfermann, "Alte Totenlieder der Kirche," *Bibel u. Liturgie,* 9 (1934-1935), 55-59, where fourteen different texts are cited for the Communion, among which only one other (n. 14) contains a similar repetition. In the Dominican Missal, moreover, we find our *Communio* without verse and without repetition; *Missale O. P.* (1889), 86*, 89*, 91*.

[38] Albertus Magnus, *De sacrificio missæ,*

In realty the Communion chant should ordinarily have been dropped, since it was meant to accompany the Communion of the people, not that of the priest. Thus it was not incorrect to regard the *communio* as more or less a symbol of the Communion of the people, which should have taken place, and therefore to put it after the Communion of the priest. But then a further step was taken, and it was looked upon as a thanksgiving *post cibum salutarem;*[39] it was even called *antiphona post communionem,*[40] or simply *postcommunio.*[41] Finally came a new development when, even if Communion was distributed to the faithful, the Communion song was not intoned till after the Communion was over,[42] just as is generally done with the Communion verse in our own day.[43]

Meanwhile the *Agnus Dei* had become the real Communion song,[44] This held true at least for the Communion of the priest, to which, during the high Middle Ages, the extra distribution of Communion could be added without much of a pause being necessary. But on great Communion days other songs were soon added, excepting always Good Friday and Holy Saturday, when Communion was received in profound silence.[45] Thus, towards the end of the ninth century there appears in the Pontifical of Poitiers[46] for Easter Sunday a festive antiphon with the heading: *Ante communionem,* which was in use on such occasions during the entire Middle Ages and beyond, especially in many French churches; the song ran as follows:

III, 23, 1 (Opp., ed. Borgnet, 38, 162), remarks the change in the designation; cf. Sölch, *Hugo,* 150.

[39] Rupert of Deutz (d. 1135), *De div. off.,* II, 18 (PL, 170, 46) and others after it. Sölch, *Hugo,* 150.

[40] Cf. Innocent III, *De s. alt. mysterio,* VI, 10 (PL, 217, 912). Cf. too the Expositio "Introitus missæ quare" (9-10th cent.) ed. Hanssens (*Eph. liturg.,* 1930), 46; *Cantus post communionem quare celebratur? Ut ostendatur vere gratias agere populos.*

[41] Innocent III, *loc. cit.,* title of chapter; Durandus, IV, 56, 1.

[42] Dominican Missal of the 13th century; Sölch, 151. The Rituale of Soissons openly opposes the development of such a practice: Martène, 1, 4, XXII (I, 612 f.); *Communio,* as the name indicates, is to be sung *in hora communionis.*

[43] When the *Graduale Romanum* (1908), *De rit. serv. in cantu missæ,* n. 9, prescribes that the *Communio* is to be sung *sumpto ss. sacramento,* the priest's Communion is clearly meant, not that of the faithful. This is not only fully in accord with the historical purpose of the Communion chant,

but also with the rubric of the missal, which is not at all ambiguous. The missal, speaking of the Communion of the faithful at a solemn Mass, says: *Interim a Choro cantatur Antiphona quæ Communio.* Meanwhile . . . *Ritus serv. in cel. missæ,* X, 9. Of course the present short *Communio* is hardly sufficient to fill the time when the distribution of Communion is prolonged. This is true in spite of its prolation by neums, for these are different from the neums of the *Introit,* quiet and melodically unpretentious, as befits the dignity of the moment (Ursprung, *Die kath. Kirchenmusik,* 32). It would seem that the addition of the corresponding psalm would be as legitimate as the use of other chants. Cf. the similar case at the *Introit, supra,* I, 327.

[44] *Supra*—In Milan also as O. Heiming, *Liturgie u. Mönchtum,* 3 (1949), 84, remarks, the *Transitorium* is a later production, while the Roman *Communio* has become the *Confractorium.*

[45] References in Browe, "Mittelalterliche Kommunionriten" (*JL,* 15, 1941), 60 f.

[46] A. Wilmart, "Notice de Pontifical de

Venite populi, sacram immortale mysterium et libamen agendum. Cum timore et fide accedamus. Manibus mundis pœnitentiæ munus communicemus. Quoniam Agnus Dei propter nos Patri sacrificium propositum est. Ipsum solum adoremus, ipsum glorificemus cum angelis clamantes, alleluia.[47]

In other places a part of the choir Office was inserted. In the Cathedral of Soissons around 1130 the canons sang Sext on Easter Sunday during the Communion of the faithful.[48] In a Hungarian cathedral of the eleventh-twelfth century of this same day it was Vespers that was said, and care was taken that its close would coincide with the *Ite missa est* of the deacon.[49] According to John of Avranches (d. 1097) Vespers was to be inserted on Holy Thursday during the Communion, since its closing oration was identical with the post-communion.[50] Other songs, psalms, hymns or antiphons which seemed suitable were also used, either according to strict regulation or according to choice,[51] which is in line with our present-day practice, even aside from the fact that even on festive occasions the greater proportion of Communions are given at the early Masses, which are *missæ lectæ* where Communion songs even in the vernacular can be freely developed.

On the other hand the Communion verse became solidly anchored in the Roman Mass by the practice of having the priest read it from the

Poitiers" (*JL,* 4, 1924), 75.

[47] Martène, 1, 4, 10, 6 (I, 432); cf. *ibid.,* 4, 25, 26 (III, 488 f.). Numerous references from the 11-15th centuries in Leroquais, III, 422; see Wagner, *Einführung,* I, 122.—In the Rite of Lyons the song is inserted at High Mass after the first *Agnus Dei;* Missale of Lyons (1904), page XXXVIII; cf. Buenner, 256; 281-284.—In Milan also it is heard to this day on Easter Sunday; *Missale Ambrosianum* (1902), 189. It was still in use at Vienna as well as at Tours (Martène, 4, 25, 26), in the 18th century; de Moléon, 17; 29. Nor was the hymn unknown in either England or Germany; Buenner, 282. In regard to Münster i. W. where is evidence in the Ordinarius II (1489), ed. by Stapper (Opuscula et Textus, ser. liturg., 7-8), 69.—It goes back to a Byzantine hymn of Maundy Thursday (Δεῦτε λαοί); Buenner, 282, with reference to P. Cagin (*Paléographie musicale,* V, 185. Cf. also the invitation before Communion in the liturgy of St. James: Μετα φόβου θεοῦ (The Byzantine liturgy of the 9th cent. adds και πίστεως και ἀγάπης προσέλθετε; Brightman, 64, 341).

[48] Browe, "Mittelalterliche Kommunion-riten" (*JL,* 15, 1941), 51, n. 13; cf. *ibid.,* 60.

[49] G. Morin, "Manuscrits liturgiques hongrois," *JL,* 6 (1926), 57.

[50] John of Avranches, *De off. eccl.* (PL, 147, 50). This arrangement was for a long time observed, among others, by the Premonstratensians; Waefelghem, 210. The insertion of a canonical hour after Communion, independently of a Communion of the people, was not unheard of, even irrespective of the traditional Vespers of Holy Saturday. In Vienna about 1700 Lauds were inserted at the Midnight Mass on Christmas; de Moléon, 14 f. The Missal of Zips in the 14th century testifies to the same practice; Radó, 71. Something similar was customary about 1410 at Valencia; Ferreres, 207. In the present Dominican rite, too, Lauds is wedged in before the end of Mass; *Missale O.P.* (1889), 19; see N. M. Halmer, O.P. in *Divus Thomas,* 27 (1949), 253-256.—In the latest rubrics for the restored Easter Vigil (Jan. 11, 1952), an abbreviated form of Lauds is inserted in the Mass after Communion; *AAS,* 44 (1952), 63.

[51] Examples in Browe, *Mittelalterliche Kommunionriten,* 61. Texts in the ver¬

missal. This custom was already to be found long ago at private Masses[60] even though for a long time it was not universal. For the Mass celebrated with chant it seems not to have become very common until quite late, since the corresponding direction is still missing in most of the Mass plans even of the late Middle Ages.[61]

Even if the Communion song as it stands in the Roman Missal is but a tiny part of what was originally intended, it must be stated that even the original plan of this song in the Roman Mass represented the result of an evolution that was markedly peripheral. The principle of psalmody was kept, but there was no tendency to prefer one of the Communion psalms, or even the "praise" and alleluia psalms.

There was no intention to establish at this point a Communion song in the narrower sense, but instead, much as in the case of the other songs in the Roman Mass, to set up an ecclesiastical song of a general character which could present the festal thoughts as the occasion demanded. From all this it can be seen how far the Roman Mass was from evolving a special Communion devotion.

Even in regard to the prayers in the part of the Mass around Communion, we have already shown [54] that the early medieval Roman Mass *ordo*, in comparison with other liturgies, displayed the utmost poverty.

So when we consider only the Communion antiphons of the present time we find that on the Sundays after Pentecost verses are simply taken from the psalms in order of the psalter, from Psalm 9 to 118.[55] On the ferias of Quadragesima, if we except the later formulas of Thursday, Psalms 1 to 26 are used in regular progression from Ash Wednesday to Palm Sunday.

If the antiphon was taken from the Book of Psalms, then the corresponding psalm followed. In the other cases, the psalm used was the introit psalm,[56] which could have but little relevance to Communion. However, for festive seasons and on feast days some reference to the thought of

nacular were not excluded in such cases. As Bishop Urban of Gurk decreed in an enactment promulgated after 1564, "a hymn or psalm should be sung in the vernacular" after Communion to help the devotion of the faithful (*ibid.*).

[60] This was emphatically stipulated, just as in the case of the Introit, by the *Capitulare eccl. ord.* (Silva-Tarouca, 207).

[61] A Minorite Missal of the 13th century supplied with careful rubrics has the celebrant *cum ministris* reàd the Introit, but makes no similar remark either at the Offertory or the Communion; Ebner, 313 f, 317. Still, the practice occurs at the same time in the rite of the Dominicans (Guer-

rini, 244) and is taken over by the Benedictine *Liber Ordinarius* of Liége (Volk, 9).

[54] *Supra*, p. 294.

[55] Above I, 331. The only large break is from the 11th to the 15th Sunday, which happen to come in the fall and have been given antiphons that (outside the 14th Sunday) have reference to the harvest and (heavenly) bread; cf. Hesbert, S. LXXIV f.

[56] This rule in Bernold of Constance, *Micrologus*, c. 18 (PL, 151, 989 B).—It holds true also in a part of the old manuscripts. On the other hand, the rule is pitted by many exceptions especially in the manuscript of Corbie; see Hesbert, n.

the day was sought.[57] This draws closer again to the ideas connected with Communion. Thus, on the Sundays after Easter, we can listen to our Lord challenging Thomas: *Mitte manum tuam et cognosce loca clavorum*, or the call of the Good Shepherd: *Ego sum pastor bonus;* or in Advent we can hear the prophet's cry: *Ecce Dominus veniet et omnes sancti eius cum eo.* And besides, even our missal contains a small number of Mass formularies whose creators obviously had in mind to give a more eucharistic touch to the Communion verse. We refer to the Masses for the Thursdays of Lent, which originated in the eighth century. For the second and third Thursdays phrases are taken from our Lord's promise of the Eucharist (John 6:52; 6:57); according to one tradition these verses were linked with the Communion Psalm 33.[58]

15. Silent Prayer after the Reception

After the priest has received and distributed Communion, several actions in the interest of good order still remain, especially the ablutions, which he again accompanies with silent prayer. In the very nature of things this prayer is not concerned with the performance of the actions, in themselves of no importance, but with that which has just happened, namely the Holy Communion. The prayers are similar both in origin and in character to the preceding prayers that prepared for and accompanied the Communion. And here again we discover that originally these prayers were intended for the faithful as well as for the priest; both found nourishment for their personal devotion from the same source.

The first prayer, *Quod ore sumpsimus*, which is found already in the oldest sacramentaries,[1] we also encounter in the prayer book of Charles the Bald, where it bears the superscription: *Oratio post communionem;*

2, 4, 16, 22, 29, etc. On Candlemas (n. 29), e.g., the *Nunc dimittis* is used.—The *Capitulare eccl. ord.* (Silva-Tarouca, 206 f.). does not adhere closely to the rule, as, for example, on the Feast of the Virgins when, in place of the *Quinque prudentes* it permits either the Introit Psalm 44 or Psalm 45; cf. *ibid.*, 205, 1. 19 ff.
[57] See the Table of Communion verses according to the Cod. Sangall., 399 (10th cent.) in Pietschmann (*JL*, 12, 1934), 142 ff.; 68 Communion verses are not taken from the Psalter, as opposed to only 39 of the Introit, 14 of the Gradual, and 17 of the Offertory; cf. Wagner, *Einführung*, I, 118, according to whom the verses named comprise the greater bulk of the Communion verses in this manuscript. In

the Missal of today the number of non-psalmodic Communion verses has again grown considerably.
[58] Hesbert, n. 44; 50.—The antiphon *Acceptabis sacrificium iustitiæ* of the first Thursday is perhaps inspired by the same thought. In the same manner are to be judged the antiphons on the fourth and sixth Thursdays, which are derived from Psalm 118, the Psalm of praise of the (New) Testament that has become the Sunday Psalm and that also was the Communion Psalm on Maundy Thursday. Somewhat more foreign is the fifth Thursday, with Psalm 70; 16-18.
[1] Also already in the Leonianum: Muratori, I, 366; further references in Mohlberg-Manz, n. 1567.

this version reads: *Quod ore sumpsi, Domine, mente capiam, ut de corpore et sanguine D. n. J. C. fiat mihi remedium sempiternum. Per eumdem D. n. J. C.*[2] Later on, we find it as the prayer for communicating clerics.[3] Since it is evident that this prayer is spoken by the priest not with a loud voice, but softly,[4] it is to be considered here as his personal prayer, as a private prayer coming before the *post-communio*. We find it in the majority of medieval Mass plans, as a rule in the plural form of the original text,[5] and not seldom also with the closing formula, *Per Christum D. n.,*[6] which has been dropped from the text of the Roman Missal.[7] In a twofold antithesis the plea is made that the internal[8] efficacy of the Sacrament might tally with this sacramental reception in time.

Our second prayer after Communion, namely, the *Corpus tuum Domine*, which (in keeping with its origin in the Gallic liturgy[9] displays a somewhat different character, also served for the private devotion of the faithful. It is found in the Communion Devotions of Monte Cassino at the end of the eleventh century.[10] It also appears as early as the tenth century as a fixed part of many Mass arrangements, and in contrast to the

---

[2] Ed. Ninguarda, 116. The variant *ut de corpore et sanguine D. n. J. C.,* that was supposed to suppliant the *et de munere temporali* (see below), which was no longer understood, is also in the printed Missals of Rouen and Lyons; de Moléon, 65; 315; likewise in Sweden (Yelverton, 21); and also in today's Dominican Missal (1889), 22, which has only this formula after Communion. A Missal of the 16th century of Orleans has *et corpus et sanguis D. n. J. C.;* de Moléon, 201.

[3] *Supra*, p. 369.

[4] In as far as it did not become, for a time, a permanent *Postcommunio;* see below, p. 424.

[5] The plural form is knowingly set down by Bernold of Constance, *Micrologus*, c. 23 (PL, 151, 995) with this reason as a premise: *Postquam omnes communicaverunt, dicit;* here it is the only prayer after Communion. The Mass-arrangement of Rouen (13-14th cent.) : Martène, 1, 4, XXXVII (I, 678 C), and the *Missale parvum Vedastinum* (Arras, 13th cent. ; edited by Z. H. Turton [London, 1904]) in Ferreres, 202, have the prayer in the singular form; see moreover, Lebrun, I, 546, note a. —The formula is parallel to *Deus qui humanæ substantiæ* of the Offertory section which has likewise retained the plural form of the original oration and moreover the concluding form of the same.

[6] See, e.g., Köck, 130.

[7] Since the formula is couched in the terms of a wish *(capiamus)* it is not firmly attached to any definite form of address. The more easily, then, can it be combined with the formula that follows under the conclusion of *Qui vivis*, i.e., as though addressed to Christ.

[8] The *pura* before the *mente* is missing quite often in the text of the *Postcommunio* in the old Sacramentaries and even in its use in this part of the Mass until into the 13th century (cf., e.g., Köck, 127; Ebner, 326) ; originally it was a question only of a contrast of *ore* and *mente*.

[9] The prayer appears first as a *Postcommunio* in the Gothic Missal of the 7th century (Muratori, II, 653) : *Corpus tuum, Domine, quod accipimus et calicem quem potavimus, hæreat in visceribus nostris, præsta, Deus omnipotens, ut non remaneat macula, ubi pura et sancta intraverunt sacramenta. Per.*—It is not to be denied that the version to be mentioned below (n. 16) which is likewise a *Postcommunio*, is of similar antiquity.

[10] Wilmart (*Eph. liturg.*, 1929), 325.—The same Communion devotion contains, among the prayers that follow the receiving of Communion, the prayer *Domine Jesu Christe Fili* (see above, p. 369), besides some formulas that appear rarely or not at all in liturgical books.

other formula we considered above, it appears here in the singular, the very trait of private prayer. Among the earliest witnesses[11] is, significantly, a Mass *ordo* from nearby Subiaco,[12] to which we can add other Benedictine *Ordines*[13] and also others from Italy, especially the Franciscan Missal which was to be decisive for the later development.[14] This prayer also gained a wide though not general acceptance elsewhere. In France, even the original plural form was retained for some time,[15] partly in conjunction with a different version of the second part,[16] going back perhaps to a Mozarabic origin.[17] Frequently this prayer also showed other more or less marked expansions or variations.[18] Sometimes, too, instead of the Gallican mode of address to Christ, it had the ordinary form of address, *Corpus D. n. J. C. quod sumpsi*,[19] so that the *Per Christum* could also be added at the close.[20] But such changes did not become common.

In regard to its contents, this prayer goes a step beyond the preceding one. It does not feature the contrast between the outer sign and the inner efficacy; instead, the Sacrament Itself appears almost as the grace: through that which It contains, It is so pure and so holy that in a certain

---

[11] Aside from the second version to be mentioned immediately (n. 16).

[12] 11th century, Ebner, 339.

[13] Ebner, 299; 302; 338; Fiala, 216.

[14] Ebner, 317.

[15] Missale of Remiremont (12th cent.): Martène, 1, 4, 9, 9 (I, 424 D).

[16] In the Missal of Troyes (about 1050): Martène, 1, 4, VI (I, 534 D), the formula reads: *Corpus Domini n. J. C. quo pasti sumus et sanguis eius quo potati sumus, adhæreat in visceribus nostris et non nobis veniat ad iudicium neque ad condemnationem, sed proficiat nobis ad salutem et ad remedium vitæ æternaæ.* The same version of the second part but in the singular, in the Sacramentary of S. Aubin in Angers (10th cent.; Leroquais, I, 71) and in that of Paris (10th cent.; Netzer, 247). Somewhat expanded in a Missal of lower Italy about 1200 in Ebner, 323 f.; in the Cistercian Missal of the 13th century; Ferreres, p. LI; 203; in the Missal of Westminster, ed. Legg (HBS, 5), 520 f.; in the Missal of Fécamp (about 1400): Martène, 1, 4, XXVII (I, 642 B); finally in a larger number of Mass-books of the 12th-15th centuries of northeast Spain; Ferreres, p. LXII, CXII, 190, 210 f., where the conclusion reads: *remedium animæ meæ et animabus omnium fidelium vivorum et defunctorum.*

[17] Férotin, *Le Liber ordinum*, 242. Here, as against the version in the Missal of Troyes (preceding note), the formula already shows certain elaborations.

[18] In German Mass-books: *quod ego miser accepi:* Köck, 131; Beck, 310; v. Bruiningk, 88; Hoeynck, 376; cf. de Corswarem, 142. In Spanish Mass-books: *quod ego indignus et infelix sumere præsumpsi;* Ferreres, 190; 202; cf. Martène, 1, 4, XV (I, 593 D). In Styrian Mass-books: *Sanctum corpus tuum, Domine, quod indignus accepi;* Köck, 128, 130; see also *ibid.*, 127, the still more strongly expanded form of the Seckau Missal of the 12th century, which in turn is again expanded in the Sacramentary of Boldau in Hungary (about 119), ed. Kniewald; *Theologia*, 6 (Budapest, 1939), 26. In the Pontifical of Mainz about 1170 the first part is entirely reshaped; Martène, 1, 4, XVII (I, 602 D): *Corporis sacri . . . perceptio.*

[19] For Italy see Ebner, 147; 335; cf. 299; 323 f.; 326; Muratori, I, 94. A further example in Brinktrine, *Die hl. Messe*, 268 (Vat. lat. 6378; 13-14th cent.).—Missal of Westminster, ed. Legg (HBS, 5), 520. Cf. Augsburg Missale of 1386: Hoeynck, 376.—*Liber ordinum*, Missal of Troyes and the further variant sources above, note 16.

[20] So in the Augsburg Missale of 1386; Hoeynck, 376.

sense It need only remain in us in order to push aside and burn up all stain of sin.[21]

Besides these two formulas, which were seldom found together in earlier times, and even then not often in the order they have today, a great number of other prayers and texts on which the priest could nourish his devotion after the reception of the Sacrament were current during the Middle Ages.[22] We have remarked before that the prayers *Domine Jesu Christe Fili* and *Perceptio* which precede the reception and which in another manner beg for the efficacy of the Sacrament, frequently also had a place after the reception.[23] Other prayers of similar content also appeared. Thus in the eleventh-twelfth century we find this formula a few times:

> *Domine Jesu Christe fili Dei, corpus tuum pro nobis crucifixum edimus et sanguinem tuum pro nobis effusum bibimus. Fiat corpus tuum salus animarum et corporum nostrorum et tuus sanctus sanguis remissio omnium peccatorum hic et in æternum. Amen.*[24]

Frequently other formulas of the post-communion type, or even actual post-communion texts were used.[25] The Mass *ordo* of a Parisian manuscript has as many as thirteen orations following Communion.[26]

[21] The older text; *ubi pura et sancta intraverunt sacramenta* (see above, n. 9), that prevails into the late Middle Ages brings this picturesque manner of speech into stronger focus. It is somewhat varied in the Rhenish Missal of the end of the 13th century described by F. Roedel, *JL*, 4 (1924), 85: *ubi tua sacrosancta intraverint sacramenta*. In today's version the personal element has come to the fore.

[22] A long but otherwise rare prayer of thanksgiving in the Sacramentary of Fulda (Richter-Schönfelder, n. 27): *Deus noster, Deus salvos faciendi, tu nos doce gratias agere . . .*—Still at the end of the Middle Ages the idea prevailed that one could here choose and insert prayers in conformity with one's own personal devotion, at least if one said them quietly; Browe, "Die Kommunionandacht" (*JL*, 13, 1935), 50 f.

[23] *Supra*, p. 348-349.

[24] Missal of Remiremont (12th c.): Martène, 1, 4, 9, 9 (I, 424 C); Sacramentary of Echternach (1st half of the 11th c.): Leroquais, I, 122; cf. *ibid.*, 307; II, 340; Missal of Seckau (12th c.): Köck, 127; Admont MS. of the 14th c.: Franz, 111, note 4.—The first part of the above formula likewise introduces a Communion prayer in the Bobbio missal (Muratori, II, 780); in the second part there is an echo

of the prayer in the Sacramentary of Vich (11-12th c.): *Fiat nobis hoc sacramentum . . .* (Ferreres, p. XCVI).—A Sacramentary towards the end of the 9th century from Tours offers the formula: *Sumentes ex sacris altaribus*: Leroquais, 1, 49; Martène, 1, 4, 9, 9 (I, 423 B).—In the missal of St. Vincent the *Corpus tuum* is paraphrased: *Post communionem . . .*; Fiala, 216.

[25] Mass-*ordo* of Amiens, ed. Leroquais (*Eph. liturg.*, 1927): 544: *Præsta quæsumus.*—Sacramentary of Moissac: Martène, 1, 4, VIII (I, 541 B): *Da quæsumus.* —Missa Illyrica, *ibid.*, IV (I, 517 A): *Conservent; Custodi; Præsta Domine Jesu Christe.*—Italian Mass orders of the 11-12th century: (Ebner, 297:) *Huius Deus*, (158, 348 and Fiala, 214:) *Prosit*, resp. *Proficiat nobis*; Brinktrine, *Die hl. Messe*, 291: *Conservent.*—This last formula also in Strengnas, Sweden: Segelberg, 259.— For England, see Sarum Missal: Legg, *The Sarum Missal*, 228: *Hæc nos communio*; cf. Martène, 1, 4, XXXV (I, 670 f.); Ferreres, 203; Missal of York, ed. Simmons 116. The same oration also in Vorau: Köck, 133.—An Eichstätt missal (Köck, 7) has: *Concede quæsumus o. D. ut quidquid.*

[26] Martène, 1, 4, 9, 9 (I, 426 f.).

Here we must also reckon the *Agimus tibi gratias* that appears occasionally during the late Middle Ages.[27] Even earlier a *Gratias tibi ago,* one of the treasures of private prayer, was widespread. Its apparently original form is found in the Missal of Remiremont in the twelfth century; it runs as follows:

> *Gratias ago tibi, Domine Deus Pater omnipotens, qui me peccatorem satiare dignatus es corpore et sanguine Jesu Christi Filii tui Domini nostri. Ideo supplex deprecor ut hæc sancta communio sit in arma fidei, scutum bonæ voluntatis ad repellendas omnes insidias diaboli de corde et opere meo et illuc me mundatum introire faciat, ubi lux vera est et gaudia iustorum.*[28]

That this version goes back to even earlier days is seen from the fact that the Communion Devotions of Monte Cassino, dating back to the eleventh century, presents a form of the prayer more than twice this length,[29] and this, in turn, after further expansions, found its way into our missal in the section *Gratiarum actio post missam* under the title *Oratio S. Thomæ Aquinatis.*[30]

In many instances during the Middle Ages a prayer such as these was followed by the canticle *Nunc dimittis* as a further expression of joyful thanks.[31] Without doubt it fits the occasion perfectly. It is also used in the Byzantine liturgy as part of the conclusion of Mass.[32] With a remarkable

[27] Missal of Toul (14-15th c.) : Martène, 1, 4, XXXI (I, 652 D) ; *Alphabetum sacerdotum* (about 1500) : Legg, *Tracts,* 49; Ordinary of Coutances (1557) : *ibid.,* 66. Further examples in Lebrun, I, 545, note e. —In all of these cases, as we shall see, there follows the *Nunc dimittis.*

[28] Martène, 1, 4, 9, 9 (I, 424 D).—A prayer with this beginning in Italian sacramentaries of the 11-13th cent.: Ebner, 4, 17, 281, 295, 307; cf. 158.—A text-form that alters especially the second portion: *precor ut non veniat mihi ad iudicium,* etc., in Norman-English texts of the later Middle Ages: Martène, 1, 4, XXVIII (I, 645 D) ; Legg, *Tracts,* 228; Maskell, 190; Ferreres, 190, 202.

[29] Wilmart (*Eph. liturg.,* 1929) 324, with *Gratias tibi ago Domine sancte* in the beginning. Likewise in the Missal of St. Vincent (Fiala, 215).

[30] Brinktrine, *Die hl. Messe,* 269, who did not yet know of the Communion devotion of Wilmart, but did have in mind another 12th century manuscript of Monte Cassino with the same prayer, refers to the fact

that Thomas was reared in this monastery until 1236.

[31] Missal of Toul (above n. 27) besides the witnesses mentioned with it; Missal of Evreux-Jumièges (14-15th cent.) : Martène, 1, 4, XXVIII (I, 645 E). In a Missal of Rouen this song of praise follows the washing of the hands (which was accompanied by the *Lavabo*) ; *ibid.,* XXXVI (I, 637, note d). The use of *Nunc dimittis* is also verified on German soil; Martène, 1, 4, XXXII (I, 657 E) : Köck, 134 (n. 347) ; Franz, 595; 753. Among the Dominicans the song of praise was forbidden in 1551 as well as the *O sacrum convivium* and all additions after Communion except the *Quod ore. Monumenta O. Fr. Pr. historica,* 9 (1901), 322; Browe, "Die Kommunionandacht" (*JL,* 13, 1935), 51. The Missal of Valencia about 1411 has a petition to the Mother of God, *Domina nostra, advocata nostra* to follow upon the *Nunc dimittis;* Ferreres, 201. Gabriel Biel likewise testifies to the addition of the Marian antiphon *Bendicta filia;* (see below) ; Franz, III, n. 4.

[32] Brightman, 399.

feeling for form, the *Kyrie* and *Pater noster* were used to bridge the passage from the *Gloria Patri* at the end of the canticle to the postcommunion which was used as a conclusion,[33] or else a special concluding oration was added.[34] With the latter, this complex of prayers belongs to a Communion devotion dating back, seemingly, at least, to the twelfth century.

In the same spirit of tarrying meditatively over the great mystery of divine condescension, we often find in the same place the sentence from St. John, *Verbum caro factum est et habitavit in nobis*[35] or the antiphon *O sacrum convivium*,[36] to which Swedish missals add the versicle *Panem de cælo* and the oration of the Blessed Sacrament.[37] More frequently the

---

[33] Missal of Toul and the two related witnesses, *supra*, n. 27.

[34] Vorau Missal (15th cent.; Köck, 134): *Perfice in nobis, quæsumus Domine, gratiam tuam, ut qui iusti Simeonis expectationem implesti . . . ita et nos vitam obtineamus æternam. Per Christum D. N.* This arrangement of prayers beginning with *Nunc dimittis* forms the core of the Communion thanksgiving prayers published by A. Dold, "Liturgische Gebetstexte from Cod. Sangall. 18," *JL, 7* (1927), 51-53. In the manuscript of St. Gall that is probably to be dated about the middle of the 13th century (37) three other formulas precede; one beginning with the cited *Corpus Christi quo repleti sumus et sanguis* (a variant form of our Communion prayer *Corpus tuum Domine* as in the Troyes Missal; cf. above, n. 16; Dold's harking back to the antiphonary of Bangor is unnecessary), a free and shortened version of *Gratias ago* (above, p. 404), and the prayer *Domine Jesu Christe fili Dei vivi, corpus tuum crucifixum* (*supra*, p. 403). At the conclusion a further formula *Omnipotens sempiterne Deus propitius* is added to the oration *Perfice*. These two orations are found as Postcommunions in the Sacramentary of Fulda; (Richter-Schönfelder, n. 200; 2185).—In the still simpler form, as the Vorau Missal presents it, we have in all likelihood a Communion devotion designed particularly for private use that was in existence before the 13th century. In its make-up it is reminiscent of the Communion devotion of Monte Cassino, even though there is but little resemblance as regards the texts of the prayers.

[35] This phrase that we have met with in the Communion devotion of Monte Cassino (above, p. 369) is found since the 11th century above all in the central Italian Benedictine monasteries, as in the Sacramentary of Subiaco of 1075; Ebner, 339; cf. 323, 338. Often it is combined with a preceding threefold *Deo gratias* and is itself said three times with the addition: *Tibi laus, tibi gloria, tibi gratiarum actio in sæcula sæculorum, o beata Trinitas* (cf. the Communion devotion named); thus in the Pontifical of the library of Casanata of lower Italy (about 1100); Ebner, 331; cf. *ibid.*, 302, 311, 344, 348 f.; Fiala, 215. The Carmelite Ordinal of 1512 (Zimmermann, 84) has only the *Tibi laus;* likewise the present-day *Missale O. Carm.* (1935), 319. A Sacramentary of St. Peter's in Rome adds in its stead: *Et vidimus gloriam ejus.* Ebner, 336.—Towards the end of the Middle Ages the Johannine phrase appears in all sorts of places; see for France, Martène, 1, 4, XXXII f., XXXVI (I, 657 D. 661 C, 675 A); Legg, *Tracts,* 49; Lebrun, I, 542, note b; for Germany: Köck, 53; 70; 130; Beck, 271; Franz, 111, n. 4.

[36] Missal of Riga (about 1400); v. Bruiningk, 88, n. 5. Commentary of John Bechofen (about 1500); Franz, 594 f. Cf. the Dominican prohibition mentioned above, note 31.

[37] Missal of Strengnas, Sweden, 1487): Freisen, *Manuale Lincopense,* p. LI; likewise the Breviarium of Skara (1498; *ibid.,* XXXI), which in addition has two strophes of the hymn *Jesu nostra redemptio* as a preliminary. The hymns *Jesu nostra refectio* and *O salutaris hostia* were put to similar use in the North; Segelberg, 259.

Marian encomium, *Benedicta filia tu a Domino quia per te fructum vitæ communicavimus*[38] appears, or else a passage from the Passion of St. Agnes.[39] Other texts appear only occasionally.[40]

The prayers which thus serve to nourish and support the devotion of the priest after the reception of Communion as a rule coincide, in whole or in part, with the movements the priest makes while cleansing and arranging the vessels which have come in contact with the Sacrament. We must now turn our attention to both of these, the reservation and the ablutions.

16. Reservation. Ablutions

It is almost self-evident that some sort of preservation of the Sacrament after the celebration of the Eucharist was necessary from the start, since It had to be on hand for the sick. This preservation was nothing

[38] Seckau Missal (first half of the 14th cent.) : Köck, 130; cf. 71; Missal of Riga (about 1400) : v. Bruiningk, 88, n. 5. In Germany the use of the antiphon must have been well spread about the turn of the Middle Ages, since Gabriel Biel and Berthold of Chiemsee speak of it; Franz, 111, n.4.—Already in the 13th century it is present in Sarum, where however it was dropped later; see Legg, *The Sarum Missal*, 228, with the reading *Benedicta a filio tuo, Domina*. A prayer to Mary, *Sancta Maria genitrix D. n. J. C.*, also in the Sacramentary of Boldau, as an appendage to the prayer mentioned above, n. 18; Kniewald, 26; cf. Radó, 44.

[39] *Jam corpus eius corpori meo sociatum est et sanguis eius ornavit genas meas.* Apparently only in south Germany since the 14th century: Köck, 71; 130; Beck, 310. —Often also found with the beginning *Mel et lac.* Köck, 53; 70; 79; Franz, 111 n. 4; 753; Radó, 102. Cf. above, p. 352.

[40] A prayer beginning *Domine, suscipe me* in the Missal of Riga (v. Bruiningk, 88, n. 5) recalls Byzantine hymnody. Many a scriptural phrase is here incorporated; the promise, John 6: 55 in the monastic Missal of Lyons of 1531; Martène, 1, 4, XXXIII (I, 661 C) ; the doxology, Apoc. 7: 12 and the plea for a blessing, Ps. 66: 7 (*Benedicat nos Deus;* with the rubric *signando se calice*) in the Mass arrangement of Bec; *ibid.*, XXXVI (I, 675 A.B.). Also more or less freely formulated words

of meditation, thus in the Missal of Regensburg about 1500 (Beck, 271) : *Consummatum est et salva facta est anima mea. Hæc sunt convivia quæ tibi placent, o Patris Sapientia;* cf. Köck, 70. Or in the Missal of Valencia (before 1411) (Ferreres, 202) : *Hæc singulariter victima* (cf. above, I, 275, n. 21). A prayer for the grace of Viaticum: *Rogo te, Domine Jesu Christe, ut in hora exitus mei,* in the Vorau Missal of the 14-15th century: Köck, 133. For the rest, purely private prayers are rare. Cf. the same picture above in the Communion devotion of Monte Cassino.—We prefer not to delay over the Apologies as they occur, e.g., in the Missa Illyrica.

[41] This use of the prayers to accompany the actions is already noticed in the rubric of the Sacramentary of the 12-13th century from St. Peter's in Rome (Ebner, 336) : *ablue digitos dicendo: Quod ore . . . Corpus tuum . . . Verbum caro factum est . . .* It is also emphasized by Gabriel Biel, *Canonis expositio*, lect., 83, for the prayers mentioned by him, *Verbum caro factum, Lutum fecit, Nunc dimittis, Benedicta.* He remarks at the same time that the prayers are not prescribed, but left to the devotion of the celebrant.—On the other hand, the Ordinal of the Carmelites, 1312 (Zimmermann, 84), expressly stipulates: *deinde* (after the first ablution) *iunctis manibus inclinet ante altare dicendo: Quod ore.*

very special in itself, because the faithful were permitted to keep the Body of the Lord in their homes.[1] But the question arose, what should be done when, after the needs of the communicants have been fulfilled, a large portion of the sacred species should be left over. According to the custom of Antioch during the fourth century, the deacons were obliged to take the particles remaining after the Communion of the faithful into the sacristy at once;[2] what happened after that is not mentioned. But from various isolated ordinances of that period we can gather that the case when a large amount of the consecrated gifts remained after the Communion posed quite a problem. The Sahidic ecclesiastical *canones* warned the responsible clerics not to place too much bread and wine on the altar, so that the punishment meted out to the sons of Heli for their disrespect to the sacrifice might not fall upon them.[3] In some places, basing their action on Leviticus 8:32, they burned what was left.[4] In other places it was thought more seemly to bury the remainder in the ground.[5] Seldom was there the possibility of doing what was done at the pilgrim church in Jerusalem, where the remaining particles were used for Communion on the following day.[6] Elsewhere, innocent children were called in on certain days and given the sacred species,[7] or else—a practice that was certainly

---

[1] Of the method of reservation we know very little. It is possible that the tower-shaped and dove-shaped vessels (*turres, columbæ*) made of precious metals, which were listed in the registry of gifts in the *Liber Pontificalis* during the 4th and 5th centuries (*Liber Pont.*, ed. Duchesne, I, 177, 220, 243) have some relevance here; see Beissel, 310 f.; Andrieu, *Les ordines*, III, 73, note 3.

[2] *Const. Ap.*, 13, 17 (Quasten, *Mon.*, 231). Cf. Chrysostom, *Ep. ad Innocentium*, I, 3 (PG, 52, 533).

[3] Brightman, 463, 1. 6.

[4] Thus the Commentary on Leviticus II, 8 (PG, 93, 886 D; Brightman, 487), ascribed to Hesychius of Jerusalem (d. about 450). In the West since the 7-8th century this method of disposal was often prescribed for Hosts that had become unfit for consumption. Fire was considered the purest element, one that purified without needing purification itself. Even Durandus (d. 1296), IV, 41, 32 f., still speaks of an *incinerare*. Sometimes the ashes were preserved as a relic. However, this procedure was attacked by theologians since the 11th century. Numerous evidences in Browe, "Wann fing man an, die in einer Messe konsekrierten Hostien in einer

anderen Messe auszulteilen?" (*Theologie und Glaube*, 30 [1938], 388-404), 391 ff.

[5] The practice existed in the Byzantine Church at the time the schism started; proofs in Browe, *loc. cit.*, 389 f.—The Arabian Canons of Nicea (5-6th cent.) provided burial in case of vomiting and consider it as reverential a treatment as the parallel treatment of the remains of the Martyrs (Mansi, II, 1030; Browe, 390).

[6] Humbert of Silva Candida, *Adv. Græcorum calumnias*, n. 33 (PL, 143, 952 A) refers with praise to this method used in Jerusalem: *nec incendunt nec in foveam mittunt, sed in pixidem mundam recondunt et sequenti die communicant ex eo populum.*

[7] Evagrius Scholasticus (6th cent.), *Hist. eccl.*, IV, 36 (PG, 86, 2796 A), testifies to the practice in Constantinople, and Nicephorus Callisti (d. about 1341), *Hist. eccl.*, 17, 25 (PG, 147, 280), adds his own witness, reporting from the experience in his own childhood. Further data regarding Constantinople in Browe, 393 f. The same was stipulated by the Synod of Mâcon (585), can. 6 (Mansi, IX, 952): On Wednesdays and Fridays call the children and administer to them the *reliquias conspersas vino.*

more natural and obvious—the clerics themselves partook of the remaining particles at the end of the divine service.[8]

Reservation was thought of only for the sake of the sick. The amount of time which seemed admissible for the preservation of the species for this purpose was measured in various ways. It is the Byzantine custom even today to consecrate the Sacrament for the sick for the whole year on Maundy Thursday. This practice was already known to the West Syrians in the seventh century, and by the year 1000 had also become established in England. In the West, the custom was rapidly overthrown, and was also attacked in the East. Among the Uniate congregations it has long since disappeared.[9] In England about the year 1000 Abbot Aelfric of Eynsham struck at the practice by insisting that the Hosts reserved for the sick must be renewed every week or two,[10] and this regulation was generally retained during the centuries that followed.[11] Among the Carthusians during the thirteenth century the renewal of the species was molded into the structure of the Sunday high Mass,[12] and the same happened in other places also. In Soissons every Sunday at the priest's Communion the deacon was supposed to bring the vessel (containing the Blessed Sacrament) which hung over the altar to the celebrant, who put in a new Host and consumed the old.[13]

All through the Middle Ages reservation was considered only in relation to the sick. Hence, in the pertinent decrees we find mention made of

---

[8] Thus in the West there were different enactments from the 9th to the 13th century prescribing that the remaining species be consumed either by the clerics who were present, or by the celebrating priest himself. The latter, e.g., in Regino of Prüm, *De synod. causis,* inquis., n. 65 (PL, 132, 190 A). Further data in Browe, 394 f. The same method is still in force at present in most oriental liturgies, where it is even part of the rite to have something of both species remaining; Hanssens, III, 527-533. Particularly pronounced in the East Syrian Rite, *ibid.,* 528, 529 f.; Brightman, 304 f., 586 f.

[9] Browe, Die Sterbekommunion (*ZkTh,* 1936) 235 f.

[10] B. Fehr, *Die Hirtenbriefe Aelfrics* (Bibliothek der Angelsächsischen Prosa, IX; Hamburg, 1914), 30, 62, 179; Browe, *Die Sterbekommunion,* 235.

[11] A stricter rule is reproduced in Regino of Prüm, *De synod. causis,* I, 70 (PL, 132, 206 A; cf. *supra,* n. 8) : The renewal must take place *de tertio in tertium diem.* Still Regino is content himself with the renew-

al *de sabbato in sabbatum; ibid.,* 71 (206 B). The like stipulation in Ivo of Chartres, *Decretum,* II, 19 (PL, 161, 165) : *de septimo in septimum mutetur semper.* A weekly renewal is provided for in the Cluny Constitutions of the monk Udalrich, I, 8; II, 30 (PL, 149, 653 C; 722 f.). On the other hand, the *Liber ordinarius* of Liége (Volk, 100; cf. *ibid.,* 98 line 24) is content with a renewal of the species on each Communion day, i.e., about once a month. (Cf. Browe, *Die häufige Kommunion,* 68 ff.). Until the last centuries the interval permitted was variously estimated; Corblet, I, 570-572.

[12] Martène, 1, 4, XXV (I, 612 E) : The deacon places a new consecrated Host in the *capsula* after the Communion of the priest and then communicates himself from the old one.

[13] Martène, 1, 4, XXII (I, 612 E). The practice in Bayeux was the same: *ibid.,* XXIV (I, 630 B), and also in the old Cistercian rite; see the detailed account in Schneider (*Cist.-Chr.,* 1927), 162-165.— In the case of Soissons we clearly have a

only one or two Hosts.[14] All the rest of the faithful communicated with the priest at Mass and partook of the Hosts which had just been consecrated. The one exception was Good Friday, which was, until near the end of the Middle Ages, a favorite Communion day;[15] following the oriental model, Communion then took place within the *missa præsanctificatorum*, using Hosts consecrated the day before. On other occasions the practice of purposely consecrating and reserving a larger number of Hosts for later distribution was unknown all during the Middle Ages.[17]

But even in early times it was unheard of that Communion was distributed after Mass.[18] In the Byzantine Mass of the Greeks this is the ordinary practice.[19] On the other hand, wherever (as in Rome and Gaul)

very strange custom for here the celebrant used for his Communion only the Host consecrated on a previous occasion (aside, of course, from the particle deposited in the chalice). This remarkable practice was followed in Spain and Belgium into the 17th century, and also elsewhere, and was declared by individual theologians as permissible, while others (like de Lugo, *De sacr. eucharistie*, XIX, 5, 76 [Opp., ed. Fournials, IV, 240 f.]) rejected it. Browe, *Wann fing man an*, 399 f.

[14] Still in the visitation accounts from the Diocese of Ermland from the beginning of the 17th century, in which the number of particles provided was regularly noted with exactness, there were at most only from four to eight; G. Matern, "Kultus and Liturgie des allerheiligsten Sakramentes in Ermland," *Pastoralblatt für die Diözese Ermland*, 43 (1911), 80; Browe, *loc. cit.*, 404; *ibid.*, 401-404 further data.

[15] P. Browe, "Die Kommunion an den drei letzten Kartagen," *JL*, 10 (1930), 56-76, especially 70 ff.

[16] It is reported from Jerusalem, as we have seen above, as an exceptional practice in the 11th century that the Hosts which were left over from an earlier Mass were used in a following Mass. In the West about the same time we have the first testimony of a similar practice from Cluny, together with the fact that such a procedure was avoided elsewhere; Udalricus *Consuet. Clun.*, I, 13 (PL, 149, 662 B). In other monasteries even in the later centuries scrupulous care was taken that by and large no more hosts were consecrated than were necessary for each occasion. It was taken for granted as long as the faith-

ful went to Communion only on a few feast days, that in parish churches this was don as a matter of duty, as the Synod of Osnabrück, 1571, still provides (VII, 6; Hartzheim, VII, 715). Browe, *Wann find man an*, 396 ff.

[17] For that reason the receptacle for the preservation of the Eucharist, the oval cavity in the back of the Eucharistic dove that in many places hung over the altar, was only 4-6 cm. (1.5-2.1 inches) long. However, the diameter of the pyxes in the 14-15th century varied between 8 and 11 cm. (about 3.1-4.3 inches). The vessel might be large enough to suffice for a single Communion for the major part of a medium sized congregation (at Easter several days were provided for). Not till towards the end of the 16th century did the ciborium come into more general use as at present; Braun, *Das christliche Altargerät*, 328-330. Think of a General Communion stretched out to two or three succeeding Sundays, and you can see how easy it was to take the next step and no longer consider it of importance that the Communion be taken from the corresponding consecration.

[18] A hagiographic notice from Alexandria in H. Delehaye, *Anal. Bolland.*, 43 (1925), 28 f.—Gregory the Great, *Dial.*, III, 3 (PL, 77, 224).

[19] Brightman, 396. Among the Nestorians the practice mentioned above of consuming the remains of the Sacrament after the celebration, developed to the point where the priest himself, in cases when the faithful did not communicate, would postpone his own Communion and partake only after the celebration. Hanssens, III, 528.

the non-communicants left the church before Communion,[20] there was no reason why, even on great Communion days the distribution of the Sacrament should not take place within the Mass. This was true at least till the eighth century. But a changed attitude is noticed already in the Carolingian reform. True, it was presumed that the faithful would remain only till the *completio benedictionis sacerdotalis*, but this was now identified with the final prayers of the newly-accepted Roman Mass.[21] The result was soon seen. Not only on occasions here and there, but even on the greater Communion days, Communion was distributed after Mass at least to a great number of communicants.[22] Evidences for such a usage begin to grow more numerous since the twelfth century.[23] In the year 1256 the *Ordinarium* of the Dominicans directs the priest, that in general, when people are present who are waiting for the end of the Mass, the Communion should then be postponed *usque post missam*, but this should not be done on Maundy Thursday.[24] Still, Communion remained united with the Mass.

A certain perplexity in regard to the exact time when the faithful were to receive is seen even earlier. Therefore, some exponents of the liturgy insisted that the right moment for it was before the post-communion, because the latter presupposes the Communion of the faithful. Even the Roman Ritual, which first appeared in 1614, proposes the same reason in a pertinent admonition, but then, with a genuine regard for the cure of souls, it leaves room for distributing Communion before or after Mass *ex rationabili causa.*[26]

After the Council of Trent the tendency to separate the Communion from the Mass moved forward by leaps and bounds, since the appreciation of the liturgical pattern did not keep step with the zeal for the sacramental life. At first, this held true only for Communion on greater feasts and for general Communions, but later it spread to other occasions also, so that by the time the eighteenth century had faded into the nineteenth,

---

[20] Above, p. 341.

[21] Nickl, 57 f.—In Rome in the 12th century the announcement of the occurring festivities, etc., were no longer made before, but after the Communion; *Ordo eccl. Lateran.*, ed. Fischer, 87, line 9. Nevertheless an exception in the contemporaneous *Ordo Rom.* of Benedict, n. 24 (PL, 78, 1038 C).

[22] *Ordo Angilberti* (about 800): Bishop, *Liturgia historica*, 373.

[23] Browe, "Wann fing man an, die Kommunion ausserhalb der Messe auszuteilen?": *Theologie u. Glaube*, 23 (1931), 755-762. An example of the 12th century from Rome is the Communion of the neophytes that occurs daily *post finem missæ*

during the Easter and Pentecost octave; *Ordo eccl. Lateran.*, ed. Fischer, 73.

[24] Guerrini, 248.

[25] Walafried Strabo, *De exord. et increm.*, c. 22 (PL, 114, 950 f.) ; Bernold of Constance, *Micrologus*, c. 19 (PL, 151, 990) ; Durandus, IV, 54, 11.—Sometimes we find the distribution of Communion taking place before the priest's chalice Communion; Udalricus, *Consuet Clun.*, II, 30 (PL, 149, 721) ; *Liber ordinarius O. Præm.* (Waefelghem, 89-91) ; Köck, 131; cf. Ebner, 311. —In the Byzantine Mass also the priest, before his own chalice Communion, gives the sacred species of Bread to the deacon; Brightman, 395 line 12.

[26] *Rituale Rom.* (1925), IV, 2, 11.

Communion outside of Mass had become the general rule.[27] But during our own century a reverse movement has gradually gained ground.[28] Moreover, an increasing number of voices are being heard in favor of using for Communion substantially only those Hosts which were consecrated at the same Mass, so that the connection between sacrifice and repast might again gain its full, natural expression.[29] This aspiration has been heartily praised and encouraged by Pius XII.[30]

When the Communion is ended and the remaining sacred particles have been reserved there follows what we might designate by the comprehensive term, the ablution rite.

We are accustomed nowadays to think in this connection only of the washing of the fingertips that touched the Body of the Lord, and of the purification of the chalice, which should be freed from the remains of the Precious Blood by twice pouring wine (and water) into it. But even the Roman Missal of the present day designates something else as the first act of this rite when, speaking about the first ablution after Communion, it uses these words: *se purificat.*[31] The *ablutio oris* is, in fact, the most ancient part of the ablution rite. While for everything else we do not hear of any express prescriptions until much later, we find Chrysostom already advocating, and himself carrying out, the practice of taking a bit of water after Communion, or eating a piece of bread, so that whatever remained of the sacred species might not be ejected from the mouth along with the spittle. This practice was previously unknown in Constantinople, and was one of the charges leveled against the saint.[32] A similar practice is still in vogue amongst the Copts even today; after Communion they take a swallow of water which they call "the water of covering" because by it the Sacrament will be "covered,"[33] In the West, too, the *Regula Magistri*

---

[27] Browe (*Theologie u. Glaube,* 1931), 761 f.

[28] In countries like Austria, Germany, France and Belgium, where the liturgical movement has been in full swing since the dawn of the century, Communion has been generally restored to its rightful place within the Mass for the past two decades or more. Yet there are Sisterhoods that even to this day insist on the distribution regularly before the Mass; see an example in *Gloria Dei,* 2 (1947-48), 169. Elsewhere the old practice is still more general; e.g., in Italy, U. S. A.

[29] J. Gülden, "Grundsätze und Grundformen der Gemeinschaftsmesse in der Pfarrgemeinde" (*Volksliturgie und Seelsorge* [Colmar, 1942], 111; J. Pinsk, "Ex hac altaris participatione," *Liturg. Leben,* 1 (1934), 85-91; A. Lemonnyer O.P., "Communions a la Messe" (*Cours et Confér-*

ences, VII [Louvain, 1929]), 292 f. Similar suggestions already in the 18th and 19th centuries, in Trapp, 96, 109, 299. An obstacle to the practical carrying out of this method is the shape of the ciborium, which does not lend itself to being cleaned as simply as the paten.

[30] Encyclical letter of Nov. 20, 1947, *Mediator Dei* (II, 3) : *AAS,* 39 (1947), 564 f.

[31] *Ritus serv.,* X, 5; also in the text of the *Ordo missæ.*

[32] Palladius, *Dial.,* c. 8 (PG, 47, 27); Photius, *Bibliotheca,* c. 59 (PG, 103, 109 A).—The custom is still found in the Byzantine liturgy. For this *ablutio oris* the remainder of the ζέον is used, mixed with a little wine, and a bit of bread from the prosphora. The Slavic term for this is "zapiwka," after-drink.

[33] G. Graf, *Ein Reformversuch innerhalb der koptischen Kirche im 12. Jh.* (Pader-

in the same sense permits the reader at table to take a drink of wine before the reading on Communion days *propter sputum sacramenti*,[34] and the Rule of St. Benedict has a similar ordinance.[35]

Although in the beginning of the Middle Ages the custom was not generally widespread, still it was mentioned repeatedly. Two examples can be cited from the life of Louis the Pious (d. 840), who took a drink immediately after Communion; the first time it was offered him by Alcuin himself, on a pilgrimage in Tours;[36] and the second time on his deathbed.[37] And it was not entirely unknown even in the Roman pontifical liturgy.[38] At Monte Gargano, after the faithful had communicated they were accustomed to drink from a certain well next to the church.[39]

If we thus see greater stress put on this cleansing of the mouth than we would expect, we must remember that before the change from leavened to unleavened bread the Sacred Host had to be chewed.

Nevertheless, the custom continued and, in fact, burgeoned out after the aforementioned change of matter.[40] It is the time when all our ideas about reverence for the Blessed Sacrament were beginning to blossom. In 1165 Beleth favored the custom; he would have liked to see it introduced

born, 1923) 85; *idem.*, "Liturgische Anweisungen des koptischen Patriarchen Kyrillos ibn Laklak" (*JL*, 4 [1924]), 126.

[34] C. 24 (PL, 88, 992 D).

[35] C. 38: *accipiat mixtum priusquam incipiat legere propter communionem sanctam.* Cf. in this regard I. Herwegen, *Sinn und Geist der Benediktinerregel* (Einsiedeln, 1944), 254.

[36] *Vita Alcuini*, c. 15 (MGH, Scriptores, XV, I, p. 193, 1, 9): *cum post communionem corporis Christi et sanguinis manu propria eis misceret.*

[37] Thegan, *Vita Chludowici*, c. 61 (MGH, Scriptores, II, 648, 1, 1): *Iussit . . . communionem sacram sibi tradi et post hœc cuiusdam potiunculœ calidulœ haustum prœberi.*—See the reference in Martène, 1, 4, 10, 15 (I, 440 f.).

[38] In the Ordo of S. Amand (Andrieu, II, 168), obviously following Roman custom, a ceremony of this sort is mentioned; at the end of the stational service the assistant clergy receive *pastillos de manu pontificis,* whereupon another drink is handed them. The *Capitulare eccl ord.* (*ibid.*, III, 109; cf. III, 71), also makes mention of a drink, taken from three cups; after the pope's return to the secretarium, the remark is made concerning the assistant clerics: *et accepta benedictione de manu ipsius confirmant ternos calicis,* that is,

from three chalices.—On the other hand, it is surprising that the first Roman Ordo makes no mention of anything of the kind at the end of divine service; perhaps, however, we have a somewhat secularized development of the practice in the strange usage, probably reserved for solemn feasts, of a special invitation which, according to the later recension of the Ordo is extended to certain designated persons before the Communion; three court officials approach the throne of the pope *ut annuat eis scribere nomina eorum qui invitandi sunt, sive ad mensam pontificis per nomenculatorem, sive ad vicedomini per notarium ipsius,* whereupon the invitation is immediately carried out; *Ordo Rom.* I, n. 19 (PL, 78, 946). This banquet, having outgrown its sacred sphere, continued with increasing abandon even to the 15th century in the Cathedral of Bayeux; G. Morin, "Une ordonnance du Cardinal Légat G. d'Estouteville," *Beiträge zur Geschicht der Renaissance und Reformation,* J. Schlecht zum 60. Geburtstag, (Munich, 1917), 256-262.

[39] Martène, 1, 4, 10, 15 (I, 441), out of a manuscript dated about 1000.

[40] P. Browe, "Mittelalterliche Kommunionriten, 5. Die Ablution": *JL*, 15 (1941), 48-57.

everywhere, at least at Easter.[41] It had been the practice in monasteries even before this. We come upon a first mention of it in the prescriptions of William of Hirsau (d. 1091).[42] Also among the Cistercians it was customary for the *sacrista* to offer wine to every communicant when he had left the altar after having received Holy Communion under both kinds.[43] We see the same thing being done in other orders after the chalice was no longer received, with the express admonition: *Ad abluendum os diligenter, ne aliqua particula hostiæ remaneat inter dentes.*[44]

The reason given naturally held good for the priest as well as for the rest of the communicants. Innocent III issued a decretal (1204) for the priest: *Semper sacerdos vino perfundere debet postquam totum acceperit eucharistiæ sacramentum.*[45] But since the thirteenth century the custom of giving the faithful wine after Communion became more and more general. The practice then amalgamated with the last remnants of the practice of the lay chalice in which, in fact, only wine that had been mixed with a little of the Precious Blood or "consecrated" by contact with a particle, was presented.[46] Hense, the transition went in part unnoticed. The new practice was merely an enfeebled continuation of the other.[47] But in some

[41] John Beleth, *Explicatio,* c. 119 (PL, 202, 122). He would have a *parvum prandiolum* of bread and wine on this day for all immediately after Communion. The advice was in fact followed in some churches, as two examples from the 13th and 14th centuries in Browe, 49, show. Further data also for later times in Corblet, I, 621; cf. 594 f. In Oisemont (Somme) a duty was imposed even as late as 1619 to provide cereals and wine for the days of the Easter Communion (621). In general, however, the bread was soon dispensed with. In passing, we might mention that Beleth thinks the reason Mass was said at a late hour on ferial and fast days was that in this way a *prandium* could be taken immediately, just as on feasts. In the same sense but more emphatic an apparently later but unknown author in Martène, 1, 4, 10, 15 (I, 441).—However, there was also a contrary tendency. In Regino of Prüm, *De synod. causis,* I, 195 (PL, 132, 226) and in the Decretum Gratiani, III, 2, 23 (Friedberg, I, 1321), a wait of several hours before a meal is prescribed on Communion days because of the *residua Corporis Domini;* this appears as a demand—rejected—for every Communion, in authors such as St. Thomas, *In IV Sent.,* 8, 4, 3.

[42] William of Hirsau, *Const.* I, 86 (PL, 150, 1019 C) : the priest drinks the wine, which the server poured out at a private Mass for the ablution of the chalice and the fingers, from the Mass chalice, *quamquam de eodem calice etiam communicantes mox debeant vinum bibere.*—It is strange that the other Benedictine *Consuetudines* of the same period apparently say nothing of the practice.

[43] *Liber usuum* (after 1119), c. 58 (PL, 166, 1432).

[44] *Ordinarium O. P.* about 1256 (Guerrini, 247) : *Liber ordinarius* of the Liége monastery of St. James (Volk, 99). Similarly a rubric at the Ordination Mass of French Pontificals (14th to 16th cent.) : V. Leroquais, *Les Pontificaux* (Paris, 1937), I, 47 ; II, 54 ; cf. I, 129.

[45] *Corpus Jur. Can.,* Decretales Greg., 1, III, 41, 5 (Friedberg, II, 636). Cf. Good Friday in the *Pontificale Rom. Curiæ* of the 13th century (Andrieu, II, 563, line 5 ; PL, 78, 1014 B).

[46] Browe (*JL,* 15, [1941]), 51 f.

[47] This is seen, e.g., in the fact that now simply some wine was given to children after baptism instead of the usual Baptismal Communion. In individual cases perhaps the wine of the ablution of the chalice and the fingers was used for this purpose;

instances the modification was brought to the attention of the faithful.[48]

The reform synods of the sixteenth century often demanded that the drink be given not from a chalice, but from a vessel differently shaped, so as not to occasion any wrong conception. With this special restriction the practice is still found imbedded in the Roman Missal.[50] For the same reason, the vessel was not to be presented by the priest.[51] To keep the custom intact and to insure themselves that there was sufficient wine ready for the feast days, many foundations were established for this purpose almost everywhere towards the end of the Middle Ages and the beginning of the modern era.[52] Even today there are survivals of this last reminiscence of the communion chalice, which in turn had absorbed the old custom of the *ablutio oris*.[53]

see *Ordo eccl. Lateran.*, ed. Fischer, 73 line 13. Even Emperor Joseph II, on May 14, 1783, protested against an "abuse" prevalent in the Swabian provinces of Austria—the practice of giving newly baptized children a sip of the ablution wine on the eighth day after their christening, *Gesetzammlung über das geistliche Fach von dem Tage der Thronbesteigung bis 1783* (Vienna, 1784), 126 f. Older examples in J. Hoffmann, *Geschichte der Laienkommunion*, 165. The old administration formula or some other suitable one was used for the occasion, e.g., *Hæc ablutio calicis sit tibi salutaris et ad vitam æternam capessendam. Amen.* E. Martène, *Voyage littéraire*, II (1724), 141. The Exsequiale of Augsburg 1850, has the priest say *Prosit tibi ablutionis huius perceptio ad salutem mentis et corporis in nomine Patris . . .*; Hoeynck, 126. In other cases, however, wine was given that was simply blessed; see references that reach into the 16th and in part into the 18th century in Browe, *Die Pflichtkommunion*, 140-142. My confrere and teacher, O. Seywald, S.J., born in 1845 at Weitensfeld near Gurk in Carinthia, tells me that in his youth the practice still existed there of giving the child some wine when it was brought home from baptism. L. Andrieu, *La première communion* (Paris, 1911), 72, testifies to a similar practice still surviving in Champagne. It is also customary in some places today among the Carinthian Slovenes to put some crumbs dipped in wine into the mouth of the child (Chr. Srienc).

[48] The Synod of Lambeth (1281), can. 1 (Mansi, XXIV, 406), directed the priests

to teach the people that they received the Body and Blood of Our Lord under the species of bread and what they received from the chalice, on the contrary, was nothing sacred, *sacrum non esse.* As Browe, "Mittelalterliche Kommunionriten" (*JL*, 15, [1941]), 26, thinks, it was probably in opposition to this that the Synod of Exeter, 1287, permitted the people to be taught that they received the Blood of Christ from the chalice (Mansi, XXIV, 789). Cf. also Browe, "Die Sterbekommunion" (*ZkTh*, 1936), 219 f.

[49] Browe, "Mittelalterliche Kommunionriten" (*JL*, 15, [1941]), 56; Braun, *Das christliche Altargerät*, 552-557.

[50] *Ritus serv.*, X, 6. Similarly also in the Roman Pontifical, De ord. presbyteri, where however a chalice different from the one used by the officiating bishop is required. According to the Ordo of Peter Amelii, n. 11 (PL, 78, 1280 B) three large chalices should be in readiness at the third Mass on Christmas: one for the consecration; one *cum quo papa vinum bibit;* and one for the Communicants, to whom the server, after Communion administers the wine. The administration from one chalice also in French cathedrals about 1700; de Meléon, 127; 246 (others, *ibid.*, 409 f.). Cf. also *infra*, n. 53.

[51] Browe, 56. *Ibid.*, 55, an example from Deventer, where a *poculum publicum* instituted by the town is provided, to be administered by a *minister Senatus.* Cf. also Ordo of Peter Amelii, n. 11 (preceding note) ; *Cæremoniale ep.*, II, 29, 3 f.

[52] Examples in Browe, 54-57.

[53] Thus at every solemn Communion of

As at the *ablutio oris* or *purificatio,* so even more at what we call the ablution in a narrower sense, namely, the cleansing of the chalice and the fingertips that have come in contact with the Body of the Lord, the earliest standard set was the feeling of the individual *liturgus.* Whatever was thought proper was done as a rule after divine service, as is usually the case in the oriental rites even today. First of all, there is the cleansing of the chalice. The older Roman *Ordines* do not as yet contain any special provisions in this regard.[54] It is not till the ninth and tenth centuries that we find any express directions about this in the West. The purification of the chalice was handed over to the deacon or the subdeacon, if they were present; otherwise, the priest himself had to take over the task.[55] There must have been a special place in the sacristy or next to the altar where the water used for this purpose was poured out.[56]

Here mention is still made only of water, but we find that even in the eleventh century, monastic prescriptions called for wine for the purification.[57] It was considered praiseworthy to wash the vessel not only once, but three times, as was customary amongst the Premonstratensians,[58] and as is particularly recorded about Blessed Herman Joseph (d. 1241).[59]

Later, the purification of the chalice was combined with the purification of the tips of the fingers. Seldom is there mention of a special purification

---

the monastic congregation in the Carthusian order; *Ordinarium Cart.* (1932), c. 27, 14; cf. c. 29, 26. Among the Dominicans at present on Maundy Thursday; Sölch, *Hugo,* 148. I myself witnessed this practice as a theological student, almost every year from 1909 to 1913 on Maundy Thursday at the Cathedral of Brixen; a Master of Ceremonies stood beside the altar and served the wine from a chalice, the rim of which he cleansed each time with the prescribed *mappula.* Elsewhere the old tradition is traceable until 1870. F. X. Buchner, *Volk and Kult* (Forschungen zur Volkskunde, 27; Düsseldorf, 1936), 39. In Münster in Westphalia the practice was kept up on Maundy Thursday until the first World War; besides that, there is talk of a small bread that was distributed to the people; R. Stapper, in the memorial booklet, "Aus Ethik und Leben" (Münster, 1931), 88. See the bibliographical references in Browe, 57, n. 60. Notices of the practice in France, in Corblet, I, 261 f.

[54] Cf. *Ordo Rom.* I, n. 20 (PL, 78, 947 A; Stapper, 29): when the altar chalice is empty, it is immediately given to an acolyte, who in turn brings it back to the sacristy.

[55] Regino of Prüm (d. 915), *De synod. causis,* inquis., n. 65 (PL, 132, 190 A). The *Ordo Rom.* VI, n. 12 (PL, 78, 994) that also came into existence in Germany in the 10th century, impresses upon the archdeacon that he must take extreme care, *nimis caute,* that nothing of the sacred species remains in the chalice and on the paten.

[56] So, too, in the 9th century the *Admonitio synodalis* (PL, 96, 1376 B).

[57] Udalricus, *Consuet. Clun.,* II, 30 (PL, 149, 721). Statuta antiqua of the Carthusians: Martène, 1, 4, XXV (I, 635 B): in the High Mass the deacon takes the chalice, *vino lavat et sumit tantummodo quando communicat, alias vinum dimittitur in sacrarium.* In the *vita* of the emperor St. Henry (d. 1024) it was already taken for granted that wherever possible the ablution of the chalice was not thrown away; c. 34 (MGH, Scriptores, IV, 811): *qua [missa] completa, sicut semper facere consueverat, ablutionem calicis sumere volebat.*

[58] See the *Liber ordinarius* of the 12th century: Lefèvre, 13 f.; cf. Waefelghem, 95 f.

[59] *Acta SS,* April, I, 697 F; Franz, 105 f.; Lentze (*Anal. Præm.,* 1950), 143.

of the paten.[60] A washing of the fingers after the sacrifice is already mentioned in the life of Bishop Bonitus of Clermont (d. 709), of whom it is
related that the sick made efforts to obtain some of this ablution water.[61]
The same is recounted about a certain monk from Monte Cassino around
th year 1050.[62] The first Roman *Ordo* also speaks of the washing of the
hands of the pope as soon as all had communicated: *sedet et abluit
manus;*[63] similarly, in the tenth century in the sixth Roman *Ordo*, which
was intended primarily for Germany.[64] This is nothing else than the hand-
washing which is still customary in the pontifical rite, but which at that
time and in many places, even as late as the twelfth and thirteenth centuries, was considered a sufficient ablution; the only direction stressed in
regard to it was that the water was to be poured out in some fitting
place.[65] Meanwhile, however, especially in monasteries, even greater care
was exercised in regard to this ablution. The fingers were first cleansed
with wine, using either another chalice[66] or else the Mass chalice.[67] After
this, the fingers were washed with water at the *piscina* set up near the

[60] This is the case, among others, in John
of Avranches, *De off. eccl.* (PL, 147,
37 B): the subdeacon should help the
deacon *ad mundandum calicem et patenam.*
In some religious Communities, among
others the Premonstratensians, a rinsing
of the paten was prescribed, done with
wine; Waefelghem, 95, with n. 3. Also the
Missal of Riga (about 1400) entitled the
prayer mentioned above, p. 406, n. 40 *Domine suscipe me* with the rubric: *Ad ablutionem patenæ* (v. Bruiningk, 88, n. 5).

[61] Life by a contemporary biographer
(Mabillon, *Acta sanctorum O.S.B.,* III,
1, 92); Franz, 106.

[62] Leo Mars., *Chron. Casinense,* II, 90
(PL 173, 697): *ex aqua qua post missarum sollemnia manus ablueret.* Franz,108.

[63] *Ordo Rom.* I, n. 20 (Andrieu, II, 106),
older recension; but the later recension
(PL, 78, 947 C) also mentions among
those to whom the pope administers Communion: *qui manutergium tenet et qui
aquam dat.*

[64] *Ordo "Postquam"* of the episcopal Mass
(Andrieu, II, 362; PL, 78, 994 C). Cf. in
the 9th century the *Admonitio synodalis*
(PL, 96, 1376 B), that required a *vas
nitidum cum aqua* in the sacristy or alongside the altar, in which the priest might
wash his hands after Communion.

[65] Ivo of Chartres, *De conven. vet. et novi
sacrif.* (PL, 162, 560 D); Innocent III,

De s. alt. mysterio, VI, 8 (PL, 217, 911).
Also the work dependent on Innocent, Wilhelm of Melitona O.F.M., *Opusc. super
missam* (about 1250), ed. van Dijk (*Eph.
liturg.,* 1939), 347. Likewise Durandus
(d. 1296), IV, 55, 1, repeats the statement of Innocent III.

[66] Udalricus, *Consuet. Clun.,* II, 30 (PL,
149, 721 f.): the deacon does it first,
then in the same chalice the celebrating
priest, who then drinks the ablution. John
of Avranches, *De off. eccl.* (PL, 147,
37 B). Further documents from the monasteries in Lebrun, I, 545.—According to
the *Ordo eccl. Lateran.* (Fischer, 86, line
37) wine is poured over the fingers of the
bishop *in perfusorio argenteo;* the deacon
then takes the wine.

[67] William of Hirsau (d. 1091), *Const.* I,
86 (PL, 150, 1091; *supra,* n. 42). Similarly in the *Liber usuum O. Cist.,* c. 53
(PL, 166, 1127): the priest has wine poured into the chalice after his Communion,
*recepto calice respergat digitos suos in ipso
calice, quem ponens super altare eat ad
piscinam abluere in ipsa digitos aqua. Quibus tersis . . . redeat ad altare sumere
vinum quod dimisit in calice. Quo sumpto
interum aspergat calicem vino.* Even more
plainly is the ablution of the fingers by
the priest connected with the first ablution
of the chalice in the Ordinal of the Carmelites about 1312 (Zimmermann, 83 f.).

altar,[68] or in some other manner,[69] and then were dried. Only then[70] was the ablution wine taken from the chalice.[71] Thereafter, wine was again poured into the chalice, i.e., the Mass chalice for certain, and then drunk.

A special *ablutio oris*, consequently, became superfluous, since it was bound up with the ablution of the chalice.[72] While, as we have said, it was thought satisfactory in some places to use only wine to cleanse the chalice, it was generally considered necessary, for obvious reasons, to use water too, at least for the fingers,[73] and thus to adhere to the traditional method of washing the hands. The *Ordinarium* of the Dominicans, introduced in 1256, contains for the first time, at least for the occasion when no *honesta piscina* was to be had, the advice *(melius est)* to wash the fingers with water over the chalice, and then to drink this water along with the wine that had been previously used for cleansing the fingers.[74] This manner of

[68] The construction of such a *piscina* alongside the altar is demanded among others by the Synod of Würzburg of 1298, can. 3 (Hartzheim, IV, 26) and by the Cistercians in their General Chapter of 1601 (Schneider, *Cist.-Chr.*, 1927, 376). Even at present, as we recall, the priest goes to the epistle side for the ablution.

[69] *Ordo eccl. Lateran.* (Fischer, 86 f.).

[70] At Tongern about 1413 this was done before stepping to the *piscina;* de Corswarem, 141.

[71] Accordingly it became customary to drink the ablution of the fingers only after wine began to be used in the function, i.e., since its assimilation to the ablution of the chalice, or its adoption by it. And here also the practice varied. In the life of St. Heribert of Cologne (d. 1021; Vita by Rupert of Deutz, d. 1135) there is an account of a woman who had a way of securing for herself the wine with which the bishop according to custom washed his fingers after Communion (c. 19; PL, 170, 410; Franz, 109); consequently it was not consumed by the celebrant.—French churches held fast to this older method of cleansing the fingers, in part still in the 18th century; an acolyte brings a special ablution vessel to the altar (de Moléon, 230; 291) or the priest goes over to the *lavatorium* (ibid., 315); cf. Martène, 1, 4, XX, XXII (I, 609 A, 613 A).—However, that the ablution was regularly consumed by the end of the twelfth century is clear from the fact that numerous Synods since 1200 impress upon the priests that in case of a bination, they may not

take the *ablution digitorum* of the first Mass.,K. Holböck, *Die Bination* (Rome, 1941),' 102. Cf. also the pertinent statement by Simmons, *The Lay Folks Mass Book,* 303-307. We might note in passing that even today we have a twofold practice, for outside of Mass we are content with the ablution of mere water, which then is disposed of in the manner in earlier times.

[72] Clearly the meaning and purpose of the *ablutio oris* is still kept in view in the Pontifical of Durandus (Andrieu, *Le Pontifical Romain*, III, 348; cf. 371, line 37) where the administration of Communion to the newly ordained is inserted *post primam oris ablutionem, priusquam digitos lavet,* obviously because of the formula that must be said while administering it.

[73] Still, e.g., John Burchard about 1500 in his Mass-order mentions during Mass only the ablution of the fingers with wine (Legg, *Tracts,* 164). This presupposes washing the hands in the sacristy afterwards.

[74] Guerrini, 244; cf. Sölch, *Hugo,* 149. In the Dominican Ordinarium mentioned *(loc. cit.,)* there is also for the first time a more definite instruction regarding the use of a small cloth to dry the fingers, our purificator: *intra calicem reservetur, et cum explicatur calix, reponatur super altare a dextris in loco mundo.* Nothing is said about drying the chalice with the same cloth; sometimes another cloth was used for the purpose, as the monastic Consuetudines of the 11th century indicate. Braun, *Die liturgischen Paramente,* 212 f.; cr. de Corswarem, 125; 128. According to

procedure was propagated only gradually, but finally became normal.[75] In the pontifical *ritus* of today it has been added to the ancient manner of washing the hands.[76]

However, until the very end of the Middle Ages there was no uniform practice in these matters. According to Gabriel Biel, for instance, it was left to the choice of the priest to have the ablution of the fingers either right after the Communion or only after Mass.[77] On the other hand, English Mass books of that same period gave very careful and circumstantial rules in this regard, although varying in details.[78]

A custom had been spread in Germany since the fourteenth century, which reminds us of the blessing of the senses with the Eucharist which had been in vogue a thousand years earlier. After the ablution of the fingers, the eyes were touched, and these words uttered: *Lutum fecit Dominus ex sputo et linivit oculos meos et abii et lavi et vidi et credidi*

a later practice, the priest had to place the chalice upon the paten; thus, e.g., according to the later Sarum Mass-books: *ponat . . . super patenam, ut si quid remaneat stillet;* Martène, 1, 4, XXXV (I, 671 A); Maskell, 194. This custom also in the *Statuta antiqua* of the Carthusians: Martène, 1, 4, XXV (I, 635 B); as someone from Valsainte has kindly told me, this was done by laying the rim of the cup on the paten, so that any drops that remain might flow thereon. In accordance with the latest edition of the *Ordinarium Cart.* (1932), c. 27, 13, the chalice is merely tilted and whatever is thus gathered together is then swallowed.—In any case the use of the purificator gained ground but slowly. A Jesuit traveling from Italy to Poland in 1563 affirms that it was not in use either in Germany or in Poland; Braun, 213. But it was required by the Missal of Pius V, and so its use became general.

[75] The Benedictine *Liber ordinarius* of Liége, which otherwise often copies the Dominican Ordinarium word for word, does not have it (Volk, 96). The Ordo of Stefaneschi (about 1311), n. 53 (PL, 78, 1168 f.) also has the pope perform the ablution with water over a dish after the consumption of the wine ablution of the fingers. The water is then poured out *in loco puro.*

[76] *Cæremoniale ep.,* II, 8, 76.

[77] Gabriel Biel, *Canonis expositio,* lect., 83.

[78] A Sarum Missal of the 15th century (Legg, *Tracts,* 266) offers the following procedure: After the chalice Commu-

nion, the priest has the deacon on his right side pour in the wine; after consuming it he says: *Quod ore.* Then he has wine poured over his fingers, drinks that and says: *Hæc nos communio;* then water in like manner, whereupon he prays at the middle of the altar before the crucifix: *Adoremus crucis signaculum per quod salutis nostræ sumpsimus exordium,* and the further prayer *Gratias* (see above, p. 404). Finally he goes to the *sacrarium* and washes his hands. Cf. Ferreres, 202 f.—According to a manuscript of the 14th century, which presents approximately the same procedure, the priest prays the *Lavabo* verse, Ps. 25: 6 (Legg, 268) during this last function of washing his hands; this verse is also found elsewhere in this place; see Maskell, 197; Martène, 1, 4, XXXI, XXXVI (I, 652 D, 675 B). Thus at Linkoping in the 14th century and later; Segelberg, *Eph. liturg.,* 65 (1951), 259. A survey of the different ablution rites in England at the turn of the Middle Ages in Maskell, 190-197.

[79] John 9: 11, in the form of the *Communio* for the Thursday of the fourth week of Lent. The Regensburg Missal about 1500 (Beck, 271) with the following rubric: *Lingendo digitos dic . . .* (and other formulas ensuing).—Freising Missal of 1520: Beck, 310; Augsburg Missal of the 15th century: Franz, 753. Mass-*ordo* of Gregorienmünster (14-15th cent.): Martène, 1, 4, XXXII (I, 657 E). The earliest testimony (without rubric) I find in the Seckau Missal of the first half of the 14th century

Deo.[79] It was a custom which could easily have lead to superstition and abuse,[80] but it later disappeared.

Special prayers were not generally composed for the ablution.[81] The prayers which today accompany the ablution are (as we see from their history) only outwardly connected with it.

It is remarkable that the oriental rites—even those outside the union—in spite of their greater indifference in regard to the care of the Blessed Sacrament, have also come to have a special ablution rite which, at least in some points, is quite close to our western one. Amongst the Syrians as early as the sixth century we find an ordinance which demands that the water used in purifying the sacred vessels should be poured out in a decent place.[82] Amongst the West-Syrian Jacobites the rite of ablution is even more detailed and framed with many prayers, and includes, besides the washing of the vessels, a repeated ablution of the fingers and a wiping of the chalice with a sponge.[83] A sponge is also one of the appurtenances of the Byzantine liturgy.[84] The Copts also have several traditional ablutions.[85]

17. The Post-Communion

Even the earliest expositions of the liturgy, after speaking about the Communion to which all the faithful are invited, do not forget to admonish them to make a thanksgiving.[1] Basing himself on Timothy 2:1, Augustine distinguishes four sections of the Mass; as the last of these he places the

---

(Köck, 130) where Ps. 12:4b (*Illumina oculos meos*) and Ps. 85:17 (*Fac mecum signum*) are added. Later examples from Styria, Köck, 53; 59; 65; 71; 133. Also a formula in a Passau Missal of the late 14th century: Radó, 102, and in an Odenburg Missal of 1363: Radó, 109. The words of Ps. 12:4b with the rubric: *Madefac oculos* in a Missal of Riga (v. Bruiningk, 88, n. 5). Also in the German commentators of the 14th to 16th cent. the custom is mentioned; Franz, 111 (with n. 4); 576.

[80] Franz, 110-112.

[81] An exception is the Missal of the 15th century from Monte Vergine (Ebner, 157) which has the priest saying at the ablution of the fingers: *Omnipotens sempiterne Deus, ablue cor meum et manus meas a cunctis sordibus peccatorum, ut templum Spiritus Sancti effici merear. Amen.*

[83] Johannes bar Cursos (d. 538), *Resolutio,* can. 3 (Hanssens, III, 532 f.); *Aquæ ablutionis rerum sacrarum in locum decentem, in fossam profundam proiciantur et occultentur.*

[83] Brightman, 106-108; cf. *ibid.,* 574 s. v. deaconess. At the beginning of the rite the consumption of the remaining particles of the Sacred Species takes place; cf. above, p. 407-408, n. 8.

[84] Its function in any case goes farther than among the Syrians; Brightman, 588, s. v. sponge.

[85] According to the practice of today the chalice is first rinsed with wine; Hanssens, III 530. A statement from the 14th century speaks also of rinsing the paten; the water used for the purpose was then drunk; *ibid.,* 532.

[1] Cyril of Jerusalem, *Catech. myst.,* V, 22 (Quasten, *Mon.,* 110; *supra,* p. 378). Theodore of Mopsuestia, *Sermones catech.,* VI (Ruecker, 38): *Permanes [in ecclesia], ut cum omnibus laudes et benedictiones secundum legem Ecclesiæ persolvas.*

gratiarum actio, the thanksgiving after Communion.[2] Chrysostom thrusts sharply at those who cannot wait for the εὐχαριστήριοι ᾠδαί, but, like Judas, hurry away instead of singing a hymn of praise with the Lord and His true disciples.[3]

There is question, first of all, of a thanksgiving said in common in the church—that is what we must naturally expect. We find this in early times in the liturgies of the Orient,[4] and regularly as follows: after a prayer of thanksgiving, generally composed of several members, another such prayer of blessing follows, whereupon the faithful are dismissed. Sometimes the hymns accompanying the Communion are so prolonged that they seem to be the first part of the thanksgiving.[5] Before the actual prayer of thanksgiving, according to the *Apostolic Constitutions,* the deacon invites the faithful to prayer: "After we have received the Precious Body and the Precious Blood of Christ, we want to give thanks to Him who has made us worthy to partake of these sacred mysteries, and we wish to plead that it shall not redound to our fault but to our salvation, to the weal of soul and body, to the preservation of piety, to the remission of sin, to life everlasting." At this, all arise and the bishop recites a comprehensive prayer in which thanksgiving merges into a renewed plea for all the intentions of the congregation and for all classes and ranks of the Church.[6] Similarly, this call to prayer by the deacon recurs later on also,[7] but in other places it has developed in various ways. In the Greek Liturgy of St. James it begins with a solemn praise of Christ,[8] and then, as in all Greek liturgies, it unfolds into a short litany to which the people respond in the usual manner with   χύριε ἐλέησον. [9] In the Ethiopian Mass, after the deacon's call to prayer, there is an exchange of prayers between priest and people, in which the latter reply three times to the priest's recitation of Psalm 144: 1, 2, 21: "Our Father who art in heaven, lead us not into temptation."[10] In all cases, the close is essentially formed by the thanksgiving prayer of the celebrant of which—in the Greek liturgies at any rate— only the closing doxology is now spoken in a loud voice and in the Byzantine liturgy this doxology is all that has survived.[11] On the other hand,

---

[2] Augustine, *Ep.,* 149, 16 (CSEL, 44, 363).

[3] Chrysostom, *De bapt. Christi,* c. 4 (PG, 49, 370).

[4] Cf. *supra,* p. 276.

[5] Thus the East Syrian Mass: Brightman, 297-301; in the Armenian: *ibid.,* 452-454.

[6] *Const. Apost.,* VIII, 14, 1-15, 5 (Quasten, *Mon.* 231 f.).—In the Euchologion of Serapion only the prayer of the celebrant is included: *ibid.,* 65 f.

[7] In the liturgy of the West Syrian Jacobites: Rücker, *Jakobosanaphora,* 53; 75.

[8] Brightman, 65. A similar prayer of praise, but from the priest, also in the Jacobite liturgy: *ibid.,* 104.

[9] Brightman, 65; 141; 397; cf. 454.

[10] Brightman, 242 f.—Ps. 144 is the Communion psalm already certified by Chrysostom; see above, p. 392; the continuation of the alternating prayer in Hanssens, III, 521.

[11] Brightman, 65 f.; 141 f.; 342 f.; 397. In the present-day Byzantine liturgy the doxology (*ibid.,* 397, 1, 13) is separated from the thanksgiving prayer (*ibid.,* 395, 1, 33).

the priest's prayer of thanksgiving in the West-Syrian Mass is assimilated to the eucharistic prayer by taking up and amplifying the introductory formula: "It is worthy and right and meet . . ."[12] In the Gallican liturgy, too, the thanksgiving consists of a lengthy call to prayer, and the priestly oration.[13]

Here again the Roman liturgy is distinguished by the special scantiness of its prayer-language. Originally it also had a double close consisting of a prayer of thanksgiving and a prayer of blessing. This prayer of thanksgiving, usually captioned *Ad complendum* or *Ad completa* in the Gregorian Sacramentaries, and *Post communionem* in the Gelasian,[14] with its ever varying formulas belongs to the very substance of the Roman Sacramentary, just like the collect and the *secreta*. The post-communion is also formed exactly like them. And hence, like them, it displays the outlines of a prayer of petition. Like them, in its older forms it turns without exception to God through Christ, and so closes with the formula, *Per Dominum*,[15] which in many medieval churches gained special stressing at this point by being recited in the middle of the altar.[16]

The parallelism of the post-communion to the two earlier orations is broadened by reason of the surroundings in which it appears. The opening, the offertory and the communion represent three liturgical structures of closely corresponding patterns. In each case there is outward activity united with a certain local movement: the entrance, the offertory procession and the march to the Communion. In each case—and originally only at these three points—the choir of singers is busied with the antiphonal singing of the psalms. In each case—and again almost only here—there is an introductory series of silent prayers with which the celebrant nurtures his devotion. So again, in each case the singing and the praying come to a close with an oration which is preceded, mediately or immediately, by

[12] Brightman, 302.

[13] *Missale Gothicum*: Muratori, II, 519; 523 et al.

[14] The last designation also in the Gallican Missal (*Missale Gothicum*: Muratori, II, 519, etc.).

[15] Jungmann, *Die Stellung Christi*, 103 ff.; cf. 226 f. Individual departures from the rule mentioned did not turn up in the liturgy of the City of Rome until about 1000 when the old formulas came back to Rome from the Gallican atmosphere of the North; four of them now had the *Qui vivis* conclusion and henceforth presupposed that the prayer was addressed to Christ, as was the case also everywhere in the prayers that meanwhile came into use before the Communion. Later on, newly elaborated texts often chose this mode of address, e.g., the *Postcommunio* on Corpus Christi (*Fac nos*), without, however, setting any precedent or giving rise to a preponderance of this form of *Postcommunio* even in the new formulas. Even on days when the secret prayer has the address to Christ, the Postcommunion frequently has *Per Dominum* (e.g., on June 4, or June 13).

[16] Thus in the Dominican Rite: *Ordinarium O.P.* of 1256 (Guerrini, 245), likewise still today: *Missale O. P.* (1889), 22; Liber ordinarius of Liége (Volk, 97); Missale of Hereford of 1502 (Maskell, 197 f.). According to the Regensburg Mass-*ordo* about 1500 (Beck, 272) the priest kisses the Missal after *Filium tuum*, closes it, and with the words *Qui tecum* returns to the middle of the altar. Thus also an *Ordo* of Averbode, Belgium (about 1615): Lentze (*Anal. Præm.*, 1950), 145.

the liturgical greeting and the *Oremus*. And the oration itself has been formed according to the same stylistic rules.

In this instance the *Dominus vobiscum* and the *Oremus* immediately precede the prayer, for although the entire Communion cycle must be hidden in an atmosphere of prayer, even prayer of the faithful, yet the prayer here demanded is not a prayer of public and ecclesiastical character as is the *oratio communis* which is united with the offertory. How close a bond was judged to exist between the *post-communio* and the Communion cycle (and hence with the Sacrifice-Mass) can be seen from the fact that, as the later versions of the Roman *Ordo* note, the pope did not turn to the people at the *Dominus vobiscum* but stood before the altar facing East,[17] the same attitude he assumes at the beginning of the preface when he is not to turn away any more from the gifts of sacrifice on the altar. This prescription, however, was not retained for any length of time, since it had to be conceded that the sacrifice had already been completed.[18] But for the same reason the *Flectamus genua* was never said before this oration, for surely it belongs at least to the culmination of the prayers grouped about the Eucharist.[19]

Considering the contents, the theme of the *post-communio* is given by the communion just finished; and it is always the Communion of the assembled congregation that is thought of, not that of the priest alone. This rule of form was followed even in those formulas that go back only to the times when a congregational Communion was exceptional.

Relatively few formulas appear which have no connection with the Communion and present merely an oration of a more general character—a consideration of the celebration of the day[20] or some special needs.[21] The rule is that the prayer begin with a grateful glance at the gifts received. The reception of the sacrament is represented either as an item in the delineation of the petitioner: *Repleti cibo potuque cœlesti, sacro munere satiati;* or as a starting-point of the effect prayed for: *Hæc nos communio purget, Per huius operationem mysterii;* or else it is simply represented as a fact, either in the ablative form: *Perceptis Domine sacramentis;* or as an independent clause: *Sumpsimus Domine, Satiasti Domine;* or finally, it is worked into the course of thought in some other way.

---

[17] *Ordo Rom.* I, n. 21 (Andrieu II, 107; PL, 78, 948 A).

[18] In the *Ordo "Postquam"* (Andrieu, II, 362; PL, 78, 994 C) that originated in the 10th century in Germany for the Bishop's Mass, provision is made for turning towards the people.

[19] Cf. *supra*, I, 369.

[20] Thus on the feast of the Annunciation (*Gratiam tuam*); on the feast of John the Baptist (*Sumat*); frequently on the feast days of Saints (among others, Commune Apostol., Commune Doctorum); in sev-

eral Vigil Masses.—The same appears in the oldest Sacramentaries, of which the Leonianum indeed gives the formulas without title; the two first named feast-day Postcommunions in the Gregorianum (Lietzmann, n. 31, 4; 125, 3).

[21] Thus frequently in Votive Masses and the *orationes diversæ* of the *Missale Romanum* derived from them. In the present-day *missa tempore belli,*, e.g., there is a *Postcommunio* that served as a second collect in a similar Mass of the older Gelasianum, III, 57 (Wilson, 272 f.).

If we combine all the various details in these approaches to the mention of the Sacrament, we acquire an excellent picture of Christian revelation regarding the Eucharist and Communion. What we have received is called a holy gift, a heavenly banquet, spiritual nourishment, an efficacious mystery, the Holy Body and Precious Blood. Just as in the preceding prayers of the Roman Mass, the Person of our Lord is not brought to the fore as such, wherefore there is no special impetus here to address ourselves to Christ directly. The picture that is constantly presented is a picture of the sacrifice as a whole, the sacrifice that we have offered to God along with Chrst, the sacrifice in which we take part, and the petition which we direct to the Father *per Dominum nostrum*. It is the same way of looking at the Sacrament which in our own day is at the bottom of the admonition in the Roman Ritual when it advises the faithful to remain in prayer for some time after Communion, *gratias agentes Deo de tam singulari beneficio.*[22] As a matter of fact, our thanks to God is best expressed in such a manner, even though the word "thanks" itself seldom appears, for in such words we "think of" that which God has granted.

Next, to give the picture that distinctive mark which it gets by pointing to the sacramental effects of Communion, the wording of the post-communion shifts to the petition. What we expect and implore from our partaking of the Body and Blood of Christ is the progress and final triumph of its redemptive efficacy in us: *ut quod pia devotione gerimus, certa redemptione capiamus,*[23] *ut inter eius membra numeremur, cuius corpori communicamus et sanguini.*[24] As part of this, deliverance from both internal and external obstacles enters in: *et a nostris mundemur occultis at ab hostium liberemur insidiis.*[25] Our bodily welfare is also mentioned time and again in the constant recurrence[26] of the antithesis of body and soul, present and future, internal and external: *et spiritualibus nos repleant alimentis et corporalibus tueantur auxiliis,*[27] But the essential effect is inward. The Sacrament must heal and strengthen us: *salvet et in tuæ veritatis luce confirmet;*[28] it must produce in us, *ut non noster sensus in nobis, sed iugiter eius præveniat effectus.*[29] But above all, this Sacrament of fellowship is to increase love in our hearts: *ut quos uno cœlesti pane satiasti, tua*

[22] *Rituale Rom.* IV, 1, 4; cf. *Cod. Iur. Can.,* can., 810.

[23] Sources from the oldest sacramentaries in Mohlberg-Manz, n. 975; *Missale Rom.,* July 2.

[24] Gregorianum (Lietzmann, n. 58, 3); *ibid.,* further references. *Missale Rom.,* Saturday of the third week of Lent.

[25] Mohlberg-Manz, n. 295; *Missale Rom.,* Wednesday of the first week of Lent.

[26] Cf. *supra* I, 378 f.

[27] Mohlberg-Manz, n. 410; *Missale Rom.,* Wednesday of the fourth week of Lent.— The idea that the Eucharist should extend its beneficial effect to both the temporal and spiritual welfare is particularly pronounced in the older texts; see, e.g., in Leonianum: Muratori, I, 322; 328; 362; 378; 413; 420; 462.

[28] Mohlberg-Manz, n. 1080; *Missale Rom.,* Aug. 13.

[29] Mohlberg-Manz, n. 1177; *Missale Rom.,* 15th Sunday after Pentecost.

facias pietate concordes.[30] We know, however, that our own free effort is co-decisive in this matter. Hence, looking at the Sacrament, we entreat *ut quos tuis reficis sacramentis, tibi etiam placitis moribus dignanter deservire concedas.*[31] An ideal of Christian living flashes out when, after the reception of the Sacrament, we ask that we may never slip away from it: *ut (in) eius semper participatione vivamus;*[32] indeed, that we may never cease giving thanks: *ut in gratiarum semper actione maneamus.*[33] The final fruit, however, that this Sacrament must give us is life eternal, as our Lord Himself has promised: *ut quod tempore nostræ mortalitatis exsequimur, immortalitatis tuæ munere consequamur.*[34] What occurs at the altar remains in the world of symbol and sacrament, but we desire the full actuality: *ut cuius exsequimur cultum, sentiamus effectum.*[35] What we have received was grand, but it was only a pledge and first payment; boldly we desire, *ut . . . beneficia potiora sumamus.*[36] Apropos of this, it is most generally the thought of the feast which determines what special effect is emphasized in our petition. Sometimes, too, expression is given to our consciousness that the sacrament is not the only source of grace, that faith and the profession of faith also enter in: *sacramenti susceptio et sempiternæ s. Trinitatis . . . confessio* should lead us to salvation.[37] On the feasts of saints the plea is generally changed only insofar as the effect of grace is petitioned *intercedente beato N.;* but there also the intercession of the saint sometimes appears alongside the efficacy of the Sacrament: *Protegat nos, Domine, cum tui perceptione sacramenti beatus Benedictus abbas pro nobis intercedendo.*[38]

In Rome it seems that for a short time the constant variation of the post-communion was given up. The fourth Roman *ordo* has the pope after the Communion chant recite with a loud voice, *Dominus vobiscum,* and then the one oration, *Quod ore sumpsimus,* which in Rome at that time was not yet one of the private Communion prayers.[39] In its double progression,

[30] Mohlberg-Manz, n. 1395; *Missale Rom.,* Friday after Ash Wednesday; cf. the *Postcommunio* on Easter.

[31] Mohlberg-Manz, n. 110; *Missale Rom.,* Sunday within the Octave of the Epiphany.

[32] Mohlberg-Manz, n. 1113; *Missale Rom.,* Aug. 22.

[33] Mohlberg-Manz, n. 785; *Missale Rom.,* Aug. 30.

[34] Mohlberg-Manz, n. 518; *Missale Rom.,* Maundy Thursday.

[35] Frequently in the Gregorianum (Lietzmann, n. 22, 3, etc.) ; *Missale Rom.,* Commune unius Martyris and in other places.

[36] Mohlberg-Manz, n. 75; *Missale Rom.,* Dec. 31.—Regarding the meaning of this

expression cf. O. Casel, *JL,* 3 (1923), 13, and other places.

[37] In the appendix of the later Gelasianum in Mohlberg, page 257, n. 51; *Missale Rom.,* Feast of the Trinity.

[38] Mohlberg-Manz, n. 998; *Missale Rom.,* Commune Abbatum.—J. Tschuor, *Das Opfermahl* (Immensee, 1942), offers summary of the Eucharistic teachings contained in the *Postcommunio* formulas of today's *Missale Romanum.*

[39] *Ordo "Qualiter quædam"* (Andrieu, II, 305; PL, 78, 984 C). The testimony is confirmed in the Gregorianum of the Cod. Pad. (Mohlberg-Baumstark, n. 894) and the later Gelasianum (Mohlberg, n. 1567), both of which have this formula

from the food of the body to that of the spirit, and from the gift in time to the remedy which is effective in eternity, this formula in typical fashion marks the upward progress which we ought to bring to completion on the strength of this Sacrament.

and the further Postcommunion *Conservent* following the Canon; cf. above, p. 403, n. 25. See also Puniet, *Le sacramentaire de Gellone,* 214* f.; Leroquais, I, 6.— What is most likely a relic of this arrangement is found at present in the Good Friday service, where the *Quod ore sumpsimus* supplants the *Postcommunio.*

Part IV

CLOSE OF THE MASS

1. The *Oratio super Populum*

WITH THE PRAYER OF THE THANKSGIVING AFTER COMMUNION THE service comes to an end and the assembly can disperse. However, the ancients with their sense of form and order could not have been satisfied for very long with a formless dispersal. Hence a certain procedure took shape. In addition there was a second, still stronger influence and that was the consciousness of the Christian communities of their fellowship, tied together, as it were, in Christ and united anew precisely at the divine service. Even though they separated, they were still bound to one another by means of those spiritual influences which were alive in the Church.[1] We need not be surprised, then, that they wished to see these influences again become operative before their leaving one another. To the formal declaration of the close of the service, therefore, was united a last blessing, with which the Church sent her children out into the world. In the course of centuries this blessing took on various forms, dwindled away and was built up anew, was doubled and tripled,[2] shifted over into the final thanksgivings and petitions which then ended up in private prayer. And so at the end of Mass there was once again a development of various forms, and it is these we want to consider more closely.

The first closing act we come upon is a prayer of blessing by which the celebrating priest calls down God's help and protection upon the people as they go back to their work. A remnant of this is seen in the *oratio super populum* during Lent. This prayer, generally described as a prayer of inclination (or bowing), is an exact parallel to those prayers at the end of the fore-Mass which we found variously used to bless those who had to leave the divine service after listening to the readings.[3] As in

---

[1] An awareness of this even at the present is vividly voiced by E. Fiedler, *Christliche Opferfeier* (Munich, 1937), 90; the Christian, he says, should feel as if he ought to shake hands with all who are pouring out of church.—See the chapter "Collective Participation" in A. Chèry, *What Is the Mass?* (trans. L. C. Sheppard; London, 1952), 97-104.

[2] In the oriental liturgies, too, there developed other blessings or blessing prayers along with the prayer of inclination common to all. Such was especially the case in the Egyptian liturgies; see Brightman, 187 f., 243 f.

[3] *Supra*, I, 468 ff.

that case, so here also the prayer is preceded by a call from the deacon admonishing the people to bow before the Lord to receive, the blessing. Then follows the prayer of the celebrant in the form of an oration which is answered with *Amen*. In this shape the prayer appears as a fixed part of the Mass in the ancient Roman liturgy as well as in the Egyptian and Syrian liturgies of the Orient;[4] and since we find it in the earliest sources for these liturgies, as also in other sources of the fourth century,[5] we can conclude that the tradition goes back at least to the third century.

In Egypt the admonition of the deacon runs as follows: Τὰς κεφαλὰς ὑμῶν τῷ κυρίῳ κλίνατε.[6] It is therefore exactly the same cry as in our Roman liturgy: *Humiliate capita vestra Deo.*[7] In the Orient the prayer is most generally much developed.[8] In the West-Syrian liturgy every anaphora has its own blessing prayer. In the oldest one, the anaphora of St. James, we read: "God, great and wonderful, look down upon Thy servants who have bowed their necks before Thee, stretch out Thy strong hand filled with blessings and bless Thy people, protect Thy inheritance, so that we[9] may praise Thee now and forevermore" . . . .[10] It is characteristic of this blessing that the personal object is not designated as "us," as if the celebrant includes himself, but instead it is "Thy servants," "Thy people," *populus tuus, ecclesia tua, familia tua,* etc. This stylistic law has been observed almost without exception in the corresponding formulas of the Leonianum, while in the Gregorianum, to which the *Super populum* formulas of the Roman Missal go back, the law governs only a portion of the prayers.[12] A further distinction of the prayer with which the faith-

---

[4] In the Byzantine liturgy the admonition of the deacon was gradually discontinued. The prayer of blessing was retained as εὐχὴ ὀπισθάμβωνος. Hanssens, *Institutiones*, III, 521 f.

[5] *Const. Ap.*, VIII, 15, 6-11 (Quasten, *Mon.*, 232 f.).—Euchologion of Serapion (*ibid.*, 67); here the χειροθεσίη over the people is preceded by the blessing of natural things that had a place in the Roman Mass at the end of the canon.

[6] Brightman, 186 line 33; cf. *ibid.*, 142.

[7] This coincidence with Egyptian practice (cf. *supra*, I, 55 f.) shows that what was found in Rome was ancient tradition. In the sources the present Latin wording does not appear till about 800 in the Ordo for Lent of the city of Rome (Andrieu, III, 261; PL 78, 949 B). The Gallican version has already been noticed above, p. 296. Everywhere in Scandinavia except in the diocese of Upsala and in the missal of Abo (Turku) the deacon's admonition is written: *Inclinate capita vestra Deo;* cf. E.

Segelberg in *Eph. liturg.*, 65 (1951), 259. —But the deacon's summons is presupposed in Roman texts from the very start. For the people bowed at the prayer; this is evident from not a few formulas of the prayer of blessing, where the congregation is described as *prostrata, supplex, inclinantes se,* etc.; see the references from the Leonianum in A. Baumstark, *JL*, 7 (1927), 20, note 97. Cf. also *infra*, note 15.

[8] See the comparative survey in L. Eisenhofer, "Untersuchungen zum Stil und Inhalt der römischen oratio super populum" (*Eph. liturg.*, 52 [1938], 258-311), 302-309.

[9] Eisenhofer, 300, conjectures that originally this was "they": ἔκλιναν.

[10] Brightman, 67.

[11] In 154 out of 158 instances. In the other four cases the formulas involved are really in the wrong place. Eisenhöfer, 262-269, especially 267.

[12] Only 13 out of the 25 original formulas. Those that were added for the Thursdays

ful were dismissed lies in this, that the gifts petitioned—protection in peril, spiritual and corporal welfare, preservation from sin—were all implored not as in other orations, in a general way, but for the whole indefinite future: *semper, iugiter, perpetua protectione,* etc.,[13] much as we conclude the formula of blessing which we have at present: *Benedictio . . . descendat super vos et maneat semper.* That temporal wants are not seldom given mention here is understandable, considering the place these prayers occupy, the frontier between the Church and the world. However, in the formulas of the Gelasian Sacramentaries, in contrast to those in the Leonianum, a certain spiritualization of the petitions has taken place.[14] How highly the Roman people valued this blessing can be seen from an event in the year 538. Pope Vigilius had conducted the stational service on the feast of St. Cecilia in the church of that saint and had just given out Communion; then suddenly an envoy of the emperor arrived to take the pope into custody and lead him to Byzantium. The people followed him to the ship and demanded *ut orationem ab eo acciperent.* The pope recited the oration, all the people answered *Amen,* and the ship got under way.[15]

One thing that seems strange about the *oratio super populum* which is still retained today is that it is only to be found in the Lenten season. That was exactly the case already in the Mass book of Gregory the Great, whereas in the Leonianum it is found in every formulary of the Mass, and in the Gelasian books it is at least scattered throughout the year. Beginning with Amalar and down to our own time there have been various attempts to explain why the *oratio super populum* is confined to Lent: Quadragesima was said to be a time of greater spiritual combat, which therefore required more blessings;[16] this oration of blessing was a substitute for Communion (for one was expected to receive daily at least in this season),[17] a prayer dedicated to the non-communicants;[18] or a

---

are taken from older texts and thus follow the old rule; Eizenhöfer, 286 f.; cf., too, L. Eisenhöfer, Zum Stil der oratio super populum des Missale Romanum: *Liturg. Leben,* 5 (1938), 160-168.
[13] C. Callewaert, "Qu'est-ce que l'oratio super populum?" (*Eph. liturg.,* 51 [1937], 310-318), 316.
[14] Eisenhofer, *Untersuchungen,* 283, 297 f.
[15] *Liber pont.,* ed. Duchesne, I, 297.— Moreover, the blessing formulas of the Leonianum frequently contain turns of expression to bring into bold relief the longing the people have: *suppliciter et indesinenter expectant* (Muratori, I, 339), *supplex poscit* (362), *benedictio desiderata* (441), and others. The frequency of these blessings and the procedure they followed is certified already in Ambrosiaster, *Quœstiones Vet. et Novi Test.* (about 370-

75 in Rome), q. 109 (PL, 35, 2325): *Nostri autem sacerdotes super multos quotidie nomen Domini et verba benedictionis imponunt;* even when one is holy, *curvat tamen caput ad benedictionem sumendam.*
[16] Amalar, *Liber off.,* III, 37 (Hanssens, II, 371 f.).
[17] Bernold, *Micrologus,* c. 51 (PL, 151, 1014 f.).
[18] H. Thurston, *Lent and Holy Week* (London, 1904), 190.—However, it is especially to be noted that some few formulas do expressly presuppose the Communion of the one receiving the blessing. In the Leonianum there are 14 out of 158; in the older Gelasianum 9 out of 71; see statistics in Eisenhöfer, *Untersuchungen,* 265; 282. Here we must also count the formulas of Ash Wednesday and

substitute for the *eulogiæ* which one received at other times,[19] or the oration was originally used only as the oration at Vespers and not till later on was it taken into the Mass, which in Lent was celebrated after Vespers.[20] Finally an important fact is noted, a fact we have already verified elsewhere in the history of the liturgy, that especially in Lent an older tradition still continues to survive.[21]

This point without question deserves consideration. It is possible that the old blessing of the people, the *oratio super populum* as it is still called at present, could have been preserved in Quadragesima just as a series of venerable customs have been retained in the last days of Holy Week. But it will still be a mystery why the most celebrated days of Lent, the Sundays, form an exception, and why the series is broken off already at the Wednesday in Holy Week.[22]

Here it will be necessary to consider the institutions of public ecclesiastical penance in the closing years of Christian antiquity. Not long after the end of the fifth century public penance must have been limited at Rome to the time of Quadragesima, in contradistinction to the former system of having it all through the year.[23] Only Sundays, even in Quadragesima, were never regarded as actual days of penance.[24] The end of the time of penance for the penitents was Holy Thursday, the day they were reconciled. The penance therefore embraced those very days to which, in our missal as well as in the Gregorian Sacramentary, an *oratio super populum* is assigned. But if we want to be more exact, we must point out that Quadragesima at the time of Gregory the Great began only with the first Sunday of Lent, so that the time of public penance opened the following Monday.[25] In addition, the Thursdays of Lent and the Saturday before Palm Sunday were aliturgical; that is, they did not as yet have

the Thursday of the first week in the present-day missal, formulas that were already to be found in the Gregorianum of the 8th century, whereas both must have been lacking in the primitive Gregorianum; see Eisenhöfer, *Untersuchungen,* 288 f.

[19] Honorius Augustod., *Gemma an.,* I, 67 (PG, 172, 565); Sicard of Cremona, *Mitrale,* III, 8 (PL, 213, 144).—There is no evidence that at Rome during the period under consideration there was a regular distribution of the sacred bread such as took place in Gaulish regions; cf. below, 549 f.

[20] Fortescue, *The Mass,* 390 f. See the refutation in Baumstark (following note).

[21] A. Baumstark, "Das Gesetz der Erhaltung des Alten in liturgisch hochwertiger Zeit" (*JL,* 7, 1927), 16-21, especially 20.

[22] If the surmise advanced by Baumstark,

op. cit., 21; is of any value, that the invitation *Humiliate capita vestra Deo* and the corresponding demeanor were considered incompatible with the joyful character of the Sunday, it could simply have been omitted, as is done in other instances, e.g., the Ember days of Pentecost where the *Flectamus genua* and the rite that goes along with it are dropped. Besides this, there is as yet no explanation why the Wednesday of Holy Week was made the terminus.

[23] Cf. Jungmann, *Die lateinischen Bussriten,* 13 f.

[24] For that reason it has been customary since the 7th century not to reckon them in the 40 days.

[25] Jungmann, *Die lateinischen Bussriten,* 48-51.

any Mass, and consequently no *oratio super populum*. So if we do not count these days on which the blessing was added only later with the further development of Quadragesima, we find that the *oratio super populum* on the remaining days in the Sacramentary of Gregory the Great displays two peculiarities. In comparison with the older sacramentaries it consists of entirely new formulas, evidence therefore of a reorganization.[26] And in no case—as occasionally happened otherwise[27]—does it presuppose a Communion on the part of the recipients of the blessing, which is again understandable if we keep the penitents above all in mind. But another circumstance forces us to come to the same conclusion. The history of penance shows not only that in Rome, just as elsewhere in the closing years of Christian antiquity there was an *ordo pœnitentium*, but also that the penitents during their time of penance were obliged to receive regularly the blessing of their bishop—of which there is no trace in the rich liturgical sources if the *oratio super populum* is not regarded as such. All this forces us to the conclusion that Gregory the Great, in the new arrangement of the *oratio super populum* seen in his Sacramentary, took into account the conditions of the penitential discipline. During the year he permitted the oration of blessing to be dropped; it had already been missing sporadically in the Gelasian formularies, without any clear principle apparent for its use or non-use. But during Quadragesima he retained it, since during that time the penitents at least were obliged to receive a blessing on each occasion.[28] True, the *oratio super populum* was still what the name implied, a blessing of all the people, who were to spend these forty days, especially in that age of constant and dire need, as a time of penance and prayer, and the words of this blessing and petition remained, as before, broad and general, embracing all temporal and spiritual wants; but the core of the penitential assembly was formed by the public sinners, who perhaps at that time had still to step forward at the call of the deacon, kneel, and receive the imposition of hands,[29] then remain in deep prostration with the rest of the faithful while the pope pronounced the oration of blessing.

However, this function of the *oratio super populum* in the discipline of penance seems not to have been continued for long. Among those formulas

[26] Eisenhofer, *Untersuchungen*, 288 f.

[27] *Supra*, n. 18.

[28] Jungmann, "Oratio super populum und altchristliche Büssersegnung," *Eph. liturg.*, 52 (1938), 77-96. The thesis that I defended in *Die Lateinishen Bussriten*, 15 ff., 38 ff., 296., 313, without the necessary checks and that herefore drew attacks from several critics, is here handled with the proper reservations and verifications. Cf. also Eisenhofer, *Untersuchungen*, 293 ff., who in consequence of his detailed analysis with full justice rejected the hypothesis I previously proposed regarding the development of the *oratio super populum* from a private Penance Blessing, but considers the possibility that the penitents might have been included already before Gregory the Great, and asserts that such is certainly in harmony with the sombre character of so many of the formulas (295 f., 297 f.).

[29] Cf. Jungmann, *Die lateinischen Bussriten*, 20 ff.

which were entered in the Gregorianum in the seventh and eighth centuries we again find, as already remarked,[30] those which speak of the Communion of the recipients of the blessing. The Frankish commentators make absolutely no mention about any relation to public penance, wherefore even its limitation to the Lenten season was in some instances broken through.[31] And it could not be otherwise, because the Gregorian Sacramentary, which was originally intended for the pontifical service, where alone the blessing of the penitents came into question, was now used in the ordinary divine service. Since then the *oratio super populum* has again became simply an oration of blessing which is kept during the holy season of Lent as a piece of ancient tradition. Soon, in fact, it was not even regarded as a blessing at all, since no one except the celebrant paid any attention to the admonition to bow the head.[32] So when a missal from Huesca in 1505, although not daring to suppress the oration, did however direct that it be said *submissa voce,* thus relegating it to a secondary position,[33] we cannot quarrel about the consistency of such a measure.

2. The Dismissal

Just as at the close of the fore-Mass, once the prayer of blessing had been said over those who were told to leave, there follows (at least according to some of the sources) a formal dismissal, so all the more there probably must always have been such a dismissal at the end of the entire service. One cannot expect much more than the word with which the one presiding at every well-ordered assembly ordinarily announces the close, especially when the farewell blessing has just preceded. Such announcement of the conclusion was common in ancient culture, at times even using the word *missa.*[1] In Christian usage the corresponding formula often acquired a religious or a biblical cast. Chrysostom witnesses to the use at

---

[30] *Supra* n. 18.

[31] The Carolingian commentary on the Mass, *Primum in ordine* (PL, 138, 1186 A) notes that *orationes sacræ communionis* are said *et benedictio super populum* before the *Ite missa est.*—The 10th century Sacramentary of S. Remy at Rheims (ed. Chevalier, p. 345) presents a *benedictio super populum* in the standard Mass-*ordo* after the Postcommunion: *Domine sancte Pater, omnipotens æterne Deus, de abundantia misericordiarum tuarum* . . . It is the first of the formulas that the later Gelasianum presents under the title of *Benedictiones super populum* (Mohlberg, n. 1569) ; cf. *supra.*

[32] In the 10th century this bow was customary at least insofar as the faithful bowed at every oration said at the altar; see above I, 370 f. Even in 1090 the *oratio super populum* was considered as an actual bestowal of the blessing; cf. Bernold, *Micrologus,* c. 51 (PL, 151, 1015), according to whom then a different final blessing became more and more customary only in *aliis temporibus.* The Benedictine *Liber ordinarius* of Liége (about 1258) still prescribes for the *collecta super populum* the same bow *(inclinent versi ad altare caputia removentes)* as for the solemn Pontifical blessing (Volk, 103).

[33] Ferreres, 248.

[1] *Supra,* I, 173, n. 37.

Antioch of the cry of the deacon: Πορεύεσθε ἐν εἰρήνῃ [2] which was also customary in Egypt[3] and has there remained customary.[4] Similarly in Byzantium it runs: 'Εν εἰρήνῃ προέλθωμεν.[5] Among the West Syrians the religious tone is even stronger: 'Εν εἰρήνῃ Χριστοῦ πορευθῶμεν;[6] in fact, in the Syrian form of this liturgy, the cry—which is here made by the priest—is followed by a silently spoken prayer of blessing.[7] In all the Greek liturgies the cry is followed by the answer of the people: 'Εν ὀνόματι κυρίου. [8] Turning to the West, we find a similar method in Milan, where the invitation to leave, *Procedamus cum pace* is answered by *In nomine Christi*.[9] A longer formula, which indicates the ending of the service only retrospectively, is found in the Mozarabic Mass: *Sollemnia completa sunt in nomine Domini nostri Jesu Christi. Votum nostrum sit acceptum cum pace. R. Deo gratias.*[10]

Our form of dismissal, *Ite missa est*, in contrast to all these is more laconic, but true to the essential genius of the Roman liturgy. While the *Ite* corresponds exactly to the πορεύεσθε of the Egyptian liturgy, the *missa est* added thereto is somewhat unique. Here the word *missa* still has its original meaning: dismissal, conclusion.[11] When it was incorporated into the formula, it must have been so widely used with this meaning that it became in particular a technical expression for the conclusion of an assembly, because otherwise a phrase like *finis est* would rather have been employed. The word had this meaning at least as far back as the fourth century,[13] while, on the other hand, this meaning was no longer

[2] Chrysostom, *Adv. Jud.*, 3, 6 (PG, 48, 870). Likewise *Const. Ap.*, VIII, 15, 10 (Quasten, *Mon.*, 23): 'Απολύεσθε ἐν εἰρήνῃ Cf. Lk.. 7: 50 and other places.

[3] Thus, namely, in the Egyptian church order, i.e., the 4th century Egyptian version of Hippolytus' *Apostolic Tradition* (Brightman, 193).

[4] Brightman, 142, 193, 244, 463 l. 6; Hanssens, *Institutiones*, III, 526.

[5] Brightman, 343.

[6] Brightman, 67.

[7] Brightman, 106; Hanssens, III, 525; 527.

[8] Brightman, 67, 142, 343. In other liturgies the summons remains without any answer.

[9] *Missale Ambrosianum* (1902), 183. *Benedicamus Domino* is then added.—The invitation mentioned, along with a like answer, is also found at the conclusion of the Roman blessing for a journey; see *Brv. Rom.*, Itinerarium.

[10] *Missale mixtum* (PL, 85, 567 B).

[11] The dismissal presented in the Stowe Missal (ed. Warner; HBS, 32) 19, is outwardly similar: *Missa acta est. In pace.* But here *missa* is already used with the meaning of "Mass." The formula is probably an attempt to amend the Latin dismissal formula which was no longer understood at the time (9th cent.).

[12] Cf. *supra*, I, 173. See Fortescue, *The Mass*, 399-400.

[13] That becomes most evident from the fact that the word survives in the Byzantine court ceremonial in the form μίσσα or μίνσα with the meaning, "Dismissal from the audience and the session"; Dölger, *Antike u. Christentum*, 6 (1940), 88-92; cf. the entire study "Ite Missa est": *ibid.*, 81-132. In church use, too, the word *missa* for dismissal from divine service is verified since the end of the 4th century, among others in the *Peregrinatio Aetheriæ*, c. 25, 1 f.; cf. Jungmann, *Gewordene Liturgie*, 36; 38. The hypothesis of Th. Michels, "Ite Missa est—Deo gratias," *Per hanc lucis viam*, 8 (Salzburg, 1929), Benediktiner-kolleg), who assumes that the formula is

current even in the early Middle Ages. So even if the first literary evidence for the *Ite missa est* is found in the Roman *ordines*,[14] we will not be blundering if we hold that this formula is as old as the Latin Mass itself.[15] A corroborating argument is found in the fact that similar formulas were prevalent in the everyday social life of the Romans. After a funeral the assembled mourners were dismissed with the word *Ilicet = Ire licet*.[16] According to the bronze tablets of Iguvium (Gubbio in Umbria) from the last century before Christ, the conjoined blessing of the people and cursing of the strangers closed with the cry: *Itote Iguvini*.[17] Other formulas were stipulated for the conclusion of gatherings in political life.[18]

The dismissal in the Roman Mass is given emphasis and at the same time a religious framework by being introduced with the *Dominus vobiscum* and answered by the *Deo gratias* of the people. In substance the *Dominus vobiscum* merely takes the place of the vocative of address which ought otherwise to precede the imperative *Ite*.[19] Even at high Mass this *Dominus vobiscum* is pronounced by the celebrant, so that the deacon appears only as his organ when he announces the dismissal. The *Deo gratias* with which this announcement is answered is an exact parallel to that which the people (according to the liturgical sources of the early Middle Ages) also answered the announcement of the coming feast days.[20] It is therefore only an acknowledgment that the message has been received, but is imbedded in that fundamental Christian sentiment of thanksgiving.[21]

At Rome the *Ite missa est* was originally used at every Mass[22] no

an abbreviation of a more complete *Ecclesia missa est,* is, to say the least, superfluous; but see also the refutation by Dölger, 117-120; the rejection by D. Casel, *JL,* 9 (1929), 174.

[14] *Ordo Rom.* I, n. 21 (Andrieu, II, 107; PL, 78, 948); *Capitulare eccl. ord.* (Andrieu, III, 109); Ordo of S. Amand (*ibid.,* II, 167).—A clue in any event already in Avitus of Vienna, *Ep.* 1 (PL, 59, 199; *supra* I, 173, n. 37).

[15] Cf. Dölger, *op. cit.,* 107 ff., who concludes that the formula must have been in use already in the year 400, but that a dismissal "with this or an almost similar formula" must already be presupposed in Tertullian, *De an.,* c. 9 (CSEL, 20, 310) when he says of the end of the Mass: *post transacta sollemnia dimissa plebe.*

[16] Thus, according to Servius, we are to understand the passage about the *novissima verba* in Virgin, *Aeneid,* VI, 231. Dölger, 123 f.

[17] Dölger, 130 f. Thus, according to Apuleius, *Metamorph.,* XI, 17, the concluding

invitation at the Isis celebration: λαοί ἄφεσις, which is rendered by the Humanists as *populis missio.* However, the Greek text has been attacked by critics. Dölger, 124-130.

[18] Senate sessions at the time of the Roman Republic were concluded with the words: *Nemo vos tenet.* The committees at the time of the emperor were dismissed with: *Nihil vos moramur, patres conscripti.* Livy, II, 56, 12 gives the dismissal formula, spoken by the tribune: *Si vobis videtur, discedite Quirites.* Dölger, 122.

[19] Above, I, 361. Untenable is the explanation, as Gihr gives it, 798, according to which the greeting is there only "in order to maintain between priest and people an active, lively intercourse."

[20] *Supra,* I, 420 f.

[21] *Supra,* I, 420.

[22] Both the older *ordines* (*supra,* note 14) and the later ones mention only the *Ite Missa est;* see *Ordo sec. Rom.,* n. 15 (Andrieu, II, 226; PL, 78, 976); Ordo *'Postquam'* for a Bishop's Mass, (Andrieu,

matter what its character,[23] and probably also at the end of other services.[24] On the other hand, the *Benedicamus Domino* could have been a concluding formula of the Gallican liturgy. For although there are apparently no signs of it in Roman sources before the year 1000,[25] we find traces of it considerably earlier in Frankish territory. The *Ordo Angilberti*, of about the year 800, in describing the order of Communion on high festivals, mentions that after the *completio missæ* the people left *laudantes Deum et benedicentes Dominum*.[26] In an *ordo* for the sick from about the same time we read after the giving of Communion: *Tunc data oratione in fine dicat sacerdos: Benedicamus Domino. Et respondeant omnes: Deo gratias, et expletum est.*[27]

In the eleventh century, however, an adjustment was made between these two formulas, such as we have at present: the *Ite missa est* is used whenever there is a *Gloria;* the: *Benedicamus Domino* on the other days.[28] But efforts were made to find a deeper reason for this merely outward division. The days with *Ite missa est* are days of a festive character, when the entire populace is assembled, so that the invitation to leave at the end of service has a meaning, while the days with *Benedicamus Domino* are days when only the *religiosi*, the pious whose life is more especially devoted to spiritual service, are present; wherefore the priest, without turning around, urges them, and himself with them, to continue praising God.[29] That this explanation for the present-day arrangement does not reach deep enough is seen from the use of the *Benedicamus Domino,* amongst other times,[30] on the Sundays of Advent and from Septuagesima on.[31] Besides, if people had been so sensitive about the communal character of each celebration, then we would have had to omit many other things, at least at private Mass, for instance, the *Dominus vobiscum*. The *Benedicamus Domino* was as much a formula of departure for the assembled faithful as the *Ite missa est*. Hence, like it, it receives the

II, 32; PL, 78, 994).

[23] The Roman Ordo for Lent (Andrieu, III, 260 f.; PL, 78, 949) certifies it for Ash Wednesday and the Lenten season.

[24] However, it will be difficult to follow Dölger, 95, in finding a reference to it in the so-called Litany of Beauvais; cf. above I, 390, n. 70.

[25] It appears about the middle of the 12th century in the *Ordo eccl. Lateran.*, both in the Office and in the Mass (ed. Fischer, p. 1 and *passim;* see the Register, p. 165); cf. Ordo of Benedict, n. 8 f. (PL, 78, 1029 f). The surprising stress given to the formula makes it evident that it had hardly had time to become familiar.

[26] Bishop, *Liturgica historica*, 323.

[27] Theodulf of Orleans, *Capitulare,* II (PL,

105, 222 C). Amalar, *Liber off.*, IV, 45, 5 (Hanssens, II, 541; cf. III, 445), witnesses to the *Benedicamus Domino* and *Deo gratias* as the regular conclusion of the Office.—Cf. also the *Benedicamus Domino* in the Milanese liturgy, *supra*, n. 9.

[28] Bernold, *Micrologus*, c. 19 (PL, 151, 990). The same rule held at Rome in the 12th century; *Ordo Eccl. Lateran.* (Fischer, 3 l. 30; 65 l. 20).

[29] Bernold, *Micrologus,* c. 46 (PL, 151, 1011). Similarly Durandus, IV, 57, 7.

[30] Cf. also the *Benedicamus Domino* in Theodulf, above, n. 27.

[31] Hardly opposed to this is the reason suggested by Bernold, *Micrologus,* c. 46 (PL, 151, 1011 D), that the latter application occurs *pro tristitia temporis insinuanda*.

response *Deo gratias*.[32] But here the dismissal is given a religious turn, just as the acknowledgment of the message receives a religious expression in the *Deo gratias*. However, we must admit that when the lines were drawn for the use of the two formulas, considerations like those referred to above, especially the solemn character of certain festivals, played a part.[33] Also when the divine service was continued, as at the midnight Mass of Christmas, when Lauds followed, or on Maundy Thursday and the vigils of Easter and Pentecost, preference was given to the invitation to praise God, *Benedicamus Domino*.[34] Since the *Ite missa est* was considered an expression of joy, it had to disappear from the Requiem Mass. So we find that since the twelfth century the *Requiescant in pace* begins to supplant it.[35]

When the herald in olden times announced the conclusion of an assembly, he did so with a corresponding raising of his voice. The judge, the official of the state, remembering his dignity, speaks in a moderate tone, but the herald lets his cry resound loudly over the whole assembly. It could not be much different in the case of a dismissal from divine service.[36] As a further step, the *Ite missa est* must soon have been provided with a special singing tone. Already in the tenth century there must have been various melodies which were richly adorned with melismas; for this time also marks the appearance of tropes, the expanding texts which set a syllable to each note of the melody.[37] On the other hand, there seem

---

[32] Kössing, *Liturgische Vorlesungen*, 593, had already called attention to it.—The decision of the Congregation of Rites, Oct. 7, 1816 (*Decreta auth. SRC.*, n. 2572, 22), that the celebrant at a solemn Mass was to say softly not the *Ite* but the *Benedicamus* and *Requiescant*, is probably to be explained by the prayer-like character of these two formulas.

[33] Batiffol, *Leçons*, 303, refers to the combination of the *Ite missa est* with the *Gloria* and conjectures that the *Ite missa est* like the *Gloria* originally belonged to the Bishop's Mass. Dölger, 91 f., adds that such inclusion in the Bishop's Mass would be understandable, if not only the expression *missa*, but also the formula *Ite missa est* were a part to the imperial court manners, from which, since the time of Constantine, a few practices passed over to the bishops with the transfer of the privileges and honors. But this is all just a matter of assumptions. It is to be especially noted that there are no traces of the *Benedicamus Domino* in the pre-Carolingian Roman liturgy.

[34] Bernold, *Micrologus*, c. 34, 46 (PL, 151, 1005; 1011) ; cf. John Beleth, *Explicatio*, c. 49 (PL, 202, 56).

[35] Stephan of Baugé (d. 1139), *De sacr. altaris*, c. 18 (PL, 172, 1303); John Beleth, *Explicatio*, c. 49 (PL, 202, 56).

[36] Dölger, 132, recalls Cassian, *De inst. cœnob.*, XI, 16 (CSEL, 17, 202), and the Commentary of Smaragdus (d. 830) c. 17 of the rule of St. Benedict: *levita . . . elevata voce cantat: Ite missa est* (Dölger, 119 f.; otherwise, however, the text in Migne, PL, 102, 837 C).

[37] Blume-Bannister, *Tropen des Missale*, I, p. 407-416. A trope of this kind that appears in the 12th century in Seckau reads: *Ite, Deo servite, Spiritus Sanctus super vos sit, iam missa est. Deo potenti nobis miserenti, ipsi demus dignas laudes et gratias; loc. cit.*, 411. The same trope among others in the Regensburg Missal of 1485 which contains a series of other tropes and *Ite missa est* melodies; Beck, 240 f. From the fact that no corresponding trope text is given for the *Deo gratias* it became clear that the wording presented

to have been no tropes for the *Benedicamus Domino* in the Mass.[38]

The *Ite missa est* has kept another sensible expression of its function as a call to the people: just like the greetings, it is pronounced with face turned to the people. Hence this cry has always remained a manifest closing point of the service.[39]

3. Leaving the Altar

In the first Roman *ordo,* when the deacon had sung the *Ite missa est,* the seven torch-bearers and the subdeacon with the censer begin to move and precede the pope to the *secretarium.*[1] The *Ite missa est* was therefore the real conclusion of the Mass. Among the Carthusians even today the priest leaves the altar immediately after these words.[2] There is only a short ceremony, perhaps accidentally omitted from the first Roman *ordo:*[3] the kiss of the altar as a farewell salute, the counterpart of the kiss of greeting at the beginning of Mass.[4]

This or a similar farewell salute is also customary in other liturgies. Amongst the West-Syrian Jacobites we also find the kiss, which is followed by a three-fold farewell of highly poetic beauty. It begins: "Remain in peace, holy and divine altar of the Lord. I know not whether I shall return to you again or no. May the Lord grant that I may see you in the church of the First-born in heaven.[5] In this covenant I put my confidence."[6]

In the Roman Mass in the Frankish area an accompanying word was also added to this kiss of the altar, just as was done at the beginning with the kiss of greeting; these are the only kisses of the altar customary at that time. The Sacramentary of Amiens in the ninth century ordains: *Expleto officio sanctum osculatur altare dicens: Placeat tibi sancta Trin-*

---

was to be sung by the priest (or deacon). —In Croatian country parishes the trope *Ite benedicti et electi* (Blume, p. 412) is still sung today. D. Kniewald, *Eph. liturg.,* 54 (1940), 222.

[38] Blume, *loc. cit.,* quotes no *Benedicamus* tropes. The Regensburg missal just mentioned gives only one melody, without tropes, for the *Benedicamus Domino;* Beck, 241.—On the other hand, the *Benedicamus Domino* at the end of the Office is not only supplied with tropes already in the 11-12th centuries but is already the object of early and tentative polyphonic efforts. Ursprung, 120 f.

[39] In many French Cathedrals in the 18th century the deacon turned to the north at the *Ite missa est;* de Moléon, 11; 169; 429. Here the same sort of symbolism that determined the deacon's position at the

reading of the Gospel seems to have come into play.

[1] *Ordo Rom.* I, n. 21 (Andrieu, II, 107; PL, 78, 948).

[2] He does add the *Placeat* (but this serves as a private prayer), and at the foot of the altar, according to a later prescription, he says a *Pater noster.*

[3] So also Dölger, *Antike u. Christentum,* 2 (1930), 193.

[4] Above I, 314 f. The explanation frequently put forward, that the priest in kissing the altar must first himself accept the blessing (and similarly in other instances the greeting for the people) from Christ, goes to pieces in view of the fact that this kissing of the altar occurs also in the Mass of the Dead, where no blessing follows.

[5] Hebr. 12: 23.

[6] Brightman, 109.

itas.[7] This prayer, which in the following centuries was used everywhere, although not universally,[8] was of Gallic origin, as is plain from the fact that it is addressed to the Trinity.[9] It is a very natural idea when leaving the table of sacrifice to beg once more for God's gracious glance on that which happened there. Here again the dual meaning of the offering appears: honor to God's majesty, that our actions may find gracious acceptance, and a plea for our own needs and those of others, that they may be graciously heard.

As the only prayer after Communion, the *Placeat* is recited in the middle of the altar, because it is an accompaniment to the act of kissing. Since this is a personal action of the priest, the prayer is kept in the singular. As a counterpart to the *Oramus te Domine* which is attached to the altar kiss at the beginning of Mass and which is likewise a plea for the priest's own person *(peccata mea)*, the *Placeat* is also distinguished by the fact that it is recited with a deep bow, the hands resting on the altar, and in a quiet voice.[10] In the Mass books from the eleventh to the thirteenth century the *Placeat* is often joined by a second prayer which more clearly shows the relationship to the altar kiss: *Meritis et intercessionibus omnium*

---

[7] Leroquais (*Eph. liturg.*, 1927), 444. The prayer has the exact wording as today, but the concluding formula is missing (the expressions used in the conclusion of the prayer also in the apologia *Deus qui de indignis; ibid.*, 440 f.). Thereupon follows only a prayer after the removal of the vestments.—Likewise in union with the kissing of the altar in the Sacramentary of Le Mans (9th cent.): Leroquais, I, 31; in the Sacramentary of Fulda (10th cent.): Richter- Schönfelder, n. 28; in the Sacramentary of Ratoldus: PL, 78, 245 B.—The explicit connection with the kissing of the altar is almost universal in the older texts; see also Bernold, *Micrologus*, c. 22 (PL, 151, 992): *osculatur sacerdos altare dicens*. Likewise the contemporary Missal of St. Vincent (where, exceptionally, the text is expanded by the addition of a mention of the dead, etc.); Fiala, 216. An example from the 14th cent.; Ebner, 175.

[8] In Germany in the 14th century a more emphatic recommendation was needed, one, moreover, that was supported by a legend; Franz, 511. The prayer is missing also in several English Mass arrangements, e.g., that of York (Simmons, 116).

[9] The Sacramentary of S. Denis (11th cent.): Martène, 1, 4, V (I, 528 B), has the Gallican ending: ... *propitiabile. Per te Trinitas sancta, cuius gloriosum re-*

gnum permanet in sæcula sæculorum. Spanish Mass arrangements since the 11th century present the ending: ... *propitiabile. Rex regum qui* (several MSS. expand: *in Trinitate perfecta) vivis;* Ferreres, 208; 210. But ordinarily the prayer ends with *Qui vivis;* thus in the Mass arrangement of Sées (PL, 78, 251 A), and in the Missa Illyrica: Martène, 1, 8, IV (I, 517 B), and so, too, at the end of the Middle Ages, e.g., *Alphabetum sacerdotum*: Legg, *Tracts,* 49 f.; Ordinarium of Coutances: *ibid.,* 67. —The conclusion *Per Christum* is found in Bernold, *Micrologus*, c. 23 (PL, 151, 995), and appears to have been customary in Italy since the 11th century if the citations in Ebner, 229; 302; 317; 324; 331; 339 ("as now") are to be referred also to the conclusion. Also in German Massbooks, Beck, 272; 311. By using the *Per Christum* conclusion, the Roman Missal adopts the same compromise that it did in the case of the *Suscipe sancta Trinitas* (above, p. 46 f.); in fact these two prayers are kindred in type, especially in the prominence given to the *offerre pro.*

[10] It is only exceptionally that there is explicit mention during the Middle Ages of the bowed position at the *Placeat*, e.g., in the Augsburg Missal of 1368 (Hoeynck, 376) in the *Alphabetum sacerdotum* (Legg, *Tracts*, 49).

sanctorum suorum misereatur nobis omnipotens Dominus.[11] This prayer, which as a rule appears only where the kiss of the altar is previously mentioned, obviously parallels the notice of the altar relics in the *Oramus te Domine* at the beginning. Often it was expanded to the form: *Meritis et intercessionibus istorum et omnium sanctorum.*[12] As a consequence of these additions, the special meaning of the altar kiss as a farewell salute had become somewhat clouded by the end of the Middle Ages.[13]

4. The Closing Blessing of the Priest

At present when the bishop leaves the cathedral after a pontifical high Mass, he passes through the ranks of the faithful blessing them while they genuflect to receive his benediction. Something similar took place at the close of the Roman stational service, as recounted in the first Roman *ordo.* When the pope had left the altar after the *Ite missa est,* with the thurifer and the seven torch-bearers going on ahead and accompanied by the deacons,[1] the bishops stepped forward and said, *Iube domne benedicere,* whereupon the pope answered, *Benedicat nos Dominus.* The same was done by the priests, then by the monks.[2] Next the *schola* approached and intoned the same petition and answered with a loud *Amen.*[3] As the entourage advanced, the noble banner-bearers *(milites draconarii),* the light-carriers, the acolytes who had charge of the doors, the cross-bearers and the other officials of the divine service did the same.[4]

[11] Mass-*ordo* of Séez: PL, 78, 251 A; cf. the related Mass arrangements: Martène, IV, XV (I 517 B, 594 C); 1, 4, 9, 9 (I, 424 E). Ebner, 20; 139; 158; 164; 169; 311; 331; 349; Köck, 135 (three examples). Two cases still of the 15th century; Ebner, 158; Köck, 136.—Two Cistercian missals of the 13th century from Tarragona: Ferreres, 210. The prayer also accompanied kissing the altar in the Cistercian ritual of the 17th century: Bona, II, 20, 4 (905); Schneider (*Cist.-Chr.,* 1927), 265.—The formula preceding the *Placeat:* Ebner, 189.—In individual instances this prayer appears alone without a preceding *Placeat:* Sacramentary of Modena (before 1173(: Muratori, I, 95; Seckau Missale about 1170: Köck, 135 (n. 479).—In a Venetian MS. at the end of the 11th century the sentence is combined with several parallel formulas: Ebner, 20.

[12] *Vetus Missale Lateranense* (about 1100): Ebner, 169. Likewise in the Cistercian Missal since the 13th century (preceding note); also already in the Missa Illyrica: Martène, 1, 4, IV (I, 517 B).

With regard to the *istorum* cf. *supra* 60.

[13] But it is remarkable that in the Mass-*ordo* of Regensburg about 1500 a new farewell kiss should appear; before closing the book the priest kisses the cross in the Missal; Beck, 272.

[1] Cf. Ordo of St Amand (Andrieu, II, 167).

[2] Thus far also the *Ordo sec. Rom.,* n. 15 (Andrieu, II, 227; PL, 78, 976), but with the variant *vos* instead of *nos.* Cf. also Tertullian, *De test. an.,* c. 2 (CSEL, 20, 136), where this phrase is used as a Christian dictum: *Benedicat te Deus.*

[3] That each of the groups came forward for the blessing is the interpretation found in the Frankish abstract of *Ordo Rom.* I (Andrieu, II, 227; PL, 78, 984). According to the *Ordo "In primis"* for Episcopal Mass (Andrieu, II, 336; PL, 78, 990), the schola asks the blessing last of all and responds with a loud *Amen.* This is not indicated in the papal Mass.

[4] For the above in general, *Ordo Rom.* I, n. 21 (Andrieu, II, 108; PL, 78, 948).

Such a blessing on leaving was a very ancient episcopal practice.[5] In the northern countries, even if it was not always the practice, still it became customary at least upon acceptance of the Roman liturgy.[6] It was first of all the privilege of the bishop. It was in the northern countries precisely that old laws, that the simple priest was not allowed to give the blessing[7] at public service,[8] were not forgotten. The Carolingian legal codes stressed this prescription anew because they wished to protect the superior position of the episcopate.[9] But, besides this, a second interpretation was abroad and already partly anchored even in the *canones;* this too, denied the priest the right to bless even at the final blessing of the Mass, but only *præsente episcopo.*[10] Accordingly, in the Gallican Mass of the seventh

[5] *Aetheriæ Peregrinatio,* c. 24, 2 (CSEL, 39, 71) : *Et post hoc* (at the end of the daily morning service, after the oration of blessing over the people) . . . *omnes ad manum ei accedunt et ille eos uno et uno benedicet exiens iam, et sic fit missa.* The *ad manum accedere* could mean that the bishop in passing placed his hands upon the individuals who knelt along the way; cf. Council of Laodicea, can. 19 (Mansi, II, 567), where the penitents after the Mass of the catechumens, before their departure approached ὑπὸ χεῖρα, i. e., for the imposing of the hands; cf. above, I, 477, n. 18.—Ambrose, *Ep., 22,* 2 (PL, 16, 1020). —This by no means excludes the possibility that a kissing of the hand is meant, as Dölger, *Antike u. Christentum,* 3 (1932), 248; 6 (1940), 98, assumes.

[6] Cf. *supra,* notes 2 and 3.

[7] This was decided with special firmness by the Synod of Agde (506), can. 44 (Mansi, VIII, 332) : *Benedictionem super plebem in ecclesia fundere . . . presbytero penitus non licebit.*

[8] The priest's right to bestow a blessing privately *per familias, per agros, per privatas domos* was recognized already at the Council of Riez (439), can. 5, al. 4 (Mansi, V, 1193).

[9] Benedictus Levita, *Capitularum collectio,* III, 225 and *Add.,* IV, 71 (PL, 97, 826; 898) ; Herard of Tours, *Capitularia,* n. 78 (PL, 121, 769). It is quite possible, however, that the precise point against which these renewed prohibitions were directed was that the solemn Gallican pontifical blessing, which some of the bishops had incorporated into the Roman Mass, was being employed also by priests *(benedictionem publice fundere).*

[10] In the first Council of Orleans (511), can. 26 (Mansi, VIII, 355) it was decreed: ... *populus non ante discedat, quam missæ sollemnitas compleatur, et ubi episcopus fuerit, benedictionem accipiat sacerdotis.* In virtue of this decision and in accordance with the older phrase of the development of the law (in the Gallican Mass) only one concluding blessing of the bishop, who might be present, was permitted (cf. above, p. 296 f.). The canon was passed on in the medieval collection of laws, but already in the Hispana (before 633) it appears with a variant that changes the meaning: *ubi episcopus defuerit* (if no bishop is present one should receive the blessing of the *sacerdos* = the priest) which, as a matter of fact, was in accordance with can. 7 of the II Council of Seville (619;; Mansi, X, 559) and a documented practice at about the turn of the 6th century. J. Lechner, *Der Schlussegen des Priesters in der hl. Messe* (Festschrift E. Eichmann; Paderborn, 1940) 654 ff., 658 f. Already at the beginning of the 7th century pseudo-Jerome, *De septem ordinibus ecclesiæ* (PL, 30, 148-162; respectively, 152-167), bids for the same interpretation; Lechner, 666-672. — With what concern the 7th century regarded the special privilege of the bishop in this matter of blessing is seen clearly in the listing *"De gradibus in quibus Christus adfuit"* which is found, *inter alia,* in the missal of Bobbio (ed. Lowe: HBS, 58, p. 178) : Christ exercised the episcopal office when he raised his hands over the disciples and blessed them. Regarding the theological rapport of this view with other matters, see W. Croce, "Die niederen Weihen und

century, there was a practice of a closing priestly blessing after the *Pater noster.*[11]

It was but natural that the defenders of the Gallican tradition and the rights (there included) of the priest should not want to abandon this right of the priest to bless, especially since it was possible as always, to rest their claim upon the desire of the people and their spiritual needs.[12] In the transition to the Roman Mass, i.e., at first to the Gelasian Sacramentaries, a prayer of blessing *super populum* at the end of Mass was to be found in a large portion of the Mass formularies, and this was even preceded by a formal invitation to receive the blessing. At the same time a transfer of the blessing to the real end of the Mass could be welcomed, because the exit of the non-communicants right after the *Pater noster* would have looked almost like a universal flight from the house of God. But when the further transition was made to the Gregorian Sacramentary and only the post-communion remained as the *ultima benedictio,*[13] many would not see therein a proper substitute and therefore, insofar as the *oratio super populum* was not kept in the ordinary plan of the Mass,[14] they began to fix their attention on the gesture and phrase of blessing as they were prescribed by the Roman *ordines* at the recession from the altar. This manner of blessing must then have become widespread by the end of the eleventh century.[15]

Apropos of this, however, it is surprising that the true liturgical sources do not mention this new closing blessing until considerably later. For the liturgical texts not only of the eleventh century but even those of the twelfth are almost entirely silent about the matter.[16] This is quite understandable, though, because first, the blessing was not given till "after the Mass"—and even today in many churches there are various additamenta "after the Mass" which are not to be found in any liturgical book; and because, secondly, liturgists still regarded the action as not justifiable and would rather not talk about it. But because occasionally even in the later Middle Ages there were *ordines* of the Mass— and among them some which describe the close of the Mass in exact detail—which leave out any reference to a blessing, we are forced to infer that the blessing was really not given in many places. And this is true especially[17] in monastery

---

ihre hierarchische Wertung," *ZkTh,* **70** (1948), 297 f.

[11] *Supra,* p. 294 f.

[12] Lechner, 662; 672; 683 f.

[13] *Supra,* p. 343, n. 11.

[14] *Supra,* p. 432.

[15] We must agree with Lechner, 679 f., that the final priestly blessing goes back to the time of Charlemagne, even though his more detailed explanation is incomplete, as indicated.

[16] The Sacramentary of Brescia at the close of the 11th century is an exception, with

the direction, *finita missa,* to bless the people: *Benedictio Dei Patris et Filii et Spiritus Sancti descendat super vos.* For the rest, the Italian Mass-books even at the turn of the 12th century make no mention of the blessing; see, e.g., Ebner, 334-336.

[17] Not exclusively. In England none of the four Mass-arrangements from the end of the Middle Ages presented by Maskell, 202 f., has a blessing of the people. Two of them have the phrase *In nomine Patris* . . . follow immediately upon the *Placeat,*

churches, where many private Masses were said and consequently there was no need of a blessing. In this sense the Dominican *Ordinarium* of 1256 concludes the Mass *ordo* with the remark: *Et si consuetudo patriæ fuerit et extranei affuerint hoc expectantes, det benedictionem secundum modum patriæ*.[18] The silence especially of the monastic Mass books at the end of the Middle Ages must be understood, as a rule, as implying that the blessing was omitted. The Benedictines,[19] Cistercians,[20] Premonstratensians,,[21] and Dominicans[22] did not incorporate the final blessing in their Mass-plans until later, and the Carthusians have not done so even to this day.[23]

On the other hand, another final blessing at the Sunday high Mass was to be found precisely in monasteries; namely, a blessing of the reader at table for the coming week.[24]

The citation of a special formula of blessing was generally superfluous, because ordinarily the form used was the form common in that particular country, the same as that always in use at private blessings.[25] Consequently,

a phrase probably combined with the making of the sign of the cross on one's own person; cf. below, n. 31. In some French cathedrals also there was no final blessing at the High Mass even as late as 1700; de Moléon, 159, 169; cf. 200.

[18] Guerrini, 245. The same note also in the Carmelite Ordinal (about 1312; ed. Zimmermann, 84); also in a Carmelite Missal of 1514 (according to Eisenhöfer, II, 223).

[19] The concluding blessing is still lacking in the Missal of the monastery of Fécamp about 1300 and 1400; Martène, 1, 4, XXVI f. (I, 638, 642); in the Lyons monastic missal of 1531; *ibid.*, XXXIII (I, 661 D). In this connection it is worth remarking that the Benedictine *Liber ordinarius* of Liége (Volk, 97), which otherwise generally repeats the Dominican Ordinarium word for word, passes up the above-mentioned note as superfluous.

[20] As Bona, II, 20, 4 (905), remarks, the blessing was first introduced *paucis abhinc annis* (his works appeared 1671); cf. Schneider (*Cist.-Chr.*, 1927), 266 f.

[21] The bestowal of the blessing is included in the *Liber ordinarius* for the first time in 1622; Waefelghem, 98, note 0.

[22] A Dominican Missal that appeared at Venice in 1562 still has no concluding blessing; Ferreres, 213.

[23] A writing of the 15th century alleges as the reason for this, because they have no congregations; Franz, 595.

[24] Regula s. Benedicti, c. 38: *Qui ingrediens post missas et communionem petat ab omnibus pro se orari, ut avertat ab ipso Deus spiritum elationis.* He himself begins three times: *Domine labia mea aperies*, whereupon he receives the blessing.—Later this blessing was at times incorporated in the liturgy of the Mass; see already the Sacramentary of Fulda (Richter-Schönfelder, n. 29), as an appendix to the Mass-*ordo;* a few versicles are said over the reader and then the blessing formula: *Dominus custodiat introitum tuum et exitum tuum et auferat a te spiritum elationis.* Cf. Udalricus, *Consuet. Clun.*, II, 34 (PL, 149, 725 r.); *Missale Westmonasteriense* (about 1380), ed. Legg (HBS, 5), 524, and the editor's commentary (HBS, 12), 1506 with reference to the Monastic Consuetudines of the 11th century. See also the *Liber ordinarius* of Liége (Volk, 97, 1. 16), where the blessing follows the *Placeat*; the Missal of Monte Vergine (15th cent.; Ebner, 158), where it follows the *Ite missa est.* Cf. Köck, 59; Radó, 56; de Moléon, 135; 392; Schneider (*Cist.-Chr.*, 1927), 267 f.

[25] *Ordinarium O.P.* of 1256 cited above. Two Minorite Missals of the 13th and 13-14th centuries (Ebner, 317, 351) give only the blessing without indicating any accompanying formula; so also the Augsburg Missal of 1386 (Hoeynck, 376).

where the texts of blessings are mentioned, we find the most diverse formulations.

However, the connection with the blessing as it was described in the Roman *ordo* and as it became ever more strongly anchored in the episcopal service, remained clearly evident. The liturgical commentators pay more and more attention to this episcopal blessing.[26] As far back as the middle of the twelfth century, even in Rome, this blessing was no longer given on leaving, but imparted from the altar.[27] At the beginning of the fourteenth century we find it in a heightened form.[28] It is the same ceremonial that has become customary at episcopal pontifical Mass and also in the episcopal private Mass.[29] Even in the later Middle Ages this Roman method of imparting the blessing had often become current also outside of Rome and Italy.[30] Thus, the living model of the episcopal rite could gradually have encouraged the sacerdotal blessing, all the more so in northern countries, since the episcopal blessing given in this place—perhaps generally on less festive occasions—did not have the solemn form of the Gallic pontifical blessing, which was always reserved to the bishop. But we also recall at once the simple *Benedicat nos Dominus* of the Roman rubric booklets when, in the accounts of the sacerdotal blessing that now begin to be more plain and outspoken, we find frequent mention made of the priest blessing himself[31] or when, in addition, formulas appear which begin with the same words (and by degrees become more expanded)[32]

---

[26] Sicard of Cremona, *Mitrale,* III, 8 (PL, 213, 143) ; Innocent III, *De s. alt. mysterio,* VI, 14 (PL, 217, 914) ; cf. Durandus, *Rationale,* IV, 59.

[27] *Ordo eccl. Lateran.* (Fischer, 87, 1. 18).

[28] Ordo of Cardinal Stefaneschi, n. 53 (PL, 78, 1169 D) : beforehand the pope should sing *cum nota: Sit nomen Domini benedictum.*

[29] *Cæremoniale episc.,* I, 25; I,29, 11. In the solemn pontifical Mass, when no sermon was preached after the Gospel, the *publicatio indulgentiæ* (cf. above, I, 494), the announcement of 40 days or 100 days indulgence, occurs here in connection with the blessing.

[30] *Liber ordinarius* of Liége (about 1285; Volk, 103, 1. 32). About the same time Durandus mentions this bestowal of the blessing in his Pontifical beside the Gallican Pontifical blessing, and he considers it a less solemn method used by the bishop when he imparts the blessing at the end of the Office or a Mass that was not celebrated by himself. On the contrary, this final blessing in the Mass would not be necessary, if the solemn pontifical bless-

ing mentioned before had been given. Martène, 1, 4, XXIIII (I, 623 C) ; Andrieu, *Le Pontifical,* III, 655 f. Cf. too Durandus, *Rationale,* IV, 59, 7.

[31] Thus in the Sarum Ordinary of the 13th century (Legg, *Tracts,* 228) : confession of one's faults with *In nomine Patris . . .*; likewise in the later texts of the Sarum: *ibid.,* 268 and Martène, 1, 4, XXXV (I, 671 B). There is no particular notice at all here of a blessing of the people.

[32] Missal of Paris of the 14th century (Leroquais, II, 182) : *Benedicat nos Deus omnipotens P. et F. et Sp. S.;* Missal of Toul (about 1400; Martène, 1, 4, XXXI ([I, 652 E]) : *Benedicat nos divina maiestas et una Deitas, Pater . . .*; German missals of the 15-16th centuries (Köck, 136; Beck, 310; cf. 272) : *Benedictione cælesti benedicat nos divina maiestas et una Deitas . . .*; the Mass arrangement "Indutus planeta" (Legg, *Tracts,* 188) : *Benedicat nos et custodiat omnipotens Dominus Pater . . .*; Mass-*ordo* of Bec (Martène, 1, 4, XXXVI ([I, 675 D]) ; *Dominus nos benedicat . . .* (with broader execution) ; a Franciscan missal of the 13th century (Leroquais, II,

or which in some other way modestly include the one imparting the blessing.[33] Formulas or variants that employ the word *vos* appear comparatively seldom: *Benedicat vos*,[34] *Benedictio . . . descendat et maneat super vos*, and so forth.[35] The formula in use today, *Benedicat vos omnipotens Deus, Pater et Filius et Spiritus Sanctus,* appears (amongst other places) at the Synod of Albi (1230).[36]

Here and there, however, the solemnity of the concluding sacerdotal blessing began gradually to increase, taking on forms which, according to modern ideas, belong to the episcopal rite. There are introductory versicles, which have been used even in the thirteenth century as a specialty of the episcopal rite:[37] *Sit nomen Domini benedictum . . .* and *Adiutorium nostrum in nomine Domini.*[38] The words of blessing are accompanied

129) : *In unitate Sancti Spiritus benedicat nos Pater . . .*

[33] *Alphabetum sacerdotum* (Legg, *Tracts,* 51) : *Et benedictio . . . descendat super nos . . .* Custom of Tongern in the 15-16th centuries (de Corswarem, 144) : *Benedicat et custodiat nos et vos divina maiestas . . .*

[34] Cf. nevertheless the above, n. 16.

[35] Salzburg Missal of the 12-13th centuries: Köck, 135.

[36] P. Browe, *Eph liturg.,* 45 (1931), 384. The formula is also in the Ordo of Card. Stefaneschi (about 1311), n. 71 (PL, 78, 1192 A).—Durandus gives two other blessing formulas with *vos;* Durandus, *Instructiones et constitutiones* (ed. Berthelé, p. 77; Browe, 384, n. 4.: *In unitate Sancti Spiritus benedicat vos Pater et Filius; Benedicat et custodiat vos omnipotens Dominus P. et F. et Sp. S.* A missal from Metz dated 1324 (Leroquais, II, 208): *Benedicat vos divina maiestas, una Deitas . . .* In Germany about 1450 we have the witness of Egeling Becker for the formula: *Cælesti benedictione benedicat vos et custodiat vos P. et F. et Sp. S.*; Franz, 549. Similar forms were also typical in the Scandinavian countries: Segelberg, *Eph. liturg.,* 65 (1951), 260.

[37] Durandus, IV, 59, 7.—Gabriel Biel, *Canonis expositio,* lect. 89, finds himself confused by the fact that even priests use this versicle.

[38] Salzburg Missal of the 12-13th century: Köck, 135; South German Mass-orders of the 15th and 16th centuries: Beck, 272; 310; Franz, *Die Messe,* 754.—But (mostly

with a reversal of the order of the two versicles) also in French Mass-arrangements since the 14th century: Leroquais, II, 182; 208; de Moléon, 200; Legg, *Tracts,* 50; 67; Martène, 1, 4, XXVIII; XXXI (I, 645 E, 652 E).—A yet more solemn form is presented in the monastic breviary of Rouen (Martène, 1, 4, XXXVII ([I, 678 f.]) : the two versicles are preceded by a prayer of praise: *Te invocamus, te adoramus, te laudamus, o beata Trinitas!* Thereupon follow four orations, then other versicles and the double blessing formula: *A subitanea et improvisa morte et a damnatione perpetua liberet nos P. et F. et Sp. S., Et benedictio Dei omnipotentis P. et F. et Sp. S. descendat et maneat super nos. Amen.* Similarly the *Alphabetum sacerdotum* (about 1415) : Legg, *Tracts,* 50 f.; cf., too, the Ordinarium of Coutances (1557): *ibid.,* 68; in all three instances the benediction rite comes after the last gospel.—A Missal of Rouen offers an older form of the rite (Martène, 1, 4, XXVI, n. ([I, 638 E]) : the blessing in a simpler form precedes and only the oration follows upon the gospel. A weakened version also in the rite of the private Mass of the Monastery of Bec: *ibid.,* XXXVI (I, 675).

[39] Thus already in a sacramentary of the 11th century from Bologna (Ebner, 17) and still about 1500 in Burchard of Strassburg (Legg, *Tracts,* 167). Even the Missal of Pius V still provided for a triple blessing by the priest at a *missa sollemnis,* to be made in three directions (in the Ritus serv., XII, 7; Antwerp edition of 1572).

not with a single sign of the cross, but with three[39] or even four[40]—towards the four points of the compass. In pronouncing the blessing a chant tone is used.[41] In all these matters the missal of Pius V and its revision by Clement VIII (1604) have indicated retrenchments and clear restrictions.

On the other hand, the consciousness that there ought to be some difference even in the final blessing between the bishop's way of doing it and the priest's was manifested in various ways also in the Middle Ages. The bishop made the sign of the cross with his hand, while the priest was to use some blessed object. It had been the custom in some places already in the eleventh century to place relics on the altar during Mass[42] or a particle of the true cross, and to use these to impart the blessing at the end of Mass.[43] Durandus advises the priest to make this sign of the cross with a crucifix or with the paten or with the corporal.[44] This manner of giving the sacerdotal blessing, especially with the paten or with the corporal, is frequently attested since the fourteenth century, at first in France, and then also in Germany.[45] The chalice and paten, indeed, generally remained uncovered on the altar till the end of Mass.

While these methods of imparting the final blessing have disappeared, yet one peculiarity which, aside from the words, distinguished it from the sacerdotal blessing otherwise used outside of Mass, has been kept: before giving the blessing the priest raises his eyes and hands towards heaven.[47] This gesture is explained by the medieval allegorism, which saw in this blessing the last blessing of our Lord before He ascended into heaven[48] when He blessed His disciples, *elevatis manibus* (Luke 24:50).[49]

[40] John Bechofen (about 1500), who advocates the simple sign of the cross; (Franz, 595); Bursfeld missal of 1608 (Gerbert, *Vetus liturgia Alemannica*, I, 406).

[41] According to Eisenhofer, II, 224, in France still in the 18th century.

[42] Shrines for relics were the first objects that one dared place on the altar; see above I, 258.

[43] P. Browe, "Der Segen mit Reliquien, der Patene und Eucharistie," *Eph. liturg.*, 45 (1931), 383-391.

[44] Durandus, *Instructiones et constitutiones*, ed. Berthelé, p. 77; Browe, 384, n. 4.

[45] Browe, 385 f. Also a blessing of individuals with the corporal was quite customary after Mass: it was either laid on the face or fanned in front of the person, a practice that Henry of Hesse (d. 1397) mentions with some disapproval; *ibid.*, 385 f. An extraordinary veneration for the corporal, which often deteriorated into superstition, is verified already since the 10-11th centuries; Franz, 88-92.

[46] A Persian missal of the start of the 14th century (Leroquais, II, 182) : *cum calice vel patena*. Likewise the ordinarium of Coutances, 1557) : Legg, *Tracts*, 67. Data from England in Browe, 386.

[47] This rite provided for in the *Missale Rom., Ritus srv.*, XII, 1, remains restricted to the bestowal of the blessing in the Mass, at least according to Ph. Hartmann - J. Kley, *Repertorium Rituum* (14th ed.; Paderborn, 1940), 625. Otherwise M. Gatterer, *Praxis celebrandi* (3rd ed.; Innsbruck, 1940), 333. The rubrics have no further directions about this. The attitude mentioned is nowhere prescribed in the Roman Ritual for the blessing of the people and objects.

[48] Amalar, *De eccl. off.*, III, 36 (PL, 105, 1155 B) ; Bernold, *Micrologus*, c. 20 (PL, 990) ; Durandus, IV, 59, 4.

[49] Cf. above I, 91.

The final blessing was sometimes given before kissing the altar and reciting the *Placeat,* sometimes after. In general the determining factor seems to have been the priority of the respective development. In France, where the *Placeat* had been incorporated earlier, the blessing generally followed.[50] On the other hand, in Germany, where the *Placeat* was introduced only later, the blessing was as a rule given before.[51] This latter sequence was for a time the prevailing one also in Rome.[52] It is found even in various editions of the Roman Missal, e. g., in those of 1474, 1530 and 1540.[53] The inversion, as fixed in the missal of Pius V, must have originated from the notion that, if blessing and prayer were to follow the dismissal, then surely the blessing which at one time was itself called a *missa* must necessarily stand at the end.[54] The same feeling lay at the root of the practice in the church of Rouen where, in the dying years of the medieval era, when the final blessing had been magnified into a form of great solemnity, this blessing was placed after the last Gospel.[55] In regard to the formula to be used, for a long time—as we have already said—there was no fixed rule. In the printed editions of the *Missale Romanum* of 1530 and 1540 we find a choice between two forms; they were essentially the ones which had been recommended by Durandus. In the printed editions of 1505, 1509, 1543, 1558, 1560 and 1561 only one of them is given, *In unitate Spiritus Sancti, benedicat vos Pater et Filius,* which was eventually displaced in favor of the formula we have at present.

The editions of the Roman missal printed in 1558 and 1560 also presented a special form of blessing for the Mass of the Dead: *Deus, vita vivorum, resurrectio mortuorum, benedicat vos in sæcula sæculorum.*[59] But here, too, the later *Missale Romanum* asserted the general principle that all blessing of the living should be omitted in Requiem Masses. German missals of the declining Middle Ages introduced in the Mass *ordo* a blessing for the departed, even outside of Masses of the Dead. As in the office the oration and *Benedicamus Domino* are followed by *Fidelium animæ,* so also in the Mass following the post-communion and the dismissal first a blessing for the dead was given and then the blessing of the living.[60] In

---

[50] Durandus, IV, 59, 8; Martène, 1, 4, XXVIII; XXXI (I, 645 E, 652 E); Legg, *Tracts,* 67; cf. 228.

[51] Bernold, *Micrologus,* c. 21 f. (PL, 151, 991 f) ; Beck, 272; 310 f.; Hoeynck, 376; Franz, 576; 754. Latter arrangement also in the Minorite missals in Ebner, 317; 351.

[52] Ordo of Stefaneschi, n. 53 (PL, 78, 1169 D).

[53] R. Lippe, *Missale Romanum,* 1474, Vol. II (HBS, 33), 114 f. Louis Ciconiolanus' *Directorium divinorum officiorum,* which appeared in Rome in 1539, leaves the choice to the priest; *in suo positum est arbitratu.* Legg, *Tracts,* 212. The present

usage was instituted in the revision of the Roman Missal under Pope Clement VIII (1604).

[54] Gavanti gives a more external reason, hardly an apposite one: "The Mass that has begun with the kissing of the altar, should also end with the same."

[55] Missale of Rouen and *Alphabetum sacerdotum,* above, n. 38.

[56] Lippe, *loc. cit.*

[57] Above, n. 36.

[58] Lippe, 115; also see Ferreres, 212.

[59] Lippe, 115.

[60] Regensburg Missal of 1500 (Beck, 272): *Et animæ omnium fidelium defunctorum*

the Roman missals at Rome this blessing of the dead did not have a place. But the *Requiescant in pace* at Requiem Masses, which seems like a shortened form of this blessing, appears to have sprung from a similar source.[61]

5. The Last Gospel

It is certainly remarkable that at the close of the Roman Mass a gospel pericope should be read. But if we go back to its origin, we find that this reading harmonizes with the series of dismissal rites and more particularly with the blessings. The prolog of the Gospel according to St. John, with the exalted flight of its ideas and the profundity of its mysteries, was accorded an extraordinary esteem even in the early Church. Augustine quotes the saying of a contemporary of his that this text ought to be placed in gold letters at some prominent place in all the churches.[1]

The prolog of St. John is rightly regarded as a summary of the Gospel, the divine power of which is, in a measure, concentrated there. Just as sacred symbols, words or pictures were used as pledges of divine protection, just as blessings were and still are imparted with holy objects, cross, chalice, paten, or (in the Orient) with *dikirion* and *trikirion*, so in the course of time the beginning of the Gospel of St. John began to be used as an instrument of blessing. It might be that the written words were carried on one's person, or that they were recited or listened to. Naturally it could happen that, in place of that Christian trust in God which, inspired by the sacred word, looks up to Him in humble petition, superstitious and magical practices would creep in.[2] In the year 1022 the synod of Seligenstadt noted that many lay people and especially women placed great store in daily hearing the Gospel *In principio erat Verbum* or special Masses *de s. Trinitate* or *de s. Michaele*. In future this was to be allowed only *suo tempore* and insofar as it was asked out of reverence for the Blessed Trinity, and *non pro aliqua divinatione*.[3]

But alongside this misuse of the holy text there was still room for the proper and Christian use of it. The beginning of the Gospel of St. John was read in the sick-room before dispensing the last sacraments,[4] or after baptism over the newly baptized child.[5] A particularly favorite use, dating

---

requiescant in sancta Dei pace. Likewise the Augsburg Mass-*ordo* from the second half of the 15th cent.: Franz, 754; Freising Missal about 1520: Beck, 310; Missal of the Bursfeld Benedictines of 1608: Gerbert, *Vetus liturgia Alemannica,* I, 405 f.
[61] An immediate derivation is not possible because of the time interval—the *Requiescant in pace* appears 300 years earlier.
[1] Augustine, *De civ. Dei,* X, 29 (CSEL, 40, 1, p. 499).
[2] Cf. A. Jacoby, "Johannisevangelium":

Handwörterbuch des detutschen Aberglaubens, edited by Baechtold-Stäubli, IV (1931-32), 731-733.
[3] Can. 10 (Mansi, XIX, 397 f.).
[4] Missal of Remiremont (12th cent.): Martène, 1, 7, XVII (I, 911 A). Also according to the present-day *Rituale Rom.,* V, 4, 24, John 1: 1-14 is one of the favorite selections that should be read when visiting the sick.
[5] Rituale of Limoges: Martène, 1, 1, 18, XVIII (I, 215 A).

back to the twelfth century, was as a blessing for the weather,[6] just as later the introductions of the four Gospels (for the four points of the compass) were used, and are still used, for the purpose. Just as during the summer—from Holy Cross (May 3) to Holy Cross (Sept. 14)—this blessing in some form or other is given even today, in many dioceses every Sunday, and in some places every day after the parish Mass,[7] so it might have happened that the prolog of St. John, as a pericope of blessing, became more and more a permanent part of the end of Mass. In his explanation of the Mass which appeared about 1505, the Augustinian hermit John Bechofen speaks about the reading of this Gospel as a *laudabilis consuetudo,* and he grounds the custom on the argument that reading or hearing the Gospel is a direct attack on the devil, who is trying to rob us of our union with God and to harm us in soul, body and goods.[8]

The first evidence of the Gospel of St. John at the end of Mass—it is a question here primarily of private Mass—is found in the *Ordinarium* of the Dominicans, which was fixed in 1256: The priest may recite it when unvesting or later, together with the oration *Omnipotens æterne Deus, dirige actus.*[9] This custom must have rapidly found favor in the Dominican order, for members of the order working in the Armenian mission introduced the last Gospel, among other things, into the Armenian Mass, and with such effect indeed, that in spite of the break-down of the union in 1380 it remained in the liturgy even of the schismatics down to the present[10]—an example of missionary latinizing which, to the Middle Ages (which were not renowned for their historical sense), seemed only natural.

In the West, however, it had not become common everywhere even at the close of the Middle Ages.[11] When, in the year 1558, the first general

[6] A. Franz, *Die kirchlichen Benediktionen im Mittelalter,* II (Freiburg, 1909), 52, 57 f.

[7] A daily blessing of the weather at the end of Mass is still customary in the diocese of Salzburg and in parts of Carinthia; cf. the Ritual of Gurk (1927), 160. The Joannine gospel passage always forms the start of this blessing.

[8] Franz, *Die Messe,* 595.

[9] Guerrini, 250. The Dominican Bernard de Parentinis about 1340 speaks of an optional reading of the Gospel of St. John; Franz, *Die Messe,* 595, n. 2.

[10] Brightman, 456.

[11] The Gospel of St. John is provided for about 1285 in the *Liber ordinarius* of Liége (Volk, 102), here also only for the private Mass. Durandus, IV, 24, 5, mentions it in passing but does not describe it at the end of Mass (IV, 59). Later it appears in several French Mass orders: Mar-

tène, 1, 4, XXXI; XXXIII; XXXVII (I, 652 E, 661 D, 678 D); Leroquais, III, 12; 57; 70; 107; 113, etc.; Legg, *Tracts,* 50, 67. According to the late medieval Missal of Sarum in England (Martène, 1, 4, XXXV ([I, 761 C]) it is said *redeundo* by the priest, just as today in the Rite of Lyons (Buenner, 258) and also in the Roman rite at the Pontifical Macc (*Cæremoniale episc.,* II, 8, 80). In Germany about 1494, as Balthasar of Pforta wrote, the Last Gospel was not in general use; Franz, 588; cf. 595, 727. In the description of 79 Styrian Missals of the 12-15th cent. made available by Köck, the Last Gospel is mentioned only once (p. 191). Still it is verified at the turn of the Middle Ages in the Mass-arrangement of Regensburg (Beck, 272) and Augsburg (Franz, 754) and by John Bechofen (*supra*). For Scandinavia it is mentioned in the breviary of Skara (1498): Freisen, *Manuale Lin-*

chapter of the Society of Jesus, convened to choose a successor to St. Igna-tius, expressed the desire to make the rite of the Mass uniform within the order, the last Gospel was one of the points that still hung in balance even in Rome itself.[12] A last Gospel was indeed decided upon for the order's rite, but it was left free to choose Luke 11:27 f.: *Loquente Jesu ad turbas* (the pericope which recounts the happy cry of the woman in the crowd: "Blessed is the womb that bore thee"), or the prolog of St. John.[13] On the other hand, the Carthusians have not yet taken the last Gospel into their rite even today,[14] just as they have not inserted the last blessing.

Oftentimes the last Gospel was rounded off liturgically by reciting an oration after it, and as a rule this latter was introduced by a few versicles.[15]

Already in the thirteenth century the prolog of St. John was not com-monly regarded as the only possible last Gospel,[16] although this is seldom indicated in earlier sources. But with the increasing possibility of using another Gospel reading, the thought suggested itself with ever greater force that the last Gospel, besides having the character of a final blessing and sacramental, might at the same time be a commemoration in which the main text of a second formulary could be taken up in this place in the Mass. This notion was all the more natural because even in the six-teenth century the *missa sicca* was still current custom. At such a "mass,"

copense, p. XXXI, and in the missal of Trondheim (1519) : *ibid.,* p. LXI; still these seem rather to be exceptions; see Yelverton, 21.

[12] As Bona, II, 20, 5 (908 f.) remarks, the *Missale Romanum* which was approved at Rome and appeared 1550 in Lyons, still had no Last Gospel, while the reading of the same in the Ceremonial of the Roman Master of Ceremonies, Paris de Grassis (d. 1528), was left to the choice of the celebrant.

[13] *Decreta Congr. gen.* I, n. 93 (Institu-tum S.J., II; Florence, 1893, 176).

[14] So likewise the Castile Cistercians; see see B. Kaul, *Cist.-Chr.,* 55 (1948), 224. Several French churches about 1700 also did not have it, or they let the priest re-cite it on his return from the altar; de Moléon, see in the Register, p. 522., s. v. Evangile.

[15] In the *Liber ordin.* of Liége (Volk, 102) it is the Oration *Protector in te speran-tium* (today on the 3rd Sunday after Pentecost) ; likewise in the monastic Mis-sal of Lyons of 1531; Martène, 1, 4, XXXIII (I, 661 D). In the Carmelite Ordinal of 1312 (Zimmermann, 89) the Oration *Actiones* is added. With four ora-

tions and various versicles in the Breviari-um of Rouen; Martène, 1, 4, XXXVII (I, 678) ; still these four orations, as the Mass Ordo of Bec (Martène, 1, 4, XXXVI ([I, 675]) shows, were joined to the Communion prayers even without the concluding Gospel (cf. above, n. 38) ; or as the Missal of Rennes (15th cent.; Leroquais, III, 70) directs, a *memoria de beata Virgine vel de dominica vel de quo-dam sancto vel de mortuis* was to precede the Last Gospel.—The *Ordinarium O.P.* of 1256 (Guerrini, 250), and likewise also the Missal of Bursfeld of 1608 (Gerbert, *Vetus liturgia Alemannica,* I, 406) uses after the concluding Gospel, the Oration *Omnipotens sempiterne Deus* (today on the Sunday within the octave of Christ-mas). Cf. Ordinarium of Coutances of 1554: Legg, *Tracts,* 68.—The Augsburg Missal of the 15th century (Franz, 754) adds to the concluding Gospel, as to the Gospel of the Fore-Mass, the blessing *Per istos sacros sermones.* Similarly the Pre-monstratensian Ordo of Averbode (about 1615) ; Lentze (*Anal. Præm.,* 1950), 149.

[16] Durandus, IV, 24, 5: some read the Gospel of St. John at the end of Mass, *vel aliud.*

at which the priest officiated without chasuble,[17] and which was generally added to the regular Mass, the celebrant as a rule read the entire proper text of the second formulary, along with other Mass prayers (except the canon), or else only the Epistle, the Gospel and the *Pater noster*.[18] Then, as the *missa sicca* gradually disappeared after the Council of Trent, it did not involve too great a change to keep at least the proper Gospel of the second formulary as an appendage to the first Mass.[19] It did not take long to make such a proposal. In the missal of Pius V a special addition of this kind was proposed first of all for those formularies of the *proprium de tempore* which were hindered. In 1920, in the new edition of Benedict XV, this was extended to all those Masses which have an *evangelium stricte proprium*, as, for example, the Mass formularies of the Blessed Mother or an apostle.[20]

It cannot be denied that through such directions a progressive change in the character of the last Gospel and a refinement of its function is revealed. The note of blessing draws into the background. It is the content of the pericope, even that of St. John, that comes to the fore. More recent exponents of the Mass no longer mention the benedictional character of the last Gospel; they try to portray the Johannine pericope, with the mystery of the incarnation therein contained, as the real epilog of the entire Mass, the concluding paragraph by which the Mass is brought back to its "eternal root" or source.[21] The prolog of the "good tidings" has thus become the epilog of the sacrifice by which those tidings are renewed. Naturally a convincing reason for the necessity of such an epilog is not forthcoming. In consequence there is something incongruous, something discordant about this last point of the Mass-liturgy.[22] This is shown also by the fact that there is no actual "proclamation" of the Gospel, no public reading of it. True, the Gospel is introduced with the same forms as the Gospel of the fore-Mass, a greeting, an announcement, with an acclamatory response; while the faithful are accustomed to rise and cross themselves with the priest as at the Gospel of the fore-Mass.[23] But this greeting and announcement and acclamation, like the reading itself, are all done

---

[17] In the 15-16th cent. the Gospel of St. John was frequently read after the chasuble was removed. Leroquais, III, 107; 135; 227; Legg, *Tracts*, 67.

[18] J. Pinsk, "Die missa sicca," *JL*, 4 (1924), 90-118, especially 104 f.

[19] Along the same lines see G. Malherbes, "Le dernier évangile non-Johannique et ses orgines liturgiques": *Les Questions liturgiques et paroissiales*, 25 (1940), 37-49.

[20] Additiones et Variationes, IX, 3. More clearly defined by a decree of the Cong. of Rites, March 29, 1922; *Decreta auth. SRC*, n. 4369.

[21] Kössing, *Liturgische Vorlesungen*, 598 f. One could describe this also as a sort of doxology about him who became man for and among us, a sort of Christ-doxology at the end of Mass, similar to that at the end of the canon.

[22] In the new Easter Vigil Mass the Last Gospel is left out: *AAS*, 43 (1951), 137.

[23] The Regensburg Missal about 1500 notes that he makes the sign of the cross upon the altar and then upon himself *in fronte et in corde;* Beck, 272. About the same time the genuflection at the *Et Verbum caro factum est* is insisted upon, and the demand is supported by a genuinely me-

only in a semi-audible voice. Evidently, then, these are only imitations designed to create a worthy frame around the priest's reading. In fact, the reading itself has not the formal character of a lesson; it is normally recited by rote, like a sacred text which is always handy. At the end of the Middle Ages, "in many countries," as the *Hortulus animæ* (published at Strassburg in 1503) averred, the Gospel of St. John was recited by all present, a practice which obviously was planned to strengthen its function as a blessing.[24] In the pontifical high Mass the bishop speaks these words while leaving the altar; he merely makes the sign of the cross on the altar, to show that he receives the word of the Gospel from the altar, from Christ, from God.[25]

6. Final Blessings Sanctioned by Particular Law

When we keep in view the living liturgy, that is, not only the shape it has insofar as it accords with the universal prescriptions of the *Missale Romanum*, but beyond this, the factual performance as it exists in different places, we are forced to state that often the Mass celebration does not come to an end with the last Gospel. The urge to bless and the desire to receive the blessing of the Church has called still other forms into being.

We spoke before about the blessing of the weather which in many places still follows the Mass during the summer months, in forms which have developed since the Middle Ages in various ways in the different bishoprics.[1] Insofar as the blessing is added to the Mass day after day, it consists as a rule only of a prayer (that the priest either recites at the foot of the altar or leads the people in reciting) and of a blessing with the Blessed Sacrament or with a particle of the cross, accompanied by the words of the blessing of field and meadow.

In other places during the whole year, especially on Sundays and feast-days, the blessing is given to all the faithful with the monstrance;[2] either

dieval *exemplum.* Franz, 576, n. 7.—In England it must have been customary to kneel and kiss the ground at *Verbum caro factum est;* cf. E. Peacock (ed.), *Myrc's Duties of a Parish Priest,* EETS-OS, 31 (1868), 1, 1665 ff. Cf. also Lydgate's poem "On Kissing at Verbum caro factum est" in H. N. MacCracken (ed.), *The Minor Poems of John Lydgate,* EETS-ES, 107 (1910).

[24] Franz, 719.

[25] Cf. above I, 444 f. This symbolism is clearly indicated already in one of the earliest references regarding a Last Gospel, namely in Durandus, where this particular sign of the cross is used as a proof to show that the Gospel book must always be taken from the altar.

[1] Regarding this cf. P. Browe, "Die eucharistischen Flurprozessionen und Wettersegen," *Theologie u. Glaube,* 21 (1929), 742-755; Eisenhofer, II, 447 f.

[2] A blessing with the Blessed Sacrament at the end of the Mass became customary in the 14th century first of all on the Feast of Corpus Christi; in the 15th century in the Thursday Masses frequently established for the veneration of the Blessed Sacrament. The first mention of this in a Thursday Mass comes to notice in the year 1429 at Ingolstadt. The blessing was generally combined with the hymn *Tantum ergo.* At the word *Benedictio,* a sign of the cross with the monstrance was formed, thus giving the word a sort of outward interpretation. Besides this, a blessing was

the monstrance is exposed during the whole Mass, as is still the custom on many occasions in southern Germany,[3] or it is removed from the tabernacle at the end of Sunday high Mass and after a brief period of adoration is raised in benediction.[4]

Then there are forms to be used when the blessing is not only given to the entire congregation as a unit but in a certain manner is intended more or less for each one singly. In the primitive Church we find the individual imposition of hands,[5] but as this requires a great deal of time, it is used nowadays almost only when necessary for the performance of a sacrament, as in confirmation and ordination. The most widespread form for giving a blessing that touches each individual in the assembled congregation is sprinkling with holy water. Frequently, especially in many south German country parishes, this sprinkling with holy water is the actual end of the Mass. Immediately before he leaves the altar, the priest passes through the ranks of the faithful, swinging the aspergillum and reciting the psalm with the prescribed antiphon *Asperges;* in this way the faithful take home with them in a visible form something as their share in the blessings of the Church. This has been the practice for centuries.[6]

Somewhat distantly related to the sprinkling with holy water is the distribution of blessed bread, the *eulogiæ*, which survives in the oriental liturgies and also in France even today. In the Byzantine liturgy the custom has an especially elaborate form. After the closing prayers the priest steps out of the sanctuary and hands out the so-called ἀντίδωρα.[7] These are the pieces left from the host-breads from which are taken the particles used for consecration. The name *antidoron*, ἀντίδωρον, is usually explained in the sense that this gift is meant to take the place of the real and' infinitely greater gift of the Eucharist.[8] The ἀντίδωρον is thus a

frequently given also at Mass during the Sequence *Lauda Sion* at the words *Ecce panis angelorum.* Browe, *Die Verehrung der Eucharistie im Mittelalter*, 151 f.; 181-185.

[3] Cf. above I, 122 f.

[4] This latter method is frequently followed where one wishes to restrict the Mass of Exposition and yet avoid a complete break with tradition. Thus the Diocesan Synod of Vienna, 1937, combines a far-reaching restriction of these Expositions with the hint that it is still permissible to impart the blessing with the Blessed Sacrament at the end of the Mass according to the method prescribed in the ritual; *Die Erste Wiener Diözesansynode* (Vienna, 1937), p. 36.

[5] *Supra,* I, 477.

[6] According to the ecclesiastical customs of the village of Biberach, as they were listed

in 1530, the priest on definite occasions first had to give the blessing at the end of the Mass with the monstrance and then had to sprinkle the congregation with holy water. A. Schilling, "Die religiösen und kirchlichen Zustände der ehemaligen Reichsstadt Biberach unmittelbar vor Einführung der Reformation," *Freiburger Diözesan-Archiv*, 19 (1887), 154; Browe, 185. The original place for the sprinkling with holy water in church, as is known, is before the divine service in parishes on Sundays. Here the early indications of a sprinkling can be verified already in the 8th century. Eisenhöfer, I, 478-480; cf. Braun, *Das christliche Altargerät*, 581-598.

[7] Brightman, 399; cf. Pl. de Meester, *La Liturgie de s. Jean Chrysostome* (3rd ed.; Rome, 1925), 135.

[8] Thus Brightman, 577; Mercenier-Paris, 253, n. 1. On the other hand, Baumstark,

substitute for Communion, although nowadays it is also taken by the communicants.[9] Essentially the same custom prevails amongst the Armenians[10] and Syrians. Among the East Syrians the distribution of the *eulogiæ* belongs to every liturgy;[11] among the West Syrians it is restricted to Lent and the vigil Masses. The bread used at this function need not have any relation to the Eucharist, but it is given a special blessing immediately before the distribution.[12]

That appears also to be in accord with the original conception of the *eulogiæ*. It may be that we have here a survival of that blessing of natural gifts which in the ancient Roman liturgy since Hippolytus is found at the end of the canon,[13] but elsewhere, even quite early, at the end of the entire celebration.[14] The gifts in many cases were ones that the faithful themselves had brought or even offered up, and which they now received back as tangible transmitters of the divine blessing.

In the West this custom of the *eulogiæ* at the end of Mass developed most vigorously in the area of the Frankish realm.[15] It is seen first in the sixth century.[16] In the ninth century it appears in full light in the direction stipulating that after Communion on Sundays and feast days priests should take this bread, which is to be blessed beforehand with a special formula, and distribute it to non-communicants.[17] From then on the custom was gen-

Die Messe im Morgenland, 179, renders ἀντίδωρα by "countergifts" (to the faithful in place of the previous customary bread offering).

[9] Thus the monks on Mt. Athos. R .Pabel, *Athos* (Münster, 1940), 23; cf. 27.

[10] Brightman, 457.

[11] Brightman, 304; A. J. Maclean, *East-Syrian Daily Office* (London, 1894), 291.

[12] A secularized form of the distribution of the Eulogia also among the Copts; see Baumstark, *loc. cit.,* 179.

[13] *Supra,* I, 29; II.

[14] In the Euchologium of Serapion (Quasten, *Mon.,* 66) after the prayer that concludes the Communion of the Faithful, there follows a "prayer over the oil and water that was offered" and then the final blessing over the people. Likewise in the *Testamentum Domini,* I, 24 f. (*ibid.,* note; Rahmani, 49) ; cf. Baumstark, *Die Messe im Morgenland,* 178.

[15] A. Franz, *Die kirchlichen Benediktionen im Mittelalter,* I (Freiburg, 1909), 247-263; Nickl, *Der Anteil des Volkes an der Messliturgie,* 68-71; Browe, *Die Pflichtkommunion im Mittelalter* 185-200 ("Der Kommunionersatz: Die Eulogien") ; G. Schreiber, *Gemeinschaften des Mittel-*

alters, 213-282, especially 229 ff., 262 ff. Cf. also the materials in Corblet, I, 233-257.

[16] Gregory of Tours, *Hist. Franc.,* V, 14 (PL, 71, 327 B) : *Post missas autem petit* [*Merovech*], *ut ei eulogias dare deberemus.* Cf. *ibid.,* IV, 35 (PL, 71, 298 B). These liturgical eulogias are to be distinguished from the private eulogias that are frequently mentioned at that time; cf. Franz, *op. cit.,* I, 239-246; Nickl, 69 f.; Browe, 187 f.

[17] Hincmar of Reims, *Capitula presbyteris data* (of th year 852), c. 7 (PL, 125, 774) : *Ut de oblatis, quæ offeruntur a populo et consecrationi supersunt, vel de panibus, quos deferunt fideles ad ecclesiam, vel certe de suis presbyter convenienter partes incisas habeat in vase nitido et convenienti, ut post missarum sollemnia, qui communicare non fuerunt parati, eulogias omni die dominico et in diebus festis exinde accipiant.* The prayer of blessing cited afterwards is in its essence the same as that offered in today's *Rituale Romanum,* VIII, 16. A pertinent prescription also in the almost contemporaneous *Admonitio synodalis* (among others, PL, 96, 1378 B). Cf. also the corresponding Visitation

eral throughout the West for centuries.[18] It died out earliest in Germany, where Wolfram von Eschenbach in 1209, writing in *Willehalm*, a translation of a French epic, speaks about the bread that *"alle suntage in Francrîche gewîhet wirt"*—bread that was blessed every Sunday in France.[19]

The custom was so closely associated with Communion, being regarded as a substitute for the benefit of non-communicants, that when the change to unleavened bread was made, the *eulogiæ* at first were also changed and took the form of hosts. But since the twelfth century cognizance began to be taken of the danger that lurked in having both Communion hosts and *eulogiæ* look alike, and so a distinction began to be made not only in the form of the bread but often also in the manner of distribution.[20] Then, too, the idea which was still much in prominence towards the end of the twelfth century, namely, that the *eulogiæ* were a substitute for Communion,[21] gradually vanished, and so this blessed bread became simply a "sacramental which was dispensed like holy water."[22]

In this sense the custom of the *panis benedictus, pain bénit*,[23] survived for a long time in France and Switzerland, in the rural districts, especially in Burgundy and Brittany, where it still exists today. A family of the parish, chosen in fixed rotation, is designated to furnish the bread for a certain Sunday which that family therefore regards as its own particular feast. On that Sunday the family, accompanied sometimes by relatives and friends, transports the bread to church.[24] Before the beginning of Mass or before the offertory, or else at the end of Mass, it is brought up to the altar to be blessed and divided into small pieces and so distributed to all present. If those who receive it do not intend to communicate they eat it

---

Question in Regino of Prim (above, p. 9, n. 45) and a related decision for monasteries already in the *Capitulare monasticum* of 817, n. 8 (MGH, Cap., I, 347). In monastic circles the *eulogiæ* were distributed in the refectory; see Udalricus in PL, CXLIX, 711, 723; William of Hirsau, PL, CL, 1014-1015. Cf. Leclercq, "Le Pain Bénit Monastique," DACL, 13: 460; Franz, *op. cit.*, I, 247 ff.

[18] In Italy the practice is still presupposed about 1320. In England a confession questionnaire about 1400 asks "Have you taken your Sunday meal without blessed bread?" In Spain in 16th century liturgical books there are still texts for the blessing of the bread brought by the faithful; Browe, 189 f., 194 f.—The custom was retained the longest for the days of the Easter Communion and in many monasteries besides, and in such cases it was clearly marked as a substitute for Communion. Browe, 191-194.

[19] II, 68, 4 f.; Wolfram of Eschenbach, *Werke,* edited by Lietzmann, II (Altdeutsche Textbibliothek, 15), 54.
[20] Browe, 198 f. Cf. the parallel case regarding the ablution chalice, *supra*, p. 414.
[21] John Beleth (see above, p. 325, n. 23); Sicard of Cremona, *Mitrale,* III, 8 (PL, CCXIII, 144). Durandus, IV, 53, 3, calls it *communionis vicarius.*
[22] Browe, 194.
[23] Also called *panis lustratus, panis lustralis;* in old English it was known as *gehalgod hlaf* (hallowed bread). Cf. U. Seres, "Le pain bénit," in *Les questions liturg. et parois.*, 1933, 248 ff.
[24] G. Schrieber, *loc. cit.*, 278 f. Here also more details from various descriptions of the practice during the past century. Sometimes a definite number of breads is provided, three, twelve, fourteen (273 f.). In the district of Metz, bread was distributed on Sundays (274), but on feast days cake. A candle generally went with the offer-

at once.[25] Bringing the bread to the altar before the offertory seems to show a certain connection with the former offertory procession, but the original idea of the blessed bread is best retained where the distribution takes place at the end of Mass.[26]

7. The Prayers of Leo XIII

The additions to the Mass-liturgy described above have sprung more or less organically from the closing of Mass; namely, from the notion that before the conclusion of the divine service the Church should once again show its power of blessing. But in the nineteenth century—though only at private Mass—prayers were added of which we cannot affirm any such inner relationship. They are intercessory prayers in time of stress, pleas for the great needs of the Church, appeals in which the people should share and which therefore are recited with the faithful in their own language.

More than once in the course of our study of the Mass-liturgy and its historical development we have come upon this notion of intercessory prayers, and precisely intercessory prayers for the needs of the Church, to be said by the people in common. They had their original place at the end of the readings or lessons, in the General Prayer of the Church. When this General Prayer was dropped from the Roman liturgy at the turn of the fifth century, its popular components acquired a fresh and rich development in the *Kyrie* litany, while the priest's intercessory plea entered more deeply into the innermost sanctuary of the canon. Then, as the *Kyrie* litany was reduced to a manifold repetition of the *Kyrie* invocation and modified into a melodic song for the choir, the need for supplication in times of dire trouble produced anew, since the ninth century, a mode of expression in conjunction with the Lord's Prayer, at first after the embolism, later before it.

And finally, in the later years of the Middle Ages, prayers for wants and peace were injected into other places, especially after the *Dona nobis pacem*.[1] In the latter cases we are dealing only with common prayers to be

ing of bread, as was the practice already in the Middle Ages.

[25] Paul Claudel in one of his poems, *La Messe La-Bas* (15th ed., Paris, 1936), 103, dedicated a section between the *Ite missa est* and the Last Gospel to this popular custom: "The part of the Mass the youngsters in France like best of all is when, near the end, the server sallies forth from the altar with a large basket full of bread from which one has only to grab . . ." In the Mass arrangements of the Middle Ages the blessing of the bread is mention-

ed only rarely, thus in the Missal of Evreux-Jumièges; Martène, 1, 4, XXVIII (I, 646 A), and in the Westminster Missal (about 1380), ed. Legg (HBS, 5) 524; in both cases it is at the end of the Mass.

[26] The double character of the old rite is displayed in its purest form when, as reported to me from a congregation in the neighborhood of Besançon, the bread is brought up after the Gospel, then into the sacristy where it is cut into pieces and lastly distributed after Communion.

[1] See above, p. 292.

recited by the clerics assembled in choir, but the *literati* who knew Latin were expected to join in.[2]

Oriental liturgies which were faced with a change in the language of the people, like the Byzantine-Melkite, the West Syrian and the Coptic after the ultimate victory of the Arab element, did not hesitate, despite their otherwise conservative attitude, to translate into the new vernacular not only the readings but also such litanies (corresponding to the intercessions) which the deacon was accustomed to recite alternately with the people;[3] they are now recited in Arabic. Except for some tiny ventures in the earliest period,[4] a similar accommodation has not been made in the Western liturgies. In the Roman liturgy in the centuries that followed, there was even less occasion than elsewhere for such an adoption of the vernacular, as long as a Latin culture dominated the West and thus gave assurance that the Latin prayers would at least be faintly echoed in the congregation. For very different reasons, conditions had not become any more favorable in the nineteenth century when the desire arose for such a prayer for needs. Even in the middle of the century every effort was still directed towards emphasizing the boundary-lines between priest and people, as can be seen from the 1857 prohibition to translate the *Ordo missæ*.[5] True enough, Leo XIII urged the faithful to pray aloud during Mass, but it was the praying of the rosary in the month of October, a prayer that in its ultimate significance, but not in its concrete form, displays a certain relevance to the action of the Mass and even to the step-by-step movement of the liturgy. So if an intercessory prayer was to be recited by all the people for the needs of the Church, then in accordance with the stand taken by the liturgists at that time, this could have a place only before or after Mass.

The kernel of the prayers which we recite after private Mass had been in use even before Leo XIII. In 1859, when the danger to the Papal States grew ever more serious, Pius IX ordered prayers for the area of his secular dominion. The prescription continued even after the Papal States had fallen. When Leo XIII made his last efforts to set aside the laws of the *Kulturkampf* in Germany and to win back the liberty of the Church, on January 6, 1884, he extended these prayers to the whole Church.[6] Even after the liberty of the Church was essentially won back here, the prayers nevertheless remained. In their new form, as we have it today,[7] they were

---

[2] *Supra*, p. 293 f., p. 339 f.

[3] Baumstark, *Von geschichtlichen Werden*, 102.

[4] *Supra* I, 335, n. 11.

[5] *Supra* I, 161.

[6] *Acta S. Sedis*, 16 (1883), 239 f. The oration closes here: . . . *et omnibus sanctis, quod in præsentibus necessitatibus humiliter petimus, efficaciter consequamur. Per.*

[7] It was published in the diocesan papers and church magazines, e.g., *Irish Ecclesiastical Record*, 3rd ser., 7 (1886): 1050. There is nothing to be found in the *Acta S. Sedis*, 19 (1886). Two slight changes were silently made in the prayers about 1900: *beato Joseph* replaced the unusual *Josepho* and *eumdem* was added to the *Per Christum D. N.*

broadened to include a purpose which undoubtedly must be dear to the heart of the Church at all times: in the oration, among other things, the words *pro conversione peccatorum* were added.

Measured by the ceremonial form of the Roman Mass-liturgy, it is indeed striking that these prayers are recited kneeling at the foot of the altar. It had been customary for the priest to give expression to the humble and suppliant petition of such prayers by means of a low bow. But since such a bodily bearing was no longer customary among the faithful, and it is with the faithful that the priest is to say these prayers, nothing was left but this kneeling together, an attitude of prayer for which there were precedents even at the altar.[8] This kneeling position at the end of Mass had been prescribed in the liturgy of the Carthusians long ago, in their *Statuta antiqua* (before 1259); according to this direction the priest, after laying aside his vestments, is to recite the *Pater noster* at the foot of the altar *flexis genibus*.[9]

As regards their construction, the prayers of Leo XIII follow in all essentials the laws of form of the Roman liturgy. Whereas earlier examples of similar prayers in need regularly began with psalms, here the more popular element of the Hail Mary[10] was chosen; with the petition which is a part of it, this prayer is recited three times, and then the *Salve Regina*[11] is added to further enforce the tone of supplication. As we know, the effort to give the liturgical celebration a Marian note in the high Middle Ages led to the practice of concluding the canonical office, or at least certain hours of it, with a Marian antiphon. A prayer of praise addressed to the Blessed Virgin was sometimes added also in the Mass, either after Communion[12] or at the close.[13] The *Salve Regina*, too, some-

---

[8] *Les questions liturgiques et paroissiales,* 6 (1921), 63, rightly emphasizes that this prescribed genuflection for all times of the year is in contradiction to the rules otherwise obtaining in the Roman liturgy.

[9] Martène, 1, 4, XXV (I, 635 C). The present-day *Ordinarium Cart.* (1932), c. 27, 19, demands *Pater* and *Ave.*

[10] This is not the first appearance of the *Ave Maria* in the liturgy of the Mass. It was taken into the prayers at the foot of the altar (Stufengebet), e.g., at the end of the Middle Ages; see above I, 297 f., n. 30, 33. The combination of Lk. 1: 28 and Lk. 1: 42 occurs as an insertion in the intercessory prayer after the consecration in the Greek liturgy of St. James (Brightman, 56) and (without *Dominus tecum*) as an offertory hymn in the oldest MSS. of the Roman antiphonary (Hesbert, n. 5, 7, *bis*, 33), that is, in the basic text of the antiphonary at the beginning of the 7th cen-

tury. The addition of the name of Jesus and the petition *Sancta Maria . . .* originated from the popular practice of the Middle Ages and is confirmed today in its present form through the breviary of Pius V, 1568. Cf. H. Thurston, "Hail Mary," CE, 7: 110-112.

[11] The *Salve Regina* must have originated in the 11th century in the monastery of Reichenau; for more details about its history see A. Manser, "Salve Regina": *LThK,* IX, 137 f. Cf. also Wm. Martin, "The Salve Regina," *Liturgical Arts,* 16 (1948), 41-48.

[12] Above, p. 406.

[13] Two Mass arrangements of the late Middle Ages from Normandy added to the Trinitarian formula of the concluding blessing: *Et beata viscera Mariæ Virginis quæ portaverunt æterni Patris Filium.* Martène, 1, 4, XXXVI f. (I, 675 D, 679 A). According to the Pontifical of Durandus the

times formed the close of the *ordo* of the Mass.[14] The versicle *Ora pro nobis* then leads over to an oration, as is ordinarily done according to traditional usage after a psalm or an antiphon. And the oration gathers together our prayers and formulates our pleading. Here again the old stylistic rules of the Roman method of prayer are at work: in view of the intercession (already sought) of the Mother of God, with whom are ranged the great protectors of holy Church, we beg of God's grace the internal welfare and the external freedom and growth of the Church, and we close the prayer with the *Per Christum*.

Finally, to this addition other further additions were made, and again we cannot affirm that these additions have any intrinsic relationship to what has gone before. Leo XIII himself, in 1886, when issuing the new form of the oration, added the invocation to the Archangel Michael.[15] There is no question here of a second oration but rather of an isolated invocation, something very unusual in the Roman liturgy.

Another independent composition, of an entirely different character, strikingly in contrast with the final words of the preceding prayer, *in infernum detrude*, is the threefold cry: *Cor Jesu sacratissimum, miserere nobis*, added under Pius X. However, here is not a matter of regulation but of permission granted by the Congregation of Indulgences, dated June 17, 1904.[16] If, however, a certain obligation has arisen in this matter, as it seems it has, it must be derived from the custom that has been established.

The publication of the prayers of Leo XIII included the direction that they be said with the people, but no official text in the vernacular was prescribed. As a result almost every diocese uses its own version. This is true not only in Germany but elsewhere, too.[17] Obviously such a state of

---

priest may still add the prayer, *Salve sancta parens* at a Mass that he celebrates in the presence of the bishop, but only after the bishop has given the final blessing. Martène, 1, 4, XXIII (I, 620 C) ; Andrieu, III, 647.

[14] According to a French monastic missal of 1524 (Leroquais, III, 268) the *Salve Regina* or another antiphon, along with the appropriate oration, was said after the Gospel of St. John. Similarly also in the Cologne rite of the 16th century; Peters, Beiträge, 188.—The Carmelites added it during the 14th century (it was not yet in the ordinal of 1312). The *Missale O. Carm.* (1935), 323, inserts it, with its oration, between the final blessing and the Last Gospel. B. Zimmermann, "Carmes," DACL, II, 2170 f. Cf. the problem answered by the Congregation of Rites on June 18, 1885; *Decreta auth. SRC*, n.

3637, 7.—The Missal of Braga (1924), 336-338, includes after the Last Gospel a *commemoratio b. Mariæ Virginis* that varies according to the seasons of the Church year.

[15] The opening words of the invocation are similar to the Alleluja-verse in the Mass for the feast of the Archangel on May 8 and Sept. 29.—Bers, "Die Gebete nach der hl. Messe," *Theol.-prakt. Quartalschrift*, 87 (1934), 161-163, vehemently combats a legend making the rounds that this prayer was introduced by Leo XIII after a dream or vision (!) of the powers of hell.

[16] *Acta S. Sedis*, 36 (1904), 750; F. Beringer, *Die Ablässe*, I (14th ed.; Paderborn, 1915), 194.

[17] On the difficulties of translation see the article by R. E Brennan, "The Leonine Prayers," *American Ecclesiastical Review*, 125 (1951), 85-94, especially 89 f.

things did not help to endear the prayers to either priest or people. Insofar as they had to be added[18]—and they had to be added even on feasts that excluded every commemoration!—these prayers not seldom underwent that same "liturgizing," that same reduction to an exchange between priest and server, that same fusion with the Latin of the rest of the Mass-liturgy that forced other textual elements which were originally conceived in the vernacular—like the phrases before the distribution of Communion—back into a Latin mold.

In France, Italy, and elsewhere for the past few decades another prayer in the vernacular has become customary at the end of Mass and Benediction. This prayer consists of a number of laudatory sentences recited singly by the faithful after the priest. It is called "The Divine Praises." It begins with the praise of God: "Blessed be God," then touches on the most important mysteries of faith in the form suited to the religious thought of the time, and ends with the words, "Blessed be God in his angels and in his saints."[19] In this way the close of the Mass acquires a final harmony which re-echoes in the *Benedicite* of the priest.

8. Recession

When all the final obligations have been taken care of, the priest leaves the altar. In the Mass celebrated without levites, the priest—according to present-day practice—himself carries the chalice, with the paten on top and a veil covering it, and the burse with the corporal, back to the sacristy, while the Mass-server as a rule precedes him with the book. At a high Mass the sacred vessels remain on the credence table.

This order, which appears to us so natural, is of relatively recent date.

---

[18] Regarding the extent and limits of this obligation and details of ceremonial an elaborate system of rubrics has arisen; cf. Brennan, *loc. cit.*, especially 90 ff.

[19] The "Divine Praises" originated in Rome, the work of Fr. Aloysius Felici, S.J., who presumably publicized them in 1797 as a means of combating blasphemy. It is as *Laudes in Blasphemiarum Reparationem* that they appear in the official collection of indulgenced prayers, *Enchiridion Indulgentiarum,* (Vatican City, 1950), n. 696. The first grant of indulgence was made by Pius VII, July 23, 1801. Cf. A. P(aladini), "De laudis 'Dio sia benedetto' historia, progressu et usu,"*Eph. liturg.,* 63 (1949), 230-235. It was not long before the prayer came into quasi-liturgical use: in Italy frequently after Mass, as also in France; in America and Spanish and Portuguese lands after Benediction of the

Blessed Sacrament. The Congregation of Rites made it its concern several times: in connection with Benediction (March 11, 1871; *Decreta auth. SRC,* n. 3237), inclusion of an invocation of St. Joseph (Feb. 23 1921; SRC, n. 4365), and of an invocation in honor of the Assumption (Dec. 23, 1952; *AAS,* 45 [1953], 194).

[20] Where it is customary it is permitted to add the Divine Praises or prayers indulgenced for the faithful departed (S.C. Indulg., June 17, Aug. 19, 1904; SRC, n. 3805).—Dom Bede Lebbe, *The Mass: A Historical Commentary* (Westminster, 1949), 168, mentions the time-honored custom which exists in Ireland of reciting after Mass a *De profundis* with the verses and prayer *Fidelium Deus,* a practice which appears to go back to the troublesome days of the 17th century.

That the chalice and paten should carried in the manner customary today could not have been considered, as we have seen, until the time when the paten was reduced in size. A German Mass-plan about the year 1000, in describing the end of the high Mass, directs the subdeacon to carry the (uncovered) chalice, and an acolyte, the paten.[1] But after that both chalice and paten are taken together. However, because even at the close of the Middle Ages our chalice-veil did not yet exist,[2] the priest—according to the Mass-*ordo* of Burchard of Strassburg (1502)—placed the chalice and paten in a small bag which he then tied, put the burse with the folded corporal on top of the bag, and carried the two into the sacristy, while the server preceded him (according to this *ordo*) carrying the book, the pillow, the cruets, the box for the hosts, the altar candles and the elevation candle.[3] The present arrangement, therefore, dates back only to the time of Pius V.

At the recession the priest begins the canticle *Benedicite*, the song sung by the three young Hebrews in the Babylonian furnace (Dan. 3:57-88). This, and the prayers that go with it are now found in the Roman missal no longer as part of the text of the *Ordo missæ* but in the *Gratiarum actio post missam* which is prefaced to the missal. The pertinent rubric[4] is therefore today considered as merely directive.[5] On the other hand, medieval Mass books which include this canticle and the other closing prayers that follow it, after they became customary about the year 1000, regularly group them with the preceding texts without indicating any distinction.[6] This song of praise, which was recited at the recession and which from the very start was united with Psalm 150, was on about the same level with the psalm *Judica* which was said at the beginning of Mass, and it was recited or sung by the celebrant, together with the assistants, at the altar, as the oldest witnesses from about the tenth century expressly remark.[7] Even here the psalmody was followed by a number of versicles and the oration *Deus qui tribus pueris*. But, soon after, various expansions begin to appear.

Between the *Benedicite* and Psalm 150, Psalm 116 *Laudate Dominum omnes gentes*, was sometimes inserted,[8] or the ancient hymn *Te decet laus*

---

[1] *Ordo "Postquam"* for episcopal Mass (Andrieu, II, 362; PL, 78, 994).

[2] In the archdiocese of Cologne it was first prescribed at the Synod of 1651. Braun, *Die liturgischen Paramente*, 214.

[3] Legg, *Tracts*, 169.

[4] Cf. also Ritus serv., XII, 6.

[5] Cf. *supra*, I, 275 f.

[6] Cf., e.g., the facsimile of an 11th century central Italian Sacramentary in Ebner, 50. Still in a part of the Mass-arrangements, although not in the oldest (see *infra*), the priest is ordered to say the prayers *exuens se vestibus;* thus e.g., Bernold, *Micrologus*, c. 23 (PL, 151, 995).

[7] Mass arrangement of Séez (PL, 78, 251 A) : *Expletis omnibus episcopus rediens ad sacrarium cum diaconibus et ceteris cantet hymnum trium puerorum et Laudate Dominum in sanctis eius.* Then follow, without a preceding *Pater noster*, ten versicles, among them those ordered by the present *Missale Romanum*, and then the first oration, which however is somewhat elaborated. Similarly in two related witnesses; Martène, 1, 4, IV, XIV, XV (I, 517 f., 582, 594), where, however, in the rubric given, twice after *et ceteris* is added a restrictive: *quos (quibus) voluerit.*

[8] The 11th century central Italian Sacra-

was appended.[9] Later we find that they sometimes added the *Nunc dimittis*.[10] At the head of the versicles which were subject to a great deal of shifting, we find the *Pater noster*[11] and the *Kyrie*,[12] and as an addition to the oration *Deus qui tribus pueris,* which for centuries has been used even in other circumstances as an adjunct to the canticle of the Three Young Men,[13] we find a second oration, *Actiones nostras.*[14]

Much later, and only occasionally, do we find the oration (in the third place in our day) which refers to the victorious suffering of St. Lawrence.[15] Some have suggested that this rather strange oration is to be traced back to the practice of the pre-Avignon popes, who were accustomed to celebrate daily Mass in the papal chapel of the Lateran's *Sancta sanctorum* dedicated to St. Lawrence.[16] The facts, however, contradict this opinion.[17] The oration from the Mass of St. Lawrence would have been adopted whenever they began to put greater emphasis on the character of the canticle as the song of the three young men in the fiery furnace, with whose fate St. Lawrence's had such a likeness. That was evidently the case after the song was framed with the antiphon *Trium puerorum cantemus hymnum,* which appears for the first time in 1170 in the pontifical of Mainz.[18] For in the medieval texts the Laurentian oration has a different position than in the Roman missal, either immediately after the oration

mentary already mentioned: Ebner, 50; 299.—Missa Illyrica: Martène, 1, 4, IV (I, 517 C); *Liber ordinarius* of Liége: Volk, 102.

[9] Missal of St. Lawrence in Liége: Martène, 1, 4, XV (I, 594 C).

[10] Mainz Pontifical (about 1170): Martène, 1, 4, XVII (I, 602 E); Missal of Toul: *ibid.,* XXXI. Regensburg Missal about 1500; Beck, 272. Cf. the use of the same song of praise after Communion, *supra,* p. 404.

[11] Missa Illyrica: Martène, 1, 4, IV (I, 517 C).

[12] Bernold, *Micrologus,* c. 23 (PL, 151, 995); Missal of St. Vincent: Fiala, 216; *Liber ordinarius* of Liége: Volk, 102.

[13] Mohlberg, *Das fränkische Sakramentarium Gelasianum,* n. 841, 891, 1146 and the further findings reported, *ibid.,* p. 317 f., 335.

[14] Missa Illyrica, *loc. cit.;* cf. also Martène, 1, 4, XIV f., XXXII (I, 582 D, 594 C, 658 B); Bernold, *Micrologus,* c. 23 (PL, 151, 995); Fiala, 217. In two Roman documents this oration alone is added to the first: in *Vetus Missale Lateranense* (Ebner, 169) and in the Mass-*ordo* of the papal court chapel about 1290, ed. Brinktrine (*Eph. liturg.,* 1937), 209.

[15] Blew MS. of the Sarum Manuale (14th cent.): Legg, *Tracts,* 268; Missal of Toul (about 1400): Martène, 1, 4, XXXI (I, 653); Pressburg Missale D (15th cent.): Jávor, 120; Regensburg Missal about 1500: Beck, 273.

[16] H. Grisar, *Die Römische Kapelle Sancta Sanctorum* (Freiburg, 1908), 23; adopted also by Baumstark, *Missale Romanum,* 145.

[17] The Canticum, contrary to a remark of Eisenhöfer, II, 227, was current in Rome before the Ordo of Stefaneschi, therefore, as a matter of fact, before the Avignon period; see Roman sources cited above, n. 14. To these belongs also the Mass-*ordo* of the papal chapel of this time, that developed from the Ordinarium of Innocent III. The oration *Da nobis quæsumus* is not mentioned in it, nor in the Ordo of Stefaneschi, n. 71 (PL, 78, 1192 B), where about 1311—and this precisely in Avignon —we find the last phase of the development in the papal court chapel, where, too, only the two orations *Deus qui tribus* and *Actiones* appear.—In other Italian sources of the 11-13th century, in Ebner, 317, 331, 334, 349, all we find is the prescription to say the *Benedicite.*

[18] Martène, 1, 4, XVII (I, 602 E).

Deus qui tribus pueris,[19] or separated only by the oration *Ure igne Sancti Spiritus* which is intrinsically akin to it.[20] These orations were intended to petition help against the most dangerous enemy, the enemy within us. In this tradition the oration *Actiones nostras* was not at first provided.[21]

On the other hand, the versicles which even at present precede the orations endeavor to take up the tone of praise and above all to continue the theme started in the verse *Benedicite sacerdotes Domini Domino,* the stirring call to priests whose very first duty it is to hymn the praises of God. Hence such versicles as *Sancti tui benedicant tibi, Exultabunt sancti in gloria.*[22] One series of sources, in fact, provides only that part of the canticle itself beginning with the verse cited above.[23] In the concluding orations there was less room for such a tone of joy, since they were prayers of petition.[24]

The idea of a psalmodic song of praise at the end of Mass is so natural that there is hardly any need of a special explanation, more particularly when such a song of praise at the recession (as is the case in the oldest witnesses) is only the counterpart of the psalm of longing which has accompanied the accession to the altar.[25] We should rather wonder that the song of praise at the end did not, like the psalm at the beginning, remain an integral part of the actual liturgy to be recited at the altar. Hence if legal-minded reformers in the centuries following,[26] intending to give more prominence to these prayers, cite from the old Spanish church a

---

[19] Toul, Pressburg, Regensburg (see above, n. 15).

[20] Blew MS. This MS. shows, in addition to the three mentioned, three further Orations; see *infra,* n. 24.

[21] It was incorporated only into the Missal of Pressburg where it is the final oration so that it does not interfere with the thought of the other two formulas. The two traditions are brought together in another way by Burchard of Strassburg in his Mass-*ordo* (Legg, *Tracts,* 170 f.) : to the two orations *Deus qui tribus pueris* and *Actiones* anciently current in Rome, *Da nobis* is added only externally. This sequence was retained in the Missal of Pius V.

[22] In the Missa Illyrica (*loc. cit.*) too: *Sacerdotes tui, Domine, induantur iustitiam.*

[23] *Vetus Missale Lateranense* (about 1100) : Ebner, 169. Late medieval Mass-orders from Normandy (Bec, Rouen): Martène, 1, 4, XXXVI f. (I, 675 D, 679 A) ; Ordinarium of Coutances (1557): Legg, *Tracts,* 69. It is therefore unnecessary to refer for this versicle to the chapel

of the Sancta Sanctorum and its relic treasure, as do Grisar (above, n. 16) and F. Cabrol (R. Aigrain, *Liturgia* [Paris, 1935], 554).

[24] In single instances a pertinent attempt has been made here, thus in a preceding oration of the Missa Illyrica, *loc. cit.* (517 E) : *Deus quem omnia opera benedicunt.* The Ordinarium of Coutances (Legg, *Tracts,* 70) has an oration with the character of a *Postcommunio* in the third place : *Purificent vos,* a very natural solution. The Blew MS. of the Sarum Manuale offers besides the three orations relating to fire *(Deus qui, Ure, Da nobis),* three others : *Infirmitatem nostram, Deus qui conspicis, Protector in te sperantium;* still such an accumulation is rare. The missal of Braga (1924) emphasizes the tone of joyful thanksgiving by ushering in the *Benedicite* with the *Te Deum* (p. XCII; 338).

[25] Cf. Mass-*ordo* of Séez (PL, 78, 251 A, respectively 246 A). Cf. *supra,* I, 94.

[26] Bernold, *Micrologus,* c. 22 (PL, 151, 992) ; Sicard of Cremona, *Mitrale,* III, 8 (PL, 213, 144 A).

canon which does indeed treat about this canticle of ours, but which actually has an entirely different connection in view,[27] we may not exchange such a canonistic underpinning with the actual reason for the origin of this recessional prayer.[28] The canticle *Benedicite* and Psalm 150 are eminently suited to the purpose. In view of what has occurred at the altar, all creation seems to us to resound in wordless jubilee and to sing the praises of Him who has so richly favored the world and mankind.

Then, too, the canonical hours have been drawn on occasionally to prolong the praise of God. In the Lateran basilica during the twelfth century, after the *Ite missa est* of a pontifical high Mass, sext was begun, and only after it was finished did the bishop return to his seat, *hymnum trium puerorum cantando cum eisdem ministris.*[29] A similar thing is still done in many cathedrals at the present.

Next comes silent prayer and meditation. It is no discovery of modern piety that the time after Mass and Communion, when the crowd has dispersed and quiet has settled over the church, is a time for the priest—and the same holds for the faithful—to give himself to more than vocal prayer. Monastic Mass-plans of the thirteenth century, after indicating the recessional prayers, add this direction for the priest: *Terminatis vero omnibus potest orare sacerdos secreto prout ei Dominus inspiraverit.*[30] In the spirit of olden prescriptions[31] the canon law at present warns the priest that just as he prepared himself for the sacrifice by prayer, so he ought not to forget to make a proper thanksgiving afterward, *gratias Deo pro tanto beneficio agere.*[32] This is in accord with a long-established ascetical practice.[33]

For this, of course, the liturgical books can offer nothing else but more prayer texts. In the Roman missal the appendix to the real recessional

[27] The IV Council of Toledo (633), can. 14 (Mansi, X, 623) : *in omnium missarum sollemnitate* the *Benedicite* must be sung immediately, but what is meant here is the Canticle that belonged to the Mass of the Catechumens in the Gallican liturgy; cf. above, I, 47.

[28] As also in Eisenhöfer, II, 227.

[29] *Ordo eccl. Lateran.* (Fischer, 87, line 20).

[30] Dominican Ordinarium of 1256 (Guerrini, 251) ; *Liber ordinarius* of Liége (Volk, 102).

[31] *Rituale Rominum*, IV, 1, 4; already in older editions.

[32] *Codex Iur. can.*, c. 810.

[33] Already in Bk. IV of the *Imitatio Christi*, c. 1,24, there is an indication that the devotion after Communion ought to last a half hour or so. Etienne Binet (d. 1639) directed his attention to the matter of how long the eucharistic Presence endures after Communion (he judges an hour) and then combines with his ascetical considerations some even broader calculations; H. Bremond, *Histoire littéraire du sentiment religieux en France*, I, 141 f.—Demands for a quite prolonged thanksgiving after Communion are also to be found recurrent in St. Alphonsus de' Liguori, *Dignity and Duties of the Priest* (ed. Grimm, rev., 1927), 228; *True Spouse of Jesus Christ* (ed. Grimm, rev., 1929), 577: "I say 'at least for half an hour,' for an hour is the proper time for thanksgiving." Similar reflections appear to have been made during the period of the pseudo-Isidore Decretals, though they were concerned less with the time of thanksgiving than with the continuation of the fast; the priest who in the morning consumed the remnants of the people's Communion, it was said, should remain fasting until noon, etc.; cf. Decretum Gratiani, III, 2, 23 (Friedberg, I, 1321).

prayers, the *Orationes pro opportunitate sacerdotis dicendæ*, contains such texts, of which particularly the first, captioned as *Oratio s. Thomæ Aquinatis*, is very old.[34] The prayer following, which is called *Oratio s. Bonaventuræ*, actually comes from the pen of that doctor of the Church.[35] For the rest, the series of prayers here presented has in recent years been enriched in many ways. Missals of the Middle Ages now and again contain at the end an addition of private prayers of a similar sort.[36] But here a distinction between private and public prayer, while not absolutely excluded, is even harder to make than in the present missal, since indeed some of the Mass prayers themselves were still in the stage of private prayers.

When we look farther back and try to get a picture of the first thousand years of the Mass-liturgy, we must admit that generally with the *Ite missa est* not only communal divine service but also personal devotion were terminated, so that the Mass in the Roman liturgy, even when the older oration of blessing was still customary, came to a relatively rapid and abrupt end, and there could be but little talk of a special thanksgiving for all the great things which God had granted in Christ and in His Church. What was momentarily received in the Sacrament was only a sacramental corroboration of the presence of that grace in which our Christian life is imbedded. If the realization of this were revived in the celebration, the work of the entire day could actually become a sufficient thanksgiving for this new hour of grace, as many a *post-communio* sets forth.[37] But with the increasing separation of a gradually fixed Mass-liturgy on the one side and of personal piety, ever seeking new roads, on the other side, and with the growing accentuation of the Eucharist as an all-embracing and all-illuminating gift of God, it was but natural that a *gratiarum actio* should become a requirement even after the εὐχαριστία. The more conscious practice of meditative prayer, which was known to the ancient monks only in the form of the *lectio divina*, was also bound to lead in the same direction. For no moment is so opportune for meditating on what we have received and what we possess, as the moment when the last prayers of Mass have died away. Although we are less shocked than our forebears were when the faithful who have work to do take the *Ite missa est* more or less literally, even when they have been to Communion, still for clerics at least a good solution would be to use the few moments of quiet prayer after the sacred action as an opportunity to allow the spirit of the Eucharist to permeate our innermost soul more and more.[38]

---

[34] Cf. *supra*, p. 404 f.

[35] M. Grabmann, "Der Einfluss des hl. Bonaventura auf die Theologie und Frömmigkeit des deutschen Mittelalters," *Zeitschrift f. Aszese u. Mystik*, 19 = *ZkTh*, 68 (1944), 20.

[36] The missal of Valencia (before 1411) has an additional prayer after the *Placeat*,

namely, *Sit, Jesu dulcissime, ss. corpus tuum.* Ferreres, 209.

[37] *Supra*, p. 424.

[38] Cf. in a like sense the explanation given by Pius XII in his encyclical *Mediator Dei* of Nov. 20, 1947: *AAS*, 39 (1947), 566-568.

INDEX

A. Sources

I. Christian Sources

Canones Apostolorum (Funk) II—10[52].

Canones Basilii (Riedel) I—238[26], 258[33], 262[5], 460[28], 476[7]; II—37[41], 44[16], 62[108], 76[1], 115[1], 118[16], 276[4], 388[108].

Canones Hippolyti (Riedel) I—15[37], 197[11].

Constitutiones Apostolorum (Funk, Quasten) I—32[19], 35f., 51[5], 57[29], 119[51], 195[1], 203[55], 243[51], 246[14], 262[5], 296[27], 334[10], 347[6], 350[12], 352[22], 364[17], 368[43], 374[6], 393, 394[3], 411[52], 423[10], 443[5], 448[40], 457[7], 476[6,9,11], 481[7], 483[20]; II—5[11], 157[5], 54[62], 76[3], 93[16], 109[47], 113[21], 114[27], 125[59], 128[3,4], 133[26], 136[41], 154[15], 171[7], 173[19], 192, 200[34], 219[6], 221[16,17], 222[22], 226[41,42], 227[4], 230[19], 231[31], 235[47], 238[7], 250[11], 276[6], 279[13], 283[29], 297[23,27], 321[1], 344[4], 386[92], 388[102,107], 392[4], 393[17], 407[2], 420[6], 428[5], 433[2].

Didache I—11f., 13[28], 16, 17[46], 18, 19[56,60], 22, 25[16,17], 30[8], 170, 191[51], 213, 216[26], 352[24]; II—154, 264, 297[24].

Didascalia (Funk, Quasten) I—32, 195[1], 218[40], 241[31], 245[3]; II—19f.

Doctrina Apostolorum I—245[3].

Peregrinatio Ætheriæ I—41, 170, 174[38], 262[2], 263[8], 318[3], 398, 408, 429[52], 443[7], 445[19], 457[7], 477[16], 481[9]; II—133[26], 433[13], 440[5].

Sahidic Ecclesiastical Canones (Brightman) I—475[6]; II—388[107,108], 407.

Testamentum Domini (Rahmani, Quasten) I—235, 368[43], 433[81], 468[58]; II—4[10], 5[11], 114[27], 147[44], 276[6], 363[23], 380[58], 386[92], 388[105], 453[14].

—Arabian Testamentum Domini (Baumstark) II—241[20], 250[14], 380[59], 388[106].

—Syrian Testamentum Domini (Quasten) II—388[105].

Traditio Apostolica of Hippolytus of Rome (Dix, Hauler) I—13[29], 14[36], 15f., 19[60],

26ff., 195, 245[3], 247[20], 393[14], 422[5], 441[124], 456, 457[7], 473[74], 475[4,5], 480, 482[15]; II—5, 76[1], 111[6], 119[24], 125[57], 132, 145[37], 147, 187, 192, 195, 220, 224, 226, 235, 261f., 265, 301[46], 322[4], 360[2], 366[34], 380[44], 382[58], 386[94], 388[108].

II. Non-Roman Liturgies

1. Egyptian Liturgies

Serapion's Euchologion (Quasten) I—31[15], 33ff., 171[23], 408[28], 476[8], 477[16], 480[3]; II—4[10], 102[2], 109[47], 116[9], 132, 135[39], 191[24], 193[31], 195, 218[2], 219[5], 238[1], 241[21], 276[6], 301[46], 420[6], 428[5], 453[14].

Egyptian Church Order II—276[6], 433[3].

Papyrus of Dêr-Balyzeh I—41; II—193[31], 222[23,27].

Coptic Liturgy (Brightman, Renaudot) I—41, 325[24], 366[36], 367f., 405, 407[18], 423[13], 424, 430[60], 445, 447[34], 449[53], 457[13]; II—4[10], 37[41], 114[26], 145[37], 202, 204, 222, 250ff., 251[20], 274[79], 276[6], 279[10], 284[40], 286[49], 297[22,26], 328, 380[59], 389, 393, 411, 419, 453[12].

—Coptic Anaphora of St. Gregory Nazianzen I—42; II—334[13].

Ethiopian Liturgy (Brightman) I—42, 352[21], 366[36], 384[42], 405[10], 406[18], 423[11], 443[7], 445[20], 486[52]; II—35, 77[5], 118, 145[37], 160[8], 200[34], 203[7], 204, 222[27], 235[47], 261[14], 276[6], 286[49], 299[34,35], 356, 380[59], 382, 388[108], 393[15], 420.

Greek Liturgy of St. Mark (Brightman) I—42, 362[9], 395[15], 406[14], 423[12]; II—54[62], 82[2], 125[59], 135, 148[3], 149[10], 151[16], 159[2], 193[31], 195, 198[22], 222[24], 223f., 234[42], 248[2], 250f., 282[25f.], 294[5], 299[34].

—Papyrus fragments I—42[27]; II—241[23], 251ff.

See also Index B: Alexandria; Egyptian Liturgy.

b) Mass Ordos of the Séez Group

281^{33}, 297^{29}, 302^{29}, 315^{32}, 316^{33}, 319^{15}; II—49^{33}, 56^{71}, $63^{112,116}$, 69^{152}, $884^{0f.}$, 347^{15}, 402^{13}, $406^{38f.}$.

c) Pontificals

Cambrai (Martène 1, 4, I) I—282.
Codex Casanatense 614 (Ebner) I—297^{33}, 319^{13}; II—236^{52}, 237^{54}, 269^{54}, 272^{66}, 309^{33}, 310^{40}, $319^{41f.,45}$, 326^{23}, 405^{35}.
Donaueschingen (Metzger) I—311^{84}.
Durandus, see Index A: III, 3, c, Pontificals, below.
Egbert (Greenwell) II—$260^{2,7}$.
Freiburg (Metzger) I—486.
Hungarian (XI–XII cent.; Morin) II—260^{8}.
Laon (Leroquais) II—89^{51}, 212^{66}, $291^{80,83}$.
Mainz (Martène 1, 4, XVII) II—56^{70}, 67^{140}, $72^{11,14}$, 84^{16}, 87^{31}, 164^{21}, 236^{52}, 269^{54}, 291^{84}, 327^{32}, 349^{27}, 353^{14}, 359^{61}, 402^{13}, $461^{10,18}$; (Martène 1, 4, XVIII) II—295^{13}.
Naples (Ebner) II—56^{71}.
Narbonne (Martène 1, 7, XIII) I—209^{10}; II—281^{23}, 323^{11}, 363^{23}, 370^{22}.
Poitiers (Morinus, Martène) I—300^{16}, 302^{25}, 386^{51}; II—27^{2}, 146^{33}, 397^{46}.
Roman Pontificals of the Middle Ages (Andrieu) I—$198^{12f.}$, 274^{19}, 373, 388^{60}, 411, 459^{22}; II—13^{67}, 324^{17}, 370^{25}, 413^{45}.
Romano-German Pontifical (Andrieu, Hittorp) I—66, 95f., 224^{85}, 386^{52}; II—305, 390^{117}.
Salzburg (Andrieu) I—93^{1}; II—390^{117}.

d) Roman Ordos

John the Arch-Chanter: Ordo (Silva-Tarouca) I—65, $76^{7,9}$, 105, 201, 222^{70}, 236^{19}, 298^{2}, 345, 357^{48}, 384^{40}, 407^{22}, 455^{94}; II—42, 61^{104}, $78^{13f.}$, 90, 104, 115^{30}, 142^{21}, 288, 315^{30}, 333^{7}.
—Capitulare Ecclesiastici Ordinis (Silva-Tarouca; Andrieu) I—201, 298^{2}, $323^{12f.}$, 324^{17}, 326^{23}, 331, 341^{44}, 343^{52}, 345^{67}, 356^{44}; II—5^{16}, $42^{4f.}$, $90^{4f.}$, 104^{16}, 107^{42}, 129^{7}, 161^{10}, 238^{7}, 258^{50}, 267^{40}, 288^{60}, 304^{6}, 314^{15}, 315^{80}, 319^{40}, 321^{2}, 326^{24}, 333^{3}, 337^{24}, 342^{6}, 379^{33}, 383^{65}, $395^{27f.}$, 399^{52}, 400^{56}, 412^{33}, 434^{14}.
—Breviarium Ecclesiastici Ordinis (Silva-Tarouca) I—199^{18}, 201, 206^{70}, 262^{4}, 298^{3}, 324^{19}, 326^{23}, 356^{44}, 421^{10}; II—

$42^{4f.}$, 82^{1}, 90^{5}, 129^{7}, 267^{40}, 319^{40}, 333^{6}, 342^{6}.
Ordo "Qualiter Quaedam"; Ordo "In Primis"; Ordo "Postquam", see respectively Ordo Romanus IV; V; VI, below.
Holy Week Ordo of Einsiedeln (Duchesne) II—333^{6}, 337^{25}, 338^{36}.
St. Amand (Duchesne; Andrieu) I—66, 70^{11}, 72^{20}, 124^{119}, 196^{6}, 201^{35}, 209^{9}, 236^{19}, 240^{36}, 267, 326^{23}, 332, 338^{23}, 339^{32}, 341^{44}, 342^{49}, 343, 356f., 357^{48}, 368^{46}, 421^{10}, 432^{70}.
Engelbert [Ordo Angilberti] (Bishop) II—343^{11}, 410^{22}, 435.
Ordo Romanus Antiquus [Vulgatus] (Hittorp) I—66, 70^{12}, 240^{36}, 284^{51}, 300^{16}, 310^{80}, 369; II—200^{33}, 322^{3}.
Ordo . . . Ecclesiae Lateranensis (Fischer) I—66^{39}, 69^{10}, $106^{15,17}$, 107^{21}, 199^{23}, $203^{53,55}$, 204^{56}, 240^{36}, 303^{32}, 343^{55}, 359^{61}, 362^{11}, 369^{47}, 371^{69}, 419^{3}, 427^{41}, 441^{127}, 452^{63}, 456^{1}, 457^{11}, 472^{63}, 494^{21}; II—7^{30}, 8^{35}, 36^{32}, 44^{16}, 60^{99}, 62^{106}, 64^{125}, 76^{35}, 79^{15}, 129^{6}, 131^{22}, $272^{66f.}$, 306^{12}, 308^{24}, 310^{43}, 319^{41}, 324^{17}, 338^{32}, 339^{47}, 340^{49}, 342^{7}, 377^{23}, 386^{95}, 410^{21}, 414^{47}, 417^{69}, 435^{88}, 443^{27}, 463^{29}.
Ordines Romani of Mabillon (PL 78):
—Ordo Romanus I (VII cent.) I—66, 67^{1}, 69^{9}, 76, 83^{45}, 196^{6}, 197^{9}, 200^{33}, $267^{22,24}$, 290^{1}, 291^{5}, 296^{27}, 298^{2}, 314, 318^{5}, 323^{12}, 333^{61}, 340, 344, 356^{43}, 357^{48}, 362^{8}, 364^{21}, 368^{47}, 371^{60}, 407^{22}, 410^{43}, 411^{48}, $415^{70f.}$, 420^{6}, 430^{58}, $432^{70,73}$, 433^{78}, 443^{8}, 444, 445^{17}, 447^{34}, $449^{50f.}$, 460^{56}, 481^{15}; II—6^{25}, 27^{4}, 30^{22}, 37^{59}, 43^{11}, 50^{41}, 53^{52}, $61^{105f.}$, $62^{106,108}$, 64^{122}, 79^{15}, 103^{11}, $104^{15f.}$, 129^{6}, 138^{46}, 146^{40}, 258^{50}, 267^{40}, $304^{2f.,5}$, 305^{8}, $307^{18,22}$, 310^{59}, 311f., $312^{2f.,7}$, $315^{20f.}$, 316^{27}, 319^{40}, 326, $333^{2f.,6}$, 336^{16}, 337, 342^{6}, 344^{4}, 352^{3}, $383^{65f.,69}$, 386^{93}, 394^{21}, 396^{30}, 412^{33}, 415^{54}, 416, 422^{17}, 428^{7}, $434^{14,22}$, 435^{23}, 437, 439^{4}; (IX cent.; Stapper) I—67^{3}, 70^{12}, 356^{43}, 360^{8}, 415^{71}, 432^{70}, 433^{78}, 484^{25}; II—315^{21}, 342^{6}, 415^{54}.
—Ordo Romanus II (IX–X cent.) I—66, 69^{10}, 72^{19}, 76^{9}, 83^{45}, 358^{60}, 360^{2}, 364^{21}, 414, 418^{31}, 420^{6}, 428^{48}, 432^{74}, 436^{93}, 447^{33}, $448^{37,42,46}$, $449^{51,53}$, $451^{66f.}$, 452^{75}, 453^{78}, 470^{50}; II—27^{4}, 47^{27}, 53^{52},

b) Further Mass Ordos

B. Names, Things, Formulas

Mass, arrangement of, I—121f., 269[28], 388, see also Table of Contents; as dedication, I—186f.; as recollection, I—176f.; "boxed", I—131; composition, I—126f.; daily, see Mass, daily; essence, I—175ff., first, see First Mass; hours of, I—247f.; in prisons, I—208, 213[3]; interpretations, I—86f., 108f., 115f.; see also Index A: III, 2, h; III, 3, d; in the consecration, I—184; meal, I—178; multiplication of, see Multiplication of Masses; names, I—169ff.; nuptial, see Nuptial Mass; of the catechumens, I—261, 474; of the faithful, I—474; ordos, see Index A: III, 2, b; III, 2, d; III, 3, b; prayers, see Prayers of the Mass; Presence of Christ, I—177ff., 183, 186; private, see Private Mass; series, I—130f., 134; stipends, I—134, 153[62], 191[48], 232; III—24ff., 26, 167; word, see *Missa*.

Mass, daily, I—117[31], 216f., 221f., 231ff., 247; of the faithful, I—221ff.; on week

Appendix

5. The Commingling[1]

IN THE PRESENT-DAY ROMAN LITURGY THE FRACTION IS FOL-
lowed at once by the commingling: the separated particle is dropped into the
chalice with an accompanying prayer that had been used in a similar way already
in the papal Mass of the eighth century. Thus in the present-day ceremony of the
commingling there is a survival of that ceremony in which the celebrating pope,
just before his Communion, broke off a particle from his own Host and dropped it
into the chalice. But the Roman liturgy of that time also had a commingling at the
same spot in which we have it today. Originally, this rite was only in the non-papal
liturgy of the churches in the environs of Rome. By an acolyte, the bishop sent the
priests of the vicinity a particle of the Eucharist as an expression of the ecclesiastical unity, as a token that they belonged to his *communio*. This particle was called
the *fermentum*. The priests dropped it into the chalice at this part of the Mass. The
practice is ancient indeed. It answered to that awareness, so keen in the ancient
Church, that the Eucharist was the *sacramentum unitatis*, that this Sacrament held
the Church together, and that all the people of God subject to a bishop should, if
it were possible, be gathered around that bishop's altar and receive the Sacrament
from his table of sacrifice.

In France, the *fermentum* was unknown. However, the Frankish editor of a widely
used Roman Ordo saw that in the ordinary Mass of a priest a commingling always
took place at the *Pax Domini*, whereas in the papal Mass things were done differently. In any case, he concluded that a fraction must take place beforehand since
a first commingling had to take place *before* the *Pax Domini*, and a second, as the
First Roman Ordo clearly demonstrated, before the Communion.

Naturally, one of the other of these was soon dropped, although for a time there
was some confusion and hesitancy as to which one should be retained. It was not
long before the first of the two gained the upper hand. Symbolism was probably a
determining factor in this decision, because thus the commingling, which was to
represent the Body of Christ returned to life, preceded the peace greeting of the *Pax
Domini*; for indeed our Lord first rose from the dead, and only then did He bring
peace to heaven and earth.

Here we find a symbolic interpretation for the old practice which came about with
the combining of the two commingling rites. What was the original meaning of the
second commingling rite which took place at the Communion? A careful examination of the evidence in the *Ordines* as well as in the Oriental rites has recently shed
some light on a previously little known area.

---

[1] This chapter was newly edited by Father Jungmann himself for a later edition. The re-editing
was necessitated chiefly because of the important findings of the Dutch liturgist Johann Peter
de Jong with reference to the rite of commingling.
We refer here to his last published word on the
subject: "Le rite de la commixtion dans la Messe
Romaine dans ses rapports avec les liturgies syri-
ennes": Archiv fur Liturgiewissenschaft 4 (1956)
245-278; 5 (1957) 33-79.—Rev.

We find ourselves confronted with a twofold origin. First there was the Roman (and general) practice which was linked with the reception of Holy Communion under both species. In the early Church it was thought to be of real importance that the faithful receive the Wine as well as the Bread, and of course they found themselves face to face with the difficulties that are bound to accompany the practice. For the most part (with the exception of Egypt) the early Christians wanted to avoid consecrating more than one chalice. So the solution was adopted of taking other vessels of plain wine and "sanctifying" them. That is to say, they somehow "consecrated" them either by pouring some of the Precious Blood into them or by dipping one of the consecrated particles into them, "mixing it in." Or sometimes both were done. But the last mentioned practice seems to be what is referred to in the *Ordo Romanus Primus*.

According to this *Ordo*, the Pope returns to his cathedra after the fraction. The consecrated Bread is then brought to him on a paten. He consumes part of it and drops the rest into the chalice while he says the commingling prayer. Then he drinks of the Precious Blood. What now follows is especially noteworthy. The Archdeacon also receives part of the Precious Blood, and after the Communion of the bishops and priests, pours the rest together (it seems) with the Particle into another chalice with wine. From this the people will receive their Communion, and should there not be enough, more will be added.

As we learn from the *Ordo* of St. Amand, there could even be more such chalices and each priest had to take one of them, make the sign of the cross with a consecrated Particle over it, and drop the Particle into the chalice. It was certainly a rite of this kind which is referred to in the legend of St. Lawrence as described by St. Ambrose where Lawrence is described as the holy deacon to whom was entrusted "the consecration of the Blood of the Lord."

THE SYMBOLISM

But this explanation does not alone suffice. For this commingling was also carried out in the chalice of the priest which held the Precious Blood. And the priest accompanies it even today with the words: *fiat accipientibus nobis in vitam aeternam*—" may there be accomplished (this commingling and consecration) for life everlasting to us who receive it." Why is this rite here as well?

Here symbolism had a part to play, a symbolism which came from the Orient from the Syrian liturgy. With the Syrians, at least since the fifth century (Theodore of Mopsuestia), there was a great enthusiasm for the idea that at the words of consecration the *death* of the Lord was represented, especially in the *separation* of the Body and Blood. But in the Communion we should receive the food of immortality; therefore, the *Resurrection* must also be expressed by the sacramental species. This took place by *reuniting* the Body and Blood. The Sacred Host was sprinkled in the form of a cross with a few drops of the Precious Blood and a Particle was mixed with the Chalice. Thus there was expressed in this rite the idea that the Blood and with it the soul returned to the Body in the resurrection. This also corresponds to the formula with which the rite was accompanied: "It is united and sanctified and completed in the name of the Father and of the Son and of the Holy Spirit."

The accompanying formula in our Roman Mass also reminds us of this oriental parallel. Since the words were not intended to be spoken aloud, they are not mentioned in the older sacramentaries but are rather to be found in the *Ordines* and run as follows: *Fiat commixtio et consecration corporis et sanguinis D.N.J.C accipientibus nobis in vitam aeternam. Amen.* "May there be accomplished the commingling and consecration of the Body and Blood of Our Lord Jesus Christ for life everlasting to us who receive it." We may certainly assume that in Rome a similar formula served to accompany and illustrate the commingling of the Particle of the Blood with the wine of the different Communion chalices. Still, the words "us who receive it" in the form that has come down to us remain strange on the part of the priest, who certainly receives the Precious Blood from the altar chalice itself and not from one of the secondary Communion chalices. The commingling must have had a meaning of its own independent of the "sanctifying" of the secondary chalices. It must now have had the same meaning it had in the Syrian liturgy: the symbolic expression of the unity of the Body and Blood of the Lord, in other words, the presentation of the Resurrection. The carrying over of such a practice from Syria to Rome could easily have been achieved especially at that time when a number of popes came from Syria.

The above-mentioned formula which was said at the commingling continued in use, unchanged, especially in Italian Mass books. In the preparation of the reform of the missal at the Council of Trent, theological doubts were raised against this formula, for on the face of it, its meaning—leaving aside the word *consecratio* for a moment—clearly was: let there be a commixture of our Lord's Body and Blood, (let it bring) us recipients to life everlasting. Thus, the formula could be construed as though, in consequence of it, the Body and Blood of Christ would be united to each other only after the commingling, and not already at the consecration of the two species, so that the Utraquists had grounds for arguing that Communion under one kind was insufficient. So the change to the present reading was proposed: *Haec commixtio . . . fiat accipientibus nobis in vitam aeternam*, here there is no longer any possible question of a commingling taking place beyond the visible performance; it is now merely the expression of a wish that this external ceremonial commingling may avail us for salvation. It has been established that this is the only change in the Tridentine Missal that was aimed at the Reformers. The word *consecratio*, which stayed in the text in spite of the objections brought against it, and in spite of the fact that it was missing in some medieval texts here and there, must be rendered by "hallowing" in the sense that through the commingling a sacred token or symbol is effected in the sacramental species and mediately in the Body and Blood of Christ a symbol of the Resurrection.

Elsewhere, in Carolingian territory, at least since the ninth century, a second formula was rife. This one presented, in a somewhat more verbose vein, the thoughts that were stressed in the Missal of Pius V. It was in general use in Northern France and in England till the reform of the missal, and in the Dominican rite is used even at present. It runs as follows: "May this most sacred commingling of the Body and Blood of Our Lord Jesus Christ be for all who receive it salvation (*salus*) of mind and body and a salutary preparation for obtaining eternal life."

The thought of the Resurrection, which, among the Syrians, had been linked first with the Fraction and then with the commingling, was associated with the latter also by the Carolingian commentators on the liturgy. It was even stressed by the fact that the rite of commingling (as we said above) was inserted not immediately before the Communion, but already before the *Pax Domini*. So the idea of the Resurrection in this relationship remained as an element in the explanation of the Mass all through the Middle Ages and even down to the present. On the other hand, the fraction was not until somewhat more recent times linked to the Passion of Christ, as signifying Christ's death, a signification on which later theologians, even post-Tridentine ones, placed a great deal of importance.

It must have been the attitude of Amalar which ultimately decided the anticipation of the commingling ceremony. According to him, this ceremony, along with the accompanying phrase, ought to be placed before the *Pax Domini*, in the short pause after the conclusion of the embolism during which the fraction of the Host and the crossing of the chalice would already have occurred; for it was not till after His Resurrection that our Lord appeared to His disciples and saluted them with His greeting of peace. Thereafter only the partition of the Host was anticipated, being linked with the concluding formula, *Per Dominum*, in lieu of a pause. The crossing then was joined to the *Pax Domini*, for this latter was by degrees interpreted as a formula of blessing.

However, only in one portion of the post-Carolingian Mass plans did this commingling follow immediately; but it was this arrangement that was adopted in Italy and therefore also the one definitely fixed in the Missal of Pius V.

By far the greater portion of the Carolingian Mass plans contained a different arrangement. True, they did not hold to the original Roman pattern, where the commingling was linked to the Communion itself or, at any rate, followed the kiss of peace. But the commingling often occurred after that *Agnus Dei* in those churches where it had already become customary for the priest to recite it. And so the priests kept the sacred particle in their hands during the *Agnus Dei* with the purpose (as Durandus says) of making their prayer more efficacious since they were holding the Lord Himself in their hands. In this case, then, we have a secondary reshifting which likewise rests on Amalar's solution and which in the main has disappeared since 1570.

Since Amalar had indicated for the rite of commingling a place at the *Pax Domini*, the very spot where, according to the practice of the ancient Church, the space-encircling unifying force of the Eucharist had been represented by the admixture of the *fermentum*, our modest rite had gained an additional significance beyond its original meaning of representing the intrinsic unity of the Sacrament under two kinds and the Resurrection, borrowing from the farther-reaching significance of its sister rite the symbolism of Communion of church with church. The accompanying *Pax Domini* could easily add support to these latter ideas. On the other hand, The rite of fraction and commingling, as now in use in the Roman Mass, has lost some of its importance, since it does not occupy a place in the pause mentioned above and, as a consequence, appears simply as an accompaniment to the close of the embolism and the *Pax Domini*, texts which have no immediate relevance to the rite. Thus few celebrants will find it possible to keep in mind the significance of the venerable rite. And for the other participants, the rite has hardly any purpose at all, since it is perceptible only to those close to the altar. Besides, the ancient song that formerly accompanied the fraction, the *Agnus Dei*, did not follow the change of position of the rite as we have it now, but continued to occupy the position of the older fraction, as we shall see. Scarcely anywhere else has the transparency of the liturgical procedure suffered so much by later contraction and compression as here in the purlieu of the fraction and commingling, although the elements of the ancient tradition have been faithfully preserved.